O'BRIEN GUIDE TO
IRISH GARDENS

SHIRLEY LANIGAN

Illustrated by Aileen Caffrey

THE O'BRIEN PRESS
DUBLIN

For Michael, Mary Kate and Michael
who still like books

First published 2001 by The O'Brien Press Ltd.,
20 Victoria Road, Dublin 6, Ireland.
Tel: +353 1 4923333; Fax: +353 1 4922777
E-mail: books@obrien.ie
Website: www.obrien.ie

ISBN: 0-86278-632-0

British Library Cataloguing-in-Publication Data
A catalogue record for this title is available from the British Library

1 2 3 4 5 6 7 8 9
01 02 03 04 05 06 07

The O'Brien Press receives
assistance from

The Arts Council
An Chomhairle Ealaíon

Editing, typesetting, layout and design: The O'Brien Press Ltd.
Illustrations: Aileen Caffrey
Maps: Design Image
Cover separations: C&A Print Services Ltd.
Printing: The Guernsey Press Ltd.

122887

€19.00

ACKNOWLEDGEMENTS

I have so many people to thank for helping me with this book, people who generously gave me their time as I wandered around Ireland.

I should start with Sally O'Halloran of the National Botanic Gardens, Dublin, who was hugely generous with information. Patricia Barrow in County Louth was another helpful informant. The people who run the Private Gardens of County Wexford Trail – Helen and Bryan Miller, Dr Austin O'Sullivan, John and Irene Roche and their colleagues – are probably the most helpful guides on the island, closely followed by the women who run the South Tipperary Garden Trail. In Cork, Carla Blake was kind as was Catherine MacHale. Sandro Caffolla of Design by Nature in Laois also deserves a thank-you. The women at the Drogheda Tourist Office set the standard to which all tourist office staff should aspire.

I am grateful to Adrian Burke and his family in Castlebar and to Mrs MK Moore in County Down for their much-appreciated hospitality.

Thank you to Shay Healy and Paddy Friel. Thanks also to Ray and Lorna.

Then there are the gardeners who accompanied me around their gardens in all sorts of weather – mostly wet – to give me the full tour of their enviable gardens: Lorna MacMahon, Robert Gordon, Rosemary Brown, Rubel and John Ross, Christine Fehily, Brian Cross, Mr Acheson Aiken, Alexander Mattei, June Welsh, David Gilliland, Seamus O Gaoithin, Mary Simpson, Lady Jessica Rathdonnell, Nora Burgess, Mary and John Walsh, Doreen Moody, Jimi Blake, Elizabeth Kennedy, Ned and Liz Kirby, Mary Tarry, Deborah Begley, the Boyce family, Mary Jennings and Christopher Hone, Deirdre Ryan, Dick Mallett and Eve Kennedy, Mary Byrne, Dermot Kehoe, Betty Timmerman Damiaans, Hannah Weimar, Mary Lynch (and Liz Kavanagh).

Koraley Northen and Angela Jupe at the GLDA and are owed special thanks for the abundance of information they gave me.

I would like to thank Michael O'Brien, Íde ní Laoghaire and all the staff at the O'Brien Press. Rachel Pierce was endlessly patient, enthusiastic and hard-working and I am grateful. To my other editors, Susan Houlden, Mary Webb and Eoin O'Brien I also extend warm thanks, and to Lynn Pierce and Caitríona Magner. Thanks are also due to Gráinne Devaney, Gráinne Farren and Jorid Lindberg.

My two great families helped me enormously, particularly Mum, Paddy, Billy, Dor and Mick, and Mary, Zoë, Billy and Gráinne. Thank you Niall for resuscitating the computer on countless occasions.

Finally, the biggest thanks of all to Michael, Mary Kate and Michael who deserve a break now.

PICTURE CREDITS

Front cover: National Trust (main picture); Jimi Blake (top left).

Colour Section 1: Jimi Blake, p.1; Terence Reeves-Smyth, p.6 (top); Tim Allen, p.7 (top); Rosemary Brown, p.7 (bottom left). **Colour Section 2**: Chris Hill, National Trust, p.1; National Trust, p.2 (both); Rita O'Lynn, p.4 (bottom); Roger Kinkead, National Trust, p.5 (top); Mike Williams, National Trust, p.5 (bottom); Robert Thompson, National Trust, p.8.

Many thanks to the garden owners who also contributed photographs.

CONTENTS

Foreword by Mary Davies
Introduction
How to use this guide
Notes on garden-visiting etiquette

FOREWORD

To say that Irish gardens are the best in the world would seem a proud boast. But there are many qualities that have made them a mecca for visitors for more than 200 years. Long before the present boom in gardening, travellers praised the 'big house' parks and their elegantly planted woods, with rustic summerhouses and seats along winding paths, set into the romantically beautiful Irish landscape. They marvelled at the exotic flowers and fruits grown in the glasshouses and gazed admiringly into the carefully tended walled gardens with their neat rows of fruit bushes, vegetables and flowers – enough to supply the owners and their guests with produce throughout the year.

Many of these gardens attached to large estates have survived, some relatively intact. Others had fallen into decay due to lack of money and manpower, but have recently undergone major restoration, overseen by professional landscapers and horticulturists. EU funding has been a blessing and the results have been both dramatic and satisfying; woodland areas have been renewed, herbaceous borders replanted and once utilitarian walled gardens have found new life as pleasure grounds.

To these older gardens has been added a wealth of delightful newer ones, large and small, situated in all parts of Ireland. These gardens have been created by the labour of private individuals, many of them self-taught, who combine an enthusiastic love of plants with artistic vision and skill. They take great pride in their gardens and often enjoy the challenge of participating in national competitions. At the same time they welcome the visitor wholeheartedly, so that more gardens than ever before are open to the public either regularly or on an occasional basis.

Irish gardens would not, however, be as internationally renowned as they are if they did not have so many factors in their favour. Ireland is famously 'green', thanks to the mildness and dampness of the climate – extremes of temperature and drought are rare. Growth is luxurious and rapid. Many of the soils are acidic, suiting a wide range of different species. Plants from all over the world, from the Mediterranean to China, from New Zealand to South America, combine happily in these benign conditions. Tree ferns and groves of myrtles in Kerry, towering 100-year-old rhododendrons in Donegal, Canary Island echiums growing wild on the cliffs of Howth, County Dublin – all these are sources of envious amazement to visitors from beyond these shores.

The Irish landscape has reached the twenty-first century relatively unspoiled. The many gardens set in the countryside can still take full advantage of their surroundings, whether it be the dramatic sea inlets of Cork and Kerry, the mountains of Wicklow, the drumlin hills of County Down or the wide, undulating, lake-studded vistas of the midlands. The sense of peace and quiet that enfolds Irish gardens, often even those in built-up areas, is an important part of their charm.

So much has been written about the best-known Irish gardens in recent years that it might be thought difficult to say anything new. But Shirley Lanigan, a self-described 'obsessive gardener', has traversed the highways and byways of the four provinces and brings a fresh approach as she records her finds in lively style. The 303 gardens featured in this book range from County Waterford's magnificent Mount Congreve, with twenty-five gardeners to tend its 630 varieties of camellia and 350 Japanese maples, to tiny, gracious Fairfield Lodge set in the urban bustle of south County Dublin. Parks that open daily, such as St Stephen's Green, Kilkenny Castle grounds and Belfast Botanic Gardens, take their place next to gardens that may be open only once or twice a year. Each of the gardens, distinctive and unique as they all are, has its own particular portrait painted, sometimes warts and all, but always with a sympathetic eye.

The gardens are arranged by county, with directions, opening hours and other necessary information. Each county has its own short introduction, and ends with details of gardening clubs, garden centres and nurseries, designers, craftworkers, country markets and other relevant local businesses. Shirley's personal choices – ten favourite gardens, twenty best nurseries, etc. – enliven the pages, as do the photographs, drawings and maps.

The enthusiasm Shirley Lanigan shows for the gardens – and their owners – is infectious. The avid and experienced garden visitor will be stirred to new activity; the beginner will be ensnared. Readers of this book will not only find themselves compulsively reading on from page to page, they will also experience a great urge to set forth to the gardens, large and small, famous and unknown, she so lovingly describes. Gardens, other people's as well as our own, are above all places to be enjoyed. This most comprehensive guide can only enhance the pleasure of every visitor.

Mary Davies, 2001

INTRODUCTION

I remember the day well. It came after two months of sleeping in a different bed every night and solo travel, fried breakfasts seven days a week and a too-intimate knowledge of service station sandwiches. The rain was pouring from the heavens and I was searching for a garden in West Cork. As the car made its way gingerly up yet another pot-holed *boreen*, a horrible scraping sound told me the day was about to take a turn for the worse. Climbing out of the car, I picked my way back down the hill between treacherous fissures and found the steaming exhaust pipe in the middle of the road, brought it back and put it on the back seat like a wounded animal. With something approaching horror, I realised that I was more upset at the thought of not reaching the garden than of being stranded 150 miles from home with a dying car.

Limping to a garage in Skibbereen, a ten-to-one bet from a bemused mechanic that the car might just hobble on for another three days before collapsing came as wonderful news. In business again and insanely happy, I made my way back to the *boreen*, found the garden and it was glorious – even in the monsoon-like rain that West Cork specialises in. Gardens can do that to otherwise sensible people, and for me there is no mood so black and no day so miserable that it cannot be improved significantly by a walk around someone's gorgeous garden.

This book is the result of two years dedicated to visiting gardens throughout Ireland, north and south. I aimed to visit every garden I possibly could so that I could give a personal description of each. But Ireland is in the middle of a gardening frenzy. New gardens open to the public all the time, sometimes in an informal, quiet and unannounced way. There are certainly gardens I have missed, but with a final tally of over 300, I have found many, many more than I thought I would, and sometimes in the most unexpected places – in schools, beside the most traffic-clogged motorways in the country, in housing estates as well as grand estates, out on the coast, up in the mountains, behind sweet shops and hotels and attached to churches and ruins. And they are all great places, some of unquestionably good taste, others interesting and quirky, and some far from what one might expect. But they are all interesting because they are each the fruit of someone's imagination and work; all loved, or at least loved at one time.

Gardening brings out the best in people. On my travels I have sometimes arrived unannounced, rightly expecting the dogs to be set on me, only to be met by welcomes, cups of tea and slices of cake – often enjoyed in hand while taking a guided tour around the garden. Other times I was sent on my way with a particularly good seedhead in my pocket, until eventually seedlings and divisions of all sorts covered the floor of the car, busily respiring and steaming up the windows. Other times it was slips of some choice shrub in a plastic bag with strict orders to 'make sure and get it in the ground quickly'. One thoughtful woman dispatched me with a pot of basil on the dashboard to mask the smell of wet oilskins for the rest of the journey. Towards the end it felt like driving a portable greenhouse. As a result of my travels, gardening friends now litter the island and I am reminded of them through the pots of rooted cuttings and seedlings around my back door.

I am grateful for all that, but mostly I am grateful for the fact that these generous people open their gardens and welcome us in. It is not an easy thing to do to expose one's work to scrutiny, and not always forgiving or fair scrutiny at that. As a visitor, always remember that one person's passion for a magnificently manicured, high-maintenance look is another's over-tidy nightmare. You will not always find what you expect to see or even want to see, but sometimes that might be a good thing. Be generous towards others' tastes. Enjoy these gardens. I certainly did.

Shirley Lanigan
JANUARY 2001

How to Use this Guide

Using this guide is very simple. I have divided the island into provinces, each of which is further divided into individual counties, arranged alphabetically. Within each county chapter the gardens are also listed alphabetically. At the end of each county chapter I have listed gardening and horticultural clubs, garden centres and nurseries and garden-related stockists. The maps illustrate garden locations within each province, enabling the visitor to get to the approximate location from where the directions given in each garden's own entry can be followed. Loosely arranged throughout the book are boxes on gardening-related items that do not readily belong within the main text.

INDIVIDUAL GARDEN ENTRIES
Each garden entry begins with a rubric, detailing, in symbols and writing, all relevant information. This includes the name of the house and/or garden and its address.

CONTACT
A contact name is given either for the owner or a designated person who should be contacted when booking a visit. Telephone numbers*, fax numbers and, where applicable, e-mail and website addresses are given. If it is stated that appointments must be made either by telephone or letter, please follow this proviso.

Please note: the prefix for Northern Ireland if you are calling from outside the region is: 048; the prefix for calls made within the region is: 028.

OPENING HOURS
Opening hours are given as the gardeners outlined them. When exact months, days and times are given, these apply without exception. In other cases an entry may read 'open during the summer months by appointment only' – such entries apply to gardens where the owner is happy for visitors to come at any time between May and October, but they nevertheless require that visitors make contact and arrange a suitable time before arriving.

ADMISSION
This is marked by one of two entries: **No entrance fee** or **Entrance fee**. Usually reductions will apply to children, OAPs and groups, so it's worth telephoning in advance to check. If the admission or part of it goes to charity, this is noted.

CHILDREN
Some gardeners prefer not to have child visitors. There are many reasons for this: the garden may not be suitable for children due to the existence of water features or substantial drops in ground level. Whatever the reason, it is in the interest of your child's safety to obey this stipulation.

SPECIAL FEATURES
Some entries have a note referring to **Special features**. These call attention to an interesting feature, sometimes unrelated to gardening, for instance, an historic house or castle, a petting zoo, a museum, craft or gift shop or produce for sale. These extra

features should help you to plan your day more easily, especially if you are bringing the whole family along.

OWNERSHIP

Properties owned by Dúchas, The Heritage Service (the Department of Arts, Heritage, Gaeltacht and the Islands) in the Republic and by the National Trust in Northern Ireland are noted. Affiliations to other organisations, for example, Landmark Trust, county councils, FÁS, are also noted.

DIRECTIONS

Directions to the gardens were compiled from gardener's instructions and my own experiences.

PLANTS FOR SALE

The Plants for Sale symbol is: 🏵

Buying plants, particularly unusual or hard-to-get varieties, is an important part of a garden visit for many people, so a note has been made of those gardens where plants may be bought. 'Plants occasionally sold' means that a small number of plants propagated from the garden will be available from time to time, usually on open days.

REFRESHMENTS

The symbols for refreshments available are: ♨ and ⑩

Gardens which have a restaurant/café serving full meals are denoted by this symbol: ⑩. Gardens offering more modest refreshments are denoted by this symbol: ♨. Groups should note that it is always wiser to book meals and refreshments in advance, even when the garden has a full restaurant. Many gardens are isolated and special provision may need to be made for large groups.

WHEELCHAIR ACCESS

The symbol for wheelchair access is: ♿

When the wheelchair symbol is supplied, this means that the garden is either fully or partially wheelchair-accessible. This information has been supplied at the owner's instruction. However, wheelchair-users should *always* telephone in advance to discuss with the owner the extent of accessibility. Gravel surfaces can vary widely and wheels can more easily negotiate some than others. Speaking to the owner will clarify whether or not the garden is suitable for your vehicle.

DOGS

The symbol for dogs allowed is: 🐕

Very few gardeners allow dogs, sometimes out of fear of the damage they might cause, sometimes because there are dogs or cats living in the garden. Some gardens allow dogs on leads however, and these are all marked with the dog symbol. All gardens allow guide dogs, but be sure to inform the owner before you arrive.

ACCOMMODATION

The symbol for accommodation available is: ⌂

Accommodation is sometimes available and ranges from basic camping facilities to full hotel or country house accommodation. Ring the owner for full details.

Notes on Garden-Visiting Etiquette

Garden visitors can show their appreciation to their hosts by observing a few rules and by employing good manners at all times when visiting other people's gardens:

- If a gardener requests that an appointment be made, please make one, otherwise you could arrive to a locked gate or interrupt someone hanging wallpaper.
- Don't be put off as an individual if only groups are admitted. Round up some friends and make a day of it.
- Children should be brought to gardens only when it is stated that they are welcome. Sometimes a garden simply isn't suitable due to water, cliffs or other features that could prove dangerous. If they are welcome, please supervise them well; a private garden is not a playground.
- It should go without saying that plants should never be dug up or have branches, flowers or seedheads 'borrowed'. 'Just one little bit' is still theft. Already the grounds of some of the grander hotels with gardens have been closed to the public due to extraordinary plant losses from Sunday visitors 'just taking a bit of a plant'. If you really covet a plant, a polite request will usually be met with generosity and a cutting or off-shoot.
- Always obey signs and respect privacy.
- If there are picnic facilities, bring home your rubbish.
- An honesty box provided by the gardener should always receive attention, and with the appropriate amount of appropriate currency.
- Only expect facilities where they are advertised. Many gardens are private homes and when you ring to book they will advise you of the nearest hotel, café or garden with restaurant and toilets, which you can use either before or after your visit.
- It is only if garden visitors maintain a reputation for respectful and unobtrusive behaviour that owners will continue to open their gates. Too many gardens have closed because gardeners, despairing of visitors' bad behaviour, give up and return once more to signs marked Private: No Entry. These are sad losses for us all and we should all do our best to avoid such outcomes.
- Finally, if you enjoy a garden, tell the gardener. It will always be appreciated.

MAP KEY

1. Stephenstown Pond Trust
2. Millhouse Gardens
3. Newcastle House
4. Rockfield Gardens
5. O'Grady's Garden
6. Listoke House and Garden
7. Beaulieu House and Garden
8. Carrigglas Manor
9. Rockfield Demesne
10. Tullynally Castle
11. Loughcrew Historic Gardens
12. Ballinlough Castle and Gardens
13. Grove Gardens
14. Butterstream Garden
15. Glebelands House
16. Glebewood Cottage
17. 51 Woodview Heights
18. Woodfield
19. Belvedere House and Garden
20. Ballindoolin House and Garden
21. Larchill Arcadian Gardens
22. Hamwood House
23. Celbridge Abbey
24. Lodge Park Walled Garden and Steam Museum
25. Coolcarrigan House
26. Birr Castle Demesne
27. Portrane House
28. Emo Court Garden
29. K Gardens
30. The Japanese Gardens and St Fiachra's Garden
31. Gash Gardens
32. Heywood Garden
33. The Sensory Garden
34. Hardymount
35. Lisnavagh
36. Tobinstown Garden
37. Joe Buckley's Garden
38. Jenkinstown Woods
39. Ballon Garden
40. Altamont Gardens
41. Martina Lynch's Garden
42. Rosybower
43. Butler House Garden
44. Kilkenny Castle Park
45. Shean Garden
46. Ram House Garden
47. Knockbawn
48. Ashbrook
49. The Bay Garden
50. The Watergarden
51. Kilfane Glen and Waterfall
52. Mount Juliet
53. Woodstock
54. The Three Bridges
55. Woodville
56. Berkeley Forest
57. Sandy Lane
58. Kilmokea Manor House and Garden
59. John F Kennedy Arboretum
60. Heatherset
61. Johnstown Castle
62. Shortalstown

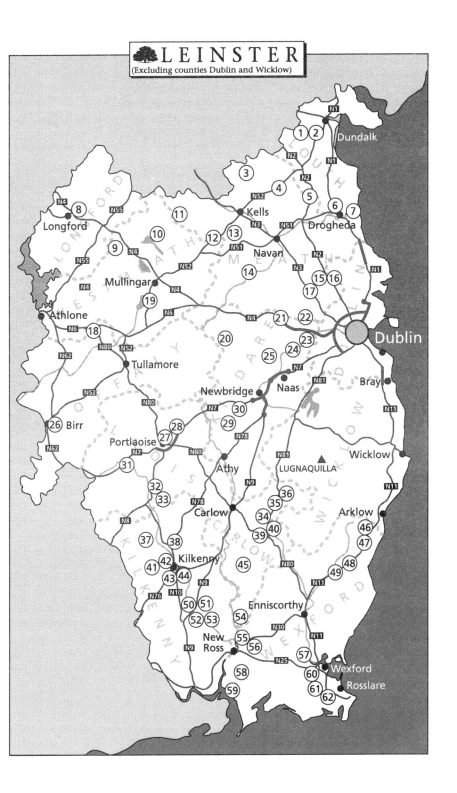

COUNTY CARLOW

Carlow is one of the smallest counties on the island, bordered on its eastern side by the Wicklow Mountains and, further south, by the Blackstairs Mountains in Wexford. Most of the county is good farming land: fertile, well-worked and cultivated. The countryside is notable for its tidy, winding, hedged roads and well-maintained farms. There are a large number of gardens open to the public in the county, ranging from old estates, like Altamont, recently acquired by the State, to small private gardens. They are all worth visiting and within easy reach of each other for a daytrip.

ALTAMONT GARDENS

Tullow, County Carlow; Tel/Fax: +0503 59444 ▪ **Contact**: Pauline Dowling ▪ **Open:** Thursday–Sunday, 10.30am–6.30pm; times are due to change, so telephone in advance; guided tours available if booked in advance ▪ **Entrance fee** goes towards garden upkeep ▪ Supervised children welcome ▪ Member of Dúchas ▪ **Directions:** leave Tullow on the N81 and turn left at the sign for Altamont. The garden is also signposted on the main Carlow–Wexford road (N80).

Altamont has a history which goes back to the sixteenth century, at least. The riverside site has housed monastic settlements, a nunnery, as well as several families who have been gardening and building through the centuries. The house seen today is Georgian, built on a foundation of immensely thick walls, with arrow slit windows which date from an older castle.

The garden is the creation of gardeners from the end of the nineteenth century onwards, chiefly Fielding Lecky Watson and his daughter, Corona North. The Watson family were Quakers who came to County Carlow in the 1640s. Fielding Lecky Watson moved into Altamont in 1923. After serving in the Second World War Mrs North came to Altamont and began to work the garden. She died in the late 1990s, leaving the Irish garden world worried about what would happen to her wonderful County Carlow creation. However, as she herself had planned, Altamont was taken over by Dúchas, The Heritage Service. Despite complaints from some quarters about that State body's expenditure and the resources it puts towards the gardens in its care, Altamont would appear to be in safe hands.

There has been consolidation and restoration of existing features. A new double border, recently created in the walled garden in remembrance of Mrs North, sits on the site of an older border. Friends of Mrs North from all over the Irish gardening world donated the plants for the new feature. This is a fascinating place, filled with plants such as a lilac (*Syringa*) bought from the nursery at Altamont twenty years ago by a woman in Castleknock, County Dublin. The tree became too big for its suburban home and was donated back to Altamont for the new border. Another special plant is the salvia given by a County Wexford gardener who obtained it from Fernhill (*see* County Dublin) with the information that it arrived there via someone's walking holiday in South America. A little hellebore came from Helen Dillon (*see* County

Dublin). She had been given it by David Shackleton of Beech Park (*see* County Dublin), and he in turn had received the plant from the famed Lady Moore, wife of Sir Frederick Moore, Director of the National Botanic Gardens in the late nineteenth and early twentieth centuries. Indeed, Lady Moore crops up in all sort of places around the border in the shape of *Iris* 'Lady Moore', *Agapanthus* 'Lady Moore' and *Acanthus* 'Lady Moore'.

Many of the plants in the new borders have strong links to the history of Irish gardening, including a ligularia found by the plant hunter Dr Augustine Henry, and an unnamed rose from Belvedere (*see* County Westmeath). More recent finds, such as a Tibetan rose

Swans on the ornamental lake at Altamont in County Carlow.

collected by Seamus O'Brien and a collection of grasses given by Jimi Blake of Airfield (*see* County Dublin), represent the younger Irish gardening community. The beds are divided simply by colour: long bands of yellow helianthus, chrysanthemum, cone flowers and creamy *Campanula thrysoides* run into the front rows of blue and purple nepeta, salvia, aconite, delphinium and echinops. Dahlias, cosmos and penstemon, like the little Irish cultivar 'Evelyn', which came courtesy of Berna Purcell of Burton Hall (*see* County Dublin), supply reds, pinks and plums to the scheme.

The two well-stuffed, wide beds are held up on ledges of warm-coloured granite and separated by pea gravel paths and granite steps that came to Altamont compliments of the Dublin quays, from where they were removed to accommodate the Millennium pedestrian bridge across the Liffey.

The house and garden are reached by a short, wide avenue of beech trees underplanted with varieties of mountain ash (*Sorbus*) and thousands of daffodils. A big *Rhododendron augustinii* stretches ten metres up the side of the house. This was named for Augustine Henry, the Irish plant collector (*see* box, p.41). To the garden side of the elegant old building is a goldfish pool set into a slab stone terrace of iris and angel's fishing rod (*Dierama*), one of the most elegant of flowers. Yews, shaped into domes or eggs, march down the hill on either side of the Broad Walk and into the main body of the garden. The scent of snow-white *Rosa* 'Mme Hardy' along here is gorgeous. The old French rose, along with other old varieties, is interspersed with dusty-pink double opium poppies, and in spring over forty varieties of snowdrop sheet the bed. The path continues, through a golden yew arch with 'Mickey Mouse' ears and 150-year-old clipped box, toward the Lake Walk and a white-flowering handkerchief tree (*Davidia involucrata*).

Most gardeners know that a huge number of the plants grown in this country today are not native to Ireland. But we know precious little about the men, and they were mostly men, who brought the abundance that we enjoy in our gardens today to Ireland and Britain. Yet their names are scattered liberally around every garden, from William Lobb, remembered through the beautiful, scented, pink *Rosa* 'William Lobb', to John Tradescant, immortalised in the name of tradescantia, and Robert Fortune, remembered through *Rhododendron fortunii*. Since the seventeenth century when the father-and-son team of John Tradescant senior and junior made their explorations to Russia and North America, there has been a long chain of plant collectors, explorers and hunters who have scoured every part of the globe for the seed and seedlings of exotic annuals, perennials, shrubs and trees that gardeners at home could enjoy. We have much to be thankful for.

These were brave, tough, pioneering and sometimes quite mad people. My personal hero is David Douglas (1799–1834), the Scot who led a short life of almost impossible hardship in the name of horticulture and botany. Working chiefly in North America and Canada, Douglas endured endless miseries, living for long periods on trading posts, missionary stations and out in the wilds. He was attacked by bears, lost in blizzards, deprived of food. All his belongings were stolen several times. In the course of his long expeditions he was forced to cross icy rivers by stripping off and carrying his clothes over his head. Added to these were ambushes by Indians and shipwrecks. Lastly, he endured a grisly death at the age of thirty-five when he was gored by an escaped bull while collecting samples on the island of Honolulu. Douglas is responsible for bringing countless numbers of plants to Europe, including the Monterey pine (*Pinus radiata*), *Limnanthus douglasii*, *Abies grandis*, *Garrya elliptica* and the flowering currant *(Ribes sanguineum)*, seen so often in our gardens. I cannot look at its lovely little flowers without thinking of poor Douglas.

Ireland benefited eventually from the work of all the plant collectors, from Sir Joseph Hooker to Frank Kingdom Ward and George Forrest, because many Irish gardeners and landowners subscribed to various plant-hunting expeditions, receiving plants and seeds in payment. But there are two plant hunters in particular that Ireland claims 'ownership' of. The first is Thomas Coulter, an Irishman who also collected in the Americas, largely for Trinity College. In the 1830s and 1840s Coulter collected species of cacti and conifers and sent many thousands of herbarium or dried samples back to Dublin. His name will always be remembered, however, through *Romneya coulteri*, a superb shrub with big open white flowers, which he found in New Mexico. The other is Augustine Henry, the most famous of the Irish plant collectors (*see* box, p.41).

The pump-house walk leads past and under a range of rhododendrons, down to the 'bund', a marl or clay wall around the lake, spiked with the bright orange of thousands of Welsh poppies (*Meconopsis cambrica*), and creeping periwinkle (*Vinca*). The raised wall which holds in the lake seeps in places, so the surrounding ground is damp and perfect for candelabra primulas. Good shelter also permits a number of young tree ferns to grow well here.

It is a pleasure to walk around the lake and look across the lily-strewn water at the trees. Thomas Pakenham declared the *Pinus sylvestris* the 'best specimen of Scots pine in the country' (*see* Tullynally Castle, County Longford). The weeping silver birch and a Kilmacurragh cyprus (*Chamaecyparis Lawsonia* 'Kilmacurragh') are also remarkably good-looking specimens. A bog stream travelling from a half a mile away fills the large lake. During the Famine, over 100 men were employed for two years to dig it out by hand. One hundred years later a smaller team, made up of Mrs North and her husband Garry, would drain and clear the lake. They took out a metre and a half of mud, roots, reeds and sixty fallen trees in a matter of months, before filling it again and restoring it to its former glory.

A little path leads from the lake to the Ice Age glen, over the stream into the oak collection. Mrs North began an arboretum and shrub area here with an arbutus-edged pool guarded by a statue of the god Lugh, a formidable-looking creature.

The Glen is home to over 100 varieties of rhododendron and a number of sessile oaks (*Quercum petraea*), over 500 years old, growing by a fast-flowing stream. Many of the rhododendrons came as seed from the plant-hunting expeditions of Frank Kingdom Ward to the Himalayas (*see* box, The Plant Hunters, p.5). In spring this area fills with wild daffodils, and in May sheets of bluebells and ferns take over. The name Ice Age glen refers to the huge stone outcrops and overhanging boulders that create a wild and primitive look. At the bottom of the garden the River Slaney runs wide and straight, cutting through mature woods. Stone stairs known as 'The One Hundred Steps' lead from the river bank back up to the garden. Built by Fielding Lecky Watson, they were either designed or influenced by William Robinson (*see* box, p.182). At the top of the hill, in the sheep-filled field, sits a little temple, from which there are views of the Wicklow and Blackstairs mountains, and back to the lake and house. A tall Wellingtonia was planted, according to legend, to commemorate the Battle of Waterloo. (Wellingtonia is the name given to the *Sequioadendron giganteum*, one of the tallest trees in the world. In 1852 the seed collector, William Lobb, brought specimens of seedlings to England from the forests of northern California. The duke of Wellington had died the year before and it was felt that this was the sort of impressive plant by which he should be remembered, so it was called Wellingtonia.) A fine golden oak shares the field with the Wellingtonia. Follow the track and it will lead you to a new feature: a bridge over the stream, complete with swans, a white wisteria and rose walk, and cushions of hardy geranium. The way then travels under the Nun's Walk. This is an avenue of beech trees underplanted with small wild daffodils, primroses in spring and cyclamen and ferns later in the year. The trees are now, unfortunately, over-mature, which means that they may not be standing for much longer. All the more reason to go and see them soon.

Attached to the walled garden in Altamont is an excellent small nursery, which sells plants propagated from the special plants in the Mrs North borders as well as from all over the garden.

BALLON GARDEN

Ballon Village, County Carlow; Tel: +0503 59144 ▪ **Contact:** Statia or Maurice O'Neill ▪ **Open**: mid-May–end July, Sunday 2pm–6pm; bank holidays, telephone in advance to confirm opening hours ▪ **Entrance fee** ▪ Children welcome ▪ **Directions:** situated at the edge of Ballon village on the Bunclody Road (N80). Turn right onto a small private road. The garden is a few hundred metres along on the left.

The entrance to Mrs O'Neill's garden is marked by three silver birches underplanted with low-growing evergreens, heathers and autumn crocus (*Colchicum*). To the side is a wall of trees, including snake-bark maples *(Acer rufinerve),* over a run of pink geraniums and more white colchicum.

The garden was an old orchard when Statia O'Neill began to work it fifteen years ago. At one time there were nearly fifty fruit trees on the site; some of these were kept at the front of the house by the drive, but she cleared most of them to make way for the garden.

'Statia is great with plants,' says Maurice, her husband. 'We have lots of people who call to her with bits of mystery leaves and flowers to identify and she always knows what they are. She can also get anything to grow.'

The process of gardening is what interests Mrs O'Neill; she is less concerned with minor details, like the size of the garden: 'I suppose it's about three-quarters of an acre,' she replied, when asked, in a tone which suggests that this might be the first time she has put her mind to the question.

'I started with the orchard and began to pull out the trees, which I replaced with spuds. By degrees they came out too and other vegetables went in, and then by degrees the vegetables dwindled and the ornamentals began to take over.' Today the garden is almost all ornamental planting, from specimen trees and flowering shrubs to herbaceous perennials.

The garden has no land shelter at all and strong winds which sweep straight down from Mount Leinster cut viciously through it. Mrs O'Neill dealt with this by planting a shelterbelt which softens the edge of the winds a little, protecting the more tender plants. The front of the garden enjoys some extra protection from the house, which makes it a very sunny, dry, gravel garden that soaks up the warm weather. Self-seeding plants of angel's fishing rod (*Dierama*), carex grass and creeping thyme grow out of the local white-bleached granite. Beds of astrantia and Cape daisies (which came from a recent visit to South Africa) contribute to the hot climate look. Sprawling camellias, broom, evening primroses and white species roses hang out over the walls. Granite millstone tables and sculptural stone features have been artfully placed around the area.

The garden spills onto the road, taking over the ditch, and sneaking further out towards the other side of the road.

A long, castellated wall of box hedge runs the length of the garden by the house. Maurice is responsible for these inch-perfect green battlements. Across the lawn from the box wall there is a long mixed bed, full of the bright lime leaves of honey locust, Japanese hydrangea (*Gleditsia triacanthos* 'Sunburst'), roses, purple smoke tree (*Cotinus coggygria*), lemon mint, cut-leaf beech, philadelphus and lysimachia, commonly known as loosestrife. At the end of the bed a steely-blue cedar (*Cedrus atlantica* 'Glauca') shelters from the worst of the Carlow winds.

Pay a visit to Maurice's box nursery where he sells well-shaped box in cones, balls and corkscrews in various sizes, as well as smaller plants for hedging.

Hardymount, Tullow, County Carlow; Tel: +0503 51769 ❋ **Contact:** Mrs Sheila
Reeves-Smyth ❋ **Open:** during the Wicklow Gardens Festival, Sunday 2pm–6pm
(see local press for annual dates); other Sundays, May to September; 2pm–6pm, by
appointment only; groups most welcome ❋ **Entrance fee** donated to cancer research ❋ **Directions:** drive into Tullow from Dublin on the N81. Turn left at the
bridge and right after the Statoil petrol station. Then turn right at the crossroads.
The garden is 600m along on the right, with a granite-walled, white gateway.

Hardymount announces itself with a short but impressive drive past a low spreading
cherry, a fine Spanish chestnut (the second biggest specimen on the island), and
other mature trees. But the real reason to visit Hardymount is the walled garden,
tucked in behind the house, through a door in a wall.

'I grow what I like,' says Mrs Reeves-Smyth of her wonderful walled garden.
Unlike some gardeners, who will practically bar the gates to visitors arriving after May
or June, Sheila Reeves-Smyth puts her work and effort into a garden that will give
pleasure for the length of the summer and into autumn. Hardymount is a sight worth
seeing right up to late autumn.

When you arrive at the gate, you are met by a sea of flowers. It is a giddying sight –
swathes of lilac-coloured *Erysimum* 'Bowles Mauve', the perennial wallflower; tall,
purple, poisonous monkshood (*Aconitum*); yellow daisies; downy variegated mint;
pom-poms of blue agapanthus; rich plum scabious and penstemon vie with each
other for attention, and the visitor knows that this is going to be a great experience.

California tree poppies (*Romneya coulteri*), with big fried-egg flowers, and acanthus combine well alongside purple geranium, Chinese foxgloves and Persian shield
(*Strobilanthes dyerianus*). Loose runs of nasturtium are scattered in numbers reminiscent of Monet's garden at Giverney. They create an exuberant, loose feel and also tie
the beds together.

An old sundial sits between tall verbascum, peony and elegant Japanese anemone.
Next to these, rich red salvia and hellebores grow around espaliered apple trees. The
surrounding stone walls are lined with lilies and alliums. Big clumps of red-hot pokers
(*Kniphofia*) look great. This is a plant that can look a bit silly in ones and twos but
makes a strong banded run of colour when it is grown, as Mrs Reeves-Smyth grows it,
in masses. A ten-metre-long bed of roses, tradescantia and Welsh poppies (*Meconopsis cambrica*) mixes blue and yellow, and is a perfumed delight to walk along.

Grass paths lead between beds of herbs, sucha as lavender, mint, sage, sweet pea
and asparagus; beds which both look and smell good. Shovels stand in the vegetable
beds among beetroots, beans, potatoes, artichokes and leeks, ready to dig out lunch or
dinner at short notice.

Beside these a wisteria walk is further improved with an underplanting of foxgloves and peach-coloured hollyhocks.

Trellis, espaliered apples and the wisteria tunnel all create a pleasing division of
the space and structure in the walled garden. Each little area feels private and secluded. But the overall picture does not look contrived or 'designed'. Hardymount is
well cared for but not overly manicured, a relaxed country garden.

LEINSTER • COUNTY CARLOW

Rathvilly, County Carlow; Tel: +0503 61104 ▪ **Contact:** the Rathdonnell family ▪ **Open:** 10 May–end July, Sunday 2pm–6pm; by appointment only at all other times during the summer ▪ Groups and supervised children welcome ▪ **Entrance fee** donated to riding for the disabled and goes towards garden upkeep ▪ **Directions:** driving out of Rathvilly in the Hacketstown direction, at the end of the village take a sharp right. The garden is signposted from here.

A little cherub holds up a bird-bath in the garden at Lisnavagh.

Lisnavagh house and garden were designed in 1850 by the noted English architect Daniel Robertson, famous for his work in Powerscourt in Wicklow (*see* also Johnstown Castle, County Wexford, and Carrigglass Manor, County Longford). Over the years the gardens at Lisnavagh have been added to and subtracted from, most notably when half of the house was demolished in the 1950s because of the high cost of window taxes. The house seen today, although still a fine building, is only one wing of the original construction. Lady Jessica Rathdonnell is the garden's current guiding force. She began her gardening career when she moved to Lisnavagh, and in her hands the garden is being developed sensitively.

'I married the garden,' she says, not entirely joking. 'When I came to it there were eight gardeners working here. Now there is just me and one man to help.' This is a story one hears in big gardens all over the country.

The garden covers about ten acres and the visit starts close by the house with a line of topiarised yews that look like aliens. Nearby, mixed borders stand on low granite ledges. These are crammed with plants, both herbaceous and shrubby, including a Judas tree *(Cercis siliquastrum)*, and embothriums. Lady's mantle *(Alchemilla mollis)*, planted under a white-flowering *Hydrangea paniculata* 'Grandiflora', spills onto the path. Roses, sedum and clerodendrum, with delicate white flowers and red berries, also live on these ledges. The old kitchen flags, pulled up when the 1950s demolition took place, were put back into service as garden paving around the house and also in the spaces between the stuffed ledge beds.

The track begins to move out from the house, past a big cotoneaster and a drimys that was a gift from Mrs North of Altamont. The trees get bigger out here and include an impressive Wellingtonia *(Sequioadendron giganteum)*, and a good paulownia. Jessica Rathdonnell's knowledge of paulownias is well known and she has written on the subject in *Irish Garden* magazine. Young rhododendrons are scattered through this informal woodland, but the plant that commands attention is the tall eucryphia drenched in flower. Years ago, the writer Hubert Butler saw it and declared that it might just flower itself to death. Nearly two decades on it's still going strong.

On the edge of the garden, before the parkland begins, an arched yew walk that saw some years of neglect is now being restored. Close by, a rare tree from China, *Idesia polycarpa*, stands out, with red stems and big heart-shaped leaves.

The pool and rock garden is something of a surprise. This is a little walled garden safe from the deer and rabbits that the rest of the garden falls prey to from time to time. There is also a swimming pool. Unusually, the pool does not dominate as the rectangle of aqua-blue normally tends to. Instead it is set into a limestone-flagged courtyard and the eye is not drawn to the water but to a big rockbed behind it. Another distraction from the pool is the massive *Gunnera* or 'industrial rhubarb', with leaves two metres across. Along the ground, shiny bergenia leaves and thyme soften the lines of stone by the pool. Irises, and any seedlings that care to, are allowed to take over whatever small crevice they find. In the corner is another great specimen of clerodendrum with bright, white flowers. One could happily lock the gates behind and just move into this little garden.

SHEAN GARDEN

Garryhill, County Carlow; Tel: +0503 57652 ▪ **Contact:** Mrs Emily Smyth ▪ **Open:** May–June, Sundays, 2pm–6pm; groups by appointment only ▪ **Entrance fee** donated to charity and goes towards garden upkeep ▪ Supervised children welcome ▪ Teas may be arranged for groups, by appointment only ▪ **Directions:** from Fenagh take the Borris Road and at the second crossroads turn left by Donoghue's Plant Hire. Then turn left at the Y-junction and take the next left. The house is third on the right.

The Smyth family has lived in this farmhouse for 400 years but, as with many farmhouses, the garden is young, created by the current Mrs Smyth. Gardens were not always at the top of the agenda of hard-worked farmers' wives in the past. The one-acre plot is an informal country garden, divided into different compartments by hedges, small trees and flowering shrubs. Mrs Smyth, like many gardeners, works the place herself and would not welcome help. She likes to be in control of new seedlings and whatever developments might sprout up. Helpers tend not to differentiate between weeds and wanted seedlings.

There are some pretty features in Shean garden, like a little bed of irises around a small statue. Emily Smyth picks out the colour in a dusty blue ceanothus growing by the house by using a similar shade of blue pot for her violas and hypericum. She is not a snobbish gardener and just likes plants that look good, regardless of their rarity: purple-fringed mimosa leaves marry well with less exalted, lavender-coloured buddleia flowers. *Clematis tangutica,* with flowers like yellow fairy caps, shares a raised granite bed at the side of the house with a yellow dahlia and a sweet pepper bush. Yellow *Paeonia lutea* and leptospermum flank the pergola near the house.

The garden is full of great standing stones that were turned up by farmers ploughing in the adjoining fields. With the help of family and neighbours, Emily placed the granite stones around the garden, where they look ancient and monumental. Down the drive, a collection of shrub and rugosa roses, like *Rosa* 'Roseraie de l'Haÿ', have been grown for their tough habit and good hips. The snowbell tree (*Styrax japonica*), eucalyptus and a tulip tree (*Liriodendron tulipifera*) are sited among these and beside more standing stones, in an attractive display that will become better as the trees grow and begin to dominate the stones.

Glynn, County Carlow; Tel: +051 424550 ▪ **Contact:** Mrs Brigid Ryan ▪ **Open:** all year, every day ▪ **No entrance fee** ▪ Children welcome but must be supervised due to the abundance of water ▪ **Special features:** teas may be booked by prior arrangement ▪ **Directions:** take the New Ross Road (R729) from Borris and go straight through Glynn. About 200m from the church on the Borris side is the downhill gateway to The Three Bridges, on the left-hand side.

The Ryans's eccentric garden is set on the fast-moving River Aughavaun and the ancient Three Bridges bridge that gives the garden its name. The bridge is the meeting place of three townlands and three counties: Waterford, Kilkenny and Carlow. The garden is built around and based on the water. The Three Bridges is on the site of an old bog which was 'too wet even for the animals,' says Mrs Ryan, whose friends and family thought the land completely impossible to use for anything, let alone a home and garden. Bravely, the Ryans took the site on, working all the hours God gave, and they have produced a pretty river garden.

The site is long and narrow, sloping down to the river. Beds full of tobacco plant (*Nicotiana*) and arum lilies are cut randomly into the lawn between a network of paths and steps, drops and ledges, down to the river. Nicotiana is Mrs Ryan's favourite flower. She grows it in a variety of colours and it returns the compliment by scenting almost the whole garden with sherbet perfume at the height of the summer. Runs of cotoneaster, pittosporum and philadelphus march down the hill to the water. There are small stone-edged beds of borage, love-lies-bleeding (*Dicentra*) and purple and blue clary sage (*Salvia sclarea*), so-called because of its alleged abilities to repair damaged eyesight. More tobacco plants, in various pinks, whites and pale-greens, are scattered through the other flowers.

The river is Mrs Ryan's pride and joy and, as a bonus, is filled with brown trout. She enjoys the fish as a spectator sport from the comfort of a grassy slope planted up with euonymus and periwinkle (*Vinca minor*). An old French rambler, *Rosa* 'Albertine', grows over a trellis and bench by the water. By the bridge a big hebe, knotted through another pink rambler, *Rosa* 'Dorothy Perkins', tumbles down to the river, and a large bottlebrush shrub (*Callistemon*) enjoys having its feet in the water.

On the other side of the river are banks of mop-head hydrangea, spring bulbs and dahlias, growing around large outcrops of rock. Mrs Ryan is particularly proud of the dahlias. They are very old and came from Borris House close by. The house is long gone but the dahlias continue to enjoy the high life in this lovely spot.

Tobinstown House, Tullow, County Carlow; Tel: +0503 51233 ▪ **Contact:** Nora Burgess ▪ **Open:** May and June, Sundays and bank holidays, 2pm–6pm; by appointment only at all other times ▪ **Entrance fee** donated to charity and goes towards garden upkeep ▪ **Special features:** iris nursery and fancy fowl collection ▪ **Directions:** situated on the R727 between Carlow and Hacketstown, near Tobinstown Cross (signposted).

Nora Burgess is a charming woman who works a farmhouse garden in the middle of the family farm. The garden is set at the top of a drive, past a big field of cows, with views clear across County Carlow to the Wicklow Mountains. Unusually for a farm-house garden, it dates a long way back – to the 1860s.

At the entrance to the garden is a welcoming bed of clove-scented pinks (*Dianthus*), roses and minuscule pink cyclamen, under hydrangea and variegated *Euonymus fortunei* 'Silver Queen'. The house itself is smothered in Boston ivy (*Parthenocissus tricuspidata*) creeping out onto the gravel, with a splayed creeping rosemary (*Rosmarinus officinalis* 'Prostratus') at the base, also snaking onto the drive.

Nora adores irises, and a dedicated bearded iris bed stands on its own – a rectangular island in the middle of the lawn. She also breeds them for sale (*see* Nurseries and Garden Centres, p.13).

Four topiarised yew bushes, in the shape of spaceships or flying saucers, dominate the lawn. These are similar to the yew 'creatures' in Lisnavagh a few kilometres away. Nora's yews date back to the beginnings of the garden, 150 years ago.

A gravel path runs around the lawn, bordered by a little granite rockery. Beside the path a dome of clipped beech on a granite perch reaches seven metres. This was once a standard beech tree, but it fell seventy years ago and the stump sprouted. So the family started clipping, it kept growing and they kept shaping. It's a handsome object lesson in what can happen if one waits before taking a decision to clear up after a loss or disaster in the garden. This great tree sits into and lords it over a mixed bed, including two old roses, 'Mme Alfred Carrière' and 'Chapeau de Napoléon', one creamy white, the other rich dolly-mixture pink, both sweet and heavily scented.

This garden is informal and cottagey, but Nora says she is becoming more formal as time goes on. In fact, the latest area in the garden includes quite an element of formality. The new garden is reached by a stone-stepped slope through the trees, past monkshood (*Aconitum*) and hellebores, by a little fenced paddock of sheep.

Down here is a small garden, quite invisible from the rest of the garden. This came about due to a universal problem: a gardener's inability to say 'no' to a new plant. 'I had far too many plants. So this little flower garden takes up the extra,' Nora explains. The central focus is a summerhouse employing the old windows from the Shillelagh Workhouse. Pink and plum are the predominant colours in the planting: pink and ruby-coloured penstemon, cosmos and roses, all looking very pretty together.

Here too is the formality mentioned earlier, the entrance guarded by two white variegated *Pittosporum tenuifolium* 'Irene Paterson'. A pine standing among the tidy rows of sweet pea, lettuce and pansy was allowed to stay, to make sure the formality didn't become too formal. The paths in the little garden are made of blonde granite sand that brightens the area and throws up a soft light.

Tobinstown is another garden with a collection of swanky hens and ducks – Peking Bantams, little white Call ducks and, most important to the garden, black Cayuga ducks that Nora is convinced eat all her slugs right up until July, when they are so fat that they simply cannot fit any more. Many gardeners can only dream of being slug-free until July, so they might benefit from Nora Burgess's secret to successful pest control – a pair of ducks!

GARDENING CLUBS AND SOCIETIES

CARLOW FLOWER CLUB

Contact: Margaret Collins (Secretary), Eastwood, Bagenalstown, County Carlow.

Meets on the last Tuesday of the month, from September onwards. Club activities include garden talks, demonstrations on growing plants and all aspects of flower arranging. Flower and plant shows are held annually and summer garden trips are organised. New members are always welcome. For details of the changing venues contact Margaret Collins.

TULLOW FLOWER AND GARDEN CLUB

Founded ten years ago, this club meets on the first Tuesday of the month at the Mount Wolsey Golf and Country Club, just outside Tullow. In June the meeting is held at a garden venue. No meetings are held in July and August. An annual trip is organised for May, usually within Ireland but occasionally to Britain. The Tullow club is active, with a good social side, and they always welcome new members. Go along to a meeting to find out more.

NURSERIES AND GARDEN CENTRES

ARBORETUM GARDEN CENTRE

Rathvinden, Leighlinbridge, County Carlow; Tel: +0503 21558.

ASHLAWN GARDEN CENTRE

Borris Road, Bagenalstown, County Carlow; Tel: +0503 21175.

NORA BURGESS IRISES

Tobinstown House, Tullow, County Carlow; Tel: +0503 51233.

Nora Burgess sells sixty varieties of bearded iris by mail order. Contact for list or visit by appointment only.

MORGAN'S GARDEN CENTRE

Green Road, Carlow, County Carlow; Tel: +0503 43092.

MAURICE O'NEILL BOX PLANTS

Ballon, County Carlow; Tel:+0503 59144. (Visit by appointment only.)

RATHWOOD HOME AND GARDEN CENTRE

Rath, Tullow, County Carlow; Tel: +0503 56285; website: www.rathwood.com

GARDEN ACCESSORIES

McCALL'S WOODWORKING LTD.

Rathvilly, County Carlow; Tel: +0503 61552; e-mail mccall@iol.ie

Garden furniture. Contact for brochure.

STONE DEVELOPMENTS LTD.

Old Leighlin, County Carlow; Tel: +0503 21227; e-mail: stonedev@ indigo.ie

Garden benches and tables, paving, ornaments, windowsills and pier caps.

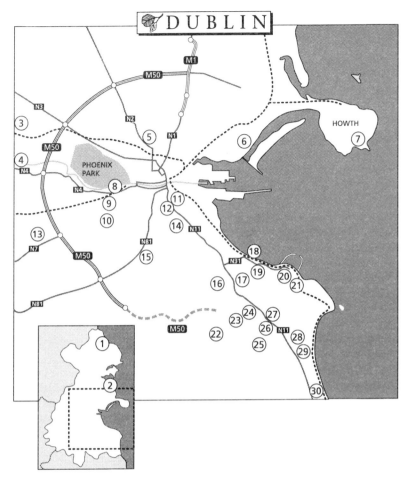

MAP KEY

1. Ardgillan Demesne
2. Talbot Botanic Gardens, Malahide Demesne
3. Beech Park
4. Primrose Hill
5. The National Botanic Gardens
6. St Anne's Park
7. Medina
8. War Memorial Gardens
9. Royal Hospital Kilmainham
10. Drimnagh Castle
11. St Stephen's Green
12. Iveagh Gardens
13. Kilmatead Gardens
14. The Dillon Garden
15. St Enda's Park and Pearse Museum

16. Airfield Gardens
17. Aurora
18. Deepwell
19. Fairfield Lodge
20. Kensington Lodge
21. Grasse Cottage
22. Glenasmole Lodge
23. Burton Hall
24. Rathmore
25. Fernhill
26. Knockcree
27. Shanganagh
28. Rathmichael Lodge
29. Springmount
30. Corke Lodge

COUNTY DUBLIN

Lying between two extended arms – Howth and Dalkey – and close to sea and mountains, Dublin enjoys a perfect setting. The city is a fairly compact, walkable place, which is just as well because it is becoming difficult to negotiate by car. Traffic clogs the road system from one end of the day to the other. Naturally, the capital is filled with touristy places to visit, like Trinity College for the Book of Kells, Guinness's brewery and Georgian squares that can be viewed from open-topped buses. There is a wealth of other great venues, such as the Irish Museum of Modern Art (IMMA) at the Royal Hospital, Kilmainham, the nearby Kilmainham Jail and the Phoenix Park, home to Dublin Zoo, Áras an Uachtaráin, herds of deer and polo grounds. Closer to the city centre is the Hugh Lane Gallery, the newly restored National Museum at Collins's Barracks on the quays, the exquisite, almost untouched Victorian Natural History Museum, the National Gallery, the Abbey and Gate theatres and the Casino in Marino.

The bars are glorious, varied and numerous, and there is a huge number of good restaurants scattered throughout the city. Apart from the vast Phoenix Park, there is a big network of smaller parks in the city and suburbs: St Anne's Park in Raheny with its rose gardens; St Stephen's Green, a much-loved, handsome park that dates back to the 1600s; and the National Botanic Gardens in Glasnevin, which will fill as much time as the visitor can give. A large number of private gardens are open to the public under the umbrella of the Dublin Garden Group and there are also plenty of individuals who open their gardens independently. Bear in mind when touring gardens within County Dublin to try to work visits in the opposite direction to the traffic – travel to the outskirts early in the day when the traffic is moving inwards, and vice versa.

AIRFIELD GARDENS

Airfield Trust, Kilmacud Road Upper, Dundrum, Dublin 14, County Dublin; Tel: +01 2984301; e-mail: airfield-trust@iol.ie ▪ **Contact:** Jimi Blake ▪ **Open:** Easter–September, Tuesday–Saturday, 11am–3pm (ring beforehand to check); groups by appointment only, tours can be arranged ▪ **Entrance fee** ▪ Supervised children welcome ▪ **Special features:** wildflower meadow; sheep and cattle herds; pet cemetery; honey and vegetables for sale ▪ **Directions:** travelling from Clonskeagh and the city centre via Goatstown, turn right from the Goatstown Road onto Taney Road at the Goat Grill pub and restaurant. Take the first left (Birches Lane) and go to the T-junction. Turn onto the upper Kilmacud Road and the entrance is the first gate on the right. From Stillorgan and the N11, turn onto the Kilmacud Road and pass St Benildus's College on the left. Airfield is also on the left.

Airfield was built as a small farm and cottage dwelling in the 1830s. In 1860 and again in 1913 it was extended to make a more comfortable house with a finer garden. However, the gardens went into decline in the 1950s. The city and suburbs began to wrap around the house, gardens and farm, turning it into an island of neglected green. In 1995 the Airfield Trust was set up to restore the place. A huge amount of work has been carried out over the past five years and the gardens have not only been restored but also expanded. They opened to the public for the first time in 1999.

The garden work is carried out by the enthusiastic Jimi Blake, whose dedication is admirable. The centrepiece at Airfield is the walled garden, which, after several years of work, once again includes big herbaceous borders, a pond, rose and herb gardens, as well as espaliered and wall-trained fruit trees. Hornbeam hedges were planted four years ago to divide the larger garden into the smaller rooms that now fill the walled area. Hornbeam is a good choice for hedging as it is fairly fast-growing and makes a tight deciduous barrier and backdrop.

The pond is filled with arum lilies and surrounded by buddleia, ceanothus, lavender and *Verbena bonariensis*. The herb garden contains all the usual culinary and medicinal herbs, like dill, rue, blue-spired Russian sage *(Perovskia)*, lovely, smelly curry plant and chives.

Big mixed borders, one of which faces southwest, are held in train by box hedges. Tipping out over the box are the most gorgeous frothy mounds of white phlox, *Rosa* 'Lady Hillingdon', *Rosa* 'Mme Isaac Pereire', *Rosa* 'Boule de Neige' and *Rosa gallica*; all great roses with terrific scents and exotic names.

Other fine plants are the echiums, one of which had been beheaded, fortuitously creating a mop-top shape. There are some great rarities, like *Acca sellowina,* an unusual shrub that has beautiful red-and-white edible flowers. Next door is an un-named thistle brought from Tibet by Seamus O'Brien, formerly of Beech Park (*see* County Dublin). Another fine plant is *Rehmannia elata,* with a pink flower like penstemon, that gives a good account of itself from June right up to August. The garden also boasts heavily flowering solanum, eupatorium and the Korean shrub *Tetradium daniellii*, which has fine white flowers, interesting fruit and a great shape.

Other features in the garden include a dry shade garden called Tot's garden, named for Laetitia Overend, one of the sisters who lived and worked the garden earlier in the twentieth century. A little pet cemetery sits in here, filled with tiny headstones which mark the resting places of various dogs, cats and newts belonging to the Overend sisters (*see* box, Pet Cemeteries, p.154). The greenhouse has been well restored to hold the fruits of Jimi Blake's own plant-collecting travels, particularly in Australia, from where he brought a *Melaleuca armillaris*, a more refined version of the ordinary bottlebrush plant (*Callistemon*).

Great work has been put into marking the millennium at Airfield – a hot border was planted and restoration work was carried out on the old orchard, rejuvenating the trees. A two-acre wildflower meadow was planted in conjunction with Sandro Caffolla of Design by Nature (*see* County Laois). Thirty-four varieties of wild flowers, including field scabious, camomile, cowslips, and lesser celandine, ox-eye daisies, mallow, hypericum and ragged robin, now flourish in the meadow. Because the field being used for the project is wood-edged and has a damp area and a dry, droughty spot, the variety of plants being sown is very wide – there are woodland plants, damp and shade-lovers as well as sun-worshippers.

Finally, a farm walk that includes the wildflower meadow has been created, leading past the sheep and the Jersey, Aberdeen Angus and shorthorn cattle.

Airfield is a fine countryside visit set well within the city boundaries. The peace and quiet are remarkable and it is with something of a shock that one hits the noisy Kilmacud Road outside the gate.

ARDGILLAN DEMESNE

Balbriggan, County Dublin; Tel: +01 8492342 ▪ **Contact:** Brenda Kenny ▪ **Open:** daily, November–January, 10am–5pm; February–March, 10am–6pm; April, 10am–7pm; May, 10am–8pm; June–August, 10am–9pm; September, 10am–8pm (subject to change, phone in advance) ▪ **No entrance fee**, tour charges ▪ Supervised children welcome; please note, dogs on leads ▪ **Special features:** tours of the gardens are given from June to August on Thursdays at 3.30pm, or at other times by appointment; garden museum; castle may be viewed (Tel: +01 8492212) ▪ Managed by Fingal County Council ▪ **Directions:** travelling north on the N1, take the turn off for Balrothery. The demesne is very well signposted from here.

The Reverend Robert Taylor built a fine country manor overlooking the Irish Sea at Ardgillan in north County Dublin in 1738. His descendants continued to live there until 1962. In the 1980s the house and 194 acres of parkland and gardens were taken over by the Parks Department of Fingal County Council. The formal gardens were restored in 1983 using the 1865 Ordnance Survey map of the demesne. The planting is chiefly of roses, with species and old varieties around the sides and climbers and ramblers on the pergolas and central walks.

The restored Victorian green-houses at Ardgillan Demesne in north County Dublin.

The Victorian greenhouses have been restored and house a big vine and trained peach. Unusual inner free-standing walls punctuate the two-acre walled garden. These are whitewashed and niched to attract the maximum amount of sun, and to allow air circulation behind the fruit trees. The shelter afforded by the walls and surrounding mature woodland renders the climate in the walled garden particularly soft. A tender specimen of *Dodonaea viscosa* 'Purpurea' has survived since 1992.

This garden houses an educationally laid out herb garden and some very pretty *potager* beds. The sheds are being rebuilt to house a garden museum. In addition, there is an Irish garden in development, where the aim is to display a collection of native plants – plants gathered or found here and those bred by Irish gardeners and collectors.

There are five miles of paths through the woods, parkland and gardens. Three features not to be missed are the yew walk, the lady's stairs and the ice house. The stairs is a quaint pedestrian footbridge which crosses the Balbriggan road and the Dublin– Belfast rail line, supposedly to allow ladies cross to the sea for bathing. It is, as you might expect, haunted by one of those ladies! The ice house was recently uncovered (*see* box on ice houses, below).

ICE HOUSES

Ice houses were subterranean storage rooms, set within the grounds of large country houses, and filled with ice. This was imported from abroad, usually from Norway, or collected from frozen lakes, rivers and ponds during the winter. The ice was cut into blocks and stored between layers of straw in these cool underground sheds or houses in order to provide cold storage for meat, other foods and drink for the household throughout the year.

ST ANNE'S PARK

Mount Prospect Avenue, Clontarf, Dublin 9, County Dublin; Tel: +01 8338898 ▪
Contact: Mr Mick Molloy ▪ **Open:** every day until dusk ▪ **No entrance fee** ▪
Please note, dogs on leads ▪ **Special features:** International Rose Trials in July; lectures; guided tours; rose clinics during the trials.

Covering 300 acres – almost half the size of the Phoenix Park – St Anne's is a huge suburban park. Previously owned by the Guinness family, today it is cared for by the City and run by the Parks Department of Dublin Corporation.

In the 1970s a man called Leslie Mitchell, of the Clontarf Horticultural Society, began the push to create a rose garden on a grand scale in St Anne's. The result is one of the finest gardens of its type on the island. The rose garden covers fourteen acres and holds over 25,000 rose bushes in hybrid teas, floribundas, patio and ground-cover varieties, together with old garden cultivars. Other interesting features at St Anne's include a walled garden with a quaint clock tower, a pond and herbaceous gardens, sunken gardens, rockeries, yew and chestnut walks and a millennium arboretum.

The sheer size of the park makes it problematic. As with many big parks, St Anne's is not a place to be visited alone. For great stretches the walks are isolated and out of sight of the main features, playing grounds and surrounding houses. Visit it in company and during the busier times of the day and year.

The International Rose Trials held in July are a good opportunity to enjoy the flowers. Guided tours, talks, lectures and clinics on rose care are given at this time of year by well-known gardeners, such as Gerry Daly.

AURORA

6 Stillorgan Park, Blackrock, County Dublin; Tel: +01 2889463 ▪ **Contact:** Deirdre Ryan ▪ **Open:** groups of six or more only, by appointment only; specified open days in aid of St John of God's in July (see local press for details) ▪ **Entrance fee** donated to charity ▪ **Special features:** teas can be booked by prior arrangement ▪ **Directions:** travelling south on the N11, turn left at the Blake's Cross junction in Stillorgan and go to a small roundabout. Take the left-hand slip road. Travel down Stillorgan Park for about 200 metres. The house and garden are on the right-hand side. *Note:* the house numbers on this road are erratic and hard to follow, so eyes peeled.

Mrs Ryan's is a perfect town garden and a model in how to garden a long, narrow site. She works it so that it blooms and presents a decent show from February right up to November. In grand-scale gardening it is possible to enjoy specific areas, like a spring garden, June border or an autumn garden. The size means that it is not necessary to affront the eyes with the straggly growth of the June border when it has gone over in September, and the spring garden can be ignored when the small bulbs that cheered up a dull February are hibernating in the summer. In a small garden, however, every part has to give a good account of itself all of the time because every part of the garden is being seen every day. Small-garden gardeners have to work harder and Deirdre Ryan has it down to a fine art.

Leading up the house and wrapped around a long, slim lawn are lines of flowering shrubs, some common and some special, as well as a herbaceous border that looks good at the end of October but which also carries plenty of bulbs for the spring. The colours are mainly light and pale: white acanthus and aquilegia, pink phormium, silver artemisia and a silver, velvety-textured weeping pear. Pruning the pear gives extra space underneath for ground planting. White phlox runs through the border at several points. Mrs Ryan loves phlox. A ceanothus on its second flowering in late October sits behind a red acer and the fried-egg flowers of the California tree poppy (*Romneya coulteri*). *Rosa* 'Aloha', well-trained up an arch, flowers from May to the end of October. This is a particularly good plant that flowers in a great variation of pink shades over each bloom's life. Mrs Ryan recommends it for gardeners with allergies or aversions to pesticides or herbicides because it is resistant and doesn't need spraying.

Yellow coreopsis and variegated pittosporum complement each other, as does a great pampas (that she had to take an axe to when it got too big) looming over *Papaver* 'Patty's Plum'. A pink geranium noses through the gold-green leaves of *Hellebore argutifolius*. Geranium is a useful plant to grow through small shrubs or other herbaceous plants whose own flowers arrive at a different time of the year.

In the back garden an array of pots gather around the back door as though they are about to storm the house. Agave, grasses, box, a red acer and steely-white phormium are just a few of the pots' residents.

The space around the door gets smaller and smaller as helichrysum, fuchsia, a pink pelargonium that grows like a tree up the wall, crinodendron and *Abutilon megapotamicum* encroach. The pelargonium is actually allowed to stay out over the winter in this very mild, sheltered spot. A little farther out a peach rose called 'Breath of Life' grows up through a purple beech in a clever colour combination.

Sitting in the centre of the back garden is a pond, circled by paths of rough granite slabs and plantings of ferns and a showy, white-veined thistle. Also here are masses of *Primula denticulata*, ligularia and Moroccan broom. Above the pond, a plum tree that was recently pruned hard has *Clematis* 'Marjorie' growing through it. Sit on a little rough granite bench under the tree and you can study the knot of tulips, fritillarias and snowdrops that bloom in springtime.

Mrs Ryan employs the principle of growing one tree that you really like until it reaches the maximum height and size you want, then grubbing it out, chopping it down and replacing it with another favourite. She believes in trying new things – a variegated fatsia, which everyone told her wouldn't survive, is doing well in her busy garden. So too is a big mass of twining campsis, *Clematis armandii*, passion flower and 'New Dawn' roses, which all climb up a pergola by the house in an impossible-looking but handsome tangle. The campsis had been in the ground for nineteen years before it started flowering, four years ago. Patience paid off.

BEECH PARK

Clonsilla, County Dublin ※ **Contact:** Cathy Burke; Tel: 086 8522886 ※ **Open:** Easter–September, Sunday–Tuesday, 2pm–5.30pm; at other times telephone for a booking; groups by appointment only ※ **Entrance fee** ※ **Special features:** the largest private collection of herbaceous plants in the country ※ **Directions:** travelling from Clonee or Blanchardstown, go over the railway crossing in Clonsilla. Look for a new gate directly to the right (if closed please follow the wall until you reach the next gate).

Beech Park is, without doubt, one of the most famous private gardens in the country. For most of the twentieth century it was lived in by the renowned Shackleton gardening family, cousins of Sir Ernest Shackleton, the Arctic explorer.

A walled garden in Beech Park can be traced back to 1740. Until the 1940s it comprised of vegetable and fruit patches edged in box. But then David Shackleton put his mark on the garden, pulling out the box hedges and replanting the one-and-a-half-acre garden completely to accommodate his collections of alpine and southern hemisphere plants, rare dwarf trees and shrubs. The garden was passed on to Jonathan and Daphne Shackleton, who continued the work, adding vast numbers of herbaceous plants to the collection. At the height of its fame the garden held over 4,000 different varieties of plants.

The Shackletons have now moved on to start a new garden (*see* Lake View Gardens, County Cavan). In the meantime the renowned Clonsilla garden marches on, in the hands of new owners who are continuing the gardening tradition. A great number of the original plants are still to be found in the garden and the collection is being added to all the time.

Two raised beds – one of peat and loam for acid-loving plants, the other with grit and a coarse structure for alpines – considerably increase the range of plants that can be grown in Beech Park. It is a beautiful garden, laid out in a grid of straight, crossing paths between deep beds of tall herbaceous plants, shrubs and small trees. But it is first and foremost a collection and a collector's paradise, filled with unusual, rare and special plants.

Seamus O'Brien worked the garden between 1997 and 2000, having come from the glorious subtropical garden of Glanleam in County Kerry. He was involved in collecting expeditions to Tibet and China. The Tibetan trip was made specifically to collect seed for Beech Park.

Beech Park holds the largest private collection of herbaceous plants in the country and the fourth largest in these islands, according to the famous English gardener Graham Stuart Thomas. The collection includes many rare plants not even in the *Plant Finder*. The garden also houses the national collection of *Dierama* (angel's fishing rod), with *Dierama pulcherrimum* 'Blackbird', a gift from noted gardener Helen Dillon (*see* the Dillon Garden, County Dublin), the Irish *Dierama* 'Puck' and a new variety they hope to name after Beech Park. The largest collection of oriental poppies in the country also lives here. The celmisia collection is in the process of being restored. Furthermore, there are collections of herbaceous lobelias, hellebores, and a sizeable collection of snowdrops, including *Galanthus* 'David Shackleton', which was raised by the famous man. There are forty types of phlox in the garden, some from the great gardens and some found by Shackleton over the years in cottage gardens around the country.

There is a concentration on old Irish cultivars, with plants like *Agapanthus* 'Lady Moore', *Elaeagnus* 'Quick Silver', sea-holly (*Eryngium alpium* 'Slieve Donard') and a *Chaenomeles* (Japanese flowering quince), which has been named for Mrs Corona North of Altamont (*see* County Carlow). A specimen of the Trinity College betula, with its lovely washed bark, is also found here. The place is full of plants named for the garden, like *Penstemon* 'Beech Park', raised by Shackleton in the 1960s, and *Helianthemum* 'Beech Park'. *Omphalodes luciliae*, a very hard plant to grow, was brought to Beech Park by David Shackleton.

A multi-branched acer has been attractively grazed down by cattle to a lovely shape. This is not, however, a recommendation to let cattle loose on young trees! The results are more likely to be a stump and tears than this pretty shape. A rare old rose called 'Fortune's Double Yellow', rediscovered only recently in a garden called St Catherine's in Celbridge, County Kildare, was brought to Beech Park, where it was propagated in the greenhouse and now grows vigorously. This glasshouse is being rebuilt and restored around the rose.

The north border, at eight metres deep, is probably one of the deepest in the country. This is shaded and damp and gets only a meagre ration of sun. Here they grow Himalayan poppies as well as primulas collected on the Tibetan trip, like *Primula alpicola var.* 'Luna', massive *Hosta sieboldiana* with leaves one metre long, ligularia and astilbe. I love the deep violet-coloured *Primula florindae,* introduced in 1924.

The tall spikes of *Delphinium* 'Alice Artindale' have grown here for a long time and *Geranium pratense* grows huge in its double form beside an onopordum that shoots four metres into the sky. Deep under the canopy in the north border a *Dicksonia antarctica* nestles in the shade. This was originally a seedling from Glanleam (*see* County Kerry).

There are hardy orchids, rare ferns, the pink, wild form of *Rosa moyesii* and sultry, dark-stemmed *Anemone rivularis*, seeding itself into every available space.

On the west wall plums and greengages are grown. The east wall holds pears. Peaches enjoy the warm, brick south wall and on the north plums manage nicely. A ginkgo that was planted in the 1920s over a well looks as though it is floating over the water.

Looking back to the many bleak newspaper articles lamenting the dreadful loss of a great Irish garden when the Shackletons moved on in the mid-1990s, it is satisfying to see that news of the demise was greatly exaggerated. Beech Park is a garden with a future as well as a past. It continues to be a genuinely good-looking garden, well laid out, handsome and filled with great plants.

BURTON HALL

Sandyford Industrial Estate, Sandyford, County Dublin; Tel: +01 2955888/087 2340068; e-mail: burtonhg@iot.ie ✳ **Contact:** Berna Purcell ✳ **Open:** 1 May–November, every Wednesday, 2pm–5pm; by appointment only at any other time; an open Saturday is also held in May (ring in advance for details); groups by appointment only ✳ **Entrance fee** ✳ Supervised children welcome ✳ **Special features:** plants for sale Monday–Friday, 10am–4pm; teas may be arranged for groups; educational courses ✳ Managed by the Hospitaller Order of St John of God ✳ **Directions:** set in the middle of Sandyford Industrial Estate. It can be accessed from Brewery Road roundabout, near the entrance to Leopardstown Race Course.

Burton Hall is a two-acre walled garden that somehow managed to avoid being flattened by its overbearing commercial surroundings. This is an extraordinary garden to find in the middle of the offices and factories of an industrial estate. Having seen long years of neglect, the garden is very much in the process of restoration and work is being carried out on both the ornamental and kitchen gardens within the walls. Following plans drawn up in 1909, the Edwardian garden is being faithfully reworked. This includes restoration of the old vine and peach houses.

Burton Hall is a pleasant garden. Wide paths cut through herbaceous borders, with mad mixes of colour provided by dierama, phlox, lilies, dianthus, the red climber lobster claw (*Clianthus puniceus* 'Roseus') and tradescantia, all backed by restored bay hedges with a strong, tangy scent. The yew and box hedges are also being rejuvenated.

Fruit trees are being trained over and along wide metal arches in espaliers and tunnels. These have been fairly recently planted and provide a good lesson in training techniques – spacing plants, tying in and encouraging the desired tree shape, as well as spacing and dimensions in constructing arches and tunnels.

Central to Burton Hall is the double penstemon walk. The penstemons are the chief feature of the garden and over 100 varieties are grown, interspersed with lavender. The combination makes a very colourful and attractive low border. Varieties of the penstemon seen in this bed can be bought from the nursery, along with other plants from the garden.

The St John of God order runs the garden as a sheltered training project, where courses in gardening are given and teachers and students work the garden together.

/22887
/

Woodbrook, Shankill, County Dublin ▪ **Contact:** the Dublin Garden Group, c/o John S Bourke, Fairfield Lodge, Monkstown Avenue, County Dublin; Tel: +01 2803912; e-mail: jsb@indigo.ie; or Shirley Beatty, Tel: +01 2955884 ▪ **Open:** groups only by appointment ▪ **Entrance fee** ▪ **Special features:** historic villa; architectural follies ▪ **Directions:** provided on confirmation of appointment.

Idiosyncratic is the word that comes to mind to describe the gardens at Corke Lodge. There was an arboretum here when Mr Cochrane, its current owner, took the garden in hand back in the late 1980s. The house, or villa, was built in the 1840s, one of many properties owned by the wealthiest widow in Ireland, Louisa Magan. She built a seaside villa with a Greek revival façade, surrounded by a romantic Gothic garden and woodland filled with cedar of Lebanon, evergreen oak and a cork tree grown because it reminded her of an olive tree. Louisa passed the house and garden on to her daughter, Georgina, whose sad life was said to be Dickens's inspiration for Miss Havesham in *Great Expectations*.

The house eventually ended up in the Cochrane family at the beginning of the 1900s and Alfred Cochrane redesigned the garden in the mid-1980s. He is a designer and his eye is very much in evidence throughout the garden. It is refreshing to see a place with its own particular style and this is one of a small band of gardens with a clear signature written right across it. The two-acre grounds are strewn with architectural remnants, oddments and loose ends.

The famous cork oak tree (*Quercus suber*), the oldest in the country, has a wonderfully gnarled, strange bark and looks like something from a willow-pattern plate. Whatever about its resemblance to an olive tree, it is certainly earning its keep, underplanted with the lime-coloured bracts of euphorbia. The space around the tree has been cleared effectively so that, like a fine piece of statuary, it can be seen from all angles.

A series of elliptical arches, architectural jokes, follies, ruins, half arches and mullions stand on an apron of gravel, interplanted with young eucalyptus, artemisia, fascicularia, bamboo and gardener's garters (*Phalasis arundinacea*). A rose is allowed to climb lightly through one of the arches. This is all seen through an avenue of cordylines that marches out from the house, via a little opening in the lawn, walled by low box plants. Cordylines make an unusual, well-structured, interesting and fairly fast-growing avenue, and they endear themselves further by taking up a minimal amount of space and casting very little shade.

To the side of the lawn and edging the woods are Portugal laurel (*Prunus lusitanica*), hydrangea, fuchsia, purple beech, maple, cherry, hoheria and *Betula utilis*. A little walk of creamy pampas grass is held back by a low castellated bridge leading into the woods. A huge stone arch frames the view and tugs the walker in the opposite direction. In the woods the gardening is done with a light touch. Between small openings and clearings there are mixed combinations of conifers and deciduous trees and, underneath, ferns, tree ferns and holly.

A grove of young myrtles has been planted by the house, near an island of tall mimosa, white variegated phormium, yellow abutilon and peach-coloured roses. *Allées* lead from the house through stone sentries to another stone arch folly lightly covered in ivy.

Box clipped into half circles holds back tree ferns (*Dicksonia antarctica*), grasses, stag's horn schumach, more pampas, bamboo and eucalyptus, regularly chopped or pollarded for better foliage. All of these elements are pulled together by a laurel hedge.

The garden doesn't depend on flowers. There are only occasional blooms – dots of geranium, hydrangea, pulmonaria, some roses and delicate, small myrtle flowers. It is rather a restful, cool, masculine garden in which great restraint has been shown in the marrying of an old garden with contemporary ideas.

DEEPWELL

Blackrock, County Dublin; Tel: +01 2887407 ▪ **Contact:** Ciara Gallagher ▪ **Open:** for a selected number of days in January, May, June and September, 9am–1pm; all visitors must phone ahead for an appointment; telephone for annual opening hours ▪ **Entrance fee** ▪ **Directions:** will be provided on confirmation of booking.

Deepwell is set in the middle of Blackrock, with tremendous views over Dublin Bay and across to Howth Head. It is a pleasant surprise to find such a wonderful formal garden right beside the town centre. The house was built back in 1810, but was substantially changed and renovated in the 1840s. The gardens as they stand today are a recent creation, going back only to 1995. The planting was carried out by Helen Dillon, with the overall design by Mitchell and Associates. Deepwell is formal, smart and restrained, but good flowers counteract the restraint, providing heavenly scents and big frothy gushes of flower and colour.

A view from the house at Deepwell, looking out over the formal garden and temple and beyond to Dublin Bay.

The garden falls down from the elaborate house and out toward the sea in runs of ceanothus with dusty blue pom-pom flowers, complemented by lavender spikes. Placed at intervals down the steps are pots of white Paris daisies underplanted with petunia and parsley, unusual in purely decorative planting, but so effective it should be used more as an ornamental. At the bottom of this drop, the parterre is defined and held in with a double backing of teak trellis and violet-flowered buddleia; a good combination of smart and loose. The roses in the beds are meringue-white 'Margaret Merrill' and pink 'Natalie Nypels', two prim ladies and well suited to each other. The other planting is simple and made up of white Japanese anemone, bluey-silver perovskia, big asters, catmint and sea lavender, which has a great mass of thread-thin wiry stems after flowering.

A cool, minimalist central pond and fountain stand in front of a small temple, the walls of which are softened by acanthus and *Ceanothus arboreus* 'Trewithen Blue'. The temple looks back over the garden and up toward the house, centring on the big run of steps. A late-flowering *Clematis recta* climbs over the house, with more creeping campanula under it.

Where the garden borders the sea there are some fine small trees, including a *Robinia pseudoacacia* and corokia, fronted by lamb's ears (*Stachys byzantina*) and polygonum sprawling comfortably onto the gravel. The planting is not permitted to go too wild or tall however, as the sea view is crucial to the look of the garden.

By the tennis court is a mixed bed filled with roses, canna lilies, hollyhocks and herbaceous clematis grown over tree stumps. Artichoke, echium and brilliant little Californian poppies all jumble together in happy chaos.

A golden aggregate in the paths matches the ochre colour of the house and picks up even the smallest drop of sun, lighting up the garden on a dull day. To one side of the house is a little terraced herb garden with beds of Welsh onions, rocket, nasturtium, vines and big pots of fragrant jasmine and nicotiana. To the other, around a pool, are masses of *Rosa* 'New Dawn', underplanted by Corsican campanula and a good acer planted on a bank of ivy and spring bulbs. The wall that holds up the bank is overrun with cotoneaster, pennyroyal and more ivy.

Out to the side of the garden is a fine grove of mature trees – beech and birch, with splashes of honesty and cyclamen beneath, alongside hellebores, euphorbia and lychnis.

THE DILLON GARDEN

45 Sandford Road, Ranelagh, Dublin 6; Tel: +01 4971308 ※ **Contact:** Helen and Val Dillon ※ **Open:** March, July and August, every day, 2pm–6pm; April–June and September, Sunday only, 2pm–6pm ※ **Entrance fee** ※ **Special features:** teas may be arranged for groups; member of the Dublin Garden Group ※ **Directions:** signposted off Sandford Road and situated by the church at the intersection between Sandford and Marlborough Roads.

It is hard to know where to start with the Dillon garden. The word 'shrine' might hit the mark. This is a place of pilgrimage for gardeners the country over, not a small number of whom feel a favourable comparison between a plant in their garden and a specimen in Dillon's to be an achievement worthy of medals and one that should be pointed out at every opportunity. Set in town in a not-too-huge space, it is a garden that fools the amateur into believing that they can imitate and replicate parts of it. The garden has featured regularly on RTÉ television's 'Garden Show', as Helen praises hellebores or old-fashioned roses, using her own exquisite specimens to illustrate her point to a salivating audience. So garden visitors are engaged by it in a way they never are by the giants like Powerscourt, Ilnacullin or Mount Stewart.

Once you have passed through the front, paved garden of stone slabs, scatterings of Shirley poppies, irises, sparse but handsome planting and the most wonderful 'pruned up' lollipop of holly (*see* box, Pruning Up, opposite), the main garden is reached through a gate, past bins full of the most desirable compost and leaf mulch. Visitors who have got the gardening bug bad can be seen putting a hand into these impressive bins to sift some of the lovely brown mould through their fingers. They know this is 'The Right Stuff'.

One of the most photographed and well-known vistas in Irish gardening for some time now has been the Dillons's perfect rectangle of lawn, guarded by two sphinxes and reached by a set of old stone steps. It was beloved of lawn-lovers the country over – and now it is gone. The words 'shock' and 'horror' come to mind, but Helen Dillon is nothing if not tasteful. She has replaced the gorgeous turf with a perfect, formal, cascading canal of water. Filling perfectly the rectangle that the lawn once inhabited, the canal is thirty metres long and made up of five stretches of water, divided by three cascades. A minimalist, perfect circle of unadorned water that previously stood at the top of the lawn now acts as the dot on this long letter 'i'. Helen is delighted with the whole affair and says with merriment that, 'Everyone over fifty hates it and everyone under fifty loves it.' She can in no way account for the opinion divide, but is highly amused by it.

PRUNING UP

Pruning up is a technique of shaping a shrub or small tree so that it suits the garden's requirements rather than its own. In essence it is a tortuous practice, like bonsai, that involves surgery and manipulation. It is sometimes called arborising.

Pruning up, as seen in Helen Dillon's garden, is done for several reasons, one of which is to free up soil beneath trees, giving a whole new area for shade-loving woodland plants, like spring bulbs, anemones, aconites, cyclamen, ferns, primulas, ivies and some violas.

To prune up a shrub, start by getting right into the middle of the shrub and examining all the stems to ascertain which are the strong, well-shaped limbs that will give an attractive, well-spread canopy. Once you have decided on the trunks to be maintained, the others can be cut away. Do this cleanly, using a sharp saw. Be careful to cut level with the ground or close in to the trunk.

Some of the more suitable shrubs for pruning up are lilac, viburnum, holly and pyracantha. But it is also worth trying on any tree or shrub that is getting too heavy and looks as though it might need to be taken out altogether. In a case like this, you have nothing to lose and might gain a useful feature in the garden.

The canal is flanked by two perfect flowerbeds: one is composed of blues, mauves and whites, with goat's rue, tons of campanula, delphiniums, asters, viola, clematis grown as ground creepers and roses. The other contains the vivid reds, oranges, yellows and wines of lobelia, French honeysuckle (*Hedysarum coronarium*), dahlia, cannas, cimicifuga, red-hot pokers (*Kniphofia*), heuchera, the Maltese Cross lychnis and berberis.

The two central beds can be viewed from different perspectives from the paths running behind them and bordered by beds of celmisias, dactylorhiza orchids and arisaema, trilliums and hostas. Poppies in all shades spring up through everything at the height of summer, dotting the place with every conceivable shade of dirty-pink, plum and shell. Other plants that sneak in everywhere are the violas and pansies.

The surrounding stone walls drip with a range of climbers behind good shrubs – old tea roses, a fine azara, tree peonies, potato vine (*Solanum crispum*) and more varieties of clematis.

The back of the house is covered with a huge ceanothus that looks great from the end of the garden. At the wall base there are troughs full of white petunias, trained box, argyranthemum and helichrysum, as well as alpines. Pots of annuals pour into each other like old-fashioned champagne-glass fountains.

Fine statuary, little paths in and around beds of handsome shrubs, the best garden flowers and great 'trained up' small trees that allow more plants to be squashed in underneath are all features of the flower garden. Every plant earns its keep and its spot here; all are healthy and well-tended. Trellises and pergolas, arches and walks for clematis, rose and sweet pea lead in and out of the different garden rooms. Tall foxgloves grow happily in the shade under the arches. There are alpine beds and a cold house to hold the frost-tolerant but damp-hating alpine plants, which suffer miserably in rot-inducing Irish weather.

The Dillon garden is like a box of chocolates without the unloved coconut creams; one of the best gardens in the country, worked by one of the most talented gardening couples, who are willing and happy to explain and discuss their methods with visitors. Helen Dillon, who can be seen walking around with an ever-present weed bucket, is quick to give information as valuable as gold dust to less successful gardeners.

DRIMNAGH CASTLE

The Long Mile Road, Drimnagh, Dublin 12, County Dublin; Tel: +01 4502530 ▪ **Contact:** Amanda Wilton ▪ **Open:** April–September, Wednesday, Saturday and Sunday, 12pm–5pm; October–March, Sundays, 12pm–5pm; other times by appointment only; guided tours can be arranged ▪ **Entrance fee** (castle and garden) ▪ Supervised children welcome; please note, guide dogs only ▪ **Special features:** restored Norman castle with flooded moat ▪ **Directions:** travelling on the Long Mile Road toward the city centre, Drimnagh Castle is on the left behind the Christian Brothers' school and is well signposted.

Drimnagh Castle and its newly restored formal seventeenth-century herb and box garden.

Drimnagh Castle, situated incongruously on the traffic-clogged Long Mile Road, was, until 1954, one of the oldest continually inhabited castles in Ireland. It is a magnificent example of a feudal stronghold; the only castle in the country still surrounded by a flooded moat. These days the moat is filled with fish – a bit disappointing to children scanning the water for crocodiles!

The garden is small and formal, arranged in a seventeenth-century layout. One of the finest features is the tidy, tight box hedging. This is overlooked by clipped yew, mop-head laurels and an *allée* of hornbeam. The beds have recently been replanted with herbs in simple block patterns. If you walk through the garden on a warm day the scents of lavender, sage, dill, artemisia, chives, thyme and rosemary waft in and out of each other in a clean, sharp, herby knot of smells. This is a particularly popular style of gardening at the moment, and anyone planning a herb garden should bring a camera and notebook. The whole project is being run by the admirable Drimnagh Castle Restoration Project. Denise Dunne of the Herb Garden in Forde-de-Fyne advised on the herb plans (*see* Twenty Best Nurseries in the appendices).

ST ENDA'S PARK AND PEARSE MUSEUM

Sarah Curran Road, Rathfarnham, Dublin 16; Tel: +01 4934208; Fax: +01 4936120 ▧ **Contact:** the Administrator ▧ **Open:** November–January, daily, 10am–4.30pm; February–March, 10am–5.30pm; April–September, 10am–7pm; May–August, 10am–8pm; October, 10am–7pm ▧ **No entrance fee** ▧ Dogs on leads permitted in the grounds, but not permitted within the walled garden ▧ **Special features:** Pearse Museum; nature trail and study centre; concerts during summer months; tearooms open May–September, daily; February–April and October, weekends only ▧ Member of Dúchas ▧ **Directions:** travelling up Grange Road, turn right after the Esso station on the right-hand side onto Sarah Curran Road. The park is signposted.

The park surrounding the Pearse Museum in Rathfarnham is a great suburban park. The playing fields are well used. Dog-walkers, groups of children playing and joggers busily exercising populate the grounds. St Enda's is an attractive place that feels safe and open.

Within the park, and attached to the house that Patrick Pearse used for his innovative and famous boys' school in the early years of the twentieth century, is a fine walled garden. The garden can be seen first from a clematis-draped parapet that runs out in a semicircle from the side of the classically proportioned granite house. Tall monkey puzzle and sweet chestnut trees and an initial glimpse of a yew walk are the first sights to greet the visitor. Climbing down the steps past knots of periwinkle (*Vinca*), go through the iron gate in the wall to get into the garden. The path runs past a long, deep, informal bed basking in the sun against the house wall. An auctioneer might describe this bed as 'smart-cottagey'. It is a real cracker. Big mounds of pink, apple-scented rock rose (*Cistus*) make rounded cushions beside the spiky, fire-red *Crocosmia* 'Lucifer' and endless sprawls of hardy geraniums. Pale, papery astrantia flowers are followed up by brasher, strong purple asters, and shrub rose blooms give way to round, fat, orange hips for the later summer.

At the back of the bed, and sometimes, interestingly, toward the front, are tall plume poppies and steely-blue echinops. Behind all this a huge Boston ivy (*Parthenocissus tricuspidata*) threads its way up the house wall. This bed *looks* as though it minds itself; all informal and relaxed. Unfortunately no such thing exists. In reality, enormous numbers of good gardening hours are poured into this sort of bed. Those tall rudbekias and delphiniums are held up by well-disguised stakes, and deadheading keeps the blooms coming all summer long. Cutting back, feeding, mulching and judicious weeding is the labour that keeps the bed looking so relaxed. A dais in the middle of the glorious backdrop of flowers is used for recitals and small concerts.

A gate in the far wall beckons visitors out to a stone pergola and rose walk, which leads off toward the courtyard where a yellow fremontodendron climber is accented by yellow walls. In here a central pond is decorated by pots of grass, twisted hazel and rosemary set into rough stone paving. Attractive sculpture on the edge of the woods beyond also distracts the walker.

Resist the temptation to leave immediately and stay to enjoy the rest of the walled garden. On a sunny day the paths lined by low lavender hedges could fool someone into thinking they are in a warmer country. Lavender is notorious for failing in our damp climate, but the hedges in St Enda's are bushy, healthy and strongly scented. They lead in different directions, towards gates in the walls and iron benches set among wall shrubs and climbers. In the centre of the garden the yew walk holds back perfect lawns and leads toward a circular pond surrounded by a rim of vicious red pelargoniums.

St Enda's walled garden is simply laid out, beautifully maintained and cared for, and set in a fine park.

FAIRFIELD LODGE

Monkstown Avenue, Monkstown, County Dublin; Tel/Fax: +01 2803912; e-mail: jsb@indigo.ie ▦ **Contact:** John S Bourke ▦ **Open:** May–July, Sunday, 2pm–6pm; at other times by appointment to groups only ▦ **Entrance fee** ▦ **Special features:** teas can be arranged in advance; member of the Dublin Garden Group ▦ **Directions:** a pale, pink-washed, Georgian, one-storey house at the top left-hand side of Monkstown Avenue, travelling toward the city centre.

John Bourke's plot is a perfect little garden, divided into three small rooms that wrap around the late eighteenth-century villa. Each of the garden rooms has a different feel. The first greets the visitor from the gateway, a confection of white, grey-greens and silvers: 'Iceberg' roses and box-enclosed *Artemisia* 'Powys Castle' look good enough to eat in the sunny front garden beside the California tree poppy (*Romneya coulteri*), which has distinctive, big, white flowers and bluey-grey leaves. The self-discipline of using only white and silver plants is countered by choosing good showy plants and encouraging voluminous growth. This is quite an appetiser for the main garden.

From here one enters a snug courtyard. This garden room is an education on the bringing of light to dark corners. Although quite shady, it is brightened up by the use of a beautiful golden hop (*Humulus lupulus* 'Aureus'), twining through *Rosa* 'Chinatown' and pretty yellow *Clematis tangutica*, on a north-facing wall. The young leaves of the hop have a quality of bright freshness that would cheer up the darkest space.

The finale in this little garden is reached as one moves around the house into the last 'room'. This is a long, slim area, rich with reds and golds of plants such as *Rosa moyesii*, fuchsia, vines, pieris and macleyea. A small lily pond stands elevated on a platform that looks over the garden and the borders. Beautiful statuary finishes the look of small-scale splendour. This is an incredibly well-maintained little garden. Slackness and raggy edges can be countenanced, and even sometimes look good, in country gardens and larger places, but in a smart town garden no lapse will be forgiven. John Bourke needs no forgiveness.

THE DUBLIN GARDEN GROUP

This is a group of garden owners located mainly around the south side of Dublin. All the gardens involved in the group are private and most are open to visitors in a very limited capacity only. The group is made up of superbly maintained, cleverly planted and designed gardens. They are extremely varied and each is an inspiration in its own way.

The gardens included in the group are:

    Corke Lodge
    The Dillon Garden
    Fairfield Lodge
    Graigueconna *
    Knockcree
    Knockmore *
    Lodge Park Walled Garden
    Primrose Hill
    Rathmichael Lodge
    Rathmore
    Shanganagh

See County Wicklow for gardens marked *; *see* County Kildare for Lodge Park Walled Garden. For detailed descriptions and information on each of the gardens contact either Shirley Beatty (Tel: +01 2955884) or John S Bourke (Tel: +01 2803912; e-mail: jsb@indigo.ie).

If visiting these or any other private gardens, remember that they are part of someone's home, so arrive only when expected and within the hours stipulated by the owner.

FERNHILL

Sandyford, County Dublin; Tel: +01 2956000 ▪ **Contact:** Mrs Sally Walker ▪ **Open:** March–end September, Tuesday–Saturday and bank holidays, 11am–5pm; Sunday, 2pm–6pm ▪ **Entrance fee** ▪ **Special features:** plants for sale 2pm–5pm on Saturdays, including many specifically Irish cultivars and some hard-to-get plants ▪ **Directions:** taking the main road for Enniskerry, Fernhill is between Lamb's Cross and Stepaside, on the right-hand side and well signposted.

Situated on the northeastern slope of Three Rock Mountain, Fernhill has been one of the treasures of County Dublin for many years. Covering over forty acres and containing remarkable trees, fine walks and individual gardens, it is a Robinsonian-style garden with a wild woodland feel.

The walled flower and vegetable garden is the first part of the garden seen on a visit to Fernhill. This is one of the few gardens on the island to have been continuously cultivated for over 200 years. The area is romantic – one can sense the history of the place – and filled with great flowers and plants, such as towering, three-and-a-half-metre-tall campanulas, roses, delphiniums, acanthus, alstroemeria and creeping jenny. At the height of summer the place is full of the smell of strawberries and clipped box, a perfume combination made in heaven. Roses border the vegetable and fruit cages and espaliered apples give a good backdrop to the flowers. *Tropaeolum speciosum* snakes beautifully through clipped yew. Mrs Walker, who looks after the huge garden, is one of the small band for whom this gorgeous plant is a weed that is too easy to grow. There are many gardeners who would live happily with a plague of this particular scourge.

The style in Fernhill is of just-contained wildness. There is control but it doesn't look over-tended or tidied. The less experienced gardener might think that the garden is just doing its own thing, even growing wild, when in actual fact it is like a swan – serene, unruffled and calm above the water, but being worked like billy-o beneath the surface.

The stream garden is worthy of a full visit by itself. It is laid out in such natural and easy lines that it looks as though it might always have been here, and is planted up with damp-loving and marginal plants. The path meanders through it.

Up by the fine old house, and leading out to the pleasure grounds, are two venerable trees. The Great Chestnut is one of the finest sweet chestnuts in the country, a huge tree and, at over 200 years old, a tree with a reputation. This is possibly one of the first of the species planted in Ireland. It dates from the same period as the equally venerable Large Beech spreading out magnificently over the path. These trees are contemporaneous with the original house. Mrs Walker tells of how she chased away a man who came offering to buy her house and tried to ingratiate himself by declaring that the first thing that would have to go would be the beech tree; the sort of man on whom the dogs should be set!

The Broadwalk, on which, it is thought, £10,000 was spent in 1860, is lined by trees, including three baby Wellingtonias (*Sequoiadendron giganteum*), aged only 140 years and already measuring forty metres. They could grow to ninety metres and last for another 2,000 years.

There are great runs of rhododendron in the old quarry beyond the laurel lawn, which is a wide run of laurel trimmed to look like a lawn on stilts. This is a justly famous feature.

A mile of tall wire-fencing helps keep the Sika deer out and away from the delicious food that rhododendron, exotic shrubs and good perennial flowers present for these attractive but troublesome animals. Despite this, an occasional deer does manage to steal its way into the garden, munching on only the choicest plants. According to Mrs Walker, the most recent invader had a cultivated palate and a particular penchant for *Bergenia* 'Ballawley', a very special Irish strain of bergenia. Town gardeners are mercifully spared so much of the heartache that country gardeners have to suffer, ranging from ravenous deer to rabbits, invading cattle and even, at times, escaped horses playing tag on the lawn.

Fernhill has been used many times as a sculpture trail, with a number of contemporary artists placing their works through the wonderful grounds. It is a marvellous setting in which to view art.

GLENASMOLE LODGE

Glenasmole, County Dublin; Tel: +01 4510642 ▪ **Contact:** Mrs June Judd ▪ **Open:** June–August, strictly by appointment only ▪ **Entrance fee** ▪ **Directions:** travelling from Enniskerry, drive to Glencree. Pass the reform school and German war cemetery and continue for 1km. You will then round a sharp hairpin bend back to the right, onto the old Military Road. Take the first turn left and then the next left again, and continue for about 8km until the black gates appear on the left-hand side.

This wonderful four-acre garden is set in a valley in the Dublin Mountains. The garden is bordered by the River Currach on one side and Kippure Mountain on the other. The mountainous base is evident throughout the garden in the shape of boulders. There are numerous huge rocks, and remarkably good use has been made of them. Pond gardens are worked around them; the lawns wash up against them. Great pines planted around the garden add to shelter provided by the mountains. Most of these trees are between 200 and 300 years old.

The house was originally a thatched hunting lodge in the Swiss Cottage style (*see* County Tipperary). The thatch is long gone, however, and has been replaced with slate. Granite steps around the house are edged by good planting, which anchors the house well into the rock. Old pots of geranium and crinum lilies add flower to the picture. A rich, orange-coloured, unidentified rose climbs up the house, around which some clipped box hedges bring a touch of formality.

The greater garden is largely made of rhododendron and azalea – banks and banks of them – making the place a pure glory in spring. Embothriums and eucryphia also do well in this garden, happy in the acid soil. This is primarily a woodland garden and the wood is charming, with a good fernery and an unusually perfect moss path that is kept immaculately well swept and clear of leaves, like a soft, green carpet. But it is a knobbly carpet too, which rises and falls over tree roots; one of the finest sights.

In from the path, among the trees, there are carpets of ferns and bluebells, crocosmia, geranium and fritillaries. The wood is one of Mrs Judd's favourite features, with paths leading into an arboretum containing a good collection of specimen trees. A path leads into the woods past bluish-flowering olearia and drimys, by a statue that peeps demurely out of a sprinkling of winter cyclamen. A chiming clock, set behind one of the old garden walls, adds to the charm of the fine old garden. In front of this wall are the flower gardens, with banks of blue and white hydrangea, red-hot pokers and a white bed made up of white roses, olearia, hydrangea, primula, white variegated hosta and white abutilon.

The pool house is ingeniously surrounded by flower carpet roses, lobelia and osteospermum so that the pool itself is invisible from the house. The plants here include a very big standard azara.

A mixed bed sweeps around the wall, full of lupins, hollyhocks, roses and an architectural-looking *Cornus controversa* set into the middle. A big *Vitis coignetiae* snakes up over an old window in the wall. The bed includes *Rosa* 'The Fairy', *Rosa* 'Annabell', hydrangeas, California tree poppy (*Romneya coulteri*), peony, poppies, alstroemeria and blue, hazy catmint (*Nepeta*). In the middle of the garden is a lily pond and a waterfall, fringed with Lady's mantle (*Alchemilla mollis*), lilies, primula, bullrushes (*Scirpus lacustris*), astilbe and mossy stones. Glenasmole is a peaceful and secluded garden on the edge of the bustling city.

GRASSE COTTAGE

130 Rochestown Avenue (opposite Kensington Lodge), Dún Laoghaire, County Dublin; Tel: +01 2852396 ■ **Contact:** Mr Dick Mallet ■ **Open:** all year, by appointment to groups of ten-plus only ■ **Entrance fee** donated to charities ■

Directions: take the Rochestown Avenue exit at the Cabinteely junction off the N11. At the Rochestown Avenue lights, turn left. The house is third on the left beyond the Texaco garage.

Grasse Cottage is a treat of a garden, hiding away behind a row of semi-detached houses on busy Rochestown Avenue. Mr Mallet has been gardening here for over forty-four years and his half-acre garden is a quiet oasis, peaceful and calm, filled with scent and colour. The garden is quite simply crammed with plants and it is necessary to snake in and out of beds and under shrubs to get around. This could be any size of a garden, as it is impossible to see from one end to the other.

The garden is full of lovely plants, such as a huge *Crambe cordifolia* with gypsophila-like flowers and pretty, beady seedheads, and a *Prunus serrula* that has the shiniest copper-banded bark and delicate white flowers. 'That's a tree that never gets too big for a small garden,' says Dick Mallet, 'it's a great plant, but if you're going to buy one, pick a tree without too many knots in the bark for the best effect.' Another interesting plant in the mass of old roses and herbaceous plants is an exotic-looking climbing gerbera with pink flowers. Leaf and colour contrasts are well executed everywhere: the red leaves of *Photinia* 'Red Robin' and pale, cream-coloured leaves of *Cornus controversa* 'Variegata' are a big success together.

The vegetable beds are prettily arranged and surrounded by trellised clematis and roses. This part of the garden loses nothing of its looks to production requirements. More and more we realise that vegetable beds do not have to be allotment-like, nononsense rows of food-in-waiting, but can be attractive gardens that are decorative as well as delicious.

The greenhouse is a mass of tender plants, but the centrepiece is a spectacular *Campanula pyramidalis*, a tender plant with delicate powder-blue bell flowers, grown up a tall wigwam. This garden is a real plantsman's paradise and Mr Mallet is an informative and pleasant guide.

IVEAGH GARDENS   ♿

Clonmel Street, Dublin 2 ▪ **Contact:** Margaret Gormely at Dúchas, Tel: +01 4757816 ▪ **Open:** summer months, Monday–Saturday, 8.15am–6pm; Sunday and bank holidays, 10am–6pm; winter, as before, but closing half-an-hour before dusk ▪ **No entrance fee** ▪ Member of Dúchas ▪ **Directions:** enter by Clonmel Street, off Harcourt Street, or through the grounds of the National Concert Hall, Earlsfort Terrace.

The Iveagh Gardens is one of Dublin's greatest secrets. Formerly the private garden of Iveagh House, it was donated to the State by Lord Iveagh in the 1930s. Screened on all sides by houses and tall buildings, the garden is a very secluded and peaceful spot in the middle of a busy city, providing an oasis of quiet amid the chaos and noise of the surrounding streets.

In the 1860s Ninian Niven, working for Lord Iveagh, laid out a public garden for the International Exhibition of Arts and Manufacture of 1865. The design was based on the Italianate and French style of park design and included a cascade, fountains, a rosarium with scented old roses, and rustic grottos. The most novel feature of the place, however, was the archery ground, used for competitions among both ladies and gentlemen. This sunken green, along with most of the other features, still survives.

The tiny box maze – just high enough to confound a toddler – is also part of the original design and was based on the Tudor maze at Hampton Court in London.

The Iveagh Gardens were neglected for many years and in the 1960s the green was used by brazen University College, Dublin students as a makeshift football pitch before the college left Earlsfort Terrace for Belfield. Now, however, it is in the hands of Dúchas, The Heritage Service, and has been restored. Because so much of the charm of the place was its slightly dilapidated, rather faded grandeur, the restoration work was done with a very light hand.

One of Dublin's best kept secrets – the Iveagh Gardens, a Victorian beauty hiding behind St Stephen's Green.

KENSINGTON LODGE

Rochestown Avenue, Dún Laoghaire, County Dublin; Tel: +01 2803577 ▪ **Contact:** George and Eve Kennedy ▪ **Open:** by appointment only; groups welcome ▪ **Entrance fee** donated to charity and goes towards garden upkeep ▪ Supervised children welcome ▪ **Special features:** gardening courses; flower-arranging (telephone for details of upcoming events); teas can be booked by prior arrangement ▪ **Directions:** from Stillorgan, leave the N11 at Foxrock Church and drive towards Deansgrange and Baker's Corner. Turn right there and travel for 300m. The garden is signposted on the left-hand side.

The Kennedys of Rochestown Avenue have been working for thirty-eight years on their three-acre garden. The husband-and-wife team of Eve and George is now aided by a daughter and son. Theirs is a varied garden, with a history going back 200 years.

Kensington Lodge is split into two distinct areas: the walled garden, covering an acre to the rear of the house, and the front garden, covering two acres of lawn, large mixed beds and specimen trees. Dividing the two areas is a courtyard and a big garden room in which Eve holds her gardening and flower-arranging classes. Planters, pots and troughs galore fill the courtyard and the busy working area. Everything in the garden is grown from seed and from their own propagation, and a walk through the courtyard takes you to a propagator's paradise. Trays and trays of covetable little seedlings, cuttings and plants being potted are to the gardener what a shop full of the best Belgian chocolates are to the chocaholic. This is a flower-arranger's garden. Eve Kennedy has been an arranger for many years and there is more than one agenda being worked to here, with plants grown not only for their value in the garden but also for the variety of leaf and flower for arranging.

The old walled garden behind the house was originally the home of the vegetables. Now the vegetables share the space with a handsome flower garden filled with plants such as blue-flowering peas and choice delphiniums like 'Alice Artindale'. Box hedging holds in the fine flower borders. In the vegetable beds older varieties and heritage seed vegetables are grown. George is the master of the vegetable patch. As well as old varieties of seed, he grows a number of varieties with anti-carcinogenic properties, and all the work is carried out organically.

Beside a white border is their millennium border or, more precisely, the Dublin Millennium Border. This is a strong-coloured border of rich reds, aubergines and purples, featuring plants like *Heuchera* 'Chocolate Ruffles' and sedum. Little paths wander through the tall beds of spicy-scented *Rosa* 'Souvenir de la Malmaison' and 'Empress Josephine'.

To the front of the house the mood is very different from the cottagey, old-fashioned walled garden. Here runs of lawn divide punchy, striking beds of shrubs, trees and grasses. One of the cleverer features here is a central bed in the lawn. This was developed in order to drain off the lawns that at one time were prone to becoming waterlogged. The solution was to make a damp, boggy garden for large candelabra primula *(Primula florindae)*, a strong red version of French honeysuckle *(Hedysarum coronarium)* and a mat of wet-loving plants, like hosta and ligularia. During the winter this bed is fed by rainwater as the lawn drains into it.

The sculpture bed is filled not with stone nymphs and Greek gods, but with architectural plants like pampas, cordyline and phormium, used for their bold shapes and strong textures. The specimen trees include a sephora from New Zealand, with light, fringed leaves, tulip trees *(Liriodendron tulipifera)*, a sequoia and a southern beech *(Nothofagus)*.

Walking through the garden with either of the Kennedys, you will enjoy a very informative tour filled with good tips on subjects such as mulching and propagation. One thing they swear by is placing thick layers of damp newspaper on the soil, covered with a layer of manure or farmyard muck, to choke weeds. An advantage of using papers like this is that it keeps moisture in the soil, while using up newspaper in an environmentally sensible way. The paper eventually rots down and is amalgamated into the soil by the worms. Just don't use shiny or glossy paper.

KILMATEAD GARDENS

Kilmatead House, Naas Road, Clondalkin; Tel: +01 4594339 ▪ **Contact:** Mary Jennings, Christopher Hone or Finlay Colley ▪ **Open:** for charity open days in July (telephone for details); otherwise by appointment only between May and September ▪ **Entrance fee** ▪ Children welcome but must be supervised because of the water ▪ **Special features:** teas may be booked in advance ▪ **Directions:** situated off the N7 between the Green Isle Hotel and City West flyover, on the Naas side of Camac Valley Caravan Park. Travelling from Naas, take the first left onto a laneway after the footbridge at Kingswood. Follow the signs for Carbery Nursery. Travelling from Dublin, drive past the entrance and continue on under the City West flyover (a highly landscaped junction). Take the left turn off the dual carriageway. Cross the flyover and then follow the directions as if from Naas.

Kilmatead is made up of two separate gardens centred on the ruins of an early eighteenth-century gunpowder mill. There were once nineteen mills between this spot and Clondalkin, and there is an enormous amount of history attached to the ruins and the whole area. The family in both house and gardens has lived on this land for 350 years and the lands once formed part of the old Corkagh Estate. The two gardens together make up an area of about five acres. Some of the ground is in woods and orchards, while the rest is laid out in complementary formal flower gardens, bog gardens and shaded wood gardens.

Mary Jennings began gardening on her site in the early 1990s. Finlay Colley's next-door garden has been in development since 1960. Mary works away from home for up to five months of the year and Finlay works every day of the year in his garden, attached as it is to his specialist nursery. So the two gardens couldn't have more different, yet complementary, personalities. Together they make up a charming extended garden visit.

When Mary began gardening on the handsome, tree-surrounded site, she started by putting in a small herbaceous border close to the old house. The bed then grew out in an arc, to become the long sweep of graded colour it is today. The border starts with blues: 'Blue does well in this garden,' says Mary, walking past the different shades of galega, catmint, purple mallow and *Campanula lactifolia*. From blue, shades of white take up the line, with papery catanache, astrantia and veronica. Mixed in with these is ruby-coloured scabious which she says is hard to place, although it looks good here. The bed then moves along to yellows and reds, with geum, red monarda, oriental poppies and watsonia, which grew from seed Mary brought home from Mauritius. In the yellow area pale, buttery day lilies, anthemis and yellow verbascum soften down the effect again. Scattered along the bed are plants grown from South African and Ethiopian seeds. Mary loves to grow from seed and has a flair for it, but generally the plants don't overwinter, so she grows them as annuals and enjoys getting a season or two from the tender plants, not minding when they succumb to the Irish frost or damp.

The long bed was arranged so that it incorporates a view over a low hedge to a big man-made lake and an inviting wooded island, with colonies of arum lilies along the water's edge.

Leaving the open garden by way of an iron arch brings one into the spring garden and woods. In the spring this is a sea of anemone, hosta and Solomon's seal (*Polygonatum*), grown under the tall ash, cherry and chestnut. Not many slugs annoy the hosta plantations under the trees because it is so dry. 'This is a hard place to work because it is shaded and north-facing,' says Mary, 'so if something seeds here I leave it have its way.' One plant that enjoys the awkward conditions is a pretty little oxalis, which is spreading like wildfire under the tree canopy. A stone pool in the woods was part of an original garden, so this was simply cleared out and planted with giant cowslips and drumstick primulas. A little spitting dog fountain is also a relic from the old garden.

Mary's husband, Christopher Hone, built the humped bridge over the stream in the wood garden as well as the other iron features scattered around. I admired the big clematis growing under the bridge, only to be told that it had been planted to climb up and over it!

Emerging into the open, the path leads past the little waterfall from an underground spring and a damp stream garden of *Digitalis lutea* and dierama, stipa and lobelia. Mary loves grasses, but they are slow to grow in this area. Her biggest headache however is the marauding rabbits who eat everything. Where the rabbits fail, squirrels step in, efficiently harvesting the big old walnut tree.

This area leads around to a wood of Portugal laurel (*Prunus lusitanica*), where Mary's small son holds teddy bear picnics, and out past a big weeping beech, sweet chestnut and a mulberry. The way leads on to Finlay Colley's garden via a laneway with a great wall of the sweet moss rose, Rosa 'William Lobb'. Mr Colley says that, at forty years old, his garden is quite young. His aunt started it and as a young boy he began by helping her with her new garden, eventually taking it on himself. His is a garden for lovers of herbaceous perennials. The garden spreads out around the house in splashes of colour and bloom.

The first flowers to catch the eye at the height of summer are the big double opium poppies. 'They're nothing special,' says Mr Colley. Next door is the pretty little *Dahlia merckii*: 'Very handy. I just leave it alone and it comes up every year.' Among his favourites in the great mixed beds is *Campanula thyrsoides*, an unusual, pale yellow flower, rather like an orchid. Red scabious (*Knautia macedonica*) is living happily in his garden beside a *Paeonia* 'Bowl of Beauty'. Mr Colley says he doesn't go in for colour planning and that he 'just plonks things in the bed', but that obviously completely discounts his innate good taste.

The gunpowder mills are a centrepiece of his garden and here, by the old, many-times blasted walls, is where some of his favourite plants live, such as francoa and the simple white paper flowers of *Rosa* 'Penelope'. *Eryngium veriifolium* dipped in steely-blue and *Lamium orvala*, an exotic relative of the nettle, are rare and lovely. Dotted through the place are the most wonderful perennials, such as gayfeather (*Liatris*), *Anthemis tinctoria* 'Sauce Hollandaise', a particularly pale lemon daisy flower, and *Artemisia lactiflora* 'Guizhou', which has purple shot through its veins and stately spikes. Another little gem is *Stylophorm diphyllum*, a rare yellow poppy. *Semiaquilegia ecalcarata* is very subtle, with a dirty pink, delicate flower. In the ruins of the powder mill is a good tree fern that is nicely framed in the space. This garden is just full of great perennials, many of which Mr Colley sells in his nursery next door.

The most interesting series of little sunken streams runs around the garden just below the turf. He created them very simply: 'I just flooded the lake nearby and let the water come into the garden in its own way.' He spread chalk where the water travelled and when the water receded he simply dug where the marked channels had run. The effect is both unusual and attractive. The sound of gurgling water travels around the garden with the walker and the ground by the little streams is ideal for an occasional spot-planting of damp-loving plants like hosta.

Mr Colley's garden is lovely in itself, and an articulate advertisement for the plants he sells in the nursery.

KNOCKCREE

Glenamuck Road, Carrickmines, County Dublin; Tel: +01 2955884 ▪ **Contact:** John and Shirley Beatty ▪ **Open:** 1 April–31 July, daily, 2pm–6pm, by appointment only ▪ **Entrance fee** ▪ Supervised children welcome ▪ **Directions:** leave Foxrock village by the Brighton Road. Turn right onto the Glenamuck Road and travel for about 1km. Knockcree is on the left.

The garden at Knockcree is based on a huge outcrop of granite laid down 75,000 years ago in the last Ice Age. This two-acre garden with neutral soil is, quite simply, moulded around the rock, so much so that even the lawn wraps around the large boulders standing proud of the turf. The garden has been insinuated into the attractive but tough landscape in such an impressive manner that it appears to be totally natural, an effect increased by John and Shirley Beatty's clever fading of the garden out into a rough gorse boundary. The boundary between the garden and the Dublin Mountains is almost imperceptible.

The garden has a collection of alpine plants, good herbaceous plants, azaleas and great flowering shrubs, including several varieties of rhododendron and mock orange (*Philadelphus*). Mock orange is a lovely, early-flowering summer shrub with white, scented flowers which one is always tempted to bring into the house as cut flowers, but which never fail to drop all their petals the minute the door closes behind them.

Shirley Beatty is a firm believer in close planting. There is no soil to be seen between any of the plants in her garden. 'I think plants are happiest close together. It keeps the weeds down and the moisture in,' she explains. She is also the sort of sensible gardener who leaves well enough alone. A pretty self-seeding thistle in among the *Anemone rivularis* was not pulled out just because the gardener didn't put it there. She also leaves *Geranium maderense*, a plant she calls 'a weed', to seed itself around because it too looks right, as does *Astrantia* 'Margery Fish'. Astrantia is something many of us fight with in the seed tray in an attempt to get it to germinate. Mrs Beatty also has a real love for geraniums, particularly the Schiaperalli-pink *Geranium psilostemon*, which scatters itself freely around the garden.

The house is wrapped in white *Clematis* 'Marie Boisselot', its flowers as big as soup plates, as well as the big, cabbagey, pink *Rosa* 'Mme Caroline Testout'. The Beattys came to the garden thirty years ago when there was nothing here but a big *Cotinus* 'Notcutt's Variety', which doesn't flower but looks good nevertheless. They have carried out stunning amounts of work to create the garden that graces the place today. My abiding memory is not of the glorious and varied plants and shrubs in the borders, but of a single *Rosa glauca*, about a metre in spread, growing happily on 'the smell of an oily rag' on top of the great rock that stands in the middle of the garden.

Particularly pleasing is the knowledge that Shirley Beatty propagates from her fine stock of plants, selling these attractive babies at the weekly Kilternan branch of the country market (*see* Country Markets in the appendices). No wonder the crowds there are legendary.

MEDINA   ♿

Thormanby Road, Howth, County Dublin; Tel: +01 8324720; Fax: +01 8320026 ✼ **Contact:** Karl Flynn ✼ **Open:** May–September, Saturday–Sunday, 2pm–6pm; small groups and strictly by appointment only ✼ **Entrance fee** donated to charity ✼ Supervised children welcome; please note, guide dogs only ✼ **Directions:** at the Marine Hotel at Sutton Cross, turn right at the sign to Howth Summit. Drive for about 3km until the summit appears at the top of the hill on the right. Medina is ten houses along from the summit, on the right. The name is on the gate.

Karl Flynn came to his house at the very top of Howth Head twelve years ago. He has taken pictures of his garden every week since then, creating a remarkable record of the growing, developing garden. He began working on the garden before he even moved into the house, slowly transforming it from a typical long stretch of grass with lines of predictable shrubs into the extraordinary exotic jungle it is today. The garden covers about one third of an acre. The main garden is to the rear of the house, rising steeply up from the building toward Howth summit, almost into the clouds. There is not much depth of soil before reaching solid Howth stone. 'I have to use a pickaxe on the ground,' says Karl. He maintains that the steps up through the garden 'just made themselves' – stone steps lying in wait under the thin veneer of soil is the attractive side of working on almost solid rock.

Looking at the massed exotic plants that now grow in jungle-like proportions in the garden, it's hard to conjure up a picture of barren rockland. An obliging neighbour with horses supplies Karl with manure and this helps to improve the rocky, acidic nature of neutral soil. Karl's tree-sized echiums particularly appreciate this treatment. 'I got one echium plant originally and now I have thousands. They come up everywhere,' he says uncomplainingly.

In the front garden, among the white abutilon, giant feather grass (*Stipa gigantea*) and rich, red-flowered broom (*Cytisus* 'Killiney Red'), there are straight lines of cordylines. In fact there are cordylines right through this garden. 'As you can see I like the cordylines. I loved them before I ever started gardening,' Karl says. Medina is something of a cordyline sanctuary and he has moved in many plants condemned from other gardens.

Karl loves foliage plants and the garden is a magnificent display of leaf colour and texture. Tree ferns from Heligan in Wales are growing beautifully in the mist and cloud of Howth Head. Sharp-pointed astelias, like silver swords, grow under a snakebark maple, and they look as though they were made for each other. What flowers are here are subtle – colonies of wild cowslips and the soft purple-blue of mint bush (*Prostanthera rotundilfolia*). 'This is not a colour garden,' he says, accurately. Masculine is the word that best describes the garden. Cleverly arranged varied foliage from a mix of hardy exotics make up the backbone of the planting.

A tall, peeling eucalyptus hangs over his Japanese-influenced area. 'I've taken some of the ideas from Japanese gardens, like the stepping stones which make the walker slow down.' A red arch leads out of this area, with a mimosa and *Clematis tangutica* knotted over it. Karl admits that 'keeping the restraint in here is hard. I might want to keep it empty, but the plants have other ideas. They grow wild, so every so often I have to get in and hack them back.'

In the main body of the garden one perfect cone of golden Leyland cypress (*Cupressocyparis leylandii*) stands out. There used to be twelve of these marching up the garden, taking up almost the whole area. Karl began taking them out one by one over the years. His method is simple (*see* box, below).

TAKING OUT AN UNWANTED CONIFER

Top the tree to about head height. Get a spade and pick-axe and, working in a circle about half a metre (two feet) out from the trunk, lop off the roots. Next, climb into the middle of the tree and shake it hard. If there is no movement, go back to lopping off roots. Fill the trench with water and when it is soaked, climb back into the tree and continue shaking. The tree should then come out fairly easily.

Medina has won awards on several occasions from the judges of the Shamrock All Ireland Gardens Competition. For four years on the trot it has won Best Pond, and has taken second place in the Patio Section for three consecutive years. But despite the extreme good looks of the garden, Karl is very much a part-time gardener. He works it at weekends and only in the growing season. 'I don't take care of my plants. They look after themselves or die. I'll give them one season, and after that they're on their own. I go for seeds and plants grown in Ireland, not Holland, because they are a bit more likely to survive neglect and hard weather.' He is an organic gardener with no time for herbicides and pesticides. If black spot arrives, he leaves it.

The wonderful pond, the Japanese garden, a secret garden and an interesting woodland walk at the very top of the garden under a *Rhododendron ponticum* and privet canopy all go to make up this exquisite garden.

THE NATIONAL BOTANIC GARDENS &

Glasnevin, Dublin 9; Tel: +01 8377596/+01 8374388; Fax: +01 8360080 ▓
Contact: Donal Synnott, Director ▓ **Open:** all year except 25 December, daily, 9am–6pm; summer Sundays, 11am–6pm; winter weekdays, 10am–4.30pm; winter Sundays, 11am–4.30pm ▓ **No entrance fee** ▓ **Special features:** courses; lectures; occasional events, contact for details; guided tours available for a charge ▓ Member of Dúchas ▓ **Directions:** situated on the north side of the city on Botanic Road. *Note:* if possible take a bus or taxi to the Botanic Gardens because it is very difficult to find parking outside the gates. Buses: nos. 19, 19A and 13 leave from O'Connell Street.

Founded in 1795 by the Dublin Society (later to become the Royal Dublin Society), the Botanic Gardens in Glasnevin constitute Ireland's foremost botanical and horticultural institution. For over 200 years it has played a vital role in the conservation and distribution of rare, imported and unusual plants throughout the country. All the great gardens around the island have been involved in the division and sharing of plants with the Botanic Gardens, which has been a great force for good in the world of Irish horticulture since its foundation. Education has played a part of the work of the Botanic Gardens since the last days of the 1700s, when six boys were taken on as apprentices, to be paid *if* their work was considered satisfactory. Since then research and demonstrations of good planting and gardening techniques have been carried out at Glasnevin.

The plant collections are a delight, arranged in geographical and scientific groupings in a landscaped setting on the banks of the River Tolka. The layout incorporates rock gardens, alpine yards, rose gardens, order beds, herb and vegetable gardens, a pond, herbaceous and shrub borders, wall plants and an arboretum.

The four glasshouses include the Victoria House, built specially to house the giant Amazon water lilies beloved of generations of small children. Other houses contain succulents, palms, orchids, ferns and alpines. The curvilinear houses, built by Richard Turner in 1848 and with additional work carried out by himself and his son William twenty years later, are justly world famous. They have recently been magnificently restored. Comparing the Palm House, which awaits restoration, with the already restored curvilinear range with its delicate cream paintwork, lacy iron veins, warm granite base and the 1870-planted Chusan palm (*Trachycarpus fortunei*) beside it, one can see how glorious the Palm House will be when restored. Interestingly, it was decided to use cream – a specially developed shade called 'Turner White' – for the restored paintwork rather than the original white, as the white paint on the Victorian houses had oxidised to a similar creamy colour soon after application.

AUGUSTINE HENRY

Augustine Henry (1857–1930) is the most famous of the Irish plant collectors. Having completed his training as a doctor, he began his working life as a customs official in China where he became fascinated with the local plants used for medical purposes. From there his interest in botany and horticulture grew and he began to send samples of plants, seeds and young plants to Kew Gardens in England. As his work took him further into China, including the Yunan region, he continued to send samples back to London. In twenty years of working in the East he collected over 150,000 dried plant specimens, returning these to Europe along with samples of the scores of living plants discovered by him.

Upon returning to Europe, he began a career of writing books on trees, and took up a seat as Chair of Forestry in the Royal College of Science in Dublin. Among the plants introduced by him are:

Rhododendron augustinii, an evergreen shrub with funnel-shaped, lavender-blue flowers;

Vitis henryana, also known as *Parthenocissus henryana*, the Chinese Virginia creeper;

Lilium henryi, a turkscap with a fiery orange-scented flower.

In addition to these and other lasting legacies to the world of horticulture, Dr Henry left his forest herbarium (collection of dried plants) to the National Botanic Gardens in Dublin, where it is still used and studied today.

The Botanic Gardens have been a favourite haunt of Dubliners for many years. A wide range of people visit them – from painting groups studying and sketching the summer borders, to school classes being hauled along for a good walk and fresh air, to students studying the well-labelled plants and families out for a Sunday walk.

PRIMROSE HILL

Lucan, County Dublin; Tel: +01 6280373 ■ **Contact:** Robin Hall ■ **Open:** February, daily, 2pm–6pm; June–beginning August, daily, 2pm– 6pm; groups welcome, by appointment only ■ **Entrance fee** ■ Supervised children welcome ■ **Directions:** in Lucan village, turn into Primrose Lane, which is signed opposite the AIB bank. The garden is at the top of the lane, through black gates. *Note:* buses must park in the village as they will not fit up the drive.

Primrose Hill is one of the most charming gardens in the country. Attached to a fine Regency house attributed to James Gandon, it is a plantsman's garden, created over the past forty years by the Hall family. That said, it has the look of a garden from another age; an old-fashioned, quirky, personal and colourful place, full of fine herbaceous plants and flowers.

The impressive, hardworking Robin Hall tends this stuffed-to-capacity garden. His mother, Cecily, began the garden in the 1950s when she took on the long-neglected site, turning it into a garden dedicated to flowers with a particular leaning towards old-fashioned cultivars. The garden now has one of the largest collections of small flowering plants in the country, a famous collection of snowdrops (*Galanthus*) that can be seen during the spring, (*see* box, snowdrops, p.108), many varieties of lobelias and an arboretum, currently in development, covering five acres.

The beds in the walled garden are beautifully laid out. Red lobelia and magenta *Salvia grahamii*, yellow santolina, big Scotch thistles and papavars in a whole range of shades do battle with each other to glorious colour effect. Good, gutsy plant combinations stand out everywhere. *Rosa moyesii* sits in the centre of a border beside fine campanula and *Crocosmia* 'Lucifer'. Strong colours make for a richer blend of shades. Golds and pinks, purples, yellows and plums mix in and out of each other attractively, making this garden solid proof that gardeners can get away with a lot more than they might think.

Tiny, pale yellow sisyrinchium, tiger lilies and swathes of hellebore flowers brighten up a dark corner. Some gardeners fear that bold planting will produce a brassy, blousey look, but as long as the vibrant colours are well broken up by good clumps of foliage and green, a brave gardener can use a tremendously wide palette of colour. Plants live cheek-by-jowl in these beds and the weeds have no chance of taking up residence because their more cultivated brethren have accounted for every little bit of space.

As you tiptoe over the little stone paths you encounter dangling barriers of angel's fishing rods (*Dierama*). This is an assault course of flowers, with Japanese anemone self-seeding everywhere in the paving cracks, pushing and shoving in competition for those spaces with tall verbena and steely-white eryngium. Arctic beech, tree peonies underplanted with gardener's garters and varieties of birch overlook the flowerfest. An aged vine, intertwined with honeysuckle, grows on a sunny wall and its gnarled trunk is a lovely sight. Close by, in a shady spot, the fernery holds a collection of various lacy fronds, and in front of it the ground is carpeted with golden oregano, which gives off a wonderful smell when stepped on. A little formal garden with statuary was being worked on when I visited.

The garden opens for a short time in February so that the well-known collection of snowdrops can be visited.

RATHMICHAEL LODGE &

Ballybride Road, Shankill, County Dublin; Tel: +01 2822203 ▪ **Contact:** Mr and Mrs Hewat ▪ **Open:** May–July, by appointment only; groups welcome ▪ **Entrance fee** donated to charity ▪ Supervised children welcome ▪ **Directions:** leave the N11 (travelling towards Bray) by the Loughlinstown roundabout, turning left. Take the first right at the petrol station and continue to Rathmichael Church. Turn left at the church gates onto Ballybride Road. Rathmichael Lodge is the third house on the left.

Rathmichael Lodge, with its back-to-front garden, is not easy to find, but it is worth the journey. Only about fourteen kilometres from the centre of Dublin, it could be out in the furthest wilds.

The garden is very cottagey and is strong on roses of every description, from great swathes of *Rosa filipes* 'Kiftsgate' sent into bat against the trees, to the beds and borders filled with various old and shrub roses. An array of the sweetest-smelling blooms, like *Rosa* 'Mme Isaac Pereire', *Rosa* 'Margaret Merrill' and the compact little dusty-pink *Rosa* 'William Lobb', send gorgeous perfume around the garden. Flowers are the passion in this exuberantly planted plot – *Papaver orientale* 'Patty's Plum', big explosions of gypsophila, lilies, day lilies, mock orange (*Philadelphus*), delphiniums and tall, thistle-flowering globe artichokes all vie for notice. The flower borders create a sea of colour and scent out in the middle of the countryside, with the Dublin Mountains in the near distance. A shell arch leads out of the flowers to the fields and hills beyond the immediate garden.

Mrs Hewat is the flower gardener while her husband is set on an expansionist mode. He has created a millennium walk of Turkish hazel (*Corylus colurna*). To the front of the house a gravel garden boasts marvellous, tall echiums, whose towering and exotic plumes of flower are proof of the sheltered aspect the garden enjoys, at the foot of the mountains and close to the sea.

RATHMORE

Westminster Road, Foxrock, County Dublin; Tel: +01 2895101 ▪ **Contact:** Mrs Mary Simpson ▪ **Open:** June–July, daily; by appointment only ▪ **Entrance fee** donated to charity ▪ **Directions:** turn from the N11 onto Westminster Road in Foxrock. Rathmore is the house on the right-hand corner of the first left turn.

As I arrived, Mrs Simpson was tearing alstroemerias and red tropaeolum out of the front bed, complaining of the dreadful weeds, and I was jealous. As you walk around the garden it is clear that Mrs Simpson doesn't know how not to grow plants exceptionally well, even when she doesn't want to. The front bed is full of beautiful plants, like the steely-blue *Hosta* 'June', which Mrs Simpson says is slug-resistant in comparison to its greener relatives. *Actaea rubra* with brilliant red berries lives next door and in among these is more of the cheeky alstroemeria, a 'weed' that would be welcome to take over in less well-endowed gardens.

Moving around the house to get to the main garden at the back, one needs to step lightly around the ranks of troughs and pots. In the back garden, the beds are bursting with colour, with herbaceous *Clematis integrifolia* in full bloom late in June beside purple roscoea, self-seeding meconopsis and tall wands of *Verbena bonariensis*, double scabious and French honeysuckle (*Hedysarum coronaria*). Specimen trees include a good *Cornus controversa* 'Variegata'.

One of Mrs Simpson's favourite plants here is the underrated *Astrantia maxima*, a watery-pink, frilled flower. This is a shy, easy-to-pass bloom that only shows itself as a truly gorgeous flower when inspected closely. Mrs Simpson is an enthusiastic gardener who really loves her plants and will scramble around a pergola of clematis to pull out one perfect bloom so that she can inspect it at close quarters.

There are secret paths in between tall shrubs and behind a trellis covered in roses, climbers and light, floating, lilac-coloured thalictrum. Back here the problem is too much catmint (*Nepeta*), which Mrs Simpson wants to thin out – another enviable problem.

In the middle of the blooms of rose and lobelia is a fine statue. Mrs Simpson has a story about the arrival of this little beauty that is so convoluted, roundabout and unlikely that it is obvious that the statue was destined to come and grace this attractive small garden.

Military Road, Kilmainham, Dublin 8; Tel: +01 6129900; Fax: +01 6129999 ▩
Contact: Mary Condon ▩ **Open:** all year, Tuesday–Saturday, 10am–5.30pm; Sundays and bank holidays, 12pm–5.30pm; closed Mondays and 23–26 December ▩
No entrance fee ▩ **Special features:** Irish Museum of Modern Art; bookshop; guided heritage tours can be arranged ▩ Member of Dúchas ▩ **Directions:** travelling along St John's Road West by Heuston Station, turn left onto Military Road. The entrance to the Royal Hospital is about 200m along, on the right-hand side of the road.

Built by James Butler, Duke of Ormond, in the 1690s, and modelled on Les Invalides, the retired soldiers' hospital in Paris, the Royal Hospital in Kilmainham is one of the city's most striking buildings and today is home to the Irish Museum of Modern Art (IMMA).

The restoration of the gardens attached to the building began twelve years ago and was completed in 1999. The work centred on the Master's Garden, which stands below the hospital on a shelf looking over the River Liffey to the Phoenix Park, which was also laid out, as a deer park, by the Kilkenny duke. The garden was an important feature of the 1695 design. This was to be a place 'for the greater grace of the house' and for the recreation of the retired soldiers.

The gardens are formal, in keeping with the French-style building. This formal style involves avenues of pleached limes running out from a central pond. Paths dissect each other, running diagonally across the garden. The planting is sparse, as much back-up colour to the hard landscaping as a focus in itself. Box hedges, lollipop hollies, fine statuary and soft-coloured golden gravel add to the cool, ordered look.

A wide sweep of sandstone steps marked by large lead urns leads down to the garden from the viewing terrace above by the hospital. A group of big chestnuts sits on an intermediary ledge – a shady place in the summer to sit and admire the gardens.

A view across the central pond in the Master's Garden at the Royal Hospital Kilmainham.

LEINSTER • COUNTY DUBLIN

12 Shanganagh Vale, Cabinteely, Dublin 18, County Dublin; Tel: +01 2825207 ❊
Contact: Anna Nolan ❊ **Open:** one weekend in August, telephone for details ❊
Entrance fee donated to Our Lady's Hospice ❊ **Directions:** from Dublin, travel on
the N11 past Cabinteely. Take the first left turn after the Esso Eglinton service
station. Follow the house number marker 1–14.

In a way it would be fun not to give the number of Anna Nolan's house and just tell
visitors to find the garden themselves, but it would almost be too easy. This gem
announces itself from the outset with a little apron of tasteful planting fronting the
house. Mrs Nolan's neighbours are lucky.

This is a perfect, tiny town garden that earns its keep all year round. Anna obviously revels in the challenge of small-spot gardening. I visited the garden the day after
builders had completed some work on the house. No cement mixer, butane stove,
left-over bricks or tools were anywhere in evidence. There was not even a muddy foot-
print on the exquisite turf, just a perfect garden. Seemingly they saw the pristine
garden and knew without being told that this place was to be treated differently. They
respectfully told her: 'We're minding the garden, missus.'

The front garden shows intelligent use of the little space by using fine pea gravel,
scree, low-growing, ground-hugging, tufty plants and clumps of spring snowflakes
(*Leucojum vernum*). The temptation to get down on hands and knees is strong. There
are spring bulbs at the beginning of the year and, later, angel's fishing rod (*Dierama*)
in variety, variegated daphne, alstroemeria, thalictrum, tiny aquilegia and an
unnamed old watsonia in orange with white spots.

This smartness continues at the back of the house with a completely different
garden. The back garden signals the end of minimalism and hard landscaping and the
beginning of a lush jungle of bloom and foliage. A mind-boggling range of herbaceous
plants, small trees, ferns and grasses vie with each other for attention in the well-
tended, well-fed beds that wrap around the garden. The back beds get all the sun and
here blue agapanthus, verbena, phlox and thistles are stationed. Dotted both here
and in the shadier spots are hostas and lilies, which do well anywhere. A lush patch of
green-tinted arum lilies (*Zantedeschia* 'Green Goddess') grow through yellow
hakonechloa grass in a head-turning combination. The reds in the shadier part of the
garden work well. Mrs Nolan doesn't like the glare of red out in the full light of the
sun, so the *Dahlia* 'Bishop of Llandaff' and *Crocosmia* 'Lucifer' comport themselves
in a more seemly way in soft shade. This is an idea for anyone with a fear of using
strong reds or hot colours.

Close to the house an unusual *Codonopsis convolvulacea* with violet bell-flowers
climbs through a berberis. Unusual black salvia, which could be an *Addam's Family*
favourite, with silver, hairy leaves and a velvety-black flower, lives in the greenhouse.

The miniature garden is made up of Lilliputian gunnera, the tiniest hosta, called
'Thumbnail', a mini thalictrum only a few centimetres high, and tiny astilbe in stone
troughs. 'I love the big things and I love the little things and I love putting them
together,' Anna says enthusiastically. Her enthusiasm has paid off recently: she won
second prize in the Garden for All Seasons category of the Shamrock All Ireland
Gardens Competition 1999.

Rathmichael, County Dublin; Tel: +01 2822032 ☀ **Contact:** Catherine O'Halloran
☀ **Open:** May–end July, strictly by appointment only ☀ **Entrance fee** donated to
Festina Lente charity ☀ Supervised children welcome ☀ **Directions:** travelling from
Bray, drive up the Old Connaught Road, pass the Old Connaught Golf Club and
continue a short distance. The garden is on the right-hand side, with a gate lodge
to mark it.

The house at Springmount is covered in heavily berried orange cotoneaster, wisteria
and jasmine. The windows hold well-filled boxes and pheasant berry (*Leycesteria formosa*) grows out of the gravel drive. All this bodes well for what the garden promises.
Secret stone steps surrounded in honeysuckle, vinca and ivy lead up to the secluded
woody garden that backs the house. Hebe and mahonia light up the area under the
canopy of pines. By the drive is a big bank of bergenia, lavender, aubrieta, Welsh poppies, cowslips, common primroses, small rhododendrons and azaleas. There are ferns
through the aubrieta, campanula and mind-your-own-business (*Soleirolia soleirolii*).
This is an attractive, busy bank, not big or showy but absolutely lovely.

Climbing up through a combination of one-third stone step, one-third box hedging and one-third mind-your-own business, the way leads in under an arch of
Clematis 'Duchess of Edinburgh', through a garden gate and into a big 'Wow' of a
garden. Spreading out in front is a vision of rolls of box hedge, like a line of police
trying to hold back a riotous crowd of herbaceous flowers and shrubs. The first bed is
largely composed of white and silver foliage plants: white roses, white-flowering
myrtle, pulmonaria, weeping pear, *Clematis viticella* 'Alba Luxurians' with greeny-
white, frilled flowers, *Anemone japonica* and Paris daisies, all knotted together. The
greyish leaves of a backing hedge of cotoneaster foil them nicely. A peach-coloured
rose arches over a fine iron bench further along the bed, which at this point begins to
colour, sweeping up around the garden and off into the surrounding woods.

More cotoneaster hedging runs into yew, and another step up in the garden leads
to a bench, royally guarded by urns on a little stage, and a sweep of steps snowed
under by self-seeding nasturtium, aubrieta and Lady's mantle (*Alchemilla mollis*).
Good repeat planting is used in the garden and strong foliage plants dotted along the
beds give backbone to the more fleeting good looks of flowers. Further up the path is
another iron bench under a canopy of bamboo, from where one can look back through
the central axis of box, paths and sundials and on to Killiney Hill and the sea. A fountain and raised pond, surrounded by lush hosta and fern leaves, backs this part of the
garden. It is a verdant, cool spot.

From here another path leads down to an eye-catching bed of *Centaurea montana*,
fat, juicy, flowering fuchsia, penstemon, sedum, lavatera, asters and more carpeted
steps, a laurel-encircled summerhouse and a little rose garden, all against a backdrop
of mature trees. Smart, terraced lawns lead up to the house, past rose beds held in
with box and a rocky wall bed with roses and wall planting of saxifrage, houseleeks and
a little jasmine.

This garden has the best of everything – a series of heights and drops, views of the
sea, the proximity of the mountains, a surrounding of mature trees and a talented and
tasteful gardener.

St Stephen's Green, Dublin 2 ▪ **Contact:** Margaret Gormely at Dúchas, Tel: +01 4757816; Fax: +01 4755287 ▪ **Open:** all year; Monday–Saturday, 8am–dusk; Sundays and bank holidays, 10am–dusk; Christmas Day, 10am–1.30pm ▪ **No entrance fee** ▪ **Special features:** children's playground; garden for the visually impaired; concerts during the summer months ▪ Member of Dúchas ▪ **Directions:** the main entrance is opposite the junction of Grafton Street and South King Street; entrances also at the Merrion Row, Earlsfort Terrace and Harcourt Street corners of the Green.

St Stephen's Green is a much-loved public park, home to a thousand lunchtime sun-worshippers in summer and to duck-feeding children at all times of the year. The park dates back to the medieval period, when it was used as a common.

In 1663, Dublin Corporation decided to develop St Stephen's Green, building houses within the park and laying out a parade ground and walk as well as a place of public entertainment, which famously housed a grand fireworks display in 1749. In 1815 the iron railings and the granite, chain-linked bollards on the broadwalk outside the Green were erected. The Green was then locked to the public, a move which provoked general discontent. In 1877 Sir Arthur Guinness, Lord Ardilaun, rowed into the fray, declaring that he would pay for the Green's development as a public park himself. Work began: an artificial lake with a substantial waterfall and rockery was created; formal flowerbeds and fountains were laid out and erected and a pretty superintendent's lodge was built. Finally, in 1880, the transformed St Stephen's Green was opened to the grateful public.

Only once was the Green involved in important historical events, when Countess Markievicz and the Irish Citizen Army occupied it during the 1916 Easter Rising. Afterwards the superintendent was praised by his superiors for continuing to feed the birds in the Green – at the risk of getting shot. Six waterfowl were killed and seven park benches were destroyed in the crossfire, but the superintendent survived.

The park still looks much as it did in the time of Lord Ardilaun. At the centre are the formal flowerbeds and two elaborate fountains. The beds are used for colourful

The castle at Malahide Demesne, home to the Talbot family from the 1180s until 1973.

summer bedding – petunia, wallflower and tulips. The lake is the real central feature of the garden, with its bridges, islands and rockwork, all well covered by mature shrubs. The water in the lake is pumped from the Grand Canal.

Despite the sheltering barrier of trees and shrubs, which filter out much of the pollution, there is still enough environmental damage to prevent many specimens of plant from being grown in the Green. A significant number of the trees are London plane, a species tolerant of pollution. Most of the Wych elms were lost to Dutch elm disease. Sycamore is planted widely, along with evergreen holm oak.

The big rockery is currently under restoration, and a garden for the blind, with aromatic shrubs and herbs labelled in braille, is a fairly recent feature. There is a good children's playground, and the bandstand is used for music and performances throughout the summer.

THE TALBOT BOTANIC GARDENS, MALAHIDE DEMESNE

Dublin Road, Malahide, County Dublin; Tel: +01 8462184; Fax: +01 8463620 ▪ **Contact:** Anne James ▪ **Open:** May–September, daily, 2pm–5pm ▪ **Entrance fee** (separate charge for castle) ▪ **Special features**: historic castle; tours on Wednesdays at 2pm, or by appointment at other times ▪ **Directions:** driving from Fairview to Malahide, turn right at the sign for Malahide Castle. The entrance is on the left.

The castle at Malahide was lived in continuously by the Talbot family from the 1180s, when the lands were granted to Richard Talbot by the English Crown, until 1973 when the last of the family, Lord Milo de Talbot, died. He left the castle and lands to the Parks Department of Dublin County Council (the demesne is now managed by Fingal County Council).

Despite the lengthy history of the demesne, the gardens are very young, having been created by Lord Milo between 1948 and 1973. He was a learned gardener who set out to create a garden full of tender and less common plants, many of them from Tasmania, New Zealand and Australia; all countries with which he had close connections.

The variety of plants in Malahide is limited by the alkalinity of the soil. This prevents the growing of rhododendrons and other acid-loving plants. In Malahide, visitors with alkaline soil in their own gardens for once need not be green-eyed at the numbers of plants on show that they can't grow themselves. Genera well represented in the gardens include euphorbia, crocosmia, hebe, pittosporum, escallonia, olearia and clematis. Great sweeps of lawn, snowdrop carpets in spring, shrubberies, groves of trees and specimen trees are placed handsomely and in abundance around the demesne.

The gardens are divided into the greater or pleasure garden and the walled garden. The pleasure garden is made up of varied rides and paths, in which almost 5,000 species of tree can be identified with the help of a guiding leaflet. The walled garden covers almost four acres and is divided into herbaceous and mixed beds, a spectacularly densely planted pond and the Australian garden, which is currently being developed using plants from that continent in strict and formal arrangements. The greenhouses and alpine beds complete the walled garden, which for many visitors is the high point of the visit.

Islandbridge, Dublin 8; Tel: +01 6770236/+01 6472498 ▪ **Contact:** Robert Norris ▪ **Open:** all year, Monday–Friday, 8am–dusk; Saturday–Sunday, 10am–dusk ▪ **No entrance fee** ▪ **Special features:** two book rooms containing the names of 49,400 Irishmen who died in the First World War, the rooms may be viewed by prior arrangement; guided tours may be arranged in advance ▪ Member of Dúchas ▪ **Directions:** the gardens may be entered from Con Colbert Road, by the South Circular Road at the Phoenix Park end, or from the bridge to Parkgate Street, from where it is signposted.

The War Memorial Gardens is one of the lesser-known fine gardens in the country, though it is thought by many to be one of the most beautiful memorial gardens in Europe. Designed by the renowned architect Sir Edwin Lutyens (1869–1944, *see* Heywood Gardens, County Laois), it was built in the 1930s.

The gardens suffered for years from a national tendency to ignore the First World War, despite the deaths of thousands of Irishmen in that war. They were neither visited nor tended for many years. Today, however, the place is well maintained and visited a little more often.

The memorial is divided into large garden rooms. The main feature is a raised lawn enclosed by granite piers and book rooms, where the names of all those who died are listed. There are pergolas, a pair of mirroring sunken rose gardens and formal ponds. It is a very handsome garden, with restrained planting, in a fine site overlooking the River Liffey, the boat clubs on the opposite bank and the old Magazine Fort.

MARLAY DEMESNE AND REGENCY WALLED GARDENS
Grange Road, Rathfarnham, Dublin 16; Tel: +01 2054700.

The walled gardens at Marlay, restored with the assistance of an ERDF grant, under the Great Gardens of Ireland Restoration Programme, opened to the public in April 2001. They contain a number of recreated Regency-style buildings: an *orangerie*, bothys and the arbour, which afforded shade for the ladies of the house during their afternoon walks. Authentic Regency plants are used throughout. Guided tours of house and gardens available.

GARDENING CLUBS AND SOCIETIES

ALPINE GARDEN SOCIETY OF IRELAND

See appendices.

CASTLEKNOCK AND DISTRICT GARDEN CLUB

This club has been in existence for twenty-five years. It meets at 8pm on the fourth Wednesday of each month in St Brigid's National School, Castleknock. Activities include lectures and talks from visiting experts, summer outings and trips. An autumn show is held annually.

CLONTARF HORTICULTURAL SOCIETY

Contact: Olive Keogh, 4 Kincora Road, Clontarf, Dublin 3.

Clontarf Horticultural Society was established in 1954, making it one of the oldest in County Dublin. Meetings are held between October and May, on the last Thursday of the month, at 8pm in St John's House, Seafield Road, Clontarf. Members and non-members may attend. In June and September shows are arranged.

DUBLIN FIVE HORTICULTURAL SOCIETY, THE

Contact: Mr Tony Boston; Tel: +01 8474585.

DUBLIN NATURALISTS' FIELD CLUB AND FLORA SOCIETY

Contact: David Nash, 35 Nutley Park, Dublin 4.

EUROPEAN BOXWOOD AND TOPIARY SOCIETY

Contact: Geoffrey Willis, Greenmount, Glenamuck Road, Kilternan (attached to Kilternan Nursery, which specialises in topiary).

This society is in its infancy in Ireland. With a small number of members, it does not yet have a structured lecture and meeting arrangement.

FOXROCK AND DISTRICT GARDENING CLUB, THE

One of the most successful clubs in the country. Since its foundation ten years ago, it has acquired such a reputation that its 200-member capacity is well filled and there is always a queue to join. The club meets from September to May, on the fourth Tuesday of the month, at 8pm in the Foxrock Church Community Hall. Visitors can attend meetings for a fee.

HOWTH AND SUTTON HORTICULTURAL SOCIETY

Contact: Mr Karl Flynn, Medina, Howth, County Dublin.

The society was founded in 1943. Apart from an active programme of monthly meetings from autumn to spring, shows are held in April and September. They welcome new members.

IRISH GARDEN PLANT SOCIETY

See appendices.

NORTH DUBLIN HORTICULTURAL SOCIETIES' ASSOCIATION

Contact: Tony Boston; Tel: +01 8474585.

ROYAL HORTICULTURAL SOCIETY OF IRELAND

See appendices.

NURSERIES AND GARDEN CENTRES

ATLANTIC HOMECARE

Unit 4/6, Stillorgan Industrial Estate, Blackrock, County Dublin; Tel: +01 2952926.

Unit 419, Blanchardstown Retail Park, Blanchardstown, Dublin15; Tel: +01 8215699.

Royal Liver Retail Park, Bluebell, Dublin 12; Tel: +01 4503388.

BAGGO GARDENING

118 Cork Street, Dublin 8; Tel: +01 4542299.

BALDONNELL CROSS GARDEN CENTRE

Naas Road, Dublin 22; Tel: +01 4573222.

BEECH VISTA NURSERY GARDEN CENTRE

Main Street, Ashbourne Road, Finglas, Dublin 11; Tel: +01 8342953.

BONSAI SHOP

Powerscourt Townhouse Centre, Clarendon Street, Dublin 2; Tel: +01 6793456.

BRENNAN'S GARDEN SHOP

17 Lower Camden Street, Dublin 2;
Tel: +01 4750029.

BYRNE'S, HARRY, GARDEN CENTRE

Castlepark Road, Sandycove, County
Dublin; Tel: +01 2803887.

CARBERY NURSERIES

Kilmatead, Naas Road, Dublin 12; Tel:
+01 4592668/087 2473549.

CLONDALKIN GARDEN CENTRE

Boot Road, Clondalkin, Dublin 22; Tel:
+01 4573390.

COLGAN, MAURICE AND MAUREEN

2 Mooretown Road, Swords, County
Dublin; Tel: +01 8403685.

From May to the end of July the Colgans,
known locally as the couple to whom Elvis
wrote personal letters in the 1960s, sell
herbaceous plants from their garden in
aid of charity.

COLOUR GREEN GARDEN CENTRE

Carr's Lane, off Malahide Road, Bal-
griffen, Dublin 17; Tel: +01 8674319/
+01 8325565.

CONNEFF, SYDNEY

3 Ardagh Court, Blackrock, County
Dublin; Tel/Fax: +01 2887625 ※ Mail
order service available all year (catalogue £1).

Sydney Conneff supplies many of the
great gardens of Ireland, as well as the
keener amateurs, with over 400 unusual
and quality herbaceous perennials. He
works largely through mail order, and in
addition to the main catalogue a bulb list
is available.

COOLQUAY NURSERY AND GARDEN CENTRE

The Ward, County Dublin; Tel: +01
8351289.

CORKAGH NURSERIES

Naas Road, Baldonnell Cross, Dublin
22; Tel: +01 4592336.

DACUS PLANTS

PO Box 5326, Dim :apgjaore; e-mail:
dacus@indigo.ie.

Rare and alpine plants by mail order. A
catalogue is available from the Post Office
Box above or via the Internet site. Mr
Dacus stocks many seeds from the wild,
particularly from Chile, the Himalayas,
China and South Africa.

DRIMNAGH GARDEN CENTRE

11 Rafter's Road, Drimnagh, Dublin 12;
Tel: +01 4556082.

ENNIS, PADDY, GARDEN CENTRE

90 Terenure Road North, Dublin 6; Tel:
+01 4924176.

FLOWER CENTRE, THE

754 Howth Road, Blackbanks, Dublin
5; Tel: +01 8327047.

FOREST NURSERY

Forest Road, Swords, County Dublin;
Tel: +01 8407843.

FOUNTAINS AND DÉCOR

Kingswood Cross, Naas Road, Dublin
22; Tel: +01 4591724.

GARDEN SHOP, THE

Main Street, Cabinteely, Dublin 18; Tel:
+01 2851469.

GARDEN STYLE

15 Main Street, Baldoyle, County Dublin; Tel: +01 8321640.

GARDENWORKS

Mablestown, Malahide, County Dublin; Tel: +01 8450110.

GARDEN WORLD

Ballyboden, Dublin 16; Tel: +01 4932554.

GRANGE GROWERS

The Grange, Kilternan, County Dublin; Tel: +01 2955650.

HARDY PLANT NURSERY

Ridge House, Ballybrack Crossroads, Ballybrack, County Dublin; Tel: +01 2826973/088 2785614.

One of the most exciting places to buy hardy perennials in the country. The plants can be bought either by mail order or on one of the nursery's open days. Write to the address above for a catalogue.

HERB GARDEN, THE

Forde-de-Fyne, Naul, County Dublin; Tel: +01 8413907; herbs@indigo.ie

Organic herb garden, with over 200 varieties of herbs, organic vegetables and salads. They also sell herbs, salads, vegetables and herb-related items at the food market in Meeting House Square, Temple Bar, Dublin, every Saturday. Send a SAE for details and plant lists.

HOMEBASE GARDEN CENTRE

Omni Park Shopping Centre, Santry, Dublin 9; Tel: +01 8621435.

Nutgrove Avenue, Rathfarnham, Dublin 14; Tel: +01 2983197.

JONES'S FRUIT FARM AND GARDEN CENTRE

Donabate Road, Swords, County Dublin; Tel: +01 8401781; Fax: +01 8402705.

KILTERNAN NURSERIES

Old Post Office, Kilternan, County Dublin; Tel: +01 2955597.

KINSEALY GARDEN CENTRE AND FLORIST

Malahide Road, Kinsealy, County Dublin; Tel: +01 8460984.

LISSENHALL NURSERIES

Lissenhall, Swords, County Dublin; Tel: +01 8402700.

MACKEY'S GARDEN CENTRE

Castlepark Road, Sandycove, County Dublin; Tel: +01 2807385; www.mackeys.ie

MAHONEY'S NURSERIES

Old Rush Road, County Dublin; Tel: +01 8439088.

MALAHIDE NURSERY

Opposite Malahide Demesne, Malahide, County Dublin; Tel: +01 8450110.

MARIAN NURSERY

New Haggard, Lusk, County Dublin; Tel: +01 8437445.

MR MIDDLETON'S

58 Mary Street, Dublin 1; Tel: +01 8731118.

MURPHY AND WOOD GARDEN CENTRE

Hill Hire Centre, Johnstown Road, Cabinteely, County Dublin; Tel: +01 2854855.

NEWLANDS GARDEN CENTRE

New Road, Clondalkin, Dublin 22; Tel: +01 4592013; Fax: +01 4593658.

OBELISK NURSERY

St Augustine's Park (off Carysfort Avenue), County Dublin; Tel: +01 2881771.

PHOENIX PARK GARDEN CENTRE

Castleknock, County Dublin; Tel: +01 8383326.

ROLESTOWN GARDEN CENTRE

Off the Rathbeale Road (R125), Swords, County Dublin; Tel: +01 8405780.

SCALPWOOD NURSERIES

Enniskerry Road, Kilternan, Dublin 18; Tel/Fax: +01 2954636.

SEABROOK, MR STAN

16 Sarto Road, Sutton, County Dublin; Tel: +01 8322254.

Specialises in fuchsia and rare herbaceous plants. Telephone for an appointment or for information on plants for sale.

SOUTHSIDE GARDEN CENTRE

Kilternan, County Dublin; Tel: +01 2954353.

TALLAGHT GARDEN CENTRE

Belgard Road, Tallaght, Dublin 22; Tel: +01 4610266.

THREE GATES GARDEN CENTRE

25 Drogheda Street, Balbriggan, County Dublin; Tel: +01 8414914.

WINDYRIDGE GARDEN CENTRE

110–114 Rochestown Avenue, Dún Laoghaire, County Dublin; Tel: +01 2852796.

WOODIES DIY GARDEN CENTRES

Malahide Road, Coolock, Dublin 5; Tel: +01 8485923.

Ballydowd, Lucan, County Dublin; Tel: +01 6210766.

Dublin Industrial Estate, Glasnevin, Dublin 11; Tel: +01 8307222.

Sallynoggin Road, Sallynoggin, County Dublin; Tel: +01 2840200.

Seatown, Swords, County Dublin; Tel: +01 8408822.

Belgard Road, Tallaght, Dublin 24; Tel: +01 4596944.

Burtonhall Road, Sandyford Industrial Estate, Sandyford, County Dublin; Tel: +01 2959722.

GARDEN DESIGNERS

GARDEN AND LANDSCAPE DESIGNERS' ASSOCIATION (GLDA)

73 Deerpark Road, Mount Merrion, County Dublin; Tel: +01 2781824; Fax: +01 283 5724.

Designers with the letters GLDA after their name are full members, as listed in the association's 1999 brochure. I have restricted information on garden designers to GLDA full members whose work has been assessed and has met the requirements of a panel of horticultural experts. Contact the association for an updated list of full members.

GLENN CRAIGIE, ANDREW AND LISA MURPHY, GLDA

Landscape Restoration Design, The Rookery, Powerstown, Clonee, Dublin 15; Tel: +01 8217046 (office hours).

Most work is carried out in Dublin and Leinster. Andrew Glenn Craigie has been designing and making gardens for eighteen years.

GORDON T LEDBETTER

74 Highfield Road, Rathgar, Dublin 6; Tel: +01 4970439.

To view Mr Ledbetter's public work, see the overall design of the National Garden Exhibition Centre in Kilquade in Wicklow (*see* County Wicklow). He also designed the Water and Woodland and the Victorian Rose Garden in the NGEC.

SANIO, GABRIELE, GLDA

Microenvironments, The Coach House, 32 Monkstown Road, Monkstown, County Dublin; Tel: +01 2844007.

An award-winning designer working throughout Ireland. See her designs in *Irish Garden* magazine.

GARDEN COURSES

DUBLIN SCHOOL OF HORTICULTURE

67 Rollins Villas, Sallynoggin, County Dublin; Tel: +01 2847387/+01 2809602; e-mail: dacus@indigo.ie

The Dublin School of Horticulture has recently started to run night classes for the RHS General Examination in Horticulture. The course is aimed at serious amateurs and those thinking of entering the horticulture world professionally. This is a well-recognised basic qualification and a good starting point for anyone wishing to formalise their horticultural knowledge.

In 1999/2000, classes were held at the Presentation College in Glasthule. The course runs two evenings a week (Monday and Wednesday) for twenty-four weeks.

KENNEDY, EVE

Kensington Lodge, Rochestown Avenue, Dún Laoghaire, County Dublin; Tel: +01 2803577.

Eve Kennedy holds occasional part-time and weekend gardening courses. Contact for details.

GARDEN ACCESSORIES

AMAU CERAMICS

Blackrock Market, Blackrock, County Dublin.

ARCHITECTURAL HERITAGE

Terenure Lodge, Terenure Road, Dublin 6; Tel: +01 4907034.

ARTEFACTION

12–13 Lime Street, Sir John Rogerson's Quay, Dublin 2; Tel: +01 6776495.

BALLYGRIFFIN PATIO CENTRE

Carr's Lane, Malahide, County Dublin (beside Colour Green Garden Centre).

CHRISTY BIRD, ARCHITECTURAL SALVAGE

31–32 South Richmond Street, Portobello, Dublin 8; Tel: +01 4754095.

COWSHED, THE

DIY and Garden Centre, Sandycove, Glasthule Village, County Dublin; Tel: +01 2300303.

DECK CLAD

Kingswood Cross, Naas Road; Tel: +01 4595492.

Old glass bricks, stone pieces, salvaged railings and fencing, strange bric-a-brac for gardens, as well as the usual railway sleepers, street lights and troughs.

DESIGNER STONE LIMITED

144 North Strand Road, Dublin 3; Tel: +01 8366065.

Hand-dressed flagstones and tiles for indoor and outdoor use.

EGG DEPOT, THE

34a Wexford Street, Dublin 2; Tel: +01 4756506.

Cut flowers, garden accessories and window-boxes.

FORMALITY GARDEN DESIGN

5 Old Dunleary Road, Dún Laoghaire, County Dublin; Tel: +01 2808071.

HABITAT

6 St Stephen's Green, Dublin 2; Tel: +01 6771433.

HILLS HIRE CENTRE

Johnstown Road, Cabinteely, Dublin 18; Tel: +01 2853676.

Garden tools and machinery.

LENEHAN'S HARDWARE

124 Capel Street, Dublin 1; Tel: +01 8730466 (also branches).

NORTON PEAT SALES

48 Francis Street, Dublin 8; Tel: +01 4540666.

ORIGINAL ARCHITECTURAL SALVAGE COMPANY

South Gloucester Street, Dublin 2; Tel: 086 8207700.

PATIO CENTRE, THE

The Hills Centre, Johnstown Road, Cabinteely, Dublin 18; Tel: +01 2853398; website: thepatiocentre.com

PORTER, STEPHEN, ARCHITECTURAL SALVAGE

Quarry Road, Dún Laoghaire, County Dublin; Tel: +01 2857709.

SHANGANAGH MARBLE AND STONE CENTRE

Crinken, Bray Road, Shankill, County Dublin; Tel: +01 2825811.

STONEBROKERS, ARCHITECTURAL SALVAGE

Greenbanks, Old Quarry, Dalkey, County Dublin; Tel: +01 2857709.

COUNTY KILDARE

Kildare is the centre of the horse industry in Ireland. Racecourses, sales rooms and stud farms of some of the biggest names in racing stretch across the county. The National Stud, just outside Kildare town, is among these and opens to the public. Driving through the flat expanse of the Curragh, you will see racehorses being exercised in groups, especially in the morning. Kildare is an obviously wealthy county, made up of fertile brown clay farmland. There are plenty of places to visit, from the Palladian splendour of Castletown House in Celbridge, to the gardens and museums of Lodge Park, Larchill and Ballindoolin. An unusual attraction is the small Quaker museum in Ballitore, a village built by Quakers and made famous in the *Annals of Ballitore*, written by Mary Leadbeater (1758–1826). Stroll along the banks of the Royal Canal between Kilcock and Maynooth or visit Robertstown, a pretty village run through by the Grand Canal. In the grounds of the university church in Maynooth is a bicentennial garden commissioned to commemorate the 200th anniversary of the college in 1995. Composed of plants named in the bible, it is worth a visit. The university is also the site for the Annual Maynooth Garden Festival (*see* box, p.57).

BALLINDOOLIN HOUSE AND GARDEN

Carbury, County Kildare; Tel: +0405 31430; Fax: +0405 32377; e-mail: sun-dial@iol.ie ▨ **Contact:** Mrs Esther Molony ▨ **Open:** beginning May–end September, Tuesday–Sunday, 12pm–6pm; by appointment only at any other times ▨ **Entrance fee** ▨ Children welcome; please note, only guide dogs allowed ▨ **Special features:** small collection of rare-breed farm animals; nature trail; museum; restaurant in main house (Tel: +0405 32400 for bookings) ▨ **Directions**: just south of the Dublin–Galway road on the R104, about 5km from Edenderry. Signposts direct you from Moy Valley and Kinnegad.

When the Molony family inherited Ballindoolin in 1993, they inherited not just a house and garden but an enormous amount of work. Built in 1821 by a Dutch family, the Bors, Ballindoolin and the surrounding 250-acre demesne had seen better days. The Molonys took up residence on the understanding that they would bring the house and garden back to life. And so, fifty years of neglect and wild growth were swept away enthusiastically, revealing another jewel to add to the many grand gardens retrieved from choked wildernesses around the country. Work finished on the garden in 1999 and it has been open to the public since then.

The garden is a success but that success was hard won: 'We had to dig down through two feet of soil before we found the original paths,' says Esther, laughing now as she looks back on the slave labour the team willingly undertook. But despite the Herculean task completed she takes no credit, handing all praise to Daphne Shackleton and her young head gardener, Thomas Hopkins.

When Esther Molony and the family started work, the walled garden was a mass of sycamore saplings and saving it was a mammoth task, but as Esther explained: 'One great thing about the walled garden was that the cattle had not been left in so the excellent old espaliered apple trees had survived well.' These gnarled trees, like knotty candelabras, are the backbone of the design for the new walled garden. Daphne Shackleton (*see* County Cavan) incorporated them into her arrangement when she produced her reworking of the 1821 walled garden. This is a formal working walled garden, which feeds the restaurant in the main house but is also decorative in itself.

Within the walls, the area has been divided into squares: one in soft fruit, one in herbs, another as a nuttery, two lawns and the rest in vegetables. To one side a melon pit awaits restoration. Double borders running under the apple trees cut the garden in two. They are well laid out, mostly made of low-growing plants, which will not interfere with the shaped trees. These are beds that look good throughout the year, starting with spring bulbs, which, as they fade and die back, are replaced by emerging hosta and hardy geranium leaves. Over these, with arms outstretched, stand the remarkable century-old fruit trees. On the west wall is a fine, formal knot bed made of clipped box wrapped around David Austin roses. Austin English roses have the habit and big cabbage-like good looks and scent of old roses, but they have the health and robust constitution of modern roses. They are therefore more resistant to aphid, blackspot and rust attack than older varieties.

The main border stands in front of a warm south wall. Measuring 100 metres long, this bed is planted in colours which were inspired by Gertrude Jekyll (*see* box, Gertrude Jekyll, p.58). Cool shades, such as mauves and blues, start at the outside of the bed. The scheme hots up toward the middle with oranges and yellows, and cools down again toward the end of the bed. It's an attractive border and looked well even at the very end of September, when I visited, despite a pretty dreadful storm three days before. A Michaelmas daisy border travels off at an angle from the main border. This is an exercise incorporating daisy-like flowers, such as aster, anthemis, rudbekia, argyranthemum and felicia, in a mass of colours tied to a simple flower shape.

Now that the walled garden is up and running, fighting the weeds has become the task of the moment, but Thomas Hopkins is working the design wonderfully.

Beyond the wall is a strange Victorian rockery, part of which was put together by Victorian 'vandals' who obtained their stone from statues and monuments. Their finds are scattered through the rockery, clearly and shamelessly visible. From the top of the rockery there is a fine view of a shamrock-shaped ruined dovecote.

Beginning at the rockery, you can follow a two-kilometre nature trail through the

200-year-old wood that Christopher Bor began planting in the 1760s. The trail is well signed with informative notices pointing out the trees and wildlife (a leaflet with this information is also available).

Finally, a small collection of rare-breed farm animals – pigs, chickens, goats, hens and ducks of all description – will add to the day out for children. The animals are a hugely important part of the set-up in Ballindoolin. The day I visited, the drawing-room of the old house had been turned into a hospital nursery, complete with incubator, for a gang of tiny ducklings in need of a bit of snug. I encountered them as they were being ferried into the house by 'jumper express', courtesy of Mrs Molony's daughter!

GERTRUDE JEKYLL

Gertrude Jekyll (1843–1932) has been described as 'perhaps the greatest artist in horticulture' and, for several reasons, this description of the English garden designer, writer, artist and craftswoman is appropriate. She began life as a student of art, and when she moved on to gardening she brought her love of painting and colour to bear on her designs. Particularly devoted to the work of JMW Turner, she was heavily influenced by his use of colour. Turner reduced Newton's seven-colour spectrum to three primary colours – red, yellow and blue. Likewise, in a Jekyll-created or inspired flower border, red is the central and most powerful colour around which range yellows, oranges and golds, moving out to blues, purples, whites and greys.

Gertrude Jekyll created her first garden in Munstead Wood in Surrey, England, in 1878. In 1889 she met the architect Edwin Lutyens and the pair worked together on numerous gardens until her death in 1932. They specialised in the design and planting of memorials to the Great War.

Her work and the influence of her work ranges far and wide in these islands, and she designed around 250 gardens on this side of the Atlantic alone. She also wrote several books on garden design, which are still popular and in print almost seventy years after her death.

CELBRIDGE ABBEY

Clane Road, Celbridge, County Kildare; Tel: +01 6275508; Fax: +01 6275062 ▪ **Contact:** Tony or Maria O'Toole ▪ **Open:** all year, Monday–Saturday, 10am–6pm, Sundays and bank holidays, 12pm–6pm ▪ **Entrance fee** donated to the Hospitaller Order of St John of God ▪ Supervised children welcome; please note, only guide dogs allowed ▪ **Special features:** model railway; garden centre; guided tours of the historic abbey; a garden club meets here on the first Monday of each month, contact administrator for details ▪ **Directions:** leave Celbridge by the Clane Road. The abbey is a few hundred metres out of the town on the left-hand side, well signposted.

Celbridge Abbey is a wonderful garden for a children's outing. One of the first things to greet you is a fine old chestnut tree surrounded by and decorated with quirky monster and alien sculptures. This immediately sets the tone. More pieces of art are hidden in the woods or under trees and they are all child-centred.

The gardens are attached to the abbey, built in 1697 by Bartholemew Van Homrigh, Lord Mayor of Dublin and father of Vanessa, made famous through the letters of Jonathan Swift. Swift (1667–1745) was Dean of St Patrick's Cathedral, Dublin, and was one of the finest satirists in the English language. His best-known work is probably *Gulliver's Travels*. He shared an interest in gardening with his friend, the English satirist Alexander Pope, who created a famous garden in Chiswick, outside London. There is a Swiftian theme to Celbridge Abbey because of Swift's connection with Vanessa Van Homrigh, who laid out the original gardens, and Swift, a regular visitor, would have known these gardens well.

The river walk is quite magical, with weirs, little stone bridges and sluices. Signs set out along the banks tell children about the wildlife to be seen and the life cycle of the river. There are small stone bowers and benches for sitting. Indeed, Vanessa's Bower is thought to be where Henry Grattan, a later inhabitant of the house, composed his famous 'Declaration of Rights' speech.

The riverside planting is wild and woody and the whole feel of the gardens is informal. Pretty herbaceous beds with paths are sited near the café and house. There is a ninety-one-metre-long model railway for children, complete with a scaled-down model of the local Hazelhatch Station, which will satisfy train fans. The whole venture is the work of the Hospitaller Order of St John of God, who are running it as a public garden, garden centre and coffee shop in which the work is carried out jointly by able-bodied and less able-bodied workers.

COOLCARRIGAN HOUSE

Coolcarrigan, Coill Dubh, Naas, County Kildare; Tel: +045 863512; Fax: +045 8341400 ■ **Contact:** Hilary Wilson Wright ■ **Open:** April–August, by appointment only ■ **Entrance fee** ■ Supervised children welcome; please note, dogs on leads ■ **Special features:** 1,000 species of shrubs; lunches can be booked by prior arrangement ■ **Directions:** drive from Clane to Prosperous and continue to the crossroads by the Dag Weld pub, from where Coolcarrigan is signed. Go through Coill Dubh. Pass the church and the garden is a short distance along on the left, marked by black gates.

The Wilson Wright family has been gardening at Coolcarrigan for five generations. The present owner, John Wilson Wright, is the most recent member of the family to continue the gardening tradition. Today, his interest and knowledge is pooled with that of his gardener, Rory Finnegan, in the working of this gorgeous space.

Coolcarrigan is a classic Victorian garden with a rockery, lily pond, herbaceous borders, lawns, greenhouses and a collection of shrubs and trees. A visit begins with the border in the more intimate area around the house. Mr Wilson Wright's wife, Hilary, planted this handsome bed. Blue delphinium spires, bell-like campanula, geum, dahlia, blue *Clematis integrifolia*, California tree poppies (*Romneya coulteri*) and a host of other border flowers that bloom from mid-summer to autumn fill the bed. There is a striking example of the native evergreen strawberry tree (*Arbutus unedo*), with tiny white flowers, edible fruit and a bark like a huge cinnamon stick.

A long, well-maintained greenhouse is divided into separate, smaller houses. One is home to healthy-cropping vines and peaches. But the stars are next door in the shape of a collection of passion flowers, which includes the gorgeous red banana passion flower (*Passiflora antioquiensis*). This plant has slender, rich pink flowers that frill out like tutus. Another variety is the bizarre-looking *Passiflora quadrangularis*, which has wavy filaments like purple- and cream-striped jellyfish tentacles. In here there are also succulents and a pineapple guava with edible and fairly tasty flowers. Kiwi plants bear fruit but they don't ripen.

Out from the greenhouse is a naturalistic, almost village green-style pond cut straight into the turf. The planting around the rim is sparse and for the most part restricted to a simple grass edge. A few lilies decorate the water, but here too restraint has been shown and the main body of water is left clear to reflect the sky and trees. In the surrounding damp lawns wild orchids grow in almost weed-like numbers. Indeed, scattered throughout the grounds several varieties of wild orchid thrive, including pyramidal orchids (*Anacamptis pyramidalis*), the common spotted orchid (*Dactylorrhiza fuchsii*) and the common twayblade (*Listera ovata*). For naturalists, the wildlife in the gardens includes red squirrels, spotted fly-catchers and stoats; we glimpsed a few red squirrels as we walked through the woods.

While the main garden at Coolcarrigan is based on limestone, there is one area where the soil is acid because of a flanking bog. The peaty bed here has been planted with rhododendron, azalea and spring bulbs for an early-year show of colour.

But the important features at Coolcarrigan are the woods, arboretum and the long walks through the grounds. For five years the arboretum benefited from Mr Wilson Wright's working relationship with the well-known British plantsman Sir Harold Hillier, whose knowledge contributed hugely to the seriousness and significance of the Coolcarrigan tree collection. The collection amounts to around 100 maturing specimen trees, like ginkgo, embothrium and varieties of sorbus.

At Coolcarrigan, John Wilson Wright is pouring heart, soul and finance into both the upkeep and advancement of the garden. It is fairly rare and encouraging to come across someone working away as an unaided private individual on such a large garden.

**The beehive huts in
St Fiachra's Garden
in County Kildare.**

Kildare, County Kildare; Tel: +045 521617/522963; Fax: +045 522964; e-mail: stud@irish-national-stud.ie; website: www.irish-national-stud.ie ■ **Contact:** Frieda O'Connell ■ **Open:** 12 February–12 November, Monday–Sunday, 9.30am–6pm; last admission, 5pm; at any other time open only to groups, and strictly by appointment only ■ **Entrance fee** is combined ticket for Japanese Gardens and Irish National Stud ■ Please note, guide dogs only ■ **Special features:** self-guided tours in ten languages; guided tours ■ **Directions:** situated on the edge of Kildare town, signed clearly off the N7 and from all parts of Kildare county.

In 1906, after a highly successful trip to Japan, Colonel William Hall Walker of Tully in Kildare brought a Japanese gardener, Tassa Eida, back to Ireland to create a Japanese garden on the Kildare plains. Eida worked with forty men for several years to develop the garden until he left for home in unfortunate circumstances. He returned to Japan with Kildare-acquired tastes for drinking and backing horses; his relationship with his master had become strained and unhappy. Eida may have left his money in Kildare, but he also left behind him a lovely garden.

The Japanese Garden at Tully is an impressive and attractive garden, its miniature landscape heavily laden with symbolism and meaning. However, the symbolism is optional and the garden can be enjoyed simply as a garden. It is a well-designed space, full of mature shrubs, trees, topiary, waterside planting, paths and statuary. Visitors follow a winding path, travelling up and down rocky outcrops and past trees with cleverly exposed root runs. By making choices in direction along little side paths one can visit different areas of the garden, each of which portrays a time in the life cyle of man. A charming little teahouse, the site of occasional Japanese tea-making ceremonies, sits smartly in the centre of it all, surrounded by remarkable bonsai. In fact, some of these bonsai have been in the garden since 1906.

Although it is not a huge garden it is one of the busiest in the country, with over 130,000 visitors a year. If you want to avoid the crowds, time your visit carefully – go on an out-of-season Monday or Tuesday. The garden does not depend on flowers and plants that need to be seen in the summer, so a trip off-season will be just as rewarding, and perhaps even more enjoyable, particularly in early autumn when the maples begin to colour. The structure of the garden, combined with the many and various textures and shades of foliage, are its attractions.

Attached to the Japanese Garden is the larger St Fiachra's Garden. This is a woodland Irish garden designed by Martin Hallinan of University College, Dublin and dedicated to St Fiachra, the Irish saint who is known in France as the patron saint of gardening. This garden has achieved an artless and natural feel. The design is made up of simple walks through plantations of native oak, ash and willow and around lakes which are fed from springs discovered in the area. The water in the lakes has been trained over small waterfalls and there are nicely sited rock pools.

Simplicity is again the keyword for the planting by the lakes. The woods are underplanted with spring bulbs, wild garlic and wood anemone. These are all plants which will spread and naturalise under the light canopy. Fossilised tree trunks are placed like sculptures throughout the garden, giving an air of history and something ancient to the place. Set by the lakes there are replicas of three beehive huts, reminiscent of the monastic cells in which St Fiachra and his monks would have lived. Inside one of the cells is the unique Waterford Crystal Glass Garden with plants and ferns made from crystal.

While you are at the Japanese Gardens you can also visit the Irish National Stud (admission is included in your ticket price). This combination makes it a good trip for all the family.

K GARDENS ❀ ♿

Booleigh, Nurney, County Kildare; Tel: +0507 26189 ✹ **Contact:** Mr PJ Kirwan ✹
Open: Easter–end October, Monday–Sunday, 9.30am–6pm ✹ **Entrance fee** ✹
Special features: garden tours can be arranged; teas can be booked in advance ✹
Directions: leave the Athy–Kilcullen road by the right turn marked for Nurney.
Turn right off this road at the sign for K Gardens.

For the curious, K is for Kildare and for Kirwan, and why wouldn't PJ Kirwan name the garden after himself having created and worked all five acres of this high-mainte-nance garden on his own? His achievements were appropriately lauded when the K Gardens came second in the Kildare and Wicklow category of the Shamrock All Ireland Gardens Competition 1999.

The garden is made up of a series of big rooms linked together with trails and paths. There are also walls of ruler-straight beech and hornbeam with arches cut into them. These provide backdrops for several of the gardens, and, as well as giving the re-quired privacy within each of the gardens, the tall, tidy hedges afford a windbreak, slowing down and redirecting the winds that whistle over the open Curragh.

A long path leads through a selection of gardens, each one different from the last. The path starts at the flower garden. This is filled with argyranthemum, cornflowers, cosmos and many of the daisy-type flowers, set between runs of bamboo and phor-mium. Continue along through a range of lime walks, pond gardens, winding shrub walks, primula ponds, a country flower garden full of cottage plants and a big rock garden with raised beds.

Touring the garden is quite a feat, and thankfully the place is liberally scattered with benches and chairs, affording a welcome rest for the exhausted but determined visitor.

Mr Kirwan's rose garden, containing over 2,000 bushes, won the All Ireland Rose Garden category in the Shamrock All Ireland Gardens Competition 1998. It is full of neat beds of roses, surrounded by a tall leylandii hedge (*Cupressocyparis leylandii*), looking as it should but rarely does in most gardens: neatly clipped, like an architec-tural living green wall.

Finally, the last in the series of gardens is a very different, very cool, mature garden of trees. This large area features eucalyptus, oak, cherry, blue spruce (*Picea pungens*), and a particularly handsome four-trunked betula with a fine creamy bark, which PJ washes in the winter to keep it at its pale and interesting best. There are fine-looking mounds of heather and low shrubs rising out of the manicured lawn and leading the eye toward the taller trees. The restraint shown in this garden, in comparison to the enthusiasm in all the other areas, is remarkable.

The interesting point of K Gardens is how each of the different styles has been rec-reated. It's like a set of illustrations on different garden styles where the temptation to link the parts together has been resisted so that the styles can be studied without distraction.

LARCHILL ARCADIAN GARDENS

Kilcock, County Kildare; Tel: +01 6287354; Fax: +01 6284580; e-mail: delascasas@indigo.ie ▪ **Contact:** Michael or Louisa de Las Casas ▪ **Open:** 1 May–end August; 12pm–6pm, seven days; weekends in September; groups any time by arrangement ▪ **Entrance fee** ▪ Supervised children welcome ▪ **Special features:** rare-breed animals; lecture hall; gift shop; old-fashioned playground ▪ Member of Dúchas, the National Trust and Landmark Trust ▪ **Directions:** take the Dunshaughlin Road from Kilcock and travel 5km. Look for the signposts on the right.

Looking across the lake at Larchill Arcadian Gardens in County Kildare. This fortress was used by the family, along with another little island folly called the Temple, to stage mock battles.

Larchill is an unusual place, the only surviving example of a mid-eighteenth-century *ferme orné* or ornamental farm on the island. A *ferme orné* is a decorative landscape made up of walks and rides laid out around a park. Along the walk's length there were framed views, monuments of different sorts, and ornamental plantings of trees and sometimes flowers. Larchill was built between 1750 and 1780 and it amounts to sixty acres of parkland, woods and pleasure grounds; the lake alone covers eight acres.

There are ten follies set into the parkland, all dating back to the eighteenth century and situated along a circuit of beech trees with views of the Wicklow Mountains in the distance. These follies are strange and unusual in comparison with the more often seen layout of Gothic arches and mock castles. Set on an island in the lake is a 'fortification' known as Gibraltar, due to the shape of the rock. This is complete with battlements, turrets and gun ports on which the family used to fight mock wars. Wonderful! The other folly out here is a classic circular temple. I'm not sure if the Gibraltar folk fought with the Templars, but it's worth a thought.

There are also boathouses and a gazebo, which was once used as a plunge pool. But some of the most interesting features are the bizarre animal pens and houses, including moated piggeries and little castles on top of which the resident goats stand, surveying the rest of the farm. Hen-houses have gangways, walkways and look-out points, all castellated and self-regarding stuff for the pompous-looking fowl that reside there. It's very posh and very daft; children will adore it.

Meanwhile, the walled garden at Larchill is charming and has benefited from a great deal of restoration work over the past few years. There is a good herb and vegetable garden, with lovage and comfrey as well as flowers in among the artichokes, sage, leeks and beets. The flowers and herbs are arranged prettily and in strong patterns. The style is very much that of a French *potager,* as pleasing as it is useful. New, young box edging has rejuvenated a little lawn and brick-path edging gives the area a smart look. Young fruit trees trained on wires divide the spaces between the smaller gardens within the larger walled space and a fine rose walk.

A loggia at one end of the walled garden, with a little Gothic stained-glass window set into it, is called the Dairy. Possibly this was once part of an ornamental dairy (*see* Killruddery, County Wicklow). A herbaceous border runs the length of the walls, leading off from the dairy. At one corner a delicate old shell tower is, unfortunately, deteriorating, but still pretty in a faded sort of way. An intriguing set of steps leads up to the tower, which is off bounds to visitors.

The atmosphere in this walled garden is lovely. It has been restored and rescued and is now well in hand, but nevertheless is a bit quirky and otherworldly as befits a garden attached to something as whimsical as a *ferme orné.*

WHITE GARDENS

The craze for the Perfect White Garden started with the famous Vita Sackville-West and her garden at Sissinghurst in Kent, England. That garden has spawned a thousand imitations, but a white garden is notoriously difficult to get right for any decent length of the year; it is as much an intellectual exercise as a gardening project. Finding a good succession of white-flowering plants that complement each other throughout the summer and will do well in a particular area, climate and soil is, to some, akin to finding the Holy Grail.

The planting will require some evergreens, ground cover, shrubs, a backbone of perennials and some showy annuals. White anemone, crocus and snow flakes are the mainstay at the beginning of the year, and as these die back the white tulips, grape hyacinths and white creeping nettle take over. Choices for the summer and autumn could include the silver-leaved lamb's ears (*Stachys byzantina*) and white *Lychnis coronania,* which has furry silver leaves and simple flowers. *Campanula persicifolia* is as easy to grow as it is pretty in a summer border. White pansies and oriental poppies, like *Papaver orientale* 'Black and White', white iris, anemone, rose and daisies will glow beside the sharp leaves of artichoke and eryngium's thistle-like flower.

Perhaps it's not surprising to hear quietly defensive mutters about white gardens 'not being all that good-looking anyway' as defeated gardeners give up the ghost and let the colour slink back in. But, of course, white gardens *are* that good and we all love to see them when they work.

Three good examples of white gardens that will inspire are: Lodge Park in Straffan, County Kildare, the moon garden at Kilfane Glen and Waterfall, County Kilkenny, and Drenagh in County Derry.

Lodge Park, Straffan, County Kildare; Tel: +01 6273155/6288412; Fax: +01 6273477; e-mail: garden@steam-museum.ie ■ **Contact:** Mr and Mrs Robert Guinness ■ **Open:** June–July, Tuesday–Friday and Sunday, 2.30pm–5.30pm; August, Tuesday–Friday, 2.30pm–5.30pm; other times by arrangement ■ **Entrance fee** ■ Supervised children welcome ■ **Special features:** steam museum ■ **Directions:** Straffan is signed from Kill on the N7, and from Maynooth on the N4. It lies approximately 8km from both places.

Lodge Park is another garden that is good for a family visit. The museum will interest children and non-gardening members of the troop, and a Thomas the Tank Engine section in the gift shop should keep certain parties happy.

The gardens date back to the 1770s but they were restored in the early 1980s. The walled garden is divided into rooms by beech hedging. A long walk covers its length, with small gardens leading off the path as it makes its way down to a *rosarie*. In the middle of the garden a small greenhouse with a charming entrance is full of wonderful canna lilies, an exquisite red banana passion flower (*Passiflora antioquiensis*) and banana plants. Outside is a little pond with a lizard-like spout, fronted and edged with Paris daisies, small fuchsia bushes and gardener's garters, a redbrick path and a rose arch.

Organisation is the keyword in the smart *potager* or kitchen garden, and here small brick paths surround beds that are regimentally edged with chives, parsley and dead-straight lines of red-stalked Swiss chard. Other beds are lined with hummocks of pinks (*Dianthus*) and Lady's mantle (*Alchemilla mollis*), Cape daisies and catmint (*Nepeta*), all under espaliered fruit trees. A pergola of sweet pea divides this area from the soft fruit, borage and ornamental squashes. To one side is a clever yew and box walk where the yew is trained into standard clubs which march along the path parallel to the wall, like extras from *Alice in Wonderland*. They hold back a series of flowering shrubs and big herbaceous plants. Among the plants in this south-facing border are trachycarpus, corokia and three-metre-high bronze phormium.

A huge beech hedge with a gateway set into it forms an internal barrier within the walled garden. Gates always entice, and this one leads off towards a tall herbaceous border and on down toward a nude goddess in a little bower.

Another interesting little area is a square lawn with a small stone urn backed by a curtain of beech and underplanted with geranium. Two mixed flowerbeds lead toward this arrangement. Even those of us working on postage stamp-size gardens could copy this neat garden room. Over the vitus-clad wall can be seen a clock tower on top of which a huge weather vane pig – the family crest – swivels in the wind.

The last room within the well-divided walled garden is a particularly good white garden (*see* box, White Gardens, p.64) with white agapanthus, sedum, lamb's ears, phlox, stock, anemone, white borage, rock roses, agave in pots and potentilla.

The pots in the courtyard leading in to the restaurant are particularly smart, one holds an azara, trained as a standard, with black pansies underneath it.

GARDENING CLUBS

MAYNOOTH FLOWER AND GARDEN CLUB, THE

Contact: Felicity Satchwell (Secretary), Maybrook, Maynooth, County Kildare.

The club meets in Maynooth College at 8pm on the third Tuesday of the month, from September to June. Talks vary between floral art and gardening topics. One weekend trip (usually within Ireland) and two half-day garden visits are arranged in the summer. The club has a healthy membership and new members are welcome. Visitors may attend meetings for an admission charge.

NEWBRIDGE FLOWER AND GARDEN CLUB

The club divides its activities between flower-arranging and gardening. It meets on the second Monday of each month in the Parish Centre, Newbridge, at 8pm, from September onwards. Go along to find out more.

NURSERIES AND GARDEN CENTRES

CELBRIDGE ABBEY GARDEN CENTRE

Clane Road, Celbridge, County Kildare; Tel: +01 6275062.

CLANE GARDEN CENTRE

Dublin Road, Clane, County Kildare; Tel: +045 868149.

COURTYARD GARDEN CENTRE, THE

82 Leinster Street, Athy, County Kildare; Tel: +0507 32484.

DERRYLEA TREES

Monasterevan, County Kildare; Tel/Fax: +045 525757; e-mail: dertrees@ eircom.net (By appointment only.)

DUNSHANE NURSERY

Brannockstown, Naas, County Kildare; Tel: +045 483633.

FLEMING'S GARDEN CENTRE

Tonlegee, Athy, County Kildare; Tel: +050 731681.

GARDEN WORLD GARDEN CENTRE

The Square, Maynooth, County Kildare; Tel: +01 6289465.

GUILFOYLE'S GARDEN CENTRE

Grey Abbey Road, Kildare, County Kildare; Tel: +045 521579.

JOHNSTOWN GARDEN CENTRE

Johnstown, County Kildare; Tel: +045 879138.

LEIXLIP GARDEN CENTRE

Mill Lane, Leixlip, County Kildare; Tel: +01 6243730.

NEWBRIDGE GARDEN CENTRE

Moorefield, Newbridge, County Kildare; Tel: +01 2953988.

O'KEEFE'S GARDEN CENTRE

Ballymore Eustace, Naas, County Kildare; Tel: +045 864410.

ORCHARD GARDEN CENTRE

Old Lucan Road, Celbridge, County Kildare; Tel: +01 6288903.

THORNHILL GARDEN CENTRE

Maynooth Road Celbridge, County Kildare; Tel: +01 6276901.

GARDEN DESIGNERS

ANGELA BINCHY, GLDA

Gormanstown Studios, Kilcullen, County Kildare; Tel: +045 481303.

Angela Binchy confines her work to projects within a ten-mile radius of Kilcullen. She works frequently on gardens and landscapes for stud farms and, in some cases, these designs may be viewed (contact her for details). The most public of her commissions is the Irish Rural Garden at the National Gardens Exhibition Centre in Kilquade in Wicklow. She is a founder member of the Garden and Landscape Designers' Association of Ireland.

GARDEN ACCESSORIES

JOHNSTOWN CONSERVATORY CENTRE

Johnstown, County Kildare; Tel: +045 897305.

COUNTY KILKENNY

Kilkenny is a hugely popular destination with weekenders and holidaymakers in general. The city of Kilkenny is home to the venerable St Canice's Cathedral, which has the only complete cathedral close in the country. Rothe House is one of the last remaining medieval merchant's houses on the island, and Kilkenny Castle houses the Butler Gallery, one of the country's finest contemporary art galleries. The Cat Laughs comedy festival in June has recently joined Arts Week in August as a summer highlight. The county is known for its good farmland. There are some pretty tied villages, like Inistioge – location for a number of recent films and home to Woodstock Gardens. The crafts trail between Bennetsbridge and the city provides guests with plenty of shopping opportunities in the shape of well-made pottery, glass, leather goods and jewellery.

BUTLER HOUSE GARDEN

Patrick Street, Kilkenny city, County Kilkenny; Tel: +056 65707 ▪ **Contact:** the Manager ▪ **Open:** Monday–Sunday, 9am–5pm ▪ **No entrance fee** ▪ Supervised children welcome; dogs must be kept on leads ▪ **Directions:** entrance is through the courtyard of the Kilkenny Design Centre on the Castle Road in the centre of the city, directly opposite the gates of the castle.

This is a modest-sized town garden attached to Butler House, a big Georgian residence built as a dower house for Kilkenny Castle and which now operates as a hotel. The castle can be seen over the stone and brick walls of the garden, adding a stately atmosphere to the place.

Until recently the garden was in a state of slow deterioration, beds were slipping into the stranglehold of bindweed and other perennial weeds. In 1999 a new design was drawn up by Arthur Shackleton. Work has since been completed and the result is a smart, formal garden that suits the old house. Shackleton's design is centred on a raised circular pond cut from Kilkenny limestone. Radiating out from this, like spokes on a bicycle wheel, are crunchy gravel paths, each lined with runs of box hedging encasing wedges of lawn. There were lavender walks in the old garden and these have been reinstated against a sunny south-facing wall. To the side of the garden the orchard has been enlivened with an underplanting of spring bulbs, and the meadow grass under the trees is allowed to grow tall through the summer.

New shrub borders running along the outer walls are filled with flowering and easily cared for ceanothus, hypericum, mock orange, *Sambucus nigra* 'Guincho Purple', broom (*Cytisus*), buddleia and white rugosa roses. A ledge above one of the old garden paths is home to a long peony border with double flowers in shades of white, pink and ruby; all plants rescued from the old garden. This bed, too, is wrapped in young box walls. An outdoor theatre and summerhouse, used for recitals and readings, have been set into a sunny wall, guarded by two big, white abutilon shrubs.

Here's a puzzler for aficionados of table quizzes: *What is the link between Butler*

House and Lord Nelson? Answer: *The seating around the new pond is made from the base stones of Nelson's Pillar.* When the monument was blown up in1966 the undamaged stones found their way out of storage and down to Kilkenny, where they sat for many years. They were eventually requisitioned by Mr Shackleton and his team and cleverly turned into a bizarre but attractive seating arrangement around the pond.

JOE BUCKLEY'S GARDEN

38 Woodview, Freshford, County Kilkenny; Tel: +056 32603 ▪ **Contact:** Joe Buckley ▪ **Open:** June–September, by appointment only ▪ **Entrance fee** donated to charity ▪ Supervised children welcome; please note, dogs on leads ▪ **Directions:** set in the village of Freshford.

Mr Buckley's small town garden is quirky and different. He has his own style of gardening and his enjoyment of the place is obvious as he talks about working his plot. The use of materials closest to hand is a big feature. Because it is surrounded by tall beech trees, courtesy of an estate next door, Joe Buckley designed his smaller garden with an emphasis on trees also. His trees are smaller: holly, birch and ash.

Paths throughout were made from unearthed stones, dug up over the years. The same source provided him with the edging that weaves along the paths, holding back the borders. Low, home-made hazel hurdles are used to hold back beds of vegetables and to stake flowers. The whole place is full of artificial stone troughs made from cement (*see* box, below) and pots filled with little bonsai trees. Nothing goes to waste, and a small colony of 'stone' mushrooms, made from the left-over cement mix, peep up from under the leaves of pulmonaria and ferns at the bottom of a raised bank. Artfully placed mounds of stone are dotted around the garden like small sculptures. These catch the eye, sometimes from under a slim run of silver birches or sometimes creating a focus at the bottom of a path.

Joe Buckley has a good imagination. He lives in a small modern house in the middle of a village, but when he found himself wishing for something different he went ahead and created it: 'I got the idea for a little cottage when I visited County Clare, and so I came home and looked at my own shed and I couldn't get the idea of that cottage out of my head.' He proceeded to turn the shed into his own quaint cottage, wreathed in roses and honeysuckle. The interior is home to all manner of strange objects: old garden tools, pictures, tin advertisements, bottles of 'stuff' and other unidentified items. Out in the garden, under heaps of weaving *Clematis montana*, sit farm implements, such as harrows and ploughs.

Joe Buckley has taken a very ordinary, small suburban garden and turned it into something individual, intimate and attractive in a manner that owes nothing to gardening trends and fashions.

MAKING YOUR OWN STONE TROUGHS

Make up a cement mix in the quantity you require, using four parts fine white sand to half part white cement and half part ordinary cement and three parts water. A powdered dye can be added for a colour effect. Pack the wet cement into differently shaped boxes, basins and bowls, sitting a similar but slightly smaller box or basin on top to hold the shape until the cement is dry. When set, tip out carefully. Once drainage holes have been drilled in the base of the finished trough or bowl, you can then plant up your new containers.

JENKINSTOWN WOODS

Jenkinstown, County Kilkenny ▨ **Open:** all year round, all hours ▨ **No entrance fee** ▨ **Special features:** bluebell wood; picnic area ▨ Managed by Coillte ▨ **Directions:** on the road from Kilkenny city to Castlecomer, 6km from the city on the left. Look for the signposts.

Jenkinstown is a Coillte-run forest park set in the grounds of Jenkinstown House, with a network of paths for dog-walkers, Sunday strollers and joggers. However, for one period in the year, during the month of May, it becomes one of the best bluebell woods in the country, with a glorious sea of violet running beneath the trees. It is a sight well worth the drive. The car park is set within the old, sloped walled garden, which has a big circular dovecote with a picnic shelter underneath.

KILFANE GLEN AND WATERFALL

Thomastown, County Kilkenny; Tel: +056 24558; Fax: +056 27941 ▨ **Contact:** Mrs Susan Mosse ▨ **Open:** April–May, June and September, Sunday, 2pm–6pm; July–August, Monday–Sunday, 11am–6pm; groups welcome ▨ **Entrance fee** ▨ Supervised children welcome ▨ **Special features:** sculpture trail – an appointment can be made for Wednesday evenings to see 'Air Mass'*, time the visit for one hour before dusk; guided tours by appointment; groups may book refreshments by prior arrangement ▨ **Directions:** situated 3km off the main Dublin–Waterford road (N9), signposted to the right 3.5km from Thomastown.

Kilfane Glen is a beautifully restored romantic garden that was originally created by the Power family in the 1790s. Many of the features of the classic romantic garden are found within the thirty-acre plot: woodland, a glen with its own perfectly placed artificial waterfall, a *cottage orné*, hermit's grotto and a meandering river crossed at several points by little rustic bridges. Over the years the garden was neglected and forgotten, becoming swallowed up by choking *Rhododendron ponticum* and laurel. In the early 1990s Kilfane was rediscovered, dug out and restored by Susan and Nicholas Mosse (well-known for his pottery). They cleared out the laurel and scrub and replanted the woods with ferns, masterworth *(Astrantia)*, foxglove *(Digitalis)* and other woodland plants.

Down in the glen, at the centre of the garden, is the *cottage orné*. Razed to the ground in the middle of the nineteenth century, it was painstakingly rebuilt by the Mosses using an 1821 print as a guide. The interiors of the little thatched cottage were designed by the late Sybil Connolly. Connolly is best known as Ireland's first fashion designer or couturier, but she also designed gardens and interiors *(see* Swiss Cottage, County Tipperary). The walls of the cottage are planted with honeysuckle, jasmine and climbing roses in peat pots, in a manner faithful to the original planting.

Outside the cottage, and visible through the leaded windows, an artificial waterfall pours out over a cliff. The ancient pumps were found to be in working order and were clanked back into commission to send water tumbling into the glen for the first time in nearly 200 years.

Another feature in the garden is the blue orchard. Here, circles of crab apples have been underplanted with grape hyacinths *(Muscari)* and bluebells, and the facing wall backs a blue bed of agapanthus, monkshood, delphinium and aubrieta.

Mrs Butler's Bridge, one of several rustic stone bridges over the little river that runs through Kilfane Glen in Kilkenny.

A stone gateway leads into the pool garden, where the artist Barrie Cooke's clematis wall holds up *Clematis* 'Mrs Cholmondeley', *Clematis* 'Star of India' and *Clematis tangutica*. The formal pond, filled with fish, is a favourite venue with the Mosses's many cats. It looks down on the all-white moon garden. Tender angel's trumpets (*Datura arborea*), tall, waving bugbane (*Cimicifuga*) and white under-bellied New Zealand flax (*Phormium tenax*) add a little 'oomph' to the more usual white and silver border plants. Susan Mosse says her preferred time in this little garden is in the late evening when the whites glow and it all looks ghostly.

The latest features added to the garden include a bamboo walk, a sort of Hall of Mirrors hidden in a laurel walk, and the vista. This is a view of Slievenamon through a clearing in the trees where a wildlife pond is being prepared.

A contemporary sculpture trail is also in the process of being created. Two of the finest British sculptors, Bill Woodrow and David Nash (known for his ecological work), have made pieces for the garden. So too has William Pye, whose copper water vessel is set into the vista. This brims with water, reflecting the surrounding trees. Set beside it is Lynn Kirkham's living willow bench. But the glory of the sculpture trail is the American artist James Turrell's 'Air Mass'* (*see* rubric, p.70). From the outside this is a huge galvanised metal cube. Inside, the visitor is put through an incredible visual experience, looking up at the sky through a square opening in the ceiling. It is designed to be seen at dawn or dusk.

The next planned feature is a modern folly, from British designer Paul Bradley. This will be a pristine glass room set into the middle of an oak circle in the woods – as if you needed another reason to visit Kilfane.

KILKENNY CASTLE PARK

The Parade, Kilkenny city, County Kilkenny; Tel: +056 21450; Fax: +056 63488 ▪ **Contact:** Pat Comerford ▪ **Open:** October–March, 10am–5pm; April–September, 10am–9pm; groups welcome ▪ **No entrance fee** ▪ Supervised children welcome; please note, dogs on leads ▪ **Special features:** tearoom and restaurant open May–September; free guided tours of the park are available at 3pm on Sundays during July and August; art gallery; bookshop; playground (including swings for children with disabilities); historic castle ▪Member of Dúchas ▪ **Directions:** situated in the middle of the city. Look for the signposts.

This thirty-five-acre park, set high over the banks of the River Nore, belongs to Kilkenny Castle, the former seat of the Butlers of Ormonde. The Butlers were one of the chief families in Ireland, arriving here with the Normans in the twelfth century. They ruled much of the southeast up until the nineteenth century, contributing such luminaries as James, the first Duke of Ormond, and Black Tom (a favourite of Queen Elizabeth I) to Irish history. The Butler family lived in Kilkenny until 1935 when they vacated Kilkenny Castle, selling it to the State in the 1960s for a nominal price of £60.

A castle has stood on this site since the twelfth century, and the gardens have seen many upheavals and changes over the years. Only some of the details of the original gardens have survived, but descriptions of James, first Duke of Ormond's garden in the late seventeenth century still exist (*see* also Royal Hospital Kilmainham, County Dublin). As an ally of Charles II, James spent years in exile in France, where he became interested in the French style of gardening as practiced by André Le Nôtre, garden designer to the French monarch and aristocracy. Returning with the Restoration of the monarchy in 1660, James restyled his Kilkenny residence, rather incongruously, as a French château with a garden to match. That arrangement included grottos and extravagant waterworks; these are long gone. Time marched on, tastes changed and today the gardens are largely the result of work carried out in the middle of the nineteenth century by the renowned Irish garden designer Ninian Niven (*see* Hilton Park, County Monaghan, and the Iveagh Gardens, County Dublin).

The gardens are divided into two distinct parts: a formal terraced garden to the north and parkland to the south. The terraced garden is made up of a sunken lawn planted with formal rose beds. Hybrid tea roses make up the bulk of the flowers, but there are also some old varieties, like *Rosa rugosa*. These beds surround a big limestone fountain set within a cruciform network of paths whose arms lead out to seats and benches. The garden looks up to the castle, which stands on a raised platform of stone balustrades climbed by *Rosa* 'Dorothy Perkins'.

In the park, long runs of lawn are broken by large shrubs and parkland trees. A small wooded area opens onto a rather romantically neglected lily pond, grandly termed 'the boating lake'. A wild garden has recently been planted up in the park and is developing. Other attractions are the well-equipped children's playground and, close by, a small ancestral burial ground for the Butlers and their dogs.

MARTINA LYNCH'S GARDEN

5 Hillcrest, Granges Road/Dunningstown Road, Kilkenny city, County Kilkenny; Tel: +056 65847 ▪ **Contact:** Mrs Martina Lynch ▪ **Open:** mid-June–beginning of August, by appointment to groups only ▪ **Entrance fee** partially donated to various charities ▪ **Special features:** occasional plant sales; refreshments may be booked by prior arrangement ▪ **Directions:** driving from Kilkenny city on the Granges

Road, turn left onto a small slip road called the Dunningstown Road. Travel 2km beyond the 30mph sign and turn left into Hillcrest. Martina Lynch's garden is the fifth house along on the right.

Martina Lynch has been working her one-acre site for ten years. I get the impression that she has hardly taken a day off since the JCB left it in a flat, compacted mess of wet rock and hard ground. The garden is a jam-packed place worked by a woman with a flair for growing plants and an eye for arranging them well.

Smart order rules at the front of the garden. Conifers and double-flowering mock orange (*Philadelphus*), callistemon and other flowering shrubs wrap around the perimeter and shelter the garden from the prevailing winds. Surprises tucked between the shrubs, like a tall, rose-pink poppy (*Meconopsis napaulensis*), are particularly enjoyable precisely because they are not loudly declared and shown off.

Right up against the house is a rockery made of stone from the quarry over the hill. In spring it is filled with Welsh poppies (*Meconopsis cambrica*), saxifrage, and aubrieta. These add colourful splashes to the permanent dwarf conifers, like fat, mop-top Norway spruce (*Picea abies*) and *Thuja plicata*.

The garden really moves into high gear once you pass through the tall wooden gate that divides the front from the back – a gate erected to protect Martina's six ducks who live in the large back garden, eating slugs and looking decorative. Hordes of pots occupy the wide patio to the back of the house. As well as those holding plants such as bougainvillea, there is a big water tub housing three goldfish and a large water lily. This is an idea worth considering for a tiny patio garden with no room for a pond. Step off the patio into a jungle of flowers, shrubs and grasses. Big cordylines dominate one bed beside an iron archway draped with a heavily flowering, creamy-white *Rosa* 'Iceberg' and *Clematis* 'Marie Boisselot'. 'Iceberg' has no great scent, but it more than makes up for that by blooming profusely. Beyond the arch is a great mass of love-in-a-mist (*Nigella damascene*), in every shade from silver-white through palest blue and right up to a rich shade of cobalt.

Martina apologises for the size of the huge mullein (*Verbascum olympicum*), which forces you to squeeze past as you pick your way through the plants on narrow gravel paths: 'I planted that in the border several times and it refused to grow, but it insists on taking up space out here. The family say I don't have a garden but an obstacle course.'

At the very bottom of the garden are her delphiniums. Martina grows the tall spires in every shade of blue and purple and sells them at the local country market when the women of the city pounce on the gorgeous flowers within minutes of the stall opening. But she grows them in such numbers that her own garden is still a mass of elegant blue flowers. As the beds of crinodendron, salvia, phormium and pheasant berry (*Leycesteria formosa*) expand, Martina regularly steals chunks out of her ever-decreasing lawn. I am betting that if I return in a year or two there may be no lawn left at all!

MOUNT JULIET

Thomastown, County Kilkenny; Tel: +056 24455; Fax: +056 24522 ■ **Contact:** the Manager ■ **Open:** daily, 9.30am–6pm, by appointment only ■ **No entrance fee** ■ **Special features:** hotel, restaurant and bar; golf course; riding school; leisure centre ■ **Directions:** turn left at the top of the square in Thomastown and follow the signposts to Mount Juliet, about 4km away.

Mount Juliet is a fine old estate and now one of the country's major golf courses and hotel complexes. The parkland has been largely remodelled in order to accommodate the golf course. However, within the demesne there is still a fine double herbaceous border situated in the old walled garden, which is close to the golf clubhouse and leisure centre. The border was designed by one of the few female garden designers of the early twentieth century, Mrs Solly-Flood.

A circular opening or gateway in the wall leads onto a broad grass path that divides the border. Blues, pinks and creams melt together in a haze of soft colour that is very easy on the eye. Tall delphinium, phlox, aster, hesperis, peony and a host of other plants in substantial blocks weave in and out of each other in a show that is at its very best in late May and June.

There is also a rock and water garden close by the main house, and a woodland walk through beech, ash and oak trees, underplanted in places with naturalised spring bulbs, moss and fern.

ROSYBOWER

Hillcrest, Kilkenny city, County Kilkenny; Tel: +056 22253 ▪ **Contact:** Olive O'Shea ▪ **Open:** mid-May–mid-July, by appointment to groups only ▪ **Entrance fee** donated to the Alzheimer Foundation ▪ Supervised children welcome ▪ **Special features:** teas can be booked by prior arrangement ▪ **Directions:** drive from Kilkenny city on the Grange Road. As the main road bends to the right, turn left onto a small slip road called the Dunningstown Road. Travel for 2km beyond the 30mph sign and turn left into Hillcrest. Olive O'Shea's garden is the second last garden on the left.

I had passed Mrs O'Shea's garden many times and had always enjoyed the good-looking gravelled front garden with huge scarlet oriental poppies growing from silver limestone gravel picking up the colour of the red front door. So I was delighted to hear that Olive O'Shea was planning to welcome visitors into her pretty garden. Olive is a fanatical gardener who has put several hours' work a day into the plot since she started it from scratch eight years ago.

Arriving at the front of the house, the nose is greeted by a collection of roses basking in the sun, including a delicious marshmallow-smelling *Rosa* 'Gertrude Jekyll', among the well-shaped box plants in pots. ('Gertrude Jekyll' is a rose whose scent is so strong that experiments have been carried out on it for perfume production.) Scattered through the gravel are cheerful Cape daisies and pale shell-pink everlasting sweet pea (*Lathyrus*). Olive explained that the sweet peas are not actually supposed to be pale shades, but as mutants go they are great.

Visiting Rosybower on a warm summer day, it is not immediately obvious that this garden is on a difficult site on the shoulder of a windy hill. The garden gets whipped by vicious gusts for much of the year; winds strong enough to knock walls, as they did in the 1997 Christmas storms. Battling with gales, the healthy plant growth is chiefly due to Olive's clever placing, arrangement and care of her plants rather than the luck of a sheltered site. In addition, the garden owes much of its good looks to Olive's husband, John, whose well-made wooden summerhouses, ponds and paths are everywhere. There are three ponds. The largest of these is sheltered by *Pittosporum tenuifolium* underplanted by Lady's mantle, the tall fairy wands of francoa, penstemon and a peeling eucalyptus, which Olive's cat appreciates as a climbing and scratching post. But the flower-arranger in her feels the eucalyptus leaves are too top heavy, dangling unhelpfully in arrangements. Olive regularly gives flower-arranging demonstrations so she has an insatiable appetite for foliage, flowers and seed heads. One of her favourite flower-arranging plants is the shrub *Luma apiculata* 'Glanleam Gold', which sports pretty fronds of small, waxy, variegated leaves, tiny white flowers and edible berries.

Despite my enthusiasm for the front garden, Olive says the garden doesn't really start until one goes out back – a half-acre rectangular area, well divided into plots of flowering shrubs, ponds and beds looking over Kilkenny city on the plain below. A path around the perimeter wanders past runs of sweet honeysuckle and tall, white hollyhocks, variegated ivy and *Parthenocissus*.

This path leads down to the 'bower' of Rosybower, a beautifully constructed summerhouse with an old slate roof and comfortable cushioned seats, a place regularly used for leisurely entertaining. A yellow border of evening primrose, rock rose (*Cistus*), golden variegated ivy, *Hedera* 'Paddy's Pride' and potentilla leads from the bower down to a stone bench and provides a picture for the guests to look at and enjoy. Down here, memories of her grandfather's garden come courtesy of a big patch of hardy cranesbill, and *Rosa* 'Schoolgirl' recalls the day Olive's daughter started school.

Further along, blue spikes of veronica and a bushy callistemon, heavy with strong pink bottle-brush flowers, hem in a secluded spot 'for cups of tea and a quick sit-down'. Out on the grass is a pheasant berry (*Leycesteria formosa*), unusually grown as a specimen. This was so called because it was grown on the great estates to keep the shoot birds fed and provided with shelter or cover, ensuring they remained on-site for the coming season's shoot. The dangling flowers, often compared to elaborate earrings, turn into shiny ruby berries.

Rustic arches lead into what was the vegetable garden, now taken over by giant feather grass (*Stipa gigantea*) and *Rosa* 'Sally Holmes', a rose Olive loves because of the variety of colours each flower goes through over its life. It graduates from coral orange to pale peaches-and-cream as it goes from bud to full-blown bloom. In here there are more seats and tables set with candle sconces so the family can sit out on warm evenings.

A big phlomis was planted in by the house wall for the wonderful evening smell it sends in through the windows. Beside it is a tall run of goldenrod (*Solidago*). Olive hates to see its tall, gold flower spikes beginning to flower because they signal the end of the summer. She needn't fear – this garden is a treasure, regardless of the season.

THE WATERGARDEN

Ladywell Street, Thomastown, County Kilkenny; Tel: +056 24690 ▪ **Contact:** Mike Holey or Aviva Walsh ▪ **Open:** Easter–Christmas, Sundays, 12pm–5.30pm; Tuesday–Friday, 10am–5pm; closed on 24 June ▪ **Entrance fee** donated to the Camphill Community, but admission free if using tearooms ▪ Children welcome but must be well supervised because of the river; please note, dogs on leads ▪ **Directions:** situated on the edge of Thomastown, on the road to Bennettsbridge. Well signposted.

The Watergarden is a little garden that was started many years ago by a man who began working on his own small, river-banked garden and quickly ran out of space for his growing plant collection. So he did the obvious: borrowing the unused ends of his neighbours' gardens, he continued to build a snake-like plot, incorporating and reclaiming the boggy bits from the line of village gardens that edge the river. He worked these into one long garden secreted away behind the village of Thomastown.

The garden has since been taken over by the Camphill Community. The community is a network of small groups set up to enable able-bodied and disabled people to live together outside of institutions. Everyone works and contributes according to their abilities. They run farm enterprises, crafts workshops and garden centres around the country. In the Watergarden the Camphill workers have widened the paths for easier wheelchair access. The miniature watermill has been restored and the river restocked with a variety of ducks.

Planting is informal and cottagey, with masses of mock orange (*Philadelphus*), shrub roses, columbine (*Aquiligea*), hostas and marginal plants, like flag iris, lysimachia and ferns, by the river. All the work is carried out organically.

The community also runs a small nursery which stocks many of the plants featured in the garden. They sell these at reasonable prices. Good quality home-made lunches and teas are available from the tearoom, which has an outdoor eating area from where the garden can be observed and admired.

WOODSTOCK ♿ 🐕

Inistioge, County Kilkenny; Tel: +056 52699/086 8580502; e-mail: cmurphy@ kilkennycoco.ie ▪ **Contact:** Claire Murphy or John Delaney (086 8849785) ▪ **Open:** all year round; groups welcome ▪ **Entrance fee** (car charge) ▪ Supervised children welcome; please note, dogs on leads ▪ **Special features:** guided tours can be organised; Inistioge village is very picturesque and has been the location for several films ▪ **Directions:** situated 2km west of the village, up a steep hill to the left of the two village churches.

Woodstock House was the seat of the Tighe family for several hundred years until it was burnt down during the Civil War in the 1920s. What was once described as one of the finest gardens in the country, with an important collection of exotic plants, became a disintegrating giant. Although dilapidated and wild, it was still beautiful in a faded way.

Recently, under the Great Gardens of Ireland Restoration Programme, work began on bringing Woodstock back to something of its former glory. Since then, under the watchful eye of garden expert Finola Reid, a spectacular monkey puzzle avenue, one of the longest in Europe, has been restored. New, young monkey puzzles (*Araucaria araucana*), planted where older specimens have fallen, look like tiny babies beside huge parents.

Other avenues of trees that were all but invisible under the tangle of rhododendron, laurel and bramble have been opened up and re-gravelled. One of these leads off at an angle from the monkey puzzle walk and a sense of space and grandeur has been created from what, until about a year ago, looked like a tattered mess of trees.

All over the pleasure grounds clearances have revealed gardens not seen properly for nearly a century: the yew walk and kitchen gardens, only barely discernible up to recently, may now be saved and restored. A box parterre has already been replanted outside the walled garden leading up to where a circular Turner-designed greenhouse once stood (for Richard Turner, *see* National Botanic Gardens, County Dublin). The dovecote is still in a good state of repair, while nearby are the skeletons of rows of cold frames, melon-houses, greenhouses and sheds. The bathhouse, a strange-looking item that was invisible under soil and build-up for years, is now clearly seen, and the big Victorian rockery has also been laid bare.

Sunken lawns in front of the house have been regrassed. Long woodland walks wind their way through the huge estate, leading in one case to a Gothic teahouse perched in the trees, with a panoramic view over the valley, woods and river below. It is easy to go back in time and imagine enjoying tea up here, with servants ferrying the tea tray and cucumber sandwiches up the hill!

Although the once-famed collection of trees has become sadly depleted over the years from storm damage and neglect, it is still worth visiting to see the monkey puzzles (*Araucaria araucana*), Monterey pines (*Pinus radiata*) and the massive *Sequoiadendron giganteum*. It is to be hoped that funding will continue to be made available to consolidate what has been done at Woodstock.

GARDENING SOCIETIES

KILKENNY HORTICULTURAL SOCIETY

Contact: Olive O'Shea, Hillcrest, Kilkenny, County Kilkenny; Tel: +056 22253.

The Kilkenny Horticultural Society is one of the oldest in the country, dating back to the early 1900s. It is affiliated to the Royal Horticultural Society of Ireland (RHSI), so members are regularly notified of RHSI events. Meetings are held from February to November, on varying Tuesdays, in the Clubhouse Hotel on Patrick Street, Kilkenny. The society runs a full programme of talks, lectures and demonstrations. In the summer months regular day trips and short outings to visit gardens are arranged. An annual dinner is also held.

NURSERIES AND GARDEN CENTRES

CORLOUGHAN GARDEN CENTRE

Fiddown, County Kilkenny; Tel: +051 643331.

DARVER NURSERIES

Jenkinstown, County Kilkenny; Tel: +056 67028.

GARDEN CENTRE, THE

John Street, Kilkenny, County Kilkenny; Tel:+056 22034.

HENNESSY'S GARDEN CENTRE

Carlow Road, Clara, County Kilkenny; Tel: 1850 278287; e-mail: info@hgc.ie

MULLINAVAT GARDEN CENTRE

Mullinavat, County Kilkenny; Tel: +051 885159.

SOS GARDEN CENTRE

Callan Road, Kilkenny, County Kilkenny; Tel: +056 64000.

COUNTRY MARKETS

COUNTRY MARKETS

The Market Yard, Kilkenny city, County Kilkenny ▪ **Hours:** Friday and Saturday mornings, 9am–12pm.

The country market (*see* appendices for countrywide details) is held in Kilkenny city every Friday and Saturday morning. This is the place to pick up plants from an ever-changing array of herbaceous plants and shrubs, indoor plants, bedding and herbs, tomato and courgette plants. The star attractions of the county market however are the cut flowers. There is always a good selection of whatever garden flowers are in season, selling for reasonable prices. Gardeners reluctant to raid their own plots to beautify the house will find this particularly useful. The sellers are usually the growers and are willing to give advice on the correct care for the plants they sell. These, like the flowers, tend to be old-fashioned garden plants. Much of the produce is organic. Foragers should turn up as early as possible because those in the know will always arrive by 9.30am to snap up the good stuff. As a bonus, there are also stalls selling organic vegetables, chicken and sometimes duck eggs, cakes, bread and jam.

GARDEN COURSES

LAVISTOWN HOUSE STUDY CENTRE

Lavistown House, Lavistown, County Kilkenny; Tel/Fax: +056 65145; e-mail: courses@lavistownhouse.ie; website: www.lavistownhouse.ie ▪ **Contact:** Roger and Olivia Goodwillie ▪ Accommodation is available for weekend courses.

Set in its own informal gardens, with ponds, woods and a walled vegetable garden as well as a farm with Kerry cows, sheep and pigs, Lavistown has been an attractive venue for part-time and weekend courses for over twenty-one years. Many of the courses are garden-related. The 2000 brochure included courses on design, pruning and propagation, as well as on discovering bats, exploring the Burren and its plants, and mushrooming. Conducted garden tours are available.

GARDEN ACCESSORIES

KILKENNY ARCHITECTURAL SALVAGE AND ANTIQUES

The Old Woollen Mills, Bleach Road, Kilkenny; Tel: +056 64434 ▪ **Contact:** Robin Maharaj.

A big selection of old slates, flagstones, stone troughs, cappings and outdoor garden items.

NAIM – HOLY LAND URNS

Main Street, Ballyhale, County Kilkenny; Tel:+056 68198; Fax: +056 66160; e-mail: naim@indigo.ie

Frost-proof mixed clay indoor and outdoor terracotta pots in all shapes, sizes and shades.

LEINSTER • COUNTY KILKENNY

COUNTY LAOIS

Laois is a small county, right in the heart of the midlands. The Slieve Bloom Mountains border the county on the west, where there are some excellent walks and hikes, while the navigable River Barrow and Grand Canal flank the east. Because of its history as one of the first counties to be settled by English 'planters', Laois is full of well-planned, pretty estate villages. Stradbally, home to a huge annual Steam Rally, is one of these. Durrow and Abbeyleix, built by the de Vescis, are also well laid out. Morrisey's in Abbeyleix is one of the country's most loved and nostalgic pub (and undertakers), and a few doors along the main street is a sensory garden. A little outside Portlaoise is the curious-looking Rock of Dunamaise, an unusual forty-five metre outcrop with the ruins of a medieval castle and an earlier Iron Age fortification lording it above the surrounding flat countryside. Emo Court, the Gandon-designed seat of the Earls of Portarlington, was recently acquired by the State and can be visited. The villages of Rosenallis and Mountmellick have strong Quaker roots, including the first Quaker school in Ireland.

EMO COURT GARDEN

Emo, County Laois; Tel/Fax: +0502 26573/056 21450 ▨ **Contact:** Mavis Duggan or Pat Comerford ▨ **Open:** all year, every day, during daylight hours ▨ **No entrance fee** ▨ **Special features:** tours of the garden depart from the car park at 3pm every Sunday between July and August; tours at other times by prior arrangement; historic house can be visited, mid June–mid September, Tuesday–Sunday, 10.30am–5pm, for an admission charge ▨ Member of Dúchas ▨ **Directions:** 2.5km from the village of Emo, accessed from the Kildare–Portlaoise road (N7).

Emo Court was built in 1790 for the Earls of Portarlington and forms the second largest walled park in Europe after the Phoenix Park in Dublin. The gardens were first laid out in the eighteenth century, but development continued until the middle of the nineteenth. Emo's parkland and arboretum are a pleasant and interesting place to wander in, and make a complete change from a flower-filled garden. Their charm is in substantial features like a fine sweep of lawn, a view across the park to a grove of trees or over the huge man-made lake and woodland walks.

Since the demesne was taken into state care in the early 1990s, a great deal of work has been carried out on the gardens. Close by the house are rolls of manicured lawns. These are crossed and lined by smart avenues of yew cones. A major job of restoration has been done over the past year on the yew avenues; each plant has been rejuvenated, reshaped and tied-in. The elegant railings near the house were painstakingly restored by Dúchas, The Heritage Service. To appreciate the work involved, take a look at the badly decayed rails awaiting restoration under the trees to the side of the house.

Running from the front of the house to what was once the main entrance to Emo, but is now a blank gate, is the estate's most famous feature – the longest avenue of Wellingtonia (*Sequoiadendron giganteum*) in the country. At just under 150 years old, these are mere babies, and they will still be growing when Emo is on its umpteenth restoration. An ornamental game larder stands by the garden entrance. The ceiling hooks are visible through the decorative windows, so that visitors can inspect the 'bag' off the estate's most recent shoot.

From here one arrives at an area called the Clucker. This is a wooded area where rhododendrons and azaleas thrive in a pocket of acid soil. The path runs past a vener-able-looking Monterey pine and down to another yew walk. This walk is under heavy restoration. The yews were almost completely strangled by laurel and it is satisfying to see the progression of the new growth as the laurel is pulled out and the hard pruning takes effect. This path eventually leads back out toward the lawns and then beyond them, to the Grapery, a name of unknown origin, where special trees like sequoias, weeping beech, *Picea smithiana* and black (*Pinus nigra*) and Corsican pines grow.

The path through the Grapery runs down to a pair of ornate golden gates, possibly made by Richard Turner (*see* National Botanic Gardens, County Dublin). The walled garden has an attractive bell tower and split-level gardener's cottage dating back to the seventeenth century. The cottage is also under restoration.

The centrepiece of the restoration work has been a complete overhaul of the twenty-five-acre ornamental lake. Nineteen acres are under water and there are three islands. In the past two years the whole lake was drained. Tons of silt and build-up, reeds and rushes were dragged out, and then it was refilled and once more trans-formed into a pristine lake complete with fishing stands and new walks. A temple stands by the sluice gates. This was a teahouse folly, built in the 1850s. Someone once said that you know you have too much money when you start building follies. Six full- and part-time workers are doing the massive work being carried out on Emo. Would that there were the money and manpower for folly building!

GASH GARDENS

Castletown, Portlaoise, County Laois; Tel: +0502 32247 ■ **Contact:** Mary Keenan ■ **Open:** May–October, Monday–Saturday, 10am–5pm; Sundays, 2pm–5pm; groups by appointment only ■ **Entrance fee** ■ **Directions:** the garden is 1km off the main Dublin–Limerick road at Castletown.

In 1986 this remarkable garden was a cow paddock. This is some-thing to ponder as you walk through the big double wooden gates that lead from the farmyard into the delicious surprise of Gash garden. Over fifteen years Noel Keenan single-handedly laid the garden out; today it is maintained by his daughter, Mary.

A gazebo sits snug among the flowers at Gash Gardens in County Laois.

Gash covers over four acres of flowers, clever planting and unusual features. The most impressive of these features is the moon house, a little cave set in the base of a large rockery. It peeps out through a circular stone opening into which the visitor sits and watches a cascade of water coming from above. The rush and noise created from the crashing water is invigorating but the moon house is only one, albeit the most spectacular, of many water features at Gash. Ponds, streams and rivulets cover the garden, travelling in all directions, feeding the roots of damp-loving primulas and meconopsis, hostas, gunnera and astilbe.

Threaded through the garden is a collection of special and specimen trees, including *Metasequoia glyptostroboides*, *Liquidambar* and *Cornus kousa*. This place is full of bold statements, as seen in the three, white-barked Himalayan birch (*Betula utilis var. jacquemontii*) underplanted with red heathers – an extraordinarily striking combination of colours.

Ranged around the garden are huge, natural-looking rockeries and alpine beds, substantial herbaceous, rose and mixed beds, laburnum walks and a damp and shaded fernery. Spreads of giant grasses, like *Stipa gigantea* and bullrushes, wave and dance in the breeze. A rarely seen *Clematis rehderiana* with little nodding, creamy-green bells, acquired from Wisley, the headquarters of the Royal Horticultural Society in London, is flowering happily up a host tree.

One of the most recent creations is a mixed maple walk, with some Spanish chestnut, beech and species roses, down by the River Nore. It travels for a quarter of a mile along the water. This came about from a simple desire to go for walks by the river and, as it was difficult to get there through the fields, a river walk seemed like the sensible answer. Once the trees were planted, a stream gave the idea for a water garden, which was followed by a bower, and then finished off perfectly with three small waterfalls.

There is so much to be seen in this garden, it deserves several visits at different times of the year. Gash came third in the Garden for All Seasons in the Leinster category of the Shamrock All Ireland Gardens Competition 1999, as well as first in the Midlands category in 1996 and 1998.

HEYWOOD GARDEN &

Ballinakill, County Laois; Tel: +0502 33563 ▪ **Contact:** Pat Shortis (1pm–1.30pm) ▪ **Open:** all year, daily, during daylight hours ▪ **No entrance fee** ▪ Children should be supervised as there are substantial drops in garden levels ▪ **Special features:** guided tours of garden at 3pm every Sunday in July and August, at other times by appointment (fee charged) ▪ Member of Dúchas ▪ **Directions:** 7km southeast of Abbeyleix, off the R432 to Ballinakill (in the grounds of Ballinakill Community School).

The formal garden at Heywood is one of a very few on this island designed by the English architect Edwin Lutyens (*see* the War Memorial Gardens, County Dublin). Heywood is a small but spectacular garden, set in the middle of the rolling Laois countryside. The garden has been known and hugely admired by garden visitors for years. Over the past number of years, however, a great amount of detective work has been carried out and an older, larger garden, which had been almost completely forgotten, has been discovered by the park superintendent Paddy Friel. The discovery has added hugely to the interest of an already fine garden.

**Lutyens's sunken garden and fountain,
complete with spouting turtles, at Heywood in County Laois.**

Lutyens's garden is a little gem, created at the beginning of the twentieth century on several levels of an embankment standing out from the old site of long-gone Heywood House. The gardens are divided into small rooms of various sizes, from secret sundial and iris gardens to little herbaceous gardens wrapped in yew hedging, with hide-and-seek hedges all making for a great sense of mystery and secrecy.

The main area of this formal garden is a sunken, circular, terraced garden with a central lily pond surrounded by spitting lead turtles and a wonderfully daft-sized fountain shaped like a huge champagne glass, way out of proportion to the little pond. Herbaceous perennials, low shrubs and roses which run around the circular garden in two terraces, each backed by walls and ledges, make up the bulk of the planting. There is a handsome summerhouse in grey, lichen-covered, split limestone, where you can sit and enjoy the view. Set into the tall outer walls are cleverly placed circular windows, each framing a perfect vista, like landscape paintings on a drawing-room wall. The views include rolling parkland, distant church spires and the village nearby. The compositions are worthy of Constable.

Heywood is a fine garden, almost domestic and intimate in scale, and, being walled, it soaks up sun in the summer. Leaving the formal circular garden, the path leads through a fine wrought-iron gate to a short avenue of pleached limes and a pergola on a high ledge above and overlooking the lake, woods and wider pleasure ground. The wall to the side of this holds niches for pieces of sculpture. Moving off the path, an expanse of lawn is surrounded by more low stone walls backing herbaceous borders. Visitors with children should note that this low wall masks a steep drop on the other side, because the whole garden is on a raised terrace overlooking the parkland.

Heywood's new discovery awaits you down in the woods: this is a wonderful late eighteenth- and early nineteenth-century romantic garden created by Mr Frederick Trench, a tenant of the original house and the man responsible for the first gardens at Heywood. His garden was made up of trails or rides past a series of features: a lake walk, an old subterranean bath house, Gothic follies peeping out from beyond woods and hills, rustic and quaint stone bridges and serpentine pools and streams. It is a charming garden slowly being uncovered and worked upon by Dúchas; they should be commended.

PORTRANE HOUSE

Carlow Road, Portlaoise, County Laois; Tel:+0502 21403 ▪ **Contact:** Mrs Joan Tyrrell ▪ **Open:** during the summer months, by appointment only; groups welcome ▪ **Directions:** travelling into Portlaoise from Dublin, turn left at the Catholic church and the garden is on the right, marked by a vet's sign.

Portrane is a good town garden just off the busy road in Portlaoise. It is well known, not just to garden visitors, but to hundreds of Portlaoise newly-weds who have used the gorgeous garden as the backdrop for their wedding photographs. Mrs Tyrrell has been working here for thirty-four years, perfecting the informal mixed garden.

Close by the house is an old courtyard used to great effect, filled with pots of shrubs, perennials and annuals, in front of creepers and climbers which decorate the stone and limed walls. Mrs Tyrrell is a woman who grows great plants well. Her canna lilies, dahlias, tall, white-tinged pink flowers of *Gaura lindheimeri* and oak-leaved hydrangea (*Hydrangea quercifolia*) are placed and combined with taste.

The sheds surrounding the courtyard are weighted down with a mass of variegated *Euonymus* 'Silver Queen', purple clematis, roses and ivy. In the summer, there are bright orange splashes of nasturtium everywhere. A base planting of geranium and bergenia, white flowered creeping vinca, pots of hosta and acer stand up against a whitewashed wall.

Every place in Mrs Tyrrell's garden is an opportunity for planting. Even the tennis court was brought into service as an opportunity to plant roses and climbers on the chain link fence. Low retaining walls hold up lawns, and lines of big rough granite mushrooms decorate both grass and the island beds.

A tall bank rises high above the house, full of flowering shrubs and perennials, almost in the nature of a hanging garden. Narrow mountain-goat trails lead up through the flowering lavatera, picea and holly, golden yew and white lychnis. In the gravel there are little tufts of golden thyme, cyclamen, creeping mint and tall *Verbena bonariensis* with floating tiny purple flowers, catmint and cotoneaster. These are all plants that will self-seed with disgraceful abandonment if happy.

This is a well-designed garden, with good structure and great flowers.

THE SENSORY GARDEN

Dove House, Main Street, Abbeyleix, County Laois; Tel: +0502 31325 ▪ **Contact:** Paul O'Toole or Miriam Hyland ▪ **Open:** May–September, Monday–Friday, 10am–4pm; Saturday–Sunday and bank holidays, 2pm–6pm; goups by appointment only ▪ **Entrance fee** donated to charity ▪ Supervised children welcome ▪

Special features: *pétanque* (*boules*) court; a vibrating stone (called the 'humming stone') for people with hearing difficulties; guided tours can be arranged; nursery ※
Directions: situated on the main street in Abbeyleix.

The Sensory Garden is set within the walled gardens of the Brigidine Convent in the middle of the picturesque village of Abbeyleix. Work started in 1996 when the Sisters of Charity gave the land to the town. An inspired thought led to the gift being turned into a community garden. Head gardener Paul O'Toole has led a team of eleven able-bodied and disabled people in the creation of a series of garden rooms that make up the Sensory Garden.

A Sensory Garden is just that, designed to appeal to all the senses. In the Abbeyleix project the concentration is on appealing to blind and visually impaired visitors. This involves braille-labelled beds, easily negotiated paths, and plants chosen for their leaf texture and scent as much as for flower and colour.

The backbone of the garden is a circle of mature common limes underplanted with spring bulbs, with a path running under the circle. The smaller gardens are set within and around the circle. There are secret gardens, a rose pergola and a fernery in an old wall. A High King's chair was built for children, with a laurel-edged path leading into it, hiding the chair within its evergreen leaves. A little teahouse, based on the design of the bandstand in St Stephen's Green, sits in one corner of the garden. There is also a small sculpture garden, a *potager* with a snug lime arbour, and nearby a hornbeam maze is growing up nicely around a loving seat.

At the top of the garden, the longest herbaceous border in County Laois is maturing well. Many of the plants in the border were kindly donated by the Botanic Gardens in Dublin.

On an historic note, a rill or sunken directed stream that flowed through the town can still be seen in the garden, where it wanders along by the paths and beds. A trail is being created through the town so that the rill can be spotted at different points. Water systems like this are now very rare. The only village in which I have seen a network of these is Glenarm in County Antrim where they proudly maintain a well-preserved system.

A *pétanque* or *boules* court was created in the middle of the garden and the locals, led by an intrepid group of French players and coaches in the locality, use this on summer evenings. It is good to see gardens being used and enjoyed by so many people.

GARDENING CLUBS AND SOCIETIES

CULLAHILL/DURROW FLOWER AND GARDEN CLUB

A new club that runs a mixed programme of gardening and floral art talks and demonstrations. Meetings are held at 8pm on the first Monday of the month in the Cullahill Community Centre (except January, July and August). Visitors and new members are welcome. Apart from demonstrations, plant sales and talks, summer garden visits are arranged for members and friends.

PORTLAOISE GARDEN CLUB
Contact: Mary McEvoy; Tel: +0502 20131.

STRADBALLY FLOWER AND GARDEN CLUB

The club meets between 8.00pm and 8.30pm on the first Wednesday of every month, except July, in St Joseph's Hall on the Main Street in Stradbally. The meetings cover a mix of gardening and floral art subjects. In the summer months garden visits are arranged and occasional plant sales are organised. New members are welcome to join at any time.

Nurseries and Garden Centres

BALTH CLUAIN GARDEN CENTRE

Mountrath Road, Portlaoise, County Laois; Tel: +0502 61661.

Specialises in native Irish plants.

DESIGN BY NATURE

Monavea Cross, Crettyard, County Laois; Tel: +056 42526/087 2937143; e-mail: wildflow@indigo.ie ▪ **Contact:** Sandro Cafolla*.

Design by Nature has been involved in the collection, conservation and dispersal of native wildflower seed throughout Ireland for the past ten years. Almost-extinct plants have been rescued, and collections of woodland, wetland, cornfield and esker species are being collected and preserved. As well as working with seed, they advise on eco-systems and best practice in the management of natural habitats.

An informative seed catalogue, combined with a manual for growing wildflower seed, can be obtained from the above address. The cost of the catalogue will be reimbursed on purchasing seed, and, for anyone interested in but ignorant of how wildflower seed should be dealt with, it is invaluable. Seeds are sold by the kilo, 500 gramme, 250 gramme and 100 gramme weights in a range of different mixes, designed to suit the site being chosen to grow wildflowers. A seed mat measuring approximately two metres by 0.45 metres, holding thirty-two species, can be bought for small gardens. They also stock ranges of cards using wildflower designs, complete with little seed packs.

* Sandro Caffola has worked as a garden designer in the past and still occasionally designs natural, wild and native-species gardens.

DUNNE'S GARDEN CENTRE

Dunmore, Durrow, County Laois; Tel: +0502 36277.

EMO GARDEN CENTRE

Emo, Portlaoise, County Laois; Tel: +0502 46632.

IRISH COUNTRY GARDEN PLANTS

Upper Irey, Ballyfinn, County Laois; Tel:+0502 55343.

A specialist nursery run by Assumpta Broomfield, co-creator of the new border at Altamont (*see* County Carlow). A wide range of hard-to-find, rare and old cultivars, specialising in herbaceous plants. Telephone before visiting. Contact for a seasonal list.

IRISHTOWN GARDEN CENTRE

Portlaoise Road, Mountmellick, County Laois; Tel: +0502 24864.

LAWLOR'S GARDEN CENTRE

Bridge Gardens, Durrow, County Laois; Tel:+0502 36101.

POWDER'S FLORIST AND GARDEN CENTRE

Ballytegan, Portlaoise, County Laois; Tel: +0502 21557.

County Longford

Longford is one of the smallest counties in Ireland, set in the flat, limestone heart of the midlands. The River Shannon, along with Loughs Ree, Forbes and Gowna, border the county, which is also dissected by the Royal Canal. Naturally, Longford is known for cruising, boating and fishing; Gowna and Ree are among the best pike fisheries in the country. The little villages of Ardagh and Castle Forbes are pretty and historic. Ardagh features in Oliver Goldsmith's play 'She Stoops to Conquer', and is also said to be where St Patrick appointed St Mel as one of the earliest Irish bishops, on the site of the now roofless cathedral.

CARRIGGLAS MANOR

Longford, County Longford; Tel: +043 4516; Fax: +043 45165; e-mail: info@ carrigglas.com ▪ **Contact:** Tricia Flynn ▪ **Open:** May–September, Monday, Tuesday, Friday, Saturday, 11am–3pm ▪ **Entrance fee** ▪ **Special features:** costume and lace museum; house tours at 12pm, 1pm and 2pm on open days; teas and lunches can be booked by prior arrangement; gift shop ▪ **Directions:** situated just off the Longford bypass on the Ballinalee–Granard road (R194).

Carrigglas Manor is a most romantic place with a great history, including associations with Jane Austen, who is thought to have modelled Mr Darcy in *Pride and Prejudice* on Thomas Lefroy. Lefroy, when not stealing poor Jane's heart, had the Gothic revival house designed and built by Daniel Robertson in 1837 on the site of an older house (for Robertson, *see* Powerscourt, County Wicklow, Johnstown Castle, County Wexford and Lisnavagh, County Carlow). Fortunately, the building and improvements carried out by the Darcyesque Lefroy did nothing to interfere with the stable block, which had been built in 1790 by James Gandon. The idea of Gandon designing a stable block is wonderful, rather like having Norman Foster or Sam Stephenson in to design a new carport for one's house.

Carrigglas has been under restoration by the Lefroy family for some years. Work was first started about ten years ago by Tessa Lefroy on the pretty cottage garden near the famous stable block, a short distance from the more austere house. Tessa created an old-fashioned informal flower and water garden on this spot. This is a very easy garden to love. A series of ponds dominates the little area, surrounded by rough slabstone paths, sprouting purple-spiked bugle (*Ajuga reptans*). The flowers are all good old-fashioned stock, like crocosmia, marigolds, love-in-a-mist (*Nigella damascene*) and a mix of old roses. When I visited, three big black ducks stood on a stone in the middle of the water, posing like living sculptures. 'They're always there and they just show off,' said a little girl who lives nearby, throwing her eyes to heaven.

Above the pond garden is a stone terrace. This is known as the Italian garden, and is guarded by two exhausted-looking stone lions. It has been taken over by creepers and self-seeding Lady's mantle (*Alchemilla mollis*), lamb's ears (*Stachys byzantina*),

The 'Big House' – Carrigglass Manor in County Longford, built by Thomas Lefroy, who is thought to have been the model for Mr Darcy in Jane Austen's *Pride and Prejudice*.

digitalis, roses, poppies, lupins and *Sisyrinchium* (a member of the Iris family), with blue summer flowers, hardy geraniums and more love-in-a-mist in all its shades, from steely-white to rich peacock blue, and the Persian shield (*Strobilanthes dyerianus*). Paths lead along the garden and over streams bridged by stone flags.

In June and July the roses that scatter through the beds are at their best. They include two Old French varieties, *Rosa* 'Mme Isaac Pereire' and velvety-purple *Rosa* 'Reine des Violettes', which flowers repeatedly through the summer and is known for its scent. This garden is a wild oasis on the edge of the parkland: a meandering jungle – perhaps not for the obsessively tidy gardener, but cultivated with a light touch. A woodland garden was started a decade or so ago and it has taken off well. Spring bulbs multiply at a satisfying rate and carpet the place. 'It is as near as I can get to the Robinsonian style of gardening,' says Tessa Lefroy. With these gardens well in hand, Tessa continued her restoration and moved on and up to the big house.

Carrigglas Manor House is no place for fluffy flowerbeds. The Gothic grey limestone austerity requires a formal garden and so work is now underway to reinstate the Victorian parterre. Outlines of this lost garden were enterprisingly discovered and redrawn with the help of aerial photographs, which showed the vague indentations of the old paths in the grass. Digging will continue until the original levels are reached. This sort of work, half archaeology, half gardening, is always exciting and will yield up an interesting new garden for Carrigglas. Meanwhile, a *potager* is being worked on and it is hoped that it will open in 2001.

Finally, a walk called the Ladies' Mile circles the park, past the pets' graveyard and, according to Tessa, covers (as 'Ladies' miles' were wont in those days) about half a mile – not too taxing for any lady.

GARDEN CENTRES

ABBEYLARA GARDEN CENTRE

Abbeylara, Granard, County Longford; Tel: +043 86125.

LONGFORD GARDEN CENTRE

Clonbolt, County Longford; Tel: +043 46911.

KITCHEN GARDEN

CASTLE FORBES

Kitchen Gardens, Castle Forbes, County Longford; Tel: +043 46263 ▪ **Contact**: Bridget O'Toole, head gardener ▪ **Open:** Monday–Saturday, 1pm–5pm.

The working kitchen garden at Castle Forbes produces fruit, vegetables and cut flowers, both for the house and for sale to the public.

IRISH GARDENS

COUNTY LOUTH

Louth is a small county on the route between Dublin and Belfast. To schoolchildren it is well-known as the home of Mellifont Abbey, the first Cistercian monastery in Ireland, and of the famous round tower and high cross at Monasterboice, close by. The two principal towns of the county are Drogheda (although the Louth–Meath border designates a small portion of it to County Meath) and Dundalk. Drogheda has a well-organised heritage tour that takes in its historic sites, such as St Peter's Church where the head of St Oliver Plunkett can be seen. In addition, a tombstone dating to 1520, depicting the Black Death in all its horror, is in the church's graveyard. The tour also takes in places associated with Oliver Cromwell and his infamous siege of the town. Dundalk is a rapidly changing town but, like Drogheda, retains much evidence of its past. Small coastal villages, like Blackrock, are marvellous places to stroll and enjoy the beautiful views of the Mourne Mountains, which dominate the scenery throughout the county. The Cooley Peninsula, running out to Carlingford Lough, is also a good place to walk and drive. The land is naturally hilly and varied, edged by drumlin country to the west and the granite foothills of the Mournes to the east. There are some good gardens to be seen in the county, and in Termonfeckin, An Grianán (the Irish Countrywomen's Association (ICA) Horticultural College), runs full-time courses.

BEAULIEU HOUSE AND GARDEN   ♿

Beaulieu, Drogheda, County Louth; Tel: +041 9838557 ✹ **Contact:** Mrs Sidney Waddington ✹ **Open:** 4 May–9 November, Monday–Thursday, 9am–1pm; closed August and bank holidays ✹ **Entrance fee** ✹ Not suitable for children ✹ **Special features:** the historic Beaulieu house may be visited May–July, Monday–Thursday, 9am–1pm; first two weeks in September, Monday–Thursday, 9am–1pm ✹ **Directions:** the garden is on the right turn for Baltray off the Drogheda–Termonfeckin road, 2km from Termonfeckin.

Beaulieu House was built in 1628 and refurbished between 1710 and 1720, and bears the distinction of being the first non-fortified house of its kind. The style of the red-brick house is unusual for Ireland and looks as though it might have been borrowed from northern France or Holland. In fact, the bricks used to build it came from the Netherlands. The drive up to the house is short, wide, impressive and also in keeping with the Franco-Dutch style, fairly singular in County Louth or indeed in the Republic as a whole. The walled garden is set close by the house and is bordered by a mature wood. The Dutch artist Van der Hagan, who painted several canvasses which can be seen in the house as well as an allegorical work on the ceiling of the drawing room, was also reputed as a designer of walled gardens. It is thought that the walled garden at Beaulieu may have been his work, and if so it dates back to no later than 1732.

To get to the garden you take a path, bordered by golden yew and fuchsia, which passes a temple-like building and a delicate old greenhouse with a small grotto and fernery. The garden is a gem and is remarkably well-tended by Mrs Waddington, now in her eighties; a tiny, delicate-looking, but determined woman. She works and maintains Beaulieu with minimal help in a way that gardeners a third of her age would have difficulty managing.

On stepping into the walled garden the visitor is greeted by a huge border. Ranked flowers include white galtonia, variegated mallow, asters, phlox and rust-coloured phormium. Plants like exotic *Cautleya spicata*, which has red stalks, red-veined leaves and vivid yellow flowers, and the Maltese cross (*Lychnis chalcedonica*) in a shade of red that scares off more timid gardeners are just two of the bolder plants in the south-facing border. At eighteen metres deep, this bed holds an enormous number of plants in beautiful combinations of leaf and flower: white agapanthus beside cream and green variegated sage, waves of anemone and the honey bush (*Melianthus major*) are thoughtfully mixed. Big pink crinum lilies and sea lavender, like sprays of gypsophila, are another gorgeous combination. A sundial – at least a month out of date and going along at its own pace – stands among the flowers. Losing a month in Beaulieu is quite understandable.

The path by this *tour de force* leads down toward a rustic summerhouse that looks like something the 'crooked man' from the nursery rhyme might have lived in. It is fronted by a knot garden of box, roses, purple heliotrope and antirrhinum. Two huge Irish yews, nearly 300 years old, hide a shady foxglove and hellebore garden to the side of this formal bed. Mrs Waddington planted an eucryphia here in the 1950s and every year she photographs it for her Christmas card. To get the best angle for her pictures she has to lie flat on the ground beneath the tree; I hope recipients of the cards appreciate the effort. 'It's almost too full of flowers,' she says, in a worried way, of this great tree with its branches sagging under the weight of blossoms. A fig tree beside the eucryphia has been denuded of fruit: 'The tree rats [grey squirrels] got them all,' she explains.

Both border and knot garden stand on a ledge that then drops down to a lower level where the fruit and vegetable garden is sited. The bank is covered in meadow grass, hardy cranesbill geraniums and other wildflowers. Down below, paths lead under rose-covered arches and trellis with trained apple trees into the vegetable and working kitchen garden.

An interesting point about Beaulieu and Listoke (*see* below) is that, as long-time swapping neighbours, they carry a lot of the same flowers, yet the gardens are hugely different. It is worth visiting them together to compare and contrast.

LISTOKE HOUSE AND GARDEN

Ballymakenny Road, Drogheda, County Louth; Tel/Fax: +041 9832265; 087 2213369 ▪ **Contact:** Mrs Patricia Barrow ▪ **Open:** April–September, every evening, 5pm–8pm, and weekends, check for 'Open' sign on the gate; book in advance for an appointment; also on charity open days (see local press for details) ▪ **Entrance fee** donated to Chernobyl Children's Project ▪ Supervised children welcome ▪ **Special features:** teas available on open days or by prior arrangement; picnic area ▪ **Directions:** situated 2.5km from Drogheda on the Ballymakenny Road, on the right-hand side. Stone entrance.

Listoke is a typical Edwardian country garden, with a grass tennis court overlooked by a fine summerhouse, greenhouses, lawns, herbaceous borders and woodland walks. The family even hold Edwardian tennis parties for charity, and the players run as best they can, laden down in long skirts, many layers and flannels, using small-headed, heavy, wooden racquets. Mrs Barrow's aim is to maintain the garden's true style as that of a private garden which opens to the public rather than a public garden bending too much to the demands of public taste.

She started gardening here twenty years ago, having inherited a garden in dire need of reclamation. Arising from her experiences, Mrs Barrow has two simple and direct rules for a successful garden. Firstly, she believes in the virtues of a well-kept, smartly edged lawn. A tidy lawn against a border full of loose, billowing flowers does several things: the flowing border looks to the untrained eye as though it might all have just 'happened'; the smart grass edge however states quietly but firmly that the gardener is in control. It also makes the flowers look more voluptuous and abundant. Mrs Barrow's second rule is that colour in the borders must be muted and soft. She doesn't like bright colours and will not allow them into her garden. Only local stone, gravel and brick are used in the hard landscaping and so the walls, paths and features in the garden knit in together and look harmonious.

A large summerhouse or garden room, overhung by a weeping elm and a mulberry tree, looks out over the garden. The veranda is arrayed with pots of double nasturtium. An Edwardian greenhouse has recently been sensitively restored and planted with peaches, figs and hothouse flowers for the house.

Beyond the greenhouse is an arboretum. 'This area was under grass twenty years ago and we had no idea of what was here before that, so I thought I would love an arboretum.' An arch of normally ugly *Cupressocyparis leylandii*, the most hated of hedging, leads into the arboretum. Mrs Barrow has it looking beautiful, well-tended and neatly shaped. The arboretum is also the testing ground for paulownia, catalpa, *Pinus montezumae* and different varieties of beech to see how they will do in her garden.

A huge mock orange (*Philadelphus*) leads the way out of the arboretum into the summer border. This is a feast of flowers with three-metre tall, deep blue *Lobelia syphilitica* and *Anemone* 'Honorine Jobert' – Mrs Barrow's favourite plant. 'Honorine Jobert' is a well-known perennial, hardy and with beady buds on long stems, it produces simple daisy-like white flowers at a time of the year when there is not much white in the garden. These anemones also make good cut flowers and, once they like a spot, will thrive and spread despite all neglect. Could more be asked of a plant? From the summer border the path moves off to a laburnum walk that is underplanted with *Geranium* 'Johnson's Blue'.

Mrs Barrow is currently embarked upon restoring the wood, which will become a spring area with anemones, native bluebells and snowdrops fighting for attention. She was pleasantly surprised to locate the original woodland walks – stone-edged cinder paths lying under half a metre of soil. These have now been restored.

MILLHOUSE GARDENS

Channonrock, Iniskeen Road, Dundalk, County Louth; Tel: +042 9374354 ▪ **Contact:** Mrs Mary Campbell ▪ **Open:** mid March–end September, Monday–Friday, 2.30pm–7pm, Saturday by appointment only, Sunday 2.30pm–6.30pm; groups should book in advance ▪ **Entrance fee** ▪ Not suitable for children ▪ **Directions:** take the Carrickmacross Road out of Dundalk and travel 9.5km. Turn right at Conlon's pub. The garden is well signposted.

The Campbells have been farming at Millhouse for generations, but Mary Campbell is the first person in the family to garden on the site. In the past, farms did not always support good gardens, or gardens of any description, and Mary's twelve-year-old garden was an orchard before she started work on it. As she took out old fruit trees she replaced them with stone-edged beds of mixed shrubs and small trees. These include varieties of juniper, cedar, thuja, picea and other evergreens, which give a permanent structure to the two-acre garden. Cape daisy, sedum, thalictrum and other perennial flowers highlight the scheme in spring and summer.

Wide, rolling lawns curve around beds of herbaceous plants and shrubs. Mary Campbell is a flower-arranger and that interest is clearly evident in the variety of leaf textures, colours and shapes in her choice of plants and in the way she combines them. Many of the shrubs have variegated foliage: the blue cedar (*Cedrus atlantica* 'Glauca') has strong pink *Geranium* 'Ann Folkard' flowers laced through it; the dark green spines of monkey puzzle trees show up the pale blooms of a *Clematis montana* and purple *Clematis* 'Jackmanii' winds around a yellow rose.

The gazebo, made from 'rubbish and salvage just lying around', is a lesson in how to make use of found objects. One other good feature of this garden is a mature old beech tree standing on its own flat slate plateau, with a bog oak 'Loch Ness Monster' swimming past in the grass.

O'GRADY'S GARDEN

Coolfore, Monasterboice, Drogheda, County Louth; Tel: +041 9826368; e-mail: o-gradymatt@hotmail.com ▪ **Contact:** Frances O'Grady ▪ **Open:** May–September, by appointment only ▪ **Entrance fee** ▪ **Special features:** flower-arranging demonstrations and talks, contact for details; teas arranged on request ▪ **Directions:** travel north on the Drogheda–Belfast road (N1) for 8km. At the Monasterboice Inn take the turn marked for Collon. Travel 1.5km and then take the secondary road to the left. After another 1.5km turn left into a laneway. The garden is at the end of the lane, marked by big gates.

Frances O'Grady is well-known locally as the owner of *the* garden to visit in County Louth. She is also familiar to RTÉ viewers for her flower-arranging slots on afternoon television. Her garden covers two acres of shrubs, herbaceous plants, alpines and rare plants. It looks across at the round tower at Monasterboice and Mount Oriel, where, in the village of Collon, the Williamite army camped during the Battle of the Boyne in 1690.

The garden is divided into two areas. In the first there are specimen shrubs and trees, flowering cherries, laburnum, rowan, willow, red oak, walnut, daphne and crinodendron. Scree, alpine and rose beds, along with a good herbaceous border, make up the main garden. A second garden contains vegetables, fruit trees and flowers for cutting. Tender plants, like kiwi and vines, grow in the tunnel and there is a wildflower border.

In the most recently created part of the garden, situated on a north-facing slope, a woodland area and pond have been planted with wet-loving plants, like hosta and ligularia. The land around is acid and so an obvious place for lime-hating plants, such as rhododendron and azalea. A natural spring fills the large, unlined pond. Because of this, the ground surrounding the pond is very wet, providing a perfect home for varieties of wild orchid, loosestrife, meadow sweet and ferns.

This is going to become a surprise garden in the future as the ten-year-old spruce forest matures around it. The garden will continue to interest as it matures, and, as such, it will merit several visits to see the progression.

STEPHENSTOWN POND TRUST

Stephenstown Road, Knockbridge, Dundalk, County Louth; Tel: +042 9379019 ※ **Contact:** Reception ※ **Open:** November–April, daily, 9am–5pm; April–October, daily, 9am–dark ※ **Entrance fee** car park charge, payable on exit ※ **Special features:** playground; craft shop; carp fishing facilities; Agnes Burns's Cottage, now a visitor centre with exhibits on the life of Agnes, who was sister of Scottish poet Robert Burns and lived there for a time (separate admission fee); interactive fauna display ※ Children welcome; please note, dogs on leads ※ Managed by FÁS ※ **Directions:** turn left off the Ardee–Dundalk road (N52). Knockbridge is 8km south of Dundalk.

The pond at Knockbridge is a beautiful natural water feature surrounded by oak and hawthorn, willow, bullrush, yellow flag iris and lilies. There are signs posted around the perimeter describing the pond life, animals and plants found on the site. While, strictly speaking, the Stephenstown Pond project is not a garden, it should be of interest to anyone thinking of creating a natural or wild garden.

NURSERIES AND GARDEN CENTRES

CASEY'S NURSERY AND GARDEN CENTRE
Dundalk, County Louth; Tel: +042 9371475.

DROGHEDA GARDEN CENTRE
Bachelor's Lane, Drogheda, County Louth; Tel: +041 9836029.

DUNDALK GARDEN CENTRE
Dublin Street, Dundalk, County Louth; Tel: +042 33606.

DUNLEER NURSERY AND GARDEN CENTRE
Dundalk Road, Dunleer, County Louth; Tel: +041 6851155.

FOREST GLEN NURSERY
Drogheda, County Louth; Tel: +041 9836596.

HAGGARDSTOWN GARDEN CENTRE
Heynestown, Dundalk, County Louth; Tel: +042 9337627; e-mail: hgcentre@eircom.net

AN GRIANÁN GARDEN CENTRE
Termonfeckin, County Louth; Tel: +041 9822119.

MELLIFONT ABBEY GARDEN NURSERY

Collon, County Louth;
Tel: +041 9826216.

Mostly a wholesale nursery but they also sell retail plant plugs. Mail order catalogue available.

GARDEN DESIGNERS

PATRICIA BARROW

Ballymakenny Road, Drogheda, County Louth; Tel: +041 32265.

For an example of Mrs Barrow's work see her garden at Listoke House.

GARDENING COURSES

AN GRIANÁN

ICA College of Horticulture, Termonfeckin, Drogheda, County Louth; Tel: +041 9822158.

An Grianán runs several recognised courses in horticulture, including one- and two-year Diploma courses. Contact or write for details. There are also several demonstration gardens and plots to be seen (see An Grianán Garden Centre, p.92).

GARDEN ACCESSORIES

AMAU TERRACOTTA

27 Mount St Oliver, Drogheda, County Louth; Tel: +041 9846772.

Hand-thrown terracotta pots in all sizes. Painted, glazed and rough terracotta sold through the Blackrock Market in County Dublin as well as from the Drogheda base.

COUNTY MEATH

Meath is a county of gently undulating farmland. The neatness that goes with its prosperity gives it a certain charm. But Meath's attraction for visitors is historical. Sites such as the neolithic tombs of Newgrange, Knowth and Dowth, the Hills of Slane and Tara, and the cairns or passage tombs at Loughcrew draw tourists and students of archaeology from all over the world. Slane village is quaint and worth visiting, but it can be a traffic bottleneck at peak holiday times. The Bru na Bóinne interpretive centre permits one to see Newgrange and Knowth. This is one of the busiest centres of its kind in the country and, as a result, it can be very congested at the height of the season when hordes of people descend on it. In addition, at peak times of the year access to the sites themselves is not guaranteed. Pre-book and visit off-season to best appreciate the spectacle.

BUTTERSTREAM GARDEN

Kildalkey Road, Trim, County Meath; Tel: +046 36017; Fax: +046 31702 ※ **Contact:** Jim Reynolds ※ **Open:** April–September, Monday–Sunday, 11am–6pm; groups welcome, by appointment only ※ **Entrance fee** ※ **Directions:** within 1km of Trim, on the road to Kildalkey.

A sign at the front gate of Butterstream reads: 'Children on a tight lead please. No dogs. Gentlefolk will not, and visitors should not, help themselves to the garden plants.'

Butterstream is a garden well known to every garden visitor I meet. Created by the remarkable Jim Reynolds over the past thirty years, it is a testament to his talent. He says it all started with the acquisition of 'a few hybrid tea roses' and visits to the really grand-scale gardens, such as Mount Stewart and Rowallane (*see* County Down), Ilnacullin (*see* County Cork) and Birr Castle (*see* County Offaly). A vision of what could be achieved was planted in his mind, and those few roses found themselves joined by more roses, other species and then arranged into certain styles until, finally, they found themselves metamorphosed into Butterstream.

Two outlandishly sized, long canals are the most recent addition to the garden that was carved out of a field on the Reynolds's farm. They are monumental, and perfectly illustrate Jim's sense of fun and cheekiness. Flanked by two lime *allées*, they finish off in cascades over stone steps down toward twin classical summerhouses set in a smart courtyard.

From this extraordinary introduction to the garden, the path leads out through an arch cut from a huge regimental beech hedge and onto the summerhouse lawn. The lawn in question is softly surrounded with gradations of pink and purple hydrangea. The perfume from pots of lilies drifts past whoever might find him/herself relaxing in a Lloyd loom chair, with a Foxford rug strewn over their lap, wondering if there is honey for tea, in this most Edwardian of summerhouses.

This area of billowing, informal style serves to heighten the impact and punch of

the next garden, the regulated, clipped, trained box and yew that make up the obelisk garden. There are occasional touches of colour in the shape of pale pink roses and campanula, but the emphasis is chiefly on the tight, regimented green shapes. The path leads on and out through a laurel hedge climbed over by a *Tropaeolum speciosum*, to the pool garden and to Jim's much-photographed, Tuscan-inspired pergola. The striking plants in this garden are the mop-head hornbeams, and box shaped into tall corkscrews in big tubs and pots.

Laburnum tunnels lead to herbaceous borders that look good enough to eat and are full of the best garden plants, like opium poppies, goat's rue (*Galega officinalis*), delphiniums, honesty and alliums.

Rapunzel's romantic tower, which overlooks Jim Reynolds's gardens at Butterstream, County Meath.

Architectural-looking bear's breeches (*Acanthus mollis*) foil lighter thalictrum with fluffy flowers on top of tall stalks. Huge clumps of tall fennel and golden rod provide the backdrop. In mid-summer this border is a riot of flowers and hard to study properly in one visit. Pollen-laden bees drag themselves up out of the flowers in this bee delicatessen.

Looking back in the direction from which one has walked, the sense of division between each of the gardens is quite clear. From this point it is impossible to see the beech-hedged gate or the long canals or the twin summerhouses. The seclusion and privacy within each garden is almost complete. So even on busy visitor days, a walk around can still be a fairly quiet, unbustled affair.

The white garden and tower form the centre of Butterstream. This room is an exercise in silvers and greys: Paris daisies tumble out of terracotta pots, artichokes with spiky silver foliage contrast with soft white-flowering hydrangea, shiny variegated pittosporum leaves, clematis and cream-coloured phlox. Old roses are held and hemmed in to good manners by sharp box walls. Clipped box is one of the recurrent themes throughout the garden, used time and again to rein in and give a solidity to looser, more transient plantings.

Order and neatness are important in a kitchen garden. This is because, unlike the rest of the garden, there will always be bare patches and empty spots in the vegetable beds when, for example, a crop may have been harvested or recently sown seeds have yet to germinate. Therefore, a good-looking kitchen garden relies on permanent structure. Here that structure comes in the shape of bay obelisks and iron arches. The bay trees provide the kitchen with leaves for flavouring stews and stocks, as well as looking statuesque in the garden, and the arches look good bare or clothed in runner beans. Rows of rhubarb forcers and chimney pots add to the permanent decoration in this section, idling by the hedge in the summer or being used in the rough stone-edged beds in late winter and spring.

Towards the end of the visit is the stream garden. This is a shady spot where massed hellebores, bergenia, viola and different ferns, including the tatting fern and *Dryopteris affins* 'Cristata the King', a particularly gnarled and convoluted plant, thrive in the damp shade provided. A head of *Medusa*, with her unmistakeable snake hair, glares out at the passers-by, possibly hoping to turn any plant-stealers to stone!

Despite the virtuoso performance that is Jim Reynolds's garden, Butterstream is nevertheless the creation of a self-taught gardener and the result of trial and error. That fact should give enormous encouragement to beginner gardeners. Jim strongly recommends that new gardeners find themselves a nurseryman or woman who will sell them the sort of plants they will be able to grow on their site, whatever their own talent or lack of it. But take care to avoid the nurseryman/woman who tries to force on you the plants *he/she* wishes to sell.

GLEBEWOOD COTTAGE AND GLEBELANDS HOUSE

Ratoath village, County Meath; Tel: +01 8256015/8256219 ▪ **Contact:** Arthur Lardner or Carmel Heslin ▪ **Open:** Easter Sunday–end September, Wednesday–Sunday, 2pm–6pm; groups welcome ▪ **Entrance fee** covers both gardens ▪ **Special features:** guided tours and teas by appointment; toilet facilities ▪ Supervised children welcome ▪ **Directions:** the gardens are in Ratoath village, look for the signpost opposite the church.

GLEBEWOOD COTTAGE

Glebewood Cottage took second prize in the Meath, Louth and Westmeath category of the Shamrock All Ireland Gardens Competition 1999. That will come as no surprise to visitors.

The garden is only in existence since 1990, designed and built by architect Arthur Lardner and his colleague, gardener Noel Kennedy. Mr Lardner is an admirer of Edwin Lutyens, the English architect. Lutyens's work is well known to gardeners because of his long working relationship with Gertrude Jekyll, the late nineteenth-century garden designer. (For examples of Lutyens's work in Ireland, *see* Heywood Garden, County Laois, and the War Memorial Gardens, County Dublin).

Nine years ago, Mr Lardner began to create a garden around the Lutyens-style cottage he had recently built. That garden is now a long way from the flat field he started with. It is, as he describes it, 'a dynamic space created to give a sense of flow, height and movement.' The work began by introducing a variety of heights and levels to the flat space by building ramped walks and tracks, banks with palisades, hollows and hills. This new landscape was then ready for planting.

The trees planted included elegant trees, like the snake-bark maple *(Acer rufinerve)*, and the Antarctic beech *(Nothofagus antarctica)*. The beech, unlike the acer, will not remain light and airy forever and it is destined to become a huge tree eventually. This is a masculine, foliage garden with the emphasis on shades of green, leaf texture and light cast through groves of trees. Colour and flowers are only used sparingly to dot and highlight the picture. Well-placed statuary draws the attention toward certain features and compositions.

Mr Lardner enjoys showing his garden visitors around personally. While this may be very time-consuming, he nevertheless enjoys chatting, and for the visitor it is much more informative than an unaccompanied walk. In order to accommodate his visitors he prefers people to book in advance.

As you leave the garden, having wandered up and down hills, under plantations of trees, behind walls of vegetation and into little arbours, it is almost impossible to visualise the flat field that it once was.

GLEBELANDS HOUSE

Mrs Heslin, like her talented neighbour, was a winner in the Shamrock All Ireland Gardens Competition 1999, coming third in the same category as Mr Lardner.

Adjacent to Glebewood Cottage, Glebelands House has a contrasting and complementary garden. The double-fronted house was built back in 1813 and is an elegant Georgian building. The approach to the house and garden is a short drive lined with tall beech trees. The whole garden is, in fact, surrounded by mature park trees, including some good blue cedar, larch and pine. They make a fine backdrop and give a sense of privacy and seclusion.

The garden wraps around the house, changing mood as it turns corners. A grove of tall oak, beech and lime trees dominates the front garden, lightly underplanted with sweeps of hosta, fern and bergenia. A long swing hanging from one of the tree boughs shows the garden to be a lived-in, family place.

The back garden rises up on stone ledges behind the house and features a good deal of hard landscaping, paving, flags and raised paths holding up and hemming in herbaceous and alpine planting. Central to the varying terraces and ledges is a little water feature trickling and glittering among the stones.

The raised beds behind low stone walls are full of pretty, low-growing and alpine plants and sun-loving, silver-leaved Mediterranean plants, like oxalis, saxifrage, thyme, campanula and little sedum. Soft silvers and greens blend in effectively with the stone. The whole atmosphere is of a restful garden.

Glebewood and Glebelands are two gardens very different to each other; one mature, one young and still developing. They make perfect companion visits that will fill an afternoon and inspire visitors with their different approaches to informal gardening.

GROVE GARDENS

Fordestown, Kells, County Meath; Tel: +046 34276 ▪ **Contact:** Pat or Teresa Dillon ▪ **Open:** beginning February–end October, daily, 10am–6pm; groups welcome, by appointment ▪ **Entrance fee** ▪ **Special features:** exotic animals and birds; annual bring-and-buy fowl fair; picnic area, jam and plants (particularly clematis) for sale ▪ **Directions:** Grove Gardens is halfway between Kells and Athboy on the R164, well signed from both towns and from all approaching roads.

This is the best-known clematis garden in the country, with over 300 varieties and 800 plants spread over four acres. There are also 500 roses, including a collection of old French and English roses, magnificent herbaceous borders and mature trees, all gardened by the talented and welcoming Pat Dillon.

But the signs on every road leading to Grove carry the illustration of a parrot, and, a particular sort of tulip aside, parrots and gardens do not usually spring to mind in tandem. However, once you have entered the gate and encountered the pens of exotic farm animals, emus and other birds, llamas, goats and pot-bellied pigs, it's clear from the outset that this place is more than just a garden – but more of the animals later.

The garden proper begins with the vegetable plot, which is well designed, handsome and full of healthy beetroot, peas, beans, chard and carrots. Utility is laudable, but here it has been sweetened with rows of clematis and roses that mind the vegetables. In particular, an old pink bourbon rose, 'Mme Ernest Calvat', lends a certain glamour and class to the turnips.

Leave the vegetable garden by way of a little bridged stream and a pond full of rare ducks. Follow the path that leads up to a cottage garden and massed hardy geraniums, Sweet William, hosta, tradescantia, white goat's rue and more clematis and roses.

Raised beds close by the house are filled with rampant ground cover being trampled on by white peacocks. Children will be as keen as garden visitors to keep moving on at this point. Who knows what two- or four-legged creature may be waiting behind the next rose bush. They will not have to wait long as the path goes from here under rose- and-clematis-covered trellis, past cages of snowy and barn owls and into the rose garden proper, which, of course, shares space with the clematis.

There are many eye-catching things in here, including a golden privet shot through with an unidentified pink rambling rose. Another version of this idea is a variegated elder climbed through by *Clematis* 'Lincolnshire Lady', another pink bloom. A semicircle of grass is surrounded by a great border in which a velvety, purple-flowering *Clematis* 'Polish Spirit' ranges. This variety was famously bred by a Polish monk, who is still working away in his monastic cell and his little garden outside. The vision this conjures up of a hermit-like soul working alone in his tiny cold room is attractive and adds to the romance of the flower.

While the ordinary gardener enjoys the overall spectacle, the clematis fans may study the many varieties of this great if finicky plant, and the rest of the family will be happy to visit the lemurs, wallabies and cochin hens. For the fowl fancier, birds can be bought at an annual bring-and-buy fowl fair, usually held in August. Ring the Dillons for exact dates.

CLEMATIS WILT

Clematis wilt is a disease that strikes fear in the heart of anyone who grows these exotic-looking climbers. Wilt is caused by a fungus that attacks the plant very quickly and visibly at the stem. The whole plant can keel over and die overnight, looking as though it has been cut down. Large flowering hybrids are particularly prone to the disease.

To treat it, cut back all affected stems either to healthy growth or, if the whole stem is dead, to below ground level. Spray any new foliage with Bordeaux mixture. It is thought that planting clematis in a deep hole, placing it six to seven centimetres below the pot level, will also help to guard it against developing wilt. And remember, this nasty blight is not caused by bad gardening and should not be a cause for guilt in novices.

Dunboyne, County Meath; Tel: +01 8255210 ■ **Contact:** Major or Mrs Hamilton ■ **Open:** April–August, Monday–Friday and the third Sunday of each month, 2pm–6pm; groups welcome by appointment ■ **Entrance fee** ■ Please note, dogs on leads ■ **Special features:** guided tour of house, including eighteenth-century Irish furniture specially commissioned; groups can book teas by prior arrangement ■ **Directions:** situated 3km from Dunboyne on the Maynooth road (beside Bally-macoll Stud).

The entrance to Hamwood is marked by a most ornate gate-lodge with an elaborately slated roof, tiny leaded windows and little gables. Charles Hamilton built the Big House in 1779. Today his descendant, Major Hamilton, lets visitors wander freely through his large garden, setting them off on the right path with a few quick guidelines on direction before they embark on their walk.

Start out for the walled garden by taking a wild, wooded path under the trees. Inside the walls are old rock gardens full of ferns and bergenia. The rock gardens date back to 1810. Leading out of the rockery, a little herb patch with fennel, tansy, lavender and oregano has been hemmed in with a rough stone edge or border. Ancient iron arches are wrapped in jumbles of *Clematis montana* and potato vine (*Solanum crispum*), honeysuckle and a red rose – making an eclectic knot of colour that absolutely suits the place.

Age has rendered the old greenhouses topless and the remains of the bases have been pulled into service as homes for big splashes of feverfew, daylilies and a soft, white everlasting sweet pea with a very sweet scent. Close by, a huge yellow tree peony bakes against a sunny wall. Much of the rest of the walled garden is slipping back into the wild and old fruit-training trellises can be seen weighed down under rampant vegetation.

At the front of the house are rose, peony and iris beds and a well-placed seat sheltered by an ancient wisteria arbour. This is a lovely place to sit during blossom time in May, when the fragrance of the dangling lilac flowers is at its height.

Finally, a pine walk of stately trees, underplanted with cyclamen, spring bulbs, camellias, shuttlecock ferns and ivies, marches out from the house towards the fields in a combination of cultivated and wild good looks.

Hamwood is gardened with a leisurely hand. I cannot think of another place tended as lightly as it. Better and smarter days have undoubtedly been seen by the garden, but it cannot ever have been a more charming or romantic place than it is today. The only problem is that a garden like this must be held rather than let slip any further. The next phase is dilapidation and that is too sad to consider.

LOUGHCREW HISTORIC GARDENS

Oldcastle, County Meath; Tel: +049 854 1922; Fax: +049 8541722; e-mail: cnaper@tinet.ie ■ **Contact:** Charles and Emily Naper ■ **Open:** 17–31 March, 12pm–4pm; April–September, daily, 12pm–6pm; 1 October–16 March, weekends and bank holidays only, 12pm–4pm ■ **Entrance fee** ■ Supervised children welcome; please note, dogs on leads ■ **Special features**: St Oliver Plunkett's family house and church ■ **Directions:** 5km from Oldcastle on the Mullingar Road.

The gardens at Loughcrew are unusual in a number of ways. They are as much of archaeological and geographical as of floral and horticultural interest. They have been under restoration since 1997. Since then the work has been moving at breakneck speed on this giant undertaking. The doors were opened to the public in 1999, but work is still in progress and will be for years to come. This is a fascinating garden set in splendid isolation on the edge of Meath and Cavan, where the landscape begins to change into hilly drumlin country.

The husband-and-wife team of Charles and Emily have taken the bones of an old demesne that has been in their family since 1693 and have worked on it with the help of the Great Gardens Of Ireland Restoration Programme and garden designer Daphne Shackleton (see County Cavan). The result is a very eccentric collection of gardens and garden features quite unlike any other garden in the country; a trip through a section of garden history.

On the site is St Oliver Plunkett's family house and church. The Napers are related to the saint's family three times by marriage. There is also the foundations of a seventeenth-century long house, ornamental canals, a walled garden that has yet to be worked on, a watermill, a viewing mound, an ancient yew avenue, formal gardens, an archery lawn, a variety of follies and a lake. Rather like a big cabinet of curiosities, Loughcrew is filled with singular oddities, such as the small spring and waterfall emerging from under the raised roots of a cedar tree.

The grand-scale yew walk, made up of trees of indeterminate age, leads up to a viewing mound. The point of this mound was that one would climb to the top and survey the garden and surrounding countryside. It might not seem like a hugely impressive feature, but in pre-JCB days every shovel of soil and stone had to be hand-lifted and carted into place on the growing hill. The finished result gives a fine view.

The long herbaceous border is still young but developing and filling out. Starting ordinarily enough, the border is planted at one end with standard herbaceous classics, like delphinium, aster and potentilla. But nothing else at Loughcrew is normal and it comes as little surprise that, halfway along, the border becomes an altogether more entertaining 'Grotesques' border. Choice and colourful descriptions of the plants being grown include the unfortunately named *Vestia foetida sonanacae,* described in the accompanying label as 'an unpleasant smelling shrub'. What is usually thought of as unprepossessing vinca is intriguingly described as 'beneficial for memory disorders, irritability and vertigo'. Pulmonaria, the sign informs us, is 'for all disorders of the lung, including consumption, fever and plague,' and finally pulsatilla is 'a remedy for nervous exhaustion in women'. Labelling the plants in this manner makes the bed entertaining for non-gardeners and enthusiasts alike.

The Napers are in the process of rebuilding follies around the demesne and over the next few years will no doubt continue to reveal more historical gardening curiosities on their estate.

The Loughcrew cairns and passage tombs on the Hill of the Witch are close by, prominently signed and definitely worth a visit.

NEWCASTLE HOUSE &

Kilmainhamwood, Kells, County Meath; Tel: +046 52572 ■ **Contact:** Margaret and Peter Brittain ■ **Open:** two open days a year (phone in advance for these dates); groups welcome by appointment at other times ■ **Entrance fee** donated to local animal charity ✳ Supervised children welcome ✳ **Special features:** Mr Brittain gives garden and horticultural talks ✳ **Directions:** drive to Nobber and continue on the road towards Kingscourt. The garden is on the left-hand side, about 5km from Nobber, and the entrance is opposite a derelict cottage.

There was a garden marked at Newcastle on the 1836 Ordnance Survey map of the area and the garden here today is set within the same shape. No one had worked the garden for almost fifty years before the Brittains arrived, so this is essentially a young garden in an old setting.

'We came from Dublin and our old, big town garden bringing a lot of things with us,' says Mrs Brittain. And for the past eight years the garden has been furiously worked by the pair of them. 'When we started we planted for ease, with no nice little herbaceous things because they take up too much time, but the roses have done very well for us. We had been collecting roses for years and we brought many of them with us.' They are particularly keen on filipes ramblers like *Rosa filipes* 'Kiftsgate', which they have trained through many of the trees at the Newcastle garden.

'We planted a lot of trees when we came, and as the years go by we plant more and more.' Their collection is growing at a good rate and a former meadow is the latest area to succumb to trees, becoming a small new arboretum. Meanwhile, the lake on the edge of the garden is being turned into a natural heritage area. Wildlife experts Howard Fox and Roger Goodwillie (*see* Lavistown, County Kilkenny) were brought in to study and catalogue the plant life by the water. Other experts are looking at the bats and water life.

The drive up to the garden is side-planted with tall and imposing yew trees over laurel hedging. *Tropaeloum speciosum* threads through the yew. Its bright green leaves and red flowers, followed by bluish-purple berries, show up brilliantly against the very dark green yew.

Behind the hedge is a forest to which the Brittains are constantly adding young trees, such as ginkgo. In the great demesnes and gardens of history, huge trees were sometimes chained to each other in an effort to prevent the loss of specimens that were threatening to fall. Likewise, the Brittains don't hold that falling trees must stay fallen. In one instance a nootka cypress (*Lamycyparis nootkatensis*) that was tipping over has been pulled back into an upright position with wires until its roots settle back and strengthen. Further on, an ex-paddock has been planted with rhododendron, liquidambar and three trailing Wellingtonias (*Sequoiadendron giganteum* 'Pendulum').

Down below the house a stream borders the woods. 'This was a smelly ditch,' says Margaret, until she found an old bridge lodged at the bottom of it. She then reinstated it and cleared out the stream. The bridge now leads off to the sycamore woods, which are totally carpeted with Solomon's seal.

From here the way leads up to the house through a double terrace of lawn, finishing on a set of lichen-covered steps with jasmine and fairy foxglove seeding itself into every available crack between every stone. The steps are also full of daisy, grape hyacinth, violet, columbine, sedum and fern. If all that wasn't enough to prevent the steps from being used, a rose climbing through the stone banister completes the sense of an obstacle course. Steps that can't be negotiated and banisters that can't be held – exactly as any good gardener would wish it.

Up here is another lawn, surrounded by a good floriferous mixed border leading once again toward the trees. Under the wall are catmint (*Nepeta*), salvia, *Rosa chinensis* 'Mutabilis' and the incense rose, which has very pretty tiny flowers and extremely sharp thorns. Overall there are 150 types of roses in the garden. Living up here are the 'garden hazards', otherwise known as the peacocks. 'They peck everything. They'll try anything of colour and half the time they don't even eat it,' says Margaret, exasperated. But she is not so exasperated that she would get rid of her stately looking pests.

In essence, Newcastle is a tree lover's garden. And there are trees everywhere, even in the hen-run, where a Mexican weeping pine *(Pinus patula)* and baby cedar were planted recently for the grandchildren. Finally, there's the Big Tree – the climax in the garden. I will not give the surprise away because it is worth the trip just to see this fine tree and its wonderful situation.

ROCKFIELD GARDENS

Drumconrath, Navan, County Meath; Tel: +046 52135 ▣ **Contact:** Georgina Nicholson ▣ **Open:** May–July, 2pm–6pm, by appointment only ▣ **Entrance fee** donated to charity ▣ Supervised children welcome ▣ **Special features:** refreshments can be booked by prior arrangement; toilet facilities ▣ **Directions:** from Slane village, drive past Slane Castle to Drumconrath and out onto the Kells–Ardee road as far as a pub called Donegan's. Turn left here and then take the next right at the sign for McKeever's Mill. The garden a few hundred metres along on the right. (The distance from Donegan's is 4.5km.)

Set in the County Meath countryside just as it becomes hilly and northerly, Rockfield has a lovely walled garden attached to the house rather than a long walk from it, as is usually the case. The garden is well situated on a substantial hill rising up and away from the house, which means that it can be viewed perfectly from all windows at the back of the building. Mrs Nicholson works the garden herself, apart from the help of a fourteen-year-old boy who comes in to work as grass-cutter. On the walls around the garden the work was rendered labour-saving by planting large shrub borders, which are lifted and given extra sparkle by the addition of very occasional flowers.

The chief feature of the garden is the little stream that runs along its width, banked up in several spots to make waterfalls. There are wittily trained hedges, mostly in and around the length of the stream, adding an air of secrecy and surprise. Everlasting sweet pea *(Lathyrus verna)* grows through tall box arches and beside it all a huge, white-berried sorbus dominates the side wall entrance to the garden. The west border by the sorbus has been planted up with *Rosa* 'William Lobb', golden hop *(Humulus lupulus* 'Aurelus') and white Japanese anemone. These combine in a pleasing wash of bright green, cream and white.

The stream is sided by stone walls where the wet air encourages a profusion of damp-loving ferns and willow gentian, pennyroyal and seventeen varieties of primula. Walking the length of the stream leads in to arches of box. These are noticeably tall at about three metres high, with little stone seating areas in the middle of the big green arches. The stone in this area was rescued from unwanted old weir stones in the local river.

At the top of the garden hill are three working beehives by a steep set of steps that go down toward the old greenhouse and the vegetable areas. The vegetable beds are well marked by lollipop bays. By the greenhouse door a pink-flowering actinidea and red abutilon romp away while inside the Wedgwood-blue flowers of plumbago are striking. Sitting in a sunny spot is a fine African hemp (*Sparrmannia africana*) with gigantic leaves and white flowers. This is tender and must be kept inside the greenhouse for the winter.

In the rose bed just down from the house is an underplanting of pretty blue clover: 'It's a bit of a nuisance because it spreads everywhere, but it is a good plant as nuisances go,' says Mrs Nicholson. A small lawn is planted through with many bulbs. 'They do prevent us being able to mow the grass until June, but it's worth it for the flowers.' This is a point that beginner gardeners might bear in mind when planting daffodils or any other bulbs in a lawn: the grass cannot be cut for as long as the daffodil leaves are green. The plants are busy building up strength after blooming so that they may flower again next year. When the leaves brown and die, the lawn can be safely cut again. Resist the need to tidy up the area too early and the bulbs will repay the favour.

The garden at Rockfield covers exactly one acre, but with the mature trees outside the wall it seems to stretch further. 'The great thing about a walled garden is that it stops you straying too far out,' says Mrs Nicholson.

Recently Opened Garden: Not Yet Visited

51 WOODVIEW HEIGHTS

Dunboyne, County Meath; Tel: +01 8255938 ※ **Contact:** Doreen Thornton ※ **Open:** for one charity day in June, contact in late May for the annual date ※ **Entrance fee** donated to Little Penny Dinners charity ※ Not suitable for children ※ **Directions:** travelling on the N3 from Dublin, turn left at the Clonee exit. Go through Clonee and turn left at the roundabout, signed for Dunboyne. Take the next left, also marked for Dunboyne. In the village turn left at the apartments before the primary school. Travel over a small bridge and take the left turn, signed Woodview Heights housing estate.

Doreen Thornton's garden is small, covering under one-third of an acre attached to her modern house. She has been working her garden for the past sixteen years, but only recently began to open to the public. The experiment has proved both enjoyable for the visitors and profitable for the Little Penny Dinners Charity, so Doreen is set to continue showing off her work.

The garden is divided into patios, herbaceous beds, mixed shrubs and wooded areas. Largely neutral, her soil accommodates a wide variety of plants. This is fortunate because collecting plants is one of Doreen's passions.

In her own words, Doreen 'would never exclude wildlife' from her garden. A great love of plants, allied to a dislike of anything too formal, determined the style of the garden, and as result 51 Woodview Heights is a relaxed, flowing, organic place rather than an overly smart garden. Doreen has little time for hard landscaping so plants like her beloved *Hoheria sexstylosa* or the fine acers, including a favourite golden *Acer pseudoplatanus,* rule the look of the garden.

GARDENING CLUBS AND SOCIETIES

DIG IT AND DUNG IT SOCIETY, THE

Contact: Mrs Wilkinson (Hon. Secretary), Baronstown House, Tara, County Meath.

This society meets approximately twelve times a year. Talks and garden visits are arranged each month.

DUNBOYNE FLOWER AND GARDEN CLUB, THE

Meets on the first Wednesday of each month at 8pm in the community centre in Dunboyne. No meetings are held in July or August. The programme is divided between gardening and floral art topics. During the summer several garden visits are arranged, and in December a bumper demonstration is mounted. New members are always welcome.

KELLS AND DISTRICT HORTICULTURAL SOCIETY, THE

Contact: Maeve Furlong (Secretary), Kilmainhamwood, Kells, County Meath; Tel: +046 40071.

Founded thirty-two years ago, this is a busy society with about 100 members. It meets for lectures, slide shows and demonstrations from October to March, usually on the second Tuesday of the month, in the Edmund Rice Centre in Kells. In April a members' show is held and in July they mount an open summer show. This is one of the busiest shows outside Dublin. A plant sale takes place in October. Day trips and garden visits, with an occasional overnight trip, are organised in the summer months. The year finishes up with a Christmas party. New members are always welcome.

NAVAN FLORAL ART CLUB, THE

Contact: Mary Gaffney; Tel: +046 45006.

The club meets in the Kilberry Suite, Navan Race Course, at 8pm on every second Wednesday (excluding January, June, July and August). The main focus of the club is floral art but occasional gardening talks are given, and an annual garden visit, incorporating a trip to a floral festival, is held. Non-members are welcome and visitors may attend meetings for an admission charge.

NURSERIES AND GARDEN CENTRES

BEECHMOUNT LANDSCAPING AND MOY VALLEY GARDEN CENTRE

Trim Road, Navan, County Meath; Tel: +0405 51223; for design queries, tel: +0405 51223.

BLACK'S GARDEN CENTRE

Julianstown, County Meath; Tel: +01 8351289.

BOYNE GARDEN DESIGN CENTRE

Ardcalf, Slane, County Meath; Tel/Fax: +041 9824350.

BRIDGEWATER GARDEN CENTRE

Castlekieran, Carnacross, Kells, County Meath; Tel: +046 45026.

CAROLAN'S GARDEN CENTRE

Faganstown, Slane, County Meath; Tel: +041 9824395.

CLONEE GARDEN CENTRE AND NURSERY

Dunboyne, County Meath; Tel: +01 8255375.

COOLQUAY NURSERY

The Ward, County Meath; Tel: +01 8351289.

COTTAGE GARDEN CENTRE, THE

Raystown, Ratoath Road, Ashbourne, County Meath; Tel: +01 8256678.

CURLEY'S GARDEN CENTRE

Ashbourne, County Meath; Tel: +01 8350100.

FLYNN'S GARDEN CENTRE

Summerhill, County Meath; Tel: +0405 57017.

GARDENWORKS

Piercetown, Clonee, County Meath; Tel: +01 8255375.

HILLSIDE SHRUB CENTRE

Drumbarragh, Kells, County Meath; Tel: +046 40306.

LUSK'S GARDEN CENTRE

Killyon, Hill of Down, Enfield, County Meath; Tel: +0405 46224.

MULVANY, FRANCES, CLEMATIS NURSERY

Raystown Road, Ashbourne, County Meath; Tel: +01 8256078.

RATHMORE GARDEN CENTRE

Rathmore, Athboy, County Meath; Tel: +046 32563.

RHATIGAN'S, BILLY, NURSERY

Batterstown, County Meath; Tel: +01 8259017.

GARDENING COURSES

SONAIRTE, The National Ecology Centre

The Ninch, Laytown, County Meath; Tel: +041 9827572; Fax: +041 9828130.

Sonairte is a centre for the study of ecology and the environment. They set up displays and hold lectures and courses on subjects as diverse as stone-wall building, forest gardening, composting and organic gardening. The courses range from adult weekend projects to Transition Year workshops for schools. Special interest groups can enquire regarding tailored courses.

GARDEN ACCESSORIES

FOLEY'S FORGE

Dunshaughlin, County Meath; Tel: +01 8259100; Fax: +01 8259555; e-mail: foleysforge@tinet.ie.

A selection of ironworks, rails, outdoor furniture, lamps and gates. Commissions taken for one-off pieces.

IRONCRAFT GARDEN FURNITURE

Hill of Ward, Trim Road, Athboy, County Meath; Tel: +046 32123; Fax: +046 32123.

Custom-made iron furniture, gates and railings and repairs of old ironwork. There are some lovely weather vanes on show as well as gazebos, plant supports, obelisks and benches.

WOODPECKER GARDEN SHEDS

Adjacent to Beechmount, Trim Road, Navan, County Meath; Tel: 087 2737442.

Stone and water features, garden sheds, trellis, gates and window-boxes.

COUNTY OFFALY

Offaly is a county of great variety. Tullamore is sometimes called the 'Venice of the North' because the Grand Canal dissects the county at that point. The town has an almost totally unaltered 1798 Gothic house, Charleville Castle. Shinrone is famous for blues music. Clara bog, one of the great peat bogs of Europe, will be of interest to naturalists. Architecturally, Birr town is one of the most beautiful towns in Ireland and Birr Castle is rightly renowned. The world-famous historic site of Clonmacnoise is the historical centrepiece of the county. This monastic site is another of the hugely popular Dúchas heritage sites and should be visited off-season to avoid crowds and queues. Finally, the Slieve Bloom Mountains, which border the county, are great for walking.

BIRR CASTLE DEMESNE

Rosse Row, Birr, County Offaly; Tel: +0509 20336; Fax: +0509 21583 ▪ **Contact:** Peter Hynes, Head Gardener ▪ **Open:** 1 April–31 October, daily, 9am–6pm; 1 November–31 March, daily, 10am–5pm; groups welcome ▪ **Entrance fee** ▪ Supervised children welcome; please note, dogs on leads ▪ **Special features:** telescope demonstrations during the summer; gift shop; museum; tearoom open April–October ▪ **Directions:** in the town of Birr.

The Parsons, earls of Rosse, have always been an exceptional family. They have been living in Birr since the 1620s, earning an admirable name for themselves as scientists, astronomers, philanthropists and gardeners. In the nineteenth century they built the famous 'Leviathan', then the largest telescope in the world. Massive work has since been put into re-erecting and restoring the telescope. But that was only one of the achievements of this family. They also boast the invention of the steam turbine. Exhibitions in the museum demonstrate the pioneering work of the family in the areas of astronomy, engineering, photography and botany.

A great deal of energy has gone into the restoration of the gardens in the past four years. The park covers over 150 acres, filled with trees from all over the world. The Rosses subscribed to many of the great plant-hunting ventures of the nineteenth and early twentieth centuries, including the Kingdom Ward, Wilson, Augustine Henry and George Forrest expeditions. The sixth earl travelled to Tibet himself to collect plants, and after his marriage in 1937 he and his wife Anne went collecting in China. Many of the special trees throughout the garden, which resulted from these expeditions, are labelled and easily identified, making it an educational garden trip.

Continuity is important in the Birr demesne. The tradition of handing the great garden down through the Rosse family is mirrored in the position of Head Gardener. Peter Hynes, the current holder of the post, took over from his father, Martin.

Inviting filigreed iron gates entice visitors into the formal walled garden from the park. The smallest hint of what may be seen inside is given when one spots the restored greenhouse in the distance at the end of a long path. This walled garden has a romantic story. It was largely redesigned in the 1930s by Anne to commemorate her marriage to Michael, the sixth earl. Hornbeam *allées*, older than the 1936 garden, form a 'cloister' around the inside of the walls. Michael planted snowdrops under the hornbeams as a young man while home on leave during the First World War. The cloisters have 'windows' cut into them, allowing the stroller glimpses of the parterres of box planted in complicated patterns. These incorporate the big R's for Rosse, rather like a logo. To one side of the box parterre is a rose garden of old French roses; cultivars from the 1820s to the 1890s. The list of names reads like creatures from a bodice ripping novel – 'Duchesse de Montebello', 'Belle Poitevine' and 'Petite de Hollande'. The colours here are all pinks, dusty mauves and plums, with as much emphasis on the stronger shades, and the scents are intoxicating.

From here the eye is drawn on to a delphinium border. This is a long wall bed of catmint, tree peonies, thalictrum, inula, aconitum and a number of delphiniums in blues, jewelled purples and pale lilacs. Down below this, a Greek goddess standing in a little bower is afforded some privacy courtesy of clematis and sweet pea. Topping this off are the gnarled wisteria arches, iris and peony beds, which include the famed 200-year-old Tallest Box Hedges in the World, with their strange smell – glorious when you know that what you are smelling is box, but, like Parmesan cheese, curiously unpleasant when the source of the smell is unknown.

Walking out from the walls, the path runs under the yew avenue and into the greater garden. Paths lead through the trees to each of the featured gardens, including a Victorian fernery that must be one of the most atmospheric in the country. A great deal of work has been done in restoring this area. Bridges and springs sit under the tree canopy, where the collection of ferns and tree ferns looks suitably spooky in the dark, damp green area with moss-covered wet stones, ravines, rising and falling paths. It's the height of Gothic romanticism, with the exposed roots of beech trees crawling down the side of the bank by the little goat track.

In front of the castle is a new garden feature called the whirlpool spiral, made of lime trees. First planted in 1995, this spiral travels in ever-decreasing swirls, its shape reminiscent of a galaxy of stars. It struck me that when it is mature it will be a great sight from the air. Birr has many of the usual features expected in a great pleasure garden including, not a shell house but a shell well, set deep in the woods. The mixed borders leading up to the castle and tucked in under the outer walls of mock fortifications are flowing and easy, herbaceous and informal. These are full of buddleia, echinops, white iris, tradescantia, snow-in-summer (*Cerastium tomentosum*) and Japanese anemone.

The high and low walks are equally lovely to wander along, beside and above the river. Waterfall Point looks down the spring-flowering bank to the gushing River Camcor below, and on towards a small suspension bridge that leads across to an area of cornus, acer, willow, cherry and pine trees on the other side of the river. This elegant bridge, evidence of the family's engineering endeavours, was built in 1810. Leaving the garden one passes the castle gates, also built by Mary Rosse in 1850, with three ugly monsters to guard it and a huge rose beside the portcullis.

WOODFIELD

Clara, County Offaly; Tel: +0506 31161 ■ **Contact:** Dr and Mrs Keith Lamb ■ **Open:** only to garden groups and by prior arrangement ■ **Entrance fee** donated to charity ✤ **Directions:** drive through Clara and beyond it into a right-hand bend signed for Moate and Athlone. Take this turn and continue on to a *boreen* signed for Woodfield bog. Pass this and take the next right turn (a bad road) past a blue fence. At the next bend, turn right and travel for 18m. Then turn left onto an avenue. Pass white gates and continue on into the courtyard.

There has been a garden at Woodfield since around 1733 when the house was built. Maps show in great detail that the house had a mature garden by 1765. Faded drawings show a formal box and yew lined garden. This old garden is long gone. Woodfield has had many owners and many styles imposed on it over the years. But none could claim to be more perfect than the garden built over the past fifteen years by Dr Keith Lamb, the well-known horticulturist, a man whose name comes up time and time again when gardeners talk about really talented gardeners.

His is a one-man operation, planned with a view to being easily managed. 'Low maintenance' in its currently used sense is not, however, the phrase that comes to mind when walking around this garden. Sophisticated, wild and exotic, perhaps, but not low maintenance. 'It is made up of a spring beech garden, a rock garden, a raised bed garden and *the jungle*,' says Dr Lamb. The word 'jungle' conjures up all sorts of exciting pictures, particularly when we are bordering a bog in County Offaly in the midlands of Ireland.

The garden is of indeterminate size; it wanders off in a number of directions. Leaving the front of the house, the path leads past a fragrant, winter-flowering Nepalese *Daphne bholua* and echiums that do surprisingly well in the cold midlands. Dr Lamb explains that echiums seed madly, and if the seed is left to sprout a few will usually land in a spot sheltered enough for the plant to survive and even thrive.

SNOWDROPS (*GALANTHUS*)

To the uninitiated, one snowdrop looks pretty much like another. It's necessary to get down on the ground and look up under their skirts, so to speak, to see the small differences between one variety and another. Galanthus, like orchids, lilies and roses, have their devotees who will go to any lengths and pay whatever it takes to get hold of a particular cultivar.

But with snowdrops it makes sense in a strange way because snowdrops are something special: they are the one flower that even the most uninterested non-gardener knows, notices and loves. They flower when nothing else does in dull, cold, wet February. They are pretty and they promise spring and warmth and the end of winter; that's a lot of work for one small flower. They self-seed wonderfully, especially the common *Galanthus nivalis*. The seedheads fall to the ground, beginning the cycle of growth, and after three or four years the resulting bulbs are big enough to flower. In addition, the bulbs increase underground and these two processes will lead to a fairly rapid spread of white flowers that might one day become one of those to-die-for carpets of snowdrops. Because they emerge and flower at a time when most everything else is dormant and bare, snowdrops can be grown any place in the garden where there are bare spots, in winter under trees, perennials and shrubs that cast dense shadow or cover the ground later in the year. They also make a great sight in little pots around the door and window.

Leading out toward the beech garden is a grove of trees, which includes a pretty *Acer griseum*, an American dogwood, called *Cornus* 'Eddie's White Wonder', with big white flowers, and an early-flowering white cherry hybrid found by Dr Lamb and named for the garden, *Prunus* 'Woodfield Cluster'. The beech garden stretches out and down from the house; an impressive run of beech trees that must be contemporary with the buildings. The beeches are underplanted with little yellow winter aconites, snowdrops, blue, white and yellow anemones, winter and spring-flowering cyclamens and several varieties of hellebore, *Hesperis matronalis*, bergenia and heliotrope. These winter and spring flowers are at their best before or after the beech trees lose their leaves so they make perfect companions to the huge trees under which many gardeners find it hard to plant: 'And they all look after themselves,' says Dr Lamb.

Throughout the garden there are many varieties of snowdrop. Here, among the usual strains, is the Crimean snowdrop, which reputedly came up in droves from the disturbed ground around the trenches on the Crimea; a dainty little flower. Back in by the house is the rock garden that was largely laid out by Dr Lamb's father. This garden is close to the trees, so much of it is devoted to early, spring-flowering plants because of shade cast by the trees later in the year. This is a naturalistic rock garden, far from either the 'dogs' graveyard' or 'plum bun' style of rock garden that blights many gardens and which consists mostly of a mound of soil studded with stone in a haphazard and improbable way. Dr Lamb's rock garden is laid out with style, with stones placed as though they occurred naturally. Self-seeding tiny plants and carpeting moss, snowdrops, a variety of celmisias, scillas, sedums and little irises fill up every space available between the rocks. There are far too many plants to see in a single or probably even in a dozen visits. In the centre are three pointed helmets of *Picea glauca var. albertina* 'Conica', normally six metres tall and slim, but these three were grown from shoots taken from the base of the plants and so have a more squat, interesting habit. This is a method of propagation which space-confined gardeners might find worth copying. A northeast-facing shady and damp area by the house plays home to trilliums, meconopsis and primulas. Scattered throughout are unusual and rare plants, like a pillow of long-toothed green and silver-leaved burkheya: 'It's not a thistle although it looks like one,' Dr Lamb insists. Its strange flowers grow out from the side of the plant. Two recumbent acers spread themselves out among clumps of snowflakes (*Leucojum vernum*), of which Dr Lamb has two types: one that flowers very early in January, while the other only pokes its nose above the ground in January and flowers in late spring or early summer.

Red leaves of *Photinia fraseri* 'Red Robin' and a tall variegated pittosporum light up the gloom under a huge yew that shelters rare cyclamen and a pretty, deciduous *Sephora* 'Gnome' at the edge of the rockbed. A *Mahonia media* 'Winter Sun' stands by the bed. Mahonia is a plant that can irritate at the height of the summer, looking coarse and leathery and a bit too showy. But in the winter when everything else is lying low it comes into its own, the exaggerated holly-like leaves look good and the flowers smell divine.

Further out to the edge of this part of the garden is a very tall, well-shaped pyramid of Turkish hazel (*Corylus colurna*). This is a most impressive tree that lends height without too much spread. From here, a gate leads into what was once the kennel yard, now a series of raised alpine beds overlooked by an old dovecote. Here Dr Lamb grows the acid-loving alpines not otherwise possible in the middle of his alkaline garden. 'Whenever we are invited to tea in an acid-soil area I always ask if I may bring a trailer for soil,' he explains. As a result the garden has acid soil from every part of the country; a sort of geological tour of Ireland in which his alpines thrive. Chatham Island forget-me-nots (*Myosotidium hortensia*) thrive under glass by the wall along with several more varieties of celmisia, including 'David Shackleton' and 'Argentea', a tiny cushioning plant. In another of the beds there are American cranberries, 'just enough for the Christmas dinner', and up against a south-facing wall is the scented winter sweet (*Chimonanthus praecox*).

The last garden is the anticipated 'jungle', a place that Dr Lamb says minds itself particularly well. It contains a sea of huge-leaved, exotic-looking plants, like trachycarpus, gunnera, cardiocrinum, tall cordylines, ligularia, acanthus, teasels and rodgersia. Some plants are big enough to camp under. Even the trees chosen here have huge leaves, like the whitebeam *Sorbus* 'Mitchellii'.

At the edge of it all is a crab apple tree sporting its heavy clusters of strong, red, cherry-like fruits, which hold onto the tree right over the winter, and a Serbian spruce, doing well in the alkaline soil. Under it is a plant of European wild ginger (*Asarum europaeum*), which, according to Dr Lamb, is a real reliable for a dry, shady, bad spot: 'It stays green and shiny in the darkest place.' Under the tree canopy there are plenty of other distractions, like the greenest flowering little Yugoslavian hellebore and, finally a collection of shuttlecock ferns with a whole roofless outhouse to themselves. The excuse is that this keeps them in check, but it looks like a good old-fashioned spoiling.

NURSERIES AND GARDEN CENTRES

DEERING, JOE
Derrybeg, Killeigh, Tullamore, County Offaly; Tel: 086 8162466.

GEM GARDEN CENTRE
Harbour Road, Banagher, County Offaly; Tel: +0509 51091.

WARD'S GARDEN CENTRE
Tullamore Road, Birr, County Offaly; Tel: +0509 21215.

COUNTY WESTMEATH

Westmeath is a flat, landlocked county criss-crossed and bordered by lakes, canals and rivers. The Royal Canal divides the county in two. Lough Ennell, Lough Owel and Lough Lane take up large areas, and Lough Derravaragh is said to be where the Children of Lir were turned into swans. Naturally, many of the interests are aquatic. Angling, coarse fishing and boating are all popular. The two biggest attractions in the county are Belvedere House and Garden, recently restored and opened by Westmeath County Council, and Tullynally Castle. Mullaghameen Wood is unusual among Irish woodlands because most of its 1,000 acres are planted with beech trees; beech makes a particularly elegant woodland tree.

BALLINLOUGH CASTLE AND GARDENS

Clonmellon, County Westmeath; Tel: +046 33135; Fax: +046 33331 ∗ **Contact:** Ursula Walsh, Head Gardener ∗ **Open:** May–September, Tuesday, Wednesday, Thursday and Saturday, 11am–6pm, Sunday, 2pm–6pm; closed Monday and Friday; other times by appointment only ∗ **Entrance fee** ∗ Children must be accompanied at all times ∗ **Special features:** historic property ∗ **Directions:** driving on the N52 from Kells in the direction of Mullingar, Ballinlough is 4km from Clonmellon and signed from Athboy, Devlin and Clonmellon.

Ballinlough is the seventeenth-century castle home of Sir John and Lady Nugent, a grand building standing by a man-made lake just inside the Westmeath border. The Nugent family have lived here since the fifteenth century, making Ballinlough remarkable as an estate continuously lived in by Catholics since the 1400s.

A long drive runs in by the lake revealing the dark grey limestone castle in its full glory, then it swings away and travels some distance before reaching the gardens. It was common practice from the 1700s to separate house and walled garden. Fashion dictated that a house should stand in splendid isolation within a natural parkland surrounding, away from the working gardens. The castle was restored when, after many years of neglect, Sir Charles Nugent took over the place in 1927. It was thought that the house would need to be knocked down – it had come to such a sorry state that hens had taken over and were nesting in the drawing room – but Sir Charles restored both house and lake. The garden would be attended to later by his descendant, Sir John Nugent.

These gardens have been under restoration under the Great Gardens of Ireland Restoration Scheme since 1995, and by any standard they must be seen as reason enough for the existence of the scheme. This is gardening on the grand scale. Naturalistic woods, water gardens and lake walks out in the pleasure grounds complement more structured walled gardens, fruit, vegetable, flower and rose gardens. Retrieving and restoring them to their present state has been an achievement and the gardens at Ballinlough have established themselves among the best on the island.

A stone arch by the gardener's house and some other outhouses leads into the walled garden. Covering about three acres, the area is made up of four separate walled sections. The main section is divided into rooms centering on a formal lily pond surrounded by young beech hedges, which are part of the new planting.

Alongside a magnolia walk and an old lawn tennis court, a double herbaceous border runs the width of the garden. White phlox, delphinium, campanula and aquilegia make a cheerful show in early summer, while darker, richer colour tones come later in the year from penstemon, dahlia and geum.

Pink-and-white-striped *Rosa* 'Ferdinand Pichard' and *Rosa* 'Chapeau de Napoléon', chosen specifically for their sweet scents, share the little rose garden with white philadelphus and deutzia. By including flowering shrubs in a scheme of roses the flowering season is extended.

Next door is what is called the little garden and an orchard recently replanted with apples, plums, damsons, pears and mulberries. The garden is completed by a small decorative kitchen garden full of blue-flowered borage and walls of sweet pea with swoon-inducing scent.

Through a gate (copied from Prince Charles's Highgrove Park in Gloucestershire) the path leads out of the walled garden and into a yew tunnel down to the lake walk. The water garden and rockery are set in a clearing on the edge of the woods. First created in 1916, they fell into decline and were restored in 1943, slipping again into a state of weeds and overgrowth until saved once more in the recent restoration. Light filtering in through tall trees, a natural, informal frog pond planted with lamium, rodgersia and ferns, and rough stone paths blend into an air of romantic wilderness. A series of walks through the grounds take in views of the castle, passing mature oaks, including a good specimen of the Turkey Oak (*Quercus cerris*), as well as ornamental canals and bridges over the lake.

As an interesting aside on the work of restoration: the lake was first built in 1843 to provide work for scores of destitute people during the Great Famine. When it was cleared in 1937 the work took sixteen men three months. In 1994, as part of the most recent restoration, the same job took two machine operators just ten days to double the previous depth of the lake.

BELVEDERE HOUSE AND GARDEN

Tullamore Road, Mullingar, County Westmeath; Tel: +044 49060 ✹ **Contact:** Park Superintendent or Therese McCormack, Head Gardener ✹ **Open:** April–August, 10.30am–8pm; September–October, 10.30am–6pm; November–March, 10.30am–4pm ✹ **Entrance fee** ✹ Children welcome; please note, dogs on leads ✹ Managed by Westmeath County Council ✹ **Directions:** 6km from Mullingar on the Tullamore Road.

The history of Belvedere is worthy of a Gothic novel: the Jealous Wall is the largest Gothic folly on the island and the visible reminder of the deeply unpleasant history of the vicious, quarrelsome Rochford brothers. The wall, well named, is a big mock ruin that was built by Lord Belvedere to obliterate the sight of his brother's home, Tudenham, built next door to, and bigger than, Belvedere. The brothers' lives were one long tale of horrendous carry-on, with stories of wives locked up for decades, duels, fights and casual cruelties. An intriguing sort of oppression hangs satisfyingly around Belvedere as a result of its history of familial conflicts.

The 'Jealous Wall' – a stone testament to the sad and dark history attached to Belvedere in County Westmeath.

The gardens and deserted house were taken over by Westmeath County Council several years ago and underwent serious restoration, which culminated with the opening to the public in 1999. Belvedere is now a centrepiece attraction and source of pride in the county.

The restoration work is evident throughout the grounds: from the front of the house ivy slopes drop away between tidy formal Italianate terraces of gravel, stone steps and lichen-covered balustrades holding in banks of holly and rose. Savage lions guard the steps, using shields decorated with important-looking coats of arms. Yews being retrained and reshaped add to the formal neatness and from here Lough Ennell is clearly visible, spreading itself out in front of the house and lawns. Falling away from the side of the house a wild-looking rock garden tumbles down, full of foxgloves, tall cordylines and mature trees. It is a suitably sombre backdrop for the Jealous Wall.

A seven-acre walled garden was built, not by the Rochfords but by a later owner, Charles Marley, in the nineteenth century. He and subsequent owners stocked it with a large variety of rare shrubs and trees, but it too fell into decline and has been under restoration since 1999; it opened in 2000. The work is now substantially complete. Divided into five rooms, it should be understood that the garden has been newly planted and will take some time before it fills out. A double border by the Bell Gate leads into the garden. This is backed by a wall of yew and fronted by box hedging and is designed to look good for much of the year. Spring bulbs give way to iris, catmint and grey, sharp-leaved globe artichokes, which flower like monster thistles. Dogwoods (*Cornus kousa*) and daphne provide a permanent skeleton.

A Himalayan garden with blood-red flowered *Rhododendron thomsonii* and the Himalayan blue poppy (*Meconopsis grandis*) is a testament to one of the garden's early plant-hunting owners. The rose garden carries a pink climbing rose named for the garden, *Rosa* 'Belvedere'. Orchid and fuchsia fill the greenhouses with exotic perfume and frilly blooms. Finally, a fruit, vegetable and herb garden have been completed and opened to the public.

The walks down to the lake are sided by big bushes of pale pink, tiny-flowered fuchsia, shrub roses, buddleia and eucryphia, all attractive to butterflies and bees. Mature maple and ash march from this open walk into the deeper wooded area where old cobbled paths have been uncovered, reinstated and restored. The lake itself is as grand as such a house would require, with a wildflower meadow running up to the water's edge. On the way back to the house the path passes a fine weeping beech tree and blue cedar. A network of paths runs around the 160 acres of park leading past remarkable trees, to more follies and viewing places.

ROCKFIELD DEMESNE

Rathaspic, Rathowen, County Westmeath; Tel: +043 76204 ▪ **Contact:** Sean and Imelda Daly ▪ **Open:** May–October, daily, 2pm–6pm; groups welcome by appointment only ▪ **Entrance fee** ▪ Supervised children welcome; please note, dogs on leads ▪ **Special features:** pony and trap rides; guided tours of house and park ▪ **Directions:** Rathaspic is off the N4 at Rathowen.

Sean and Imelda Daly have recently opened their classical Georgian house to the public. The house is surrounded by parkland with mature trees, ponds, shrubberies and woodlands. Guided tours through the building and grounds are given and period-costume rides on jaunting cars are a regular feature. The walled garden is organically worked and produces an array of vegetables and fruit. Rockfield is a work in progress and will be for several years.

TULLYNALLY CASTLE

Tullynally, Castlepollard, County Westmeath; Tel: +044 61159; Fax: +044 61856; e-mail: tpakenham@tinet.ie ▪ **Contact:** Valerie Pakenham ▪ **Open:** 1 May–31August, daily, 2pm–6pm; other times by appointment only ▪ **Entrance fee** ▪ Supervised children welcome; please note, dogs on leads ▪ **Special features**: guided tours of castle; tearooms open weekends, bank holidays or by appointment ▪ **Directions:** situated 1.5km from Castlepollard on the Granard Road (N52).

Tullynally Castle is the biggest castellated house in Ireland. It was built in the 1600s by the Pakenhams and the family still live here, represented by Thomas, author and tree expert. Today the castle is largely nineteenth-century Gothic in style, and is sided by a witty yew hedge, cut like battlements, from which the terraces and parkland fall away.

Austere stone rails form a barrier between a stone terrace close to the house, where the only softening effect comes from a big, venerable-looking wisteria on the house wall, and an apron of agapanthus and Welsh poppies in many shades of orange and yellow self-seeding in cracks between the flagstones.

Out from the house is a romantic landscape dating to the eighteenth century and a garden full of features. Among these is the grotto. This curiosity is a little stone bower set up on a bank tucked under a canopy of trees. It is ghostly and atmospheric with a path leading up to it that sets the mood. It is crowded with ferns, pennyroyal and outcrops of rock. This looks secretively down over the flower garden.

The walled garden, where the flower and kitchen gardens are sited, is home to a sunken lily pond with a fountain that is completely mossed over and surrounded by Lady's mantle (*Alchemilla mollis*), geranium, fern and the strongest-scented marjoram. This is a Victorian device called a 'weeping pillar'. Two Coade-stone sphinx

In the romantic walled garden at Tullynally Castle, County Westmeath.

guard the entrance to the flower garden. These were bought by Lord Longford in 1780, and known as merrymaids by the locals. Out from the flower garden is an eight-acre kitchen garden. Built in the eighteenth century, by 1840 it was already being described as 'impossibly large for these times'.

In the walled garden there were originally twelve greenhouses ranged along the long brick wall. Today there are only two left and one hot-bed house for melons and pineapples. The summerhouse, built in the 1920s, is flanked by two substantial borders. A curve in the borders forces the visitor to move along the whole length to see the contents of the beds. This is a good design, making the walker earn their reward.

Apples trained along the walls provide productive decoration. A splendid yew avenue is tied together by humped yew and box walls, knotted through with ivy and mahonia. These are called 'tapestry hedges' and make a very beautiful contrasting wall of textures and shades of green. Ivy leaves decorate the yew pins. A hot border of orange, red and gold day lilies, nasturtium and crocosmia flames out against the strong yew greens.

Past Queen Victoria's small summerhouse the track leads to the 'bridge over the River Sham', well named because it is not a river at all but a serpentine lake masquerading as a river. Even the Sham's crocodile, standing on an island in the 'river', is bogus, and the ducks and black swans showed no interest in or fear of the wooden croc. The summerhouse too falls into the same category of misnomer: Queen Victoria never visited the garden, this is a copy of one made for her.

The path leads into the Tibetan garden (on the site of an old American garden planted by Lady Longford in 1830 with acid-loving plants, such as camellia and azalea, which eventually succumbed to the lime soil in the area.) Fortunately, the more recently planted Tibetan garden has been more appropriately placed. This is an exciting project, the product of a 1993 seed-collecting trip made by Thomas Pakenham to Yunan, a province of China. Two years later the fruits of the trip were planted out – blue Himalayan poppies, yellow primula florindae and Tibetan birch. This garden is now taking shape and will become more beautiful as time goes on.

The walk goes on past a pagoda surrounded by lime-tolerant Chinese plants, like sorbus, white pine, birch and philadelphus, a gingerbread house and on down to a viewing point. There is a good half day's saunter around Tullynally, with plenty to see in the gardens and features, and also the possibility of spotting badger tracks.

GARDENING SOCIETIES AND CLUBS

MULLINGAR AND DISTRICT GARDENING CLUB

Contact: Mary O'Sullivan; Tel: +044 40220.

The club holds its meetings at 8pm on the last Thursday of the month in Mullingar Arts Centre. January is the only month when no meeting is held. Apart from the year's programme of lectures, talks, slide shows and demonstrations, a summer show takes place in August and a plant sale and club dinner celebrate Christmas. Garden visits are made in the summer months. New members are welcome and visitors can attend meetings for an admission charge.

NURSERIES AND GARDEN CENTRES

DALTON, NOEL, GARDEN CENTRE

Coole, Mullingar, County Westmeath; Tel: +044 61054.

FERNHILL GARDEN CENTRE

Ballymahon Road, Athlone, County Westmeath; Tel: +0902 75574; e-mail: fern@iol.ie

MODEL GARDEN CENTRE

Horseleap, Moate, County Westmeath; Tel: +0506 35116.

MULVEY'S GARDEN CENTRE

Roscommon Road, Athlone, County Westmeath; Tel: +0902 94288.

OLD FORGE GARDEN CENTRE, THE

Coole, Mullingar, County Westmeath; Tel: +044 61381.

O'MEARA'S NURSERY AND GARDEN CENTRE

Gaybrook, Mullingar, County Westmeath; Tel: +044 42088.
Winner of Garden Centre of the Year in 1999.

ROBINSON, BRENDAN, COTTAGE GARDEN PLANTS

Ballykillroe, Ballinagore, County Westmeath; Tel: +044 26509.

COUNTY WEXFORD

Wexford is renowned for its many beautiful views of the sea, and Rosslare is one of the most popular seaside resorts in the country. Long, quiet beaches like Carne are perfect for anyone who hates crowds, while those seeking company will enjoy the attractive seaside villages of Ballyhack, Fethard and Kilmore Quay. Alternatively, the busy, bustling towns of Enniscorthy, New Ross and Wexford are interesting to wander around. The Wexford Coastal Walk travels almost the length of the county and provides a splendid outing for a summer stroll. The Slobs are world famous for bird life, with one-third of the world's population of Greenland white-fronted geese overwintering there each year. The soil of County Wexford is fertile, largely acid, but with pockets of lime. Its coastal location, enjoying the last warm breath of the Gulf Stream, makes Wexford slightly warmer and milder than neighbouring inland counties. It is home to a substantial number of memorable gardens open to visitors, many of which are included in the annual Private Gardens of County Wexford Trail (*see* box, below).

THE PRIVATE GARDENS OF COUNTY WEXFORD TRAIL

Unlike many other garden trails around the country which are tied to a specific week or fortnight of open time, the Private Gardens of County Wexford group open their gardens for most of the summer. The standard of the gardens is exceptional and the styles vary considerably, taking in courtyard gardens, wild Robinsonian glades, historic walled gardens and informal woodland plots. A number of the gardens are domestic and relatively small in size. These gardens are very much worth a visit. They are owned by a group of generous people who help each other and accommodate their visitors to an extent that is legendary among garden visitors. Each garden is different in its opening policy, opening times and facilities. Make sure to check the opening policy of a garden before you visit. Many are situated close to each other and are happy to advise on arranging timetables for visiting groups. The gardens involved are: The Bay, Kilmokea, Knockbawn, Ram House, Sandy Lane, Shortalstown and Woodville.

ASHBROOK

Clogh, Gorey, County Wexford; Tel: +055 22356; e-mail: jking@iol.ie ▪ **Contact:** Mrs Gladys King ▪ **Open:** May–August, Wednesday and Saturday, 10am–6pm, Sunday, 2pm–6pm; telephone for appointment ▪ **Entrance fee** donated to St Luke's Hospital in Rathgar, Dublin, and goes towards garden upkeep ▪ **Special features:** specialises in plant sales of penstemon ▪ **Directions:** travelling on the N11 towards Rosslare, the garden is 800m along on the left-hand side after Clogh village.

Mrs King has been working her three-quarter-acre site for five years. She started intelligently, beginning in one small area and slowly moving out and expanding each year, so the garden ranges in age from five years to four years to three years old and so on. Working gradually like this is a very good way to start a new garden. It allows the new gardener to become accustomed to the site and to learn about the microclimate: where the nastier winds might be; where the frost pockets and sun traps are; the damp and dry spots, and so on. This useful knowledge will, in the long run, mean fewer plant losses and fewer mistakes. Dealing with one area before moving out into others also means that a new gardener learns to manage and master that area before beginning elsewhere. In Glady's's case she has worked it all herself, from design to digging, although a son working in horticulture in the UK, whose brain she regularly picks, and two willing daughters who help with weeding and grass-cutting, contribute to help gardening life run smoothly.

Mrs King's garden is composed of flowing, soft lines and an informal style that suits the hilly site. Plants rather than landscaping are the stars in this garden. Beds of well-chosen herbaceous plants, divided along colour lines, form islands with just enough room for paths between: a hot bed mixing black-leafed ligularia, yellow *Centaurea macrocephala,* physalis, orange marigolds and roscoea is vibrant and stylish. Gladys likes to theme the beds, keeping similar colours together. Up on the hill behind the house is a good white bed, with *Phlox paniculata* 'White Admiral', where the vegetables used to live.

To the front of the house an arc-shaped wall, made from local flat stone, rises out of a low bank. Above it is a good-looking mixed bed with *Erysimum* 'Bowles Mauve', thalictrum, Japanese anemone, arum lilies and willow gentian *(Gentiana asclepiadea)*. These all grow in front of a wall of box and a backdrop of larger flowering shrubs and mature ash and beech trees.

There are over seventy different varieties of penstemon in the garden. They are, very clearly, Mrs King's passion, and she is happy to talk penstemon with anyone interested in these handsome flowers.

THE BAY GARDEN

Camolin, Enniscorthy, County Wexford; Tel: +054 83349; Fax: +054 83576 ▪ **Contact:** Frances and Iain MacDonald ▪ **Open:** May–September, every Sunday, 3pm–6pm ▪ **Entrance fee** donated to the Sonas Housing Association ▪ **Special features:** garden talks arranged ▪ **Directions:** situated on the main Gorey–Enniscorthy road (N11), just under 1km from Camolin (on the Ferns side), opposite the turn to Carnew.

Ten years ago this garden was a field surrounded by ash trees. A lawn was laid in the 1990s and from there the garden started. Designers Frances and Iain MacDonald have spent the last decade working together, designing and planting what is both their garden and their shop window.

Arriving to the front of the house brings the visitor into a welcoming little garden surrounded by tall stone walls and the front of the MacDonalds's double-fronted Georgian house. Shrub roses, white anemone, sweet-smelling tobacco plants *(Nicotiana sylvestris)* and lengths of fat, clipped box melt in a mix of strong, green foliage and white- and pale-coloured flowers. Wisteria and roses cover the house lightly. Gravel

An enticing gateway lures visitors from the tiny front garden to the main flower gardens at The Bay in County Wexford.

and stone paths divide the beds and draw light into the small space. This is an inspiring design for a period house with a small garden.

Exit, however reluctantly, by a side gate and you arrive into a bigger and completely different place. In here are large, colour-matched beds swept through by expanses of grass. An island of pink geranium knots through a pink variegated phormium and next door crinum lilies and pink-tinged goat's rue mingle in a gorgeous display. It is said that good bone structure will never fail a beauty, and the bone structure here comes in the shape of small trees, like cornus, azara and lilac.

In one bed, reds, silvers and whites play together. The designer's eye is at work here. Reds and silvers go well together and in other areas of design they are constantly combined, but in the garden a reluctance to trust an otherwise good sense of colour creeps into many people. Not so in the MacDonalds's garden.

The path travels on, stepping down to a small, formal garden – a square is divided by crossed paths into four smaller squares, again sharply colour divided. The first two beds are filled with white and shell-pink roses, white cosmos and anemone and a delicate pink-and white-tinged *Gaura lindheimeri*. In another bed, plum roses with plum-coloured penstemon and wine scabious work prettily together. The fourth bed is all yellows and limes – roses, *Anthemis tinctoria* 'EC Buxton' and Lady's mantle (*Alchemilla mollis*).

The next treat is the red-hot border filled with canna, savage red dahlia, crocosmia, tiger lily, kniphofia and mad orange rudbekia. Along here also is what Frances wonderfully calls her 'funereal border' – the only one of its kind in the country – filled with serious and sombre plants, such as the little black grass *Ophiopogon planiscapus* 'Nigrescens', *Cercis canadensis* 'Forest Pansy', a shrub with dark purple, heart-shaped leaves, *Scabiosa atropurpurea* 'Ace of Spades' and *Physocarpus opulifolius* 'Diablo'.

Leading back to the house is a little courtyard garden full of pots, troughs and old stone. The house itself is covered in fine plants. As if all of this weren't enough, the MacDonalds, who try to complete one new project every year, are working on a new area – a formal yew garden, which will begin to fill out in the next few years.

BERKELEY FOREST

New Ross, County Wexford; Tel: +051 21361 ■ **Contact:** Countess Anne Bernstorff ■ **Open:** June–July, daily, 2–5pm, by appointment to groups only ■ **Entrance fee** ■ **Special features:** doll and toy museum ■ **Directions:** from

Enniscorthy take the New Ross Road. Watch for the Berkeley Forest sign 20km beyond Clonroche; keep left here and the gate is 300m on. If travelling from Kilkenny, drive toward New Ross. At the River Barrow crossing turn left and continue until the Berkeley Forest sign points to the right.

Berkeley Forest is a grand old house, standing on a long slope looking over good parkland trees and hilly fields. From the front no hint is given of the romance hiding behind its austere façade. However, through the yard, or by a windy little Gothic arched entrance to the side of the house, is a real gem – a friendly old garden with character.

At one time the garden covered four acres. Today only a fraction of the original walled area is worked. When the Bernstorffs arrived here the whole garden was derelict. They decided they couldn't possibly attempt to work that area of land, so they sensibly picked the three best walls and stuck close to them.

'The garden is as much as one demented person can throw an eye over. I only grow things that can live under those circumstances. We can't deal with fussy plants here,' says the countess, matter-of-factly. Many visitors might feel the same. Trying to juggle work, families and everything else means that few gardeners have the enormous number of hours they might wish to put into gardening. Looking at Berkeley Forest, one can see that with the right attitude and a certain ruthlessness a good garden can be achieved in between the rest of life's distractions.

The garden slopes steeply upward towards a diamond-windowed garden house with more than a touch of the fairytale about it. The little building looks as though it floats on top of a blue cloud of hydrangea, ceanothus, blue delphinium and agapanthus. A rickety herringbone-patterned brick path leads up through the blue beds to the house, which is full of little birds' nests, wisps of invading ivy and old church pews.

From up here the rest of the garden can be viewed – a picture of small lawns and shrub beds, steps edged with wild strawberries, topiary box and bolt-upright junipers standing in pairs. Box, juniper and paths create a backbone for floppy herbaceous plants. A complete absence of symmetry is apparent, but the slightly lopsided look suits the garden. Even the little path leading down the hill to a sunburst pattern of stone at the bottom of the garden is pleasantly crooked.

Paths lead off and away from the summerhouse between lamb's ears, echinops, *Eryngium giganteum* 'Miss Willmott's ghost', pineapple broom and more blue gentians. 'Miss Willmott's ghost' is said to have been spread around by the enthusiastic Miss Ellen Willmott, who saw it as her duty to spread the seeds of her favourite plant as widely as possible. Some might call it vandalism, but it is quite romantic.

All around the sides of the garden are little oddities – a collection of bonsai, stone altars, a chimney flue in the wall which might be part of an interesting barbecue, topiary hens, a sunken greenhouse, a little herb patch, standing stones and a small *George and the Dragon* sitting in a niche in the wall.

An eighteenth- and nineteenth-century costume, doll and toy museum in the house seems like an appropriate way to finish off a visit to a garden that itself has such an atmosphere of genteel old age. The museum is a must for well-supervised and well-behaved children.

Rocklands, Wexford, County Wexford; Tel: +053 23026 ▦ **Contact:** Mrs Mary
White ▦ **Open:** April–October, by appointment only ▦ **Entrance fee** ▦ **Directions:**
approaching Wexford coming from New Ross and travelling in the direction of
Rosslare, at the first roundabout continue towards Rosslare. At the second roundabout go straight through, and at the third take the left exit for the town. Opposite
the creamery and beside a filling station take the concealed left turn at the 'Rocklands B&B' sign. Travel up the lane a few hundred yards until the garden appears
on the right-hand side.

The first word that comes to mind when visiting Heatherset at any time of the year is
'exotic'. Howling late October winds did nothing to diminish the perfect, small, hillside garden when I visited it. Mrs White took first prize in the Wexford category and
third in the Containers and Tubs category in the Shamrock All Ireland Gardens
Competition1999, and she has been a regular winner down through the years.

The garden is thirty-three years old and remarkably, given the abundant growth, it
has poor and shallow soil, according to Mrs White. When she started out she had to
bring in dozens of trailers of topsoil and organic matter. Good gardens do not just
happen and this one was certainly hard won. The contours, despite their natural look,
are completely artificial, designed by Mrs White who has a strong feel for design and
plants. It is rare to see the two talents in tandem – most gardeners go in one direction
or the other. The garden has the feel of a tropical quarry, with the house perched halfway up the slope and engulfed in vegetation. At first it looks like a jungle, but on
inspection it turns out to be an intricate and clever jigsaw of great plants.

The house is set on a rock above the front garden. It floats above beds of canna
lilies and trachycarpus. I loved the perfectly straight, tall, slim cordyline growing in a
tub and reaching the height of the house. There are stone sundials and secret paths
winding through the ferny, moss-covered rock bank under the house. A little water
feature drips water from a wall into a tub full of lilies and gardener's garters, almost
like a little grotto at the base of the building. The slate steps leading up to the house
are made from a billiard table base. At the top of the steps are troughs of vinca and
pots of daisies, cerinthe, agave and impatiens in such numbers that they look as
though they might be getting ready to take over the house, or at least collapse the
balcony.

To the back of the garden, stone and slate paths lead past lace-cap hydrangea min-
gled with potato vine and roses and on towards patches of asters and a fine cornus
with ferns peeping out from underneath its skirts. Beside it, *Thalictrum delavayi*
'Hewitt's Double' floats prettily over a honey bush *(Melianthus major)*, a mix of tiny
purple-pink dotty flowers against the blue-green matt leaves of the melianthus. The
lawn has been cut into at every conceivable point by good-looking island beds, for
example, there is one with purple cotinus, a mucky plum hydrangea, rust-coloured
sedum and wine astrantia sitting under an Indian bean tree *(Catalpa bignonioides)*. A
white rose laces through the big leaves of *Geranium maderense*.

Heatherset is an ordered jungle, where tight-clipped shrubs stand next to
rampant, loose, herbaceous flowers in a show of restraint and exuberance.

New Ross, County Wexford; Tel: +051 388171; Fax: +051 388172 ✸ **Contact:**
Mr Christopher Kelly ✸ **Open:** May–August, daily, 10am–8pm; April and September, daily, 10am–6.30pm; October–March, daily, 10am–5pm ✸ **Entrance fee** ✸
Special features: exhibition centre; picnic area; play area; self-guiding trail; guided
tours available April–September (must be booked in advance) ✸ Member of
Dúchas ✸ **Directions:** travelling south on the R733 from New Ross, turn right
12km south of New Ross at the sign for the arboretum.

The John F Kennedy Arboretum was set up in the late 1960s in memory of the
Irish-American president, and lies close to the old Kennedy family home. It is huge,
covering 252 acres, and is laid out in blocks and groves of trees joined by wide paths,
runs of grass and lakes. Alongside the profusion of trees, there are 200 forest plots,
dwarf conifers and rhododendrons.

Over 4,500 species and cultivars of tree and shrub from all the temperate regions
of the world are grown here, and the plants are arranged in a well-signed and well-
labelled grid system. The arboretum is a an educational facility as well as a pleasant
day's walk for the family. The walks are divided into two main circuits, one of broad-
leaved trees and one of conifers.

Apart from the vast array of trees, there is also a great display of different hedging
plants, varieties of shrubs, conifer beds, rockeries and lakeside and marginal plantings
around the waters. The arboretum displays such a wealth of trees and plants that it is
worth taking a whole day to explore and appreciate it fully.

Murrintown, County Wexford; Tel: +053 42888; Fax: +053 42213 ✸ **Contact:** Dr
Austin O'Sullivan ✸ **Open:** all year, Monday–Sunday, 9am–5.30pm ✸ **Entrance fee**
✸ Please note, dogs must be kept on leads ✸ **Special features:** agricultural museum
and Famine exhibition; tearoom open in July and August ✸ **Directions:** coming
from Dublin on the N11, or from Cork on the N25, take the Wexford–Rosslare
bypass (N25) to the T-junction signposted for Johnstown Castle.

Impressive battlements at the entrance to Johnstown Castle announce to the visitor
that this is something special. Moving up the drive, the big limestone castle comes
into view, standing beside one of three ornamental lakes. The castle sits in the middle
of about fifty acres of parkland, pleasure grounds and woods; an enjoyable place to
walk. Legends of King John's visit to Ireland in the 1200s gave the castle its name (*see
also* Curraghmore, County Waterford), but today's building dates back only to the
1850s, when Hamilton Knox Grogan Morgan built the castle on the site of Rathlanon
Castle, the fifteenth-century home of the Esmonde clan. Johnstown is every child's
idea of what a good castle should be – a confection of turrets, arrow slits and battlements. It was designed, along with the garden, in the nineteenth century by Daniel
Robertson, who also designed the Italian garden at Powerscourt Gardens and House
(*see* County Wicklow).

The three ornamental lakes were designed to flow into each other, and cascades
between the lakes were positioned so they could be seen to best advantage from the

LEINSTER • COUNTY WEXFORD

windows of the castle's main reception rooms. The old tower house can be seen along the same axis, fronted by the falling stream. This contrived view takes in the Robertson-designed Italian garden across the lake, where statuary and a balustraded walk stretch along the water. Lines of gunnera surround the lake along with a huge, splayed Japanese cedar (*Cryptomeria japonica*), which looks as though it is growing out of the water.

The walled garden was laid out in the 1850s, but was abandoned in the 1940s. However, in the 1950s, John Fanning, a well-known horticulturist, oversaw its reconstruction. This included the planting of the yew hedging and the two main central borders. These are traditional herbaceous borders, mirroring each other and at the height of summer they are very handsome indeed. The paths in the walled garden are cruciform, and one arm leads to a long run of greenhouses, built in the 1930s to replace the original, more impressive curvilinear houses. Unfortunately, the greenhouses are now being used in a dull way, for begonias, summer bedding and propagation. In fact, too many of the beds in the walled garden are in bedding. However, in criticising it, one should remember that Johnstown, which would once have employed 200 workers, now ticks over with only four gardeners.

The glories of Johnstown are the trees. They dominate the scene, towering over the walls of the walled garden. The walks throughout the grounds march through tall avenues of beech, oak and other park trees. Among the more specialist plants are runs of rhododendrons, which are at their best for spring visits.

KILMOKEA MANOR HOUSE AND GARDEN 🌼 🗿 🐴 ⌐

Great Island, Campile, County Wexford; Tel: +051 388109; Fax: +051 388776; e-mail: kilmokea@indigo.ie; website: www.kilmokea.com ※ **Contact:** Mark and Emma Hewlett ※ **Open:** beginning March–beginning November, Monday–Sunday, 10am–5pm ※ **Entrance fee** ※ Supervised children welcome; please note, dogs must be kept on leads ※ **Special features:** art and crafts for sale; teas and light lunches available ※ **Directions:** from New Ross take the R733, signposted for 'Campile and the JFK Arboretum'. Pass the turn for the JFK Arboretum and continue for 1.5km. On reaching an S-bend, take the right turning, signposted Great Island ESB and Kilmokea Garden. Drive 2.5km until you see gates straight ahead. Take the left fork here and the entrance is on the right.

Kilmokea Garden was originally created by Colonel and Mrs David Price. It is sited on an historic site that was once an island in Waterford Harbour. In the nineteenth century, land reclamation joined the little pocket of frost-free land to the mainland. The garden was started in 1948 when the Prices created a formal garden within the kitchen garden walls of an older house. It was taken over by the enthusiastic Hewletts two years ago. Maurice O'Shea, the head gardener, has known and worked the garden for many years, thus providing an invaluable link to the garden's provenance.

Kilmokea is a romantic garden, full of surprises, fine planting and first-class design. Low walls, hedging and elaborate topiary give the garden a year-round structure. Many features in the well-divided garden would be perfect by themselves, for example, the iris garden – all formal, straight lines with beautiful blue flowers over strappy leaves around a big Chilstone urn full to brimming with flat-cut box. The precision of topiary bells, cones and mushrooms serves to make spreads of catmint, monarda and other loose herbaceous plants look even more flamboyant. An Italianate loggia steps up and away from the formal pond, crept over by Chilean potato tree (*Solanum crispum*) and lobster's claw (*Clianthus puniceus*).

On a wall at the back of the garden a plaque framed with tall white anemones commemorates Colonel David Price and his gardening achievements. There are other small pieces of statuary dotted around the garden. Herbaceous borders backed by old walls, and hedges with windows cut into them, vie with each other to look prettiest.

Self-seeding is enthusiastically encouraged at Kilmokea. Some people complain about self-seeding plants, but dealt with correctly they can improve almost any garden with a touch of informality. Desirable self-seeders, like echiums, love-in-a-mist (*Nigella damascene*), columbine (*Aquilegia*) or poppies, can be incorporated into most gardens. Simply allow them to germinate, and then decide which little plants look good in their chosen spots and pull out all the others. Everyone loves the sight of opportunistic blooms emerging from seemingly impossible situations like gravel drives and the tops of walls. Occasionally a plant will park itself beside another surprisingly complementary plant, for which the gardener can, of course, take all credit.

From the house, the view down the bordered lawn directs the eye to a gate in a wall. Behind the gate is a second garden with a fernery, beds of geraniums and paths that run under big camellias and rhododendrons and past several wooden summerhouses. Down here the battle of the big leaves rages: huge rodgersia, three-metre-tall gunnera, skunk cabbage, acanthus and bamboo make the garden look positively tropical.

Carry on through another gate and across a road to yet another garden – the real secret garden – with a wild wood and the 'horse pond'. A little boat sits moored picturesquely by the edge of the water. Once past the pond, the level of the land falls down to a glade of tree ferns, candelabra primulas and trachycarpus; it's very damp, sheltered and warm. Little feeding ponds drip into each other, overhung with ferns and *Euonymus planipes* with pretty red-quartered fruits.

Walkways and bridges have been set into the trees. Mrs Hewlett built all of these. They give the feeling of walking on gangways through a giant greenhouse. 'It was heavy work making them, but it made a big difference,' she says. The Hewletts have certainly earned their stewardship of this extraordinary garden.

KNOCKBAWN

Inch, County Wexford; Tel: 086 8907118; Fax: +0402 37116 ▪ **Contact:** Richard Lister ▪ **Open:** May–October, Monday–Sunday, by appointment only ▪ **Entrance fee** donated to charity ▪ **Special features:** dried flower garlands can be ordered ▪ **Directions:** go through Gorey on the N11, travelling north. The next village is Inch. Turn left at the Campus Oil Station on the left. Travel up this road for 1.5km. The garden is through a gate with stone pillars and a cattle grid.

The Irish Davis Cup tennis team used to practice on the tennis court at Knockbawn until the 1920s. Mr Lister is the current custodian. He doesn't play tennis, saving his energies for the task of maintaining the garden as it was intended to be maintained.

The house was built in 1894 and the garden is contemporaneous with it. The double-fronted house looks out over a meadow and a lone mature beech tree (its partner was knocked down in a storm several years ago). It is spare and restrained. The front of the house is covered in sheets of *Clematis montana*, but otherwise gives no clue as to the garden that awaits behind the long wall running out from the side of the building.

To get to the garden proper, you go through a gate at the side of the house and enter a world where one wouldn't be surprised to see those 1920s tennis players warming up in their heavy clothes. The garden is in the form of a long rectangle, divided into smaller rectangles of lawn and herbaceous beds. Tying the elements together are three-metre-high lengths of gleaming green box hedge, cut in a blunted triangular shape. Old apple trees divide the main sections of the garden from each other. The lawn, beds and gravel paths are well maintained but not manicured. The garden feels pleasantly lived in. The borders surrounding the lawns are pretty and floral, full of tobacco plants, roses, phlox, pinks, anemone and many other unpretentious garden flowers that just do the job well. All of this light, airy herbaceous planting is held up by a backbone of shrubs.

The summerhouse is a gem, tucked so well into the shrubs and flowers that only the old slate roof is visible. Look inside at the elaborate garlands Mr Lister makes from dried leaves, fruits, berries and moss. This is a true garden room, furnished and decorated for dining and admiring the flowers outside the door.

Towards the back of the garden is one of my favourite vegetable gardens, full of big marrows, pumpkins, beans, peas and old-fashioned sweet peas. These smell much stronger than the modern hybrids for which Richard Lister has no time at all. The beds are full of vegetables which he plunders in lightning raids, seldom letting any vegetables grow to full size before eating them. If visiting in the late summer enjoy the pumpkins and elaborately ornate Turk's cap squashes.

RAM HOUSE GARDEN

Coolgreany, near Gorey, County Wexford; Tel: +0402 37238 ■ **Contact:** Lolo Stevens ■ **Open:** 27 April–10 September, Friday–Sunday and bank holidays, 2.30pm–6pm; otherwise by appointment only to groups ■ **Entrance fee** donated to charity and goes towards garden upkeep ■ Supervised children welcome ■ **Special features:** teas and luscious cakes; seeds for sale; garden videos on rainy days ■ **Directions:** travelling north on the N11, go through Inch village. Turn left and inland at the sign for Coolgreany. Continue for 2.5km to Coolgreany village. The house is the first one after the bridge, on the left-hand side.

Even if there were no garden, advertising that includes the words 'luscious cakes' is its own attraction. However, cake must be earned and I cannot think of a more enjoyable way of earning a slice than by walking around Lolo's exceptional garden, winner of the County Wexford category in the Shamrock All Ireland Gardens Competition 2000. As with so many wonderful gardens, there was nothing on the site when Lolo and Godfrey Stevens moved here in 1973. The first thing they did, to what was then an old barracks and two enticingly empty acres, was to grass the whole area over. 'I did a lot of drawings and planning, and I read every gardening book I could get my hands on. Then we began cutting into the lawns, making beds and expanding,' says Lolo.

That was twenty-eight years ago. Today there is no grass left and it is impossible to tell the shape of this garden or the extent of it from any one vantage point. It is a triumph of design, made up of a great number of different rooms on different levels, tied together with a spider's web of paths, trails and walkways. The garden has been featured on television several times and wins awards regularly. "We're lucky, it's very mild and sheltered here,' is their modest explanation.

For all the structure and good design, it is the plants and flowers that really impress. For instance, wine-coloured hollyhock and pink anemone at the front of the garden make a great combination. Garlands of wisteria are trained smartly along the house roof. The old coach house is almost lost under a gorgeous, dark, plum-scented rose with a name that conjures up all sort of romantic notions: *Rosa* 'Souvenir de la Princesse de Lamballe', as well as abutilon, clematis and cotoneaster.

Crunching around on gravel paths, you need to side-step the self-seeding, encroaching plants that are allowed to take root everywhere. Particularly clever is the use of a mirrored wall in what was the piggery – it reflects light into the dark space, also reflecting one of Lolo's own sculptures. A lovely dianella with beautiful purple berries grows well on a raised dry bed just out from this.

The garden is a dream, featuring winding paths, steps up and down and tunnels of clematis, apple trees and roses. Though there are over seventy-five different varieties of clematis here, they are not to the fore, being shown off, but laced through slender trees, like lime, willow, ash and birch. *Clematis* 'Marie Boisselot' threading through a birch, and blue-flowered *Clematis* 'Ramona' over a big weeping willow are only two of the prettiest combinations. Even holding up a climber, these trees cast very little shade and allow good underplanting.

Running through the bottom of the garden, a little stream is edged by drumstick primula, rodgersia and lobelia. A path made of crunched-up slate leads into a stepped-down area with a miniature pond fringed with hostas, which thrive in the damp soil. The paths down here change, with leaf mould or bark mulch being used as they better suit the honesty- and bluebell-filled woods. A bottlebrush shrub *(Callistemon)* is growing so well that it is leaning out onto the path. In Lolo's garden, this means that the path must go. Ram House Garden is truly a plant-lover's delight.

SANDY LANE

Killurin, Enniscorthy, County Wexford; Tel: +053 28323; e-mail: ediebro@ eircom.net ▪ **Contact:** Maurice and Edie Brosnan ▪ **Open:** as part of the Wexford Garden Trail; ring in advance for an appointment ▪ **Entrance fee** donated to Goal ▪ Please note, dogs must be kept on leads ▪ **Directions:** travel 6km north from Wexford town on the N11. Turn at Kyle Cross and follow the signs to Killurin. Cross the river and continue until you reach a right turn signposted for Ballyhogue. Pass the Sycamore House pub on the left. The next lane on the left is Sandy Lane.

This garden has only been in existence since 1996. Killurin and its surrounding area are hilly and fairly unspoilt. Sandy Lane sits naturally into these surroundings – it is suitably cottagey, rural and wild around the edges, with good hedgerows and native trees.

The main accent is on plants. Mrs Brosnan grows almost everything in the garden from seed and plant exchanges, which makes her achievements all the greater. The plants are ranged about in big mixed beds, running up and down the hilly site. The site is used well, an old marl hole being pulled into service and turned into a pond; its clay bottom means that there is no need for butyl liner. As it is in a hollow, you can look down from the path over the arum lilies and rich blue pickerel weed (*Pontaderia cordata*). The various borders are good, particularly a 'hot and grey' border – a bed of hot reds and soft, hairy silver or grey foliage, with grey willow, *Salix purpurea* 'Nana', *Rosa moyseii* with red hips, soft, grey-leaved white lychnis and striped phormium.

At the front of the garden is a scree bed with miniature columbine, woolly thyme, succulents, like sedum, and other hummock-forming plants.

Trees surround the whole garden – ash, beech, sycamore and some particularly fine, large, sweet chestnut trees (*Castanea sativa*). The biggest of these trees inspired the Brosnans to buy the house in the first place. 'I saw that tree and that did it for me. We had to buy the house,' says the smitten Edie, looking happily at her tree.

The house was once famous as 'the hurley house', where the Wexford hurling team had their hurleys made. Now the boundary ash trees look more appropriate growing than cut up and stacked to dry. With Edie in charge, they will not end their days in Croke Park.

Expansion is underway at Sandy Lane – an arboretum is to be introduced, chiefly because Edie needs space for the many trees she has grown from seed. It will be interesting to watch this garden as it progresses.

SHORTALSTOWN

Killinick, County Wexford; Tel: +053 58836 ▪ **Contact:** Bryan and Helen Miller ▪ **Open:** May–September, every Sunday, 2pm–5pm; during the Wexford Garden Trail; otherwise by appointment only ▪ **Entrance fee** donated to local charities and goes towards garden upkeep ▪ Please note, dogs must be kept on leads ▪ **Special features:** groups can book teas by prior arrangement ▪ **Directions:** travelling to Rosslare from Wexford town, take the right turn off the Wexford bypass for Kilmore Quay (on to the R739). A sign for Rathmacknee Castle is the landmark here. Travel for 2.5km along the R739, and the garden is on the right.

Shortalstown is a mature garden that has been in the same family through three generations of gardening Millers. Today it is run by the wonderfully capable Helen Miller. A leading light in the Private Gardens of Wexford group, she leaves you with the impression that the country could be safely left in her hands. The garden won first place in the Garden For All Seasons in the Leinster category of the Shamrock All Ireland Gardens Competition 1999.

The first thing the visitor will notice on arriving at the garden gate is a tall, elegant eucalyptus, which was planted in 1950. Beside it, its thirty-year-old baby is following mother skyward.

Shortalstown has good vistas in all directions, looking across lawns towards featured trees and good-looking plant combinations. It feels open, but doesn't reveal itself all at once. There are surprises everywhere. Even with the sheltered Wexford climate, it was seen fit to create an even more sheltered spot in order to grow peaches and a white lobster's claw (*Clianthus puniceus*). This secret little spot is tucked in near the house, secluded behind a beech hedge.

The house itself is covered in wisteria and fronted by a big clump of crinum lilies, some myrtle, a Judas tree and walnut, all enjoying the protection afforded by the building's walls. At the front of the house a snug, damp and shady area is populated by hostas, candelabra primulas and a big tree fern. Old moss-covered stones here make the perfect home for ferns. There are many tender things in this garden, such as white-trumpet-flowered datura growing outside, Chinese foxgloves *(Rehmannia elata)*, and echiums seeding everywhere and giving a constant succession of the exotic-looking plants at different stages in their three-year grow, flower and die cycle.

Shortalstown is a garden full of variety. A big herbaceous border, substantial vegetable and fruit gardens with plenty of mixed vegetable beds, daffodil lawns in the spring, a rhododendron wood, specimen trees and a fine herb bed are only some of the sights in a well-ordered, handsome garden. As I left, the eucalyptus and its pup were due for a telling-off for daring to shed leaves on the lawn.

WOODVILLE

New Ross, County Wexford; Tel: +051 421268 ▪ **Contact:** Peter and Irene Roche ▪ **Open:** April–September, by appointment only to groups ▪ **Entrance fee** donated to the Cheshire Homes and goes towards garden upkeep ▪ **Special features:** an interesting leaflet on the wildlife to be seen at Woodville is available; teas can be booked by prior arrangement ▪ **Directions:** 3km from New Ross on the Enniscorthy Road (N30). The gate is opposite the turn off for Kilkenny over the River Barrow.

Mrs Roche was always a gardener and is a founder member of the famed Wexford Garden and Flower Club *(see* p.129), for which there is a long waiting list for membership. Mr Roche joined his wife in the garden a few years ago and they make a wonderful gardening team, even to the extent that they lead guests through the garden together, each talking about their particular favourite spots and plants.

They started work on the garden at Woodville in 1951, on what were the very bare bones of a garden attached to their house. However, most of the garden plants seen today were planted since 1963, when the work really took off. Out on the lawn stands a Fitzroy cypress *(Fitzroya cupressoides)*, named for the captain of the *Beagle*, the ship that carried Charles Darwin to the Galapagos Islands to carry out his studies. (Captain Fitzroy went a bit mad as a result of the adventure.) These lawns were once rough pasture, but have been transformed into good lawn through years of feeding, weeding and work, proving that it is not always necessary to dig, rake and re-seed or re-turf an area of green to make a presentable lawn.

Once upon a time, the railway ran below the garden on its way to Enniscorthy. When it closed down, the resourceful Roches made use of a spring originating under the railway tunnel to fill a pond that they edged with angel's fishing rods and sisyrinchium. The pond is actually a swimming pool posing as a pond – a good idea. Occasionally one sees swimming pools incorporated into gardens like this by the use of dark tiling or paint. Glaring turquoise rectangles can look out of place in a garden, and certainly in dull Irish weather.

Below this area is a wood and water garden with various ponds flowing into each other. These can be enjoyed from the vantage of rope-railed steps down a bank of astilbe, bloodroot *(Sanguinaria canadensis)*, ferns, trilliums, snowdrops and bluebells. Overhead, huge ash, oak, holly and a camellia run through by rampant clematis make a fine wood. Further up, a row of Monterey pines *(Pinus radiata)*, which Mr Roche remembers leap-frogging over when he was twelve years old, now reach a height of twenty-four-metres. This area is natural. The self-seeding plants take their own course. For all the natural and native look however, Mr Ross proudly announces that he has counted the plants of thirty-seven countries in this area. One exotic-looking plant enjoying the shade and damp here is *Veratrum album*, sometimes called the false hellebore, with its accordion-pleated leaves. This part of the garden has deposits of sand – glacial and acid – which allows the growing of rhododendrons and other acid-lovers. The rest of the garden is made up of alkaline Kilkenny limestone, unsuitable for these plants.

Towards the house, on the way to the walled garden, are some specimen trees, including walnuts and a *Crataegus orientalis*, a member of the hawthorn family, which is thornless and bears lovely fruit.

Woodville's walled garden is built close by the house. This is fairly unusual, as in the 1700s the trend was for siting kitchen gardens, outbuildings and other working parts of the estate away from the big house, and we see walled gardens built sometimes as far as a mile away from the house (*see* Kylemore Abbey, County Galway, and Bantry House, County Cork).

It takes enormous work to keep a walled garden to the standard that the Roches keep theirs. Long beds of crinum and madonna lilies, rose beds and substantial rows of peas, beans and potatoes all require work. Taking occasional shortcuts speeds the job along, for example, the Roches don't waste time lifting and drying dahlias each year. They simply add a mulch of large amounts of sheep manure to snug them in for the winter. For Peter Roche, in particular, there are more important jobs to be done than lifting and storing tubers over the winter, only to replant them the next spring. Round-topped box hedges tie the varied beds neatly together. These are far softer in appearance than the usual squared-off hedging. At the end of one hedge a topiary fox looks across the path longingly at a fat hen on the opposite hedge, the dinner he'll never eat.

The walled garden is full to bursting with great plants – lovely yellow *Rosa banksia* 'Lutea' thrives under a north wall, along with fresh and healthy-looking Chatham Island lilies, a plant generally seen struggling and looking miserable in Irish gardens. In the east border hellebores grow in profusion. A rose border features a new pergola with the violet and purple flowers of *Clematis* 'Mrs Thompson' and *Clematis* 'The President' threaded together. A 'friends' garden' close by is a sentimental spot, where the Roches put plants given to them by friends. Finally, the greenhouse, built in 1882, is full of plumbago, unusual red nerines, vines, a century-old maidenhair fern gone wild and a host of abutilon varieties.

The Roches like to show their visitors around, and it is a pleasure to listen to them talk so entertainingly about the garden and the plants they know so well. It is hard to see how they find the time to do this and still attend to the great workload that their beautiful garden demands. But they manage to make it seem effortless.

GARDENING CLUBS AND SOCIETIES

COUNTY WEXFORD GARDEN AND FLOWER CLUB

Contact: Bernie Lynch (Secretary), 5 Glena Terrace, Wexford, County Wexford.

Founded in the 1960s, the Wexford Garden and Flower Club is one of the busiest and most active horticultural clubs in the country. Membership stands at 250 and there is a waiting list to join, but non-members are welcome to attend open meetings, for an admission fee. Meetings are held at the Teagasc Farm Centre, Enniscorthy. Dates and times vary, so contact the club for details of the next meeting. Lectures and demonstrations are held throughout the year, apart from the summer months when garden trips are arranged. One six-day trip is organised each year, usually to the UK. There is also a floral art aspect to the club, but the emphasis is on gardening.

NURSERIES AND GARDEN CENTRES

AISLING NURSERIES

Ballydungan, Tagoat, Rosslare, County Wexford; Tel: +053 32108.

BEECHDALE GARDEN CENTRE

Moneytucker, Enniscorthy, County Wexford; Tel: +054 44271.

BALLYKELLY LANE GARDEN CENTRE

Rosslare Road, Wexford, County Wexford; Tel: +053 58901.

BIZZY BEES

Dublin Road, Ferns; Tel: +054 66123.

COGLEY, MICHAEL, GARDEN CENTRE

Murrintown, Kildavin, County Wexford; Tel: +053 39319.

DRINAGH GARDEN CENTRE

Rosslare Road, Wexford, County Wexford; Tel: +054 35619/087 2716202.

ENGLISH, PATRICK, FRUIT PLANTS

Raheenduff, Adamstown, Enniscorthy, County Wexford; Tel: +054 40504.

FIG TREE GARDEN CENTRE

Castlebridge, County Wexford; Tel: +053 59211.

FUCHSIA NURSERY

Ballinaboola, County Wexford; Tel: +051 428252.

GARDENER GARDEN CENTRE

Shalom, Ballybuckley, County Wexford; Tel: +054 47947.

HENNESSY'S GARDEN CENTRE

Carne Beach Road, Tagoat, Rosslare, County Wexford; Tel: +053 31208.

HYLAND'S GARDEN CENTRE

Oulart, Gorey, County Wexford; Tel: +053 36128.

KILCANNON GARDEN CENTRE

Kilcannon Industries, Old Dublin Road, Enniscorthy, County Wexford; Tel: +054 35514.

NOLAN, GER, NURSERIES

Farmleigh, Enniscorthy, County Wexford; Tel: +054 88643.

OLD CREAMERY GARDEN CENTRE

Knockbrandon, Cranford, Gorey, County Wexford; Tel: +055 28246.

PURPLE 'N' GOLD

Selskar Avenue, Wexford, County Wexford; Tel: +053 46863.

ROCHES GARDEN CENTRE

Campile, County Wexford; Tel: +051 388429.

SPRINGMOUNT GARDEN CENTRE

Springmount, Gorey, County Wexford; Tel: +055 21368.

SWEENEY'S GARDEN CENTRE

Marshmeadows, New Ross, County Wexford; Tel: +051 421396.

GARDEN DESIGNERS

MACDONALD, FRANCES AND IAIN

The Bay Garden, Camolin, County Wexford; Tel: +054 83349; Fax: +054 83576.

The best place to see the work of Frances and Iain MacDonald is at their own garden in Camolin. It is divided into rooms, each different in style.

GARDEN ACCESSORIES

CULTECH GARDEN STONEWARE

Hillcrest, Cross Street, New Ross, County Wexford; Tel: +051 421938.

Garden statuary and stonework.

FURLONG, SEAN, GARDEN STONEWARE

Kilmuckridge, County Wexford; Tel: +053 30280.

IRISH PEBBLE COMPANY

Newtown, Kilmore Quay, County Wexford; Tel: 086 8314323.

KILTREA BRIDGE POTTERY

Enniscorthy, County Wexford; Tel: +054 35107; Fax: +054 34690.

Well known for their fine terracotta pots. They have a popular sale each spring (see press for advertisements).

KINBARK PRODUCTS

Camolin, County Wexford; Tel: +054 83247.

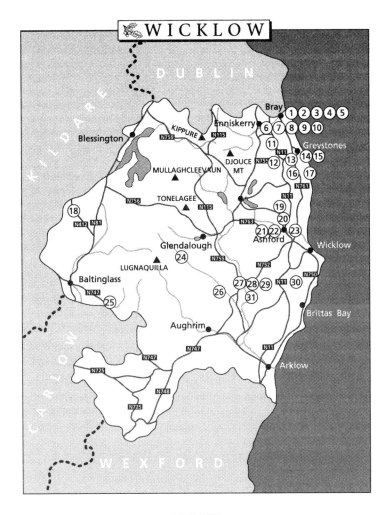

WICKLOW

MAP KEY

1. Chestnut Lodge
2. Graigueconna Gardens
3. St Joseph's
4. Festina Lente Garden
5. Killruddery House and Garden
6. Knockmore
7. Powerscourt Gardens and House
8. Valclusa
9. Rosemount
10. Ballyorney
11. Avoca Handweavers/Glencormac Estate Garden
12. Glenview Hotel
13. Style Bawn House
14. Calluna
15. Holmsdale
16. 8 New Russian Village
17. National Garden Exhibition Centre
18. Rathsallagh House
19. Wren's Wood
20. Nun's Cross School Garden
21. Hunter's Hotel
22. Rossanagh
23. Mount Usher
24. Shekina Sculpture Garden
25. Hillview Garden
26. Greenan Farm Museums and Maze
27. Kilmacurragh
28. Parnell Memorial Park
29. Tinakilly House
30. Gormanstown Manor
31. Avondale House and Forest Park

COUNTY WICKLOW

County Wicklow is a hard act to beat. On the doorstep of Dublin, it nevertheless feels like a wonderfully remote, natural place, dominated by the Wicklow Mountains, the chief component of the chain of mountains that stretches almost the full length of east Leinster. The mountains are a great natural amenity for the people of Wicklow, city-weary Dubliners and visitors from further afield. People have been mountaineering, walking, fishing, making pilgrimages and day-tripping their way through the magnificent county since the eighteenth century when tourism began to develop. Picturesque villages, such as Enniskerry, Delgany, Laragh and Avoca (better known as Ballykissangel to soap-opera fans) are scattered through the county. The seaside resorts of Bray, with its Victorian promenade, and Greystones have also long been holiday destinations for Dubliners.

Within the mountains is a series of glacial valleys, including Glenmacnass, Glendalough and Glenmalure. Wicklow rightly deserves the title of 'Garden of Ireland', as the fertile, brown, acid soil in these valleys creates some of the best gardening conditions on the island. As a result the county boasts such famed gardens as Powerscourt, Mount Usher and Killruddery. But there is a great deal more to gardening in Wicklow than these grandiose public gardens. For the past twelve years the county has played host to the Wicklow Gardens Festival, a celebration of gardening of every scale and style (*see* box, below).

THE WICKLOW GARDENS FESTIVAL

County Wicklow has justifiably been called the 'Garden of Ireland'. Much of the county is mountainous and wild, with dramatic scenery that provides an enviable backdrop to the gardens, large and small, that range across it. For twelve years the gardeners of Wicklow have banded together each summer for the Wicklow Gardens Festival. This hugely popular festival runs from mid-May to mid-July and a great number of excellent, and in many cases not otherwise accessible, private gardens throw open their gates to the public. The large heritage houses and gardens, such as Powerscourt, Killruddery, Mount Usher and Avondale, also take part in the visiting bonanza. Among the events organised for the festival are guided tours, lectures, floral exhibitions, vegetarian cookery courses, a flurry of garden parties and a floral dinner. The floral dinner is a particularly attractive event, with each course incorporating edible flowers and herbs, and floral wines and champagnes providing the refreshment.

For details and a brochure contact: Wicklow County Tourism, St Manntan's House, Kilmantin Hill, Wicklow, County Wicklow; Tel: +0404 66058; Fax: +0404 66057; e-mail: wctr@iol.ie; website: www.wicklow.ie

Kilmacanogue, County Wicklow; Tel: +01 2867466; Fax: +01 2760458 ❊
Contact: Des Carton or Donald Pratt ❊ **Open:** October–March, Monday–Friday, 9.30am–5.30pm, weekends, 10am–6pm; April–September, Monday–Sunday, 10am–6pm ❊ **No entrance fee** ❊ Dogs must be kept on leads ❊ **Special features:** restaurant; garden shop and nursery with fashionable garden accessories; gift shop ❊ **Directions:** travel south along the N11. About 4km after the turn for Bray, watch for the tall flags marking the Avoca shop on the right. Well signposted.

Avoca Handweavers is situated on the site of the old Glencormac Estate, which is owned by the Jamesons, the famous distilling family. In 1870 an eleven-acre garden was laid out for James Jameson by William Sheppard. Sheppard was a landscape gardener who worked as assistant to the Victorian garden designer Ninian Niven (*see* Iveagh Gardens, County Dublin, and Hilton Park, County Monaghan).

Today the garden is known as the home of the Glencormac cypress. Planted in 1794, it was thought to be an ordinary Monterey cypress (*Cupressus macrocarpa*), but a few years' growth showed that it was something else – a unique weeping mutant, described in a report produced for Wicklow County Council in 1977 as 'possibly one of the outstanding trees in the British Isles'. Glencormac's weeping Monterey cypress is the only mature specimen in the world, and indeed Hilliers, the well-known nursery in England, has propagated from the tree and sells the plants under the name of 'Glencormick'.

There are a number of other notable trees in the garden, including huge eucalyptus, giant redwood (*Sequoiadendron giganteum*), blue Atlas cedar (*Cedrus atlantica* 'Glauca') Scot's pine (*Pinus sylvestris*) and a grove of yews of indeterminate age. One of these yews, thought to be 2,000 years old, features in the *Guinness Book of Records*.

Water is an important feature of the garden. Meandering sunken streams dawdle around the hilly lawns between the groves of trees, so keep a close eye on children and watch your footing. The Dripping Pool, an unusual Victorian creation and part of Sheppard's design, is remarkable. According to legend, it has never once dried up since it was built in 1878.

Glencormac is a delightful garden and walk, which must have been even more picturesque when it had an unimpeded view of the Sugar Loaf Mountain – now, ironically, hidden from sight by the fine trees.

Rathdrum, County Wicklow; Tel: +0404 46111; Fax: +0404 46111 ❊ **Contact:** Reception ❊ **Open:** May–September, daily, 10am–6pm; October–April, daily, 11am–5pm ❊ **No entrance fee,** except to the house ❊ Dogs on leads ❊ **Special features:** the house, once the home of Charles Stewart Parnell, may be visited for a fee; tearooms and gift shop ❊ A member of Coillte ❊ **Directions:** 2km east of Rathdrum, on the R752 to Arklow.

Avondale House, famed as the home of Charles Stewart Parnell, was built in 1779 by Samuel Hayes, Wicklow's representative in the Irish House of Commons and the person who planted the wonderful woods to be seen in Avondale today. In 1788

Hayes presented a bill entitled 'An Act for encouraging the cultivation and better preservation of trees'. In 1904 the estate passed into the care of Coillte, the Forestry Service, and much of the land was laid out in one-acre plots for experimental tree planting. The plots are arranged in the form of a forest garden. There are three planned walks – the Pine Trail, the Exotic Tree Trail and the River Walk.

A useful colour-coded map can be obtained at the reception, marking out in detail the impressive array of special plants and trees to be seen on each of the trails. Among the groves of oak, silver fir, pine, larch, maple and beech are scattered specimens of eucalyptus, Serbian spruce, monkey puzzle, red cedar, Californian redwood, Monterey pine, Spanish chestnut and varieties of fern, foxgloves and woodland ground plants. Particularly striking is the grove of giant sequoias, an almost primeval-looking area, where the huge trees soar skywards and the dark, needle-strewn ground is soft underfoot and rippled with exposed roots. This is not a place to be forgotten easily.

BALLYORNEY

Waterfall Road, Enniskerry, County Wicklow; Tel: +01 6683791 ▪ **Contact:** Pauline Canty ▪ **Open:** strictly by appointment only ▪ **Entrance fee** ▪ **Special features:** Ballyorney House may be visited, by appointment only ▪ **Directions:** supplied when appointment is confirmed.

Ballyorney House was built in the 1800s as a dower house at Charleville, a large estate nearby in the wooded hills of north Wicklow. One arrives into the garden by a winding woodland drive – not ostentatiously long, but impressive. The house stands in a clearing, with trees running uphill behind it and the garden sweeping out to the front and into the woods and hillside. The spectacular Sugar Loaf Mountain, like a painted backdrop, stands above it all. Two sleeping lions guard the entrance to the garden, and behind them a double border is divided by a wide grass path. This double border was moved from its original location a little way off and placed here in order to frame a perfect view of the Sugar Loaf.

This part of the garden is completely wrapped around by tall and deep beech hedges, which shelter and protect the plants from the harsh mountain winds. The hedges give structure and line, but the planting in the borders is informal and mixed. Flowers and herbs, such as acanthus, dill, mint and monkshood (*Aconitum*), sit between shrubs like the wire-net bush (*Corokia cotoneaster*), honey locust (*Gleditsia triacanthos*) and various roses. Brushing past dill releases its wonderful, rich aniseed smell. In front of the taller plants, low, furry lamb's ears (*Stachys byzantina*) and hardy purple geranium sprawl onto the path to divert the walker. These beds were designed to look good all year round, because they march directly out from the house and are always visible from the building. Classic June-flowering herbaceous borders would never earn their keep in this spot.

At the far end of the path and borders is the entrance to an old orchard. The apple trees are not very productive. Rambling roses are grown up through them, an eminently sensible way of using and beautifying less than spectacular trees. There is also an old bed of rose cuttings in this secluded spot, fenced in to protect it from wandering deer – one of the great scourges of Wicklow gardeners. The views from here look back to the house through beds of waving Michaelmas daisies and tall white roses. Moving out onto a lawn, you discover that the work done on this border gives a double return – one of the beds backs onto the turf and works well as a single border from this side.

Pale shades of daffodils, snowdrops and white hyacinths growing around a central sundial start the white garden off on a good foot early in the year. Well-devised shrub beds, with clematis knotted through lilac, and roses through red-berried spindle trees (*Euonymous eurpaeus*), butt onto the lawn as it rolls down to the house. The house itself is anchored by a mass of low-growing agapanthus and a fine, yellow-flowering fremontodendron climbs the walls alongside wisteria.

A few years ago scrub was being cleared from under the trees in the woods and, by a complete accident, a stream was discovered. This threw up the opportunity of making a waterfall garden. Today the gushing water can be heard right up to the house. The stream is lush with damp-loving plants, such as gunnera and hosta, happy by the splashing water. A Japanese air has been created by the building of a red-painted bridge over the stream. This looks down on stepping stones, perfect for those who prefer getting their feet wet. Two big stone herons hide in among the ferns, ash, birch and bamboo, spying on the fish. Railway sleepers dug into the embankment hold wide gravel steps and create an inviting path down to the water. Across the stream dogwood, holly, oak and a creamy-white flowering myrtle blend into the ash wood behind. We would all love such accidents in our gardens.

CALLUNA

Church Lane, Greystones, County Wicklow; Tel: +01 287 4400 ▥ **Contact:** John and Mary Markham ▥ **Open:** to individuals and groups during the Wicklow Gardens Festival and through the RHSI Open Garden Scheme, telephone for annual dates or see RHSI brochure ▥ **Entrance fee** donated to the RNLI ▥ Supervised children welcome ▥ **Special features:** teas may be booked by prior arrangement ▥ **Directions:** approaching Greystones travelling southbound, turn right at the traffic lights at the Blacklion pub. Church Lane is the second turn left, and Calluna is the sixth house on the right-hand side.

The Markhams, like many of their fellow Wicklow gardeners, open their garden throughout the summer months for charity. 'We like to help the lifeboat service,' explains John Markham. 'I don't think we'll ever manage to help buy a whole boat. We finance the nuts and bolts.' But nuts and bolts all add up to make lifeboats, and people who open their gardens for charity are to be lauded, encouraged and admired.

The first thing to be seen on arriving at the Markhams's garden is a huge array of *Dahlia* 'The Bishop of Llandaff' ranged along the front wall of the house in a shock of rich, dark red flower and bronze foliage. This wall faces north and the soil below the house wall is bone dry, yet the Markhams keep these dahlias in tip-top shape, despite the less-than-ideal aspect of the bed. Only big pots of white-flowering argyranthemum daisies standing by the path can possibly compete with such a dramatic red. There are other good plants in this front garden, but it is not easy for them to divert attention away from the daring red dahlias, and so for the late summer at least snake-bark maple (*Acer rufinerve*), liquidambar and the prostrate *Rosa* 'Pheasant' play second fiddle to the Bishop of Llandaff.

The Markhams have been working the third-of-an-acre garden only since 1995, but looking at the varied beds, fernery, flowering shrubs, herbaceous planting and great vegetable beds it is hard to believe that the garden has had only five years' labour poured into it. John and Mary work as a team, putting in every spare hour they have. Mary picks the plants and design schemes, while John grows the vegetables, roses and dahlias: 'The really important work!' he laughs. Winning regularly at the prestigious Dún Laoghaire Flower Show with his dahlias and chrysanthemums, John Markham can afford to laugh. He also excels in the vegetable categories and can grow onions which he says 'are as big as my grandchild's head and they still taste good!' The garden is as much a competition workshop as a pleasure garden, and scattered throughout are the choicest blooms and vegetables being prepared for rosettes at upcoming summer shows.

While John is a good propagator and competition grower, Mary is a flower-arranger and many of the decorative plants in the garden feature strong foliage with contrasting leaf shapes, colours and textures, all important raw materials for flower-arranging. Drimys, camellia, holly and acanthus provide beauty in the garden and for vase and oasis indoors. This is an interesting new town garden, intensively worked and serving a great number of purposes for the Markhams.

CHESTNUT LODGE

4 Sidmonton Square, Bray, County Wicklow; Tel: +01 2868623 ▪ **Contact:** Mrs Carol Bone ▪ **Open:** mid-May–end July, by appointment only; also open for the Wicklow Gardens Festival ▪ **Entrance fee** donated to local charities ▪ Supervised children welcome ▪ **Special features:** occasional one-day garden and flower-arranging courses; teas can be booked by prior arrangement; plants for sale on charity days ▪ **Directions:** travelling from Dublin, take the third turn left off Main Street in Bray, after the Royal Hotel. Travel down this road as far as the small public park on the left. The house is opposite the park gates and has a red front door.

A state of rack and ruin ruled at the house and garden on Sidmonton Square when Carol Bone moved here in the late 1980s. Looking at it now, this is very hard to believe. This tiny garden, in front of and to the back of Carol's Georgian house, is now glorious, a place with more to interest the visitor than gardens five times its size. Every inch of space is worked hard and made to pull its weight as part of the greater whole.

Masses of clematis and roses cover the front of the house and wind themselves up the wrought-iron stair rail to the door. The eye is drawn down to the raised beds held behind railway sleepers. These are filled with impatiens, phormium, cordyline, hardy geraniums and a tree peony. Cobbles edge a run of gravel in a smart foil to the lush plants. The level of maintenance is impeccable – the cobbles look as though they are vacuumed daily. Not surprisingly, the garden took first place in the courtyard category of the Shamrock All Ireland Gardens Competition 1999.

Carol says that her aim is to try to get a little bit of everything into the garden. She manages this with style. It is not easy to get the sum of so many parts to work well in a small space, but she makes it look effortless, dividing the space so that it cannot all be seen at the same time. The trick is in the division of the basic elements, permanent and temporary. Permanence is found in gravel-and-cobble paths, trellises, stone walls, ponds, large shrubs and well-trained box hedges and statuary. Against these permanent fixtures the flowers – the transient stars – stand out, pretty touches of tumbling colour and perfume creating seasonal pictures and compositions. *Pelargonium* 'Barbe Bleue' with a rich cherry-wine colour is being trained up an obelisk and is one of the really beautiful summer sights in Carol's garden.

Pots and troughs keep a small garden turning over. These are used to hold the more showy, colourful plants that are brought out when they are looking their best and then moved backstage to be replaced by next month's favourite. In a small garden one really does not want to look at the dying-back leaves of daffodils or tulips in May when they can be moved off to the rear and replaced by daylilies or geraniums. When the sweet, heavy perfume of night-scented stock fades the plant can be whipped away and replaced by an apple mint or verbena.

The family's travels in the Far East are well documented through the garden in the form of Balinese stone heads, pots and statuary. These artefacts personalise the garden and remind Carol of great holidays as she weeds and works. My favourite statues are the two savage-looking beasts who are well chained up on either side of a little summerhouse.

An expansion programme was recently embarked upon and a neighbouring garden was requisitioned for Carol's latest project: a smart new *potager*-style vegetable garden. This in now ready for viewing.

THE BOX SYSTEM

The box system is a method of selling vegetables that organic growers have been using for several years. In return for a £5 or £10 weekly payment the customer receives a delivery of mixed seasonal vegetables throughout the year. It is a good system, providing a regular home delivery of fresh and varied vegetables. But it is not without drawbacks. Because the vegetables are seasonal there will be no tomatoes or sugar snap peas in the box in February. The contents of a box might also stretch limited cooks who have never seen a squash outside a Hallowe'en display. If you cannot supply yourself with vegetables from your own garden it is certainly worth joining a scheme for a trial.

FESTINA LENTE GARDEN

Bray, County Wicklow; Tel: +01 2720704 ■ **Contact:** Pat Howlett ■ **Open:** April–October, Monday–Friday, 10am–4pm ■ **Entrance fee** donated to charity ■ Supervised children welcome; please note, dogs on leads ■ **Special features:** horse-riding for the disabled; vegetables for sale under the box system (*see* box, above) ■ **Directions:** driving from Dublin city to Bray, turn off the M11 at the first Bray junction. Go straight through the roundabout towards the town and approach a set of traffic lights with a garden centre on the right. Turn right here and travel about 1km up the road until you see a newsagents on the right-hand side. Turn right immediately after this and follow the drive around to the right to reach the garden.

The gardens at Festina Lente are part of the old Conna Demesne, situated in the walled garden of the estate and covering just over two acres. From a state of neglect and dilapidation, they have now been completely restored and rebuilt, laid out primarily for the use of people with physical disabilities. In the reconstruction, the old walled garden has been modified to incorporate raised beds for easy inspection and access. Paved paths allow ease of movement for wheelchairs. A sensory garden incorporates plants noted for scent and texture, such as lemon verbena, lavender, curry plant, chives, rosemary and oregano; aromatic herbs are particularly important for the enjoyment of visually impaired visitors. The water features include a restored central pond and two lily ponds, all raised so the level of water is close to wheelchair height.

COMPANION PLANTING

Companion planting is a newly fashionable term to describe old methods of pest control and plant husbandry. It is thought that certain plants grown together are mutually helpful to each other. A 'companion' may reduce the chance of attack by pest or disease on its partner. Also, one plant may optimise its neighbour's growth by depositing certain nutrients in the soil which its companion plant will benefit from.

Strong-smelling alliums, like chives or garlic, are often placed alongside roses to discourage aphids. In addition to repelling pests attracted by smell, chives are thought to deter black spot and to increase the scent of roses. Planting rosemary and dill beside cabbages and other brassicas is thought to protect them from the scourge of cabbage white butterflies. Cannabis was once used for the same job, but the Gardaí might have something to say on this issue, so stick to the dill!

Companion planting is a loose term that stretches out to include planting crops that benefit each other by providing homes for pollinating insects and beneficial insects that prey on more unwelcome creatures. It also covers practices such as planting legumes, like peas or beans, to enrich the soil for the next crop to be planted. Legumes fix nitrogen in the soil, which nourishes later crops. One of the more amusing suggestions for companion planting is to plant a swathe of catmint near the strawberry patch. Cats adore it and will lie and sprawl in catmint for long stretches of time. Hopefully this will deter all but the bravest of thieving birds from the ripening fruits.

Companion planting has its avid followers but, on the other hand, there are gardeners who scorn its ideas as unscientific 'mumbo jumbo'. It is very hard to scientifically quantify the benefits of using these methods. Its adherents largely rely on personal experience and anecdotal evidence. But many companion planting practices go right back into history, in some cases to classical times, and so gardeners are happy to continue the traditions and, in the process, use fewer pesticides and garden chemicals.

The guru of companion planting is Bob Flowerdew, known to many through his appearances on BBC Radio 4's 'Gardeners' Question Time'. His books, *The Complete Book of Companion Gardening* and *Bob Flowerdew's Organic Bible* (published by Kyle Cathie), provide an enthusiastic introduction to the subject. For further information contact: The Organic Centre, Rossinver, County Leitrim (*see* County Leitrim), or The Henry Doubleday Research Association, Ryton-on-Dunsmore, Coventry, CV8 3LG, UK.

The principal feature of the garden is the reflecting double border, where one side exactly mirrors its opposite. Four beds, measuring twenty-five metres each, are interrupted by a central pond and tied together by tall cordylines. Starry blue borage mirrors borage across the path. Gayfeather *(Liatris spicata)* waves across at itself, as do big clumps of thalictrum, penstemon and golden rod. Behind this double show, a long spring border runs the length of the north wall. It is now being planted up with bulbs, early-flowering herbaceous plants, like *Dicentra formosa*, ornamental grasses, such as feathertop grass *(Pennisetum)*, and compact shrubs, like *Magnolia stellata* and *Pieris* 'Forest Flame'. Because it will be at its best in the spring, it will not compete with the reflecting June borders. Finally, a small informal herb garden using Chinese medicinal plants opens in 2001. The properties and uses of the herbs will be labelled in detail.

Like many old walled gardens, the place had some old glories of which there are now only reminders. For example, Festina Lente once held the longest run of wisteria in the country, but the long brick and stone walls are now bare, awaiting new planting. To one side of the garden is what is thought to be an old fernery, which it is hoped will be tackled and reinstated soon. But so much has been achieved already: dreadfully overgrown yew hedges are being rejuvenated, the twin lily ponds have been saved and replanted and the beds have been cleared of weeds and replanted beautifully.

Work on the garden began in 1996, and at the time of going to press it is still a work in progress. Don't expect a finished, perfect garden – it is a hive of industry and development, affording an insight into how a large walled garden can be redeveloped for use in today's world. All work is carried out using organic methods and the garden is a member of the Irish Organic Trust. Produce from the vegetable garden is sold to fund the upkeep of the garden. Anyone interested in companion planting may wish to know that they are experimenting with these methods also *(see* box, Companion Planting, p.139). Outside the walls, in an area along the driveway, two Berkshire pigs called Deirdre and Mary may be seen busily clearing ground that will in time become a wildflower garden.

GLENVIEW HOTEL

Glen O' The Downs, County Wicklow; Tel: +01 2873399 ▪ **Contact:** Reception ▪ **Open:** all year round; groups must have an appointment to visit, individuals may arrive freely ▪ **Entrance fee** donated to charity ▪ Supervised children welcome ▪ **Directions:** 8km south of Bray on the N11. The hotel is signposted clearly on the right-hand side of the road.

The gardens at Glenview cover a steep hill in front of one of the noisiest and busiest roads in the country. This difficult site has been transformed into a thing of beauty, with tables for tea surrounded by flowering shrubs, runs of herbaceous planting and mixed island beds. Being in the hills, the mist can appear at any time, and even on an August day a light mist playing around the trees and hills beyond makes the place very atmospheric.

Paths weave through the beds and shrubs, leading off beyond into the bigger trees and specimens of acer, copper beech, hoheria, Mexican orange blossom *(Choisya ternata)* and lace-cap hydrangea. It finally and naturally trails off into blackberries and dog roses as the garden sinks into the surrounding hills.

Kilbride, County Wicklow; Tel: +0404 69432 ▪ **Contact:** Margaret Murphy ▪
Open: all year round to groups, by appointment only ▪ **Entrance fee** donated to
charity ▪ Supervised children welcome; dogs must be kept on leads ▪ **Special fea-**
tures: golf driving range; plants for sale occasionally; teas can be booked by prior
arrangement ▪ **Directions:** driving south on the N11, turn off to the left opposite
Lil Doyle's pub. Pass Kilbride Church and continue on for 5km, following the signs
for the driving range. Gormanstown Manor is on the right-hand side.

Margaret Murphy started her large Wicklow garden sixteen years ago. She began by
collecting acorns from the countryside surrounding the family farm and planting
them out on the boundary. Since then she has been planting and planning a garden
for, as she puts it, 'the next hundred years'.

'I plan everything for the long term. I'm not concerned with what the garden looks
like now,' says Margaret. I cannot tell for sure what the garden will look like in a
century, but it is an attractive, if changing, infant. As Margaret doesn't know its size, I
can only say that the garden is substantial, closer to seven acres than one.

Well-designed, low withholding walls of stone and sleepers circle the big gravel
drive. Long, snaking tunnels of roses and clematis lead from the well cultivated
garden by the house into the wilder outer garden, where varied plantations of trees are
scattered through the large area. Smaller herbaceous planting fills in space at the
moment while her trees grow and mature. Margaret chiefly plans for the autumn,
winter and spring, concentrating on compositions of foliage and bark colourings to
make those times of year interesting. She particularly loves the white-barked betulas
that are dotted about in groves.

Callistemon, corkscrew hazel, *Osteospermum* 'Whirligig', tall splashes of red salvia
and puce-coloured perennial wallflowers *(Erysimum)* fill the beds around the house,
and they are bulked out with cheerful orange splays of nasturtium in summer. All of
these are held in by great numbers of railway sleepers and granite walls, which are
placed and built by Margaret. She does absolutely all the work herself.

A wide, arched pergola of golden hop *(Humulus lupulus* 'Aurelus'), Russian vine
and *Clematis tangutica*, with steps using up even more railway sleepers and crunchy
gravel, leads down to a birch walk that circles a field of lolling cattle. Mixed in with the
betulas are holly, beech, rhododendron, common elder and crinodendron, all young
but growing fast. The garden is a little wild, but Margaret likes it that way.

There are many happy plant compositions that look naturalistic and informal,
such as tall eucalyptus with purple-trumpeted potato vine *(Solanum crispum)*
threaded through them. Elsewhere eucalyptus is decorated with plum-flowered
clematis beside ruby mop-head hydrangea. Leading up to the orchard is another little
tunnel, made up of betula, lace-cap hydrangea and cherry. Oak, beech and more
eucalyptus also surround the orchard. Margaret is currently working on a plantation
of winter cherry along the driveway, another project for the distant future.

Old Connaught Avenue, Bray, County Wicklow; Tel: +01 2822273 ※ **Contact:**
Mrs Rosemary Brown ※ **Open:** May–July, by appointment to groups only ※
Entrance fee donated to charity and goes towards garden upkeep ※ **Directions:**
driving from Dublin city to Bray, turn off the M11 at the first Bray junction. Go
straight through the roundabout toward the town and approach a set of traffic lights
with a garden centre on the right. Turn right here. Go approximately 1.6km to a
Y-junction with a tree in the middle of the road. The house is to the left with green
gates. The junction is dangerous, so take care when parking.

Graigueconna has been a well-known garden for a long time. It was designed and laid
out in 1908 by Lewis Meredith, a gardener and garden writer and a relative of
Rosemary Brown. By the time Mrs Brown came to Graigueconna in the 1970s, the
garden had deteriorated along with the house, which needed considerable improvements. Initially there was precious little money to buy plants for the garden.
Consequently, as Mrs Brown began her gardening career many of the plants she
obtained came in the shape of seeds and cuttings from friends. In thirty years most of
these have grown to maturity. A once splendid garden that had degenerated into a
rough paddock is once again a beautiful place, proving in the process that bombard-
ing a garden with money is not the only way to produce a gem; a lesson particularly
relevant in these days of the exorbitant one-day makeover.

In her thirty years working at Graigueconna, Mrs Brown has put her stamp on the
garden: 'We did keep the old paths and shapes but we mostly replanted the garden,
apart from some of the original and bigger trees.' The work in the sizeable plot is all
carried out by Mrs Brown, apart from the grass cutting, which her husband
undertakes.

Arriving to the front of the house and a very pretty small garden, Mrs Brown in-
structs me lightly to 'ignore this bit because it is to be completely redone. This will all
be changed,' she says, waving her arm dismissively over a garden many would weep
for. The flowers and informal planting will be coming out in favour of a more structured garden of hebe, lavender, dwarf cistus and Lady's mantle (*Alchemilla mollis*). If
this pretty flower garden is not good enough for Mrs Brown, it bodes very well for the
garden waiting to be seen.

That garden is reached by going through a fine Georgian house and a sizeable
conservatory, brim-full of tender greenhouse inhabitants and pots of propagating
plants, lined up awaiting transplantation to the garden. Coming through the greenhouse is a good distraction because it means that when one steps into the garden
proper the first impression is almost overpowering. The long site, covering
three-and-a-half acres, is impressive in every respect.

Standing at the house looking out at the garden, the eye is drawn up along the
wide grass path that divides two deep, mixed borders. The path has its own story: 'It
was originally a railway track, on which Lewis Meredith trundled small trains and
trucks full of rocks to and from his rock garden,' explains Mrs Brown. The track was
set into a gravel path but was dismantled when the moving work was complete. The
gravel path kept sprouting weeds, so Mrs Brown decided to let them grow through it
and, with weeding and feeding, it eventually produced a well-drained grass path. The
slight camber of the original gravel path can still be seen. At the end of the path is an

old granite bird-bath rising over a circle of lime-flowering, fluffy Lady's mantle. Lying in the bird bath is the garden cat, a big white lad with black ears. The black marks point to a lack of sun lotion; I am told that white cats get sunburn, particularly on their ears.

One of the garden's borders is made up of shades of pinks and purples – rich, warm, evocative colours. Among the plants are salvia, blue cerinthe, black hollyhock, an unusual Scottish thistle that 'just turned up in the compost' and a rare *Rosa chinensis*, which flowers in single blood-red blooms for almost the whole year. Murphy and Wood Nurseries *(see* County Dublin) have been given cuttings of this, and it will soon be available to the public. The opposite border mixes yellows and golds. Swathes of golden camomile (*Anthemis tinctoria* 'EC Buxton'), Queen of the Alps (*Eryngium alpinum*) with bluey-steel-coloured stems, scutellaria, exotic-looking *Michauxia tchihaatchewii* with inside-out white flowers, and thriving abutilon vie with each other for attention. In May a white-flowering *Rosa cooperii* runs wild up an apple tree at the back of the bed and later, at the height of summer, clematis flowers through the roses, extending the flowering season and trebling the interest in one spot. Species clematis are Mrs Brown's favourites as they tend not to succumb to clematis wilt as often as large, showy, flowering hybrids.

Down past the double beds the garden changes. If the rest of the garden was enjoyable, it gave no hint of what to expect in the rockery. This is why Mr Meredith hauled the rock along his train track. He created and built it and then wrote a book entitled *Rock Gardens, How To Make and Maintain Them* (Hodges Figgis, 1908), which is based on this garden. 'The problem with the rockery, however, is that it covered one-and-a-half acres, and these days you can't keep a garden like that without a fleet of gardeners,' says Mrs Brown. So the rockery has been simplified. These days it is planted with southern-hemisphere plants and sub-shrubs or low-growing, woody plants for which she has a special regard and which grow particularly well in soft Irish conditions. A good sense of colour is apparent in the combination of red lantern-flowered crinodendron, *Photinia* 'Red Robin' and a red-budded *Osmanthus heterophyllus* 'Purpureus'.

Plants with stories are everywhere in Graigueconna, including a strange-looking, speckle-leafed *Helleborus orientalis* 'Graigueconna', named for the garden by Charles Nelson of the Botanic Gardens. Draped luxuriantly over the old rockery, a Himalayan outdoor maidenhair fern *(Adiantum capillus-veneris)* reminds Mrs Brown of the famous gardener Graham Stuart Thomas, who gave it to the garden. A dawn redwood *(Metasequoia glyptostroboides)* grows at the back of the garden. This tree was thought to be extinct and was only known to botanists through fossilised remains until a specimen was found living in China in 1941.

Mrs Brown stopped using chemicals several years ago, and as a result the number of birds, hedgehogs and other wild creatures in her garden has increased. They keep the greenflies and slugs at bay, making the garden quite an advertisement for working organically. There is no need here to resort to using old lengths of carpet as weed-suppressers or recycled Ballygowan bottles as cloches. Finally, from Rosemary Brown comes a lesson in drying a wet bumble-bee: place the wet bee in your hands and cup them together loosely for a few minutes. The warmth will dry him. Then let him out, walking him onto a dry leaf. He won't sting unless you harm him. Be brave.

GREENAN FARM MUSEUM AND MAZE

Ballinanty, Greenane, Rathdrum, County Wicklow; Tel: +0404 46000 ※ **Contact:** Jonathan or Will Wheeler ※ **Open:** May–June, Tuesday–Sunday, 10am–6pm; July–August, Monday–Sunday, 10am–6pm; September–October, Sundays, 10am–6pm; bank holiday Mondays and Easter weekend, 10am–6pm; otherwise by appointment to groups only ※ **Entrance fee** ※ Supervised children welcome; please note, dogs on leads ※ **Special features:** maze; farm implement museum; bottle museum; tearoom; souvenir shop ※ **Directions:** well signposted from Aughrim (8km) and Rathdrum (6km).

There are very few mazes in Ireland and the specimen in Greenan, covering over half an acre, is one of the prettiest. The thirteen-year-old maze, which was created by Will and Jonathan Wheeler with Lawson cypress *(Chamaecyparis lawsoniana)*, is an impressive sight and great fun. The double-pathed maze is complicated, and, although it is over-looked by a viewing platform, the escape route is not easy to make out.

In addition to the maze there are the beginnings of an arboretum at Greenan, with a handkerchief tree *(Davidia involucrata)*, silver lime *(Tilia petiolaris)*, a dawn red-wood *(Metasequoia glyptostroboides)*, snake-bark maples *(Acer rufinerve)* and plantations of oak, including holm oak *(Quercus ilex)*. A nature walk is currently being decorated by a sculpture trail, featuring works by Vincent Browne (creator of the palm tree seats in Temple Bar in Dublin), Terry Corcoran and the English sculptor Martin Constable. Attractions at Greenan also include a bottle museum, a preserved seventeenth-century farmhouse and a farm museum with a collection of horse-drawn ploughs, harrows and carts.

HILLVIEW GARDEN

Bortlemore, Kiltegan, County Wicklow; Tel: +0508 73163 ※ **Contact:** Elizabeth Jackson ※ **Open:** May–end August, Monday–Sunday, 11am–8pm ※ **Entrance fee** donated to charity ※ Supervised children welcome; please note, dogs on leads **Special features:** plants, jam and crafts for sale; groups can book teas by prior arrangement ※ **Directions:** take the second turn right off the Hacketstown–Kiltegan road. Hillview is 1.6km from Hacketstown and is well signposted.

Mrs Jackson is an enthusiastic gardener with a flair for flowers. She has been opening her garden to interested visitors for the past twenty years. It is a genuine, old-fashioned country garden covering about two acres, and she works it all herself. 'I can't let anyone else in to work it because they would root out all the good seedlings,' she says. Good gardeners are always paranoid about the treasures that an unwitting helper might destroy or throw away.

Hollyhocks fill the place and they are Mrs Kennedy's real pride and joy. Tall, sky-scraping spears in every conceivable colour, like poles of crêpe-paper flowers, are everywhere. Mrs Kennedy propagates them herself, as she does with all the plants in her garden. There are great drifts of annuals which she 'just sows from a packet'.

But the biennial hollyhocks, annual poppies and cornflowers are only a part of the garden. There is a good skeleton of permanent trees, shrubs and perennials arranged particularly well in the long beds that march the length of the plot. An example is the

LEINSTER • COUNTY WICKLOW

purple cherry tree, with tall tiger lilies growing through it. With bad eyesight one might be fooled into believing that the flame-orange flowers are borne by the tree itself. This is an effect Mrs Jackson likes and she works it wherever she can – a twisted hazel *(Corylus avellana* 'Contorta') has three-metre-high purple thalictrum and a rose campion *(Lychnis coronaria)* growing through it. Further along a copper beech is surrounded by rich gold-coloured kaffir lilies.

A reminder that the garden serves many purposes comes in the shape of two teddy-bear topiary bushes in the middle of a mixed border, which she is working on for her grandchildren. She explains that getting the ears just right is where the greatest difficulty lies. At the back of the garden are the vegetables, mulched with grit to keep in moisture and keep away weeds and slugs.

Mrs Jackson is a very friendly and knowledgeable gardener, happy to answer any amount of questions about her pleasant, classic cottage garden.

HOLMSDALE

Church Road, Greystones, County Wicklow; Tel: +01 2874270 ▪ **Contact:** Wendy and Peter Harrison ▪ **Open:** May–July, strictly by appointment only; for charity open days ▪ **Entrance fee** donated to charity and goes towards garden upkeep ▪ Supervised children welcome; please note, dogs on leads ▪ **Special features:** plant sales on open days; teas available on open days and by prior arrangement at other times ▪ **Directions:** from the Main Street in Greystones village, go 100m in the direction of Dublin and the house is on the left at the yellow junction sign before the Church Lane junction.

Holmsdale is a medium-sized town garden wrapped around a good-looking Victorian seaside villa. It is divided naturally into three distinct areas: a small front garden is linked by a carriage passage to two further gardens behind.

In the front garden a mature strawberry tree *(Arbutus unedo)* dominates the area, twisted around a big cedar. The beginnings of a collection of pittosporum, an unusual yellow *Cryptomeria japonica* 'Bandai Sugi' and a giant feather grass *(Stipa gigantea)* surround the gravel drive. This part of the garden, facing northeast, only gets morning sun, so variegated and bright foliage on many of the shrubs here brightens up the area throughout the day.

From here, the tour takes one into the side and middle garden through a little wooden gate, past a long run of tall, blue agapanthus. The garden is not big, but arranged in such a way that it constantly surprises. Mrs Harrison is too modest and says, 'It shocks rather than surprises.' In this middle garden the emphasis is on flower. Herbaceous borders are filled with early- and high-summer favourites, like aquilegia and opium poppies in every shade of plum, pink, wine and aubergine. A rampant *Rosa filipes* 'Kiftsgate' is currently taking over the outbuildings and is possibly planning world domination. Well-planted stone troughs and an old, tufa-covered shower tray decorate a little gravel garden. Deep pink *Astrantia major* 'Hadspen Blood', cyclamen, Japanese anemone and cabbage-sized pink rose look good against stone and gravel. 'That rose was sold to us as 'Constance Spry', but it's not her,' says Mr Harrison of the imposter, which he likes nevertheless.

Before reaching the main back garden more gates must be negotiated. This area is where the dogs live and the gates are there for practical reasons, but they are also pleasing aesthetically, both inviting and excluding the visitor; they arouse curiosity. At the back of the garden is a big, red tree peony *(Paeonia delavayi)*, varieties of camellia and more pittosporum. A surprise in here is a dark, ruby-leaved and flowered *Dodonaea viscosa* 'Purpurea', which is tender but, being planted in a well-sheltered area here, is doing well. The colours of a purple cut-leaf beech *(Fagus sylvatica f. purpurea* 'Rohanii') and a golden elm are gorgeous together, as is a larch with two clematis growing through it. The overriding sense in this part of the garden is of lush colour. The planting throughout is sophisticated, combining exquisite colour and texture that never clash or overpower.

HUNTER'S HOTEL

Ashford, County Wicklow; Tel: +0404 40106; Fax: +0404 40338 ✳ **Contact:** the Gelletlie family ✳ **Open**: every day, by appointment only ✳ **Directions:** from Dublin, turn left off the N11 at the Garda station in Ashford and travel 2.5km. Hunter's is on the right-hand side.

Hunter's is known to many as one of the great afternoon tea spots in the country. The garden comes upon the visitor as something of a surprise. One arrives into an ancient, unadorned courtyard and coachyard, with no evidence at all of plant life. The garden is not spotted until one passes through the hotel, emerging out into a riot of flowers and scent. The surprise is complete.

This is a very traditional country garden with a great number of creepers and climbers over the old hotel, swathes of wisteria and tiny flowered clematis knotted with sweet pea. Box beds are filled with sweet, heady patches of nicotiana and poppies. The poppies are given free rein and even allowed to grow through the box edging. This box garden is a perfect little specimen and should be inspirational to anyone with a small, square plot.

Around the lawn snakes a big bed of high summer plants and all the great border standards, like maclea, lupins and delphiniums. There are views and vistas out into the countryside in all directions, framed and marked by huge cordylines and arches. Large yew umbrellas and a little thatched gazebo overlook the River Vartry. Then, as a country garden should, it melts at the edges into native trees, hedgerow plants and the natural countryside. Sitting out in the middle of the garden, drinking in the scent and listening to the little river, one would be happy even if the tea never arrived.

KILLRUDDERY HOUSE AND GARDEN

Bray, County Wicklow; Tel: +01 2862777/2863405; Fax: +01 2862777 ✳ **Contact:** Ailbhe de Buitléar ✳ **Open:** April–September, daily, 1pm–5pm; otherwise groups by appointment only; house open May–June and September, daily, 1pm–5pm ✳ **Entrance fee** ✳ **Special features:** occasional rare plant sales, contact for details ✳ Children must be well supervised due to the ponds and canals ✳ **Special features:** tours of Killruddery House ✳ **Directions:** travelling south on the N11, take the third Bray exit, marked Greystones/Bray. Killruddery is well signposted from here.

Killruddery has been the home of the Brabazon family since 1618. The garden is unique – it is the only completely unchanged, seventeenth-century, classically

French-designed garden on the island. Its great size, austere, formal beauty and mature planting make it a singular garden that leaves a lasting impression.

The design is based on a number of large-scale features laid out along strong, geometric lines, like an illustrated lecture on seventeenth-century garden design. The twin canals measure 550-metres long. They run south from the house, framed by lines of lime trees. Like the other features, they are not too tidied or overly manicured. Behind the canals are woods, perversely called the wilderness, where the trees grow in straight, ordered, almost military lines. There is a beech-hedged pond, made up of two circles of beech, one inside the other, with a circular walk in between. The inside hedge is cut with windows through which the lily pond in the centre can be glimpsed.

A most unusual feature is the small amphitheatre, or sylvan theatre, with grass-covered seats backed by more tall beech hedging. Live performances and recitals are still held in this little place during the summer. The day I visited a quartet were practising and the music could be heard softly all around the garden.

The area called 'the angles' is the best of fun. This is a series of maze-like walks between four-and-a-half-metre-high hedges of hornbeam and lime. The walks meet at two points and radiate out from each other like an easy maze. Images of giggling aristocratic girls in ruffled skirts playing pretend hide-and-seek with their suitors come to mind, especially when music can be heard drifting across the lawn.

The rose and lavender garden is remarkable for its witty, uneven box and yew hedges, just the answer for anyone who has ever tied themselves in a knot trying and failing to get the line straight on a hedge. The box surrounds fluffy, grey, scented lavender, roses and the big fried-egg flowers of *Romneya coulteri*. This is overlooked by the recently restored *orangerie* or statue gallery, a beautiful glass structure built by Richard Turner in the 1800s. In 2000 it was completely restored and can now be viewed as part of a tour of the house. The perfume mix of tangy box, sweet rose and lavender is powerful on a warm day.

Close by is the old dairy, octagonal in shape with stained-glass windows and clothed in roses and clematis. Forget about the big house with its *orangerie* and grand rooms – I could move in to the dairy and stay forever.

KILMACURRAGH

Rathdrum, County Wicklow; Tel: +01 8374388 (National Botanic Gardens); Fax: +01 6616764 (head office, Dublin) ▪ **Contact:** Caroline Leonard or Paul Norton, Head Gardener ▪ **Open:** no restrictions – all year, all the time ▪ **No entrance fee** ▪ Dogs on leads ▪ **Special features:** historic arboretum ▪ Member of Dúchas ▪ **Directions:** situated off the N11 at Rathdrum.

Started in the 1850s, Kilmacurragh arboretum was particularly famed for its conifers. Thomas Acton planted it in conjunction with David Moore and his son Sir Frederick Moore, both of whom were curators at the National Botanic Gardens in Glasnevin, Dublin. At Kilmacurragh they planted many exotic trees which had arrived into Ireland for the first time from plant-hunting expeditions around the world. Due to the slightly milder weather and higher rainfall in Wicklow, many specimens have fared better here than their relations in Glasnevin.

For many years the garden has been neglected, but it is now in the care of Dúchas, The Heritage Service, and is undergoing a programme of slow repair and restoration.

The avenues of ghostly rhododendrons are currently being restored by a ridiculously small staff. At the moment, gardening at Kilmacurragh is more to do with the machete than the shovel and rake, as the place is painfully rescued from the strangulation of laurel and briar. However, the rewards are great. Glorious trees have been found throughout the wild garden: red-barked myrtle, podocarpus, weeping Kashmir cypress (*Cupressus* 'Cashmeriana') with silvery-fringed needles, a big pink *Magnolia campbellii* escaping over the wall from the walled garden, laurelia with aromatic leaves and self-seeding purple sycamores.

A spooky yew walk leads down to a pond that is fed by little trout-filled streams. The pond needs much work – at the moment it has young trees growing from it – but even in this state it has a great deal of charm. Its design was such that it would overflow into a decorative run-off, but it never worked. Another yew walk leads away from it and past a small, mysterious stone building.

In the front lawn grows a massive, splayed Japanese cedar (*Cryptomeria japonica*) coloured rusty-salmon from the winter cold, and a sea of snowdrops and crocuses should be seen in spring. All in all, Kilmacurragh is a charming if dilapidated garden. Its twenty-five-acre arboretum is a romantic place for a walk and there is much to be observed as the restoration work continues.

KNOCKMORE

Knockmore, Enniskerry, County Wicklow; Tel: +01 2867336; Fax: +01 2866456 ※ **Contact:** John and Rubel Ross ※ **Open:** mid-May–July and first half of September, strictly by appointment to groups only ※ **Entrance fee** ※ Supervised children are welcome ※ **Special features:** teas may be booked by prior arrangement ※ **Directions:** travelling south, leave the N11 at the turn for Enniskerry. Take the next left turn at Dargle Nursing Home. Knockmore is 400m up the hill on the left-hand side, after a very sharp right-hand turn, and sports stone pillars and black gates. *Note:* large buses cannot get through the gates.

'The Misses May lived here from 1898 until 1945, when they took what God and geography gave them and made this,' says Mr Ross, surveying his garden, which overlooks Dublin Bay. General Gerald Verney, commander of the 'Desert Rats' who fought in North Africa in the Second World War, was the next owner of Knockmore. His son Peter was a garden writer and he carried out some work on the place, but after that the garden fell into disrepair. The Rosses took over in the 1960s. John and Rubel dealt with the rot head-on and the garden is once again something the Misses May would have been proud of. This is just as well because one of the sisters is known to have threatened a haunting on future owners who failed to tend her garden.

The garden was once the site of a quarry on the Powerscourt Estate, exploited presumably to produce stone for the great Italianate extravaganza that makes up Knockmore's over-the-top neighbour. Knockmore's three acres are divided into three distinct sections: a formal area, a Robinsonian wild garden and woodland. 'Rubel is the flower person and I am the landscaper,' says Mr Ross, and thus the garden work is divided between the husband-and-wife team harmoniously.

Knockmore is a very sunny garden, built on a warm slope. The gravel garden close by the house soaks up even more rays and is full of sun-worshipping plants. Geranium and applemint knit well together in pots. *Rosa* 'New Dawn' and *Clematis* 'Étoile

Violette' climb together on the hot wall. Erodium is set into the gravel underneath a Chilean potato tree *(Solanum crispum)*, which, at only five years old, stretches six metres outwards and upwards.

One of the surprises the Rosses uncovered when they began work on the garden was a dry-stone wall bank completely overgrown with brambles. Their hard work has brought this back to its Edwardian glory. All the stone is from the quarry just beyond the cherry wood that borders the garden. Mr Ross tells me that many of the plants from the lost-and-found Edwardian bank came back spontaneously when the brambles were removed, among them aquilegias, antirrhinums and wallflowers. These give a sense of history and continuity in the garden.

The terraces are marked out by superb lavender hedging. Lavender is a native of the Mediterranean, and Irish weather is rarely warm and dry enough to sustain all of the plants in a lavender hedge. Wet weather tends to cause rot and the hedge can look uneven and gappy. At Knockmore, however, the lavender is thriving in a most un-Irish way. Stepped down from the stone terrace there are runs of *Rosa gallica* and catmint held into beds by rounded box. Next to these is the little kitchen garden, the latest addition to the garden. This is a smart affair with healthy beds of different lettuces, purple beans and fennel. The beds are all edged with alpine strawberries, mint and variegated vinca. Fennel is a great herb and a good border plant, but it has a habit of self-seeding a little too freely. Mr Ross's solution is to plant fennel after Midsummer's Day (21 June), which prevents unruly self-seeding. The double herbaceous border is classically pretty and at its best in June when blue *Campanula persicifolia*, soft grey stachys and shrub roses flower merrily. 'In here I follow the usual rule of no orange or strong yellows and everything else harmonises,' says Rubel Ross.

An unusual, half-moon-shaped sundial was 'found under a load of muck and dug out,' according to Mr Ross. It is inscribed: 'On A Quiet Day And We Being Of A Quiet Mind'. It was erected by two nieces of the Misses May in memory of a happy summer spent in the garden in 1910. Also harking back to the days of the lady gardeners is a Pekinese graveyard. When a pet died the wheelbarrow would be brought up to the veranda by the head gardener. Accompanied by the assistant gardener, two maids and the Misses May, he wheeled it, loaded with the recently departed, in procession down to the graveyard where an interment ceremony took place.

Moving out from the house, the garden begins to feel wilder and looser. Cascading ponds flow into each other and informal planting schemes surround them. An arching, rose-like shrub called *Rubus* 'Benenden' with a huge number of open white flowers and a snow drop tree *(Halesia monticola)* with white dangling flowers are very striking. The grass is allowed to grow wild on one side of the ponds and anemone, daffodils and spring bulbs spread about in a natural way.

There are an additional five acres of cherry, oak and beech wood in which Mr Ross is busy cutting paths and building bridges. The wood contains a great number of Irish sessile oak. This woodland garden was born a few years ago when Mr Ross was out one day, lost in the woods with a slash-hook. He uncovered some rock outcrops he liked the look of and, as he cleared more and more rock, the garden began to take shape. Because of the steep and tree-covered terrain, all of the work in the wood is done by hand and wheelbarrow. The rocks are tremendous in here and the path is forced to clamber around them, occasionally bridging them. In the woods is a path made for George IV, built to transport him to see the Powerscourt waterfall in 1821. Seemingly he got drunk instead and never used the path. Further along a little seat sides the path from which the Rosses were told you could once see the sea. The trees in the distance block it out, but in the winter it is just about visible.

Rubel Ross has recently written a book on the garden at Knockmore entitled *A Year in an Irish Garden* (published by A&A Farmar). I would recommend reading it before visiting this lovely place in order to fully appreciate the Rosses's addition to what God, geography and the Misses May gave them.

MOUNT USHER

Ashford, County Wicklow; Tel: +0404 40205; Fax: +0404 40205; e-mail: mount-usher.gardens@indigo.ie ※ **Contact:** Philomena O'Dowd or John Anderson ※ **Open:** mid-March–early November, daily, 10.30am–6pm ※ **Entrance fee** ※ Supervised children welcome ※ **Special features:** tearoom; craft shops; guided tours may be booked in advance; a series of specialist talks are arranged throughout the summer on a range of topics. Seats for these talks must be booked in advance. Examples from 1999's programme: 'The world of flowers at Mount Usher' and 'Eucryphia – the white knights of summer' ※ **Directions:** set within the village of Ashford, on the left-hand side if travelling south.

Mount Usher is a spectacularly beautiful garden. It covers twenty acres and is home to 5,000 different species of plants. It is a Robinsonian garden, created in the 1860s by a Dublin businessman, E Horace Walpole (*see* box, William Robinson, p.182). One of the first things to greet the visitor is the series of plaques commemorating the gardeners who have worked here and created this magnificent place. These were dedicated men who gave almost half a century of service each to the garden.

George Burns 50 years of dedicated service 1921–1971,
(Mr Burns also has an elegant *Cornus controversa* planted to his memory)
Charles Fox 45 years as head gardener,
Michael Giffney 44 years as gardener,
Miles 'Miley' Manning 40 years.

The shaded and sheltered winding paths mean that it is easy to get happily lost in Mount Usher. Indeed, the map given to visitors at the gate is frankly of no use at all, so you are better off just roaming freely. The River Vartry is the main artery of the garden, with weirs, bridges and waterfalls spread out along its length; it is the soul of the place. The views from the suspension bridge are beautiful, although it bounces as you cross it, which makes for a very strange sensation. Obey the sign: 'Bouncing on the bridge will damage it. Please do not jump.' For this reason, as well as for the dangers posed by the river, watch children vigilantly.

All the paths lead back and forward to the river, taking in huge varieties of wonderful plants and impressive views along the way. There are so many marvellous and handsome arrangements in Mount Usher that it requires several visits to take it all in. Two-metre-tall Himalayan giant lilies (*Cardiocrinum giganteum*) set in under the trees shine like a vision from out of the shade. Spring meadows sprinkled with thousands of crocuses and miniature daffodils run gently into groves of azalea and other early-flowering shrubs. Layering is what best describes the planting in Mount Usher. Compositions of trees and shrubs spread out from every point, complementing each other in ways that look completely natural.

The collection includes stunning trees, such as *Nothofagus moorei* (Sir Frederick

Moore, the curator of the National Botanic Gardens in Dublin assisted Mr Walpole in the early days of the garden), *Osmanthus burkwoodii*, *Eucryphia nymansensis* 'Mount Usher', one of the largest New Zealand red beech trees in Ireland and innumerable other great trees range through the garden. The whole collection is in the process of being catalogued for serious students.

Mount Usher is a hugely popular garden, so if you are really interested in enjoying it to the full go early in the week rather than at weekends. A leaflet detailing the seasonal highlights can be obtained from the reception.

NATIONAL GARDEN EXHIBITION CENTRE

Kilquade, County Wicklow; Tel: +01 2819890; Fax: +01 2810359 ▪ **Contact:** Tim or Suzanne Wallis ▪ **Open:** all year, Monday–Saturday, 10am–6pm, Sunday 1pm–6pm ▪ **Entrance fee** ▪ **Special features:** tearoom; nursery; garden shop ▪ **Directions:** signposted along the N11 if you're travelling from Dublin.

For the growing number of people with small gardens, it can be hard to imagine scaled-down versions of Powerscourt and Killruddery. For this dilemma, the National Exhibition Centre is just the place to visit for ideas and inspiration. It is also a convenient place to study the work of a range of garden designers should you wish to employ one.

It started out in 1993 when Tim and Suzanne decided they needed something more exciting to engage them than their existing wholesale plant nursery. This is certainly more exciting. It is a fount of ideas, styles and designs. At any one time there are nineteen gardens on display in Kilquade. They represent the work of nineteen designers as well as a number of artists, craftsmen and stockists of hard landscaping materials, such as pebbles, aggregates, stone and concrete paving.

A number of the gardens at Kilquade are replaced each year, so there is a rolling selection of designs to be seen and studied. The plants and plans are well labelled and explained in each garden, and full details are available on all the craftspeople and artists who have worked on them. I particularly loved the budget garden, with its interesting stone- and pebble-edged lawn by Richard Joyce, and the cool, contemplative green garden by Verney Naylor.

8 NEW RUSSIAN VILLAGE

8 New Russian Village, Kilquade, County Wicklow; Tel: +01 2810285; e-mail: dkehoe@eircom.net ▪ **Contact:** Dr Dermot Kehoe ▪ **Open:** mid-June–end July, by appointment only to groups ▪ **Entrance fee** donated to various charities and goes towards garden upkeep ▪ Supervised children welcome; please note, dogs on leads ▪ **Special features:** refreshments can be obtained nearby at the National Garden Exhibition Centre ▪ **Directions:** travelling south on the N11, turn left toward Kilquade at the Kilquade/Kilpedder crossroads. Travel for 300m in the direction of the National Garden Exhibition Centre. Turn left into New Russian Village. The house is fourth on the left.

Dr Dermot Kehoe is a well-known name to readers of the *Irish Garden* magazine, to which he contributes a regular garden diary. He also contributes to the journals of the

Hardy Plant Society (*see* appendices) and the Alpine Garden Society (*see* appendices). Avid garden visitors may also know his old garden in Bray.

Two years ago, Dr Kehoe began a new garden at the romantically named New Russian Village (named for its proximity to a group of houses designed by a Russian *émigré* architect). In that time the three-quarter-acre garden has been transformed into a handsome laboratory for the Kehoe plant collection. 'The garden is really about plants rather than design. I suppose I could be called a plant collector. I grow a large collection of plants, even for Ireland,' says Dr Kehoe, with no exaggeration. Herbaceous and alpine plants are his favourites and the garden is jam-packed and gorgeous.

He grows many plants not usually seen in gardens, and visitors will enjoy specimens like tall, spiked *Echium boisseri*, which stands proud of its neighbours in the large bed at the front of the house, almost putting the pretty pink bells of a neighbouring incarvillea in the shade. One gets more than a feeling of a trip around the world looking at exotics like *Seseli gummiferum*, which came from seed gathered on the rim of a volcano in Ecuador by Carl Dacus (*see* appendices). Incidentally, the English garden writer Anna Pavord named this as one of her favourite plants. Beside it is a vicious, thorny *Vallea stipularis* from Mexico, while *Dunalia australis*, a member of the potato family with a delicate blue flower and little egg-shaped seed heads, sits next door. Dermot does all the work in the garden himself, putting in about twenty hours a week to keep the place impeccably maintained. This is more than a tidy collection of plants though. I found it a pretty, pleasurable garden to walk around. While he makes no claim to design talents, the layout is attractive in an unshowy way.

The first thing to be seen in the back garden is a run of very good turf sloping uphill from the house, with a well-made stairs of wooden sleepers set directly into manicured grass. The centrepiece of the garden is an absolutely gorgeous double border that runs the length of the plot, finishing on a well-placed gap in the boundary that looks out on a hillside field of suitably attractive ponies. The double border can be seen from the house, but is properly enjoyed by climbing up a set of steps and under a honeysuckle arch. The two borders are deep, at about three metres each, and getting wider each season; the bamboo canes were out to mark a fresh expansion when I visited at the beginning of September. Tall teasel seed heads rise high above the white phlox, competing with huge, sky-trained white hollyhocks for the tallest-in-the-border prize. I loved the combination of purple-flowered artichokes and verbena, first rate *Monarda* 'Blue Stocking' and gone-over but still interesting veratrum with creamy, forked flower spikes. The tangy scent of *Nepeta grandiflora* curls along the bottom of the border through soft, pink coneflowers (*Echinacea*) and *Digitalis mertonensis* with deep pink-purple flowers. One of the rarer plants in this bed is a beauty called *Amica zygomeris* from Mexico, with a paddle-shaped leaf, pea-like yellow flowers and unusual pinkish stipules or little bracts along the stem. This is usually a greenhouse plant, but in Dr Kehoe's garden it overwinters successfully.

On the other side of the border he has combined wine-coloured scabious, sea kale and heuchera beside floaty white gypsophila. Here too there are echiums – a running theme in the garden. Along with varieties of digitalis, he uses these tall, stately flowers widely. By the boundary wall a young *Acacia baileyana* 'Purpurea' shelters alongside more exotic, big-leafed echiums and opium poppies. Further along the wall, a canopy of buddleia leads into the 'woodland walk' – not an actual wood but a pleasant, shady place. Dr Kehoe plants this little area up with hellebores, more digitalis and epimedium, rodgersia and meconopsis. This area is usually quite dry and as such hostile to these shade- and damp-lovers, so the damp conditions they love are provided by a dripping-hose watering system. Japanese painted fern, bizarre-looking arisaema and giant lilies (*Cardiocrinum giganteum*) grow in here in small numbers. 'In their natural home the giant lilies would be at least two foot taller [half a metre] but I still love growing them,' explains Dermot, happy to put in the effort that keeps these fussies happy out of their natural habitat. This woodland walk runs around the back of the garden, looking out on the fields and leading to the top of the garden from where a slope of lawn leads down to the double border. The interesting aspect of the garden is that this considerable slope only becomes apparent from this point. Dermot brought in no less than thirty tonnes of topsoil to produce a sort of plateau for the double beds.

A big poppy bed with cardoons (*Cynara cardunculus*) and grasses leads back by the lawn toward the greenhouse. Inside there are smartly laid out pots of the lovely, grotesque, black-flowering *Salvia discolor* and purest blue plumbago. The fleeting beauty Morning Glory (*Ipomoea*) is another treat in the greenhouse. It is a plant to keep a keen eye on as its flowers live for one day only from bud to drop-off.

Close to the house and patio is a new bed made up of special plants like Chinese foxglove (*Rehmannia elata*), with pretty, slipper-like, pink flowers and a salmon-coloured agastache, vivid royal blue *Salvia patens* and *Codonopsis lanceolata* with fat-flowered creamy bells. Yet another digitalis, this time *Digitalis ciliata* with sharp leaves, found its way into the bed. I love the way the rarer and more special plants have been slotted in easily beside more humble cousins. There is no sense of mollycoddling or pampering even for the VIPs in Dr Kehoe's garden, and indeed anything that doesn't mind itself after one season of special care receives short shrift. I like his style and love his garden.

NUN'S CROSS SCHOOL GARDEN

Killiskey, Ashford, County Wicklow; Tel: +0404 40700 ■ **Contact:** Stephanie McDonald (Principal) ■ **Open:** for one day a year as part of the Wicklow Gardens Festival; contact the festival office or the school for annual dates ■ **Entrance fee** goes to school upkeep ■ **Directions:** travelling south on the N11, turn right for Glendalough at the roundabout on the edge of Ashford village. After 300m take the left fork. After 1.5km take the right fork. The school is on the right, just beyond Killiskey Church.

The small garden at Nun's Cross school should be a compulsory visit for parents, teachers and anyone with anything to do with children. This is a modest but inspiring experiment in gardening with children that many, many schools could consider. Granted, Nun's Cross school is lucky to be surrounded by an area of almost three acres in the Wicklow countryside, but even a town school with a plot of four or five square metres could provide children with a fun, educational and interesting garden.

With the encouragement of Principal Stephanie McDonald, one of the parents, Wendy Nairn, has been working with the children to create a series of gardens in the grounds of the small school. Beds of huge pumpkins, sunflowers and runner beans ripen over the summer, waiting for the children to return at the end of August. Salad crops and early potatoes provide the focus for early-summer class projects. The pumpkins will be used for Hallowe'en. Sweetcorn is another crop that does well, ready for harvesting when the children return to class in the autumn. The herb beds smell of mint, rosemary, sage and oregano. Flowerbeds, fruiting hazel, betulas and ash trees decorate the boundaries.

A pretty bog garden and pond is alive with water boatmen and frogs, and even a newt has been spotted. The insect bed next door provides a home to every sort of bug, butterfly and crawly. This bed, not surprisingly, is the undisputed favourite among the children.

The project works well, with each class taking care of its own bed. As an example, the junior infants grow runner beans because five- and six-year-olds can handle big bean seeds easily in little fingers. The garden is run along the best organic principles, so compost heaps take care of all lunch leftovers. This teaches the children about the magic science that transforms messy banana skins and apple cores into lovely, black plant food. The final feature, an igloo made from living willows, forms the centrepiece of the playground. This is an inventive and practical project and really is the sort of facility that should be available to all children, particularly in towns and cities.

PARNELL MEMORIAL PARK

Rathdrum, County Wicklow; Tel: +0404 46262 ■ **Contact:** Mary Byrne ■ **Open:** all year ■ **No entrance fee** ■ **Directions:** located in Rathdrum village.

A small, landscaped public park located in the centre of Rathdrum, Parnell Memorial Park was opened in 1991 to commemorate the death of Charles Stuart Parnell. Lawns, some trees and a pond fed by small streams make up the body of the garden, and at its centre is a life-sized bronze statue of Parnell by Wicklow artist Fred Conlon.

PET CEMETERIES

Cemeteries for family pets are a fairly regular, if quirky, feature in older gardens. They are largely a Victorian and Edwardian phenomenon. In the grandest versions, pekes and pugs and the choicer sort of terrier are buried beside the family (albeit outside the sanctified ground of the family plot). An example of this is to be seen in the grounds of Kilkenny Castle, where Sandy, the companion of Elizabeth the nineteenth Marchioness, is buried near his mistress. He also had his portrait painted with her and it can be seen hanging in the Long Gallery of the castle alongside his Lady.

The more usual cemetery is a small collection of headstones found under a grove of trees on the edge of a country garden. These little places bear witness to the huge affection of gardeners for their canine, feline, avian and sometimes aquatic friends.

Some gardens with pet cemeteries include:
   Airfield, County Dublin
   Kilkenny Castle Park, Kilkenny city
   Knockmore, County Wicklow
   Powerscourt, County Wicklow
   Carrigglass Manor, County Longford
   Castle Ward, County Down
   Glanleam, County Kerry
   Camas Park, County Tipperary

Enniskerry, County Wicklow; Tel: +01 2046000; Fax: +01 2863561 ▪ **Contact:** the Manager ▪ **Open:** 9.30am–5.30pm daily, apart from 25 and 26 December, check for earlier closing times during winter ▪ **Entrance fee** ▪ **Special features:** children's play area (admission free to children under five); garden centre; Irish crafts shop; Fitzer's restaurant with terrace seating; multi-media exhibition describing the history of the house ▪ **Directions:** the gates to Powerscourt are a few hundred metres outside the village of Enniskerry, on the road to Roundwood.

Powerscourt is one of the great gardens of Europe, as well as one of the best-known and most visited gardens in the country. The eighteenth-century mansion and formal grounds were commissioned by Sir Richard Wingfield, whose descendants remained at Powerscourt for over 350 years. Set in the foothills of the Wicklow Mountains, it includes forty-five acres of formal gardens, sweeping and stepped lawns, flower gardens, lengthy herbaceous borders and woodland walks. Added to these are the walled garden, statuary, follies, rambling trails, a monkey puzzle avenue, ornamental lakes and great variety of plants. There is also the largest pet cemetery in Europe and an arboretum. One day may just not be enough time to see it all!

For all its splendours, there is one feature that no one who has visited Powerscourt ever forgets, and that is the Italian garden. Designed by Daniel Robertson in the middle of the nineteenth century and resembling an Irish version of Versailles, it took 100 men twelve years to complete. Flamboyant terraces filled with bronze and stone statues, among them *Apollo* and *Diana*, assorted cherubs and strange creatures, spread out like a gigantic stage set. The spectacle looks down over Triton's Lake, complete with a fountain modestly based on the waterworks in the Piazza Barberini in

Rome. Beyond the water are mature woods and the perfectly placed Sugar Loaf Mountain in the distance. It's wonderful stuff and shouts to the visitor: do not try this at home.

Robertson's original design was only partially carried out as his benefactor, Viscount Powerscourt, died while on an artefact-collecting trip in Italy. The work was continued by his son in a modified way, and the result is one of the most lavish gardens in the world.

One of the two famous winged horses that lead to Triton's Lake in the Italian garden at Powerscourt, County Wicklow. These zinc statues were featured in the coat of arms of Richard Wingfield.

RATHSALLAGH HOUSE

Dunlavin, County Wicklow; Tel: +045 403112 ✳ **Open:** every day, by appointment only ✳ **Directions:** on the N7 from Dublin, the hotel is signposted in Dunlavin village.

Rathsallagh is set on a 500-acre estate, including sweeping parkland and gardens. It includes mature woodland and specimen trees, including giant sequoias, tulip trees and a walled garden.

ROSEMOUNT

Enniskerry, County Wicklow; Tel: +01 2863568 ✳ **Contact:** John and Mary O'Reilly ✳ **Open:** May–July, by appointment only ✳ **Entrance fee** donated to charity and goes towards garden upkeep ✳ Supervised children welcome ✳ **Directions:** in Enniskerry village, facing the hill that leads up towards Powerscourt. Look for a green, double-fronted Georgian house on the left-hand side behind wrought-iron railings.

Mary O'Reilly's garden is hard to miss. The well-maintained Georgian house stands a little way back from the street, fronted by an intriguing modern garden – an eye-catcher in a village known for its good looks. This front garden is cleverly laid out in a minimalist fashion, with squares of gravel, beds of herbs, almost comical *Allium schubertii*, with a flower nearly 30cm across, and silver-leaved Mediterranean plants that make it seem like the sun is shining. Bay corkscrews and decorative stone balls on sticks add height and wit to the picture, while reinforced steel is a smarter class of plant support than bamboo or pea-sticks. The herbs used are borage, parsley and curry plants. It's quirky and stylish.

The O'Reillys moved into the house in 1958. 'The garden was started from a disaster area,' says Mary. 'It had to be taken from scratch.' She began by building stone walls and she continues to build them to this day, using only stone found in the garden. The stone is a unifying feature, drawing everything together. It is used to hold back beds and create raised planting areas, steps, walls and little folly-like structures. One of these is a warm, sunny snug created from an old stone wc, clambered up by a fine actinidia and roofed by a dripping wisteria. It gets the last of the evening sun and is, as was no doubt intended, a good place to sit.

Moving into the larger garden behind the house, which is wrapped around with old outbuildings and stone walls, the visitor is greeted by two Rupert Till wirework geese (*see* Garden Accessories, p.166). They stand on the lawn beside an extraordinary rusting iron ostrich made in Zimbabwe and bought in Mackey's (*see* Nurseries and Garden Centres, County Dublin). Together these decorate a long rectangle of turf better than an overstuffed island bed ever could. As well as her considerable talent for building stone walls, Mary produces trained shrubs. Lines of spindle-thin, finely shaped, corkscrewed holly, bay and box plants in the process of being worked are an education in the craft.

A well-made set of steps doubling as a fernery leads up to an old rockery, which dates from an earlier Victorian garden. The O'Reillys began clearing this area in 1999, with no idea of what was under the rubbish. As it was uncovered, new possibilities for the garden opened up. 'This is what we now gloriously call "the wood",' says Mary from the top of the steps, looking up through the rocks and trunks of mature trees stretched out ahead. The village is only a stone's throw away, but we could be lost in a forest. This is a great secluded spring area, filled with birdsong. On the ground, bulbs, like winter aconites, snowdrops, bluebells, anemone and daffodils, all flower under bare branches. Among the beech trees is the shiny, peeling copper bark of a paper-bark maple (*Acer griseum*). This was bought in Gillespies' Nursery in Newtownards, a place Mrs O'Reilly recommends highly (*see* County Down). The satiny, metallic trunk demands to be stroked.

There was a garden on this spot going back to the 1800s, and when Mary joined the ICA in Enniskerry she managed to locate the daughter of one of its old gardeners. Being able to tie in even part of an old garden's history is a great satisfaction for gardeners. The O'Reillys are doing their bit to safeguard Rosemount's future by building up an interesting collection of trees. The stars include a tulip tree (*Liriodendron tulipifera*), eucalyptus, a fitzroya grown from a cutting, acacia, strawberry trees and several varieties of oak, grown from acorns that were a present from Arnold Arboretum in Chicago. 'We have been waiting for the tulip tree to flower for twenty-five years. I think we'll have a party when it eventually obliges.' Mary should not need to wait much longer as they tend to begin flowering between twenty-five to thirty years after planting. As for the fitzroya, it is a tree for posterity, which can live up to 3,000 years.

A Tupelo tree (*Nyssa sylvatica*), which stands in the middle of the wood, marks the first frost with a display of brilliant red and orange leaves, and a number of eucryphia varieties explode into white bloom in obliging succession. The final treat is a collection of young rhododendrons, gifts from a friend with a great talent for propagating but constrained by a tiny garden – would that we all had such friends!

ROSSANAGH

Ashford, County Wicklow; Tel: +0404 40168 ▪ **Contact:** Mrs P Butler ▪ **Open:** during the Wicklow Gardens Festival; groups welcome by appointment only ▪ Supervised children welcome ▪ **Directions:** driving south on the N11, turn left at the Garda station in Ashford village. Follow this road to Hunter's Hotel. At the T-junction in front of the hotel turn right. The house and garden are through the second gate on the right-hand side.

Rossanagh was built in the eighteenth century as a dower house for a larger house nearby. At the end of the nineteenth century a garden was laid out around the house and filled with rhododendrons and azaleas. Today those mature rhododendrons provide a colourful backdrop for Mrs Butler's more recent garden, which she has been working with her son Pat since the early 1990s. The garden is sympathetic to both the house and its wider surroundings. It is a relaxing, pretty garden with several distinct areas that link easily together.

Close by the house Mrs Butler has put in an uncluttered, restrained and formal white garden made up of lines of standard 'Iceberg' roses, enhanced by white-trumpet-flowered datura and white lilies in pots. The lilies are encouraged to flower for a greater length of time through the summer with regular feeds of tomato food. The plants in the beds include helichrysum, Paris daisies, phlox and white lavender. Runs of grey-blue catmint and blue lavender scent the entrance to the garden and get the visit off to a perfect start.

Next door to the white garden is the courtyard, with walls completely covered by a huge fig tree with plenty of fruit, *Rosa* 'Rambling Rector' running wild and tonnes of blue, star-flowered *Solanum crispum* 'Glasnevin'. With its ripening fruit, the gorgeous scent of creamy roses and an entrancing shade of blue, this wall conjures up all of my favourite garden images. Leading away from the house are the old runs of azalea and rhododendron, eucalyptus and magnolia. The eucalyptus, with its pale peeling bark, is particularly lovely.

One romantic specimen of camellia in the garden gave Mrs Butler a good deal of pleasure when she found that she could date its age to over 100 years old. An elderly neighbour told her that she could remember the shrub well from a time when she rode over to visit the house as a young child, and it was already a huge tree.

A new avenue of lime trees leading down to the River Vartry is the most recent project in the garden. As it grows it gives the Butlers plenty of pleasure and it will provide the future garden, and posterity, with a fine feature to add to the rhododendron and camellia.

ST JOSEPH'S

Old Connaught Avenue, Bray, County Wicklow; Tel: +01 2821585 ■ **Contact:** Maura Sheahan ■ **Open:** 5 May–2 September, Saturday, Sunday and Monday, 12–6pm; other times by appointment only ■ **Entrance fee** ■ Supervised children welcome ■ **Directions:** driving from Dublin city to Bray, turn off the M11 at the first Bray junction. Go straight through a roundabout towards the town and approach a set of traffic lights with a garden centre on the right. Turn right here. Go approximately 1.6km to a Y-junction with a tree in the middle of the road. The modern house is on the right. Be careful, as the junction is dangerous.

This is a new garden attached to a modern house. It started out as a wood on the Old Conna demesne and had never been cultivated when the Sheahans arrived to begin work in 1990. Maura Sheahan designed, built and works the garden herself. It is a bold garden, filled to brimming with blooms. Red sunflowers, pink hydrangeas, tall frilled astrantia and a hundred other flowers compete for attention at every turn.

To enter the front garden at the height of summer is to arrive into the middle of a flower-fest of roses, barely held in by lavender hedges; a party of scent and colour. Even the wheelbarrows get pulled into service – Mrs Sheahan plants them up with annuals like aubrieta and nasturtium and moves the barrows to wherever colour is required in the garden, sort of like an emergency supply of flowers.

In the second garden, behind the house, the action continues apace with white everlasting sweet pea climbing high up into the trees and tall flowering echiums, heavy with bumble-bees. A patrol of ducks wanders through the beds, clearing up slugs. Maura Sheahan is not alone among gardeners in swearing by ducks for a slug-free garden. Ducks also look prettier than blue pellets, saucers of beer, crunched-up eggshells or any other other slug-fighters. And, of course, duck eggs are a bonus.

There is a fine white garden here, but Mrs Sheahan keeps it small as she feels you can have too much white in a garden. She has limited herself to using only really good white blooms, like galtonia, *Pittosporum tenuifolium* 'Irene Paterson', lilies, *Chrysanthemum maximum*, veronica, azara and *Rosa* 'Albéric Barbier', a rambler with creamy-white flowers shot through with the tiniest hint of pink.

Because Mrs Sheahan works the one-acre garden by herself, she puts up with no nonsense from it. A three-tiered fountain that wasn't pulling its weight as a water feature was turned into a three-tiered blue 'fountain' of lobelia and violets. 'I had so much trouble with it flooding the surrounding ground, it got to the stage where I couldn't bear to look at it any more, so I dumped the water and planted it up with annuals. Now I think they're a waste of time. Next year I'll try small perennials.' This is a busy garden, worked by a charming, no-nonsense woman and her slug-busting ducks.

SHEKINA SCULPTURE GARDEN

Kirikree, Glenmalure, County Wicklow; Tel: +0404 46128 /2838711 ▪ **Contact:** Catherine McCann ▪ **Open:** for a number of days each year as part of the Wicklow Gardens Festival; contact the festival office or the garden for annual dates; at other times, groups welcome by appointment only ▪ **Entrance fee** donated to Trócaire ▪ Supervised children welcome ▪ **Special features:** teas may be booked by prior arrangement; picnics encouraged ▪ Member of Dúchas ▪ **Directions:** travelling from Laragh, turn left at Glenmalure at the hotel and bar. Continue on for 4km. The garden is on the right, situated on a dangerous bend and marked by a green wall.

Owned and worked by Catherine McCann, Shekina is quite unique among gardens in Ireland. Set in the middle of the beautiful Glenmalure valley, it was created as a place of inspiration and reflection. The word Shekina is Hebrew, meaning 'the presence of God in a place', and there is a definite atmosphere of calm and peace in Catherine's tranquil sculpture garden.

Covering only one acre, Shekina is made up of impressively maintained greenery – beautiful lawn that bounces underfoot, surrounded by evergreen and deciduous trees and shrubs in every shade of green, moss, olive, lime, grey, purple and gold. Steps edged with little bands of cotoneaster connect different levels, patios and platforms. A lily pond, edged with shiny vinca leaves and small ferns, sits under a bank of purple acer, hypericum and wine-leaved berberis. There are two ponds and a fern and ivy-trimmed stream runs through the garden and out into the River Avonbeg. Between these, the whole place is filled with the sound of moving water.

The plants are only part of Shekina. The central feature of the garden is the collection of twelve sculptures. Catherine began to collect art for her garden in the mid-1980s, and each piece she has acquired reflects her interest in God and creation. The Shekina collection includes work by Irish and Irish-based sculptors, such as the late Alexandra Wejchert, one of the finest artists to have worked in this country over the past half century. Her *Eternal Flame*, made from gleaming stainless steel, reflects the leaves of rhododendron and ferns in its slim wave of metal. Other works include Fred Conlon's solid granite loops and circles, and a powerful piece cast in bronze by Imogen Stuart, based on a study of linked hands. Paul Page's remarkable wrought-iron screen, depicting the sun, moon, stars, clouds, rain, earth, fire and water, is reason enough to visit the garden. Each of the sculptures is given its own complete space, and each individual area is small in scale, so it is possible to feel quiet and secluded even when there are a good number of visitors in the garden. There are benches and seats set everywhere around. I lost count at twelve sitting places, including a rose-clad summerhouse.

If you'd like to find out more about this beautiful garden, Catherine McCann has written a book entitled *Time Out in Shekina*, in which the symbolism attached to the sculptures in her garden is explored. The book is available to buy from the garden or by post.

STYLE BAWN HOUSE

Delgany, County Wicklow; Tel: +01 2874969 ▪ **Contact:** Susan and John Gaisford St Lawrence ▪ **Open:** May–June, by appointment only; annual open weekends, ring for dates ▪ **Entrance fee** donated to Delgany's bid for the Tidy Towns Competition ▪ **Special features:** plant sales on open days; teas by can be booked by prior arrangement ▪ **Directions:** situated in Delgany village, opposite the Delgany Inn.

Style Bawn House was built in 1773 as a coach house. As with many of its neighbours in the quaint village of Delgany it is a picturesque house, and, along with its three-acre garden, it could form the backdrop for an EM Forster novel – very Edwardian, very pretty and very well maintained.

The garden falls down a hilly site to a tiny river below. Around the house are masses of wall shrubs and climbers, cordyline and pittosporum, a good clutter of mop-head and lace-cap hydrangeas and a wisteria completely gnarled around a pole. From here the garden begins to slope slightly. A few steps descend past a rockbed of alpine strawberries, pinks and geraniums to a patio, a fine cherry tree and a clipped bay.

Only on getting down to this level does it becomes apparent that that was not the garden, but a mere taster. The real garden begins here, marked by a small stone - *Aphrodite* chained to her rock. Leaving her behind, a set of cobbled steps descends past cotoneaster and agapanthus to a smart lily pond from where the extent of the garden can be seen properly.

The path leads past a low-growing run of cut-leaf acers and down further to the rushing Three Trout Stream. The stream is planted up in spots with gunnera, iris and willow, but elsewhere is left to cut cleanly into the turf in a wide, straight run, so the sweet chestnuts, crinodendron and other fine trees beyond can be seen to full effect. Crossing the bridge and walking along the bank, you come to a little bench under a beech tree. From here you can admire the views back by the stream and uphill to the rest of the garden. A family of ducks obliges by slipping, as if on cue, into the water.

Crossing the stream again the path continues back toward the house, through a smartly run traditional vegetable and fruit garden tied in with box hedges. The lines of French beans, leeks and onions lead in the direction of a more relaxed and loose herbaceous border set just below the house, which seems to be perched on top of the garden. The flowerbeds are full of great garden plants, like goat's rue, phlox, geranium, fennel, lilies, day lilies and verbascum, finishing off the visit to Style Bawn in a flourish of scent and flower.

TINAKILLY HOUSE

Rathnew, County Wicklow; Tel: +0404 69274; Fax: +0404 67806; e-mail: wpower@tinakilly.ie; website: www.tinakilly.ie ▪ **Contact:** Reception ▪ **Open:** every day, by appointment only ▪ **Entrance fee** donated to the Irish Wheelchair

Association ▪ Supervised children welcome ▪ **Directions:** take the N11 south to Rathnew. Tinakilly House is 500m outside the village on the road towards Wicklow town (R750).

Tinakilly House is an imposing, double-fronted Victorian country house that stands on a height above a lovely garden, overlooking the Irish Sea. The location is truly wonderful and the gardens well merit their blessed home. The house was built in the mid-1800s of local Wicklow granite and stands on seven acres of terraced lawns, mature trees, good mixed beds, water features and an extensive surrounding herb garden. The terraced lawns are joined together by runs of well-weathered granite steps softened by pale, washy-pink roses and sentries of *Crinodendron hookerianum*, the pretty lantern tree, with rich plum-pink dangling flowers.

The run of lawn at the foot of these stone steps is softened and bordered by big beds of shrubs and trees, including lovely specimens of white-flowered strawberry trees (*Arbutus unedo*) and a young sequioadendron. Along by the biggest bed, the path leads into the quaintly named Badger's Walk – a snug, sheltered spot, shaded and coloured by Spanish chestnut (*Castanea sativa*), the slim New Zealand cabbage palm (*Cordyline australis*) and an elegant silver birch that casts only the lightest of shade. I would envy the badger with a sett among these beauties.

Following the Badger's Walk leads you back up to the main drive and past a big cedar of Lebanon (*Cedrus libani*). Crossing the drive you next come upon the Beech Cathedral, a lovely woodland garden with a great circle of tall beech trees, which are reminiscent of the huge pillars of a great church.

Emerging from the woods, the way leads out to the sun, past the wisteria-clad house and formal, diamond-shaped fountain and pool. Continuing on to the other side of the house is the octagonal garden, a confection of herb beds used by the chefs for the restaurant. A working garden, this is nevertheless a very pretty area, coloured by purple chive flowers, orange marigolds and nasturtiums and scented by rosemary, thyme and woolly sage. There is something deeply appetising in seeing someone in a chef's whites filling a basket with herbs for the table, and anyone who cooks knows there is little to beat a meal made with produce picked fresh from the garden. This whole area is surrounded by a big lawn, partially enclosed by beech hedging, beech trees and Douglas firs (*Pseudotsuga menziesii*). Beyond this garden are the views of the sea and another secluded walk among more groves of lime, beech and Douglas fir. This is called the Fox's Path and it looks across the garden at the Badger's Walk.

The soil at Tinakilly is largely acid and so perfect for plants like the crinodendrons and acacias which are planted as specimens at various points around the garden.

Tinakilly House takes part in the annual Wicklow Gardens Festival and apart from opening its gates to the visiting public, the hotel hosts tours of the herb garden and an accompanying herb luncheon. Contact the hotel in early spring for the annual dates as numbers for the luncheon are strictly limited.

VALCLUSA

Waterfall Road, Enniskerry, County Wicklow; Tel: +01 2869485/087 4129608; Fax: +01 2861877 ▪ **Contact:** Duncan Forsythe ▪ **Open:** Easter–end September, Saturdays, Sundays and bank holidays, 10am–6pm; other days by appointment only ▪ **Entrance fee** donated to Camphill Community ▪ Supervised children welcome ▪ **Special features:** nursery with unusual plants for sale ▪ **Directions:** travel south along the N11 to Kilmacanogue Post Office and take the right turn here. This leads onto the Glendalough Road. Continue along it to the right fork for Enniskerry. Follow the signs for Powerscourt Waterfall. Valclusa is the last house on the left before the entrance to the waterfall.

The garden at Valclusa is over 160 years old, with the most wonderful views of the Powerscourt Waterfall and the Wicklow Mountains. It is a hillside garden, not easy to get around but worth the clamber.

Duncan Forsythe has been gardening on the site since the mid-1980s when he commenced the rescue of the garden, which was almost overgrown. He has since created a romantic grove with trees, covered alleys and stony, mossy paths edged with ferns and Solomon's seal. Streams interlace through the garden like spiderwebs, and are bridged by the tiniest bridges. Mr Forsythe had the tools out the day I visited to clear leaves from a small waterfall that was not running to his satisfaction.

The garden is situated 151 metres above sea level. Wet, mild and sheltered, it can accommodate a great collection of plants, including giant redwood *(Sequoiadendron giganteum)*, Chilean fire bush *(Embothrium coccineum)*, an extensive collection of unusual perennials, with over 100 varieties of geranium alone, and ornamental grasses. A huge, fourteen-metre-high Bentham's dogwood *(Cornus capitata)* dominates the driveway in front of the house. Mr Forsythe is proud of his sequioadendron, one of the first to be introduced into the country. It was planted in 1856, only three years after the first specimens were brought to England from America. John Anderson of Mount Usher recently measured it to be 6.6m at the girth and 42.4m high. Planted two years after the first tree in Glasnevin, the Valclusa tree is much bigger because of the extra rain enjoyed up here in the hills. Another impressive skyscraper is a thirty-six-metre-high eucalyptus nearby.

Valclusa is quite a wild garden; I felt I might be the first person to walk down some of the paths. Sometimes it's necessary to bend right down to pass under beautiful myrtles with fine orange-peeling bark and little white flowers. The garden changes dramatically with each season. In spring the carpets of early flowers and bulbs bloom in the open, before leaves appear on the trees and transform much of the garden into a snug, dark and secret place in the summer and autumn.

Mr Forsythe is a believer in working with what he has. His soil is not very fertile, but he doesn't try to improve it by bringing in huge amounts of organic matter to bulk it up or add nutrients. Instead, and more intelligently, he grows plants that don't need too much fertility; plants that enjoy the natural conditions in his garden, like his hardy geraniums and *Rosa rugosa* 'Scabrosa', which doesn't need feed or much water. This is a very green attitude, but not one likely to catch on with many other gardeners. He loves tender, scented rhododendrons and they grow well on his site, as does a lovely mimiosa *(Acacia dealbata)* from Australia with fine, thread-like leaves. The garden attracted thirty-five different types of butterfly in the summer of 1999; hebe is grown to tempt them. In many ways there is as much to interest the naturalist as the gardener in this garden.

At the very top of the site, a good climb up, is a new garden, which was put in only nine years ago. This is more open and sunnier than the garden below it. With a bench perched invitingly at the top of the butterfly-filled wildflower area, the beautiful view of Powerscourt Waterfall is the climber's well-earned reward.

LEINSTER • COUNTY WICKLOW

Kiltimon, Ashford, County Wicklow; Tel: +01 2810274 ▪ **Contact:** Alexander or Lydia Mattei ▪ **Open:** mid-April–mid-September, Monday–Sunday, 12–6pm, but telephone in advance to confirm ▪ **Entrance fee** donated to the Disabled Drivers' Association and goes towards garden upkeep ▪ Not suitable for children ▪ **Special features:** teas can be arranged for large groups only; sensible shoes needed ▪ Directions: from Dublin, travel south on the N11. Go through Newtownmount-kennedy, and opposite 'Abwood' look for a row of poplars on the right, ending with a cottage. Turn right here and go up a steep hill for 1.6km. Dunrran Castle is on the right. Wren's Wood is on the left.

The Matteis have been working on Wren's Wood since 1990, clearing stone, building walls, clearing stone, making paths, clearing stone, banking up little streams in stone, creating a standing stone garden and clearing stone! Wren's Wood is a very unusual garden, the work of a gardener with an individual slant on design and gardening. It is the product of Alexander Mattei's extreme sympathy with his wild surroundings and the raw materials to hand – the stone, the woods and the hills. The garden opened to the public for the first time in 1999 and visitors can visit alone or take an informative walk with Lydia or Alexander.

Alexander, surrounded by a family up to its knees in horticulture, never showed an interest in the subject before arriving home to Wicklow several years ago. But the place took a hold on him and produced a single-minded gardener whose stubborness has served him well in the development of this magical garden. Working with his mother, Lydia, another talented gardener, he is slowly but surely creating one of the most beautiful natural gardens in the country.

The stones, or 'gifts from God' as Alexander calls them, are everywhere. So he uses them everywhere. Trees are wrapped in organically shaped walls. Perfect raised, circular beds filled with stone stand in clearings, like huge, surreal fruitcakes. Streams criss-crossing the woody garden are bridged with stone, and dry-stone boundary walls wrap around the whole affair.

Vast numbers of oak, beech, birch, hornbeam, holly and yew have been planted throughout the garden, which covers fourteen acres of wood and wilds. Close to the house there is a domestic-scale garden with herbs, vegetables and some herbaceous planting arranged in simple stone-edged beds. Interesting topiary and hedges give shelter and structure in this area and act as a foil and backdrop for the flowers of dahlia, zinnia, rose and allium. Then, as the paths lead from the house, the trees and stones take over. A platform of stone overlooks a circle of standing stones above a drop into a valley between the trees. This valley fills with a great number of foxgloves in early summer. The tall purple-and-white giants are slowly self-seeding and sneaking down the hill. A new feature in the form of a long stone staircase, called the thirty-nine steps, is being built, drawn up the hill by the foxglove drift.

The streams, stone works and paths wind through the woods in a lazy manner and really make you wish that you could spend the whole day in this wild place. The garden is the stuff of passion, and was a well-justified winner in the Kildare and Wicklow category of the Shamrock All Ireland Gardens Competition 1999.

In 1553, Cardinal Giacomo Mattei, a patron of the painter Carravaggio and 'Protector of Ireland', bought land in Rome that was 'covered in brambles and other wild plants and moreover incapable of yielding anything.' From this he created the Mattei Gardens, which became one of the glories of Rome. It is appropriate that his ancestor should do the same in Wicklow almost 500 years later.

GARDENING CLUBS AND SOCIETIES

DELGANY AND DISTRICT HORTICULTURAL SOCIETY

Contact: Mr John Markham, Calluna, Church Lane, Greystones, County Wicklow; Tel: +01 2874400.

The society meets four times a year and holds vegetable, fruit and flower competitions. School groups are welcome to join and enter the competitions.

ENNISKERRY GARDENING CLUB

Contact: Mrs Maura Sheahan (Chairperson), St Joseph's, Old Connaught Road, Bray, County Wicklow; Tel: +01 2821585; or Mrs Mary O'Reilly, Rosemount, Enniskerrry Village, County Wicklow; Tel: +01 2863568.

The club meets on the first Wednesday of each month in the Church of Ireland Parochial Hall in Enniskerry village. During the summer months meetings are sometimes held in member's gardens. Garden trips, talks and daytrips are organised throughout the summer months. New members are welcome and visitors may attend meetings for an admission fee.

GREYSTONES FLOWER CLUB, THE

Contact: Mrs Maura Sheahan (Chairperson), St Joseph's, Old Connaught Road, Bray, County Wicklow; Tel: +01 2821585.

The Greystones club is, as its name suggests, a flower-arrangers' club, but during the summer it also arranges garden visits to venues around the country.

NURSERIES AND GARDEN CENTRES

ANNAMOE NURSERIES

Annamoe, Bray, County Wicklow; Tel: +0404 45394.

BALLLYRAINE VALE GARDEN CENTRE

Vale Road, Arklow, County Wicklow; Tel: +0402 32656.

BLAINROE GARDEN CENTRE

Unit 1, Blainroe, Wicklow, County Wicklow; Tel: +0404 62595.

BLESSINGTON LAKE GARDEN CENTRE

Russborough, Blessington, County Wicklow; Tel: +045 865403.

BOLAND'S GARDEN CENTRE

Ashford, County Wicklow; Tel: +0404 40241.

CAPPAGH NURSERIES

Aughrim, County Wicklow; Tel: +0402 36595.

CLARA LARA GARDEN CENTRE

Ballyhad, Rathdrum, County Wicklow; Tel: +0404 46849.

GAVIN'S GARDEN CENTRE

Newcastle, County Wicklow; Tel: +01 2819592.

GREENHOUSE, THE
Old Connaught Road, Bray, County Wicklow; Tel: +01 2824377.

JOHNSON, TOM, FENCING AND TREE-FELLING
Ballywaltrim, Bray, County Wicklow; Tel: +01 2863477.

OLDE COTTAGE NURSERY
Rosebawn, Tinahely, County Wicklow; Tel: +0402 38399.

POWERSCOURT GARDEN PAVILION
Powerscourt Estate, Enniskerry, County Wicklow; Tel: +01 2046014.

SEXTON, PAUL, GARDEN CENTRE
Glen O' The Downs, County Wicklow; Tel: +01 2876669.

VAN DER WEL TREES AND SHRUBS LTD.
Tinakilly, Aughrim, County Wicklow; Tel: +0402 36595; Fax: +0402 36506.

WOODSIDE NURSERY
Aughrim, County Wicklow; Tel: +0402 3610.1

WOODIES DIY GARDEN CENTRE
Bray; Tel: +01 2864520.

GARDEN DESIGNERS

CONWAY, STEPHEN
Oakdene Landscapes, Bellvue Hill, Delgany, County Wicklow; Tel: +01 2874142.

See the National Garden Exhibition Centre in Kilquade, where Stephen Conway designed the celtic stone garden. Another garden of Stephen's that can be seen by the public is the Bicentennial garden at St Patrick's College in Maynooth.

McDONOGH, FRAZER, ROCK AND WATERSCAPING
72 Glenview Park, Kilpedder, County Wicklow; Tel: +01 2819724; e-mail: rockandswaterscapes@eircom.ie

An example of the work carried out by Frazer McDonogh is the conifer garden at the National Garden Exhibition Centre in Kilquade.

TSAOUSSIS MADDOCK, MILA
Kilashee, Newcastle, Greystones, County Wicklow; Tel: +01 2819115.

In order to see some of Mila's public work, take a look at the family garden in the National Garden Exhibition Centre in Kilquade.

GARDEN ACCESSORIES

BREWERS' BARLEY MULCH PRODUCTS (AND BALLYPHILLIP NURSERY)
Kilcoole, County Wicklow; Tel: +01 2875055; e-mail: brewers@iol.ie.

Brewer's barley mulch is that wonderful, chocolate-coloured stuff used as nutritious mulch by many gardeners. A low pH makes it good for acid-loving plants. They also do lawn edging, bedding and small plants in the nursery.

FERN WOOD GARDEN & CRAFT

Blackhill, Dunlavin, County Wicklow;
Tel: +045 401306.

GROW GREEN PRODUCTS

Manor Kilbride, County Wicklow; Tel:
+01 4582261; Fax: +01 4582591. ▪
Ring in advance for an appointment.

Stocks of hen and duck runs, some in extremely quaint styles, some wonderfully
daft, like the 'Siam Duck Nest'. Dovecotes
and rabbit hutches, gazebos and summerhouses, domestic shredders and compost
bins, wormeries and weed-burners.

HEALY STONE

Tuckmill Upper, Baltinglass, County
Wicklow; Tel: +0508 81440 ▪ **Directions:** off the Hacketstown Road, on
the outskirts of Baltinglass.

A good place for reconstituted stone
statuary, follies, balustrades, pillars and
pots. They will do work to commission
(*see* the sunset field folly at Altamont,
County Carlow). This is a more affordable
alternative to finding solid stone pieces in
the architectural salvage yards.

IVERNA HERBS

Glenmalure, Rathdrum, County Wicklow ▪ **Contact:** Peter O'Neill.

Mr O'Neill grows and sells over 200 varieties of herbs, both culinary and medicinal.
Sales are by mail order only, write for
catalogue and mail order details.

MATURE MANURE

1 Kilgarron Hill, Enniskerry, County
Wicklow ▪ **Contact:** Patrick McMahon.

Mature horse manure for sale by the bag.
Watch for the sign. £1.50 a bag or £2 a
bag if you require it to be delivered.

ROUNDWOOD STORES (GARDEN FURNITURE)

Roundwood, County Wicklow; Tel:
+01 2818454.

STONE DEVELOPMENTS

Ballybrew, Enniskerry, County Wicklow;
Tel: +01 2862981; Fax: +01
2860449; e-mail: stonebb@indigo.ie

Stone garden furniture, paving and ornaments in every style and shape.

TILL, RUPERT (SCULPTOR)

Knockarigg Hill, Grangecon, County
Wicklow; Tel: +0508 82044; Fax:
+0508 82066.

Rupert Till has exhibited his wirework
pigs, dogs, sheep, foxes, horses, cows,
gorillas, peacocks and other animals
throughout Europe, Japan, the USA and
Canada. They are witty and pretty. Write
for a brochure.

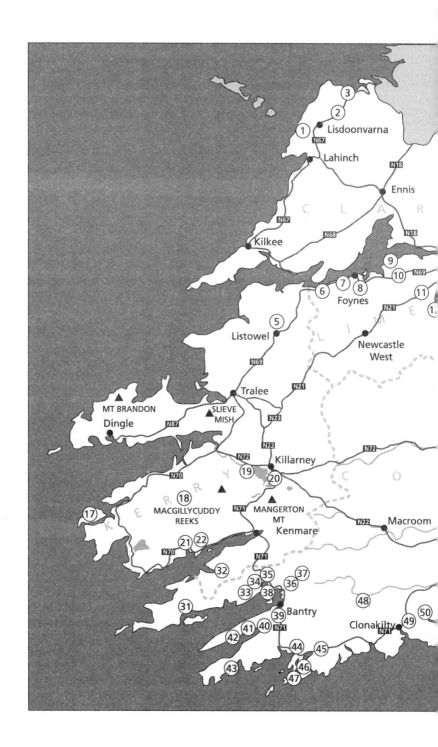

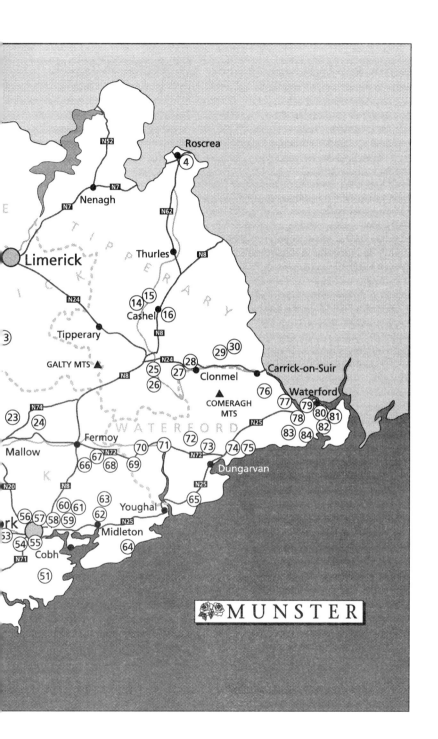

MUNSTER

1. Doolin Crafts Gallery and Garden
2. Gregan's Castle Hotel Garden
3. An Féar Gorta
4. Fancroft Millhouse
5. The Gardens of Europe
6. Glin Castle
7. Boyce's Garden
8. Knockpatrick
9. Ballynacourty
10. The Celtic Park and Garden
11. Adare Manor
12. Islanmore
13. Terra Nova Garden
14. Graves's Garden
15. Camas Park
16. Rahard Lodge
17. Glanleam House and Garden
18. Tulligelane Mastergeehy Exotic Garden
19. Dunloe Castle Gardens
20. Muckross Gardens
21. Pier Road Garden
22. The Way the Fairies Went
23. Doneraile Park
24. Annes Grove
25. Swiss Cottage
26. Slievenamon Cottage Garden
27. Inislounaght House
28. The Poppy Field
29. Heather Crest
30. Killurney
31. Rodeen Garden
32. Derreen
33. Cashelane Gardens
34. Derreenagarig
35. The Bamboo Park
36. Ballylickey Manor House
37. Larchwood House
38. Ilnacullin
39. Bantry House and Gardens
40. Carraig Abhainn Gardens
41. Kilravock Garden
42. Cois Cuain
43. Ewe Art Centre
44. West Cork Herb Farm
45. Liss Ard Foundation Gardens
46. Creagh Gardens
47. Glebe Gardens and Gallery
48. The Manor
49. Lisselan Estate Gardens
50. Timoleague Castle Gardens
51. Granig House
52. Amergen
53. Carraig Rua
54. Glenmahon
55. Clanaboy
56. Lakemount
57. Fox Covert
58. Dunsland Garden and Water Feature
59. Fota Arboretum and Gardens
60. Beechwood
61. Hillside
62. Midleton House
63. Cedar Lodge
64. Ballymaloe Cookery School Gardens
65. Bay View
66. Ballyvolane House Gardens
67. Holland House
68. Carnival
69. Ballyclement
70. Lismore Castle Garden
71. Cappoquin House
72. Maura Curran's Garden
73. Rockbarton
74. Littlewood
75. Ballymoat House
76. Curraghmore
77. Mount Congreve
78. Shalom
79. Joe and Anne Jennings's Garden
80. Sion Hill House
81. Abbey Road Gardens
82. Cois Abhainn
83. Floraville (O'Keeffes's Garden)
84. Tramore House

COUNTY CLARE

County Clare is undoubtedly one of the jewels of the country. Much of the county has been spared the taming hand of man, remaining a windswept, rough, boggy, bleak and wildly handsome place. The coastal landscape, battered by the waves of the Atlantic Ocean, is breathtaking. The Cliffs of Moher are, of course, magnificent, but there are also countless miles of cliffs and rough coastline in addition to the well-known beauty spot. There are a good number of particularly good marked walks in the Burren area, around the northwest of the county and down toward Ennistimon and Lahinch. Clare is best-known as one of the great centres of Irish traditional music, and music-lovers from all over the world gravitate to the pubs of Kilfenora, Doolin, Tulla and Labasheeda to enjoy the sessions. Bunratty Folk Park, site of medieval banquets for the past number of decades, is a big favourite with tourists. The Shannon estuary forms the county's southern border, while Lough Derg borders a large area to the eastern end of the county; it will come as no surprise that the fishing is good, both on and offshore. Depending on your point of view and style of gardening, Clare is either a fairly quiet backwater or, as the home of the Burren, a place of pilgrimage. The Burren is one of the most remarkable natural landscapes in the world, at first a seemingly barren place, it is home to an extraordinarily wide range of rare and unusual plants (see box, The Burren, p.171).

DOOLIN CRAFTS GALLERY AND GARDEN

Ballyvoe, Doolin, County Clare; Tel: +065 7074309; Fax: +065 7074511 ∗
Contact: Matthew O'Connell ∗ **Open:** Easter–1 October, everyday, 9am–7.30pm; 1 October–Easter, Tuesday–Saturday, 10am–6pm; closed for Christmas ∗ **No entrance fee** ∗ Supervised children welcome; please note, dogs on leads ∗ **Special features:** craft shop ∗ **Directions:** beside the cemetery in Doolin village, on the road to Lisdoonvarna.

This garden has been growing since 1987. According to Matthew O'Connell, 'It happened rather than being the product of conscious design.' This is an unusual statement from a man whose own reputation is firmly tied in with design. 'The design of the garden was based on common sense. For instance, if you have a problem you work around it. Use the mound rather than try to remove it,' he says.

As a busy businessman, his priority in the garden was to make working the plot as easy as possible. The second goal was to plant the garden so that it would look well all year round. This is because the garden is attached to the craft shop and so is on view constantly as a public space. These two factors determined both shape and style. Finally, Matthew had a strong desire to keep the views of the hills beyond the garden. The borrowed views or 'stolen landscape' of the Burren make his garden special.

These views mean the size of the garden is indeterminate. The actual garden covers about half an acre, but the eye is drawn further out and is happily fooled into believing the garden goes on to the horizon.

Matthew is a plant magpie and has collected a great many plants over the years. His collection now stands at around 1,000: 'And we lose very little,' he says, obviously and rightly pleased. He loves plants, both rare and ordinary. Proof of this is that he doesn't even like to lose nettles. He feels that even nettles are useful to a garden in moderation. 'There should be a place for every plant in the garden,' he says firmly.

As a working man whose garden is, to say the least, not on the main drag, he is well away from most of the country's better nurseries. However, the problems of stocking the garden were sidestepped because Matthew is a great advocate of mail-order plants: 'It's a wonder. You get exactly what you want and something else looking pretty in the garden centre never distracts you. It's a great method of buying rare and hard-to-get plants and it's cost effective.'

THE BURREN

The Burren translates from the Irish as 'great rock'. Famously described as a place where 'there is not water enough to drown a man, wood enough to hang a man, or earth enough to bury a man', it covers an area of 250 square kilometres in north Clare. Apart from occasional stunted ash or hazels, it is almost treeless, and forms a unique landscape not just in Ireland but in the world.

Its unusual make-up means that it hosts plant life from the high Alps, the Mediterranean and the Arctic side by side. Both acid- and lime-loving plants grow together in the strange, seemingly barren landscape because the carboniferous limestone rock is lightly clothed in acidic, peaty soil. The landscape is krastic. This means that over time water has seeped down into the rock rather than flowing along and over it. Sinkholes convey water down into the earth, where acid in the rainwater eats into the limestone, turning fissures already present into bigger holes and channels. During the Ice Age, this ridged and pockmarked landscape was acted on by glaciers, becoming flattened and smooth to produce 'limestone pavement'.

The coastal location of the Burren maintains temperatures high enough to prevent frost. Moisture and warmth in the sheltered cracks and fine sea mist and spray, added to the landscape, make this an extraordinary habitat. Among the plants found in the crevices of stone are *Gentiana verna*, a mat-forming evergreen perennial with dark green leaves and sky-blue flowers in early summer. From the Arctic region, the delicate-looking white star flowers of *Dryas octopetala*, a mat-forming subshrub, and the mossy saxifrage *(Saxifraga hypnoides)* grow and thrive.

The Burren is a fragile landscape, under constant threat from the feet of its many visitors. Worse still, it is in danger of being raided by unscrupulous gardeners, landscapers and builders for stone 'features'. It must be treated with great respect, and it should go without saying that plants and seeds should never be collected, or more correctly 'stolen', from here or any wild place.

A little white area wrapped in hedging contains some of his mail order acquisitions, including lesser-seen plants like *Aquilegia* 'Guinness', a black and white form of the well-loved, easy to grow flower often known as granny's bonnet or columbine. This little flower looks particularly pretty beside the grey-leaved perennial stock, with its soft cream or winter-white flowers.

Matthew has a particular love of Irish plants, like *Agapanthus* 'Lady Moore', named for Phyllis Moore, a talented gardener and the wife of Sir Frederick, the famed curator of the Dublin Botanic Gardens at the beginning of the twentieth century. He also grows the tatting fern, also known as Mrs Frizell's lady fern (*Athyrium filix-femina* 'Frizelliae'). This plant was found growing by a riverbank by Mrs Frizell in Wicklow in the nineteenth century. She gave it to the Botanic Gardens in Dublin and now this rare plant is grown in several gardens throughout the country.

I liked the yellow bed with *Buddleia globosa*, roses, peonies, kniphofia and fennel (with its yellow seedheads). The fern-like tamarisk, pale yellow with red stalks, grows well by the sea and is a plant Matthew would definitely recommend. No rule should be too strict and in this bed, complementing the yellows, is the indigo plant *Indigofera*, from which indigo dye is extracted. David Austin roses are another great favourite in the yellow bed, as well as throughout the rest of the garden. They suit the informal style and do well in the climate.

There are some interesting works of contemporary sculpture placed around the garden, including wonderful large-scale metal pieces and an interesting object made from an old milk pan filled with water and glass floats. They add considerably to the modern style of both the garden and the buildings it surrounds.

AN FÉAR GORTA

Ballyvaughan, County Clare; Tel: +065 7077023; Fax: +065 7077127 ▪ **Contact:** Brendan and Katherine O'Donoghue ▪ **Open:** June–mid-September, Monday–Saturday, 11.30am–5.30pm ▪ **No entrance fee** ▪ **Special features:** tea and garden room ▪ **Directions:** situated opposite the harbour in Ballyvaughan village.

Set in from the harbour at Ballyvaughan, this little garden is an example of using local materials to carry out work appropriate to the landscape. The O'Donoghues work four small gardens to the front and back of their two seafront cottages, one of which is a classic thatched cottage. They arrived in Clare in the 1980s to take up a life of gardening and running a tearoom. Cultivated gardens were then thin on the ground in the Burren, and the locals looked on their work with some scepticism at first, particularly the growing of purple cabbages: 'We were called the witches who grew witch cabbage,' says Brendan O'Donoghue. The witches settled in well, however.

Each of the four gardens has its own individual style, but they are linked by one thing – an abundant use of local stone, worked by the talented Brendan O'Donoghue. Good stonework is always a pleasure to admire, and here there are well-built dry stone walls, standing stones, rockeries and stone-edged ponds. Brendan and his stone works have even featured on a television programme by Charles Nelson for Channel 4, entitled 'A Growing Up Season'.

At the front of the first house there are little stone blocks stepping up and down, with simple, low, seaside planting of thrift (*Armeria*) and sedum, creeping plants and

**One of the four separate stone gardens at An Féar Gorta,
by the harbour in Ballyvaughan, County Clare.**

alpines, polygonum, cotoneaster and campanula in small clumps. Every crack in the flags has been colonised and softened by these little plants.

The next-door garden is more cottagey. For a start, the heights are different. Moving from an area of low, ground-hugging plants, this garden is filled with herbaceous plants, surrounded by tall flowering shrubs. This is the thatched cottage, complete with roses and honeysuckle around the door. There are stone troughs placed everywhere, filled with annuals and spot-colouring flowers, like small pinks or sweet, clove-smelling dianthus.

To the rear of the houses, a number of small garden rooms are joined and divided by stone walls, paths and arches. A sunken stone and gravel garden laid out with tables for tea alerts the visitor to the fact that Katherine O'Donoghue serves lovely cake and teas throughout the summer. This is a good stopping-off point to fill up before heading out to the rest of the garden. I particularly loved the herb and vegetable garden. In here peas, scallions and cabbages are planted alongside flowers and herbs in a collection of only vaguely regularly shaped beds. Boulders and rounded stones are used to edge the beds.

Beautifully constructed dry stone walls act as windbreaks on the gust-blown west coast. They are placed at all sorts of angles to each other, breaking, redirecting and downplaying the wind. They also afford opportunities for clematis, roses and ivy to grow and provide a transition between the well-planted, good-looking garden and the wild west beyond. The garden melts into the Clare landscape in a graduated way.

One big stone stands in the middle of the garden. This is a 'back stone' on which to rub a bad back. It is said that doing this will give 'the cure', and Brendan says that apparently it works. There are also various heaps of stones, which echo traditional beliefs. In the past, people wouldn't pass one of these piles, called *cloch na hamadáin* or 'the stones of the eejits', without adding a stone. Piles such as these are to be seen scattered by the roadside throughout the Burren. Local superstition is also reflected in the name of the garden: An Féar Gorta. This means 'the hungry grass' and refers to a patch of ground bewitched by the Little People. According to legend, when you step on the hungry grass you are immediately consumed by gnawing pains of hunger – a spell that relates back to the Great Famine. To avoid this, you should always carry a crust of bread in case you encounter some dreaded *féar gorta*.

GREGAN'S CASTLE HOTEL GARDEN

Ballyvaughan, County Clare; Tel: +065 7077005 ※ **Contact:** the Hayden family ※ **Open:** contact in advance for an appointment to view garden; small groups and individuals only ※ **Entrance fee** ※ Supervised children welcome ※ **Special features:** teas can be booked by prior arrangement ※ **Directions:** located on the N67 between Lisdoonvarna and Ballyvaughan.

The countryside of County Clare needs no improvement. Wild, sparsely cultivated, colourful and beautiful, it doesn't cry out for additions, which can make it harder in many ways to create a good garden here than in more tamed areas. It is all too easy to 'plant' an incongruous-looking, obviously imported garden into these wild surroundings. A more sensitive hand is required.

Mr Hayden says his garden depends as much on 'borrowed landscape' as on the work carried out within the boundaries. For example, at the front of the house a long, low fuchsia hedge is backed not by the usual beech, bay, yew or hornbeam hedging, but by the hills and huge skies of the Burren. In front of it, lying almost flat, a border of hebe, Cape daisy, peony and catmint sprawls out toward the lawn. Colour is dotted subtly along the border rather than placed in overly bold sheets. Rich, soft reds and the purple of fuchsia are the dominant colours.

Close to one side of the house is a secret garden, discovered through a discreet entrance cut into the overhanging shrubs. In here poor man's box (*Lonicera nitida*), camellia and rampant buddleia, which is found everywhere in the garden, attract large numbers of butterflies from the wild surroundings. Within this hedge is a garden of lawns, shrub roses and crocosmia, which, along with fuchsia, colonises the roadside verges of Clare and the other westerly counties. This is a particularly sensitive style of gardening, working these almost native plants and flowers into the cultivated garden. Crocosmia, with its exotic-looking, flame-coloured flowers and strappy leaves, has been combined with the matt-green leaves and frothy lemon flowers of Lady's mantle (*Alchemilla mollis*) to fringe the building, edging and softening walls. The long run of these two plants along the house makes a very strong statement.

Sorbus and betula edge the river, leading away from the house and towards a circular rockbed with an interesting and unusual pattern of stonework. Scattered over the lawns is a young collection of specimen trees. Mown paths wind through a newly planted wood of native trees, which, as it matures, will become like a little woody maze. The wood opens on to a great big lily pond, edged with more willow and fuchsia, with its own island.

Irish Seed Savers Association (ISSA)

The ISSA was set up in 1990 by Tommy and Anita Hayes. Its aim is to save seeds from endangered native Irish varieties of fruit and vegetables. The association locates, grows and then distributes these plants among gardeners, who continue to grow on and increase the stock of plants all over the country, thus giving the gene pool a chance to survive and increase.

The ISSA tries to propagate, as widely as possible, plants that would otherwise disappear forever. Fears for the future of these plants are not idle – it is thought that since the beginning of the twentieth century seventy-five percent of the genetic diversity of agricultural crops has been lost. This is because, for economic reasons, large seed merchants have drastically reduced the variety of seed available for sale and cultivation. As a result, good old garden varieties of apples, peas and carrots – sometimes, but not always, prone to certain diseases and pests – must be saved from extinction. These plants need to be saved because they are diverse, taste different, look different and add to the variety of life. They might also be needed at some time in the future if, for example, a bug or disease particular to Golden Delicious or Granny Smith threatened to empty the supermarkets of apples.

On their seven-and-a-half-acre seed garden and orchard in Clare, and at a second site in Piltown, County Kilkenny, the ISSA grows and trials rare and endangered vegetables and grains from elsewhere in the world, from countries whose climates and growing conditions are similar to Ireland's. The hope is that some ground can be made up in the area of saving and holding on to varieties of seed that have developed and improved over thousands of years of natural selection.

Open days are held at both sites annually in either July or August (contact for exact dates). The association currently has about 500 members who pay an annual subscription fee. This varies, but is always reasonable and depends on the individual member's circumstances. Membership entitles one to a biannual newsletter, including lists of seeds from which members can pick five varieties free of charge. This helps to ensure wider cultivation of these heritage seeds. This free seed distribution makes membership both laudable and ridiculously good value, as these are very special seeds and five packets of ordinary seeds will cost anything from £5 to £10 in the shops.

Contact Tommy and Anita Hayes for a membership form/catalogue or ring during office hours. Irish Seed Savers Association, Capparoe, Scariff, County Clare; Tel: +061 921866; e-mail: seedsavers@esatclear.ie

Garden Centres

GREENFINGERS GARDEN CENTRE
Clonroad Business Park, Ennis, County Clare; Tel: +065 6866506.

LITTLE ACORN GARDEN CENTRE
Tulla Road, Ennis, County Clare; Tel: +065 6821959.

LITTLE MOON GARDEN CENTRE
Mullagh, County Clare; Tel: +065 7087655

MONVANA GARDEN CENTRE
Monvana, Kilrush, County Clare; Tel: +065 9051113.

SHANNON GARDEN CENTRE
Limerick Road, Drumline, Newmarket on Fergus, County Clare; Tel: +061 363290.

Garden Accessories

DOOLIN FLAGSTONE
Luogh, Doolin, County Clare; Tel/Fax: +065 7074091.

An enthusiast for Doolin Stone, as opposed to the better-known Liscannor, John Fitzpatrick sells sawn flagstones as well as stone for garden furniture, benches or tabletops.

KINCORA SECRET GARDEN AND RESTAURANT
Doolin Road, Lisdoonvarna, County Clare ▪ Accommodation and restaurant.

A small courtyard garden and restaurant with raised stone beds full of alpines and herbaceous plants. The walls are covered in fragrant honeysuckle, and gravel walks thread through the beds and past rose beds, pots of trees and well-placed sitting places.

COUNTY CORK

Cork is both the biggest county in the Republic of Ireland and its second city. It is a vibrant, cosmopolitan, walkable place that can bewilder the visitor, built as it is on a series of islands on the River Lee with bridges crisscrossing in all directions. The hills up to Glanmire and Montenotte to the north of the city are as close as Ireland has to the streetscape of San Fransisco. Great food in the English Market off Patrick Street attracts fans from far afield as does a mouth-watering array of restaurants. The annual jazz and film festivals are justly well-known. The newly restored and expanded Crawford Gallery on Sharman-Crawford Road in the city centre is a renowned gallery, exhibiting the best of Irish and international art. Out in the wider county is the gourmands' haven of Kinsale, and a string of almost too-beautiful towns and villages, from Skibbereen, Ballydehob and Goleen to Castletownshend, stretching over to the mountains of the Beara Peninsula and Glengarriff. Finally, County Cork is an exceptionally good gardening county, with a milder climate than much of the rest of the country. Higher temperatures are delivered by the warm Gulf Stream waters and by the shelter of several ranges of hills and mountains, from the low sandstone hills around Cork city to the Sheehy and Caha Mountains on Beara, which protect the county from the worst sea gales. Other reasons for envy are the enormous number of gardens open to visitors and the busy gardening club network. Two festivals celebrate gardens in the county: the Cork Open Gardens Week and the West Cork Garden Trail.

AMERGEN

Walshestown, Ovens, County Cork; Tel: +021 7331326 ▪ **Contact:** Christine Fehily ▪ **Open:** during the summer months, by appointment to groups only ▪ **Entrance fee** donated to charity and goes towards garden upkeep ▪ Supervised children welcome; please note, dogs on leads ▪ **Directions:** travel along the N22 from Cork to Killarney. About 3.2km west of Ballincollig you'll find Sheahan's pub and restaurant; turn right here. Continue uphill and take the second turn right, which is signposted as a cul-de-sac. Drive 1.6km and you'll reach the garden, which is on the right with the name on the gate post.

'If you planted a nail here, in three weeks you'd have a crowbar,' says Mrs Fehily of the two-acre garden she has created over the last sixteen years. 'Everything we planted just took off. The soil was very good because the field had cows grazing it and fertilising it for years,' she continues, as though it were that simple. Resident at Amergen since the mid-1980s, Mrs Fehily began gardening immediately upon moving in. The slope of the land determined the shape of the garden and she used rather than fought the natural aspect of the place so that it moulds naturally into the land. The garden faces northwest and so enjoys sunsets and a fine view of Inishcara Lake (actually a res-

Scotch thistles and pink foxgloves in Airfield, County Dublin.

The Tea House surrounded by a collection of ancient bonsai at the Japanese Gardens in County Kildare. Constructed at the beginning of the twentieth century, it is still used on special occasions for Japanese tea ceremonies.

A view of the bog oak and waterfall garden at
St Fiachra's Garden, County Kildare.

The Wheelers's big double maze as seen from the viewing platform, at Greenan in County Wicklow.

Pumpkins and squashes – the autumn harvest in Richard Lister's garden, Knockbawn, in County Wexford.

The *cottage orné* at Kilfane Glen in County Kilkenny. Recreated in the 1990s, it was built on the foundations of the original rustic cottage, with the aid of prints dating back to the early 1800s and descriptions in family letters.

Sunlight filtering through the trees in the wood at Kilfane, County Kilkenny.

The architectural wisteria circle and *pecherie* at Bantry House in County Cork.

Exuberant summer bedding and smart topiary at Carraig Rua in County Cork.
Ann Law-Coffey plants over 1,000 red begonias each year in this one area
of her award-winning garden.

ABOVE: Yellows, golds and oranges in the mixed border at Hardymount in County Carlow.

LEFT: A waterlily in one of the many ponds in the exotic garden at Tulligelane, County Kerry.

The shell house, perfectly framed by the massive double herbaceous borders, at the Ballymaloe Cookery School Garden, County Cork.

An arum lily *(Zantedeschia aethiopica)* in Rosemary Brown's garden at Graigueconna, County Wicklow.

Azaleas in the wood at Annes Grove, County Cork.

The Ewe Art Centre in Goleen, County Cork – one of the many witty and unusual sculptures arranged around the pretty, informal gardens overlooking the Atlantic Ocean.

ervoir). Beyond, Mushera Mountain and Mullaghanish Mountain in the Boggeragh range are sights for sore eyes. The view costs however, and winds sweeping up from the water mean that most planting has to be placed behind the house, protected by the building and a shelter belt of birch, elder, eucalyptus and a hedge of *Rosa rugosa*. One elegant, white-barked betula planted directly into the drive in front of the house is the exception.

CORK GARDEN TRAILS

Each year Cork plays host to two garden trails. The best known is the West Cork Garden Trail, a centrepiece festival of private gardens that open to the public for varying times throughout the summer months. Some open for a very limited period, but a good number stay open for much of the summer. The trail is well organised and a colour leaflet is produced each year providing a quick guide to each garden. The trail is made up of very varied but complementary gardens, stretching from Timoleague near Bandon to Castletownbere and Goleen, close to Mizen Head. Quite apart from the gardens to be seen, the trail transports visitors through some of the most beautiful and scenic parts of the county. Contact Bord Fáilte or Phemie Rose at Kilravock Garden, Durrus, West Cork (tel: +027 61111) for further information.

The Open Gardens Trail covers eleven gardens ranging across the county, taking in the city suburbs in east and north Cork. On this trail most of the properties open only for specific open days in aid of the Marymount Hospice in Cork. For details contact the Marymount Hospice at +021 501201 or Brian Cross at +021 821052.

A sad omission from the long list of gardens that can be visited in County Cork is Ashbourne House. Ashbourne is one of the most important historic gardens in the country, and it is a particularly painful loss. It can only be hoped that some day it will be available to the nation, restored and maintained.

The garden is made up of two big borders, the short border and the long border, both divided and broken at several points by sweeps of lawn and grass paths. Hearing a description of a garden of borders, one might expect to see ranks of herbaceous planting and flowers, but these are substantial-sized shrub and tree borders filled with unusual plants, including a zelcova – an exotic relation of the elm with fine leaves that colour beautifully in autumn. The long border has a great collection of shrubs and trees, including a tender *Cupressus tortulosa* 'Cashmeriana' with leaves like fringes of long green hair. Another choice plant is the *Azara microphylla* 'Variegata', which first occurred in Cobh in the garden of the famous Victorian gardener William Gumbleton; it has golden-edged tiny leaves with fragrant white flowers. Dots of white Japanese anemone and kaffir lilies (*Schizostylis*) flower between the shrubs in little pools of colour. Acer with peeling and coloured bark, abies with upstanding cones like candles on a Christmas tree and the aptly named *Liquidambar orientalis*, loved for its fine colouring, are more than diverting; lots of flower would be overdoing it in Mrs Fehily's view. In the short border a ten-year-old blue eucalyptus has reached twelve metres and is growing fast, 'but the sky is a long way up still,' says Mrs Fehily.

Everything is given space in this garden but this is not just a collection, but a cleverly designed garden. In an opening out of the borders, a pebble beach pond was built specifically to display a southern beech by showing its reflection in the water. Around the pond there are stepping stones, black bamboo, *Elaeagnus glauca* and several varieties of pennisetum grass, including *Pennisetum orientale*, *Pennisetum aloperoiden* and *Pennisetum orientale* 'Woodside'.

Behind the house, back in the trees, is a secluded spot with a fern-sprouting moss carpet and a huge rock with a bolt-upright, self-seeded birch growing from it. A big tree fern (*Dicksonia antarctica*) grows above the rocks beside a Japanese snowbell tree (*Styrax japonica*). Styrax has white dripping flowers and egg-like seeds and puts its rhododendron and magnolia neigbours in the shade. It is a tree with a great deal to recommend it but not seen enough in gardens. In early summer this woody area is a sea of bluebells.

Nature works in echoes; trees grow in small groves or clumps. The seed gets carried off by whatever means to another spot where a new plant germinates and begins a new grove of plants. Christine Fehily employs the same principle in her design: a group of silver-barked betulas are echoed by a solitary specimen a little way off. It's like planting in drifts rather than square blocks. The effect is natural and gives a sense of glide to this substantial garden.

ANNES GROVE

Castletownroche, Mallow, County Cork; Tel: +022 26145; e-mail: hzcronin@indigo.ie ▪ **Contact:** Jane or Patrick Annesley ▪ **Open:** 17 March–30 September, Monday–Saturday, 10am–5pm; Sunday, 2pm–6pm; other times by appointment; groups welcome ▪ **Entrance fee** goes towards garden upkeep ▪ Supervised children welcome; please note, dogs on leads ▪ **Special features:** occasional garden talks and lectures, telephone for details; plants for sale from Rosamund Henley at Middle Lodge, Annes Grove (Tel: +022 26811); accommodation available in two self-catering cottages ▪ **Directions:** located 1.6km from Castletownroche, on the Fermoy–Mallow–Killarney road (N72).

Annes Grove is one of the best-known gardens on the island and rightly so. It's impossible to travel through Cork without being ordered, several times, to get up to Castletownroche and quick about it to see Annes Grove. It is a garden in the Robinsonian style and is a very good example of that style (*see* box, William Robinson, p.182), but it also incorporates an older, romantic, ornamented glen and a walled flower garden. Fortunately for the gardeners the soil is divided into acid and alkaline pockets so almost anything can be grown here, and the range of plants is exciting and varied. Richard Grove Annesley, the creator of the gardens as they are today, was a co-sponsor of Frank Kingdom Ward's plant-hunting expeditions to Burma, Tibet and Yunan, and he filled his creation with the results of these and other trips (*see* box, the Plant Hunters, p.5).

One of the first stops in the garden is the abundant walled garden, thought to have once been an eighteenth-century orchard. A knot of curved box hedges, appropriately called the ribbon beds because of their 'twisted ribbon' design, leads in towards an unusual, primitive-looking, three-legged stone sundial. Annuals like antirrhinums and impatiens sprinkle colour among the box plants. Close by, generous hazy-blue and pink-coloured double herbaceous borders divided by flagstone paths are a sight, with soft silver and pink stachys tumbling out on to the stone and tall phlox in shades of pinks and whites, while cannas and thalictrum, looking good enought to eat, take up the rear. Pergolas of wisteria radiate off from the border, leading to shaded, woody walks under cherry and eucryphia, a posh relative of the more lax-looking and more widely seen philadelphus. The shady walk makes its way to a pond area planted up with swags of hosta and tradescantia before wandering on past the water and off again to a Victorian stone fernery. (This is an arrangement of natural-looking stone ledges and mounds built to hold a collection of ferns. Ferns were a particular favourite among Victorian gardeners and Victorian ferneries, or at least their remains, can be seen widely in older gardens throughout the country.) Masses of mind-your-own-business (*Soleirolia soleirolli*) give the stone the look of being expertly covered with a very tight-tufted green carpet. Baby's tears is a tiny, mat-forming plant with serious expansionist tendencies, loved and loathed in roughly equal measure by gardeners. Personally, I love it, and its empire building does little harm here in this decent-sized space. Like the ferns, it holds moisture and glistens prettily after rain, giving the fernery a lush, fresh atmosphere.

In the middle of the shaded walk a small stone seat provides a rest before the path leads around the pond and back to the open garden and into the sun, where the warmth, colour and scent of the flower borders flood back over the visitor. At the other side of the nearby double border is a set of rickety stone steps leading up to a summerhouse on a little hill. The path to this is strewn with herbs and Lady's mantle (*Alchemilla mollis*), which in the summer throws up a limey-yellow mist of flowers above the mound of matt-green leaves below. (The leaves of Lady's mantle are singularly pretty after rain when water gathers in beads on the leaves.) The summerhouse is a ramshackle affair with leaded Gothic windows and a church-like interior. Looking back down the steps and beyond, the walled garden can be seen in its full glory: a mass of flowers set into the structure of beech and yew hedges, rose beds, big magnolia and eucryphia.

Reluctantly leaving the walled garden brings you, somewhat surprisingly, straight into the middle of the woodland and wild garden where rhododendrons grow; species here include *Rhododendron wardii* and *Rhododendron macrobeanum*. These were among the plants introduced to Ireland following the Kingdom Ward expeditions. A run of steps picks its way down under the tree canopy, past abutilon, embothrium and myrtle (*Luma apiculata*), past seas of white creeping nettle and ivy. At the bottom of the descent one feels as though not just the style of garden but the continent has changed. Only a few hundred yards back up the hill the garden was cosy and of-the-place – down here at the bottom of the valley, one could be in a rain forest. The River Awbeg snakes along the bottom of the valley, fringed by lush planting of magnolia, gunnera with leaves three metres across, rushes, skunk cabbage, candelabra primula, astilbe, dense groves of bamboo, six-and-a-half-metre high cordylines and tree palms. The air can be damp, warm and humid down in this pocket, giving an exotic feel to this part of the garden. The Awbeg winds along attractively. This was redirected, reshaped and bridged to allow visitors access to the garden on both banks; the work was carried out by soldiers posted at the barracks in Mallow during the Second World War.

The path continues along by the river, eventually emerging out of this jungle of rhododendron, hoheria and bamboo and into the open fields where there are hundreds of pheasants strutting around proprietorially. It's almost necessary to shoo them from the path. This route eventually leads to hydrangea rock. This is a huge outcrop of stone rising way above the fields and covered in hydrangeas of every colour. It's a beautiful sight to see this normally most domesticated shrub look so natural and wild. Another set of mossy, rough steps leads back into the woods to the top of the hill. Climbing up the paths, it is possible to inspect hydrangea rock from different angles. Almost all year round colour and scent can be relied on from rhododendron and azalea in this magical wood.

A hard-to-follow map will be of some small use to those with a good sense of direction. The rest of us will not get too upset on finding ourselves temporarily lost in this great garden.

BALLYLICKEY MANOR HOUSE

Ballylickey, Bantry, County Cork; Tel: +027 50071; Fax: +027 50124 ▪ **Contact:** the Graves family ▪ **Open:** May–September, Monday–Sunday, by appointment only; groups welcome by prior appointment only ▪ **Entrance fee** goes towards garden upkeep ▪ Supervised children welcome; please note, dogs on leads ▪ **Special features:** refreshments available, but must be booked in advance; meals at the poolside restaurant must also be booked in advance ▪ **Directions:** located on the N71 between Bantry and Glengarriff. The house is on the right-hand side and is well signposted.

Ballylickey Manor was built in the 1700s on the edge of Bantry Bay by Lord Kenmare as a hunting lodge. It is visible from the road, which divides it from the bay, with its creamy-coloured walls cloaked in *Clematis montana* in summer months. Today the manor house serves as a hotel and the gardens surrounding it have an Edwardian style to them. Well-tended lawns are edged by shrubs, white-flowering roses, masses of lupins, pretty, mucky, dusty poppies, salmon-coloured schizostylis and clipped box hedges. These all lead the eye along and out to a view of the sea. It would be criminal to garden in such a setting and ill-use it. Thankfully the members of the Graves family, under whose care the garden was created, are not inclined towards criminal behaviour and they have made stylish use of the sea views by keeping the planting low.

The extremities of the garden are sheltered by tall woods with dominating evergreens and pines that form a canopy over a series of ponds and woody walks. These also give a measure of shelter in the exposed seaside location and frame the garden with picture-postcard neatness. In the woods a bridge over the stream leads back out to the sunny lawns and past mature oak and beech trees fronted and fringed by big pink cosmos and pink mop-head hydrangeas. Lines of lobelia, astilbe and crocosmia, cordyline and eucryphia edge the lawns right up to a very romantic rose garden with mossy, slated walls. This little rose garden is a mass of colour with pink and white anemone fighting the roses every step of the way for dominance, along with some ferns poking out onto the stone steps. This is an adorable area within the bigger garden.

Very often hotel gardens are good-looking and well-maintained, but lacking soul. However, Ballylickey Garden feels like a loved, private family garden that happens to be open to the public. I have promised myself that my next visit will be at the height of the summer and that it will incorporate a sunny lunch at the poolside restaurant from where I will study the plants with even more enthusiasm.

WILLIAM ROBINSON

William Robinson (1838–1935), an Irish-born gardener, is arguably the most influential garden designer and writer of the late nineteenth and early twentieth centuries. His ideas on gardening have made a huge impression in Ireland and Britain.

Born in County Down, he worked as a trainee gardener in several Irish gardens, including Curraghmore where he started work as a garden boy (see County Waterford). But in 1861 he left Ireland at the age of twenty-one under what were intriguingly termed 'clouded circumstances'. These 'circumstances' involved a row with his employer, Sir Hunt Johnson-Walsh, or the head gardener (we're not sure which) at Ballykilcavan in County Laois, after which he stormed out of the job. But before he left he bequeathed them a shocking memento of his anger: he quenched the fires in the greenhouses and left all doors and vents open, thus condemning the hothouse flowers to an icy death. He then left Ireland.

Taking up work at Regents Park in London, he was, among other things, responsible for a native flower garden. He went on to become an opinionated garden correspondent for *The Times* and several gardening publications, a writer of hugely influential books, including *The English Flower Garden* and *The Wild Garden,* and publisher of his own gardening magazine, *The Garden.*

Robinson was a fierce critic of the fashionable penchant for a formal garden style with regular, flat, loud-coloured bedding of half-hardy annuals measured in ruler-precise beds. He made enemies when he scorned this style of garden as mere 'floral rugs'. Statuary, topiary, architectural and geometrical features and uninteresting shrubberies were also mercilessly attacked as 'unwelcome, unlovely and detrimental to good gardening'. He worried that gardening had moved away from the basic act of actually growing plants. To counteract this he advocated a natural style of planting, using hardy exotic plants in seemingly naturalistic ways. These were plants that would not require huge after-care.

According to Robinson, the garden should look as though it happened naturally and should not need to be worked constantly to keep it looking well. This effect can be achieved by growing a mixture of trees, shrubs, annuals, herbaceous perennials, bulbs and alpines of all shapes and sizes, planted together in as natural a plan as possible. He advocated that one should work with the natural features and vagaries of the landscape rather than imposing an obviously artificial will upon it. This included lawns which should roll and flow with the lie of the land, spiked, as in nature, with mixes of flowers and bulbs in a scattered, natural manner. Shrubs should be allowed to grow in groups. They should not be topiarised or pruned into artificial shapes. Flowers should be planted close together, leaving no bare earth between plants. Subtlety was to be prized above showy and startling colour schemes.

Robinsonian-style gardens include:
Annes Grove, County Cork
Mount Usher, County Wicklow
Derreen, County Kerry
Rowallane, County Down
Creagh, County Cork
Ashbourne House Garden, County Cork (closed to the public)
Lisselan Estate Gardens, County Cork

Shanagarry, Midleton, County Cork; Tel: +021 464785; Fax: +021 464904;
e-mail: enquiries@ballymaloe-cookery-school.ie; website: www.ballymaloe-
cookery-school.ie ▪ **Entrance fee** donated towards garden upkeep ▪ **Contact:**
Darina Allen, Susan Turner or Reception ▪ **Open:** April–September, daily; booking
necessary for large groups ▪ Supervised children welcome ▪ **Special features:** garden shop with accessories; eggs for sale; garden courses available (contact for
brochure); groups should book meals in advance; plants occasionally for sale;
accommodation available close by, contact Ballymaloe for details ▪ **Directions:**
signposted from Castlemartyr on the Cork–Waterford road (N25).

There have been gardens at Kinoith since the early 1800s when the house belonged to
the Strangman family. However, after the death of Lydia Strangman in 1952 the gardens deteriorated. In the 1970s the Allen family moved in and took over a garden that
had become a wilderness; work began on the restoration of the gardens in 1983. The
gardens at Ballymaloe have been in development since then. They are now both
well-known and well worth visiting.

A map (available free of charge) leads the visitor around a series of gardens, which
are not altogether attached to each other, so the visit is rather like a treasure hunt –
filled with anticipation and surprises. First is the latest addition to the garden – the
stream garden, which is close by the restaurant. Here, terracotta frogs and Rupert Till
ducks and geese (*see* Garden Accessories listing, County Wicklow, p.166) congregate
by the water. A planting scheme of sedges, vinca, ivy and variegated *Sisyrinchium
striatum* edges the stream and pond. From here, follow the map into what to all in-
tents and purposes is the kingdom of the hens – a big garden with an intriguing
willow-sculpture dragon made by Lynn Kirkham, which sits in the middle of the fancy
fowl. A living willow walk is growing in the dragon enclosure along with other trees.
As the trees flourish the dragon should eventually give visitors a bit of a shock when
they come upon him in the middle of a mature wood.

The map then leads the visitor out past more ducks washing themselves in pud-
dles to the fruit garden, which was designed by Jim Reynolds (*see* Butterstream,
County Meath). This is not a terribly big space, but it has plenty of good ideas to pass
on to anyone with a modest-sized plot and thoughts of an attractive, productive
garden. Wide gravel paths wrap around block beds of fruit trees surrounded by collars
of strawberries and rhubarb or pansies. Plums, pears, greengages, peaches and apri-
cots, almonds and an olive tree fill the beds. Some of the old variety apples are trained
over iron arches and underplanted with autumn crocuses and other bulbs. Little duck
scarecrows are dotted around; children will enjoy these 'defenders'.

From the fruit garden there is a walk into the woods, which lead to the well-
known, much-photographed *potager* – all herringbone-patterned paths and smart
symmetrical beds. There are no messy gaps here: tidy parsnips, leeks and celery stand
in measured lines. Marigolds and splashes of orange nasturtium cheer up courgette
beds, taking the business-like look away from the straight-laced vegetables. In here
the scarecrows are made of willow and are so pleasing to the eye that their efficacy
must be doubted.

Out on the edge of the *potager* one of the benches provided to rest poor tired feet is
surrounded by a nasturtium arbour with lines of well-behaved beans radiating away

from it in paths; it is a pleasure to sit in and enjoy the sight of tomatoes interlaced with Devil-in-the-bush, otherwise known as love-in-a-mist (*Nigella damascena*). Mop-head bay trees stand like green lollipops over the vegetables, and the whole garden is overlooked by a raised stage with walls of sweetpea. Up here, another bench stands overlooking the garden, sheltered by its backing of scented sweetpea. Next, the map leads you to Lydia's garden, named for the above-mentioned Lydia Strangman whose watercolours provided a reference for the Allens during the restoration work. Lydia's garden is a beech hedge-enclosed garden with a herbaceous walk and a pretty treehouse which overlooks several of the gardens. Beneath this is a dainty, delicate-looking mosaic, created in 1912 by the Strangmans. A sign begs visitors not to walk on the floor; please obey it.

From the treehouse you will have seen the herb garden, now it's time to clamber down to ground level where it not only looks good but the smells are intoxicating. Then out to the pond garden and the rose-clad cherry trees leading toward a Grecian folly and a pond full of classical tadpoles, simply side-planted with gunnera. This is a cool, restrained garden that serves to increase the punch of the big double border next in the line of gardens. Two beds, each measuring eighty metres long, are separated by a wide grass path. Designed by Rachel Lamb in the early 1990s, the beds are now quite mature and good to look at with all the usual herbaceous perennials, including phlox, golden rod, big red sunflowers, rudbekia, yellow dahlias, cornflowers and bells of Ireland. This all leads up to the shell house, created by Blot Kerr Wilson – an encouragement to eat shellfish if one were ever needed. A mix of usual and unusual shells make up the most wonderful geometrical patterns right up to the ceiling inside the little hexagonal-shaped Gothic house. Beside the shell house is a Celtic design-inspired yew maze. It is too young for anything bigger than a lab rat to get lost in yet, but some day, no doubt, people will have to be fished out after hours of wandering lost.

Leave the garden past a field of happy-looking pigs and *le palais de poulet* – home to the most aristocratic fancy fowl to be seen anywhere. Ballymaloe is truly a *tour de force*.

BALLYVOLANE HOUSE GARDENS

Castlelyons, County Cork; Tel: +025 36349; Fax: +025 36781; e-mail: ballyvol@iol.ie; website: www.ballyvolanehouse.ie ▩ **Contact:** Jeremy and Merrie Green ▩ **Open:** for occasional charity open days (*see* local press for details); at other times telephone in advance for an appointment; groups welcome ▩ **Entrance fee** donated to charity and goes towards garden upkeep ▩ Supervised children welcome; please note, dogs on leads ▩ **Special features:** refreshments are available, but must be booked in advance; Ballyvolane is a country house hotel so accommodation is available ▩ **Directions**: travelling towards Fermoy on the N8 from Cork city, turn right at the River Bride, just south of Rathcormack, on to the R628. Look for the signposts directing you to the house.

This is a large, mature country garden with bluebell woods, a rhododendron and azalea wood, a fine walled garden, lakes and parkland. The house was built in 1728 and remodelled in 1847 and the garden likewise. So the garden layout as it is today is based on a Victorian garden. The Greens have been working on the garden for the last eighteen years, but work 'really hotted up in the last ten years,' according to Jeremy. Planting for when he is dead is what Jeremy Green says he is doing. He is modest

A view of the house at Ballyvolane in north Cork.

about his achievements, but what he has done will not be underestimated by visiting gardeners. The garden had been left untended for several decades before he and his wife, Merrie, took it over. But the work is moving along swiftly now. Hundreds of young rhododendron and azalea were recently planted around the lawn edges, tucked under the mature trees. But as with all large-scale gardens, the understanding is always that future members of the Green family and their visitors will be the people to enjoy the results of today's work.

The house stands above a sloped meadow and park leading down to three impressive interlinked lakes set under old groves of beech and oak trees. When they started, there were two lakes already in existence and the Greens then added a third. These spill into each other in a surprisingly natural-looking way, providing a beautiful scene that can be appreciated from the house. But, if you want to take a bit of exercise, the walk down to the lakes is a pleasant stroll.

To one side of the back lawn is the kitchen garden. Half of its walled area is being worked at present. Kitchen gardens are for many owners something of a millstone: too big to tackle without a sizeable gardening staff. The Greens work a small ornamental kitchen garden within the larger walled area, producing tasty, home-grown herbs for the table and gorgeous flowers for the house. It operates effectively and looks good and makes more sense than working a larger area in a slip-shod manner. There are long, fragrant mixed borders and beds of flowers for cutting and wandering through. The vegetable garden next to the flowerbeds is a hive of industry. Varieties of lettuce, artichokes, Swiss chard, beets, carrots and all the other staples needed for the house line out along the plots. The final and best feature in the walled garden is a rounded beech hedge *allée* that frames the grazing cows in a paddock beyond the garden. This leads back to another flower border with some flowering shrubs. Myrtle, *Cornus kousa* and buddleia give a solid fabric to the flowerbeds and the structure they provide when the herbaceous plants have gone to ground in the winter is invaluable.

The atmosphere in Ballyvolane is simple, uncluttered and substantial, combining park and woodland walks with shrub-enclosed lawns and a floral and productive walled garden. It is a place that will instruct gardeners well.

Glengarriff, Bantry, County Cork; Tel: +027 63570; Fax: +027 63255; e-mail: bambooparkltd@eircom.net ▪ **Contact**: Claudine Caluwaerts ▪ **Open**: Easter–31 October, Monday–Sunday, 10am–7pm; groups welcome ▪ **Entrance fee** goes towards garden upkeep ▪ Supervised children welcome; please note, dogs on leads ▪ **Special features:** bamboo products for sale; picnic facilities; access to beach ▪ **Directions:** set in the village of Glengarriff, the park is well signposted.

Set on a warm, south-facing slope and surrounded by myrtle, rhododendron and rock, the eight-acre Bamboo Park in Glengarriff is a young garden, with several years to go before it reaches anything like its real potential. However, one day the bamboo groves will give 'the feel of walking through the bamboo forests of Vietnam,' as Claudine Caluwaerts tantalisingly describes the future in west Cork. Groves of *Dicksonia antarctica* are now handsome but some day, perhaps in ten or twenty years, they will make a breathtaking sight. That day is some time off, but the young planting is still worth seeing as it matures.

The idea for a bamboo park came about when the Caluwaerts visited the Bambouserie near Anduze in the south of France several years ago. So began the Glengarriff park as an experiment where the survival of some species will be monitored. The outcome for plants like *Trachycarpus wagnerianus* and *Trachycarpus tacil*, a native of northern India where it is endangered, will be interesting for the County Cork garden. More usual specimens, like Chusan palms (*Trachycarpus fortunei*) and *Phoenix canariensis,* grow easily in these southern parts of Ireland, thriving in the warmth and damp. A tree known to us all through Hollywood films as the LA sky duster (*Washingtonia robusta*) will be observed to see how high it can stretch up. Finally, the honey palm (*Jubaea chilensis*), which has a coconut-flavoured seed, is not expected to fruit in Cork for a couple of centuries yet, as it is one of the slowest maturing palms in the world.

These young specimens have been planted in groves between wide gravel paths. Lines of bamboo, ferns and trachycarpus will fill out and trail off into the woods, where myrtles, hydrangea and rhododendron underplanted with wild garlic lead on out to the sea. Avenues of eucalyptus facing bamboo make a loud rustle of leaves, like the sounds captured in a seashell, as one walks through them. Out by the real sea, thirteen stone pillars edge the garden on its coastal side and the views over the water to the island of Ilnacullin and the seals bathing on rocks are tranquil.

For the foreseeable future, while the Bamboo Park matures, the Caluwaerts have opened their other garden, usually not available to the public. This is a fine old garden, planted in 1910. Sunken streams are set into rising and falling tree-strewn lawns with tall pines casting only light shade on the vegetation below. Alongside these are fifteen-metre-high, stick-thin eucalyptus and mimosa and tunnels of white and blood-red camellia and *Griselinia littoralis* 'Bantry Bay'. The centrepiece in the garden is a wide, shallow, irregular stone stairs that rises up through the woods. This leads onto crunchy paths of old beech nuts, dappled by light leaf shade cast by the beech trees overhead, where spring bulbs start the year with soft colour.

Finally, deep in the middle of the garden is a bog garden of astilbe, rodgersia and arum lily beside the sunken stream, which is crossed by flat slab-stone bridges. For now, the bamboo park is two gardens for the price of one. Enjoy them both while you can.

Bantry, County Cork; Tel: +027 50047; Fax: +027 50795 ▪ **Contact:** Egerton and Brigitte Shelswell-White ▪ **Open:** March–October, Monday–Sunday, 9am–5pm; groups welcome ▪ **Entrance fee** goes towards garden and house upkeep. A fee is charged for entry to the house and garden or to the garden alone and the price varies accordingly, but children go free ▪ Supervised children welcome ▪ **Special features:** groups should book meals in advance; gift shop; Spanish Armada exhibition centre ▪ **Directions:** located on the N71 to Cork, Bantry House is just under 1km outside of Bantry town, on the left-hand side, and is well signposted.

Bantry House has been in the White family since the mid-1700s when Richard White bought it from the Earl of Anglesea. (The house built, for Lord Anglesea, known then as Blackrock House, was designed in the early 1700s by an unknown architect.) White continued to buy land in and around Bantry Bay until the family was the biggest landowner in Bantry and Castletownbere. In the 1940s Bantry House opened its gates to the curious and interested, becoming the first stately house in Ireland to do so. As a result, the Shelswell-Whites (as the family is now named) are well accustomed to accommodating visitors and they do it in an informal but expert way. Theirs is one of the finer gardens in the country, imaginatively restored and revamped by the enthusiastic family and their big team of workers after almost sixty years of neglect. The garden is being restored under the Great Gardens of Ireland Scheme and the work being done is a credit to both scheme and family. The whole restoration is being overseen by English designer Peter Teasdale who has been involved with the garden for several years. The restoration at Bantry stared in earnest in 1997 and will continue well past 2001.

It's hard not to be charmed by this house and garden. It is quite unusual: handsome on a grand scale as befits the seat of several generations of lords Bantry, but it is also idiosyncratic and, despite its formality, a quirky sort of place. Mr Shelswell-White carries out the work of ticket and brochure-seller in a wonderfully haphazard way in an entrance hall filled with Pompeiian mosaics and accumulated treasures of several hundred years, with Marian Finucane talking away on a little radio in the background.

Meanwhile, in the garden work is ongoing and gargantuan. I arrived on a day when the chaos of a great garden being brought back to glory was in full swing. Great slabs and bridges were being put in place by gangs of workers in the mixed woods on the garden hill walk. A bamboo grove has been planted along this path, giving a slightly Japanese feel. From here it is a long walk of nearly a half a mile up to the five-acre double walled garden where fig trees were being planted (with the addition of a bucket of animal blood to fertilise) as one of the advance jobs in its restoration. The walled garden is reputed to have been one of the finest in the country in its heyday in the nineteenth century – the produce for the house was as decorative in the garden as it was useful in the kitchens.

On arriving into the garden one of the first features encountered is an unusual new hedge of hornbeam, copper beech and holm oak over a bank of aconites, cyclamen and snowdrops. Almost unbelievably, this spot, right beside the house, was once the ash and rubbish tip, and over three tonnes of rubbish was cleared before the hedge and flower planting could begin.

New box plants have been placed in the delicate and intricate Italian Garden, which is set beside the house, providing a beautiful view from the upstairs windows of the house. The old plants had succumbed to a mystery rust and fungus problem. (Although the head gardener of a great garden is rarely heard confiding to Gerry Daly about leaf canker or rust, it is always comforting for lesser gardeners to know that problems also land on the great and good.) Within the box hedges is a circle of wisteria with knotty trunks that are as appealing as the dangling flowers and feathery leaves. At around 100 years old, the circle is made of two varieties of wisteria, one Japanese and one Chinese, curling clockwise and anti-clockwise around the circle to meet in the middle. They surround an eccentric-look-

Bantry House enjoys one of the most blessed positions of any garden on the island, overlooking Bantry Bay in West Cork.

ing, fossil stone-encrusted water feature and pond, or *pecherie*, in which fish were once kept decorously until their presence was required at the dinner table.

On the north terrace, at the front of the house, a line of fourteen circular beds is being recreated. These look out over Bantry Bay. Alternating Phoenix date palm and yucca with two varieties of box, one golden and one plain, combine to make up circles of green and gold linked with additional weaving bands of coloured aggregates: a high-brow, low-maintenance garden. Continuing around the the other side of the house is the rose garden, edged with cordylines and stone urns. This is being re-worked using old varieties of roses – another work in progress.

Diana's bed, close to the house, was the first of the garden features to be completed in the current restoration. The circular bed surrounding a little statue of *Diana,* goddess of the hunt, is filled with the matt bluey-grey leaves of melianthus, box, white agapanthus, silvery-blue thistles, tall alliums and hakonechloa grass. This is a strong, fairly modern combination of plants. In the spring a mass of bulbs, mainly colchicums, adds to the mix of tall and striped grasses like *Panicum* 'Hamelyn', a grass with good bottlebrush seed heads.

For most visitors the glory of the garden is the Stairway to the Sky or Hundred Steps, which is close by the Italian garden. This is a monumental-scale staircase, cut into the hill that rises up to the side of the house. The lined terraces bordering the stairs are currently being regrassed. These run off the stairway in ledges – until recently these were banks of overgrowth and rough. At the top of the stairway the view out over the garden, bay and headland beyond is not to be beaten, except maybe by the view from the top of the old carriage drive, which was once the main road into Bantry House and is a short walk up from the steps. The fine view on a clear day is particularly remarkable because, when on ground level, the garden is so diverting that one tends to forget how beautiful the surroundings are. A book on Bantry House, written by Nigel Everett, is well worth looking at for a more detailed history of the area, family and events related to Bantry House through the centuries (*see* www.homestead.com/irisharcadia).

Glanmire, County Cork; Tel: +021 4884489 ▪ **Contact:** Ned Kirby ▪ **Open:** May–October, by appointment to groups only ▪ **Entrance fee** goes towards garden upkeep ▪ Supervised children welcome ▪ **Special features:** refreshments can be booked by prior arrangement; plants for sale occasionally ▪ **Directions:** from Cork go through Glanmire village and travel 1.6km. Turn left at sign for Sarsfield Court, past the hospital, straight through the crossroads and after 0.5km turn left. The garden is on the left, a further 0.5km on.

The Kirbys have an appealing, relaxed attitude to their garden. Soccer goalposts were being erected as I arrived to visit in the early autumn. Mrs Kirby said it was the end of the visiting season and so she could hardly object to her boys playing football – it's a rare, dedicated gardener for whom the need to protect visitors from stray balls is the only reason to ban footie on the lawn. Too many people feel they cannot begin to garden because the children will wreck or eat the results of their work, but the two can marry. Children do not need to be confined to a climbing frame at the bottom of the plot. If introduced to the garden in an engaging way, most children will show consideration for the dahlias and they might even take to growing things themselves. Planting carrots and eating the raspberry crop grown together is, to use a dreadful phrase, proper quality time.

Sheltered from the road by a high beech hedge, the Kirbys's garden is a suntrap. Tucked in against this tall hedge is a sun-soaked bank of mixed shrubs and flowers, heathers and grasses, including a very pretty *Dahlia merckii*, a delicate, small, pink-flowered cultivar with a subtle style alien to many of its louder relatives. Down from this bank is a smart area with stone pots set into gravel. Chives, grasses and catmint grow easily from the gravel and variegated white and green sage spills out over the path. The sense is of controlled chaos in soft, powdery colours. Giving good-looking plants the leeway to sprawl and spread for as long as they look pleasing is a real talent and much in evidence in this spot.

In front of the house are two beds facing one another with a circle of grass between where a birdbath provides the focal point. This stands over a collar of Lady's mantle (*Alchemilla mollis*) and horned violet (*Viola cornuta*). One of the two beds is low and herbaceous with lamb's ears (*Stachys byzantina*), more catmint, lobelia and blue agapanthus lollipops. Behind it are tall shrubs and small trees with plenty of variations in leaf colour and texture.

The house is hidden under ivy, cotoneaster, climbing lobster claw and rich yellow fremontodendron. Under all this is a big run of variegated ground elder (*Aegopodium podagraria* 'Variegatum'). This is usually one of the worst thugs in the garden, spreading with worrying enthusiasm. It will grow anywhere and even thrives in dry shade. But the Kirbys have it fenced in by the driveway, so its cream and green leaves can be enjoyed while the rest of the garden need have no fear of being annexed. The back of the house looks out on a field full of cows, seen through a cottagey gateway set in the beech hedge and mounted with a sign threatening a thirty shilling fine for tampering with it – so behave! There are mounds and hummocks of creeping hardy geraniums spilling out on to the gravel path alongside sun-soaking celmisias and eryngium. Deep gravel paths by the side of the house hold back banquettes of clipped cotoneaster and golden privet shaped in a bulging, well-fed cone.

The garden is still very much a work in progress. A new area taking in a field to the side of the garden is being developed, centering on a natural pond. This will double the size of the garden and provide a host of new possibilities for the Kirbys over the next few years.

CARNIVAL

Conna, County Cork; Tel: +058 59184 ※ **Contact:** Carla Blake ※ **Open:** under the annual Cork Hospice Garden Scheme, contact the hospice for annual dates; apart from that, open through the summer by appointment only to groups of fifteen or more ※ **Entrance fee** donated to charity ※ Supervised children welcome ※ **Special features:** teas may be booked by prior arrangement; plants for sale occasionally; wildlife is abundant ※ **Directions:** travelling on the Cork–Dublin road (N8), north of Watergrasshill turn onto the R628 signposted for Tallow. Travel through Aghern to get to Conna. In Conna, travel through the village. On the outskirts of the village is a small factory and housing estate. Carnival is a few hundred yards beyond these. It is a yellow cottage marked by exuberant flowering shrubs planted along the road-side wall. If you are travelling from Tallow to Conna, the garden is on the left-hand side just outside Conna.

Carnival is not a garden that can be easily missed. The front fence is trailed over by a big evergreen flowering quince (*Chaenomeles*) with waxy flowers, clematis and a gor-geous tangle of roses, cotoneaster, aquilegia, wild garlic and bluebells. Carla Blake's garden is a real sparkler. For anyone who loves plants it's like arriving in a happy, col-ourful heaven, and Carla herself is such an enthusiast that talking to her adds hugely to the visit. The Blakes arrived in Conna in 1977 and the first task on the one-acre site was to harness it for vegetable production. Carla's husband, a survivor of the Japanese prison camps in the Second World War, brought a passion for growing food to their plot of land. But the soil was completely 'run-out', as Carla explains, and had been so over-used that it would grow potatoes no bigger than marbles. The pair set to work adding huge amounts of manure and compost to the starved soil. The garden has been a productive place ever since, a true testament to the phrase 'the fruits of one's labours'. Carla is a well-known cookery writer, contributing for years to the *Irish Press* and now to the *Irish Examiner*, so much of the food grown in the garden is used for her cooking experiments.

Carnival is completely informal and relaxed. 'It's not a chequebook garden. It's an environmentally friendly autograph garden,' says Carla, referring to the way her garden has been built, over the last thirty-four years, from gifts of plants, cuttings, slips and seeds from gardening colleagues. Added to these are Carla's 'volunteers', the plants that self-seed and make themselves at home, plants like hollyhocks, poppies, aquilegias, honesty and violas. 'Informal' means that the garden is a place where vege-tables and purely decorative plants lean against and complement each other. Aspara-gus beds beside benches provide as pretty a sight as any froth of gypsophila. One view leads along a path to a decorative obelisk of 'Leaping salmon' roses and a mass of tulips, alliums, sweet peas and delphiniums sharing their limelight with decorous, kitchen-bound artichokes. Nearby a big clump of purple sage with dusty leaves sof-tens and mutes spiked onion leaves next door. Airy fennel grown under plum trees to-gether combine function and good looks. A clematis arch knots together the romantically named *Clematis* 'Capitaine Thuilleaux', *Clematis* 'Lasurstern' and *Clematis* 'Voluceau' in contrasting purples and blues. Elsewhere a rustic pergola of *Clematis* 'Ville de Lyon', 'Jackmanii' and 'Mrs Cholmondeley' mixes blue and lavender. Phlox and roses like 'Zephirine Drouhin' add splashes of creamy pink. A purple-berried billardiera clambers up the house wall and *Clematis* 'Miss Bateman' and 'Early Sensation' also camouflage the building. Nearby, creamy azara and contrasting dark shiny pyracantha adorn the shed.

Bird-boxes and feeders on every available tree and wall mean that the garden is full of birds sporting about. Two big cordylines and a great splayed *Cornus controversa* border the path that leads from the buildings through the main garden. Roses, clematis and two fine specimens of osmanthus, one white and one yellow, supplement these. The jungle-like planting is interrupted by sunny, sheltered, gravelled openings with benches and brightly coloured osteospermum and other sun-loving plants lolling in these unexpected expanses.

Carla Blake is well liked in the village of Conna, as a plaque by a small pond in the centre of the garden testifies. The people of Conna presented this to her for services rendered to the community – Carnival has raised £34,000 for local charities since 1987. This dripping pool is surrounded by rough stone and planted naturally with ivy and *Ajuga reptans*, purple *Euonymus fortunei* 'Silver Queen' and pittosporums. Beneath these fat carp swim lazily about in the water and nearby a little Buddha sits and bestows his goodwill on a bed of creeping jenny. Glass bell cloches decorate another spot. Two small stone sentries mark the way into a good-looking bed of hesperis, honesty, rosemary and hosta. Glazed pots are set down everywhere, adding a bit of extra colour or a seasonal touch to different areas.

Rows of healthy young plants stand lined up around the side of the garden waiting for their turn in the ground. The chance to see the work in progress as well as the finished garden is always interesting for visitors. The garden moves out toward the surrounding fields where boundaries of sycamore, pink broom, mahonia and corokia wrap the space up well. Carnival is a cottagey garden with a modern twist and it doesn't look back to the past too slavishly. Carla borrows some elements of older garden styles to add to her own individual and contemporary look, creating a unique space that is a joy to explore.

CARRAIG ABHAINN GARDENS

Durrus, Bantry, County Cork; Tel: +027 61070 ▪ **Contact:** Hazel and Eugene Wiseman ▪ **Open:** 1 March–30 September, Monday–Saturday, 10am–7pm; closed Sundays and bank holidays, except during the West Cork Garden Trail when it opens seven days a week; groups by appointment only ▪ **Entrance fee** donated to charity and goes towards garden upkeep ▪ Children need to be well supervised around the river and ponds; please note, dogs on leads ▪ **Directions:** set in the middle of Durrus Village, behind Wiseman's shop.

Wiseman's shop is choc-a-bloc with hardware, beach balls, videos and newspapers, sweets, socks, cornflakes and everything. In 1982 Hazel and Eugene Wiseman bought the shop and what could be loosely described as a garden to the rear: 'It was a real no-go area,' says Eugene, 'so we just started clearing it and putting in paths. But then we realised the potential here and we got more serious and started gardening properly.' It didn't take long before the people from the West Cork Garden Trail found out about the Wisemans and encouraged them to join the other gardens that open to the public, and so Carraig Abhainn took off.

Don't let the town setting deceive you. This is a substantial, two-acre garden that stretches along behind the shop and house with the river laid out beside it along its length. Surprises are a feature in the garden, like that of a twelve-metre-long mural of Mediterranean scenes executed on a pillared portico that stands in front of an Italianate pond. Groves of gunnera, hosta, creeping nasturtium, trees and flowering shrubs are cut through by sets of steps, gravel and bark mulch paths. Specimen trees, a phormium walk and mixed beds all wander in and out of each other. Strange statuary and giant rocks planted over with alpines are dotted along the path edges. But these are really only like the appetiser in a good meal. The main course is at the bottom of the garden: the delectable river.

Carraig Abhainn is a remarkable river. The name means 'river rock', and in the water natural pools gather between rows of huge, elongated barriers or humps of rock that have been rounded by the constant flow of water. It's the sort of water feature that will send the owners of ordinary ponds (with peeing cherubs and pump-driven waterfalls) home to root out the crow bar and pick-axe. There are bridges with seats perched on them from which to catch sprays of fresh air and charged ions from the mini rapids below. Blue lacecap hydrangeas dangle over one such seat, adding an iridescent light to the shady, fresh spot. The path continues out to a really wild section of the river and it becomes more of a scramble at this point. A set of stone steps brings you down to the edge of the white water and another view of pools, torrents and foamy runs of water between the rocks. A seat is set here within easy reach of wild strawberries – have manners and resist them!

CARRAIG RUA

Upper Rocklodge, Carrigrohane, County Cork; Tel: +021 4870178 ※ **Contact:** Mrs Ann Law-Coffey ※ **Open:** June–August, by appointment to groups only; also opens for occasional charity days (see local press for details) ※ **Entrance fee** donated to charity ※ Not suitable for children ※ **Directions:** from Cork turn right at the end of the Carrigrohane Road. Pass the Anglers' Rest pub and continue on the road to the Muskerry Golf Club. Pass a petrol station on the left and take the first left uphill. After the Pitch and Putt club, turn right onto a tarmac drive into two houses and follow the red-stone signs for Carraig Rua.

Mrs Law-Coffey has been working the garden at Carraig Rua for ten years. In 1999 she won the Munster Garden for All Seasons category in the Shamrock All Ireland Gardens Competition. The garden is laid out on the steep side of a valley in the hilly area of Carrigrohane, so the views beyond the garden are striking and deeply complementary to it. Tree-tops stretch out beyond the garden, uninterrupted by buildings or other distractions. It is a beautifully placed garden. Within the garden the dominant feature is a huge rock, the Carraig Rua (red rock), which is set in the middle of the garden and provides a backdrop for much of the planting. 'This was all one level when I started out but I wanted to change the levels completely,' explains Mrs Law-Coffey, and so she did, turning the garden into a series of ledges with stone and sleeper steps and narrow paths linking them together. 'I like to open up paths. They allow me to get right in to see the plants properly and they also open new views along the garden.'

The house was built to serve the garden. Every window looks out on a particular view or angle of the different beds, across at the red rock or down to a knot garden made of over 1,000 begonia plants. Two natural springs feed a pond that stands in front of the house amid hostas, baby's tears, echiums and some natural stone sculptures.

There are several remarkable features in this garden, one of which is the scroll garden. Running for about 100 metres across the garden, this is a young bed made of over 1,000 box plants arranged in intricate patterns. It stands on a carpet of gravel backed by a stone wall with quince, apple, peach and loganberries underplanted with nerines. To the other side is a bank of 140 hydrangeas edged very practically by lettuce. Using something as useful as lettuce in this otherwise purely decorative bed is an excellent idea. Above the scroll garden, on the next ledge up, is a rose walk made up of bands of 'Sexy Rexy', 'Bright Smile' and rich red 'Trumpeter'. On the arches that divide the varieties are 'New Dawn' and 'Iceberg'. This walk leads towards one of the stone wall boundaries covered in *Rosa* 'Abraham Darby' and 'Golden Showers'. From here the garden turns upward through a camellia and azalea slope, known as the spring garden, toward the impressive carraig rua, which is moss-covered and embraced by a big *Clematis montana*. At the highest point in the garden is a flat plateau of well-maintained lawn backed by a recently laid out border. This is a long, layered bed with lilies at the back and hostas and white daisies in front, all backed by *Liriodendron* and *Cornus kousa*, both flowering exotically white. This whole garden is wonderfully well-manicured and ordered.

Out of it a gateway leads into another garden and a completely different world. A mature oak and beech wood provided the bones for this, a truly secret garden. Mrs Law-Coffey keeps this second garden well divided off and separate from the main area. In here, under huge trees, are young rhododendrons and a light scattering of ferns, tree ferns and azaleas. The light cast by young beech leaves is soft and limey and when the rhododendrons are in flower early in the summer the light is magical. At the top of the steep hill in this wood garden is a small stone tea house, set beside a holly that is twisted daintily around itself and around the 'Queen Beech', so-called 'because it's forked,' explains Mrs Law-Coffey. Lock the gate and leave me in this wild place with nothing to be seen but trees out to the horizon.

CASHELANE GARDENS

Cashelane House, Reenmeen East, Glengarriff, County Cork; Tel: +027 63051; e-mail: bettyfrancine@eircom.net ▪ **Contact:** Betty Timmerman Damiaans ▪ **Open:** during the West Cork Garden Trail and on occasional charity days for the Missionaries of the Sacred Heart (see local press for details); at any other time by appointment to groups only ▪ **Entrance fee** ▪ Supervised children welcome ▪ **Special features:** picnic facilities; path leading down to the sea; plants for sale occasionally ▪ **Directions:** travelling from Bantry to Glengarriff, go as far as the Golf Links Hotel. The entrance is opposite a pink house. From Glengarriff to Bantry, drive to the Bay View Hotel and the garden is the next on the right.

Betty Timmerman's garden is one of the big group of West Cork gardens which open for the garden trail every summer, allowing thousands of tourists and garden visitors to feast on their beauty. It is set in the middle of Glengarriff, above the sea and looking over at Ilnacullin and the Caha and Sugarloaf Mountains beyond Bantry Bay. The garden covers four-and-a-half acres and is worked by Betty, her daughter Francine and a wonderful man called Joe. Between the three of them, someone is in the garden all day, everyday. It has been worked in this manner for twenty years. 'There was a garden here when we came but it was very overgrown so we started to open it out,' explains Betty. She did more than that. Cashelane is a remarkable informal garden, filled with flowers and colour and something to see all year round, and looking out on one of the most beautiful views in the world. The large plot has its own woodland and a cool, shady area of fern, silver birch, holm oak, rhododendron, Chilean fire bush (*Embothrium coccineum*), camellia and myrtle (*Luma apiculata*), which is widely grown in the southwest where it enjoys the warmth bestowed by the Gulf Stream. Betty's myrtles are grown in an intriguing semicircle or bower, into which one sits, the walls being made of the slim, smooth cinnamon-coloured tree trunks and the roof made of glossy, dark-green leaves and sweet white flowers that carpet the floor as they fall.

The house, looking out across the bay, is surrounded by a wide circle of mature pines towering over the wood garden, which is at its height in May when rhododendrons in every conceivable shade fill the place with flower and, in some cases, scent. *Rhododendron* 'Beauty of Littleworth', with funnel-shaped white flowers, and a particularly striking pale yellow *Rhododendron campylocarpum* are real beauties. The driveway is surrounded by a mix of different osteospermums, their daisy-like flowers gleaming brightly and hanging down over a rough stone bank. The house provides both backdrop and supporting walls for a great amount of planting: little blue corydalis, veronica and oxalis hug the ground, while clematis, roses and potato vines scale the walls. Out from the house the garden wanders off in a lazy, meandering way through shrubs, herbaceous plants, small trees and sloped lawns that wash around a huge stand of gunnera or 'industrial rhubarb'.

To one side of the garden is a pond so natural I refused to believe it was man-made, but Betty says it is only in the garden seven years, 'and we have loads of frogs in it but I can't get fish to stay because the heron comes in and eats them.' The frogs live in around the rough edges obligingly planted up with sheltering ferns, iris, hosta and day lilies, which have spread and seeded around the perimeter.

Betty Timmerman paints as well as gardens and her artist's eye is evident in the way she groups plants, like lime-green variegated *Hosta sieboldiana* beside red phygelius and reddish turtle head (*Chelone obliqua*). Elsewhere mauve erysimum with golden bracts of euphorbia bring out the best in each other. Another attention-grabbing combination is *Acer platanoides* 'Crimson King', a tree with wine-coloured leaves and yellow flowers, alongside a *Viburnum tinus*, which flowers white and produces bluey-black fruits in autumn, and a huge, red-flowering leptospermum.

Betty is a gardener with a magic touch with plants – she is undoubtedly one of the blessedly green-fingered. She even has a 'sickbed': 'Everything that is sickly I put in here in the shelter to mind it until it can be transplanted again, and it works!' declares the life saver, while I think guiltily of the scores of miserable specimens I convinced myself would be better off having food and water withheld. Betty Timmerman and Cashelane have much to teach their visitors!

Baneshane, Midleton, County Cork; Tel: +021 4613379; e-mail: nswilliams@eircom.net ■ **Contact:** Neil and Sonia Williams ■ **Open:** May–August, by appointment only; groups welcome ■ Children must be well supervised due to the pond ■ **Entrance fee** donated to charity and goes towards garden upkeep ■ **Special features:** teas available by special arrangement; unusual plants for sale ■ **Directions:** travelling from Cork city, take the slip road into Midleton off the bypass. Opposite the Texaco garage, turn right and cross the flyover. Turn left at the T-junction and after 1km take a right turn. The garden is sixth on the right.

Cedar Lodge is a four-year-old garden that Mr Williams started from a flat grazed field. Described as 'a plantsman's garden', it is full of rare and unusual plants. As the former owner of the well-known Carewswood Garden Centre in Castlemartyr, Mr Williams has a wealth of knowledge and understanding of plants and it is a treat to wander in and out of the beds spotting one remarkable plant after another. His garden covers almost two acres. It is divided into different areas and within each area there are individual beds which will give the beginner invaluable tips about good spacing of plants and the arrangement of heights and types of plant together to create the best effect.

To the front of the garden, within the beech hedge boundary, there are a number of serpentine beds of different sizes, mostly low and herbaceous, with small shrubs and evergreens providing a skeleton to hold up the fleeting beauties of the herbaceous flowering plants. Behind this, the pale pink house is complemented by pinkish gravel harbouring powdery-blue ceanothus and variegated vinca around the base of the building and supplemented by seasonal pots of pink tulips. Walking out from the house there are stone banks with little sprouts of aubrieta, primroses and *Cotoneaster* 'Gnom' dotted along in repeating alternate placing. The main bed runs around the perimeter of the garden, filled with a number of brooms, peonies, white delphiniums, echiums and hellebores living in the light shade cast by tree ferns (*Dicksonia antarctica*). This bed weaves in and out so that it is necessary to walk its length in order to discover the dactylorhiza, Chatham Island lilies and Japanese painted ferns.

To the back of the house is an elaborate figure-of-eight pond with a cascade, bog garden and raised rockbed, all of which can be seen from the terrace behind the house through a quirky, well-placed window set into a hedge. Dripping down the rocks are Corsican mint, spikes of *Cimicifuga racemosa* and clumps of little white poppies. An arched walk of roses and clematis is the latest addition to the garden, planted with a mix of *Clematis* 'Comtesse de Bouchaud', *Rosa* 'Étoile de Hollande' and wisteria. The walk runs the length of the back garden by the lines of onion, lettuce and beans of the vegetable plot. The order and perfection of the whole garden reflects the great number of hours put into it by the Williams family.

Woodleigh Park, Model Farm Road, Cork city; Tel: +021 4541560 ■ **Contact:** Mrs Aileen Kennedy ■ **Open:** March–October, strictly by appointment only; for Cork Open Gardens Week (*see* local press for annual dates); groups welcome ■ **Entrance fee** donated to charity and towards garden upkeep ■ Supervised children welcome ■ **Directions:** turn right on to the Western Road at Dennehy's Cross leading onto the Model Farm Road. Turn left at the traffic lights opposite the Rendezvous pub and second on the right after Highfield Rugby Club. The garden is fourth on the left.

This small town garden proves that a huge plot is not necessary for the really avid plant collector. Mrs Kennedy's garden is a well-organised little jungle that has been worked continuously for over four decades. The tiny front garden is north-facing and a good lesson in what one might plant in that situation (albeit in the mild Cork climate). It is filled with willow gentian, ferns and variegated Solomon's seal with creamy-green leaves that light up a shady area. An acer is underplanted with a scattering of cyclamen and *Melianthus major* with the pretty pink flowers of *Geranium* 'Anne Folkard' backing it sits at the front of the bed. Growing on the north wall of the house is a fine creeping *Parthenocissus henryana*, the leaves of which colour cherry red in the autumn. That there are thirty different varieties of clematis growing in the garden is worth noting for those who think they can only have climbers if they have walls. Mrs Kennedy's answer? 'I have no walls and so I have to grow my clematis through other plants. I plant them through everything – trees, shrubs, any plant that will support them.' The glory of this is that she maximises her small space and for as long as she has a free tree or shrub, Mrs Kennedy can continue to feed her clematis habit.

Another small garden trick Mrs Kennedy uses is growing canna lilies in pots. These are moved into the greenhouse when they finish flowering, to be replaced with pots of daffodils and tulips, which themselves will be moved off when they finish flowering and so on for year-round interest. Something that impressed me, particularly given that this is a small garden, is the space Mrs Kennedy has put aside for her grandchildren. Boxes of grass cuttings were waiting for the visit of a small grandchild, who, on arrival, ran to check if her favourite flowers had opened before settling down to play with the clippings.

At the back of the house a huge azara reaches up to the top of the building. 'If you saw the tiny little hole that's sitting in you wouldn't believe it,' declares Mrs Kennedy. The azara, however, seems to enjoy the squash and I think she must keep it well-tended in its small spot. The overall picture in the back garden is of variations in foliage colour. Mrs Kennedy has no great love for too much green, which she feels makes a small garden look dark and leaden. As a former flower-arranger, she has an eye for shape, form and colour and she has filled the back garden with an impressive blend of plants with contrasting leaf shapes, textures and colours. She grows hardy trachycarpus palms, a range of different pittosporums and soft-leaved, golden *Cryptomeria japonica* 'Sekkan-Sugi' for their good leaves. To one side of the long, narrow garden is a little pond. This was formerly a child's sandpit, now enjoying a second lease of life, filled with lilies, with damp-happy hostas and primulas around it. Mrs Kennedy loves ferns and has been collecting these for some years. The collection beside the pond enjoys the shade of the taller shrubs and plants. I loved Mrs Kennedy's garden because it shows the huge possibilities a modest-sized garden holds.

COIS CUAIN

Kilcrohane, County Cork; Tel: +027 67070; e-mail: marybobw@eircom.net; website: www.aseasidegarden.net ■ **Contact:** Bob and Mary Walsh ■ **Open:** during the

West Cork Garden Trail (see local press for details); at any other time by appointment only; groups welcome ▪ **Entrance fee** donated to charity and goes towards garden upkeep ▪ Supervised children welcome ▪ **Special features:** teas may be booked by prior arrangement ▪ **Directions:** travelling from Durrus, drive along the Kilcrohane Road for 13km. Pass a prominent ruined tower on the left and approximately 1.6km later take the *boreen* to the left (the garden is signposted at this point during the Garden Trail period). The garden is at the end of this *boreen*.

The Walshs's garden is set right out on the sea, on a wind-swept peninsula among the wildest of scrub and rock. On this unlikely and difficult site they have made an award-winning modern garden, which has featured on the prestigious BBC TV programme 'Gardener's World'. Mary Walsh's garden is extraordinary, but she is modest about her work and protests that the main attraction is, in fact, the sea.

Cois Cuain is a garden of wonderful plants, many of them rare, but all share one important feature: they do well by the sea. Unusually for a seaside garden, no great shelter belt has been erected to protect it from the elements. Instead, the garden falls openly down to the shore. This means that all the plants need to be able not just to survive in but to thrive in wind, and particularly salt wind, conditions. Visitors with seaside gardens would do well to bring a notepad to Mary's garden for plant ideas.

The garden is long and narrow, running parallel to Dunmanus Bay and rising up in several steps or terraces. Cois Cuain is for the sure-footed, vertigo-free visitor. An examination of the garden carries the inspector up and up on paths and steps, past huge *Agapanthus* 'Purple Cloud' over a mass of limey melianthus, grey-leaved romneya with fried-egg flowers and blue-flowering widow's tears (*Commelina coelestis*), to ever-rising levels and 'shelves'. The way the plants and rocks knot together is what gives this place its character.

On the first level there is a great number of succulents, like aeonium, an almost alien-like plant most often seen in greenhouses. Huge agave have gone wild with growth on the stone bank and yuccas flower profusely. One unusual shrub is *Cassia fistula*, a yellow-flowering plant that naturally grows in hot, scrubby places. Another level reveals an unusual pond, which was once a fairly ordinary-looking water feature: 'I used to have lilies and grasses in it, but I found it too much trouble keeping them so I got rid of them and now I have the only floating rockery in the world,' says Mary of her sculptural prowess. It looks like floating rocks working against gravity – puzzling and contemporary and one for the engineers to figure out.

The garden rises up again to another ledge, and now we are at the highest point, with another fine view of the sea. This is a warm, sunny area, smelling strongly of lemon verbena and lavender. Looking down, the house below is covered in Virginia creeper so dense that it drapes out onto the gravel like an outsized dress. What bit of space not taken up by this exuberant plant is covered in ruby-coloured *Rosa* 'Sympathie'. In a particularly favoured spot the very tender *Solanum rantonnetti* is growing well, breathing out lovely perfume from purple-blue blooms.

Back down in front of the house a New Zealand Christmas tree (*Metrosideros excelsus*), is grown for its June costume of exotic red flowers, and chocolate-smelling cosmos (*Cosmos atrosanguineus*) grows through a vellozia with dramatic long leaves. Vellozia is a sturdy plant for rough, rocky, sunny places. As we walk along, Mary whacks an echium as she passes it to make it drop seeds and produce seedlings. The great mass of rock used in the garden is all from the site, 'and whenever you try to plant something else, you find more rock,' as her husband, who does the digging, will testify. So the rock is used everywhere, along with sculptural works and pieces of driftwood that wash up on their shore. I left reluctantly as the determined gardeners were getting down to work on a new project: a willow, oak and stream garden – with plenty more rock, no doubt.

CREAGH GARDENS

Skibbereen, County Cork; Tel/Fax: +028 22121 ▪ **Contact:** Martin Sherry or Ken Lambert ▪ **Open:** March–October, Monday–Sunday, 10am–6pm; at any other time by appointment only; groups welcome ▪ **Entrance fee** goes towards garden upkeep ▪ **Special features:** guided tours ▪ **Directions:** 6km south of Skibbereen on the Baltimore Road (L59).

Creagh is a romantic, Robinsonian-style garden, meandering, natural and wild. Even visited on a day of unremitting, teeming rain, the immense charm of the garden still managed to shine through. Creagh Garden was chiefly the work of Gwendoline and Peter Harold-Barry, who bought the house and lands in 1945, although a walled garden dating back to the Regency period existed prior to this. The Harold-Barrys began and planted the garden in the style of William Robinson (*see* box, p.182), using exotic and native hardy plants in schemes that copy the way plants grow in nature.

The garden has since been taken over by Martin Sherry, who works and maintains it in memory of its talented creators.

Covering about sixteen acres, Creagh Gardens is made up of wooded walks and groves, wilderness and water, informal mixed plantings and grass walks, a walled garden and herbaceous beds. The loveliest feature in the garden is the serpentine mill-pond under a tree canopy of jungle proportions. The mass of ground-level greenery – ferns, primula and big white spikes of arum lily – is overhung by mature oak, larch and beech. Myrtle and rhododendron flowers add scent and colour to the many greens. Little gates open out and reveal inviting views of the sea.

A quaint summerhouse in Creagh, County Cork.

In contrast to the easy feel of the informal wood and water garden, the harnessed smartness of the walled garden comes as something of a shock. Fat and well-shaped manicured box hedging encloses orderly beds of vegetables and flowers and next door smart herb beds are as pretty as they are useful. One area is given over to an orchard where an audience of fancy fowl keep an eye on visitors as they walk through the fruit cages. At the other side of the walled garden is one of the best-looking greenhouses I have ever seen. Well-arranged rows of mother-in-law's-tongue, velvety-rich purple *Tibouchina urvilleana* and banana plants, cucumbers, pots of aubergines, peppers, chillies and lines of drying onions all compete for attention in this well-maintained house.

Around and outside the walled garden is the south border, a well-planted bed of herbaceous and cottage plants with white *Lychnis coronaria* 'Alba' and tall cardoons. Opposite is a low wall of alpine strawberries and ferns. A pergola is piggy-backed by more plum-coloured, dangling *Rhodochiton atrosanguineus* flowers. Usually a greenhouse plant, here it is grown outside as an exotic annual. Scattered intelligently through the gardens are vistas and features with daft names like the Baluba Hut and DiDi's Walk (DiDi was a dog). There are walks and tracks leading in every direction. Creagh is a pleasure to get lost in, a garden with an old-fashioned atmosphere being run on old-fashioned lines, including an honour system payment box. Please do not take advantage – not many people are this trusting.

DERREENAGARIG GARDEN

Glengarriff, County Cork; Tel: +027 63212; Fax: +027 63187 ■ **Contact:** Sue Nightingale ■ **Open:** for the West Cork Garden Trail (see local press for details); at other times by appointment only; groups welcome ■ **Entrance fee** goes towards garden upkeep ■ Supervised children welcome ■ **Directions:** travelling from Glengarriff to Kenmare, take the left turn for the hostel (signposted) 1.6km out of Glengarriff and go to the crossroads. Turn left and travel for 0.5km. The garden is behind a big wooden shed on the left.

When you are following instructions to get to Sue Nightingale's garden, the feeling of getting lost in the woods starts getting stronger and stronger as the route wends along through the Glengarriff woods. You will be quite sure that you have gone adrift by the time you see the tell-tale wooden shed in the seclusion of the Glengarriff hills. Sue has been gardening here since the beginning of the 1990s. It is a wild garden dominated by a roaring river that travels through and along the bottom of the site. The bulk of the garden is set on a substantial hill, eventually slipping downwards and toward the Canrooska River, the noise of which is so powerful that townspeople might call it noise pollution, but it is a wonderful sound nonetheless.

The garden covers just over two-and-a-half acres of mature pine and larch, as well as specimen trees like Mexican white pine (*Pinus ayacahuite*), southern beech (*Nothofagus*), rhododendron, pieris and drimys. Several bridged streams drip into the river. By the house is a little sunny area full of loosely tended herbaceous plants, pretty and flowery and quite different to the rest of the garden. Sue works the garden herself, mostly on organic principles. The design too is organic: 'This is not really a garden you could plan,' says Sue, 'we have a lot of rock and not a lot of soil so the shape and style of the garden really evolved itself.' Rocks sprout from everywhere and in turn the rocks themselves sprout young oak and ash trees. Adding to the abundant natural rock is a good rockery. Sue explains: 'This part of the garden is the ruin of the old house which fell down, so we turned it into a rockery.'

Walking around the garden, pet ducks and geese join the party, leading the way toward the river, which travels through the garden very fast. 'The garden down here gets completely flooded,' says Sue. With over eighty inches of rain per year, the land is wet and heavy. 'Things either die of rot or grow like trains' – a real case of sink or swim.

On the other side of the bridge the garden continues to stretch out, with specimens of tender sephora and embothrium. 'They'll either die or love it here,' she remarks matter-of-factly. A tulip tree (*Liriodendron tulipifera*) is in the ground only five years and certainly loves it – it has already grown to a height of five metres. In this part of the world tree ferns grow like weeds and a big magnolia is putting on about one metre a year. All the trees in this wood were grown from seed and the speed of growth is extraordinary. As this was being discussed, Sue's dog, Widget, was trying to eat his way through a wisteria growing on the bridge. The Nightingales are generous about sharing the garden with their many animals.

Alongside the glamorous and tender plants are the natives: ash, holly and oak. 'We do try to encourage them along,' she says. The trees out in the wood beyond the garden add to the natural atmosphere. These, combined with the sensitive way the garden planting becomes more native as it moves out toward a blurred boundary, make the garden look as though it goes on forever – if only that were so.

DONERAILE PARK

Doneraile, Mallow, County Cork; Tel: +022 24244 ▪ **Contact:** the Administrator ▪ **Open:** April–October, Monday–Friday, 8am–8.30pm, Saturday, 10am–8.30pm, Sunday and bank holidays, 11am–7pm; November–mid-April, Monday–Friday, 8am–4.30pm, Saturday, Sunday and bank holidays, 10am–4.30pm; groups welcome ▪ **Entrance fee** ▪ Supervised children welcome; please note, dogs on leads ▪ **Special features:** picnic area ▪ Member of Dúchas ▪ **Directions:** situated off the main street in Doneraile village, which is on the R581 off the Mallow–Limerick road.

Attached to Doneraile Court – the home of the St Leger family who gave their name to the famous race – Doneraile Park covers 400 acres and is a fine example of an eighteenth-century park designed in the 'Capability' Brown style (*see* box, p.214). In Doneraile there are groves of mature deciduous trees, long and winding drives and restored water features arranged pleasingly around the rolling north Cork landscape.

The waterworks are particularly attractive. This is a series of runs of water, slow moving in places and in others sped up and sent tumbling over weirs and falls, sometimes river-like and occasionally widening out to give the impression of a lake. Big trees, their exposed roots crawling down the riverbank, can be seen as part of the view from a number of well-made stone and wooden bridges. Along the paths through the woods are wild garlic, wood anemone and lords and ladies. The sound of water from streams and falls is never far away and gravel and cobbled paths add a touch of order. One good view is from the drive up to the house, looking back toward a hill that falls down in wide steps of turf onto wooden palisades and from there into a waterfall and the flat, wide lake. The house hides behind stands of mature trees and the path leading to it snakes around and under reclining pines in a wildflower and daffodil meadow.

The St Leger family has lived here since the seventeenth century, but there were earlier gardens at Doneraile. Formal French-style gardens of embroidered box hedging parterres and ornamental woods cut through with straight avenues were laid out in the late 1600s. Today, however, the gardens date mainly to the eighteenth century, as does the house. Home to a great number of eccentrics, cursed viscounts, female freemasons and one particular lady whose best friend was a cigarette-smoking goat, it is in the process of restoration and will provide a colourful guided tour for visitors in due course.

DUNSLAND GARDEN AND WATER FEATURE

Factory Hill, Dunkettle, Glanmire, Cork; Tel: +021 4354949; Fax: +021 4354949; e-mail: peterdow@gofree.indigo.ie ▪ **Contact:** Peter Dowdall ▪ **Open:** Monday–Friday, 9am–6pm; Sunday and bank holidays, 2pm–6pm; groups welcome ▪ **No entrance fee**, but a donation box is provided ▪ **Special features:** garden centre specialising in herbaceous plants and ornamental trees; the herb and vegetable garden, which featured in Peter's television programme in 2000 ('Herbal Infusion', on RTÉ 1), is now open to visitors ▪ Supervised children welcome ▪ **Directions:** from the Cork–Waterford road drive as far as the Island Gate pub. Take the first turn on the left and travel up Factory Hill. Dunsland is on the right.

Dunsland is a work in progress. A woodland garden neglected for years, filled with rhododendron and camellias, it is now slowly being restored and reinstated by Peter Dowdall. Work began on restoring the garden in 1997, but so far the wood has taken up all energy and time and so the walled garden has yet to be worked on.

As with all rhododendron woods the best time of the year to see this garden is in the spring to early summer, when the trees are in flower and underfoot a carpet of spring bulbs brightens the floor. It is a wild place, gardened with a light touch. Perched on a steep slope, the woods can be worked only with a hand-barrow and shovel because it is impossible to bring machinery into the garden, so the clearance of huge bamboo, knotweed and briars has taken great effort.

The garden is fortunate to have a natural stream running through it with lilies, bog primulas, astilbes, ferns and ligularia lining the water. All the paths in here are edged with logs, lined out on end. These are the recycled results of storm damaged trees – a good idea borne out of necessity, the steep slope and access problems.

All replanting is in keeping with the existing garden style. The trees include: acer, camellia, cordyline and ornamental cherry, sycamore, beech, a huge sweet chestnut and two mature tulip trees (*Liriodendron tulipifera*). Newly restored paths wind through a snowdrop, viola and bluebell wood. Wild wood anemone, foxgloves and ferns take over from these later in the year and the effect of wild romanticism is complete. Outside the wood a herb garden has been created. The recreation and restoration is a slow process for Peter and his assistant, Jason Donovan, but alongside the marvellous little nursery he runs, Dunsland is well worth visiting as it slowly emerges from under the many years of overgrowth and neglect.

Goleen, West Cork, County Cork; Tel/Fax: +028 39452; e-mail: courses@theewe.com; ▪ **Contact:** Sheena Wood or Kurt Lyndorff ▪ **Open:** Easter–end September, Tuesday–Sunday, 10am–6pm, telephone for confirmation if travelling a distance; groups welcome ▪ **Entrance fee** donated to charity and goes towards garden upkeep ▪ Not suitable for small children ▪ **Special features:** art courses can be arranged for groups and individuals; accommodation available for course participants ▪ **Directions:** set in the village of Goleen.

The Ewe Art Centre garden covers about half-an-acre and wraps around the art gallery and retreat, which look out at Cape Clear and the Atlantic Ocean. Kurt and Sheena have been working on their eccentric garden since 1994, and if proof is needed that they created it from the wilds and wilderness, ask to see the 'making of a garden' photos in the craft shop. Looking at the pictures of the work done is tiring in itself. The fact that there is a garden here at all is an incredible achievement.

They started by laying out a good mix of herbaceous plants, shrubs, vegetables and flowers on the re-claimed garden site. Their young garden benefitted from the huge amount of rain that West Cork enjoys, on average between seventy to eighty inches a year, and the warm climate. The result was explosive growth. As with very many new

A work from the collection of quirky sculptures found at the Ewe Art Centre in Goleen, County Cork.

gardeners, they planted very closely to get a decent effect early on, placing five plants where three would have sufficed in the long term. The planting filled out quickly and now it's a healthy jungle and the chief task is pulling out surplus plants. The wind is a constant nuisance out on the Mizen Peninsula, but as Kurt says, 'you soon learn what you can plant successfully and what will not grow well in the wind.' So gardeners with windy plots will also find visiting the garden useful.

Kurt doesn't claim to be a specialist gardener and would say that as gardeners he and Sheena simply 'muddle through'. Despite the workers not knowing the Latin names of their plants, the garden is gorgeous and for many people the creation of a good-looking garden is enough proof of expertise. What is in operation in this garden is a good eye and a personal, self-taught style of gardening. It's worth visiting for the sculptures alone, which they have cleverly placed around the garden. As fashion now tends towards using quirky and off-beat items in the garden instead of Grecian statues and spouting cherubs, the sculpture used here should undoubtedly be of inspiration to visitors. Ceramic fish being lifted out of the pond on fishing rods, little pagodas, seats and small unusual pieces are placed strategically between the plants. Coming from ponds and water features is the sound of dripping and gurgling water. I loved the pergolas, swing seats and wattlework hurdles that hold the planting up and back from the constantly encroached-upon paths. This is a garden to inspire confidence in the beginner.

FOTA ARBORETUM AND GARDENS

Fota Island, Carrigtwohill, County Cork; Tel/Fax: +021 812728/812678 ■ **Contact:** the Administrator ■ **Open:** April–end October, Monday–Saturday, 10am–6pm, Sunday, 2pm–6pm; November–March, Monday–Friday, 10am–5pm, closed Saturday and Sunday; groups welcome ■ **No entrance fee**, but a car parking charge applies ■ Supervised children welcome; please note, dogs on leads ■ **Special features:** picnic area; adjacent to Fota Wildlife Park ■ Member of Dúchas ■ **Directions:** 14km from Cork City on the Cobh Road, well signposted.

Fota, formerly known affectionately as 'Foatey', means 'warm turf' or 'warm sod', an appropriate name for a garden that basks in the mild Cork climate. The garden covers twenty-seven acres and is attached to the grand house built by the Smith-Barry family in the early nineteenth century. The favourable conditions were well used by generations of Smith-Barrys. In the nineteenth and well into the twentieth centuries they planted the finest trees and plants from all over the world, producing an arboretum of remarkable proportions as well as a range of pleasure gardens, including a fernery, an Italian garden, a walled garden and a lake. The house and land left the hands of the colourful family and moved through Cork University and some uncertain years, ending up with Dúchas, the Heritage Service, which is now in the process of working and restoring the gardens.

The restored walled garden is only three years old and is laid out in an educational manner with a collection of 160 varieties of Irish-bred daffodils – an unbeatable early spring feature. Running the length of one of the walls is a bed of monocots – plants that start life with only one seed leaf and later on bear narrow, often strappy leaves with parallel veins. Arrangements of libertia, grasses, phormium, tradescantia, iris, crocosmia and hemerocallis make up the display. Another bed holds plants from central and South America and shade-loving plants: primula, pulmonaria, hellebores, hosta, astilbe and old roses like big showy pink *Rosa* 'Comte de Chambord', *Rosa* 'de Rescht' and 'Old Pink Moss', a rose that goes back to 1700 and has a lovely, dusty pink colour.

Beyond the walled garden is the pleasure garden and the old Italian garden, which is being studied by a team of archaeologists before restoration can begin.

On the outside wall in a bed with exotics, like banana plants, are verbena, aster, anemone and hardy plumbago. Centred on the long bed is a classical folly by a massive *Magnolia grandiflora* looking out on huge stands of multi-trunked cordylines and yew hedging under restoration.

The paths lead out past perfect staged lawns into the arboretum: a large cabinet of curiosities. Advertising the location of the arboretum are two huge Canary Island date palms, which can be seen enticingly over the wall. Examples of rare trees include the two already mentioned Canary Island date palms (*Phoenix canariensis*). One of these measured eight metres in 1984 and they are a great source of pride at Fota. Close to them and the old *Orangerie*, well due for a new roof and general overhaul, is a Camphor tree (*Cinnamomum camphora*) from Japan, a Mexican Cyprus (*Cupressus lusitanica*), a myrtle (*Luma apiculata*) from Chile and a fine Turkey Oak (*Quercus cerris*), still a young tree. An evergreen oak (*Quercus ilex*) has a most impressive canopy. The Wellingtonia (*Sequioadendron giganteum*) from California measured 31x4.8m in 1984 and the spongy-barked tree continues to rise skyward. The Monterey pines (*Pinus radiata*) are also remarkable. (The cones on a Monterey pine can stay on the tree for up to thirty years.) It would be hard not to fall in love with trees walking around Fota, as the eye is pulled away from one fine specimen to something even more good looking off in the distance.

Out beyond the arboretum is the fernery, where natural-looking rock formations and deep moss provide a backdrop for a range of ferns. It is all shaded by sweet chestnut and huge *Dicksonia antarctica* tree ferns. Seeing a fernery on a dry day always feels wrong. Visit ferneries in or after rain. The leaves are at their best dripping water and in summer may be steaming a little, giving an even more exotic feel to an already tropical place. Close by, and visible from the fernery, the pond is naturalistic with a planting of lilies over its surface, and wild flowers, gunnera and grasses by the edge.

FOX COVERT

Glounthaune, Lacken Roe, County Cork; Tel: +021 4821747 ✳ **Contact:** Mrs Gobnait O'Flynn ✳ **Open:** during the summer months, by appointment to groups only ✳ **Entrance fee** donated to charity and goes towards garden upkeep ✳ Not suitable for children ✳ **Directions:** from Cork city take the first turn left off the Waterford Road at Glounthaune Church. Continue uphill, travelling under a bridge and through the next crossroads. Turn right at the Y-junction and the garden is 1km along on the right.

Mrs O'Flynn's garden is on a quiet lane just outside Cork, a garden of one impeccably arranged acre, full of colourful flowers and shrubs and held together by a lacework skeleton of white-barked betula and solid stone walls. The garden is strongly sloped and on its banks wine-coloured, tropical-looking canna lilies, melianthus and runs of orange nasturtium overlook the tree-tops of the fields beyond. Dwarf conifers and hydrangeas provide year-round interest and back up the beautifully stuffed summer beds. Some betulas are dotted among the beds, as though they simply self-seeded, and some are grouped in little groves with nothing but white and pink cyclamen and spring bulbs underneath. The effect is stylish.

Winding paths decorated by box footballs run around the building beneath short avenues of young birch trees. To the back of the house, beds run uphill, filled with strong-coloured dahlias, more cannas and other tender and herbaceous plants. Mrs O'Flynn uses these 'statement' plants to achieve an exotic look. Creepers and climbers are everywhere, up walls and over stone arches. Despite the relatively small size of the garden, Mrs O'Flynn manages to build in secret spots, little tunnels of greenery through which you have to go in order to see more and discover surprises. This is good contemporary gardening.

The Glebe, Baltimore, County Cork; Tel: +028 20232 ▪ **Contact:** Jean and Peter Perry ▪ **Open:** May–end September, every day, 10am–6pm, as part of the West Cork Garden Trail; groups welcome, by appointment only ▪ **Entrance fee** donated to charity ▪ Supervised children welcome; please note, dogs on leads ▪ **Special features:** flowers and vegetables for sale; occasional lectures ▪ **Directions:** approaching Baltimore on the N71, the garden is on the right-hand side opposite the 'Baltimore' signpost and is clearly signed.

'We're a market garden but we try to grow the plants in a pleasing way aesthetically, so we made an ornamental vegetable garden, but it's not a *potager*,' says Jean Perry, defending her garden against accusations of over-prettiness. This is certainly no twee show garden. Jean grows a full range of fine produce – vegetables, fruit and herbs – in her hard-working four-and-a-half acre garden. Glebe garden was hard won: 'We literally dug the herb garden out with a crowbar and even then some of the stone was just too tough to move. But herbs like the stony ground so it suits them,' continues Jean. She sells vegetables weekly at the country markets (*see* Country Markets in appendices for days and times), as well as to people who come to the garden and to local restaurants and vegetable shops in Baltimore.

Regarding the plants, all the lettuce is 'cut-and-come'. She harvests the leaves for sale rather than the whole plant, and they continue to renew themselves through the season. There are also ongoing experiments with outdoor varieties of tomatoes – there were fifteen varieties being grown when I visited, including a wonderfully tasty green-striped tomato called 'Green Zebra'. Purple-podded French beans, sweetcorn, pumpkin, squash and 'Painted Lady' runner beans are also undergoing experimental testing. Interestingly, these survived the autumn and winter and came through again the next year, cropping when they are usually grubbed up as an annual. Seaweed is piled on the potato beds and a variety called 'Picasso', a big white spud with pink eyes, is Jean's current favourite. It responds well to this method of growing and is also blight resistant. Jean grows flowers around the edges of the beds because they sell at market, they encourage beneficial insects into the beds and 'they are good for my soul'. I'm not sure that the third is not her main reason. Espaliered fruit trees are being worked along the beds also. Elsewhere an arch of willow over iron bedposts at the end of a bed is a good joke. The garden faces northeast. This is a far from an ideal aspect so the beds have been divided by griselinia hedge clipped into waves. These save the garden from the worst of the winds as well as providing something good to look at.

By the house is a little courtyard garden with water and herbs where, in the summer, the smell of lemon verbena wafts around. It's a pretty spot with purple-flowered hyssop, rue, a camomile lawn and a golden hop growing over a rough arch in a stone wall. An olive tree is the centrepiece of the courtyard. 'The olive tree deals with everything – wind, rain, cold, everything, – and it even fruits in some years.' The herb beds are edged with slate, which holds the gravel off the paths.

An arch of bird cherry (*Prunus padus*), one of three native wild cherry species, leads into the bigger garden: 'All the beds in here are raised because it makes them much easier to dig.' Timber edges allow Jean to use a no-dig method. She simply adds layers of mulch to the beds annually, building up deep piles of rich organic matter into which she plants. The edges mean that nobody can walk on the bed so the earth never becomes compacted and so never requires digging or disturbance. Jean believes that keeping something on the soil all the time, even simply spreading out grass cuttings, is good as it keeps the worms active and the ground warm and insulated.

Jean is an informative gardener, generous with her knowledge, so it makes sense that she would organise classes and lectures. Talks are regularly given at the garden by various guest speakers, such as Anita Hayes of the Irish Seed Savers Association (*see* County Clare).

GLENMAHON

Rochestown Road, Cork; Tel: +021 891674 ▪ **Contact:** Mrs Catherine MacHale ▪ **Open:** occasionally in the summer and by appointment only; groups welcome ▪ **Entrance fee** donated to the Cope Foundation ▪ Supervised children welcome; please note, dogs on leads ▪ **Special features:** plants for sale occasionally; refreshments can be booked by prior arrangement ▪ **Directions:** in Cork city join the Rochestown Road from the Douglas Shopping Centre roundabout. The house is a few hundred metres along on the right, opposite a shop called 'Essentials'.

Mrs MacHale's small garden is a study in elegance. It is a perfectly manicured, beautifully arranged town garden. Walking around to the sound of chimes in the trees, the place is a mass of colour and scent with plants like *Verbena bonariensis*, lilies, tall grasses, pink shrub roses and a good selection of perennials, both usual and unusual. There are sweet peas, white foxgloves and climbers draped on the house. Pots of Paris daisies provide portable dot colour wherever needed. But Mrs MacHale's garden is more than pretty flower and colour. The underlying construction into which the flowers are set is, like good bone structure, the base that gives the garden its good looks. Sweeps of weed-free lawn and well-raked gravel paths provide definite contours, hemming in billowing flower and leaf. Shapely dwarf conifers, topiary and cordylines add vertical structure and height.

The house is surrounded by pots of all sizes. A huge agave, tobacco plants and white fuchsia sharing a pot with white South African violets is just one stylish combination on the front door step. To get to the back garden you must go through the 'workshop' at the side of the house, past pots of healthy young plants waiting for their full-time homes in the main garden. The back garden is, quite simply, perfect. Box cones clipped expertly stand by a lily pond and two circular lawns. One of these lawns is surrounded by more box, which holds back several varieties of pittosporum and other good foliage shrubs. There is great texture and solidity in this planting. The other circle of lawn is surrounded by a contrasting scheme with herbaceous plants like salvia, Japanese anemone and aster falling softly over the grass. Gardening a small plot is perhaps the hardest sort of gardening. All of it can be seen all through the year in a most unforgiving way, but Catherine MacHale has perfected the art. This is a truly inspiring small town garden.

GRANIG HOUSE

Minane Bridge, Carrigaline, County Cork; Tel/Fax: +021 4887114; e-mail: lizkavanagh@eircom.ie ▪ **Contact:** Mary Lynch/Liz Kavanagh ▪ **Open:**

May–October, 2pm–dusk; at all other times by appointment only; groups welcome, by appointment only; for occasional charity days (see local press for details) ▪ **Entrance fee** donated to charity ▪ Supervised children welcome; please note, dogs on leads ▪ **Special features:** teas can be booked by prior arrangment ▪ **Directions:** travelling through the main street in Carrigaline with the Stephen Pearce pottery shop on your right, go to the top of the town and continue for 6.5km until the T-Junction. Turn right and continue for 0.75km to a pub called the Overdraught. A few hundred metres on, take the steep hill turn to the right. Travel up a few hundred metres more. The garden gates are out on the centre of the road.

'I came to this house forty-three years ago and the farmyard was right here in front of the house. There was also a piggery and an old Dutch barn,' explains Mary Lynch, as she sits on her ride-along mower surrounded by an extravaganza of flower and scent. It is far from piggeries and barns today. In between running the farmhouse, raising four boys and writing a weekly column in the *Farmer's Journal* on farm and home life, Mary Lynch began to garden. To the question of how large the garden is she just laughs: 'I haven't the faintest idea.' The question is irrelevant: 'Why would I need to know that?' Quite so, and why would I need to know? It's one of the loveliest gardens in the country, what does it matter what size it is? But it is big. Set around an eighteenth-century house that was once home to Diarmuid Lynch, one of the commanders in the GPO during the 1916 Rising, the garden could best be described as a modern country garden, worked by a knowledgeable enthusiast and guarded by Charlie, a peacock with no great love for visitors.

The main body of the garden is made up of wide grass paths trailing in and out of long twining beds. A clever and obvious tip from the garden was to make paths where there were natural tracks made by her four boys. This meant that Mary never had to put up with the 'elephant-walk' syndrome suffered by gardeners when the path laid down takes a different route to the existing short cut. It is best to accept from the outset that the short cut path always wins. The beds are layered and planted for succession so there is something to look at all year round and at all levels in every part of the garden. For instance, in one bed an unusual white bottlebrush shrub (*Callistemon*) grows over white bluebells. And dahlias have been planted right beside lupins so that as lupins die back they are replaced by dahlias.

There are several consistent features in the garden: gravel is one. The drive and wide sweep around the house are echoed in wide collars of gravel around all the beds. The plants love it. It looks great, holds down weeds, retains moisture, chases off slugs, keeps the necks of the plants dry and pulls light into the base of the beds. Like many good design ideas it started from a practical necessity: 'Laying stones at the edge of the lawns gave the mower wheel a base on which to run. Then we thought it looked good and so whenever we came down the garden we would bring a bucket of gravel and spread it further and further into the beds.'

Another theme running through the garden is sculpture – from a delicate bronze by Annette Hennessy to a big grass sundial and several surprise stone pieces set in nooks around the site. The final theme is repeat plantings. In late spring waves of blue, pink and white bluebells can be spotted under trees and shrubs throughout the garden. Sweet rocket (*Hesperis matronalis*) is another recurrent favourite and so too are spurge – varieties of euphorbia, and aquilegia. Later in the season the repeaters are the delphiniums, lupins and day lilies. These repeaters, constantly seen from the corner of the eye as well as in the fore- and middle-ground, pull the garden together into one coherent unit.

Mary also observes a few other rules: 'I don't go in for annuals. If a plant doesn't come back every year I won't have it.' Everything is raised from seed or cuttings in one of her two big polythene tunnels, then planted out with generous helpings of manure in well-prepared planting holes and left alone. No further mollycoddling is administered. No water or feed is given and everything does magnificently. She is a tough gardener: 'Every year I go around and issue death warrants to various plants. This year it's arum lilies and alstromeria and the mouse plant (*Arisarum proboscideum*).' A stock of white foxgloves is ensured by weeding out any seedlings with red veins because they flower purple and purple is not required.

A final tip: when Mary sees a new or interesting plant, she buys it, takes plenty of cuttings and/or divisions and propagates a multitude of small plants from it. When big enough these are planted out at several points around the garden in order to find where the plant will do best, therefore if there are casualties the loss is negligible. (*Note:* with regard to the two contact names, Mary Lynch and Liz Kavanagh, the latter is Mary's *Farmer's Journal* pseudonym.)

HILLSIDE

Annmount, Glounthaune, County Cork; Tel/Fax: +021 4353119 ▪ **Contact:** Mrs Mary Byrne ▪ **Open:** for charity days (see local press for details); May–end September, by appointment only; groups welcome, by appointment only ▪ **Entrance fee** donated to charity and goes towards garden upkeep ▪ Supervised children welcome ▪ **Directions:** leave Cork on the Waterford Road. In Glounthaune turn left at the church and travel up the hill, under a bridge. Hillside is 100m up this hill, on the right-hand side, first gate on the left. The name Annmount is on the pillar.

Hillside, as its name suggests, is situated on an almost vertical site that most people would run from rather than try to work. Everything about this garden is substantial, from its ample proportions to the towering trees that overlook the site. And everything slopes. Tiny drifts of cyclamen fall down the hill under the trees between spreads of bigger plants. The secret of getting flowers to naturalise on a slope is common sense. Plant the initial bulbs or corms at the top of the hill rather than at the bottom, the seed will naturally fall down and a march down the hill is almost guaranteed. Masses of vinca and mint sweep down into tall clumps of New Zealand flax (*Phormium tenax*). Steps, secreted away among the plants, lead in all directions, making it possible for the visitor to pick their way gingerly through the beds.

Mary Byrne has been working her garden for about twenty years and it has proved a popular destination for visiting gardening groups keen to see her creation. The garden covers four acres in all and she works it all herself, spending part of every day in it. This effort has paid off: Hillside has won the Shamrock All Ireland Gardens Competition twice in four years.

A scree bed by the house is filled with celmisia and dierama which, like her echiums, self-seed almost disgracefully well through the garden. Out from the house is a pink, blue and grey border, 'but the odd bit of red gets in to it' – Mary allows the results of this sort of happy accident to contribute to the picture. She is very casual about this gorgeous bed: 'It has got all the usual things: pholx, delphinium, thalictrum ...' Mary trails off, but this bed is far from usual. It is a mass of blue, purple, lavender and pink flowers that last right through the summer.

A rock garden and stream fall down the hill, flanked by what looks like a guard of honour made of squat cut-leaf acers, to a sunken, perfectly circular pond. The rock garden looks natural and the waterfall picks its way down through it to the pond. Having travelled down the garden, look back up to the house through beds of fuchsia, penstemon and grass. I love the big clump of chocolate cosmos and petrol blue-tipped cerinthe knitted together. Another striking combination is down the hill past big echiums and a flowering tulip tree: dark grass blending with the reddish purple-leaved *Dahlia* 'the Bishop of Llandaff'.

Hydrangea, rhododendron and woods have taken over at the bottom of the hill and here the look is much wilder than above. Moving back up the garden you encounter a beech tree and under it a shady new bed of ferns, meconopsis, pulmonaria and spring bulbs. This is the latest, but most certainly not the last, new project in the garden.

HOLLAND HOUSE

Coole, Fermoy, County Cork; Tel: +025 36668; e-mail: toon@eircom.net ▪ **Contact:** Hannah Weimer ▪ **Open:** for the St Mary's Hospice Scheme, telephone for annual dates; May–September, by appointment only to small groups (not more than twenty) and individuals ▪ **Entrance fee** donated to various charities and goes towards garden upkeep ▪ Not suitable for children because of water features ▪ **Special features:** teas may be booked by prior arrangement; this is a cat-lover's garden ▪ **Directions:** leave Fermoy by the Hospital Road. Pass the hospital and turn right. Travel for 5km. The garden is on the right, down a laneway bordered by tidy hedges that leaves the road beside a grey wall and cottage on the right.

You enter Hannah Weimer's wonderful, exotic jungle garden through a big gate next to a shed that is fairly smothered by the long, cigar-like leaves of *Clematis armandii*. And as you do, keep in mind that this was a plain field in 1988. Holland House is perched on the side of a hill that looks south over County Cork toward the sea. 'We grew the garden from nothing, just a single tree,' says Hannah proudly as we slither between great stands of foliage on narrow paths along the compartmentalised garden. Living in the middle of the countryside, Hannah loves the feel of the wilds in her garden. She has little time for the more manicured look, preferring lush, abundant growth. To achieve this she 'just nudges the garden along a little, encouraging self-seeding and keeping the weeds in check' in a gentle sort of way. 'I grew everything in the garden from cuttings and seeds and I don't plant too many tender things,' explains Hannah while walking between the gorgeous plants. Her garden proves that one doesn't need to fertilise a garden with money; a sense of style and a measure of good taste do the job just as well. An example of her inventiveness is the pretty area called the periwinkle drive, a simple but effective idea using easily obtained, inexpensive vinca plants to great effect. Bargains picked up at car boot sales decorate the place as well as any expensive accessory. Animals, like the three stone cats that cost £10, hidden among the herbaceous plants, are witty touches. 'I don't like expensive things,' she laughs, and she can afford to – this woman has buckets of taste.

The garden covers about half-an-acre and has been subdivided into little rooms by runs of shrubs and groves of evergreens underplanted with wild garlic or ramsons. Small paths, less than a metre wide, run in all directions through beds of shrubs, climbers and herbaceous plants, further dissecting the area. The house is insulated under a deep cover of parthenocissus, *Clematis montana* and a Chilean fire bush (*Embothrium coccineum*). 'People say these climbers ruin the house walls. I say, so what,' laughs Hannah. Picking our way along the paths, white libertia flowers and big mophead hydrangeas spill out of the beds in an untidy, gorgeous mass.

The hip-high maze of golden *Lonicera nitida* is a pleasure to wander through and is underplanted by baby blue eyes. This is backed by a semicircle of camellia and viburnum. Out in the sunny open are gorgeous plant combinations of purple penstemon, leptospermum and hebe. Elsewhere, kiwis and vinca knot together in attractive splashes. Hannah says most of these weren't planned, they simply happened along, like the tall cordyline, birch and cherry trees set into the gravel that cast little shade over the plants below and still give great height to the composition.

The gardening style might be gentle, but Hannah is not afraid of hard work. She actually enjoyed erecting a fence to keep out marauding rabbits. It took half a year to complete and had to be dug almost half a metre below the soil level – not everyone's idea of fun. But she did this, as she does all the work in her garden, by herself. Hannah is a self-taught gardener whose other passions are cats and miniature dogs, which she breeds. Both are evident throughout the garden. There are cats posted at various look-out points and much of the place was created with them in mind, with features for them to enjoy, like sprawling perches and scratching posts set among their favourite smelling catmint and roses. Contrary to the worries of some gardeners about the damage cats can wreak in gardens, the feline inhabitants of Holland House cause no trouble. Hannah rewards their discerning and good behaviour and the cats do their bit too. Forty goldfish live in the pond. They grew from an original population of five. This aquatic population explosion is due to the cats lying around openly and keeping the heron at bay. Around the fishpond are pansies, petrol-blue *Cerinthe major* and blue-flowering pulmonaria.

WILD GARLIC

Wild garlic or ramson (*Allium ursinum*) is a member of the lily family and is indigenous to Ireland and Britain. The white clusters of starry flowers over wide, strappy leaves flower between April and June in woodlands, banks and damp, shaded places throughout the country. It's easy to spot, although you will often smell it well before you see it.

When young, the leaves of wild garlic are good in green salads and they smell strongly of garlic when picked or bruised. This smell, like the smell of other alliums, acts as a repellent to certain insects. It is for this reason that chives and onions are planted beside carrots by organic gardeners and companion-planting enthusiasts – to stave off the carrot root fly as well as providing decoration.

In the wild, ramsons often grow alongside nettles and recently fashionable chefs have been combining the two in soup making, chopping the leaves into mashed potatoes, deep frying the flowers in batter for dipping into garlic mayonnaise and mashing the leaves into soft butter for a mild version of garlic bread.

Finally, the conservatory is almost overpoweringly sweet with a flowering mimosa, the perfume of which drifts into the house and leaves the visitor with a lasting memory of the garden.

ILNACULLIN

Garinish Island, Glengarriff, County Cork; Tel: +027 63040; Fax: +027 63149 ▪ **Contact:** Finbar O' Sullivan ▪ **Open:** 1 March–31 October, Monday–Saturday, 10am–4.30pm, Sunday, 1pm–5pm; April–June and September, Monday–Saturday, 10am–6.30pm, Sunday, 1pm–6.30pm; July–August, Monday–Saturday, 9.30am–6.30pm, Sunday, 11am–6.30pm; *Note:* last landing on the island is one hour before closing time ▪ **Entrance fee** ▪ Supervised children welcome; please note, dogs on leads ▪ **Special features:** groups should book teas in advance ▪ **Directions:** situated 1.5km off the coast from Glengarriff.

Ilnacullin is set into the harbour of Glengarriff in Bantry Bay, an exotic island with views out to the Atlantic Ocean and back to the mainland. This island garden is reached by boat over a short stretch of water past contented-looking seals basking on the rocks. Small outboard motor boats level with the water are the best way to travel out to the island. A leisurely trip, trailing one's arms in the water, is the most relaxing way to start the visit.

Covering thirty-seven acres, the windswept, gorse-covered, rough-looking island was bought by Mr Annan Bryce in 1910. Mr Bryce employed the famous English landscaper and architect Harold Peto to design a house and Italianate garden for him on his new island. The work of these two men, and additional works carried out by Mr Bryce's son, Rowland, and the Scottish gardener Murdo MacKenzie, gave rise to Ilnacullin: a world-class garden in a spectacular situation.

However, their work was cut out for them. While the warm Gulf Stream, huge annual rainfall and shelter belt of trees make it possible to grow exotic plants from Australia, New Zealand and the tropics with success, Ilnacullin has its difficulties. Based on solid rock, with a miserable amount of poor quality, rain-leached soil, the island is no natural paradise and it must have required plenty of imagination for Mr Bryce to believe he could create a garden on the rock in Bantry Bay. The struggle to cart huge amounts of good soil over the water and fight salt-laden winds in the early years can only be imagined.

The finest feature of the island is the Italian garden with its *casita* (tea house) and pergola made of golden Bath stone set with variously coloured marble, from prestigious Carrara to local Connemara stone. This garden is surrounded by huge pines, elegant and good-sized flowering leptospermum, myrtle, camellia and rhododendron. To the southwest the Sugarloaf Mountain rises high and frames the perfect picture. Azure tiling on the edges of the sunken pool and stone planters with venerable and famed bonsai and statuary are among the finer details. The exotic white trumpet flowers of datura, wisteria, lilies and sprawling clematis mix with a great number of fuchsias and bedding plants in the beds branching out from the rectangular lily pool.

Out of the Italian garden, the trail leads in several directions. One path with wide, rough, stone steps in banks leads to a Grecian temple on top of a hill. Up here all formality is cast off – the impression is of tempered wildness. The temple, entered past blue agapanthus and a fine big Chilean fire bush (*Embothrium coccineum*) has views out over the sea. Everywhere the rock, never far from the surface, peeps out, a reminder that this garden was gouged from an unyielding foundation. Blasting with dynamite was necessary in many places to make planting holes for the trees and shrubs.

The paths lead on through the romantically named happy valley, past fragrant pines, hydrangeas and an incredible tender tree (*Dacrydium frank-linii*) from Tasmania, a testament to the climate on the island as it will only grow in the most protected of positions. There are so many rare and unusual things in this garden, for example, trees like *Phyllocladus trichomanoides* from New Zealand. The specimen in Ilnacullin is one of the biggest growing outdoors in these islands. Flowering fascicularia

The Italian garden and *casita*, created by Howard Peto, on Ilnacullin, off the coast of West Cork.

with fire-red leaves grows out of what looks like bare rock, and pink roses tumble over the stone. There are many varieties of fuchsia, leptospermum, abutilon, hibiscus, eupatorium, clematis and cistus in the jungle of planting. (*Note:* a booklet can be bought at reception which provides a good reference to the plants grown on the island.)

Up toward the Martello tower, built at a commanding point on the island, are mounds of ferns and recumbent pines mimicking and hugging the rock. The track then moves back towards the garden by a rocky gorse- and heather-strewn outcrop called the viewing point, and down steps that lead past evidence of storm devastation in the shape of fallen trees. The way leads into the walled garden (note the sign for dogs on a lead here, please). The walled garden is only partially open. Stretches of it are cornered off and not well tended at all – evidence of staff and money shortages. Only the central herbaceous border is fully visible and it is handsome and generously planted with fine flowers, sometimes backed by espaliered fruit trees and specimen shrubs. Asters, roses, erysimum, hydrangea, cimicifuga, delphinium, *Cardiocrinum giganteum*, campanulas, verbascum and all the usual herbaceous plants stand cheek by jowl, holding each other up. But even this great border is a bit faded and in need of a bit of extra care. There are also collections of climbers in this garden, but it is not possible to see them close up because the paths leading to them are currently closed.

Overall, Ilnacullin is a truly glorious garden, but it is clear that it lacks the sort of financial backing and staffing levels necessary to allow it to really fulfil its potential. The garden created by the gardeners of history is in need of conservation and gentle development to stop it gradually becoming an old ghost.

Durrus, County Cork; Tel/Fax: +027 61111; e-mail: kilravock1@eircom.net ▪
Contact: Malcolm and Phemie Rose ▪ **Open:** during the West Cork Garden Trail
(see leaflet for dates); for occasional charity days (see local press for details); by appointment at other times during the summer, telephone to confirm visit; closed
bank holidays; groups welcome ▪ **Entrance fee** donated to charity and goes towards garden upkeep ▪ Supervised children welcome ▪ **Directions:** 1.6km from
Durrus on the Kilcrohane Road. The garden is on the right. Look for the signposts.

'We started in 1989 with plain fields,' Mrs Rose explains, standing in the middle of
her impressive garden, a garden that has been covered by numerous magazines, newspapers and television programmes and is beloved of touring gardening clubs the
country over. Mrs Rose is the full-time gardener, with her husband, Malcolm, as
part-timer. However, they share the design ideas so the garden is a joint production.

When they started on their plot, the Roses didn't know about the abundance of
rock that is now a feature of the garden. But it soon made its presence felt when digging started. Rock was never far from the surface and always in the way of where the
spade wished to go. The garden is now handsome, but it was a challenge to plant into
the rocky soil, to use it intelligently and to wrest a fertile garden from this tough landscape. 'It's a hard place to garden, but shrubs do well because once they establish not
too much care is required by them and they more or less take care of themselves.' This
is due to the fact that along with the rocks in the soil, the garden is both very wet in
winter and very dry in summer.

A *Grevillea robusta* grows well by the edge of the rockbed and *Cotoneaster horizontalis* falls down the rock in swathes. Collections of acacias and acers grow beside the
more humble pheasant berry (*Leycesteria formosa*). By the house is an oriental-style
area with gravel, a stream, Japanese anemone and a spreading mound of *Acer palmatum var.* 'Dissectum'. In a blue pot red-flowered and purple-berried *Tropaeolum speciosum* through a silver-blue pine looks well. A big grey cat lies, colour-coordinated
and camouflaged, on the grey slate table. Above this area is a spring garden of azalea
and primula with a huge acacia. Lobelia, salvia, hosta and ferns grow alongside a
natural stream in the damp. There are also Mediterranean areas with agave, eucomis
and puya growing outside beside a purple-leafed *Acacia bailyiana* 'Purpurea', another
fine-looking plant.

Walking around the garden, it is clear that the Roses are very keen on southern
hemisphere plants and in the warmth of Dunmanus Bay they can indulge their taste.
They also germinate a great number of these plants from seed. However, West Cork's
frost-free climate is hampered somewhat by salt winds. So a tall hedge shelters the
bottom part of the garden, protecting it from the spray coming up from the bay. The
hedge is not so tall, however, as to prevent a good view of the bay. The two-acre
garden is ice cream-cone shaped, with the narrow end reached through a tunnel of
white wisteria, golden hop and clematis. In here are some lovely flowering shrubs, like
California tree poppy (*Romneya coulteri*) and a collection of rowans surrounded by a
hedge of *Rosa rugosa* in this private little finish to a varied and interesting garden.

LANCELOT 'CAPABILITY' BROWN

Lancelot 'Capability' Brown (1716–1783) was the most famous of all English landscape gardeners. He is renowned for the development of the landscape park in the eighteenth century. These parks were made of serpentine walks, rides and drives in and out of small groves and wide bands or belts of trees enclosing the demesne. Raising levels, softening hills and draining boggy land created an ideal landscape in which visitors could ride or drive through a completely pleasing landscape. Cattle and sheep, employed to keep the grass down and provide the house with food, could shelter in the trees, and thus natural, practical and aesthetic requirements were all well served. Eighteenth-century philosophy espoused a natural order in which the image of the rich man in a suitably important house set at the centre of an ideal natural landscape of rolling turf, trees and, if possible, a lake or river was seen as right and proper – an order well served by a Brownian landscape.

During his lifetime Brown amassed a huge fortune through his work redesigning the parklands of the English aristocracy and landed gentry. He never visited Ireland. When asked by the Duke of Leinster to work on his estate in Ireland, Brown replied that he had 'not finished England yet'. Despite this, his influence is seen in many Irish estates of the period and since in the work of his followers and assistants.

Brown acquired the nickname by which he is now universally known through his habit of telling potential clients and landowners that their grounds had 'capabilities'.

LAKEMOUNT

Glanmire, County Cork; Tel: +021 4821052 ▩ **Contact:** Brian Cross ▩ **Open:** April–September, Monday–Sunday, 2.30pm–5pm; groups welcome, by appointment only ▩ **Entrance fee** donated to charity and goes towards garden upkeep ▩ Not suitable for children ▩ **Directions:** drive from Cork to Glanmire and at the crossroads beyond the village, turn left and go up a hill. The garden is on the left and marked by a stone wall and wicket gate at the edge of the busy road.

Gardened by two generations of the same family, Lakemount was started over half a century ago by Mrs Margaret Cross on the site of a chicken and fruit farm. Her son Brian has been gardening since the age of eight when he began by growing Sweet William seeds. He caught the bug and today Lakemount is one of the private gardens in the country with an enviable reputation. The garden has been a winner of the Shamrock All Ireland Gardens Competition many times and Brian is now a member of the judging panel. Along with the gardens of Helen Dillon (*see* County Dublin), Jim Reynolds (*see* County Meath), Lorna Mc Mahon (*see* County Galway) and Bob Gordon (*see* County Antrim), his is a garden to which one is instructed to go by many gardeners. This is a place to be visited again and again, a picture-perfect, sophisticated garden, beautiful and well groomed.

The house stands on a level above the garden on low stone walls that provide planting space for climbers while backing a bed of euphorbia, helichrysum, phormium and camellia. It is primarily a flower garden, but is cleverly divided into intimate rooms or compartments, each with a particular mood. In one, canna lilies form a two-and-a-half-metre-high wall over beds containing many shades of pink penstemon. Brian mixes colour like a master painter, and here rich purple *Verbena bonariensis* and reddish-black chocolate cosmos is only one of his luscious colour combinations. Tree ferns, acers and camellias dripping in red tropaeolum all lead up to a hosta and fern walk decorated with big granite mushrooms. A Brewer's weeping pine (*Picea breweriana*) looms over white lychnis, romneya and fuchsia.

Lakemount garden covers just two acres but the shape and style is such that it feels a lot bigger and walking back and forward one finds oneself revisiting rooms already seen from other paths and angles. Rough stone urns full of hardy geraniums stand in the middle of beds of salvia and pink anemone. Labyrinthine paths wander in all directions, dividing rooms and leading you to them with steps up and down and gates leading off in different directions. Gates create a sense of mystery in a garden. They need not be monumental or imposing. Low wrought-iron, wooden or picket fence gates, under arches of rose or honeysuckle or set into a hedge, lend a tantalising feeling of the about-to-be-discovered and of the forbidden, even if you can see over them. In Lakemount, there are gates at every turn.

The rockery garden is a room set out in slabs of Liscannor stone with mats of creeping mint, thyme and geranium between the flags. A scattering of raised beds play house to sharp, architectural red phormium, rich red berberis and lobelia. From here a set of steps – half stone, half creeping campanula – lead to another flagged area planted through with galtonia, anemone and more troughs of dianthus and hairy little pasque flowers. Ginger plants add to the exotic feel. *Dahlia* 'The Bishop of Llandaff', alstromeria and a tiny *Rhododendron impeditum* work off each other well and a tub of grass resembles a mad Muppet wig.

A refined little area edged with box walls, cones and standard wisteria is next door. This leads to a room with more topiary and ivy lollipops where a yew peacock stands among patterned stone paths in the sundial garden. A greenhouse full of pink abutilon, fuchsia and pelargonium is so densely covered in creepers that the building looks like it was constructed from leaves, flowers and glass. Finally a 'museum' of bay hedges cut with niches and windows to display small pieces of sculpture is a bit of fun.

Brian Cross is one of the few gardeners happy for his garden to be inspected at times other than May and June, declaring it to be at its best in the autumn. This in itself makes it a good visit for Irish gardeners because Irish autumn weather is frequently better than summer. Growing plants that look good when the weather is good enough for us to sit outside enjoying the display makes a lot of sense.

LARCHWOOD HOUSE

Pearson's Bridge, Bantry, County Cork; Tel: +027 66181 ▪ **Contact:** Aidan and Sheila Vaughan ▪ **Open:** during the West Cork Garden Trail (see local press for details); at other times by appointment only; groups welcome ▪ **Entrance fee** goes towards garden upkeep ▪ Children must be carefully supervised due to water features ▪ **Special features:** restaurant open for evening meals, booking necessary ▪ **Directions:** at Ballylickey turn off the N71 and take the Kealkil Road for 3.2km. At

Pearson's Bridge turn right for the garden, which is visible from the road across the river.

With the backdrop of the Caha Mountains, Larchwood has the sort of river frontage that not even the most avaricious or covetous gardener would dare to dream of, and with a keen appreciation of their surrounding the Vaughans built the whole garden around the Ouvane River. Larchwood is laid out on a hill leading down to the river, which dominates this three-acre garden.

Aidan Vaughan has spent hundreds of hours creating a variety of stone features by the river. Torrents of water race over weirs and under stone bridges, all built by Aidan. He has also built tea houses and benches along the river, from which to enjoy the spectacle of the water. This combination of water and stonework makes the garden quite singular. Intricate stone paths and beautifully made low walls frame and tie the plants into a strong structure. The planting is simple, made up of varieties of evergreens, like camellia, heather and rhododendron, grown on banks that slope down from the house to the water.

Aidan has extended his garden beyond the riverbank by building bridges to two little islands surrounded by the fast-moving white water. On the bigger of the two islands a stone path treads along and leads to a small rough bridge over to the second, smaller island. The planting on the islands is simple and natural: beech and ash trees stand over carpets of spring bulbs, including seas of bluebells which Aidan discovered, to his great pleasure, while cutting back the brambles covering the island. A white spread of anemone precedes the bluebells and aconites and violets add variety to the wood floor. The only work carried out on the islands is maintaining the path and preventing re-invasion by the brambles.

Stone steps lead off the island down into the river, where one can sit and dawdle by the water. From the islands it is possible to look across to the far side of the river where Aidan has expanded his stoneworks by creating a bank into the water. He justifies this enormous amount of work by explaining that 'the floods were eating onto the bank and so the stone edge stops that a little.' But I suspect he will always jump at the chance of new wall-building opportunities.

Aidan started working on the garden in 1981. He built it and now maintains it all himself. He has also planted a kilometre of common limes (*Tilia x. europaea*) on the bank opposite the garden leading to the village. This planting was carried out for posterity and for the enjoyment of the public.

LISS ARD FOUNDATION GARDENS

Skibbereen, County Cork; Tel: +028 22373/40186; Fax: +028 40187; e-mail: lissardfoundation@eircom.net; website: www.lissard.com ▪ **Contact:** Reception ▪ **Open:** May–October, Monday–Friday, 10am–6pm, Saturday–Sunday, 11am–5pm; entrance to the Irish Sky Garden is by guided tour only; groups welcome ▪ **Entrance fee** ▪ Supervised children welcome; please note, dogs on leads ▪ **Special features:** the Irish Sky Garden; music festival each August ▪ **Directions:** situated on the edge of Skibbereen town and well-signposted from the town.

Set on the edge of Skibbereen, the Liss Ard Foundation Garden is made up of wild and semi-tamed landscape and woodland walks, wild ponds, coppiced woods of ash and hazel and wildflower meadows. The gardens cover over forty acres and make a pleasant walk and nature trail. But the gardens have one feature that is truly out-standing: the Irish Sky Garden set in the middle of the woods. This is an incredible experience and should not be missed.

The Irish Sky Garden is a man-made crater set in an opening in the woods. From the outside it is not quite clear what the tall, grassy mound is. A long, stone-lined tunnel leads in from the ouside through the wall or mound, and at the end of this tunnel a set of steep steps leads the viewer up towards a sharp rectangle of sky in the roof and out into the middle of a large crater-shaped area. Sitting at the bottom of the crater is a strange-looking altar or bench. The visitor lies on this, head below feet, and looks up at the sky. The fish-eye effect of the circular sky edged by the neatly cut grass crater edge is a profound experience: moving and disorienting. The Irish Sky Garden makes Liss Ard worth going out of one's way to visit.

LISSELAN ESTATE GARDENS

Clonakilty, County Cork; Tel: +023 33249; Fax: +023 34605 ▪ **Contact:** Mr Mark Coombes ▪ **Open:** 1 April–30 September, daily, 8am–dusk; at any other time by appointment only; guided tours can be arranged for groups, but must be booked in advance ▪ **Entrance fee** goes towards garden upkeep ▪ Supervised children welcome ▪ **Special features:** teas and snacks can be booked by prior arrangement; golf course ▪ **Directions:** located 3km from Clonakilty town, on the N71 to Cork city.

The gardens at Lisselan are set in a valley beside the River Argideen. Covering around twenty acres, they were laid out by the Bence-Jones family in the last century follow-ing the principles of William Robinson, the famous Irish garden writer and designer (*see* box, p.182). A leafy path through the woods from the car park leads past the house to the garden. Fine specimens of huge trees – podocarpus, eucalyptus and tulip trees – line the front driveway leading up to the house, which is completely covered in Virginia creeper. A sign by the house entices the visitor to the gardens by a circuitous route through a series of old yards. Other signs warning that only golfers should enter the rose-edged balustraded parterre add a bit of mystery to this garden. Upon enter-ing and finding the sand bunkers dug into the lawn, gardeners will wince just as much as golfers will dance a jig. Bunkers aside, the place is a sheer delight.

Off to the west of the house is a wonderful shrubbery with mature pines overhead and acacia, myrtle and robinia underneath. A meandering walk called the Ladies' Mile leads through this, by the river and rhododendron woods. A long, rough-paved set of steps covered by arched trees and edged with dahlias and other flowers leads to the River Argideen, which is crossed by a white, wisteria-covered bridge. This leads over to an island with a lily-stuffed pool and then out past weirs, sluice gates and more branches of the little river to a woody walk. Winding walks along by the other riverbank are edged by flowering shrubs and bamboo on one side and primula, ferns and irises on the other. By the water there is a quaint little bamboo summerhouse with great tufts of libertia around it.

The garden culminates at the foot of the house, a fine building on a cartoon-like precipice above the garden. A dramatic rockery climbs the steep slope to the bottom of the building. Big drifts of Solomon's seal fall down the embankment beside the rock-ery. This is a bold feature. For visitors with very sure footing it's possible to climb the rockery and through it. However, you must be careful not to step on the thousands of seedlings in the paths – walking on these is like committing infanticide. There are innumerable cyclamen, primulas and ferns, baby's tears, lysimachia and dianthus – the tiny children of healthy parents in the beds. The rockery is the glory of this garden. It is one of the most beautiful features in the county, breathtaking and definitely worth travelling to see.

THE MANOR

Knockane, Dunmanway, County Cork; Tel: +023 45725 ▪ **Contact:** James and Majella Murray ▪ **Open:** by appointment only; groups welcome ▪ **Entrance fee** donated to charity and goes towards garden upkeep ▪ **Directions:** located 5km from Dunmanway on the Clonakilty Road (R599), or 13km from Clonakilty on the Dunmanway Road. First house on the left after Drinagh Cross and marked by a long wall, the yellow house is visible from the road.

The Murrays's one-acre garden is young and as such it is an interesting place for those in the design phase of their garden. Spread out on a long narrow site along a country road, it first appears to be a straightforward garden of lawn surrounded by borders, but on close inspection an altogether more ambitious garden is found behind the house.

To the front of the house is a long shrub bed with good specimens of liquidambar, plum-coloured shrub roses and laburnum, embothrium, berberis trained into columns and white broom that stands out magnificently. Mrs Murray explains that the broom is kept in good shape by giving it a 'light haircut' after it flowers, which stops it getting too leggy and lax. The wall is climbed over by a rampant Virginia creeper (*Parthenocissus quinquefolia*), a plant that is not evergreen, but as it matures the network of thread-like branches make as useful a feature as the reddening leaves of late summer and autumn. Beyond this bed is a lawn spread out like green carpet over a big rock outcrop rising about two and a half metres above the ground. Crevices in the rock have been freely colonised by sedum and aubrieta. Bright, strappy gardener's garters (*Glyceria maxima* 'Variegata') and recumbent rosemary drip down the bank. A little patio sits under the rock surrounded by de Caen anemones in the strongest, most intense shades of reds and purples and, in spring, daffodils. Up above the garden a walk of phormium and Turkish oak has been planted and will make an impressive feature in a few years.

The garden was started by the Murrays eight years ago, replacing an old farm-yard that was an unromantic mix of silage pits and a piggery. A modest enough start with lawn, shrub beds and some flowers has been overtaken by the creation, in the past two years, of an extraordinary bank of ponds, waterfalls, rough stone walls and ledges with expanses of planting behind the house. Jim Murray is responsible for the stone work, while Majella puts in the plants: tree lupins, lavatera, grasses and cordylines, all backed and topped by a wire network supporting a long run of wisteria. Enormous numbers of annuals raised by Majella are prepared for a summer life on the new bank. She is a great propagator and runs a very impressive nursery in the greenhouse, where she raises thousands of bedding and annual plants, such as the poached-egg plant (*Limnanthes douglasii*), impatiens, larkspur and pelargonium.

The whole garden faces south and gets plenty of sun, but, as Majella explains, life is not so simple. The plot sits on one side of a valley that acts as a wind tunnel, funnelling whipping winds through the garden. The growth of trees and shrubs is quite restricted as a result and many pounds worth of plants have been lost to the drying winds. Even the leylandii shelter belt they put in was slow to take in the wind. In addition, 'Our soil is poor and dry and about one foot down we hit rock so we have to plant things that suit those conditions.' Such suitable things include a bank of wild fuchsia and crocosmia. The inclusion of fuchsia, a symbol for the West Cork and Kerry areas, marries the garden with its wilder surroundings to good effect.

Finally, I loved the vegetable beds: their regular straight lines and ordered productivity are a foil to the rises and falls of the rest of the informal garden. Apples, pears, plums and gooseberries are pretty as well as productive. 'We grow enough to keep us going through the year,' says Majella, whose suggestion for an impending glut of rhubarb is to blanch the chopped stalks in sugar water before freezing. And last but not least, there is a football pitch on the lawn at the front of the house. There must be room for everyone in a family garden after all.

MIDLETON HOUSE

Midleton, County Cork; Tel: +021 4634013 ■ **Contact:** Mrs Noreen Motherway ■ **Open:** May–June, by appointment to groups only ■ **Entrance fee** donated to charity ■ Not suitable for children ■ **Special features:** teas can be booked by prior arrangement ■ **Directions:** on the main street in Midleton, by the river and visible from the bridge.

It is almost unnecessary to provide directions to Noreen Motherway's garden as it dominates the high street in Midleton, a location that has proved a mixed blessing for the Motherway family. The tour buses on their way to visit the Midleton Distillery stop on the bridge to let the tourists hang over the wall and take photographs and admire the garden. This is not everyone's idea of privacy and seclusion, but Noreen is happy to share her garden with the public. In any case, while the audience on the bridge think they can see the garden, when you actually walk around the interior it is surprisingly full of areas that are private and well out of the public gaze. The garden rises and falls several times and little sets of steps deliver you suddenly to exquisite private spaces, safe from all viewers.

The garden was first put to work when the Motherways arrived eight years ago to a plot with three plants in it: a 150-year-old yew, a trachycarpus of the same age and a fifty-year-old cordyline. Not the worst starter pack, and Noreen and her William used these three venerable trees in their design and worked around them. Between them they have managed to produce a garden that came an overall fourth in the Shamrock All Ireland Gardens Competition 1997 and first in the North Cork category in 1999. When she first moved into the garden, Noreen brought over 1,500 plants with her from her previous garden, losing only seven in the process. That is a transplant record that speaks volumes for her ability to care for plants as well as design with them.

The Motherways divided the riverside plot into different garden rooms, including a small Italianate formal garden with box, gravel and statuary. The garden is given height by a group of skyrocket junipers and, of course, the aforementioned trachycarpus and cordyline. They are not afraid to make a statement, like that made by a big bed of fiery red *Rosa* 'Trumpeter' in the Italian garden. Box is expensive to use as a hedge and not an obvious candidate for planting very densely, but the plants take a long time to fill out. Employing plenty of seaweed as fertiliser in the planting holes under the box plants helped the hedge to a maturity much greater than its six years. The Roxboro River forms one of the boundaries of the garden and that boundary has been enhanced by Noreen's creation of a little water garden with tree ferns, hostas, gunnera and other damp-loving plants, lending a touch of the tropics to east Cork.

There are good design touches everywhere, like a white hydrangea grown through a pale, silvery phormium and a pink hydrangea through a pink variegated phormium. One witty touch was the slight tweaking of the stone wall of an old six-storey mill that sides the garden by placing little stone and terracotta urns and statuary in niches. This bestows the air of an Italian palazzo or town palace on this enjoyable one-and-a-half-acre garden.

RODEEN GARDEN

Rodeen, Castletownbere, Beara Peninsula, County Cork; Tel: +027 70158; e-mail: dervillasgarden@eircom.net ▪ **Contact:** Ellen Gowan ▪ **Open:** for the West Cork Garden Trail (see local press and printed brochure for details); at other times by appointment only; groups welcome ▪ **Entrance fee** goes towards garden upkeep ▪ Supervised children welcome ▪ **Directions:** situated just over 3km out of Castletownbere on the Glengarriff Road. Follow the signs for Rodeen Country Home Bed and Breakfast.

Ellen Gowan used to run a nursery on her one-acre site and her talent with plants is obvious to visitors walking around the garden that graces her B&B. It's a talent well tested on the wild Beara peninsula, where gardening can be a rough job. 'We have to be totally green here. Worm bins, green cones, newspapers for mulching and weed suppressing, you name it, we use it. The soil is so thin on the rock we have to feed everything we can into it.' 'On the rock' is exactly how the house and garden are situated – on a steep slope overlooking Castletownbere harbour. A quick peek over the hedges at the furze and gorse in the plots to either side of Ellen's garden speaks for itself. To say she worked to create this garden is to grossly underestimate the amount of hard graft put into it. 'You couldn't move for the furze when I started in 1972. It was a real wilderness. So I began with a donkey called Morris who ate the furze for me and then the garden got started.'

Today, the garden sits happily in its rugged surroundings, melting into the wilds with fuchsia and crocosmia grown at the boundaries. Very informal, slightly wild, floral and exotic is how it might be described. The structure is flowing and organic with surprises around every corner. Winding paths lead from one bed to another, past the tallest of rock roses, echiums and Chilean fire bushes (*Embothrium coccineum*) that seed enviably around. The embothrium is 'the devil to control,' complains Ellen. Moss and gravel paths lead in and around beds of fragrant *Rhododendron* 'Elegantisima' with big white trumpet flowers. This is a variety that even those not enamoured of rhododendrons should enjoy. Nearby a big datura with an elongated tubular flower, the bottom of which looks as though it has been dipped in red paint, is a very exotic-looking plant.

All over the garden are interesting little oddities and sculptures, like a stone trough filled with scallop shells, an upside-down sign to the garden ('People pay more attention to an upside-down sign,' says Ellen) and piles of rock cores, like long walking sticks, from local explorations for copper. Two Doric columns stand guard over a herb garden of lemon-scented balm, oregano, thyme and mint. Ellen's free style permits a big bed of red poppies to live with the herbs, adding beauty and poppy seeds to the functional area. Edible plants are found everywhere. Tiny leaves of self-seeding alpine strawberries share space with ferns, sisyrinchium and Welsh orange poppies growing on what appears to be no soil at all in the surrounding low stone wall. Next door the wire net bush, a honeysuckle and a big eucalyptus tree are locked together and make a great show. Along with a snowball tree nearby, the honeysuckle is alive with bees that live in the hives at the top of the hill and busy themselves around the garden, filling up on the best flowers to produce a fantastic honey.

At the top of one flight of rough steps is a big spread of gunnera throwing up massive leaves where wild garlic finishes off its pretty, late spring show. The gunnera sits over a pond and stream, which is in fact a land drain that fills when it rains.

The garden falls down to the road with a little pine wood edged by the already mentioned 'nuisance' embothriums, acanthus and philadelphus. All this looks out over a field of horses, the wreck of an old boat, Bere Island in Bantry Bay and up behind us Hungry Hill, one of the peaks in the Sugarloaf Mountain. An idyllic setting for an idyllic garden.

TIMOLEAGUE CASTLE GARDENS ♿ 🐕

Timoleague, near Bandon, County Cork; Tel: +023 46116; Fax: +023 46523 ▪ **Contact:** Robert and Laura Travers ▪ **Open:** during the West Cork Garden Trail (see local press for details); at other times by appointment only; groups welcome ▪ **Entrance fee** goes towards garden upkeep ▪ Supervised children welcome; please note, dogs on leads ▪ **Special features:** there is a little church on the grounds with beautiful historic mosaics and stained-glass windows ▪ **Directions:** located on the edge of Timoleague, on the Kinsale–Clonakilty road.

Arriving at Timoleague Castle one is greeted by a great 1920s house with a lawn sweeping down and out toward the entrance and the site of an older, Georgian house, which is home to the gardeners: the Travers family. Fine trees, including a *Magnolia grandiflora* and *Magnolia campbellii*, rhododendrons, azaleas, a big cryptomeria and a Paulownia mark the entrance and edge of a good-looking lawn with a history. This lawn was once the oldest tennis court in the south of the country and centre of the local club, losing its status only when there was a dispute about the erection of nets. Tempers flared and the club moved elsewhere.

Moving to the side of the house and then behind it, the real garden begins. Beds full of exotic canna lilies, usually only seen in ones and twos, are gathered here in decent numbers. Good big clumps of them are set into beds on a long rectangle of lawn shaded by rows of tall cordylines. This is all set in the old moat of a thirteenth-century tower house castle that graces the garden. A gravel apron cradles crinum lilies and a mass of plants that grow up and clamber over the castle, which peeps out from beneath this growth. Daphne, witch hazel and camellias add winter and early spring interest to a good spot with an easy feel to it. Blackberries grow unhindered through the philadelphus and big clumps of anemone.

The path leads from this area to a semicircle of steps guarded by a big myrtle and a skirt of ferns, then on through dense shrubbery into a grass walk by the River Argideen, where a view of the ruins of Timoleague Abbey can be seen. The days of the narrow gauge rail that once passed by the garden are remembered in a Great Southern and Western Railway notice threatening a forty-shilling fine for trespass. The river walk down to the wilderness is peaceful and quiet, with benches for sitting beside big lace-cap hydrangea, bergenia and tender shrubs, and looking out on Courtmacsharry Bay.

Stone steps and an iron gate lead into the lower walled garden, which is a riot of flower. Lines of white shrub roses go in one direction and lines of artichokes travel off in the other, each leading away from the main double border of yellow ligularia, orange rudbekia, yet more hot red cannas, bottlebrush (*Callistemon*) and golden yew. At one end of the bed two fine *Rosa moyseii* face each other off either side of the path.

At the back of the garden a big greenhouse full of vines, plumbago and tomatoes is fronted by a run of huge pink dahlias, thirty-five metres long and three metres deep. The family refers to these as the 'Barbara Cartlands' for obvious reasons. In another wall a door leads into a second walled garden, this time filled with vegetables and fruit. There is no shortage of flowers here either, although most of them are for cutting. Lemon trees in pots with fat lemons are great to see growing outside. Lines of raspberries, sweet pea and big pumpkins sprawl out on to the paths and herbs are scattered in every direction. Squash tendrils have to be stepped over and apples dangling from the trees overhead have to be ducked under. Old-fashioned Victorian cloches are placed around the beds. The whole picture is one of good-looking chaos.

In addition to the garden and its considerable charms, there is a fascinating church on the grounds that visitors should make an effort to see; the entrance is just outside the main gate. This is the Church of the Ascension, plain on the outside but within an elaborately decorated and beautiful interior awaits, with walls covered in gorgeously colourful mosaics. Some of these were created as memorials to members of the Travers family who were killed during wars, including one young man killed during the First World War in Gallipoli. During the creation of these mosaics funds ran very low, threatening the completion of the work. A doctor friend of the Travers who lived in the village prevailed on the Maharajah of Gwalior, whose son he had once saved, to help with the work. The Maharajah agreed to help and funded one of the walls. Next door, the Church of the Nativity of the Virgin houses marvellous Harry Clarke stained-glass windows, which it would be a shame to miss.

The Travers's garden is a quirky, attractive and very welcoming place. It is a garden run by the family to accommodate all members of the family, both gardeners and non-gardeners. It has loads of character, is not manicured to within an inch of its life and is one of my favourite gardens.

WEST CORK HERB FARM

Church Cross, Skibbereen, County Cork; Tel: +028 38428; Fax: +028 38504; e-mail: herbfarm@iol.ie ▪ **Contact:** Kevin or Rosarie O'Byrne ▪ **Open:** during the West Cork Garden Trail, Tuesday–Saturday, 11am–5pm, closed for lunch; at other times during the summer strictly by appointment only; groups welcome ▪ **Entrance fee** goes towards garden upkeep ▪ Strictly no children or dogs due to the large number of poisonous plants ▪ **Special features:** a garden shop is open mid-March–end September, Tuesday–Saturday, 2pm–4.30pm. Farm produce for sale includes herb oil, vinegar sauces, etc. The O'Byrnes's basil-infused oil won the gold medal at the Great Taste Awards in London in 1988 ■ **Directions:** located 7km west of Skibbereen on the N71.

This is a small and varied herb garden, both pretty and functional. It is divided into six rooms or individual gardens, each with its own theme: cottage, formal, monastic, wild, woodland and paved. Beech hedging divides the different areas. But it is a working garden first and foremost, a herb farm and not simply a pretty garden to visit. A visit will prove invaluable to anyone wishing to create a working herb garden.

GARDENING CLUBS AND SOCIETIES

ALPINE GARDEN SOCIETY (IN ASSOCIATION WITH THE HARDY PLANT SOCIETY)

(see information on Alpine Garden Society in the appendices.)

Contact: Hester Forde, 15 Johnstown Park, Glounthaune, County Cork; Tel: +021 353855.

BANTRY FLOWER AND GARDEN CLUB

Contact: Mary Walsh, Cois Cuain, Dunmanus Bay, Kilcrohane, County Cork; Tel: +027 67070.

The Club meets on the first Monday of each month at 8pm in the West Lodge Hotel, Bantry, from September to May. Its activities are divided equally between flower arranging and gardening, and the monthly lecture alternates between the two activities. Garden visits are organised during the summer and there are weekly competitions.

BLACKROCK FLOWER AND GARDEN CLUB

The Blackrock Club meets at 7.45pm on the first Tuesday of each month in the assembly hall of the Ursuline Convent in Blackrock. Topics are divided fairly equally between flower arranging and gardening. An annual day trip is held in June and the December meeting is a social night. The society does not meet in July and August. The club holds monthly competitions leading up to an annual award for the most successful grower. New members are welcome.

CORK GARDEN CLUB

Contact: Aidan Goggin (Treasurer), Castlewhite, Waterfall, County Cork; or Catherine MacHale (Secretary), Glenmahon, Rochestown Avenue, Cork; Tel: +021 891674.

The Cork Garden Club is one of the most active in the country and there is a waiting list for membership. Lectures run for the whole year and are held at 8pm on the second Wednesday of the month in the Ashton Comprehensive School in Cork city. Lectures, monthly horticultural competitions, garden visits and club outings are arranged. Visitors may attend the monthly meetings for a small charge.

IRISH GARDEN PLANT SOCIETY – CORK BRANCH

Contact: Kay Bourke (Hon. Secretary), Parkhurst, Victoria Road, Cork.

See information on the IGPS in the appendices for full details of the activities carried out by the society. The lecture season runs from autumn to April and garden visits are arranged in May and June.

GARDENING COURSES

BALLYMALOE COOKERY SCHOOL GARDENS

Shanagarry, Midleton, County Cork; Tel: +021 4646785; Fax: +021 4646909; e-mail: enquiries@ballymaloe-cookery-school.ie; website: www.ballymaloe-cookery-school.ie ◼ **Contact:** Darina Allen, Susan Turner or reception.

Ballymaloe have run a series of one-day and half-day courses in gardening and gardening techniques for several years. The courses include topics such as pruning, planning herbaceous borders, vegetable and herb growing. The courses are generally held at weekends and some include lunch. Contact for a brochure or look up their website.

GLEBE GARDEN AND GALLERY

The Glebe, Baltimore, County Cork; Tel: +028 20232 ◼ **Contact:** Jean Perry.

Short courses and lectures on growing plants and vegetables organically, seed saving and gardening methods given by a range of speakers. The courses are aimed at groups of five to six people and can be arranged between March and June.

An example of the two-day organic growing course given includes:

Day 1: Planning the garden, soil and site, layouts, fertility, manure, fertilisers and compost.
Day 2: Propagation and plant raising, gardening practices, mulching, protecting crops, companion and decorative planting, harvesting and storage.

NURSERIES AND GARDEN CENTRES

AISEIRI NURSERIES AND GARDEN PLANTS

Clash, Ballinhassig, Cork, County Cork; Tel: +021 4771406.

ANNES GROVE PLANTS

Annes Grove, Castletownroche, County Cork; Tel: +022 26811/086 8291467.

AQUARIUS GARDEN CENTRE

Ballydehob, County Cork.

ATKIN'S GARDEN WORLD

Camden Quay, Carrigrohane Road, County Cork; Tel: +021 542811.

BALLYLICKEY NURSERIES

Ballylickey, Bantry, County Cork; Tel: +027 50996.

BALLYVOURNEY GARDEN CENTRE AND NURSERY

Ballymakeera, Ballyvourney, County Cork; Tel: +026 45355.

BAMBOO PARK, THE

Glengarriff, County Cork; Tel: +027 63570.

BANDON GARDEN CENTRE

Glaslyn Road, Bandon, County Cork; Tel: +023 42260.

BANTRY GARDEN CENTRE

Glengarrif Road, Donemark, Bantry, County Cork; Tel: +027 51027.

BEECH HILL GARDEN CENTRE

Bonnington, Montenotte, Cork city; Tel: +021 4507042.

BIRCH HILL LANDSCAPES

Old Abbey Gardens, Waterfall, Cork, County Cork; Tel: +021 4871460.

CAHERDOWNEY NURSERY,

Carriganima, Macroom, County Cork; Tel: +029 70482.

CAREWSWOOD GARDEN CENTRE

Castlemartyr, County Cork; Tel: +021 4667283; e-mail: carewgc@eircom.net.

CARMEL'S GARDEN CENTRE

Monadrishane, Kilworth, County Cork; Tel: +025 27276.

CHÂTEAU DES FLEURS

Westpark Centre, Westpark, Midleton, County Cork; Tel: +021 4652017.

COTTAGE GARDEN NURSERY

Aghaneenagh, Newmarket, County Cork; Tel: +029 60084.

DEELISH NURSERY AND GARDEN CENTRE

Skibbereen, County Cork; Tel: +028 21574.

EARLY BIRD GARDEN CENTRE

Two Pot House, Mallow, County Cork; Tel: +022 22407.

DOUGLAS COURT GARDEN CENTRE

Douglas Court Shopping Centre, Douglas, Cork, County Cork; Tel: +021 4895132.

DRUMMOND'S GARDEN CENTRE

Skehard Road, Blackrock, Cork, County Cork; Tel: +021 4359390.

DRUMMOND'S WATERSIDE GARDEN CENTRE

Douglas Shopping Centre, Douglas, Cork; Tel: +021 4366188.

DUNNES'S GARDEN CENTRE

Mogeely Road, Castlemartyr, County Cork; Tel: +021 4667427.

DUNSLAND GARDEN CENTRE

Dunsland,Glanmire, County Cork; Tel: +021 4354949; e-mail: peterdow@ gofree.indigo.ie

FUTURE FORESTS

Kealkil, Bantry, County Cork; Tel: +027 66176; Fax: +027 66046; website: www.futureforests.net.

GARDENER'S CHOICE

Wilton Shopping Centre, Wilton, Cork, County Cork; Tel: +021 4346833.

GRIFFIN'S GARDEN CENTRE,

Agharinagh, Dripsey, County Cork; Tel: +021 7334286; e-mail: griffinsgar-dencentre@ericom.net.

HM HERBS

Ballyvourney, Macroom, County Cork; Tel: +026 45490.

HILLSIDE GARDEN CENTRE

Ballyoran Road, Castlelyons, County Cork; Tel: +025 36551.

HILLSIDE NURSERIES

Kilcoolishal, Glounthaune, County Cork; Tel: +021 4354423.

HOSFORD'S GERANIUMS AND GARDEN CENTRE

Cappa, Enniskeane, County Cork; Tel: +023 39159; Fax: +023 39300.

Hosford's has a mail order service, flocks of fancy fowl and a restaurant. Lectures and demonstrations organised.

ISLAND CROSS GARDEN CENTRE
Island Cross, Little Island, Cork, County Cork; Tel: +021 4353398.

JOYCE'S GARDEN CENTRE
Navigation Road, Mallow, County Cork; Tel: +022 42997.

KILLAREE GARDENS
Killaree, Charleville, County Cork; Tel: +063 70486.

LEMON TREE
Hibernian Way, Mallow, County Cork; Tel: +022 50133.

LISSARDA GARDEN CENTRE
Cookstown, County Cork; Tel: +021 7336499.

McENALLY, ARTHUR, GARDEN CENTRE
9 Church Street, Mitchelstown, County Cork; Tel: +025 24855.

NANGLE'S GARDEN CENTRE
Model Farm Road, Cork, County Cork; Tel: +021 4871297.

OAKLANDS GARDEN CENTRE
Freemount Road, Kanturk, County Cork; Tel: +029 51081.

OLD ABBEY GARDENS
Waterfall, Cork, County Cork; Tel: +021 4871460.

O'SULLIVAN'S NURSERY
Kerry Pike, Blarney, Cork; Tel: +021 4871320.

PEPPERMINT FARM GARDEN
Toughraheen, Bantry, County Cork; Tel: +028 31869; e-mail: peppermint@ eircom.net

RATHCOONEY GARDEN CENTRE
Knocknahorgan, Glanmire, County Cork; Tel: +021 4821589.

RAVENSCOURT GARDEN CENTRE
Kerry Pike, Blarney, County Cork; Tel: +021 4871909.

ROSENHEIM GARDEN CENTRE
Hillside, Aghada, County Cork; Tel: 087 2736885.

RYAN'S ELM TREE GARDEN CENTRE
Glounthaune, Cork, County Cork; Tel: +021 4353936.

SHANAHAN'S NURSERIES
Clonakilty, County Cork; Tel: +023 33398.

SKIBBEREEN GARDEN CENTRE
Carrigfadda, Skibbereen, County Cork; Tel: +028 22444.

SOUTHSIDE GARDEN CENTRE
Gortnanoon, Crosshaven, County Cork; Tel: +021 4831617.

SPARROW GARDEN SHOP
Main Street, Castletownbere, County Cork; Tel: +027 71077.

STONEWALL GARDEN CENTRE.
Cork Road, Carrigaline, County Cork; Tel: +021 4371923.

WEST CORK GARDEN CENTRE
New Road, Bandon, County Cork; Tel: +023 44320.

WOODIES DIY AND GARDEN CENTRE
Kinsale Road, Cork, County Cork; Tel: +021 968288.

MUNSTER • COUNTY CORK

GARDEN DESIGNERS

NED AND LIZ KIRBY

Beechwood, Glanmire, County Cork;
Tel: +021 884489.

The Kirbys design, plan, construct and
maintain private gardens. For an example
of their work see their own garden at the
above address, which may be seen by
appointment.

NOREEN MOTHERWAY

Main Street, Midleton, County Cork;
Tel: +021 634031.

For an example of Noreen Motherway's
design, see her own garden on the bridge
in Midleton.

GARDEN ACCESSORIES

CLARA BOOKS AND COFFEE SHOP

Main Street, Ballydehob, County Cork.

Old and new books, old gardening books.
A good place for browsers. A tea shop is
attached to the shop.

FINISHED LOOK, THE

Main Street, Rathcormac, County Cork;
Tel: +025 36995.

Every sort of cuddly stone creature from
alligators, flocks of geese and packs of
fowl, frogs and dogs. Also a range of gods
and goddesses.

GOODWOODS ARCHITECTURAL SALVAGE

Rosebank, Old Blackrock Road, Cork;
Tel: +021 318418.

IRISH EARTHWORM COMPANY

Farnnivane, Bandon, County Cork; Tel:
+023 43645.

The Irish Earthworm Company stocks
everything that the gardener might need
to compost successfully – wormeries or
vermicomposters in different sizes from
domestic to gigantic which will work for a
school or very large garden. They also sell
worm colonies that can be added to an existing compost heap and compost holders.

COUNTY KERRY

Kerry is wild and untamed in comparison to its gentrified close neighbour, West Cork. Dominated by the Atlantic Ocean, the coast is battered by rough waters which have created dramatic and spectacular beaches, cliffs and islands. The Macgillycuddy's Reeks, Caha Mountains and two national parks in Derrynane and Killarney challenge mountain climbers and walkers. Valentia Island is home to the picturesque village of Knightstown and Glanleam Gardens, and is well worth a detour from the mainland. Another sight to visit on the island is the huge abandoned slate quarry, developed in the early nineteenth century, which supplied slate for the British Houses of Parliament as well as for Waterloo train station in London. A boat trip to Great Skellig to see the monastic settlements and thousands of nesting puffins is a rare treat for sure-footed, vertigo-free visitors.

An annual Writers' Week takes place in Listowel, which, like Killorglin, leaves the more obvious tourist towns of the region in the shade for charm, while Kenmare is noted for good food and fine restaurants. For a gentle sort of family trip take a journey on the tiny Tralee–Blennerville steam train. Other attractions worth visiting are the beaches at Ballinskelligs and Inch, traditional farms at Muckross, rare-breed animals at Farmworld in Camp and historical Staigue Fort. The ring of land around the Iveragh Peninsula, known as the Ring of Kerry, is very scenic, but to be avoided at the height of the season when lines of tour buses clog it up. There are not that many gardens open to the public in the county, but those that can be visited are, almost without exception, remarkable gardens: sub-tropical, exotic and quite different from the gardens on the rest of the island.

DERREEN

Lauragh, Kenmare, County Kerry; Tel: +064 83588 ✽ **Contact:** Jacky Ward, Head Gardener ✽ **Open:** April–September, daily, 10am–6pm; other times by appointment only ✽ **Entrance fee** ✽ Supervised children welcome; please note, dogs on leads ✽ **Special features:** tree ferns can be ordered and potted up to order; teas can be booked in advance; guided tours can be arranged ✽ **Directions:** Derreen is situated 24km from Kenmare on the R571 travelling toward Castletownbere. It is well signposted.

In the 1600s Derreen was owned by the Cromwellian William Petty, the man who carried out the Down Survey – the first great land survey of the south and west of Ireland. He wrote of his 270,000 acres in Kerry that 'for a great man that would retire this place would be the most absolute, and the most *interessant* place in the world, both for improvement and pleasure and healthfulness.' The lands moved through Petty's descendants and a series of tenants until the 1850s when the Lansdowne family, who then owned it, began to take an interest in the property and grounds.

Today, Derreen is a large woodland garden, created through the improvements carried out by the fifth marquess of Lansdowne in the 1870s on the rock, scrub and what had been called 'unprofitable land' around his house on the Beara Peninsula. Fairly unusually, the house and garden have stayed in the same family since the seventeenth century. They are now in the care of the fifth marquess's great grandson, David Bingham.

Back in 1870 the first job carried out by the marquess was to plant a windbreak of trees, including recently introduced North American Western red cedar (*Thuja plicata*) and Western hemlock (*Tsuga heterophylla*), on the rocky land around his proposed new garden. From these beginnings he went on to create a lush, green garden, one of the most beautiful on the island, which has matured into a place that could, without exaggeration, be called magical.

The garden visit begins close to the house by the Big Rock. This is a huge, flat, smooth outcrop of stone, known since ancient times as a meeting place. Now it rises out of a sea of lawn, giving the visitor some idea of the original quality of the land not far below the fine plants.

Between the sheltering trees are the tree ferns (*Dicksonia antarctica*), for which Derreen has become famous. These grow in such numbers and size that they only serve to highlight the difficulty of growing even scrawny specimens elsewhere in the country. It is almost possible to become blasé about tree ferns in Kerry generally, and at Derreen in particular. They naturalise and self-seed everywhere.

Wonderfully descriptive names, like the King's Oozy and the Little Oozy, are given to the individual gardens within the woods. On wet days, of which there are no shortages, the term *oozy* is particularly apt. One of the best areas in the garden is the Knockatee Seat, with views over the woods to Knockatee Hill. A knobbly path leads up to this site, through rocks, trees and ferns. In the middle of the woods the exposed roots of a huge eucalyptus tree have been bridged to protect both it and the walker.

Another interesting sight is the largest *Cryptomeria japonica* 'Elegans' in the world. Even growing on its side, it still reaches over eighteen metres. The charm of Derreen is its wildness. Huge barriers of bamboo cross the path, making the visitor feel that a pith helmet and machete might have been a good idea. But the wildness is contrived; the garden is well tended by Jacky Ward.

Along one of the paths a private island with a bridge leading over to it may be glimpsed. It is mysterious and out of bounds. Moving along a little, the path comes into the open for the first time. Even on a dull, rainy day and late in the evening it's a

THE GULF STREAM

Derreen, along with its neighbours Glanleam, Muckross, Ilnacullin, Creagh and the other gardens dotted along the south and west coasts, has become a by-word for exoticism. The richness and rarity of the plants found here is due in no small part to the influence of the Gulf Stream. The gardens along the western and southern coast, stretching to a lesser extent as far as Waterford, lie in the path of the warm gulf stream waters coming up from the Caribbean. The region enjoys almost twice the rainfall of the midlands – 200 centimetres (eighty inches) of rain annually is normal – and temperatures rarely, if ever, dip to freezing, usually staying above five degrees through the winter. In these climatic conditions plants which we would normally associate only with tropical islands thrive and prosper.

surprise to emerge into sunlight and be able to look across the sea to the Caha Mountains on the other side of Kilmackilloge harbour. But this is only an interlude because the path ducks back in again under the woods and trees and turns into a carpet of moss, lichen and fern. A more romantic soul might be moved to lie down on the moss and commune with nature!

William Petty was right about the feelings of healthfulness and pleasure in Derreen; feelings heightened by visiting and revisiting as often as possible.

DUNLOE CASTLE GARDENS

Beaufort, Killarney, County Kerry; Tel: +064 44111; Fax: +064 44583 ▨ **Contact:** Dunloe Castle Hotel (Reception) ▨ **Open:** March–November, by appointment only ▨ Not suitable for children ▨ **Directions:** 10km from Killarney on the Killarney–Beaufort road (R562).

I worry about the number of superlatives needed to adequately describe the settings of some of the gardens in the southwest: Bantry House sits on the edge of Bantry Bay, Ilnacullin basks in Glengarriff harbour and Valentia Island shelters Glanleam. The Dunloe Castle Gardens, looking straight at the breathtaking Gap of Dunloe, is another magnificently placed retreat.

The castle at Dunloe has confused and disputed origins. It may have been built in 1213 by the MacThomas clan, but it is also reputed to have been built by O'Sullivan Mór. Then again, yet another source claims it as a Norman keep built by Meyler de Bermingham. Whatever the facts, the garden is built on a favourable site, commanding passages across two rivers, the Laune and the Loe, and overlooking much of the surrounding lands. It has seen many onslaughts and fighting, including an attack by Cromwell's forces, who left it in ruins. Rebuilt after his departure, it continued to be lived in until the nineteenth century, when it was left to deteriorate. Dunloe had to wait until the twentieth century to be rescued. It was bought by Howard Hamilton a keen plant-lover from America, who created the garden. Once he had bought the property, he set to work at a furious pace and, with his considerable means, within only sixteen years (1920–1936) he had produced a huge collection of trees and shrubs, including rare and unusual specimens.

The garden is set in a very exposed site, so he began with a windbreak of Monterey pines, elm, sycamore and beech. The choicer plants were then bedded within the shelter belt. These include a huge number of unusual trees, which have since been catalogued by the well-known British plantsman Roy Lancaster. (The catalogue is for sale at the hotel desk.) Lancaster began advising on planting at Dunloe in the 1980s, taking over from another great name in English horticulture, Sir Harold Hillier.

The shape of the garden is a bit amorphous and, to be honest, not that relevant. This is not a place of framed views (apart from the Gap of Dunloe) and smart features. This garden is about the plants and they are arranged so that the maximum number of choice plants can be seen to advantage as one walks around.

The tower house castle of the MacThomas clan is set in the midst of the garden, overlooking the River Laune. A little stone path travels from here through newly planted camellia and hydrangea beds, down to a lower walk. Three-metre-high stone walls surround this area and mark the drop to the beech woods below. (Dunloe Garden is very unsuitable for children because of these great drops.)

Close to the main hotel buildings there are several huge mixed beds with varieties of fuchsia, hebe, cistus and lavatera interspersed with herbaceous plants. Crinum lilies, erysimum, angel's fishing rod (*Dierama*), penstemon, buddleia, hydrangea and yet more varieties of fuchsia form a low frame beneath the view of the Gap. The hotel buildings themselves are modern, low to the ground and almost bedded into the garden.

Paths lead from these buildings out to the arboretum and walled garden, both filled with specimen trees and flowering shrubs; varieties of camellia, magnolia and viburnum, along with a great number of excellent herbaceous plants and sub-shrubs. The Japanese banana (*Musa basjoo*) is a fine exotic specimen. There are Dawn redwoods (*Metasequoia glyptostroboides*), also known as the Redwood of the Dawn of Time. This tree was rediscovered in 1944 in China, having been thought extinct. The southwest's most famous tree, the strawberry tree (*Arbutus unedo*), is planted in copious numbers, as are myrtles. Myrtles (*Luma apiculata*) come from Chile, but do so well in Kerry that they might as well be natives, self-seeding happily and decorating the garden year-round with glossy green leaves, tiny, white, fragrant flowers in August and little red fruits later in the year.

There is far too much in this large garden to take in on a single visit and for many the handy 'Around the World in Thirty Minutes' leaflet, which marks out thirty of the most remarkable trees, will be a lifeline from the sheer mind-boggling spectacle of so many wonderful plants.

THE GARDENS OF EUROPE

Listowel, County Kerry ▪ **Open:** all year round, dawn–dusk ▪ **No entrance fee** ▪ Supervised children welcome; please note, dogs on leads ▪ **Directions:** coming into Listowel town centre from the Limerick–Tarbert road (N69), turn left towards Listowel Golf Club and look for the signposts. The Gardens are next to the golf course.

Between the 1940s and early 1990s the land now occupied by this garden provided Listowel with its town dump. Today the Gardens of Europe provide a powerful lesson on the better use of public space and what a town can do if minds and energy are properly applied. Paddy Fitzgibbon, a local solicitor, was not content to continue looking at a dump and spurred the local Rotary Club into action. Together they turned a big mess into a fine garden with the help of FÁS and a team of local workers. That garden was opened in 1995 and went on to win a National Landscape Award as part of the Tidy Towns Competition 2000.

The large site, covering about three acres beside Listowel Golf Course, was given to the town by Lord Listowel. It is a beautiful location, ringed by mature oak trees, and it provided a stately and mature backdrop for the planned garden. Cleaning up the site, putting a drainage system in place and importing huge amounts of topsoil preceded the more interesting and enjoyable part of the creation. (Building a garden on top of three metres of rubbish is no straightforward task, and there were many considerations to be taken into account.) Finally, the time came when Paddy Bowe, garden historian and designer, could be brought in to design an appropriate garden.

The plan was to give the garden a European feel and this was achieved by working two elements together. The first was a statue of Oskar Schiller, the man who wrote the words to the European anthem 'Ode to Joy', which was placed at one end of the garden, representative of the highest ideals of the European project. The other element was a commemoration of the holocaust and the mass slaughter of the Second World War. This was marked by placing a sculpture by Irish artist Gerry Brouder at the opposite side of the garden to the Schiller statue. This is a monumental, enigmatic and brooding work, suggesting imprisonment and freedom.

The garden running between the two works of art was designed in twelve bays or individual gardens – representative of the twelve countries that made up the European Union at the time of the garden's creation. The planting in each bay is singular and individual – different bays are devoted to camellias, roses, heathers, herbaceous perennials and sculptural plants. No attempt was made to actually represent the flora of each country however, as this would have put needless strain on any design. And even if it were possible to create a bay of plants native and specific to Luxembourg, for example, the level of tending and maintenance required would have been huge. This garden needed to be easily maintained, so the plants used are flowering shrubs and small trees, and plants that give a good account of themselves all year round. But there are some herbaceous plantings scattered through the beds also and plenty of plants, like euphorbia, hardy geraniums and spring bulbs.

The Gardens of Europe is a peaceful and handsome garden that is enjoyed and well used by the townspeople. Let it be an example to others.

GLANLEAM HOUSE AND GARDEN

Valentia Island, County Kerry; Tel: +066 9476176; Fax: +066 9476108; e-mail: info@glanleam.ie ■ **Contact:** Meta Kreissig ■ **Open:** mid-March–end October, daily, 11am–5pm; visits strictly by appointment only ■ **Entrance fee** ■ Supervised children welcome; please note, dogs on leads ■ **Special features:** three self-catering houses; guided tours available ■ **Directions:** driving from Portmagee over the bridge to Valentia Island, follow the signs to Knightstown. In the village, turn left after the Protestant church. Travel along for a short distance and Glanleam is on the right, well signposted.

Looking through the jungle-like growth of huge tree ferns at Glanleam, on Valentia Island in County Kerry.

The gardens at Glanleam were the creation of Peter Fitzgerald, the nineteenth Knight of Kerry. Glanleam is an historical garden with connections to many famed plant collectors, gardeners and gardens of the Victorian period. For fifty years, from 1830 to 1880, the knight, a popular and enlightened man, took the bare rock of Valentia Island in hand and worked to create the garden. A clever and keen gardener, he used his many connections to fill the new garden with rare and unusual plants, many of which are still growing in Glanleam today. The gardens have been substantially well kept and today are being worked and added to by the present owners, Meta and Jessica Kreissig, who open the old house to visitors when they are not engaged in preserving and restoring the gardens. Their Glanleam is a mature garden, a place where plants grow faster and taller than anywhere else on the island.

The gardens are long and narrow, made up of walks through sheltering and lightly shading trees, with occasional openings and clearings where the house, lawns and semicircular walled kitchen gardens stand. Jessica Kreissig's 'lawn-mowers', a flock of soya sheep kept for grass-cutting, graze peacefully.

The list of exotics and fine plants is long. A lily-of-the valley tree (*Clethra arborea*) grows to over twenty-three metres here. This is an extraordinary height, as they only reach about seven metres in their native Madeira. Embothriums, declared the finest specimens on the island by the gardening writer and expert Charles Nelson, also reach heights here that they never manage in Chile, their original home. In the Knight's garden there are special ferns which grow wild and self-seed well, including the European chain fern (*Woodwardia radicans*) and the rare little Killarney fern (*Trichomanes speciosum*). Because of a craze among Victorian gardeners for ferns of every description, the little Killarney fern was almost rendered extinct. The collecting hordes would descend on woodlands, digging up everything ferny, with a particular enthusiasm for anything strange, rare or weird to bring home to their cabinet of green curiosities.

On the Upper Walk is a collection of camellias that start flowering at the end of November for a late autumn/early winter picture. And down by the sea walk and a bay of postcard-perfect blue water, the early primulas, bluebells and spring bulbs smother the ground. Fuchsias thrive in Glanleam and in the summer's damp warmth they almost wilt under the weight of flowers. In an area called the Dell, deep in the garden, tree ferns grow in great numbers and in sizes that make the owners of single weakling specimens in greenhouses weep with envy.

One of the great sights is of massed myrtles (*Luma apiculata*), which grow everywhere in Glanleam. Their small leaves, glossy and dark, the bark like smooth rust and the sweet-smelling white blossoms are immensely attractive. The fruits are edible and, though generally thought to be a dull and insipid fruit, at Glanleam they taste good; Jessica Kreissig says that they still make jam from them. A fine variegated *Luma apiculata* 'Glanleam Gold', with green leaves edged in gold, originated in this garden.

At one point the walk leads to the Spring Rice garden, which is not, as one could be forgiven for thinking, a Chinese- or Japanese-inspired garden. It was created in memory of Elizabeth Spring Rice, who died in France, having been exiled there for smuggling IRA arms into Ireland in 1916. The plants here are all exotic. There are masses of agave, succulents and ginger (*Hedychium*). A circular water feature with finely wrought stonework, and little paths, steps and rills interlace this small garden which (well-behaved) children will love because of its size and scale.

A fern walk is overhung with fringed acacia leaves in another tropical-looking spot, and leads on to a walk of angel's fishing rods (*Dierama*). In the spring this site is full of bluebells and libertia. To the front of the house a gunnera walk with big skunk cabbages and more naturalised tree ferns passes by a thundering stream. The area up here will be opened so that the beautiful rock formations can be seen. A long pond is planned and a new herbaceous border will be planted by 2001.

Everywhere in the woods are the results, good and bad, of storms and tree losses. An enormous amount of tidying up is needed. The nature of the garden means that all fallen timber has to be carried from the woods by hand, making an enormous amount of work and linking Glanleam back to its history in a real way that other gardens have moved on from. With eighty-seven trees lost in one recent storm alone, that's a lot of timber to be transported manually.

While the storms take their toll, the losses open up areas of land, revealing some previously hidden features. A thirty-metre-high monkey puzzle tree (*Araucaria araucana*) was only discovered when a recent storm knocked down all around it, removing the canopy and showing it standing tall. A *Podocarpus andinus* from Argentina fell over in another storm and continues to grow, on its side. The remains of a huge fallen cordyline gave out nearly 120 seedlings that have since been put to work as a young *allée* on the upper walk. The extra light allowed in as a result of tree losses enables replacement plants to grow.

The restoration work at Glanleam continues and, as part of a current project, decorative and intricately patterned stone path edgings are being uncovered. Recent discoveries include the old drains, edged with little cobbles, and every time undergrowth is cleared more steps appear. The Kreissigs are dedicated to cultivating and expanding the garden: more than 22,000 oaks were planted in the early 1990s, along with 15,000 ash trees.

MUCKROSS GARDENS

Muckross House, Killarney National Park, Killarney, County Kerry; Tel: +064 31440; Fax: +064 33926; e-mail: killarneynationalpark@ealga.ie ▪ **Contact:** The Administrator ▪ **Open:** all year, daily, 9am–6pm; closed for one week at Christmas ▪ **No entrance fee** to park and garden; **entrance fee** charged to Muckross House and traditional farm ▪ Supervised children welcome; please note, dogs on leads ▪ **Special features:** exhibition; craft shop; self-guiding trails, including a special trail for the visually impaired; traditional farm, with black Kerry cow herd ▪ Member of Dúchas ▪ **Directions:** situated 6km from Killarney on the N71 to Kenmare.

Set among the woods and lakes of Killarney, Muckross is a truly lovely garden. If possible, arrive in a jarvey carriage. It's not cheap, but if you can afford it, leave the car out at the gates. Slowly driving toward the gardens in an open carriage, ducking under the roadside trees and seeing the woods at close quarters is a delight. When gardens like Muckross were being made, movement was at the pace of the horse and it is appropriate to move at that pace when visiting. Also, the jarveys are informative and entertaining. Children in particular will love the slow, rocking journey through the grounds and the prospect of the same journey back will act as a good carrot if the walk around the garden seems like a chore for them.

The house stands deep into the park, surrounded by smart lawns falling down toward the famous lakes. Clipped hedges and topiary cones give a formal, tidy look to

Muckross House, clad in venerable wisteria.

the front and sides. Old shrub roses lean against the building, along with an ancient wisteria whose almost architectural trunk runs up and blends in with the grey limestone of the window arches. From the terrace there are views over the lakes to the mountains beyond, and the beginnings of the arboretum with groves of Scots pine to the foreground.

A sunken garden to the back of the house contains a large bed of canna lilies, dahlias, roses, clematis and other herbaceous plants. This is a striking and lush bed. The only thing that jars in the garden are the bedding-filled beds. They look a bit flat beside the other more substantially sized perennial planting.

A set of steps out of the sunken garden leads into the rockery, which is the really great feature in Muckross. Scramble up, down and around the rocks, which sprout cotoneaster, cornus, acer and a vicious-looking *Rosa omeiensis pteracantha* with blood-red thorns and little creamy, buttery, single flowers. This rock garden has a sort of tempered wildness. It is full of knotted heathers, the native strawberry tree (*Arbutus unedo*), grey-shooted *Rubus thibetanus* 'Silver Fern' and blue-flowering *Teucrium fruticans*. There are many unusual, lesser-seen and interesting shrubs, creeping plants and trees growing on the big sprawling rock face, and the full extent or size of the rockery is difficult to see from most points within it.

Through shrubs and rocky outcrops deep within the rockery one catches constant glimpses of the manicured parkland and arboretum beyond. There are extensive plantations of rhododendrons, particularly *Rhododendron arboreum*, and azaleas throughout the parkland.

Other attractions at Muckross include a herd of small black Kerry cows. These are part of the national herd. The traditional farms, which are an exhibition of farm life and practices from the 1930s, can be visited, as can Muckross House, and a trip to Torc waterfall might also be fitted into a day's outing. As with other popular sights, if you don't like crowds try to visit off-season or at least early in the week.

PIER ROAD GARDEN

Pier Road, Sneem, County Kerry ※ **Contact:** Head Gardener ※ **Open:** all year, daily, 8.30am–12.30pm; *Note:* as this is a productive garden there is little to see between November and April ※ **No entrance fee** ※ **Special features:** vegetables and flowers on sale daily ※ **Directions:** coming into Sneem from the direction of Caherdaniel, turn at the second right off the square for Pier Road. The garden is a few hundred metres down the road on the left.

The Pier Road Garden is a little community-run vegetable, herb and flower garden set on the edge of the village of Sneem, carrying all the usual crops and some unusual food crops also. It is not over-prettified but rather is a simple working garden that anyone with a plan to start a vegetable plot should visit and note.

TULLIGELANE MASTERGEEHY EXOTIC GARDEN

Killarney, County Kerry; Tel: +066 9474461 ※ **Contact:** Carl and Kathleen Herpels ※ **Open:** mid-April–mid-October, daily, 10am–8pm ※ **Entrance fee** ※ Supervised children welcome ※ **Special features:** wild food plants; a children's fairy corner ※ **Directions:** travel 13km from Glencar, where the garden is signposted. Travel via the Ballaghisheen Pass. The garden is signposted to the right. Alternatively, turn at the white church outside Waterville and follow signs for the garden.

Set just inside the Killarney Conservation Area, Tulligelane is 'a project for heightening public awareness in neglected, uncommon and wild food plants'. Put simply, it means that any plants in the garden with white labels are edible, and most of the plants have white labels.

Mr Herpels estimates that the garden covers three acres, but it's not easy to gauge its size. He started it in 1993, mainly because his hens – the main feature of the plot up to then – were devoured by mink. Rather than risk another massacre, he began gardening. His original purpose was not to open the garden, but simply to grow plants. Now the garden is full of wildlife; it is a wilderness harnessed rather than tamed.

Tulligelane is a fascinating garden, worked organically, but with deer, hare, badger and wood pigeon ready to tuck in to the tasty proceeds at every available opportunity, it is a fortified place. A great variety of methods are used to keep the hairier visitors away from the plants. Some of the more inviting areas are completely fenced off into little rooms to save them from marauders. This means that you need to open gates into little surprise gardens, closing them carefully behind you before going in to study the place. Children will enjoy this as many of the smaller plots are to their scale.

The place is so wet. There are sunken streams and rills everywhere. Slate paths literally float on the bog, allowing one to walk through parts of the garden that otherwise might suck an unsuspecting walker down like quicksand. In other spots, grass has been planted through barely-covered industrial wire netting to hold the weight of walkers. Standing- and stepping-stones lead from one garden to another. Within enclosures there are plots of very different vegetables, like Japanese parsley (*Mitsuba*), perpetual lettuce, delicious yellow alpine strawberries and wild chicory. The greenhouses are full of huckleberries and tamarillo as well as a big collection of succulents. Marshmallow, Indian Rhubarb (*Peltiphyllum peltatum*), tree onions, and Chinese artichokes grow alongside the more usual vegetables.

Close by the house, stone sheds covered in sedum, ferns and houseleeks look like large, house-shaped plants themselves. A small watering can sits on a stool for when it's needed, but with about two metres of rain annually it can't be too overworked.

Mr Herpels is extremely knowledgeable on edible plants, but there are also plenty of purely decorative plants in the garden: a cordyline-lined path is underplanted with primula and geranium, and groves of eucalyptus, cherry and alder break up the rooms. And all the while the Macgillycuddy's Reeks loom in the background.

Tulligelane is a quirky and eccentric garden. The formalist might shudder at its organic, snaking shape – so leave the formalists at home and enjoy!

THE WAY THE FAIRIES WENT

Sneem, County Kerry ▪ **No entrance fee**, public space ▪ Children welcome but should be supervised because of the streams; please note, dogs on leads ▪ **Directions:** coming into Sneem from the direction of Caherdaniel, turn at the first right off the square towards the Catholic church. The garden is to the right of the church.

An unusual and somewhat strange little village garden set in the middle of Sneem, The Way the Fairies Went is composed of a collection of scaled-down stone pyramids and hermits' cells set among rock and slateworks. Sunken walls dug into the turf hold in streams which run around the site. There are some small groves of flag iris, bullrush and native trees, like willow.

Standing in a display case by one of the paths is a statue of the goddess *Isis*. This was given as a gift by the people of Egypt to the people of Ireland. Without explanation or obvious reason, this is an intriguing little feature in an unusual and attractive public garden.

NURSERIES AND GARDEN CENTRES

BALLYSEEDY GARDEN CENTRE

Ballyseedy, Tralee, County Kerry; Tel: +068 49499.

BLOOMING BEST GARDEN CENTRE, THE

Farranfore, County Kerry; Tel: +066 64211.

FLORIAT

Sneem, County Kerry; Tel: +064 45550.

This is a tiny little nursery run by a true enthusiast. Mr Williamson grows anything and everything, from kiwi fruit to pomegranate and vines. He is constantly experimenting with plants from seed. I found Chilean fire bush (*Embothrium coccineum*), cobnuts, crinodendron, yucca and cordylines. Standard trained fuchsias are what he loves to grow best of all and he carries an interesting collection of these beautiful, decorative shrubs.

HICKEY'S NURSERY

Gortalea, Tralee, Ballinane, County Kerry; Tel: +066 64629.

IRISH WILDFLOWERS LTD

The Wood, Dingle, County Kerry; Tel: +066 9152200; e-mail iwf@tinet.ie

LISCAHANE NURSERY AND GARDEN CENTRE

Liscahane, Ardfert, Tralee, County Kerry; Tel: +066 34222.

LISTOWEL GARDEN CENTRE

Church Street, Listowel, County Kerry; Tel: +068 22144.

MAIL ROAD CROSS NURSERY AND GARDEN CENTRE

Listowel, County Kerry; Tel: +068 49499.

MUCKROSS GARDEN CENTRE

Mangerton Road, Killarney, County Kerry; Tel: +064 34044.

RYAN'S NURSERY

Lissivigeen, Killarney, County Kerry; Tel: +064 33507.

Ericaceous and tender plants stocked in this mid-sized nursery.

ST BRENDAN'S NURSERY

Banemore, Ardfert, County Kerry; Tel: +066 33787.

Exotics grown from seed, all tolerant of Irish weather.

SEASIDE GARDEN CENTRE

PortMagee Road, Cahirciveen, County Kerry; Tel: 087 2809866.

GARDEN ACCESSORIES

LEWIS, FRANK, GARDEN SCULPTURE GALLERY

Mangerton Road, Killarney, County Kerry ▪ **Open:** mid-June–mid-August, Monday–Saturday, 9am–6pm.

COUNTY LIMERICK

County Limerick stretches west across the estuary of the River Shannon – the longest river in these islands – and borders Kerry, Cork and Tipperary to the west, south and east. The county occupies a mixture of fertile, acid and limestone land. One of Limerick's claims to fame is the N69 scenic drive, which takes in a number of historical sights, from Askeaton Abbey and Castle to the Foynes Flying Boat Museum and the Aughinish Wildlife Sanctuary and, most importantly, a wonderful collection of gardens, including the magnificent Glin Castle, home to the Knight of Glin, and the Celtic Park and Garden.

Limerick city is an important historical centre, home to the famed Treaty Stone on which the Treaty of Limerick was signed. St John's Castle is a noted sixteenth-century fortified castle, now beautifully restored. Bunratty Castle and its folk park are one of the biggest tourist attractions in the southwest, and close by the picturesque village of Adare is filled with Tudoresque villas, pretty art galleries, antique shops and tearooms. In Newcastle West the Desmond Banqueting Hall is worth seeing. This is an imposing, two-storey, vaulted building that was built in the fifteenth century for the earls of Desmond. But the city is not simply a mix of the historic and the quaint, it is also a busy shopping centre with a number of colleges, a university and a large population of young people. Near to the city is Shannon Airport, for many years the first point of call between Ireland and the United States and the birthplace of Irish coffee – a commendable contribution. Recently, Limerick also became the proud home of the Hunt Collection, with its many priceless historical artefacts and works of art by masters such as Renoir and Pissaro. The Hunt Collection was given to the Irish nation by John and Gertrude Hunt in the 1990s, and is one of Limerick's finest attractions. Each year the city plays host to the prestigious EV+A, the largest exhibition of contemporary visual art in Ireland, when artists both renowned and unknown exhibit their work throughout the city in a bewildering array of venues. This is a city that effortlessly incorporates a fascinating past and, through the eyes of modern artists, a unique view of the future.

ADARE MANOR

Adare, County Limerick; Tel: +061 396566 ■ **Contact:** Joe O'Flaherty, Head Green Keeper ■ **Open:** May–September, Monday–Sunday, 10am–6pm; groups welcome ■ **Entrance fee** goes towards garden upkeep ■ Supervised children welcome ■ **Special features:** refreshments available in the clubhouse, but must be booked in advance; hotel accommodation ■ **Directions:** situated in the village of Adare, which is located on the N21, southwest of Limerick city.

Adare Manor sits in the middle of the almost ridiculously good-looking Adare village, a place unlike any other village in Ireland. It could have been beamed in from the heart of 'Olde Englande', complete with perfect little thatched houses, tearooms and half-timbered Tudor villas. The manor itself is another unusual sight. A nineteenth-century, Jacobean-style manor house built for the Earls of Dunraven, it now plays host to the super-wealthy as one of the best hotels in the country. The gardens are formal and elegant, just right for strolling around after a suitably rich, cream-laden afternoon tea at the hotel's restaurant. The River Maigue flows right past the manor and a wide, impressive set of steps leads down from the garden to a river walk, a weir and a huge cedar of Lebanon, about which there is a great old barney going on. Some have said that it is the oldest specimen in the country, while others hotly dispute this. Meanwhile, the tree continues to charm.

The formal gardens are spread out in front of the manor in two long ribbons of box-enclosed flowerbeds divided by wide golden gravel paths. The gardens were laid out in the 1850s. Perfectly cut box knotbeds run in lines on a sunken terrace below the building. White and pink snapdragons (*Antirrhinums*) peep up in bright splashes from out of the centre pockets of box, adding colour to the well-shaped, low hedges. Huge sentries of clipped yew add height at the end of each run of knotting. There are low retaining walls with runs of more bedding plants, wide gravel paths and sweeping steps into the garden from the terrace: all good-looking, manicured and ordered. With the river view on one side and the perfect park of trees on the other, this place is tidy and neat – but it is not a garden to inspire or surprise. The flat architectural style complements but does not distract from the house.

The walled garden, which holds the golf club within its walls, is disappointing, with nothing more than a few wall-trained fruit trees, but there are a small number of apple trees unusually well draped with mistletoe, which make a fairly rare sight. Mistletoe (*Viscum album*) is something of an unusual plant, more familiar as Christmas decoration than as a living plant. It is a parasite, pushing its roots into the bark of a host tree to suck out minerals and water. It can be grown by rubbing the white berries, which contain the seeds, into the cracks of a tree's bark. Apple trees make good hosts, as do lime, willow and poplar trees.

BALLYNACOURTY

Ballysteen, County Limerick; Tel: +061 396409 ∗ **Contact:** George and Michelina Stacpoole ∗ **Open:** by appointment, to groups only ∗ **Entrance fee** goes towards garden upkeep ∗ Supervised children welcome ∗ **Directions:** driving from Limerick to Foynes on the N69, turn right for Pallaskenry and travel for about 4km until you reach the village. In Pallaskenry village, follow the signs for Ballysteen. The garden is 3km along this road, on the right-hand side. The gateway is marked by pillars topped with stone urns.

Thirty years ago Ballynacourty was 'a plain, unadorned, old farmhouse'. Today the handsome house and garden have the appearance of a place that never knew a plain or unadorned day in its life. 'If you're patient, it's amazing what you can do ...' trails off Mrs Stacpoole in response to well-deserved and gushing praise for her wonderful garden. The thirty years since moving to Ballynacourty have been well spent by the Stacpooles, turning the place into an individual, stylish, large garden. The garden is all about surprises and is laid out ingeniously, like a mad maze. The lines in this garden are architectural, and most of them are green – the green lines of hedging. Everywhere there are great big beech hedges, with the line of one tall hedge standing out and above the contrasting line and colour of a neighbouring hedge.

The visit begins when one pulls up in front of a house draped voluptuously with a massive wisteria. Just visible under its trailing branches is a loggia-cum-conservatory; it's as much Lombardy as Limerick. Starting through an arch in a big hornbeam hedge that runs out from the house, a path leads to the first of the garden rooms. A great double curve of privet hedging, tall, expertly cut and boxy, dominates this area. Privet is a fast-growing, evergreen bush that gives great height and width as a hedge. It is easy to shape and makes a good dense screen. One drawback is that every part of the plant is seriously poisonous, from the leaves to the tiny white flowers and little black berries, so it's probably not a good idea in a garden used regularly by children.

From this point at the end of the privet hedge the garden meanders in several directions: 'One Christmas George thought we'd go this way,' explained Mrs Stacpoole as she led the way into another garden in the six-acre plot. This route takes in a lavender walk that leads towards a wildflower area with grass paths cut through the buttercups, cowslips and meadowsweet. An arbour of privet stands perched on a bank overlooking a sea of daffodils and the River Shannon, which flows below and beyond the garden. Down from this is the cherry walk, which my guide compared to 'paradise' in the late spring.

Ballynacourty is an easy garden in which to get lost. Only when the path leads up a hill that overlooks the garden can the shape and plan of the garden, gates, pillars, statues, hedge walls and mature trees be seen in context. Apart from the hedges, the other feature vital to the look of Ballynacourty is the statuary, and the place is filled with ingenious-looking pieces that constantly surprise and divert the visitor. The Stacpooles also derive as much use from the natural features as those that are brought in: old wells and huge natural stone outcrops peeping out of the well-kept lawns are used like stepping stones across a green lake. In addition to looking good, these huge stones give some idea of the sort of rocky limestone out of which the garden was born.

Every year the Stacpooles buy a Christmas tree for the house, a living tree, which is planted out after the holiday: 'I hate the idea of cutting down a tree just to put it in my house for a few days,' says Michelina Stacpoole. The idea of marking each Christmas by adding another tree to the garden, which will always be there as a reminder of the holiday, is an idea worth trying for those with decent-sized gardens.

BOYCE'S GARDEN

Mount Trenchard, Foynes, County Limerick; Tel: +069 65302; e-mail: dboyce.ias@eircom.net ▪ **Contact:** Phil and Dick Boyce ▪ **Open:** May–October, daily, 10am–6pm; at other times by appointment only; groups welcome ▪ **Entrance fee** ▪ Not suitable for children ▪ **Directions:** the garden is 1km from Loughill, travelling toward Glin, off the N69 and is well signposted.

The Boyces's one-acre garden came second in the Munster category in the Shamrock All Ireland Gardens Competition 1999. The husband-and-wife team has been working on the garden since 1983, and it has the look of a place on the receiving end of much love and dedication.

The house and garden are built on the site of six labourers' cottages – a piece of history visible in the six varieties of hedging that run along the roadside in front of the present-day garden. Each short run refers to one of the old cottages. Entering from the road you'll find the first part of the garden is a perfect little alpine bed by the front gate. This faces south and bakes when the sun comes out. A small arbour with a seat within is well placed to study the bed and its low-growing contents. Close by the alpine garden, a pretty shrub of *Griselinia littoralis* 'Bantry Bay' overlooks a lily pond. This is a tender plant, but doing well in the favourable spot given it here. (Phil Boyce is a member of the Alpine Garden Plant Society (*see* appendices) and she praises the society hugely for the knowledge she has gathered as a member over the years. She also recommends that new gardeners should join this or other societies, as they are a great source of information and seed-swapping, as well as being good places to meet like-minded people. Indeed, very many of the gardeners around the country testify to the help and fun derived from joining plant, gardening and horticultural clubs.)

A herbaceous bed of delphiniums, irises and other blue flowers on one side with yellow ligularia and rudbekia, solidago and alstromeria on the other runs parallel to the hedge. There are masses of good small garden trees, like myrtle (*Luma apiculata*), and a sambucus laced through by the flowers of *Rosa* 'Nevada', which will cover the tree with its yellow-cupped, cream-coloured flowers in time. This double use of soil is something all small-plot gardeners should try to achieve. The flowers of the host tree and the roses run one after another and are in turn followed by elderberries. This gives a well-extended season of interest in a small space.

Growing shrubs as standards is a favourite trick in this garden. They 'train up' a good number of small trees and shrubs throughout the garden. This involves pruning the lower branches and making a 'tree' shape, or lollipop, out of what would normally be a multi-stemmed shrub. This is another way of expanding the number of plants that can be fitted into a small garden. A 'pruned up' shrub (see box, Pruning Up, p.26) allows a good number of shade-loving plants to be inserted in the soil below, plants like spring bulbs, winter cyclamen, ferns and hellebores. Topiary is another feature in the Mount Trenchard garden, and a golden myrtle trained as a perfect two-metre cone is one of the more unusual plants to be seen here.

In the vegetable garden, to the rear of the garden, a brick wall has been built specially for a little peach tree. This wall will give it shelter, catch the sun and, being brick, it will hold the heat to help the peaches ripen. Lemons are grown in here also, alongside cut-and-come cabbages. A display of black pansies backed by a lilac-coloured hibiscus with a wine centre is a really good colour mix.

The greenhouse is set in the middle of the garden but is not visible until one almost bumps into it, so abundant is the planting throughout this exotic Irish garden. The Boyces won Best Greenhouse in the Shamrock All Ireland Gardens Competition 1998. Their greenhouse is a small structure but is like an Aladdin's cave, with grapes, succulents, an Australian Black Boy (*Todea barbara*), *Dicksonia antarctica*, *Fuchsia* 'Annabel' with flowers like white ballet dresses, plum-coloured *Rhodochiton atrosanguineus* and a general jam of other exotics. Outside the greenhouse a new fern bed is doing well.

At the lower end of the garden is a boggy area with, among other things, a lovely Japanese pagoda tree (*Sophora*) with zigzagging branches and miniscule sweet flowers. The garden is stuffed to capacity with plants. Being lovers of new things they collect and collect and everything is described and dated on plant labels. This is an interesting practice that will give novice visitors a good idea of the size and spread different plants might reach within a certain number of years.

THE CELTIC PARK AND GARDEN

Kilcornan, County Limerick; Tel: +061 394243 ▪ **Contact:** Pat and Bernard Downes ▪ **Open:** mid-March–end October, daily, 9.30am–6pm; other times by appointment only; groups welcome ▪ **Entrance fee** goes towards garden upkeep ▪ Supervised children welcome; please note, dogs on leads ▪ **Special features:** tea-room is open for refreshments, but must be booked in advance ▪ **Directions:** turn left off the N69 after Kildimo, at the sign for the Celtic Park and Garden. Travel for 1km and turn sharp left, a further 1km along is the entrance on the right-hand side. If you are travelling from Adare village, the garden is well signposted and lies 8km distant.

Within the Celtic Theme Park at Kilcornan is a garden that can be visited either by it-self or as part of the bigger tour of the park. The centrepiece of the garden is a formal sunken room with pillars holding up roses and steps down to a big rectangular pool planted up with irises and lilies. Cordylines mark each corner of the pool like exclama-tion marks. Up from this is a large rose garden with long, informal flowing beds and over 1,000 rose plants, mostly hybrid tea roses. The rich scent that pervades this part of the garden is lovely. Winding paths through the roses make for a good walk and the whole garden is enclosed within tall, sheltering griselinia hedges. The path leads past a long herbaceous border filled with stock, geranium, crinum lilies, phlox, verbena and mint.

The Celtic garden was designed by Bernard Downes and is worked by him and his wife, Pat. It's a young garden, only twelve years old, and is still being added to. A bog garden, with varieties of wild orchids and grass of Parnassus (*Parnassia palustris*) is being developed at the moment. A big wildflower meadow on a slight hill leads up to the garden. This itself is an increasingly rare sight and is alone worth the detour.

GLIN CASTLE

Glin, County Limerick; Tel: +068 34173; e-mail: knight@iol.ie ▪ **Contact:** Bob Duff ▪ **Open:** May–June, daily, 10am–12 noon, 2pm–4pm; groups by appoint-ment only ▪ **Entrance fee** goes towards garden upkeep ▪ **Directions:** enter the village of Glin from the Foynes–Listowel road (N69). Go to the top of the village and turn right. The castle is at the end of this short avenue.

Glin Castle has been the home of the knights of Glin since the late 1700s. The Geor-gian manor, built in 1780, was transformed into a 'castle' in the nineteenth century, complete with turrets, crenellations and Gothic features. It stands by the Shannon estuary, more handsome than imposing. The drive up to the castle is not long but it is very impressive, cutting a swathe through a run of gigantic gunnera with leaves over two metres across on stalks over three metres high, dwarfing the visitor. The castle itself is covered lightly in wisteria and *Rosa banksiae* and is fronted by tidy bay cones. Close by the castle is a formal garden with classical busts perched in niches cut into the hedges.

An avenue of clipped yew pyramids and a little green garden room were the creation of the current Knight of Glin's mother in the 1930s. No colour or flowers are allowed to invade the restraint in this part of the garden. The only concession to colour is a little white, with Paris daisies in large pots by a little French door leading out to the garden. A sundial on a stone island surrounded by low-growing rock and alpine plants is wrapped in elaborate box curlicues. Walking further out from the house, a witty swagged wall covered in lichen finishes off this garden and marks the border between the formal garden and the wood or wild garden beyond.

An avenue of cordylines, the babies of a big specimen elsewhere in the garden, leads out from the lawn towards an intriguing gateway that is glimpsed through the trees. These trees march away from the house to the side of the lawn and include specimens of the lovely evergreen dogwood (*Cornus capitata*), *Magnolia campbellii* and Monterey pine (*Pinus radiata*). Madam Olda FitzGerald, wife of Desmond, the twenty-fifth and current Knight, is a keen gardener and garden writer with a particular love of trees. She is well embarked on a tree-planting project throughout the gardens.

Up in the woods above the castle, tree ferns were planted under the canopy of mature oaks. The tree ferns will give a slightly exotic feel to the area when they grow up. An early nineteenth-century grotto with an unusual curved ceiling is snug in the wood: 'The grotto was completely covered in rubbish when they found it a few years ago. We didn't even know it was here,' explains Madam FitzGerald. But once found its history came to light too: 'It was an unofficial courting couples' bower that enjoyed good business over the last two centuries among castle servants and farm workers,' she explains. Nearby a modern folly of standing stones was erected in a clearing in the oak trees. The trees here are huge, stately, venerable. They have the effect of making the stone circle look ancient, despite the fact that it is only in place a few years – images of druids and all class of strange rituals spring to mind. A great number of baby rhododendrons have been planted up in the wood and the plan is to plant magnolias with them. 'In five years' time this will be a good spot, but it is a young part of the garden yet, a work in progress,' continues Madam FitzGerald.

Out of the woods is the walled garden. This is a proper working garden, covering two acres and brim-full of vegetables and flowers: 'Because of the B&B we have to grow everything needed to feed our guests and then we need barrel-loads of flowers for the house, so we work almost all of the walled garden fairly intensively.' Cosmos, walls of sweet pea and a sea of cornflowers, nigella and other annuals decorate the beds of asparagus, Swiss chard and lettuce. Everything is grown in substantial blocks or drifts – after all, it takes a fair amount of flowers to fill a barrel. Set into the middle of the walled garden is a temple with a headless statue of *Andromeda,* which is surrounded by white roses in summer and white tulips in spring. A dog called Bucket was doing his best to eat these particular flowers in between chasing hens in and out of the beds; help that could be lived without. The walled garden, in contrast to the rest of the garden, is a sea of soft colour, billowing and abundant flowers. At the bottom of its slope is a little, rounded, wrought-iron seat where you can sit and look up the garden to views of sweet pea, clipped yew and a big fuchsia hedge grown as an arch among the flowers.

Olda FitzGerald says she always found the prospect of taking over a garden that already bore the distinct mark of a previous and talented gardener slightly unnerving. This is a fear common among many of those who inherit old, established gardens. To be both sympathetic and progressive is not easy and a great deal of self-confidence is needed. It's not a task for the faint-hearted. But the work Madam FitzGerald is carrying out, along with her hard-working gardener Tom Wall, is adding another beautiful layer to a fine old garden rather than smothering it in the aspic of nostalgia and timidity.

ISLANMORE

Croom, County Limerick; Tel: +061 397619; e-mail: kc@islanmore.com ▪
Contact: Mrs Mary Tarry ▪ **Open:** to groups during the summer, on weekdays and by appointment only ▪ **Entrance fee** goes towards garden upkeep ▪ Not suitable for children ▪ **Special features:** teas may be booked by prior arrangement ▪ **Directions:** from Limerick, travel to Croom on the Cork Road (N20). Once in the village, the garden is the first blue gate on the right, set into a long stone wall.

Islanmore is a substantial Georgian country house that was built in 1794 for a young son of Lord Dunraven. Today the house is set within eight acres and it is thought Ninian Niven (*see* Iveagh Gardens, County Dublin, and also Hilton Park, County Monaghan) laid out the garden.

Mrs Mary Tarry began gardening here in 1974, and since then Islanmore has won prizes time and again in the Shamrock All Ireland Gardens Competition. 'I would describe it as a mixture of straight paths and wild places,' says Mrs Tarry of the garden. That also includes three acres of lawns, a walled garden and substantial shrubberies. She loves the garden, but her real passion is for trees. Huge beech and oak are grouped in impressive plantations around the grounds and she constantly adds to these. 'If I won the Lotto, which I never enter, I'd buy trees,' she laughs. An avenue of huge cedars joining the house to the walled garden is her favourite feature. These large cedars are most probably contemporary with the house at just over 200 years old. As with so many of the gardens around the island, a good number of the larger and more mature trees were lost in the terrible storms of Christmas 1997. At Islanmore however, constant planting ensures the future of great trees. Among the finer specimens are mulberry, acer, walnut and a huge paulownia, which came as a sapling from Birr Castle in Offaly along with a good wellingtonia (*Sequioadendron giganteum*), beautifully underplanted with cyclamen, which are now naturalised and spreading wildly beneath the big tree. Close by is an unusual variegated oak that Mrs Tarry doesn't have a name for but from which she is propagating.

Only two acres of the walled garden's four acres are worked, but what has been done has been done well. Good mixed beds of lilies, white phlox, daisies, cosmos and asters stand in front of a backbone of shrubs, such as potentilla, acer and fuchsia.

A little path leads down to a spring garden of cherry, daffodils and a bridged stream by a fine old rockery. This rockery was totally covered over with weeds and brambles when Mrs Tarry set to work on the garden. Her hard work has completely retrieved the rockery and brought it back to handsome life.

A length of Victorian greenhouse was restored recently. This is still backed by a functioning potting shed. Emerging into the sun of the greenhouse from this snug little workshop, the sight and tart smell of tender climbers, including a huge, trained, white pelargonium rising over three metres up the back wall, rushes at the visitor. Mrs Tarry prunes the pelargonium madly and deadheads it all summer to encourage flowering. Grapes, abutilon, plumbago and a lovely waxy-flowered hoya also decorate the space. The strong, sweet smell of hoya contrasts sharply with the bitter smell of the pelargonium.

Leaving the greenhouse and moving back out into the open, Mrs Tarry talks about creating a walled kitchen garden: 'A good deal more of the garden used to be under vegetables, but the roses are now taking over. When children grow up you don't need anything like the amount of vegetables you once needed.' The rose garden takes up most of the space and has over 1,000 bushes. In here it is the roses that Mrs Tarry is most proud of and she has some precious plants, unknown varieties and roses that can't be bought or easily found, which she grew from cuttings. Mary Tarry says that roses are very easy plants to grow from cuttings and her success rate speaks for itself.

Back at the house is the fine alpine garden. This is a dry, warm herb garden with raised beds (made from an old stone wall coated in lichens) of herbs and flowers in easy loose lines with lots of lavender baking in the sun. The paths around the planting are made of old flags and filled with self-seeding thyme, little violas and nigella. When you look at this particular spot it is not hard to see how the garden has won so many prizes.

TAKING ROSE CUTTINGS

Roses can be propagated in several ways but by far the easiest and most fool-proof way is by hardwood cuttings. Take these in late summer or early autumn. You should take far more cuttings than the number of plants you require because the success rate is not always high. (Myth says that you should take an odd number of cuttings or the fairies will not allow the plants to take root, but that's really a personal decision.)

First take a flowering shoot the width of a pencil and measuring about twenty-five centimetres long. Cut the shoot cleanly above an outward-facing bud and at an angle. Remove the leaves and soft tip, again cutting at a downward angle above a bud. Make a trench about ten centimetres deep with angled sides. Stand the cuttings right-side up against one of the angled walls and back-fill the soil. Be patient. It will take a year or so for the cuttings to take root.

TERRA NOVA GARDEN

Dromin, Athlacca, Kilmallock, County Limerick; Tel: +063 90744; e-mail: terranovaplants@eircom.net; website: www.homepage.eircom.net/terranovaplants ❈ **Contact:** Deborah Begley ❈ **Open:** May–September, by appointment only; groups welcome ❈ **Entrance fee** goes towards garden upkeep ❈ Not suitable for children ❈ **Special features:** unusual and rare plants for sale in the nursery ❈ **Directions:** travel to Bruff and leave by the Kilmallock Road (R512), follow it for just over 2km. Turn right at the crossroads and follow signs for Martin Begley Glass.

Terra Nova is a brand new small garden covering half an acre, and was started in 1993. By 1999 it had already come first in the Limerick and Clare category of the Shamrock All Ireland Gardens Competition and in 2000 it took the prize for the best water feature in Ireland. Deborah Begley is a fanatical gardener and plantswoman. She grows almost all of her plants from seed and loves unusual specimens. So while this is a small plot, it is awash with treasures that will be of particular interest to plantaholics, as well as inspiring others with small gardens.

Deborah's garden is, for want of a better name, a laboratory. She has a small nursery and mail order service through which she sells some of her more interesting plants and the garden is the trial ground for those plants. If they don't work in her plot, she doesn't sell them. She is, therefore, full of well-gleaned advice for buyers. Like a growing band of gardeners with a plant habit, Deborah subscribes to seed-collecting expeditions and pores over the Internet to locate the more unusual plants. She hotly recommended the American Cottage Garden Society website as a good source for seeds, particularly for perennials and fast-growing shrubs. Once she has acquired the seeds she grows many of these tender fast growers as annuals in her garden. They provide her with a large number of big-leaved, exotic-looking shrubs which she grows effectively, with no fear of frost or short life – plants like African hemp (*Sparrmannia africana*) and the castor oil plant (*Ricinus communis*), with its great purple leaves and red, plastic-like seed pods. The frost will get them and they will die, but she will just plant more seeds for next year, in much the same way the rest of us plant lobelia and petunia. Among the more unusual things in her garden, Deborah has a particular love for arisaema – the strange-looking herbaceous perennial that has become so fashionable among experimenting gardeners over the past few years. She was waiting impatiently for arisaema seed to arrive from China when I visited. She grows a great number of varieties both in the greenhouse and outside.

The garden is not just a collection of plants. The layout is arranged well, with seating areas everywhere – for a gardener who never sits down. It has a tiny wooded area full of wood anemone, bluebells and lily-of-the-valley, and a small door leads off from here to who knows where. The stained glass in the door comes courtesy of husband Martin and his glassworks.

A little wildlife pond, well bridged and edged with canna lilies, golden gardener's garters and bullrushes, sits in the middle of the garden. This was selected Third Best Pond in Ireland in the Shamrock All Ireland Gardens Competition 1998. A great love of trees and only her half-acre to play with means that Deborah only grows small trees. At the moment her particular favourite is a Limerick-bred betula, known as *Betula* 'White Light', the work of a Mr Buckley in Birdhill. Space is at a premium and to be too soft is to disadvantage a small garden, so she is not afraid of pulling out any tree or shrub that gets too big. An over-reaching eucalyptus has just been seen off and the space will be given over to a new young specimen that will be tolerated until it gets too big for its boots.

There are masses of unusual and attractive plants in the garden, including a run of *Duchesnea indica*, the mock strawberry with red fruits that the birds don't steal. Her hardy Japanese banana will be wrapped in straw for the winter to save it from the frosts. There are some good grotesques too, like the memorable voodoo lily (*Sauromatum venosum*), which smells like a baby's bad nappy; 'The flies love it though,' says Deborah. This is a truly inspiring garden that is well worth visiting, especially for those who also work in restricted space. It is a testament to what flair, passion and back-breaking work can achieve.

Recently Opened Garden: Not Yet Visited

KNOCKPATRICK

Foynes, County Limerick; Tel: +069 65256 ✤ **Contact:** Tim and Helen O'Brien ✤ **Open:** May–September, afternoons, by appointment only; for a charity day in May, contact for annual dates; groups welcome ✤ **Entrance fee** donated to various charities ✤ Supervised children welcome ✤ **Special features:** plants for sale on charity days only; spectacular views over the River Shannon ✤ **Directions:** take the N69 from Limerick for 34.5km. About 1.5km before Foynes village follow the sign for Knockpatrick for a few hundred metres beyond the sign for Newcastle West. The garden is 1.5km from the cross and marked by a cross over the entrance.

The garden at Knockpatrick, started by the O'Brien family, has been in existence for over seventy years. Since then, three generations of O'Briens have worked and developed the three-acre garden, which enjoys an enviable situation overlooking the scenic Shannon estuary. Between them they have created a fine garden in a lovely place.

Today the garden is worked by the husband-and-wife team of Tim and Helen. When they began to garden here, Knockpatrick was very much centred on the collections of rhododendrons, camellias and azaleas that thrive in the acid soil at Knockpatrick. While maintaining these May-blooming delights, they have also been adding to and varying the planting by bringing in bamboos, tree ferns and candelabra primulas. 'We have changed it quite a lot in the last ten years because we have the time, and really we're at it all the time, adding to the plants, particularly exotics and perennials,' says Helen. Under their care it has become a very varied garden, divided into different levels with pools and water features among the plants.

For all the new plants, the busiest and best time of the year in O'Briens's garden is late May when most of the rhododendrons and azaleas bloom and they hold their annual charity day – each year in aid of a different charity. Plants are potted up and teas and cakes are prepared for the crowds that arrive to enjoy the fleeting flowers and party atmosphere. 'Every year we say this is the last year and every year we hold it again' – admirable dedication to their garden and to sharing it with others

GARDENING CLUBS AND SOCIETIES

LIMERICK GARDEN PLANT GROUP

Contact: Jenny Baker (Hon. Treasurer), Broadwater Cottage, Glenameade, Pallaskenry, County Limerick.

The Limerick Garden Plant Group is an association of gardeners with a particular love of garden plants. It is a forum for plant lovers to 'talk plants', making it a great place for anyone eager to learn and share garden knowledge. Members receive a biannual newsletter. Garden visits are arranged both to members' gardens and to others. Workshops and talks are also arranged. Annual plant sales, seed and plant swaps and exchanges are also a feature of the club.

NURSERIES AND GARDEN CENTRES

CRESCENT GARDEN CENTRE

Crescent Shopping Centre, Limerick, County Limerick; Tel: +061 229863.

D & M GARDEN CENTRE

Ballycannon, Coagh, Rathkeale, County Limerick; Tel: +069 64084.

GARDEN SHED, THE

Main Street, Kildimo, County Limerick; Tel: +061 393211.

HILBERRY GARDEN CENTRE

Hillberry Cottage, Crecora, County Limerick; Tel/Fax: +061 355692

KIELY'S GARDEN CENTRE

Friarstown, Grange, County Limerick; Tel: +061 351818.

MARSHALL'S HARDWARE AND GARDEN CENTRE

42 Upper William Street, Limerick, County Limerick; Tel: +061 416192.

McGILL'S GARDEN CENTRE (Bricks and Paving)

Castleconnell, County Limerick; Tel: +061 377233.

McLYSAGHT'S NURSERY AND GARDEN CENTRE

Ennis Road, Limerick, County Limerick; Tel: +061 452706.

MULGUEEN, BERNARD

Ballinamona, Askeaton, County Limerick; Tel: +061 393019.

O'CONNELL'S GARDEN SHOP

New Street, Abbeyfeale, County Limerick; Tel: +068 31229.

RIVERSIDE NURSERIES

Abbeyfeale, County Limerick; Tel: 086 8468174.

TERRA NOVA PLANTS

c/o Deborah Begley, Dromin, Kilmallock, County Limerick; Tel: +063 90744; e-mail: dbegley@iol.ie; website: terranovaplants@eircom.net

Send a SAE with a 50p in stamps to receive a catalogue. A wide range of plants, including many choice and unusual plants raised from seeds obtained from official seed-gathering expeditions all over the world.

VAN VEEN'S GARDEN CENTRE

Ashfort, Patrickswell, County Limerick; Tel: +061 301499.

WISHING WELL NURSERY

Monagea Road, Newcastle West, County Limerick; Tel: +069 62658.

COUNTY TIPPERARY

Tipperary is a large county, divided into two ridings – north and south – and bordered on the west by Lough Derg. The land is among the best in the country: fertile, largely lime, but with pockets of acid soil. Almost in the middle of the county is the Rock of Cashel, the most visited historical site in the country. This group of twelfth-, thirteenth- and fifteenth-century buildings includes a round tower, chapel, castle and cathedral, built on an outcrop of grey limestone that dominates the surrounding landscape in the same way as Chartres Cathedral does in flat northern France. Another important historical site is Ormonde Castle in Carrick-on-Suir, the best example of an Elizabethan manor house in Ireland. The tiny walled town of Fethard, set in stud farm country, is unusually well-preserved and boasts one of the best pubs in the country – McCarthy's. Driving in the Galtees, through the Glen of Aherloe, is a pleasure, and historic Cahir is built around another fifteenth-century Ormonde castle. Look out for the cannonball embedded in its wall. A little way out of the town, at the end of a walk by the River Suir, is the Swiss Cottage, the most well-known *cottage orné* in the country. Ardfinnan and Clogheen are pretty villages and untouched by tourism. There are a number of gardens open to the public, some of which team together each summer under the banner of the South Tipperary Garden Trail. The trail usually takes place in July and is well advertised in the local press.

CAMAS PARK

Cashel, County Tipperary; Tel: +062 61010 ▪ **Contact:** Trish Hyde ▪ **Open:** for the South Tipperary Garden Trail (see local press for annual dates); at other times strictly by appointment only ▪ **Entrance fee** donated to the South Tipperary Hospice ▪ **Directions:** 4km from Cashel on the Dundrum Road (R505). The house is on the left with a stone wall marking it.

Trish Hyde's garden at Camas Park, in the middle of the fertile land around Cashel, is well-known by garden visitors throughout the country. The garden, surrounded by parkland, covers about four acres and within it Mrs Hyde has created several completely different gardens with considerable style.

A lawn sweeps downhill from the house to a grove of mature chestnut and lime trees which, when reached, turn out to be the canopy for a wood and bog garden and a series of serpentine iris-filled ponds. These are sideplanted by spreading runs of drumstick primula and big mounds of hosta and ferns. One of the ponds finishes up beautifully in what looks like an old sheepfold with well executed stonework. This area has a cool, green, airy feel to it, well thought out and naturalistic. In a very few years it will look ageless and ancient.

Out of the wood, the path leads out into the open and up to the house and a sunny terrace. A herbaceous border, filled with pale-coloured herbaceous plants, is the centre focus in this part of the garden: phlox, honesty *(Lunaria annua)*, sweet rocket *(Hesperis matronalis)* and delphinium in multiple shades of pale blue work subtly with the blues of *Campanula lactiflora*. The bed is a wall of pinks, creamy whites and blues, alive with bees and butterflies. A big *Cornus controversa* 'Variegata' finishes the bed. This tree is called the wedding cake tree, as its variegated pale leaves, layered as they are one above another, make it look like a layered, iced cake.

With the flair of a really good gardener, Mrs Hyde then surprises the visitor with a completely different area: a walled Italian garden. Steps lead up to this small area of warm stone and gravel, with changing levels and great, hard landscaping. Pencil-thin Italian cypresses *(Cupressus sempervirens)* give a strong feel of the Mediterranean. Ground-hugging juniper and wands of waving *Dierama pulcherrimum* are grown straight out of the sun-bleached gravel. Robust evening primrose *(Oenothera)* is testament to the warm, dry aspect of this sun garden. Tiny geraniums invade the gravel, self-seeding with abandon.

Intriguingly, the walled garden was at one time two walls, the corner of a large yard that Trish Hyde simply cornered off and squared, making a treasure of a garden room. She then lightly clothed the stone in scented jasmine, *Clematis* 'Fair Rosamond', *Clematis* 'Duchess of Edinburgh' and *Clematis viticella* 'Alba Luxuriens', a particularly good white flower with green tips that look as though they have been dipped in green paint. In one corner a wisteria pergola lightly scents the benches underneath. Artemisia with silver leaves continues the Mediterranean feel.

Leaving the walled garden, the path passes a circular sundial lawn, surrounded by a semicircle of hedge-over-stone wall, like a stone and beech sandwich. This is a semi-private garden room in which to sit and look back toward the side wall of the house and its base wall planting of alpine and rock plants. Trish found a dog's grave and headstone dating to the 1870s on the site of the wall bed. Whether there was a full animal cemetery here or not is unknown, but this sort of small detective hunt threading through an old garden adds to its colour.

FANCROFT MILLHOUSE

Roscrea, County Tipperary; Tel +0505 23020 ▪ **Contact:** Angela Jupe ▪ **Open:** for one charity day per year, contact for details; otherwise by appointment to groups only, particularly mid-May–September ▪ **Entrance fee** donated to charity and goes towards garden upkeep ▪ No children permitted due to water features; please note, dogs on leads ▪ **Special features:** refreshments, including lunch, may be booked by prior arrangement ▪ **Directions:** travelling on the N7 from Borris in Ossory to Roscrea, about 8km from Borris, pass The Loft pub and service station on the right. Turn right 500m along, at the sign for Killivilla. Travel along the winding road for approximately 4km, turning at the fourth right turn (just before a blue house). Drive for 1km to a T-junction, turn left and then immediately right. Go downhill, staying right for about 0.25km. The lake and mill will be visible on the right.

'I started the garden three years ago,' declares Angela Jupe. I would find this easier to believe if she also confided that she has had the help of a battalion of workers, but this is not so. Alongside her day job as one of the country's best-known garden designers, Angela, with occasional help from a stonemason, a carpenter and a gardener working three days a week, achieved remarkable success. Set among the rough, gravely hills of north County Tipperary, Fancroft is a substantial country garden, complete with lake and spanking new walled garden, and all from scratch; I saw the 'before' photographs so I can vouch that it's true.

The new garden is set amid a great amount of old stonework. Soft orange-, rust-, ecru- and pink-coloured sandstone forms a warm-toned link through the garden. The courtyard to the front of the house looks out on a huge old stone mill, currently being transformed into a backdrop for clambering vines, which will no doubt give it an air of the Mediterranean.

The garden proper begins to the rear of the house, however. A lacy mesh of wisteria, with its feet buried into boots of catmint (*Nepeta*), covers the back wall of the solid Georgian building. An iron arch over the back door is covered by *Rosa* 'Alister Stella Grey', a pretty yellow rambler. A bench positioned to the side of this looks up along the slab-and-cobble path to the garden beyond.

The house feels as though it is surrounded by a moat due to the little millrace that runs past the back door. Angela obviously loves bridges and here, as along its whole length, the stream is crossed by a series of bridges in different styles.

Fancroft is a difficult garden in which to begin a visit, because the attention is pulled in every direction at the same time. I began my visit by crossing the smallest little stepping stone bridge onto a lawn that leads to the walled garden. In only two years, Angela has built this half-acre walled garden, using salvaged sandstone from a nearby derelict shed. Angela Jupe is no slavish adherent to historic garden styles, and hers is no reproduction Victorian kitchen garden. Instead, within the oval-shaped area is a luxurious, modern, even decadent, walled pleasure garden. Cobble and pea gravel paths run around great lush beds of overflowing blooms. To one end lies a rough, sandstone-slabbed area fronting an unusual, circular, half-stone, half-wooden tearoom or folly. The tearoom was built specifically to accommodate a particular find of Angela's – the quirky little curved windows that grace its first floor.

Around the paved area are beds of paulownia, old roses and peonies. Many of the peonies are unknown French varieties, which Angela collected on visits to French gardens over the past number of years. Other signature plants within the walled garden are the many different varieties of persicaria, a great plant that sends up hundreds of wands of flowers on tall stems above mops of long, lance-shaped leaves. There are varieties in every shade of pink, plum and white scattered through the garden, among pink *Rosa* 'Gertrude Jekyll', wine-coloured everlasting sweet pea and fashionable ruby-red scabious.

Next door, an Ali Baba pot as big as a man stands over a wide, low bed of pink dianthus, *Diascia rigescens*, purple sisyrinchium, lovely violas, hardy geraniums, honesty and circles of young box hedging. Tiny French strawberries, that Angela says 'go on all year', edge the circle. They are just asking to be picked and eaten, even in mid-October. The warm stone walls are just about visible through the climbing and rambling roses.

A perfect circular pond was created to hold water from a natural spring that rises close by. The pond is unlined, and its crystal-clear water is rightly the envy of those of us who spend our time lowering barley straw into butyl-lined, electronically pumped, foggy-watered and weed-choked excuses for ponds. Beside the pond, a circular moon window looks out to the house, and another view of the fern-edged stream with its many bridges. Next door, an opening leads onto a courtyard garden of bamboo and hydrangea. This is not a manicured and tidy garden, but a luxurious, abundantly-scented, colourful garden, where self-seeding and exuberant spreading are allowed if they look good.

The gateway from the walled garden leads onto the main paths and beds that look down to the house and lead up to the greenhouse. Out here Angela's intelligent and personal style of planting is more in evidence. She mixes plants with such flair – tall *Stipa gigantea* with blue, hazy nepeta underneath, grows alongside geraniums and multi-coloured penstemons. Fringed bergamot (*Monarda*) in fire-engine red, and yellow anthemis work for her where they might look gaudy elsewhere.

The chief feature here is the 'lavender' walk that leads up to the greenhouse. This is in fact a catmint walk. Lavender can be a difficult plant to use as hedging – the plants tend to fail in overly wet, damp and cold weather and achieving a long regular line of blue is not easy. Plants dying off render the effect 'gummy', and replacing plants is both expensive and unsatisfactory, as replacement plants take their time growing to full size. Angela uses *Nepeta* 'Six Hills Giant' – a great plant, as fragrant and pretty and a lot more reliable than lavender. The nepeta wall stands in front of lines of fruit trees being trained on wires.

The greenhouse itself is wonderful. The windows came from the conservatory of the now-demolished Jervis Street Hospital in Dublin. Inside its decorous windows are a big pineapple-scented Moroccan broom (*Cytisus battandieri*) and a tall, delicately fringed, silver-leaved acacia. A *Passiflora exoniensis* with pencil-thin, ten-centimetre-long flowers is an exotic beauty.

Back out in the open, Angela came up with an ingenious plan for a particularly difficult part of the garden. This is an area of bad, marly ground, for which she pulled out all the old packs of seeds every gardener hordes up – out-of-date annuals, packets with no labels, envelopes of collected unknown seed and free-offer seeds. She sprinkled the area with these two years ago. The result, this second year on, is a magnificent annual garden where hollyhocks, daisies, American poppies and tall yellow verbascum compete with each other for attention right up to September.

A field gate leads from this floriferous garden out to the wilder lake garden. Yet again, in the space of two years, Angela has achieved an incredible amount, creating her own lake, fed by the already mentioned millrace. Young trees, mainly varieties of oak, willow and some chestnut, were planted and are now growing away happily. These border the drive to the lake and the wildflower meadow, with snake's head fritillaries and thousands of species of crocuses. The crocuses were hard won – 7,000 were planted but almost half were lost in the first year to marauding mice. Angela confounded the hungry hordes by replanting the bulbs under a double-crossed mesh of chickenwire.

The garden at Fancroft is modern and contemporary, both in the combination of plants and in its open, informal style. While it is still young, it is already a wonderful garden, and will reward several visits over a period of years.

GRAVES'S GARDEN

Ballintemple, Golden, County Tipperary; Tel: +062 72201 ▪ **Contact:** Mr and Mrs Robert and Dorothy Graves ▪ **Open:** March–September, groups by appointment only; one open day a year for charity (see local press for annual dates) ▪ **Entrance fee** donated to charity and goes towards garden upkeep ▪ Supervised children welcome ▪ **Special features:** teas available on charity open days ▪ **Directions:** take the Dundrum Road from Cashel as far as a crossroads at Guilfoyle's pub and garage. Turn left here and go through two further crossroads. Carry on over a small bridge. Follow the river on the right past a small house on the riverbank. Graves's is the second house on the left, marked by a roadside line of old oak trees.

Mrs Graves began gardening forty years ago. She had been told that her place would never do for a garden, so she put a tennis court on her new plot. But she wanted to garden, and tennis eventually gave way to plants. So a charming country garden began life out on the flat Tipperary plain.

The road leading up to the Graves's gateway is lined with mature oaks. From early spring, buttery primroses and white anemones, daffodils, moss and wildflowers brighten the bank underneath the trees.

The garden proper covers about an acre, but it is full of surprises, with secluded areas planted up with cottage favourites and some interesting outsiders. The drive is edged with ornamental grass, thyme, viola and culinary sage – low plants to edge and soften the gravel. To one side are lawns and a small conifer wood, underrun with what Mrs Graves calls her 'wiggly paths'. These are small stone and pebble paths, rising and dropping with the ground level. They detour around tree roots and trunks, allowing visitors to get close to the plants – white, blue and pink bluebells in great big clumps. There are lots of Jacobs's ladder, crocosmia, creeping white nettle and small hellebores, clustered around tentacled stumps covered in ivy and ferns. It's a magical area, the sort of garden a child would dream up as a secret spot.

Out in the sun a mixed bed of hebe and agave stands in front of a wire-net bush that scrambles like shower-of-hail netting through a tall pine in front of the little wood. Tall grasses break up the line of pittosporum and holly and provide a background of rustling watery sounds.

Facing this, across the lawn, is another bed of soft, pink *Rosa* 'Queen Elizabeth', planted in generous numbers and underplanted with self-seeding pansies, bluebells, violas, day lilies, poppies and more spring bulbs. Purple violas and pansies are a perfect foil for the pink flowers. This bed is straddled by old apple trees that cast a dappled shade, which doesn't interfere with the roses and herbaceous plants below. Bluebells unify and link the different elements and areas of the garden in late spring and early summer, scattering the ground with dots of blue haze.

A low stone wall of aubrieta, heliotrope and mixed primroses backs another little rectangular lawn. Elsewhere good flowering, fruiting and foliaged shrubs, like skimmia, azara and cloaks of ivy, disguise functional barns and sheds. The box and the beech with great gnarled trunks are both pretty and interesting. Down toward the working heart of the garden, more secret paths tiptoe between walls of spotted laurel, pittosporum, cordylines, mahonia and dogwoods.

This is a garden that sits perfectly into the countryside – an informal, beautiful spot.

HEATHER CREST

Priorstown, Clonmel, County Tipperary; Tel: +052 33329 ■ **Contact:** Helen O'Brien ■ **Open:** during the South Tipperary Garden Trail and occasional charity open days (see local press for annual dates); at all other times by appointment only ■ **Entrance fee** donated to the Irish Cancer Society ■ Supervised children welcome ■ **Special features:** teas available by prior arrangement to groups ■ **Directions:** driving from Kilkenny toward Clonmel, turn right just after the sign for, but before the actual roundabout for, Waterford and Clonmel. This is 1km along from the Ormonde Stores. The garden is on the right, a bungalow on the corner.

Heather Crest announces itself as something special before the arriving visitor even opens the front gate. Two long, wide verges of bugle (*Ajuga reptans*), with lovely wrinkled bronze-purple leaves and vivid purple spikes of flowers, run the length of the garden on the roadside. Anyone with an interest in gardening would feel obliged to look over the beech hedge to see the garden this belongs to.

Helen O'Brien began her garden from scratch in 1985. She works it completely by herself, putting long days and evenings of work into it all year round. Wrapped around her modern home, the garden is contemporary and perfectly maintained. Heather Crest is a favourite stop for touring horticultural societies, and the Shamrock All Ireland Gardens Competition judges have stamped it with their approval several times over the years.

Sitting in the shadow of Slievenamon, the garden covers just over half an acre of flower and colour. There are lilies, climbers, clematis and roses over arches throughout the plot. The scent of heavily flowering mock orange (*Philadelphus*) blossom is almost overpowering in the early summer. Beds of purple sage, veronica, geranium, penstemon and heather are arrayed around the house in colour-matched waves.

Angel's fishing rods (*Dierama*) dangle elegantly over the carp pond. Their pink flowers are picked up by pots of purple house leeks (*Sempervivum tectorum*) and aubergine-coloured heuchera, and the surrounding rocks are scrambled over by creeping saxifrage, blue cerinthe and dark-blue *Lobelia erinus* 'Sapphire'. The fish in here are huge and well fed and know when it's dinnertime.

Parts of the garden are restrained and cool. Juniper, cedar and thuja, wide spreads of golden heather, blue-green hostas and varieties of grass create pockets of smart solidity, where variations of green and leaf textures are played with. In one area close to the house, Helen has used small cut-leaf acers, bamboo and bonsai, set into a gravel and boulder area. The gravel hems and frames the specimen plants. A dinner plate-sized white clematis scrambles through a cherry tree at the edge of this area. But the heights are kept down so that Helen can enjoy the view of Slievenamon, when and if she sits to rest at the end of the day.

In sharp contrast, there are areas in the garden of exploding exuberance. Intoxicatingly perfumed *Lilium regale* stand in front of 2.5-metre-high cardoons and waving purple verbena, with little pinkish geum flowers peeping in through their bigger neighbours. These couldn't be more in contrast to the discipline and control in the conifer beds. An arched walk of sweet pink climbing roses, with Japanese painted fern underneath, leads out to a hosta and opium poppy walk. Combinations of same-colour plants, like a dark-purple veronica, *Geranium wallichianum* 'Buxton's Blue', blue catanache and lavender, work magic together.

Helen mulches the beds with pebbles to reflect light and give an airy look to the whole place. Even on a day without sun or with watery dull light, this garden has a touch of the Mediterranean about it. Heather Crest is a gem of a garden, designed with taste and a real love of plants.

INISLOUNAGHT HOUSE ❀ ♿

Marlfield, Clonmel, County Tipperary; Tel: +052 22847 ▪ **Contact:** Mrs Evie Reilly ▪ **Open:** May–September, strictly by appointment only ▪ **Entrance fee** donated to the South Tipperary Hospice and goes towards garden upkeep ▪ Supervised children welcome ▪ **Directions:** leave Clonmel on the road to Marlfield. In the village, turn left at the green railings and travel about 100m down the road. The gates to the garden are on the right.

The Reillys arrived at Inislounaght in 1968. Apart from a few mature trees, incidentally including the tallest elm in Britain or Ireland, a few cedars and a large bay tree in the courtyard, the garden was an untended mess. So Mrs Reilly set about clearing the brambles and the hundreds of sycamore saplings that were choking the place, before she could begin the garden that graces Inislounaght today. Inislounaght house itself is an interesting place, a substantial Georgian building sided by an old Royal Irish Constabulary (Ireland's old pre-Independence police force) barracks, complete with gun placements – badly behaved garden visitors take note of these.

With the sycamores and brambles taken out, thousands of daffodils cropped up. Mrs Reilly added to these by planting large drifts of anemone and the garden was off to a good spring start.

A substantial mixed bed stands in front of the south-facing house wall. This bed reveals itself as one walks along, starting with a huge run of yellow *Rosa banksiae* 'Lutea', Boston ivy, an old rose called 'Cupid', inherited from Mrs Reilly's mother, white perennial sweet pea or lathyrus, a yellow-flowering *Acacia pravissima* and many other good flowering shrubs and perennials. Tipperary is one of the colder spots on the island in winter, but as the wall bed faces dead south it manages well. Creeping rosemary (*Rosmarinus officinalis* 'Prostratus') trails out from the base of the wall onto the gravel, and this is certainly something that requires a bit of shelter and warmth.

Beds of pink roses, dahlias, delphiniums, hardy plumbago and silver artemisia front the wall climbers, covering the climbers' bare legs and prettifying the view from eye level down. Looking back from this spot, a well-constructed stone bank stands out; this has taken the place of a dreadful old slope that Mrs Reilly couldn't work, or mow. Giving up on it, she pulled it out and built a semicircular wall into the hill, turning an eyesore into a sight for sore eyes. The late Tipperary gardener, Mrs Betty Farquhar of Ardsallagh, near Cahir, to whom Mrs Reilly and other gardeners in Tipperary say they owe a debt of gratitude, recommended the design.

Away from the house, past raised alpine beds, are the stumpy remains of the once-tallest elm in these islands. Eventually lost to Dutch elm disease, it still provides a home for geranium, bergenia and poppies. Nearby, a golden acacia (*Robinia pseudoacacia* 'Frisia') lights up the start of the woodland garden. Under the tall beech trees, white-barked betulas, surrounded by dainty winter cyclamen, allium, iris, and hydrangea were planted, creating a layered look.

The path picks its way towards Mrs Reilly's pride and joy: the stream garden. This is one of those areas that most gardeners would do desperate things to own: a stream comes into the garden under an ancient stone bridge. It tumbles down a small waterfall edged by ferns, lungwort, gunnera and a well-placed laburnum that drips yellow flowers over the water. The stream has cut off a little island from the rest of the garden; this is covered in white creeping nettle, Solomon's seal, arum lilies and ferns.

Back through the wood, another path passes a lacy acer which has red bark in the winter. The acer is taking over the pathway, and so the path must move. For Evie Reilly, hard landscaping should complement, not dominate. Her plants come first, and her garden is gorgeous.

KILLURNEY

Ballypatrick, Clonmel, County Tipperary; Tel: +052 33155 ▪ **Contact:** Michael and Mildred Stokes ▪ **Open:** during the South Tipperary Garden Trail (see local press for annual dates); May–September, by appointment only ▪ **Entrance fee** donated to Multiple Sclerosis and goes towards garden upkeep ▪ **Special features:** teas can be booked by prior arrangement ▪ **Directions:** driving from Kilkenny, take the right turn at the Ormonde Stores. Take the third right at a sign for Killurney. Turn at the first turn on the left after the school and the house is first on the left.

This is a mature-looking garden, but Mildred Stokes began it only sixteen years ago, on a one-acre site around her farmhouse. She designed it and carried out all the work herself. This included building paths, directing the stream and creating ponds, with all the stonework those jobs entail. Mildred is a real hands-on gardener. Her hard work was rewarded when the garden came second in the Tipperary category of the Shamrock All Ireland Gardens Competition 1999.

It is an individual's garden, primarily filled with herbaceous plants, as well as some mature trees and shrubs. Stone paths lead in and out of the beds and these add structure and a little mystery to the overall shape of the garden. A natural sunken stream wanders by, with small flat stones to bridge it. This leads into a pond, heavily planted with waterside plants like drumstick primula, astilbe and lilies. The sound of water, even when it is not always visible, is attractive in a garden and water trickling along can be heard everywhere in Mrs Stokes's plot.

A feeling of privacy and intimacy is achieved by the strategic placing of taller plants, which have to be skirted around in order to see some of the herbaceous plants. The effect adds a little mystery and entices the visitor into further investigation.

THE POPPY FIELD

Clonmel, County Tipperary ■ **Directions:** leaving Clonmel on the bypass to Cahir, the field can be seen on the right-hand side of the road.

The Poppy Field is a wonderful sight – a magnificent field of wild flowers, mainly poppies. The Clonmel Wildlife Wildflower Project, in conjunction with Tipperary South Riding County Council, set this up.

At the beginning of July it is a sight to behold. At first it looks to be a field of plain red poppies, but a purple haze running through it includes loosestrife and other wild-flowers. Don't crash the car. The seeds came from Sandro Caffolla of Design by Nature (*see* Nurseries and Garden Centres, County Laois, p.85). It is not a permanent feature and will not be left for much longer.

RAHARD LODGE

Dualla Road, Cashel, County Tipperary; Tel: +062 61052 ■ **Contact:** Moira and Jim Foley ■ **Open:** May–September, 2.30pm–5.30pm; one annual charity day; otherwise by appointment only ■ **Entrance fee** donated to the South Tipperary Hospice and goes towards garden upkeep ■ **Special features:** plants for sale on charity days; meals may be arranged in advance for groups ■ **Directions:** just under 1km out of Cashel, on the Dualla Road (R691).

The Foleys's house and garden is blessed with a singular, uninterrupted view of the austere and beautiful Rock of Cashel. The garden itself, which covers about two acres, is young, very colourful and flower-filled. Out to the front, facing Cashel, the main feature is a long, low mixed bed of cistus, crocosmia, ranunculus, hebes, geraniums and other compact plants. These are healthy, well cared for and beautiful. Keeping the growth low ensures that it never interferes with the exceptional views of the Rock.

The garden is divided into several areas by well-placed trees and hedges. Trellis and pergolas, covered with variegated scented jasmine, clematis and roses, are also used to cut the space into rooms and sheltered spots. Flowering shrubs and some good specimen trees, including a young ginkgo, range around the garden. The Foleys share their house and garden with their guests, and this makes the different enclosed gardens really worth their salt. It is always possible to find a quiet spot for a sit down with a book, even if the garden is being worked on or visited by others.

Both the Foleys work the garden – Mr Foley in between his farming, and Mrs Foley when she has her B&B guests tended to. They are both tremendously friendly, as well as informative about their plants.

SLIEVENAMON COTTAGE GARDEN

Cahir, County Tipperary; Tel: +052 41397 ■ **Contact:** Renée O'Meara ■ **Open:** June–August, seven days by, appointment only ■ **Entrance fee** donated to GROW

※ Supervised children welcome ※ **Special features:** groups can book teas by prior appointment ※ **Directions:** leave Cahir on the Ardfinnan Road. Turn left at Hyland's Family B&B, travel 2.5km up the hill and turn right. The house is the first turn to the right (well signposted).

Visitors to Renée O'Meara's garden are first greeted by a small herb garden. This is a desirable little spot with tumbles of sage and the fresh smells of box, lemon balm, thyme, mint and bay. The sharp, green smells are heightened at the first hint of sun. This informal, stone-edged herb garden is just the *amuse bouche* of Renée's garden.

From here a path leads out to the main course: the large flower garden. Looking like a scene from a William Leech or Mildred Anne Butler painting, it is filled with tall, white shasta daisies, delphiniums, red bergamot (*Monarda*) and variety upon variety of lily. Garden rooms linked by grass paths bring the visitor into the heart of bee- and flower-filled areas. One path leads toward a pergola covered in roses. Another visits the fishpond, two more fine herbaceous borders, an orchard and a lavender walk. The wide greengage bower is an unusual, sheltered spot in which to sit and study the beds spread out before you.

Mrs O'Meara designed the garden and works the place by herself, while her husband Tom donates grass-cutting skills. 'Herbaceous plants, particularly special and interesting varieties, are popular now and they are easy to find, but they were almost impossible to get hold of when I started gardening twenty years ago,' she says, 'so seed was the best route to good plants. I grew almost everything in the garden from seed.'

That is the only talent that Renée O'Meara claims for herself. On the other hand, she is full of praise for the good fertile soil she has been blessed with. I think most visitors will place the praise where it belongs – with the gardener.

SWISS COTTAGE ♿

Kilcommon, Cahir, County Tipperary; Tel: +052 41144 ※ **Contact:** Patricia Hassett, Head Guide ※ **Open:** mid-March–April, Tuesday–Sunday, 10am–1pm and 2pm–4.30pm; May–September, daily, 10am–6pm; October–November, Tuesday–Sunday, 10am–1pm and 2pm–4.30pm; admission to guided tours only ※ Entrance fee goes towards garden upkeep ※ Supervised children welcome ※ **Special features:** guided tours of historic *cottage orné*; riverside walk to Cahir town ※ **Directions:** leave Cahir by the road to Ardfinnan (R670) and travel for 1.5km. The Swiss Cottage is well signposted.

The Swiss Cottage is one of the loveliest small buildings on the island. Designed by architect John Nash, architect of Regent's Street in London, it was built in 1817 for Richard Butler, the Earl of Glengall. In common with so many historical sites, the Swiss Cottage suffered many years of neglect, and it fell into a state of disrepair so dreadful that the house was used as a stable in the 1980s. However, it has been rescued and restored over the past decade by Dúchas, the Heritage Service. Today it is thought to be the finest example of a *cottage orné* on these islands.

At the end of the eighteenth and beginning of the nineteenth centuries, a fashion grew up among the gentry for little houses built into a naturalistic, romantic, landscaped gardens – a fashion sparked by Marie Antoinette and her peasant village at Versailles, the Hameau de Trianon. World-weary aristocrats played at being peasants

The delectable Swiss Cottage in Cahir, County Tipperary, designed by the famous English architect John Nash for the Butler family. The cottage was built in the early years of the 1800s as a romantic retreat and plaything. No two walls or windows, doors or levels could be of equal size in this asymmetrical masterpiece.

and enjoy 'simple country living' in these pretty peasant houses, while the real peasants quietly organised refreshments and the comforts of life in the background. In the case of Swiss Cottage, this was in a below-ground kitchen.

Swiss Cottage is set in the middle of a romantic garden, on a pleasant slope down to the River Suir, which meanders along as if to order below the house. The higgledy-piggledy building was designed so that no door or window resemble any other. No wall is straight or the same length as any other.

The garden around the little house is filled with classic cottage garden plants, similar to those that would have been planted in the original garden. Thyme, hyssop, oregano, lavender, camomile and sage are grown up against the house, and the little building fills with the romantic scent of herbs through the windows and open French doors on sunny days. Meanwhile, achillea, *Campanula glomerata*, perennial sage *(Salvia suberba)*, common periwinkle *(Vinca minor)*, *Bergenia* 'Rotblum', anaphalis and *Geum coccineum* flower merrily around the trellises and porches.

Wisteria, old-fashioned French climbers and Bourbon roses, such as 'Albertine', 'Mme Alfred Carrière', 'Louise Odier', 'Cécile Brunner' and 'Mme Isaac Pereire' decorate the porches with voluptuous shades of pink. A wide belt of sheltering beech, oak and other park trees, including Florence Court yews and monkey puzzle trees, surrounds the little garden. None of these compare to the ancient yew growing beside and over the house, said to be around 1,000 years old.

An unusual wrought-iron fence around the garden divides it from the woods. In another artistic touch, it was shaped to resemble thorny rose stems.

MUNSTER • COUNTY TIPPERARY

GARDENING CLUBS AND SOCIETIES

CLONMEL HORTICULTURAL SOCIETY

Contact: Mildred Stokes, Tel: +052 33155, or Mary Walsh, Tel: +052 41020.

The society is twenty years old. It meets at 8pm on the first Wednesday of the month in the Presentation Convent, Clonmel. Visitors and new members are always welcome. The society organises regular summer garden visits, and one weekend away per year, usually at the end of May. At the end of June a Sunday outing is organised. Spring and summer shows also feature in the calendar. The society is affiliated to the RHSI.

TIPPERARY AND DISTRICT FLOWER AND GARDEN CLUB

The club is twenty-nine years old. It meets on the fourth Monday of each month, from September to June, at the Teagasc Meeting Hall in Tipperary town. The meetings cover a broad range of topics related to floral art and gardening. Visitors and new members are always welcome. In June an evening trip to a Tipperary garden is arranged. A one-day trip is also held every summer and the annual show takes place within the Tipperary Agricultural Show. Go along to a meeting to find out more.

CASHEL FLOWER AND GARDEN CLUB

Contact: Mrs Betty Flood, Ballyslatteen, Golden, County Tipperary.

The club meets on the first Monday of the month throughout the year, apart from July. Activities are divided evenly between gardening and floral art topics. Summer trips and visits to gardens around the country are organised. The meeting venue regularly changes.

NURSERIES AND GARDEN CENTRES

CLONMEL GARDEN CENTRE

Glenconnor House, Clonmel, County Tipperary; Tel: +052 23294.

DUNDRUM NURSERIES AND CELTIC PLANATARIUM

Dundrum, County Tipperary; Tel: +062 71303; Fax: +062 71526.

GLENBRIDGE GARDEN CENTRE

Davis Road Shopping Centre, Clonmel, County Tipperary; Tel: +052 24800.

JOE'S GARDEN CENTRE

Limerick Road, Tipperary, County Tipperary; Tel: +062 33660.

KILCORAN COUNTRY GARDEN CENTRE

Kilcoran, Cahir, County Tipperary; Tel: +052 41863.

McSWEENEY'S GARDEN CENTRE

Gurteenakilla, Newtown, Nenagh, County Tipperary; Tel: +067 32553.

MILLTOWN GARDEN CENTRE

Milltown, Shinrone, County Tipperary; Tel: +0505 47119.

O'DRISCOLL'S GARDEN CENTRE

Mill Road, Thurles, County Tipperary; Tel: +0504 21636.

QUIRKE, JOHN, GARDEN CENTRE

Marlhill, New Inn, Cashel, County Tipperary; Tel: +052 62334.

ROSCREA GARDEN CENTRE

Dungar House, Roscrea, County Tipperary; Tel: +0505 22748.

SAP NURSERIES

Garnavilla, Cahir, County Tipperary; Tel: +052 42222.

SLATTERY'S ROSE NURSERY

Clogheen Rod, Cahir, County Tipperary; Tel: +052 41401; Fax: +052 42772

For mail order catalogue, send £1.50 (refundable with first order).

GARDEN ACCESSORIES

BURKE'S IRONWORKS

Old Church Street, Cahir, County Tipperary; Tel: +052 42154.

Wrought-iron railings and gates.

KILCOOLEY CERAMICS

Grange, Thurles, County Tipperary; Tel: +056 34471.

Terracotta hand-thrown pots in all shapes, sizes and shades. Ring in advance for an appointment. Special commissions taken.

COUNTY WATERFORD

Waterford, famous for superb glass and crystal, is thought by its natives to be one of Ireland's most underrated counties and best-kept secrets. Waterford city has recently undergone an admirable facelift. The long quayside is a string of quirky, varied, small shops culminating in the imposing thirteenth-century medieval fortress of Reginald's Tower, where the City Civic Museum is housed. The Waterford Museum of Treasures is a marvellous exhibition space to explore, housed in a former quayside granary. Along the coast there are fine beaches, some busy, some quiet and some secluded, stretching from Cheekpoint, Woodstown and Annestown to the hugely popular thatched village of Dunmore East, Dungarvan and busy Tramore. The Comeragh and Munavullagh Mountains attract walkers, and the drive along the R767 from Carrick-on-Suir to Dungarvan is spectacular. Lismore Castle, situated in the well-preserved town of Lismore, should not be missed. The picturesque cemetery and round tower in Ardmore, on the border with County Cork, is also worth a detour. Waterford's soil is largely acid and the county enjoys a slightly warmer and sunnier climate than its northern neighbours. There are a good number of gardens to be visited in the county, including the remarkable Mount Congreve – a garden of international importance that has been bequeathed to the Irish nation. The gardeners of Waterford are an organised group who are enthusiastic in their reception of visitors.

ABBEY ROAD GARDEN

Ferrybank, Waterford city, County Waterford; Tel: +051 832081 ▪ **Contact:** Margaret and Thomas Power ▪ **Open:** during the Waterford Garden Festival; at other times by appointment only; annual charity day (see local press for details); groups welcome ▪ **Entrance fee** goes towards garden upkeep, except on the annual charity day ▪ Supervised children welcome ▪ **Special features:** teas available by prior arrangement only ▪ **Directions:** take the New Ross Road out of Waterford city. Pass the Shell garage and go through one set of traffic lights. Turn right after the Esso garage. The house is the fourth entrance on the left.

This is a pretty, surprisingly quiet garden on the edge of a busy road, featuring good flowerbeds that mix herbaceous perennials with herbs, shrubs, old roses, climbers, scree and alpine beds. The garden is run by an enthusiastic plantswoman, Mrs Power, who started out with the usual rough, bare site in the mid-1980s. She now commands a three-quarter-acre plot full of marvellous plants and good ideas. The features dotted around include a little summerhouse by the apple trees, clematis arches and wisteria over trellis. An old stone wall and outhouse form a good suntrap for a gravel garden, which centres on a wall fountain. Blue, paper-flowered Cupid's dart (*Catanache*) suits this hot spot, along with verbascum, opium poppies and irises. Pink knotweed

(*Polygonum*) creeps out onto the gravel in a loose fashion, with columbines and sisyrinchium joining in. I like the raised gravel bed beside the greenhouse, held up with weathered stone and railway sleepers and bursting with the bloom of pinks, aubrieta and more columbines.

The garden is well-made and well cared for, but there is still plenty of self-seeding allowed. A little lily pond at the end of a path is nicely edged with London pride (*Saxifraga x. urbium*), anemone and agapanthus. A boggy bed fills the natural run-off area by the pond and here hosta, astilbe, lobelia and some tree ferns sit in the shade of a big pink cherry tree with damp, happy feet. In the yard, a whitewashed wall of roses backs up waves of anemone and geum. Growing on the sheltered warmth of the wall, a tender lobster claw (*Clianthus puniceus*), pineapple broom (*Cytisus battandieri*) and an ornamental hyssop with a perfume of lemonade all combine to smell like a naughty-but-nice sweet shop. A laburnum tree that fell down in a storm several years ago was allowed to stay and now grows across the lawn on its side; leaving it was an inspired choice – like so many of the choices in this enjoyable garden.

BALLYCLEMENT

Tallow, County Waterford; Tel: +058 56155 ✳ **Contact:** Mrs Perceval-Maxwell ✳ **Open:** opens between May and August for one open day in aid of the Marymount Hospice in Cork, contact Sr Augustus at the Marymount Hospice (+021 501201) or Brian Cross (+021 821052) for details of these open days and a leaflet; groups welcome ✳ **Entrance fee** donated to Marymount Hospice and other charities ✳ Supervised children welcome ✳ **Directions:** in the village of Tallow, take the turn for Mohill. Travel for 1.5km until you reach a fork in the road. At the fork stay on the main road and continue for 4km. The house and garden are on the right-hand side and clearly visible. There is a little restored schoolhouse opposite the entrance.

Mrs Perceval-Maxwell's handsome, solid old house sits in the middle of a well-made garden amidst tidy parkland on the Cork side of County Waterford. The house stands some way back from the road on a wide sweep of gravel sided by well-executed dry stone walls. These low stone walls around the house are planted with soft and varied flowers and the building itself is leaned over by a big ceanothus, several roses and daphne. A low, long hill sweeps up behind, providing the whole garden with an almost perfect backdrop.

Mrs Perceval-Maxwell has no idea of the size of Ballyclement. For the last twenty-five years she has been working the garden by herself, too busy to bother about that sort of irrelevancy. She started out in 'a creepy, crawly way, beginning in by the house, which at the time stood in a flat, plain field.' As one horticultural achievement followed another, she moved outward, working in tandem with Liam, her gardener. She even built the paved paths in the woods herself. A self-taught gardener, Mrs Perceval-Maxwell says she 'just tries everything ... completely unorthodox, I know,' she laughs. But as is often the case, the untrained will try things that the trained have been warned never to attempt and sometimes their experiments prove successful.

To the side of the house, leading out towards a small river, is a series of paths cut through beds and lawns. The beds are mixed and filled with strong-scented *Viburnum carlesii*, varieties of azalea and camellias growing over mounds of pale, buttery wild primroses and vivid blue *Omphalodes cappadocica*. In another bed a great big patch of delicate-looking but tough-as-nails lily-of-the-valley (*Convallaria majalis*) is spreading unimpeded along the ground. Close by, the combination of red leptospermum and aubergine-coloured rodgersia leaves would make any gardener proud. Strings of drumstick primulas are imaginatively used like daisy-chain borders around the beds. The paths form little hills, like bridges, over the roots of the trees. Rough stone steps lead into a circular lawn, almost like a small amphitheatre, and from here a wide grass path goes down to the river via a big stone urn and over a flat, blue-and-silver bed of lamb's ears and grape hyacinth (*Muscari*). White-speckled lungwort, agapanthus, hydrangea and tall spring snowflakes (*Leucojum vernum*) make the loveliest white garden trailing down to the river.

Towards the back of the site is the fenced-in and wall-backed regimented vegetable garden. In here is a clear, natural, partially walled spring stream that doubles as the house's source of water.

One of Mrs Perceval-Maxwell's 'experiments' led to the discovery that rhododendrons are very easy to grow from seed, even though many consider the growing of these much-loved plants a specialist's job. Some of her early seedlings have reached six metres, including some great, large leaf varieties, and she is justifiably delighted with the results. On top of a boundary bank to the side of the garden is a new beech hedge made from the seedlings of an old beech tree that was cut down, continuing the family line. In the woodland garden is a pink-flowering eucryphia: 'It is one of only three in these isles,' she announces, proud of how well it is doing in her care.

When I visited, Mrs Perceval-Maxwell was working in the shallow, stone-edged river, planting up the banks with irises, ferns, pampas and violas. Four tall Wellingtonias (*Sequoiadendron giganteum*) stand across from the river, saved by her when the wood they once occupied was felled several years ago. The garden is now expanding, moving out to join these elegant giants.

BALLYMOAT HOUSE

Ballymoat, Dunhill, County Waterford; Tel: +051 396186 ▪ **Contact:** Mr and Mrs James and Audrey McGuire ▪ **Open:** May–September, Monday–Sunday, 11am–5pm, by appointment only; groups welcome ▪ **Entrance fee** donated to charity and goes towards garden upkeep ▪ Supervised children welcome ▪ **Special features:** groups can book teas by prior arrangement only ▪ **Directions:** travelling from Waterford to Cork, turn left off the N25 beside the Sweep garage. Keep left when the road forks and then take the first left. At the top of the hill bear sharp right for just over 2km. Ballymoat House is a primrose bungalow on the right-hand side.

In 1996 the McGuires (originally from Britain but with Irish roots) drove around Ireland before deciding where they wanted to live, and Dunhill, County Waterford, impressed them most. So they moved into the small bungalow and started a garden. By the look of it now, they have been working in it twenty-four hours a day for the last three years. They have already won the accolade of Second-best New Garden in the Country in the Shamrock All Ireland Gardens Competition, and no doubt have their sights set on further prizes.

The house is centred on two one-acre fields, which make up two distinctive gardens. In the centre of the two is the clearest pond, stone-edged, twelve metres wide and teeming with fish – a scarecrow in the likeness of a fishing Jack Charlton deters the heron from taking them. The pond is edged by lobelia, arum lilies and loosestrife. Just below it, a bog garden takes and uses the overflow from the pond. There is always an overflow from ponds, creating a damp area on one if not all sides of the pond. Even a pond not filled to capacity will dispel water into the surrounding earth when the wind blows, so it makes sense to utilise this natural moisture in the soil. Water is the unifying feature in this garden, starting at one side in a dramatic three-metre-high waterfall, leading into a stream that travels right through to the pond. The stream is bridged at several points as it meanders along the garden.

To the south of the house is a fine alpine bed, recently installed. To the other side of the house, a great vegetable garden has been unusually cordoned off by pink-tinged pampas and cordylines. The hard-working McGuires grow everything themselves from seeds and cuttings. They are self-sufficient in vegetables from this plot, as well as having plants to sell to visitors. Stone dug from the ground has given them all the material they need for raised beds, monuments and walls. Using this found stone they have made a particularly good wall behind the long herbaceous border in one of the two gardens.

The McGuires have placed wooden sculptures throughout the garden in different areas. Most memorable, however, is a strange sculpture, made from part of the famous beached Bunmahon whale, that sits in front of the house.

BAY VIEW

Clarkestown, Ardmore, County Waterford; Tel: +024 94310; e-mail: jamesmary-flavin@eircom.net ▪ **Contact:** Mrs Mary Flavin ▪ **Open:** May–end September, by appointment only; groups welcome ▪ **Entrance fee** goes towards garden upkeep ▪ Supervised children welcome; please note, dogs on leads ▪ **Directions:** driving towards Cork on the N25, turn onto the R673 at the Cross pub – the signposts at this turn point to Ardmore. The garden is 4km along on the right, look for the white bungalow.

Bay View stands on a very exposed site facing south and looking directly at the Ardmore headland and beyond that out to sea. This is an incredibly lovely location, but very windy. Mrs Flavin started to garden here in the late eighties in a determined way. She first spent two years growing potatoes on the site to clean the soil and get it ready – a good move for a new garden, with the added benefit of potatoes for dinner while the soil is being prepared. Now she has developed a lovely flower garden on this big, sloping site, where she has placed little stepping-stone paths down through the beds. These descend past a pond completely surrounded by alliums and sea kale (*Crambe maritima*), droves of day lilies, Cape daisies, lilies, blue salvia and geranium. At the bottom of the garden there are roses, tall shrubs with clematis laced through them, powder-blue *Ceanothus arboreus* 'Trewithen Blue' and other shrubs that block out the road and some of the scorching seawind. This open site, so close to the sea, is constantly sprayed with salt and so the plants chosen are plants that will tolerate salt. Up by the house Mrs Flavin keeps pots of agave, other succulents and easier floral things like nasturtium. The garden is a very informal, friendly and relaxed place worked by a keen and knowledgeable woman.

Cappoquin, County Waterford; Tel: +058 54004 ▪ **Contact:** Nicola Dorman ▪
Open: April–July, daily, 9am–1pm, except Sunday and bank holidays; groups must
book in advance ▪ **Entrance fee** goes towards garden upkeep ▪ Supervised children welcome ▪ **Special features:** castle ruins ▪ **Directions:** entering Cappoquin
from the N72, turn right at the T-junction in the centre of the town. The garden is
200m along on the left, with a stone gateway.

Cappoquin House is built on the site of, and incorporates, the walls of one of the
FitzGerald's Norman castles on the River Blackwater in west Waterford. The house
has been the home of the Keane family for the past 200 years. The garden as it is today
is the work of Lady Keane, who has been working on its design and creation over the
past fifteen years. It is a varied garden of indeterminate size, meandering off in all directions around the house. The site is steeply sloped down toward the river. The
house is set in the middle of the garden, with one of the gardens rising high above it
and accessed via a grass path wandering through huge spreads of arboreum rhododendron and varied shrubs and trees. From up here, Lismore Castle can be spotted in
the distance.

Cappoquin is an easy, pleasing and seemingly artless garden into which a great
deal of thought and care has been poured. A great effort has gone into gentle colour
mixing, particularly with the many rhododendrons and azaleas scattered throughout
the place. They have avoided the headache-inducing effect too often seen in rhododendron gardens, where glaring oranges scream at their fuchsia pink and bright
yellow neighbours. Bamboo walks lead from one section of the garden to another, past
runs of flowering shrubs and a little pond, again surrounded by several varieties of
bamboo, including black-stemmed *Phyllostachys nigra*, and a pretty white-flowered
Magnolia stellata. Up toward the rhododendrons is a pear wall where regimentally
trained fruit trees grow on the outside of the old walled garden, facing south and
enjoying the sun. Paths along the hillside pass through damp meconopsis beds,
euphorbia, more bamboo and hydrangea.

The path falls down towards a little rose garden, sheltered in under a witholding
wall that threatens to fall on top of a mix of old, Gallica, modern and Damask roses,
including *Rosa banksiae*, *Rosa* 'Dentelle de Malines', *Rosa* 'William Lobb' and *Rosa*
'Complicata'. A little stream emerges from under the wall at one end. This creates a
damp garden for big ligularia, gunnera and a little collection of snowdrops (*Galanthus*). Close by, a grove of shrubs includes a healthy little olive tree. This is a tender
plant and its vigour testifies to the very sheltered pockets in this garden. One of the
latest additions to the garden is an area of new varieties of rhododendron. These are
the bounty of a seed-collecting trip by Thomas Pakenham to Tibet several years ago
(*see* Tullynally Castle, County Westmeath).

The specimen trees at Cappoquin include a good cropping walnut tree (*Juglans
nigra*), weeping beech (*Fagus sylvatica pendula*), pale-barked birches and groves of
slim myrtles (*Luma apiculata*).

To the front of the house is a beech hedge-enclosed garden overlooking the town, a
mix of lawns, raised beds full of lamb's ears (*Stachys byzantina*), perennial wallflower
(*Erysimum*), wild strawberries and pink osteospermums twining through black grass.
This is an intimate, domestic spot in comparison with the rest of the garden. An
elegant old conservatory fronts the house. This is never heated but still holds a good

range of tender specimens, like velvety-purple tibouchina, oleander, pelargonium and ranks of succulents in staged shelves up the back, sharing the space with a big, scented, cabbagy *Rosa* 'Ophelia'. Nearby a lemon tree in a pot awaits the seductive call of a gin and tonic.

Out beyond the conservatory is the only formal spot in the garden: a smart mirroring sundial garden. Stone paths, almost white with lichen, divide the mirroring beds of dianthus, penstemon, lupin and iris, lavender and white hydrangea. Beyond the balustrades surrounding this formal spot is the bog garden, hidden under the shade of a big holm oak. A run of acers, azara, witch hazels and a huge eucalyptus pull the garden out from the house to the spring garden, where daphne and winter sweet (*Chimonanthus praecox*) scent the air.

COIS ABHAINN

Riverside, Lower Gracedieu, Waterford city; Tel: +051 857955; e-mail: pmtobin@eircom.net ※ **Contact:** Mary Tobin ※ **Open:** May–August, by appointment and to individuals and small groups only ※ **Entrance fee** donated to charity ※ Supervised children welcome ※ **Directions:** travelling down the quays towards Rice's Bridge to leave Waterford, go straight ahead instead of going over the bridge. Travel for just over 1.5 km. The house is on the left with a stone wall fronting the road.

Cois Abhainn (meaning 'beside the river') is a country garden overlooking the wide, lazy River Suir. Mrs Tobin has been working on the garden since the beginning of the 1990s and has won several prizes in the Shamrock All Ireland Gardens Competition, including third place in the Small Garden category in 1998.

Beds of shrubs, perennials, and small trees surround tidy lawns and a nice mix of flowers such as geraniums, pinks, rudbekia, peonies, lilies and lots of different varieties of crocosmia make a lovely picture. There is a lovely small arbour with *Clematis* 'Jackmanii', little white Californian poppies scattered about and pale roses in drifts and over arches. The stone wall holding up the beds is eye-catching and well built. To the back of the house are raised beds with vegetables and herbs, as well as more flowers and grasses, particularly long runs of orange nasturtiums, cabbages, lettuce, marrows, asparagus with feathery leaves, chives and Chinese chives. These productive beds are arranged prettily because they are on view from the house and as such cannot be allowed to be merely functional. Finally, around the house are the prettiest troughs of succulents and alpines, pots of lilies, abutilon and agave.

CURRAGHMORE

Portlaw, County Waterford; Tel: +051 387102 ※ **Contact:** Lord Waterford ※ **Open:** gardens and shell house open Easter–mid-October, Thursdays and bank holidays, 2pm–5pm; January, May and June, Monday–Friday, 9am–1pm; gardens, shell house and house open to groups by prior appointment, Monday–Friday, all year round ※ **Directions:** the turning for Portlaw is off the main Waterford–Cork road (N25) at Kilmeaden. In Portlaw, the gate to Curraghmore is 0.5km northwest of the village.

There has been a castle at Curraghmore since 1176 when the Norman le Poers (later Powers) settled on the site close to the Comeragh Mountains, east of Waterford city. The family has lived here ever since. The Norman heritage is loudly signalled above the unusual house by an extraordinary family crest: a huge stag with the Cross of St Hubert set between its antlers. The house itself is a remarkable sight, partly twelfth century, partly seventeenth century, with strong French influences.

As with most great houses, the gardens have been remodelled many times over the centuries. Records exist of a garden in the mid-1700s made up of great canals with cascades, formal terraces adorned with statuary and a 'wilderness' – every inch a fashionable garden of its time. The canals and terraces were swept away in the later years of that century when a romantic, less formal landscape was put in place. The wilderness is still to be seen, however. These days it is set beside an even later garden close in by the house: a Victorian reinterpretation of formal terracing with a pond and wide gravel walks flanked by clipped yews. This looks out at the park and woodland, which boasts (possibly) the tallest Sitka spruce (*Picea sitchensis*) on the island. Dramatic and intriguing nineteenth-century French statuary edges the woodland and wilder garden.

A shell house is set in the spring garden area by the lawns, and inside it is written: *In 261 days these shells were put up by the proper hands of the Rt. Honourable Cathne Countess of Tyrone 1754.* The 'proper hands' presumably means that Cathne did the job herself, and a stunningly good job it is too. The shells, many of them from tropical seas, are arranged in swirling, organic, three-dimensional patterns that are spread over every inch of the ceiling and walls of this sizeable quatrefoil-shaped house. Apart from the massive job of piecing the work together, the acquisition of these shells, some from as far off as Madagascar and the Maldives, must have been an enormous task in the eighteenth century. The colours are very well preserved and the whole work is completely intact, unlike many of the other shell houses in Ireland.

SHELL HOUSES

Shell houses were a popular feature of the romantic style of gardening, which was fashionable from the late 1700s into the early 1800s. Trade ships and extensive links with Africa, the Americas and everywhere in between gave the gentry the chance to acquire the sort of exotic, colourful shells that accommodated the fashion for decoration. These houses or grottos were frequently the creation of ladies with time to spare, providing them with an outlet for their creative talent.

Another example of a shell house can be found at Birr Castle, County Offaly. This was built over a well, designed and constructed by friends of Marian Guinness and using shells from her collection. At the Ballymaloe Cookery School Garden, Darina Allen and Blot Kerr Wilson created a shell house in the 1990s using a huge collection of exotic shells with strong geometric patterns and vivid colours.

Another feature of Curraghmore, set into the woods, is King John's bridge – a handsome stone bridge over the River Clodagh. It is reputed to have been built for King John when he came to Ireland in the twelfth century. Curraghmore has one more claim to fame: it was the training ground of the famous gardener and designer William Robinson (*see* box, William Robinson, p.182), whose work had a huge influence on gardening on these islands in the late nineteenth and well into the twentieth century. Robinson served part of his apprenticeship as a garden boy at Curraghmore before moving on to even greater things.

MAURA CURRAN'S GARDEN

Dungarvan, County Waterford; Tel: +058 41022 ▪ **Contact:** Maura Curran ▪ **Open:** May–July, by appointment only; groups welcome ▪ **Entrance fee** donated to local charities and goes towards garden upkeep ▪ Not suitable for children ▪ **Special features:** teas can be booked for groups by prior arrangement ▪ **Directions:** drive along the N25 from Waterford toward Dungarvan and 2.5km before Dungarvan you will see a large sign for Killarney. Take the turn to the right and go through two minor crossroads. After the second crossroads the house is on the right.

Maura Curran has worked her half-acre country garden by herself for the past fifteen years and although she hates the word 'design', hers is undoubtedly a well-designed garden. Her passion is for herbaceous plants, but she doesn't specialise in any particular type of planting. Precious, dainty plants that refuse to do well find themselves ruthlessly pulled out. Most of them do well, however, thanks in part to the fact that the garden is mild and sheltered: 'We can grow tender things here because we only get caught by a frost maybe one year in eight.' Those odds encourage an adventurous spirit.

The front garden is pretty. Mixed planting stretches around the lawn and drive with runs of penstemon and the yellow-budding, black-stemmed perennial *Kirengeshoma palmata*. All of this is set behind a huge bay hedge, the welcome result of suckering after a large bay tree was taken out many years ago. (Suckers are shoots arising from the below-ground roots of a bigger plant, giving rise, eventually, to separate plants. Stag's horn schumach, poplars and cherries are particularly prone to suckering.) Mrs Curran marked the millennium very appropriately by placing a working sundial in this area. Central to this front garden is a quaint-looking gate. This is a pedestrian entrance that originally belonged to the house across the road, and dates to when Mrs Curran's garden was the vegetable plot for the bigger house. Decorating the house wall is a Chinese Virginia creeper (*Parthenocissus henryana),* whose leaves turn the richest cherry-red in autumn.

A substantial skeleton of topiary runs through the front garden and Mrs Curran's tip for a successful all-year-round garden is topiary. In winter it provides a frame and something tidy and green to look at when much of the rest of a herbaceous garden is dormant and invisible. Roses over arches should always smell divine and the Iron Arch that leads from front to rear of the garden does just that. *Rosa* 'Souvenir de St Anne's' is a gorgeously scented, shell-pink Irish rose, discovered as a sport of 'Souvenir de la Malmaison' in Lady Ardilaun's garden in St Anne's in Dublin (*see* St Anne's Park, County Dublin). A little stone boundary wall peeps across at it and its companions, a red lobster claw (*Clianthus puniceus*) and a big *Clematis armandii.*

In the back garden a small pond lies tucked under a knot of melianthus and cryptomeria. The contrasting matt-green melianthus leaves against dark-green, softening-to-rust spikes of cryptomeria meld beautifully together. The lawn is surrounded by a big mixed bed of flowering shrubs, including *Eucryphia x. nymansensis,* which tolerates lime, and beside it an elaeagnus with insignificant flowers but a heavenly scent. Old roses, rudbekia, *Viola cornuta* and pink scabious splash colour along this bed. It all leads down to a summerhouse corner with phormium, azara and echiums. The scent of *Rosa* 'Compassion' plays around the outside of the summerhouse while inside a huge pelargonium called 'Lord Bute', with purple and pink flowers, dominates the banana plants, South African primulas and purple-leaved eupatorium. Useful as well as decorative, this house is also the workshop and a very good idea for space-strapped gardeners to study.

FLORAVILLE (O'KEEFFE'S GARDEN)

Ballinaclough, Fenor, Tramore, County Waterford; Tel: +051 381582 ■ **Contact:** Mary and Brian O'Keeffe ■ Open: June–September, Monday–Sunday, 2pm–6pm, by appointment only; groups welcome ■ **Entrance fee** donated to charity and goes towards garden upkeep ■ Supervised children welcome ■ **Directions:** situated off the Cork–Waterford road (N25). Turn at the junction signposted for Tramore at Orchardstown. Pass the garden centre and the garden is on the corner at the third junction along.

Mrs O'Keeffe has been gardening at her roadside garden for thirty-five years, giving cars on the way to the seaside something good to look at. Three-and-a-half decades later, she realised that she needed more to occupy her gardening skills and extended the garden across the road to take in a little haggard. The house was just a bare cottage when Mrs O'Keeffe moved here, but she loves gardening madly and so she began working it everyday herself, endeavouring to make the very windy, exposed site as perfect as possible.

It's a marvellous little garden, full of enthusiasm and colour. There are big beds of dahlias, pots and tubs everywhere, pyracantha adorning the house walls and good flowering shrubs. These include a lovely, umbrella-shaped, heavily flowering hoheria under which she has snugged a little bench to sit on. Like so many hard-working gardeners, Mrs O'Keeffe places plenty of seats about the place for resting and then never gets to sit on them. I wondered about the lack of privacy, the constant gazing from stopping cars and onlookers, but Mary O'Keeffe has dealt cleverly with that. She has created her own little secret spots, away from the gazers on the road, where she can enjoy her own garden in privacy while the day-trippers still get to marvel at the public face of this beautifully worked landscape.

JOE AND ANNE JENNINGS'S GARDEN

51 Lower Newtown, Waterford; Tel: +051 875712 ■ **Contact:** Mrs Anne Jennings ■ **Open:** during the Waterford Garden Festival (see local press); at other times by appointment only; groups welcome and preferred ■ **Entrance fee** donated to charity and goes towards garden upkeep ■ Supervised children welcome ■ **Special features:** teas may be booked by prior arrangement ■ **Directions:** driving out of Waterford city on the Dunmore Road, turn sharp right after the De La Salle College and beside Newtown College. The house is two blocks along, on the left-hand side.

Mrs Jennings is a magpie gardener – she has gathered together the gardens of her two neighbours, adding them to her own to make the garden she wanted. She is situated in the middle of Waterford city but 'just wanted a country stream', and for that ambitious project she had to acquire the other gardens. This done, she then had to wheelbarrow sixty tonnes of stone into the plot. The problems of a site which was inaccessible to machinery were not to deter her from her country stream plans, and over several years she has achieved her goal: this is the Sistine Chapel of water features. The stream now starts at the back of the garden with a soft waterfall onto and over a bed of stones, before working its way through the garden.

The three gardens were all on different levels, so it was necessary to add to one and take away from the other to get them all on more or less the same level. However, Mrs Jennings didn't completely flatten the new garden and it is still full of interesting changing levels. The divisions are good: there are some suntraps and some shady spots for plants that need shade. Tall hedges surround the garden – Mrs Jennings feels these are necessary in a town location. The hedges give a sense of privacy and peace and they blot out the sound of the traffic, but they do take up room, so under one she has put a bluebell walk, forcing the hedge to earn its living space. Little lawns and paths divide the beds of flowers and shrubs. Because it is not a huge garden, the important thing for Mrs Jennings is to make it an all-year-round space. Every element must work that bit harder than in a larger garden. One thing that earns its keep is the small crab apple *Malus* 'Golden Hornet', which offers remuneration in the form of blossoms in spring, leaves in summer and an incredible amount of fruit that stays on the tree right over the winter – almost until the next year's blossom arrives. A small white garden close to the house is the current guinea pig, and Mrs Jennings is enjoying the challenge of finding white things that will give year-round effect.

LISMORE CASTLE GARDEN

Lismore, County Waterford; Tel: +058 54424; Fax: +058 54896 ☀ **Contact:** Michael Penruddock ☀ **Open:** mid-April–September, Monday–Sunday, 1.45pm–4.45pm; groups may book by appointment at other times ☀ **Entrance fee** goes towards garden upkeep ☀ Supervised children welcome; please note, dogs on leads ☀ **Special features:** castle; set in a historic village; contemporary sculptures ☀ **Directions:** situated in the village of Lismore.

Lismore is one of the most beautiful villages in Ireland. Rising on a high cliff above the village is what even the hardest-bitten critic would have to admit is a fairy tale castle. There has been a castle on this spectacular site since the twelfth century and it has a colourful collection of past owners, including Sir Walter Raleigh and Estelle, sister of Fred Astaire. The romantic castle seen today is largely a nineteenth-century creation for the sixth duke of Devonshire, into whose family the castle passed in the 1750s.

The garden around the castle is divided cleanly into two areas: the upper garden and the lower garden. The upper garden, built on a slope, is one of the oldest walled gardens in the country, laid out in the 1600s and continuously worked since then. It is made up of venerable yew, beech and box hedges, herbaceous and mixed borders. Wide paths link the elements together and its steep slope is inlaid with several sets of stone steps. The orchard, with mown grass paths laid out symmetrically, is the first part of the upper garden seen from the entrance, moving out from the gateway on a diagonal. Beyond it is a beech hedge marking one side of a double mirroring border that climbs up the central axis. Eucalyptus and white hydrangea, abutilon and callistemon or bottlebrush shrubs reflect each other back and forth across the path. This bed opens onto the first set of steps. From here a rose and lavender double border continues up to more steps covered in fairy foxgloves, santolina, snow-in-summer and thyme. This route is dissected by a wide grass path running north to south and bordered on one side by shrubs and on the other by austere, formal nail-scissors-smart yew hedges that lead the eye down to a beautiful piece of sculpture by English artist Bridget McCrum. This is a piece in smooth marble representing a bird at a bird-bath. The top walk has views beyond the castle roofs and out to the village. Below this walk are the unusual, accordion-shaped greenhouses designed by Sir William Paxton, along with cut-flower and vegetable beds filled with artichokes, sprouts, leeks and a range of flowers. Espaliered fruit trees cover the walls. The upper garden is a model of its type, both good-looking and functional.

The lower garden or pleasure ground is linked to the upper garden by an unusual covered bridge called the Riding House. This is a quaint and crooked old building dating back to 1620. The lower garden is made up of informal gravel paths edged with small cobbles that wind around magnolia, rhododendron and azalea in a landscape that includes a famous yew walk dating to the early 1700s. Tree ferns and woodland bulbs, anemone and bluebells cover the ground under the tree canopy. This part of the garden is also built on a slope and the top walk allows one to enjoy the blooms of some of the larger rhododendrons from above. A wall along this top walk is lined with a variety of climbing roses, clematis, cottage garden herbaceous flowers and varieties of euphorbia.

In the lower garden there are a number of important contemporary sculptures, particularly a work by British artist Antony Gormley, which is set at the very end of the yew walk; a ghostly, powerful figure. Close by, in the middle of some rhododendron, is a piece by Cork-born artist Eilís O'Connell, a blue, patinated, swirling flourish of metal. These new works have been well chosen and are perfectly placed in the old garden. What I see in the use of contemporary art at Lismore is the addition of another layer of interest and variation. It shows confidence and style to marry the absolute tradition of a garden of this age with the raw, bare emotion of contemporary art at its best. It shows a garden with a future as well as a past to enjoy.

LITTLEWOOD

Stradbally, Kilmacthomas, County Waterford; Tel: +051 293122 ■ **Contact:** Mrs Beatrice Norris ■ **Open:** April–end July, by appointment only; groups welcome ■ **Entrance fee** donated to hospice charity and goes towards garden upkeep ■ **Special features:** groups may book teas and home-made biscuits in advance ■ **Directions:** leaving Stradbally, drive up the hill past the Bairead corner shop. After the sports centre take the first turn right and continue along. The house and garden are on a corner with a sign for Ballyvooney Cove opposite.

Littlewood took first place in the Waterford Category of the Shamrock All Ireland Gardens Competition 1999. This is a really perfect little country garden, cottagey and informal and full of wonderful flowers. It does not reveal itself all at once, but winds around the house, unfolding in little rooms and surprise areas.

The image that stands out most clearly from my visit is that of a carpet of blue, star-flowered pratia, like a blue-and-green lawn under a blue-painted bench that picks up the jewelled colour – a simple but inspired idea. The house itself is covered in creepers, roses and clematis and is fronted by a wide gravel apron shot through with plants intent on spreading: Cape daisies, campanula, geranium and hydrangea splay out, softening the stone and flowering cheerfully.

There are mature trees surrounding the garden, but an area to the front has been kept clear so that a view of the Comeragh Mountains and of the waterfall spilling down the mountainside way off can be seen clearly. A large hedge of griselinia with an arch cut into it leads into a secret bench garden surrounded by flowers, such as geraniums, asters and clematis. There are little grass paths tiptoeing between flowering shrubs, roses and sedum down to a rough stone path that leads on to the little pratia carpet area and the lily pond. Everywhere there are self-seeding small things set between cracks and in paths. At the other side of the garden is a vegetable garden with more cleverly waved hedges, topiary, another secret garden with beds set up on stone walls and grass paths that lead out through gates into the fields beyond, melting the garden into its surroundings.

MOUNT CONGREVE

Kilmeaden, County Waterford; Tel: +051 384115; Fax: +051 384576; e-mail: congreve@eircom.ie ▪ **Contact:** the Curator ▪ **Open:** Monday–Friday, 9am–5pm; not open bank holidays; admission strictly by appointment and with prior permission to interested individuals and groups ▪ **Entrance fee** applies to groups only and goes towards garden upkeep ▪ Children under twelve years are not admitted ▪ **Directions:** leave Waterford on the N25 heading towards Cork. Pass the Holy Cross pub on the right and at the next crossroads, marked clearly for Tramore, take the right-hand turn on to a little road. Go through one crossroads and turn left at the next crossroads – be careful as both are dangerous junctions. Travel for about 500m and the gates are on the right-hand side. Follow the signs for the Estate Office.

During my visit to Mount Congreve, my guide told me about a group of ladies who had visited the garden a few months previously. He had escorted them to one of the more spectacular spots in this magnificent garden and, after a short talk, he left them to wander at their leisure. Several hours later he heard shouts for help. Upon investigation, he found the ladies – they had become hopelessly lost. Moral of the tale: Mount Congreve is huge. Created by Ambrose Congreve over the past eighty-two of his ninety-three years, the garden alone employs twenty-five gardeners – more than the Queen of England has at any of her palaces!

Mount Congreve is more akin to one of the great estates of the nineteenth rather than the twenty-first century; it all speaks of another age. Extensive greenhouses with walls of nectarines, a mind-bending display of orchids and bromeliads, collections of rare fuchsias and almost extinct varieties of cyclamen, rare Lorraine-series begonias, benches full of thick, strappy-leaved clivia and a particularly rare, pure yellow form called 'Vico'. There are pots and pots of datura, streptocarpus, regal pelargoniums, hibiscus, gerbera grown from seed, and great stands of tall carnations, all for use in the house. Separate to the greenhouses are dedicated houses, providing table grapes and peaches. A visitor could buckle under the abundance in these greenhouses, but stepping out into the garden proper only leads to yet more impressive sights.

Boasting one of the biggest collections of rhododendrons in the world, certainly the biggest in Europe, Mount Congreve is a place of superlatives and the lists go on and on and on: 3,500 cultivars of rhododendron, 650 named camellias, 350 named cultivars of Japanese maple. This is the world's largest plant collection, assembled in the last half of the twentieth century and started by a man who decided, at the age of eleven, to begin planting and has never stopped. In his ninety-third year, Ambrose Congreve is still developing the place and his most recent achievement is the bog garden and pinetum. The collections at Mount Congreve include a lilac collection, due to be expanded by the addition of cultivars from Poland where much work has been carried out this century, and a collection of tree peonies, with many new varieties coming from China. The rhododendron and camellia collections are being updated continuously .

Four sloped acres of walled garden have been arranged into May, June, July and August borders, each filled with usual and a lot of unusual herbaceous plants, including special iris beds and great runs of hydrangea in north-facing beds. Runs of every sort of vegetable that can be grown in Ireland are interspersed with beds of asters and chrysanthemums for the house. Fruit trees fill the middle beds and the surrounding walls hold long runs of wisteria as well as the biggest *Clematis armandii* in these islands. The last marvel in the walled garden is a north-facing bed of 100 plants of Chilean bellflower (*Lapageria rosea*), sheltering from the salt winds that sometimes bluster over the wall.

The main body of garden is woodland and its beauties are the flowering shrubs, incredible runs of magnolia and camellia, rhododendron and azalea, cherry, acer, azara, eucryphia, michelia, pittosporum and prunus. The scents are sweet, even at times of the year when very little is flowering; at the height of the late spring blossoming 'overpowering' might better describe the perfume. All of these flowering shrubs and trees are overlooked by eighteenth- and nineteenth-century plantations of oak and beech, many of them with big clematis and rambling roses winding up their massive trunks. There are over sixteen miles of paths wandering in and around the plants. As the ladies mentioned above found out, it is very, very easy to get lost and there are no maps or signs. And there are surprises: every so often the paths open onto a little secret garden, a beech lawn with rolling turf planted through with spring bulbs, secluded dells and glades, a private garden room or a temple garden. One of my favourite parts of the garden is the Chinese Dell, a sunken garden set within a twelve-metre drop. This was the quarry from which stone to build the house was obtained. At the bottom of the quarry walls, planted with oriental primula, ferns and meconopsis, is a circular pond with a colourful little pagoda set on an island. Moving on from here the path leads through a forest of *Magnolia campbellii* toward an eighteenth-century ice house via a grove of tree ferns.

Throughout the garden there are swathes of bulbs. During bluebell time the carpet of blue is so dense that most of the garden looks like it's planted through water. These have been added to by thousands of snowdrops, daffodils and fritillaries. There is this sense of abundance everywhere. Plants are grouped not in the usual groups of three and five, but in groups of twenty-five, fifty and 100. One doesn't come across a single witch hazel but groves of them, not a single little Japanese acer but an avenue of them, as for the numbers of rhododendrons and camellias – get out the calculator.

The varieties are invariably rare and unusual.

The garden is filled with fine stonework. These are the output of one man who worked for over forty years doing nothing else but building low retaining stone walls, features, steps and banks. However, not all the stonework is man-made. A huge natural outcrop of stone provided the opportunity for a cascade of water, which tumbles down toward the path but finishes in two stone ponds. The damp provided by the spray makes this a home for wet-loving meconopsis and primula. Another bank of rock provided the base for a football pitch-sized rock garden, filled with treasures and a maze of little paths.

Overlooking the River Suir at Mount Congreve, which holds the largest rhododendron collection in Europe.

The youth of the gardens is something one must remind oneself of continually. Mount Congreve has the feel of a garden much more mature than its double-digit age. One of the treasures of the island, it is destined to be given to the Irish people. However, plans plans were recently mooted to run a motorway through the garden, knocking several thousand mature beech and oak trees. These are the trees which provide the shelterbelt that creates Mount Congreve's microclimate, which in turn allows the cultivation of many of its tender, rarer plants. Public concerns have hopefully put a halt to these plans.

ROCKBARTON ♿

Garrynageragh, Dungarvan, County Waterford; Tel: +058 42508 ▪ **Contact:** Mrs Valerie Leo ▪ **Open:** June–September, by appointment to groups only ▪ **Entrance fee** donated to charity and goes towards garden upkeep ▪ Not suitable for children ▪ **Directions:** travelling on the Waterford–Cork road (N25), before coming to Dungarvan take the left turn marked for the Clonee and Dungarvan Golf Club and go through the next crossroads. Turn left at the old Waterford–Dungarvan road (the coast road). Pass the community hall. The garden is second on the left with a stone wall and griselinia hedge.

Mrs Lee began gardening ten years ago, but this garden looks more mature than that. This is largely because it is saluted by a row of tall pines running along the front of the house. A smart hedge on top of a stone wall guards the house from the road. A sweeping lawn leads up toward the house, interrupted by a swirling bed of recumbent conifers, heathers, a *Cornus controversa* 'Variegata', known as the wedding cake tree because from a distance it looks like a white, layered cake, and magnolia, all underplanted with bulbs for the spring. To the other side of the drive is a pond with a gravel and scree bed around it, planted with celmisias and *Verbena bonariensis*.

The rest of the garden is reached through a fine, tall leylandii hedge, arched and clipped tightly. This also gives a good vista through the garden to the hills beyond. Mrs Lee is unhappy with the hedge, but she treats it as it should be treated: kept well clipped and in train and low enough so that the garden view continues out over it to the landscape beyond. Through the hedge is a hot border with a huge forked eucalyptus towering above it. This is a favourite in the winter. In the summer the hot colours of penstemon, roses and cimicifuga, sometimes called bugbane, a fine, wine-coloured abutilon, orange rudbekia and dark, purple-coloured pittosporum (*Pittosporum tenuifolium* 'Tom Thumb') make a wonderful colourful impact.

In the other mixed beds there are just so many fine flowering plants to enjoy: white arum lilies and white pom-pom dahlias, sweeps of monkshood, echinops, asters and purple geranium growing through Solomon's seal (*Polygonatum hirtum*). These are all knotted together under the taller betulas and eucalyptus – trees that cast only a light shade and lend their good-looking barks and silvery leaves to the mix.

SHALOM

Cork Road, Waterford, County Waterford; Tel: +051 372681 ■ **Contact:** Jim and Phyllis Nolan ■ **Open:** May–end September, by appointment only; also opens for the Waterford Garden Festival ■ **Entrance fee** goes towards garden upkeep ■ **Directions:** leaving Waterford city on the main Cork Road (N25), Shalom is just under 5km from the city on the left; look out for the signposts to guide you.

The Nolans's garden is a well-known and popular private garden in County Waterford, as well as a winner over several years in the Shamrock All Ireland Gardens Competition. The garden covers two acres that are jammed full of plants, ponds, beds, trees, decks, rock gardens and lawns: 'intensive' is the word that comes to mind. Around the house there are masses of pots and troughs filled with bedding, annuals, dahlias, tree ferns, canna lilies and tobacco plants, fuchsias and exotic things like African hemp (*Sparrmannia africana*). The amount of watering these pots and containers take would provide a modest gardener with more than enough work to be going along with, but this area is only a small part of the overall garden.

The house itself is smothered under layers of roses, clematis, honeysuckle and other rampant growers. Jim's real loves are flowering shrubs and trees however, and he has a great collection of them, including Kashmir cedar (*Cupressus torulosa* 'Cashmeriana'), acacia and some lovely specimens of eucalyptus, golden ash and azara, swamp cypress. A little way off in one of the prettiest mixes in the garden, a little island of *Cornus controversa* 'Variegata' rests on a bed of purple bugle. There is also a fine collection of the better garden trees and they are displayed well. But Jim is a practical man and the garden was never designed past the need to be able to gain easy access to the different lawns so that they can be cut without bother. This is something to remember: an attractive lawn is only as lovely as the cutting and minding put into it. Place it in an awkward-to-get-at spot and, even with the best of intentions, it will become a neglected source of irritation to the time-strapped gardener.

A rock garden by the drive is filled with hummocks of alpine and low-growing plants. The sound of water comes from all directions in this garden. Water features are placed at several key points – ponds, pools and waterfalls lie hidden behind groves of shrubs and around corners. Shalom is a busy, good-looking garden that is a must for all enthusiasts.

SION HILL HOUSE

Ferrybank, Waterford city; Tel: +051 851558; Fax: +051 851678; e-mail: sion-hill@eircom.net ※ **Contact:** George and Antoinette Kavanagh ※ **Open:** for the Waterford Garden Festival, in the afternoons; at other times, groups welcome but must book in advance ※ **Entrance fee** donated to charity and goes towards garden upkeep ※ Supervised children welcome ※ **Special features:** groups can book teas by prior arrangement; accommodation available in the period house with views of Waterford city ※ **Directions:** leaving Waterford city on the New Ross Road, the entrance to the garden is the first gateway after the entrance to Jury's Inn.

Sion Hill was once a large estate, but by the time the Kavanaghs bought it, between one carve-up and another, the area had dwindled to the five acres closest to the house. Thanks to George and Antoinette, those grounds were saved from developers' attentions and not just preserved but developed. Unfortunately, the walled garden had been sold and built on before the Kavanaghs came. Their plan is that no such fate will befall the garden in their care, now or in the future, and with that in mind they are in the process of having the remaining garden at Sion Hill House listed for preservation for posterity.

The house is at the centre of the garden, a fine Georgian building placed in direct alignment with the clock tower and Main Street of the city. The Kavanaghs appreciate this link between the house and city, and showed that appreciation by planting 20,000 daffodils on the hilly bank that runs down from the front of the house towards the river below the garden. This bank is clearly visible from the city across the river. Thus the 20,000 blooms are seen in their full glory from the city each spring, a gorgeous sight not lost on Waterford's population. The drive up to the house was once the main road into Waterford from Kilkenny, and would have led down to the river at the Ferry Bank, from where visitors took the ferry over to the town. It is a strangely shaped drive that appears to be much longer than is necessary and running at an unnecessarily shallow slope. The reason for this is that it was built as a road for carriages, which cannot negotiate steep inclines without danger to both horses and passengers.

As the garden is being restored, the Kavanaghs have been very fortunate to work with the man who gardened here for sixty-three years. He advises them on the original garden layout and plants. (His is a fascinating story. He started washing pots in the potting shed at the age of twelve, working to a series of gardeners and head gardeners as he slowly learned his craft, before becoming head gardener himself.) Period paintings and old Ordnance Survey maps were also used to uncover the old bones of the garden; they have now been found and the Kavanaghs are cutting out the original garden paths. The whole garden is in the process of change and restoration. Replanting with period plants is taking place in the herbaceous borders and hedges of species roses are being put in. The old walled garden, long gone, is to be recreated over the next few years as a traditional flower and vegetable garden. Meanwhile, in the woods over 600 rhododendrons have been planted.

By the house is a wonderful, shaded, damp pond garden, planted up with tree ferns, mature cordylines and trachycarpus over the primula, hosta and smaller ferns. Walls around the house give shelter for a melianthus that grows too well, according to Mr Kavanagh. A Wellingtonia that was planted in 1815 to commemorate the Battle of Waterloo was once marked by a plaque, which was considered lost forever. But somehow this plaque was located in Australia and is now on its way back to the garden, where it will be replaced on the tree. Sion Hill is an interesting and varied garden, both horticulturally and historically.

TRAMORE HOUSE GARDENS

Pond Road, Tramore, County Waterford; Tel: +051 386303; Fax: +051 386098 ▩ **Contact:** Eoin Dullea ▩ **Open:** October–April, Monday–Sunday, 10am–4pm; May–September, Monday–Sunday, 10am–9pm; groups welcome and may book a guided tour ▩ **No entrance fee** ▩ Supervised children welcome; please note, dogs on leads ▩ Managed by Waterford County Council ▩ **Directions:** driving from Waterford city, on the outskirts of Tramore pass a Maxol station and take the first turn right. At the roundabout take the left exit. Pass the race course and continue to the crossroads. Turn left. Pass the fire station and community hall on the left. Tramore House is just beyond these.

Tramore House dates back to the late 1800s, and like many of the other substantial houses in what was a premier Victorian holiday resort, it is an imposing house surrounded by a fine and substantial garden covering three acres. The house was taken over by Waterford County Council in the 1980s, by which time the gardens had fallen into a state of general decline. As the vegetation got a stranglehold, the garden disappeared further and further beneath weeds and overgrowth. Recently however, the County Council took an enlightened decision to restore the gardens to their full, nineteenth-century glory. The Great Gardens of Ireland Restoration Programme joined the project and garden designer Angela Jupe drew up plans for the rebirth of the Tramore House garden. The gardens are now open, but as work continues the garden keeps changing and developing.

Tramore is built on a steep hill rising up from the sea, therefore much of the garden is hilly. The slope is well used and several paths lead through the trees and tall shrubs down to a water basin and rock garden. A herbaceous border measuring forty-five metres long leads through the main body of the garden and provides colour from early June to late October. Shrub borders work to protect the plants from salt spray and sea winds. A hillside stream cascades down the steep slope into an informal pool surrounded by glistening, water-splashed gunnera and bamboo. This wilder part of the garden, with timber pavilions and stone grottos, is romantic and informal. The woods have been planted with bluebells, anemones and tiny narcisi in spring. To the front of the house, the formal gardens have been replanted with a classic combination of box, roses, catmint, lavender and clematis, and as they mature these will provide the visitor with a colourful invitation to the garden.

Tramore is very much a work in progress, but it can be interesting to see a garden at this stage of development and then return annually to watch the changes that time and hard labour have wrought.

GARDENING CLUBS AND SOCIETIES

DUNGARVAN FLOWER AND GARDEN CLUB

Contact: Mrs Flavin, Tel: +024 94310; or Maura Curran, Tel: +058 41022.

The club meets on the first Wednesday of the month at the Teagasc office in Dungarvan. The meetings are held every month except June, July and August. An annual outing is arranged every June and visits to members' gardens are a regular feature also.

REGIONAL GARDEN CLUB, THE

Contact: Mrs Anna Jennings, 51 Lower Newtown, Waterford; Tel: +051 875712.

The Regional Garden Club meets on the third Tuesday of each month at 8pm in St Stephen's School on Manor Street, Waterford. They organise garden visits, day and extended trips, lectures, plant sales and seed exchanges.

WATERFORD AND TRAMORE FLOWER CLUB

Contact: Mrs Anna Jennings, 51 Lower Newtown, Waterford; Tel: +051 875712.

The Flower Club meets in Joseph and Benildus' Church Hall, Waterford, on the third Wednesday of each month at 8pm.

WATERFORD GARDEN PLANT SOCIETY

Contact: Jim Nolan, Shalom, Cork Road, Waterford city; Tel: +051 372681.

The society meets on the first Wednesday of every month in the Church Hall, Lower Newtown, Waterford city at 8pm from October to April. Talks, lectures, slide shows and garden trips are arranged.

NURSERIES AND GARDEN CENTRES

BLACKWATER GARDEN CENTRE

Kinsalebeg, via Youghal, County Waterford; Tel: +024 92725.

DARRER'S STORES

14 Mary Street, Dungarvan, County Waterford; Tel: +058 41581.

DELANEY'S GARDEN SHOP

7 O'Connell Street, Waterford, County Waterford; Tel: +051 876236.

EDEN GARDEN CENTRE

The Spring, Dungarvan, County Waterford; Tel: +058 43420.

FAITHLEGGE GARDEN CENTRE

Faithlegge, County Waterford; Tel: +051 382450.

GARDENER'S WORLD,

Thomas Street, Waterford, County Waterford; Tel: +051 878189.

HILLSIDE GARDEN CENTRE

Ballinaneeshagh, Butlerstown, County Waterford; Tel: +051 356222.

McGUIRE'S GARDEN CENTRE

Woodstown, County Waterford, Tel: +051 382136.

ORCHARDSTOWN GARDEN CENTRE

Cork Road, Waterford, County Waterford; Tel: +051 384273.

STAM'S GARDEN DESIGN AND NURSERY

The Garden House, Cappoquin, County Waterford; Tel: +058 54787.

Specialist nursery with a nearly 100 varieties of bamboos; rarer conifers, like acrydium and podocarpus, varieties of tree ferns, banana trees, palms, grasses, eucryphias, rhododendrons and azara are also stocked (*see* Garden Designers, below).

TRAMORE GARDEN CENTRE

Carriglong, Ballykinsella, Tramore, County Waterford; Tel: +051 391176.

WOODIES DIY GARDEN CENTRE

Cork Road, Waterford, County Waterford; Tel: +051 351040.

GARDEN DESIGNERS

PETER STAM

The Garden House, Cappoquin, County Waterford; Tel: +058 54787; e-mail stam@iol.ie

A garden designer specialising in the optimum use of plants and minimal hard landscaping. Works all over the island.

GARDEN ACCESSORIES

SALVAGE SHOP, THE

Airport Road, Waterford city; Tel: +051 873260; e-mail: salvage@iol.ie

There are few places more fun than a good salvage yard and this is a particularly good one, full of old stone troughs, boxes of slates, stone capping, wrought iron railings, glass bricks, old sinks, cobbles and the strangest odds and ends that could look great in a garden – if only you could figure out what to do with them.

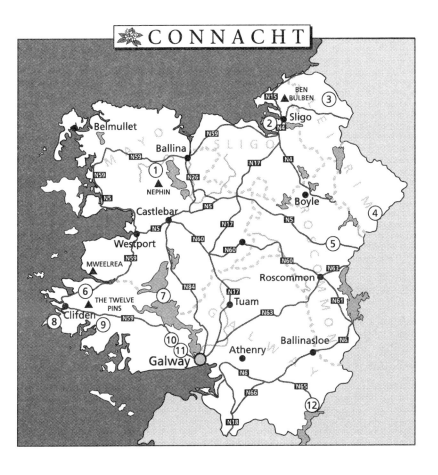

MAP KEY

1. Enniscoe Garden
2. Glenwood
3. The Organic Centre
4. Lough Rynn Estate
5. Strokestown House
6. Kylemore Abbey
7. Ashford Castle
8. Gleann Aoibheann
9. Cashel House
10. Orville
11. Ardcarraig
12. Portumna Castle Kitchen Garden

COUNTY GALWAY

Summer in Galway city, the 'city of the tribes', can be an exhausting time. Racing, film, arts and oyster festivals all blend one into the next. The weekly market next to St Nicholas's Church, with stalls of exotic foods, plants, herbs and all sorts of crafts, attracts visitors and natives alike. The city has become one of Ireland's most popular destinations – it has a young population, colourful buildings, narrow streets, many restaurants, varied nightlife and, some would argue, the best pubs in Ireland.

Within the county, Portumna Castle, a semi-fortified house, was built in the early 1600s. The walled garden has been taken over as an organic kitchen garden, which can be visited by appointment. Outside the city, on the coast, Moran's of the Weir in Clarinbridge serve wonderful oysters and seafood. Clifden, the capital of Connemara, is a busy, bustling market and holiday town, surrounded by interesting coastal and hill walks. The Connemara National Park is a good place for walking and for studying wildflowers, and it has a marvellous interpretive centre as well. Leenane, made famous as the backdrop for the film *The Field*, is a good stop-off for walkers. Out on the Aran Islands is the fort of Dún Aengus, perched precariously on a cliff overlooking the Atlantic Ocean and slowly eroding in the salt gales.

Constant exposure to Atlantic winds and heavy rainfall has shaped the land of County Galway. The soil is thin and heavily eroded in places. The Maumturk Mountains are covered with blanket bog and vegetation is sparse, apart from some sheltered areas. The imposing Lough Corrib is a great draw to fishermen, as are the scores of small rivers throughout the county. The natural beauties of County Galway are exactly the qualities that make it a very hard county in which to garden or farm. There are, however, a number of new gardens being created and opened to the public.

ARDCARRAIG

Oranswell, Bushypark, County Galway; Tel: +091 524336 ▪ **Contact:** Lorna MacMahon ▪ **Open:** one open day per year (see local press for details or telephone for annual dates); otherwise all year round, strictly by appointment only ▪ **Entrance fee** donated to the Galway Mental Health Association ▪ **Special features:** plants sold on open days only; teas available on open days ▪ **Directions:** situated off the Oughterard–Clifden road, 5km out of Galway city. Take the second turn on the left after Glenloe Abbey Hotel; the road is marked Oranswell. About 250m up the hill, the house is on the left with a limestone entrance.

'We started off with one acre in 1971. That was the usual size plot a new house had in those days. The land was scrubby. There were two trees and we had no grand plan.' So began Lorna MacMahon's garden, one of the best in the country and a favourite of amateurs and professionals alike.

Hugging into the hilly land at the southern end of Lough Corrib, Ardcarraig is a *tour de force*. The garden is divided into a series of distinctive rooms and a map is obligingly provided to make sure the visitor misses nothing. The trail begins with a front garden of heather, shrubs and spring bulbs. A formal herb garden was created from a disused tennis court. In a fascinating exercise, the beds are devoted to herbs mentioned in the works of Shakespeare and in the Bible. For instance, Biblical herbs include bee balm *(Melissa officinalis)*, which appears in Jeremiah, dill is mentioned in the Gospel of Matthew and fitch *(Nigella)* is found in Isaiah. The Shakespearean herbs include rue, rosemary and fennel, each of which is mentioned in 'Hamlet, Prince of Darkness'. The herbs are also subdivided into culinary and medicinal uses.

Next door to the herb garden and completely secluded from it, a terracotta pot garden is tucked away, very sheltered and private. There are also several woodland gardens that fill with bluebells in the spring. 'They were here before me. I just allow them to spread,' says Lorna of the obliging carpets of blue. She sees much of her gardening work as accommodating rather than manipulating plants.

The pool and primula garden is quite beautiful. In here blue *Lobelia siphilitica* takes over from the earlier flowering, deep-red candelabra primulas that seed rampantly in this wet spot. Lorna says that the damp bed takes twice as long to weed as the rest of the garden put together. The pond is natural and unlined and the whole area squelches satisfyingly underfoot. The best growth is found along the streams. These carry a lot of soil to the bottom of the garden, and the primulas self-seed with gusto in the fertile muck. The bog field garden holds plants that will put up with constant wet, including swamp cypress *(Taxodiums)*, cryptomeria, ginkgo and fitzroya.

The labyrinthine paths continue on to take in an oak garden and from there to the Japanese garden – something that anyone who dislikes Japanese gardens should see. Lorna's is a hill and pool garden of a type dating back to the 1200s. The play of shades and leaf textures with reflecting water and rock are central to this atmospheric garden. From under the trees a huge boulder stands out with the assurance of a rock that has always been there. Lorna simply uncovered it from under a blanket of soil. An antique stone snow-viewing lamp from Thailand stands by the pool. According to the story, it nearly broke the backs of a dozen strong men who foolishly (but generously) offered to help the tiny Mrs MacMahon transport it from the top of the garden down through the closely planted woodland.

Harry's garden is the most recently created garden at Ardcarraig. By 1996, Lorna had run out of room to expand the garden, so she turned to a farming neighbour. He sold her a little bit of rock and bog, intrigued by what she might do with it. The resultant plot was created as a memorial garden for Harry, Lorna's husband, using plants given to her by friends and family. The rough landscape this new garden was created from is visible from here – the very worst of gorse- and bramble-covered, hilly, rocky land. Lorna planted birch and hawthorn on the boundary to make a natural transition between the garden and the wilds beyond. She believes in maintaining a sympathy with her surroundings and knows that a perfect herbaceous border is not what is required in this landscape.

None of the contours in the garden are man-made. The land and the rocks were simply worked, without a sense of the imposing of a will on the land. This is an incredible garden by any standard, and Lorna MacMahon has never had help with it, nor would she accept any. Even as she was talking to me she was ducking in and out of a little tunnel trying to free a leaf blockage in the stream.

CASHEL HOUSE

Cashel, County Galway; Tel: +095 31001; e-mail: info@cashel-house-hotel.com ▪ **Contact:** Dermot and Kay McEvilly ▪ **Open:** May–June, Tuesday and Thursday, 2pm–5pm; otherwise by appointment only ▪ **No entrance fee** ▪ Not suitable for children under five ▪ **Special features:** horse-riding available at the hotel; tearoom (meals can be booked in advance) ▪ **Directions:** just south off the Clifden–Galway road (N59), well signposted.

Driving from Oughterard to Cashel, passing Lough Corrib, a string of smaller lakes, the ever-changing Maumturk Mountains and the indented Atlantic coast, one might question the desire to see a cultivated garden when surrounded by so much natural grandeur. However, the gardens around Cashel House hold their own admirably. Laid out around the hotel is a series of beautifully made informal gardens, big mixed beds of blue and pink hydrangeas, roses, rhododendron and fuchsia. Fuchsia is almost native along the west coast and it marries a cultivated garden to the wilder land beyond.

The house itself is covered in jasmine, ivy, clematis and roses, with some planting of antirrhinum and geranium set into a rocky base. The lines of the gardens are soft and informal. Small walks and paths covered in mind-your-own-business (*Soleirolia soleirolii*) and edged with moss-covered rocks run past rolling lawns. A long bed of flowers is spread out in front of the house, filled with viola, chocolate cosmos, phlox, canna lilies and more antirrhinums.

A fine beech walk leads up to the herb garden, which is being worked on a pronounced slope. This little section of the garden is very pretty, displaying rows of Chinese chives, all the usual herbs and some vegetables, and edged with well-shaped box balls. General de Gaulle's seat overlooks the herb and vegetable beds from a covered arbour. Both General and Madame de Gaulle holidayed at Cashel in 1969, shortly after his term as president of France ended. As the world's press chased around Ireland trying to discover where the elusive couple were, they enjoyed a royal spoiling at Cashel and stories about the trip are legion in the area.

Cashel House boasts good woodland walks, a stream bridged at several points, secret gardens and a long beach walk along a sheltered bay. Scattered throughout are elegant specimen trees, wildflowers and heather plots.

GLEANN AOIBHEANN

Clifden, Connemara, County Galway; Tel: +095 21148 ▪ **Contact:** Breandan O'Scanaill ▪ **Open:** beginning March–beginning June, Monday–Sunday, 2pm–6pm; during the Connemara Garden Trail (see local press for annual dates); at other times by appointment only ▪ **Entrance fee** donated to the Irish Cancer Society ▪ Supervised children welcome ▪ **Special features:** wildlife garden; occasional plant sales; teas can be booked in advance ▪ **Directions:** from Clifden, follow the sign for the Beach Road. Turn left after the Bank of Ireland and travel downhill to the quay. The garden is the sixth house on the right.

The handsome house at Gleann Aoibheann was built as a hunting lodge by the d'Arcy family, who were important landowners in Clifden at the beginning of the nineteenth century. It has passed through several families over the past 200 years, each of whom have added to the house and garden. Some of the older trees are thought to have been planted by the d'Arcys, but most of the garden work was undertaken at the beginning of the twentieth century, with alternate periods of development and neglect ever since then.

The garden covers two-and-a-half acres, facing south. It is sheltered from the prevailing southwest and cold north winds by a hill behind the site, making it a lot more protected than its seaside position would suggest. Warm coastal temperatures keep the frost at bay and this leaves sea spray as the only drawback, but even that is rare. Gleann Aoibheann's current owner and gardener, Breandan O'Scanaill, works the garden organically. 'I am very lucky with the garden's situation. It gets great, lush growth. A few visitors have even likened the place to Sri Lanka!' he says, obviously and rightly pleased. Jungle-like in parts, it certainly is an informal garden.

The garden is hilly, composed of sweeps of lawn interrupted by naturalistic groupings and plantings of shrubs and trees, for example, mixes of sweet chestnut (*Castanea sativa*), strawberry tree (*Arbutus unedo*), camellia and wych elm (*Ulmus glabra*). It was not always so, however: 'When I got here at the age of three it was a very formal garden and there were three full-time gardeners working it.' Now it has one, Breandan, who is busy bringing the garden intelligently into the twenty-first century. No chemicals are used at all and his dedication to nature has paid off.

A large mixed wood of birch, beech, oak, ash, hazel and rhododendron covers about one-third of the garden. This area is a miniature wildlife sanctuary, which is left to look after itself. 'I leave the old woods completely to nature. I really love the wildlife, but I try not to go in there and disturb it. I just watch it from a distance. Some people might consider big patches of nettles for the butterflies mad, but I lead guests around and explain the reasons for keeping these "weeds". And I think it's important for visitors to realise that nature is primary to the garden.'

Nature, in return, has shown its appreciation. Breandan's wood is now a populous place, home to a fox, a badger, an otter, frogs, stoats, a hare, numerous birds, bats and even a family of hawks, which Breandan says have been almost hunted out of existence in Connemara. The rewards of seeing such a collection on an almost daily basis should send many a traditional gardener down the organic path. I hope it does.

KYLEMORE ABBEY

Letterfrack, County Galway; Tel: +095 41146; e-mail: enquiries@kylemore abbey.ie ■ **Contact:** Anne Golden, Head Gardener ■ **Open:** all year round; groups can arrange in advance for specialist tours ■ **Entrance fee** ■ Supervised children welcome ■ **Special features:** shop; museum; the abbey's historic buildings and church ■ **Directions:** situated on the road between Leenane and Clifden (N59), very well signposted.

The romantic stories about Mitchell Henry and his purchase of the lands at Kylemore Abbey for his young wife Margaret are popular and engaging. She loved the area so much that he decided to build her a castle out in the wilds of Connemara. But it took far more than a dew-eyed romantic to achieve what he created at the foot of the Twelve Pins back in the 1860s. A huge and impressive demesne was imposed on this hard but beautiful landscape by hundreds of workers over a number of years, building the great Gothic pile and its splendid gardens. The Henrys's story ended sadly, however. Margaret had only seven years to enjoy her spectacular gift; while on holiday in Egypt, she died of Nile Fever. Mitchell Henry subsequently left the area and eventually sold the property. At the beginning of the First World War the Irish Benedictine nuns, who had settled at Ypres in Belgium during the Reformation, fled their war-torn base and returned to Ireland, where they bought the property and re-opened the monastery and established a girls' school. Kylemore Abbey began the slow road back to restoration.

In the gardens, reductions in manpower and money during the twentieth century led to deterioration, despite the work of a succession of gardeners. In the past few years however, with the aid of the Lawrence Collection (photographs taken at the turn of the century), the walled garden has been restored. Physical work on the garden began in 1996 with help from the Great Gardens Restoration Programme. Old paths were dug out from under great mounds of soil. Planting only began in 1999. Today, the gardens are provisionally open so that visitors can see the work in progress. It will be a work in progress for a few more years to come.

In style, the restored garden is very different from the majority of walled gardens in Ireland. There are no tall herbaceous and mixed borders, no garden rooms or surprise areas. This is a triumph of bedding, with a capital B. Victorian bedding lies in low lines of madly coloured, regimented, mainly annual flowers, in intricate and mathematical patterns. Height is achieved by strategically placed tall cordylines, phormiums, palms, pampas and tree ferns. This garden might not be in keeping with current taste, but historically it is fascinating and made more so by the use of period plants. Close scrutiny of the old photographs and the 1898 Ordnance Survey map led Head Gardener Anne Golden and her team to a successful recapturing of the ordered, proper, sometimes surprising Victorian taste that the garden was created to show off.

The walled garden of a grand house was often placed at a distance from the house, and in the case of Kylemore Abbey the garden is over two kilometres away. No one is quite sure why this long trek was made necessary, but one theory is that it was done in order that the walled garden might enjoy the dramatic backdrop of the mountains; Diamond Hill is centred dramatically on the garden wall.

THE CONNEMARA GARDEN TRAIL

Gardening in Connemara is a fast-growing interest, and this is reflected in the recently established garden trail set up by a group of enthusiastic gardeners scattered through counties Galway and Mayo. This garden trail was started in 1998, so it is still in its early years, but already, by 2001, fourteen gardeners have signed up to participate (*see* pp.290–291 for full list). In 2001 the gardens are opening each weekend from 28 April to 4 June. Each garden is different in size, scale and style: there are seaside gardens, large, formal, historic gardens, small intimate plots and fine hotel gardens.

In addition to the open gardens, in 2001 a special feature is the gardening weekend to be held 13–14 May. The event will be led by Finola Reid and is centred on the Victorian garden at Kylemore Abbey. Contact the Abbey for full details, Tel: +095 41146 .

The restored walled garden at Kylemore Abbey in Letterfrack, Connemara, built by Mitchell Henry for his young wife, Margaret. The unusual Victorian arches were recreated using photographs from the Lawrence Collection, which were taken in the early 1900s.

The remains of two glasshouses are still in the garden, and one is being restored to grow vines. Originally there were twenty glasshouses here. It is hoped that the remains of the display houses, built to display figs, bananas, palms, melons and other tropical plants, will also be restored eventually.

One interesting feature is the bothy house, where the garden boys would have lived. They had to be close to the garden at all times, as keeping the boilers stoked and the fires alight was a twenty-four-hour job. If neglected, the fires would die and the hothouses would lose the heat that kept tender plants alive. The bothy house is being restored for use as a garden museum, focussing on the work of the young garden boys and other workers who made places like Kylemore possible.

The remains of a ragged-looking floral arch stood at the centre of the garden at the start of the restoration. This has been restored to its very original, very ornate style and painted in what is thought to be the original colour, according to the memory of one of the older nuns who worked in the garden. Annual climbers are trained over its light frame.

Work has yet to extend to the vegetable and fruit gardens, where old varieties will be introduced and worked over the next few years.

There are long riverside and woodland walks at Kylemore with a good collection of trees to be seen. Mitchell Henry planted a great oak wood as well as plantations of common lime (*Tilia x. europaea*), beech, sitka spruce, common alder (*Alnus glutinosa*), wych elm (*Ulmus glabra*) and Monterey pine (*Pinus radiata*). The nuns continue to plant trees, concentrating mainly on oak.

ORVILLE

Clooniffe, Moycullen, County Galway; Tel: +091 555530 ▪ **Contact:** Gisella Price
▪ **Open:** for charity open days, contact for annual details; otherwise open
July–August, every day, but strictly by appointment only; *Note:* approach road not
suitable for large coaches ▪ **Entrance fee** donated to various charities ▪ Supervised
children welcome ▪ **Directions:** off the Oughterard–Clifden road, 9.5km from
University College Hospital. Turn right at the road marked Cluain Aoibh and con-
tinue straight for 1.5km. Turn left at the crossroads and travel for another 1.5km.
Orville is the seventh house along.

Orville has been described as a plant-lover's garden. It has taken several awards in the
Shamrock All Ireland Gardens Competition over the years, including first prize in the
Connacht category in the 2000 competition. Gisella Price designed the garden and
has worked it herself for the past twelve years. She has used the natural outcrops of
limestone, which are scattered liberally throughout the one-acre garden, to create a
number of impressive rockeries. These are the chief attraction of the garden.

PORTUMNA CASTLE KITCHEN GARDEN

Portumna, County Galway; Tel: +0509 41853 ▪ **Contact:** Ruth Carty or Mary
Rose Cormacan ▪ **Open:** May–October, seven days, 9am–6pm; group tours available Monday–Friday and weekends by appointment ▪ **Entrance fee** ▪ Supervised
children welcome; please note, dogs on leads ▪ **Special features:** working kitchen
garden; willow maze; castle; craft and plant shop on Abbey Street; craft and
garden courses available ▪ **Directions:** situated in Portumna Castle Park, on the
edge of Portumna town. Follow the signposts from Abbey Street, Portumna.

The earls of Clanricard built Portumna Castle in the 1600s on a magnificent site
overlooking Lough Derg, bordering Galway and Tipperary. The castle is one of the
finest surviving examples of an Irish semi-fortified house of this period. The gardens
at Portumna Castle are divided into two different areas: formal Jacobean gardens, laid
out to the front of the castle in a a smart design of lawns, wide gravel paths and geo-
metrically patterned beds, and a walled garden.

In the walled garden an exciting adventure has been going on since 1996, run by a
local group working with Dúchas and FÁS. Over 100 years of neglect meant that the
walled area never received the attention of chemicals, making it perfect for the creation of an organic kitchen garden. More interestingly, the decision was taken to
create, as authentically as possible, a seventeenth-century kitchen garden. Period
techniques and plants have been used on the project.

The work over the past number of years has involved a good deal of archaeological
and historical research. This began with a trawl for information about what the
garden would have looked like. Ancient seed found in the soil was analysed to discover
what plants had originally been grown in the original garden. Excavations were made
to locate and restore the original garden paths, including a turning circle for a pony
and cart.

The result is a garden that incorporates a fine vegetable plot, growing seasonal
organic fruit and vegetables. There is also a wildflower garden and a tree nursery,

where old and rare varieties of native fruit are being raised and saved from extinction in conjunction with the Irish Seed Savers Association (*see* County Clare, p.175). The herb garden not only looks good but also provides the local country market (*see* Country Markets in the appendices) and shops in the area with organic produce. A willow maze made up of twelve varieties of willow doubles as entertainment for children and a source of willow for local basket-makers. Finally, a herbaceous border has been planted with heritage plants, including gifts from some of the finest old gardens, particularly Birr Castle Demesne.

The garden at Portumna now boasts paths lined with espaliered fruit trees and underplanted with lavender. Trellises and arches over the paths play host to rambling roses, while the walls are being restored and covered with a tracery of wall-grown fruit trees. The experiment has been declared a success.

GARDENING CLUBS AND SOCIETIES

GALWAY FLOWER AND GARDEN CLUB

Contact: Lorna MacMahon; Tel: +091 542336.

The Galway Flower and Garden Club has been in existence for thirty-three years. It meets at 8pm on the third Tuesday of the month in the Westwood House Hotel, Dangan, Newcastle, County Galway, between September and June. Monthly meetings alternate between garden talks and flower-arranging demonstrations. Non-members are welcome for an admission charge. A plant stall is set up for each meeting and competitions and raffles are held. Visits to local, national and international gardens and shows are arranged each year.

OUGHTERARD FLOWER CLUB

Contact: Mary O'Malley; Tel: +091 552833.

The Oughterard Flower Club meets at 8pm on the first Tuesday of the month in the Corrib House Hotel in Oughterard. The season runs throughout the year, apart from January and February, and meetings alternate between flower-arranging and gardening topics. An annual trip is arranged for club members and their friends to an outstanding Irish garden.

GARDEN ACCESSORIES

FEATURE STONE ARCADE

33 Foster Street (off Eyre Square), Galway city.

An Aladdin's cave of stone features, slabs, standing stones, mushrooms, old and new items and unusual garden statuary.

HONAN'S ANTIQUES, Architectural Salvage

Crowe Street, Galway city; Tel: +091 631407.

THE CONNEMARA GARDEN TRAIL

The participating gardens in the festival in 2001 are as follows:

Ardcarraig

Oranswell, County Galway.

Opens for one day during the festival, telephone for details. (see full entry in County Galway.)

Schrallia Beag

Cashel, County Galway; Tel: +095 31163 ■ **Contact:** Bobby and Rosemary Carr.

One-acre hillside garden with old roses and cottage garden plants. Telephone for festival dates.

Cashel House Hotel and Gardens

Cashel, County Galway. (*see* full entry in County Galway.)

Errisbeg House

Roundstone, County Galway.

A two-acre wild and rocky garden with lots of hidden borders, heatherbeds and stands of pampas grass. Open every day during the festival.

Errislannan Manor

Clifden, County Galway; Tel: +095 21134 ■ **Contact:** Stephanie and Donal Brooks.

A three-acre garden, including a walled garden with some Victorian planting. Contact for annual festival dates.

Glasthule

Moyard, County Galway; Tel: +095 44772 ■ **Contact:** Elizabeth and Gerard Cully.

The garden covers three-quarters of an acre. This is a cottage garden with a stream, featuring rhododendrons and azaleas. Contact for annual festival dates.

Gleann Aoibheann

Clifden, County Galway. (*see* full entry in County Galway.)

Kylemore Abbey

Connemara, County Galway. (*see* full entry in County Galway.)

Lisnabruka

Ballinafad, County Galway ■ **Contact:** Pamela and Ian Reid.

This is a ten-acre natural garden incorporating mature trees planted in the 1800s. The main garden was laid out in 1910. Contact for annual festival dates.

The Quayside

Roundstone, County Galway ■ **Contact:** Tim and Mairead Robinson.

A small cliff-top garden. Contact for annual festival dates.

Rosleague Manor Hotel

Letterfrack, County Galway.

Open every day from April to October. An early nineteenth-century garden with hydrangeas and a woodland walk leading down to the ocean's edge.

Seal Cottage

Clifden, County Galway ■ **Contact:** Pat O'Connell.

A small, very exposed seaside garden on varying levels, with grass, ponds, rockeries and a wood. Contact for annual festival dates.

Zetland Hotel

Cashel, County Galway; Tel: +095 31111 ■ **Contact:** Mona and John Prendergast.

An informal country garden in a seaside setting. Contact for annual festival dates.

Enniscoe House and Garden

Castlehill, County Mayo. (*see* full entry in County Mayo.)

COUNTY LEITRIM

County Leitrim, the least populous county in the Republic, is dominated by water. The Shannon-Erne waterway runs across the county, linking the two great navigable river systems in Ireland. The canal was restored in the early 1990s and is a popular cruising route. Lough Gill and Lough Rynn are rated among the best fishing grounds in Europe by anglers and coarse-fishing enthusiasts. Parkes Castle on the shore of Lough Gill should be visited. Standing almost on the water, this plantation castle, built in the 1600s, is remarkably well-preserved. For gardeners and food enthusiasts, Leitrim brings one name to mind – Rod Alston, the man responsible for Eden Herbs and the Organic Centre (*see* below). Alston has been a pioneer of organic growing methods on this island for nearly thirty years.

LOUGH RYNN ESTATE

Mohill, County Leitrim ■ **No entrance fee** ■ **Open:** lying deserted and open to anyone ■ **Directions:** situated 5km from Mohill, on the road to Drumlish.

Lough Rynn was once one of the homes of William Sidney Clements, the third earl of Leitrim, who was famously ambushed and shot in 1878 at Cratlagh Wood in Letterkenny, County Donegal. He was one of the most notorious evicting landlords of the period. Today the house at Lough Rynn is deserted. Although the gardens look as though plans were recently in train to present them to the public, they are in serious decline. A state of genteel dilapidation has taken hold of the place.

A romantic terraced garden looks out over the lake. Fine limestone walls surround this garden and on top of the walls is a ruined Gothic summerhouse. Restored greenhouses lie empty, planting half-thought out and half-executed. All the lawns are overgrown. The picturesque boathouse is disintegrating and the stream leading into it is clogged up.

Lough Rynn is a sad sight, with nature gradually taking over, but it still has charm. In its own way it makes a good walk, taking in the ruins of Reynold's Castle by the lake. The trees in the parkland are wonderful. There are evergreen and common oaks, Scots pine (*Pinus sylvestris*), cut-leaf beech, varieties of cedar and massive monkey puzzle trees (*Araucaria araucana*), with an underplanting of rhododendron, fuchsia, holly and pheasant berry (*Leycesteria formosa*). Forgotten, neglected and deteriorating it may be, but the estate still retains a charming beauty.

THE ORGANIC CENTRE

Rossinver, County Leitrim; Tel: +072 54338; Fax: +072 54343; e-mail: organic centre@tinet.ie ■ **Contact:** reception ■ **Open:** 31 March–2 November, Monday–Friday, 11am–5pm; at other times telephone for an appointment ■ **Entrance fee** ■ Supervised children welcome; please note, dogs on leads ■ **Special features:** restaurant, meals must be booked in advance; B&B and hostel accommodation available in the locality; shop selling herbs, plants, seeds and books on organic growing methods; courses available on organic gardening and other topics ■ **Directions:** situated 3km from Rossinver on the Kinlough Road. From Sligo or Dublin, travel via Manorhamilton and Rossinver. From Enniskillen come via Belcoo and Garrison. From Donegal via Ballyshannon, Belleek and Garrison.

The Organic Centre was established in 1996 to answer a growing demand for information on organic farming, land husbandry and gardening. Set on nineteen acres of unspoiled north Leitrim limestone, the centre works in two ways. It offers a range of courses throughout the year aimed at professional gardeners, farmers, restauranteurs and interested amateurs. Also, full-time courses on organic methods are offered.

Examples of the sort of one-day courses on offer at the centre include:

■ Growing for restaurants
■ Fruit-growing for the home
■ Commercial cut-herb production
■ Starting an organic vegetable garden
■ Introduction to bee-keeping
■ Willow sculpting
■ Goat husbandry and making goats' cheese
■ Creating a wildlife garden
■ Preserving and storing fruit and vegetables
■ Hedge establishment and management

The centre also presents demonstration gardens. The demonstrations include a two-acre working kitchen garden, which is divided into plots of vegetables, herbs, fruit and flowers, grown both outside and in polythene tunnels. Examples of hedge-management and layering techniques illustrate important and disappearing conservation skills vital to the preservation of hedgerows. Domestic and commercial cropping techniques as well as composting methods can be seen in operation. There are also herb and ornamental beds with annuals and perennials, a children's play area made from willows and an array of traditional-breed hens.

A special feature of the centre is the heritage garden, planted with rare and unusual varieties of vegetables, the seed of which can only be obtained through the Henry Doubleday Research Association or the Irish Seed Savers Association (*see* County Clare, p.175). This scarcity is due to the fact that seed-merchants are selecting an ever-decreasing number of seeds to produce and sell on to the public. Old seed varieties are disappearing and need to be saved and grown more widely by gardeners to maintain a healthy, varied gene pool of seeds for posterity.

The main building at Rossinver is worth seeing. This was recently constructed in an ecologically sensitive way, using all organic materials and with an intriguing grass roof.

A Friends of the Organic Centre scheme is in place. Friends receive a regular newsletter, information on forthcoming courses and a ten-percent discount on courses, books and tools bought. Friends also gain free admission to the Henry Doubleday Research Association Gardens in Britain, at Ryton, Coventry, and Yalding in Kent.

GARDEN CENTRES

DRUMSNA GARDEN CENTRE
Dublin Road, Drumsna, County Leitrim; Tel: +078 25582.

MOHILL GARDEN CENTRE
Station Road, Mohill, County Leitrim; Tel: +078 31019.

County Mayo

Mayo is perhaps most well-known as the location of the Céide Fields. Under the Mayo bogs lie the most extensive Stone Age monuments in the world – wide-ranging networks of fields, dwellings and tombs, all over 5,000 years old. The cosmopolitan and interesting town of Westport is a good base for touring the county. Croagh Patrick, now safe from gold-miners, is an awesome sight and a challenging climb – especially if you dare to go barefoot. Mayo soil is mainly acidic and much of the land between the mountain ranges of Nephin, Partry and Mweelrea is blanket bog, with trees growing only in sheltered pockets. There are not many gardens to be visited in the county, but the landscape is powerful to behold, with its lakes, dramatic coastal areas, mountainous skylines, bogs and drumlins. Walking and hiking on the many mapped routes will reward visitors with wildflowers enough to please any gardener.

ASHFORD CASTLE

Cong, County Mayo; Tel: +092 46003 ▪ **Contact:** Reception ▪ **Open:** by appointment only ▪ **Entrance fee** ▪ Supervised children welcome; please note, dogs on leads ▪ **Special features:** one of the most luxurious hotels in Ireland ▪ **Directions:** Cong is on the edge of Lough Corrib, on the R346. The hotel is well signposted.

Ashford Castle is a nineteenth-century Gothic castellated manor house, set in extensive grounds on the edge of Cong village by the north shore of Lough Corrib, on the border between counties Galway and Mayo. Ashford is one of the grander country house hotels, but with permission the gardens can be visited.

The grey limestone moated castle stands on a big stretch of perfect lawns edged with rhododendron. A straight, wide walk leads away from the building, with views at either end of fountains and gazebos. Wide, substantial sets of stone steps with terraces between are overhung by a collection of fine trees, including a huge tulip tree (*Liriodendron tulipifera*) and varieties of oak and pine with clematis growing up through them. Everything is on the grandest of grand scales. Moving away from the building, follies and mock castles peep out to surprise.

Off this long walk is the walled garden, boasting an unusual Gothic underground tunnel entrance. This is a smart affair of hornbeam *allées* and espaliered fruit trees that run around the outside of a garden of currant bushes. A loose, informal bed of roses and lavender, artemisia and hydrangea make up a mass of blues, whites and silvers. In another of the little central areas is a good box garden with rosemary and crab apples within the low green box walls.

The grounds of Ashford Castle make for a pleasant and varied long walk.

ENNISCOE GARDENS

Castlehill, Ballina, County Mayo; Tel: +096 31809; Fax: +096 31885; Garden telephone: 088 2684390; e-mail: enniscoe@indigo.ie ▪ **Contact:** Annette Maughan ▪ **Open:** 15 April–15 September, daily, 2pm–6pm; closed Mondays; at other times groups by appointment only ▪ **Entrance fee** ▪ Supervised children welcome ▪ **Special features:** agricultural museum; genealogical research centre for the Mayo area; tearoom open May–September; plants occasionally for sale ▪ **Directions:** travelling south, the garden is 4km from Crossmolina on the R315.

Enniscoe was built in the early eighteenth century on the shores of Lough Conn, with fine views of the Nephin mountain range. There have been gardens here since then, but little remains of the early garden, and when the restoration started recently under the guidance of Mrs Susan Kellett, a debate began. The work of restoring gardens, or indeed houses, that have been in existence through a number of centuries often presents restorers with the dilemma of which period to restore to. This can be a difficult choice if records exist for several styles and periods. But in the case of Enniscoe the debate was settled: from the 1850s to the 1950s the garden was run by several generations of the family with a particular interest in gardening, and recently unearthed contemporary documentation proved useful. Added to this was a collection of late Victorian photographs of the garden. So, in 1997, the work of restoring the gardens to the Victorian period began.

There were few substantial remnants of the garden to work with, so a great deal of detective work had to be carried out, starting with an archaeological survey. The rockery in front of the glasshouses is original, as are the paths. These old paths, once uncovered from under rubble, were relined with low box hedging. Deirdre Ruttledge, who had been working on the project for four years, told me with enthusiasm that the box plants for these low hedges were propagated from the original Victorian box plants found in the old garden. These plants, after years of neglect, now found themselves as important participants in the restoration project. Box plants are notoriously expensive to buy in numbers big enough to use as hedging and edging. Propagation is a good idea if you have the time. It is also easy and a great number of cuttings can be taken from one plant.

The walled garden at Enniscoe is divided into two areas by a dividing wall. The first area to be seen is the site of work so far carried out. This is the one-acre ornamental and flower garden. The rest is currently being run as an organic fruit and vegetable garden and is not open to the public. (It is possible to buy produce from here, however.)

There is a special stone archway, like a small grotto, linking the two gardens. This very unusual, Gothic-style feature would originally have been planted throughout with ferns, making walking from one side of the garden to the other an eerie little journey. It is now in the process of being replanted with ferns and in fact, once cleared, as if impatient, it began to sprout wild ferns immediately.

The borders are herbaceous and Victorian period plants have been used wherever possible. The central beds were replanted using old photographs for guidance, and these also guided the replanting of trachycarpus and cordylines as tall architectural statements, very much in keeping with the period. In nature, the restoration work is akin to that of Kylemore Abbey, with both gardens being restored to the same period and style (*see* County Galway). As at Kylemore Abbey, the glasshouses were in a state of ruin and they are now being worked on. There are no plans to rebuild completely, but the bases will be accessible and, for anyone interested in the old workings, heating pipes and flues, these will also be displayed.

Out in the pleasure grounds paths are being reinstated and cleared to allow walks down to Lough Conn. The woods are being replanted with bulbs and spring flowers. Enniscoe provides a fascinating study of the dynamics of restoration work and of Victorian gardening styles.

GARDENING CLUBS AND SOCIETIES

CASTLEBAR GARDEN CLUB

The Castlebar Garden Club has been running for the past quarter of a century. It meets at 8.30pm on the second Wednesday of the month in the old St Gerald's College, Chapel Street, Castlebar. Gardening talks, slide shows, floral and gardening competitions are held monthly. During the summer, garden visits are held. No meetings are held in January or August.

WESTPORT GARDEN CLUB

The Westport Garden Club, at only five years old, is still a young one, but it already has a healthy membership, is very active and welcomes new members. It meets at 8pm on the first Thursday of the month, apart from January, July and August, in the Lecture Hall on the Newport Road in Westport. Lectures, talks, demonstrations, occasional competitions and trips to gardens, along with occasional charity festivals or shows, make up the programme of events.

NURSERIES AND GARDEN CENTRES

ASHLEAF GARDEN CENTRE

Sligo Road, Ballina, County Mayo; Tel: +096 70777.

CASTLEBAR GARDEN CENTRE AND NURSERY

Westport Road, Castlebar, County Mayo; Tel: +094 21792.

CONNOR'S GARDEN CENTRE

Garden Street, Ballina, County Mayo; Tel: +096 51018.

GLENROE GARDEN CENTRE

Behy Road, Ballina, County Mayo; Tel: +096 71075.

HORKAN'S GARDEN CENTRE

Spencer Street, Castlebar, County Mayo; Tel: +094 26997.

MORLEY'S GARDEN CENTRE

100 New Street, Ballinrobe, County Mayo; Tel: +092 41846.

NEW ZEALAND TREE FERNS

Cloongee, Foxford, County Mayo; Tel: +094 56960. (By appointment only.)

RAINBOW FLOWERING PLANTS

Manulla, Castlebar, County Mayo; Tel: +094 65256.

R&R NURSERIES

Swinford Road, Foxford, County Mayo; Tel: +094 56248.

SWINFORD GARDEN CENTRE

Main Street, Swinford, County Mayo; Tel: +094 51349.

THURLOUGH NURSERY

Thurlough village, County Mayo; Tel:
+094 22310.

TREELAND GARDEN CENTRE

Carrabaun, Westport, County Mayo;
Tel: +098 28122.

WESTPORT GARDEN CENTRE

Barrack Yard, James's Street, Westport,
County Mayo; Tel: +098 25324.

COUNTY ROSCOMMON

Landlocked Roscommon snakes along the mid-northwest of the country, bordered by counties Mayo, Sligo, Leitrim, Longford, Westmeath, Offaly and Galway. The county is surrounded by lakes and bounded to the east by the River Shannon, Lough Ree, Lough Boderg, Lough Forbes, Lough Kee and Lough Allen. A dozen smaller lakes and rivers are sprinkled throughout the county. Apart from water sports and boating, the chief attraction is Strokestown House, the historic Pakenham home, a period piece from around the turn of the twentieth century. This is perfectly preserved, complete with children's nursery, restored garden and, a recent addition, an important museum of the Great Famine. Boyle is home to Boyle Abbey, a well-preserved, twelfth-century Cistercian monastery, and the local people run an imaginative arts festival every summer. Lough Kee Forest Park is popular for a family day out, with serviced camping, boat hire, cruises, wooded walks, a bog garden, a rhododendron plantation, an old estate chapel and an ice house.

STROKESTOWN HOUSE

Strokestown, County Roscommon; Tel: +078 33013; Fax: +078 33712 ▪ **Contact:** John O'Driscoll, Head Gardener ▪ **Open:** April–October, daily, 11am–5pm; open all year for pre-booked groups ▪ **Entrance fee** ▪ Supervised children welcome; please note, dogs on leads ▪ **Special features:** famine museum; shop; plants occasionally for sale ▪ **Directions:** set in the village of Strokestown, on the main Dublin–Ballina road (N5).

The Pakenham family moved to Strokestown in the 1660s, having been granted 27,000 acres by King Charles II. They first built the impressive Strokestown House, then followed it by creating one of the widest streets in Europe in the little village of Strokestown. The street, forty-four-and-a-half metres (147 feet) wide, was tree-lined and grand, indicative of the grandeur of the life the Pakenhams aspired to, living between Roscommon and London. The house itself was only recently vacated by the Pakenham family, in the 1970s, and is caught in a nineteenth-century time warp with all its contents intact. Now open to visitors, it is a fascinating piece of social history.

Strokestown House conjures images of feast and famine in a remarkable way. Once at the heart of some of the most dreadful suffering experienced during the great Famine of the mid-1840s, today the outhouses and stable blocks of Strokestown House are the venue for the country's most comprehensive Famine museum. This is slightly ironic as the family's record during the Famine years was not exactly unblemished: Henry Pakenham-Mahon, responsible for clearing tenants from his estates, was eventually assassinated for his efforts.

The most recent addition to Strokestown is the restored walled garden. From the 1740s on this area was used to grow fruit and vegetables, with a smaller 'slip garden' of glasshouses attached to provide the Pakenham dining-table with fresh peaches, melons and grapes. In 1890 Henry Pakenham-Mahon converted the walled area into a pleasure garden and moved the fruit and vegetables out to the smaller enclosure. His new garden covered four acres and employed an enormous number of workers to maintain it. By 1940, however, all maintenance had stopped and sheep and cattle were allowed in to graze where the immaculate flowerbeds and borders, pools and hedges had once stood. In 1979 the property was sold out of the family and one of the biggest restoration projects in the country was undertaken, unusually by a private company (Westward Motors), in partnership with the Great Gardens of Ireland Restoration Programme and FÁS. The enterprise has cost Westward Motors an enormous amount of money and expertise, and no doubt continues to do so. The gardens were redesigned by Helen Dillon, Jim Reynolds and Luke Dodd. They were then taken over by Rachel Lamb and Caitríona White and the result is a triumph. Scraping down to the original paths, the bones of the garden were pulled expertly into place and set back together.

The walled garden is entered through an ornamental gate, made in 1914, with the words 'EK Harmon' worked into the iron lacework. This was a gift to Olive Pakenham from her fiancé, Edward Harmon. (Edward was to die in the trenches at Ypres, Belgium, shortly afterwards.)

The herbaceous border is the biggest in Ireland or Britain, according to the *Guinness Book of Records*, and is based on the original, 1890 long border. In replanting, elements of the rainbow spectrum were used, and the colours run from blue to yellow, orange, red, pink, purple and lilac. As an advertisement for organic gardening, the border couldn't be more spectacular. It includes big stands of heavily scented nodding crinum lilies, and plume poppies (*Macleaya*), reaching two to three metres in height. In August, yellows and oranges come into their own and the bed puts on a great late summer and autumn show. Huge fennel plants, ligularia with acid yellow flowers on top of black stems, red-hot pokers (*Kniphofia*), goldenrod (*Solidago*), fringed inula flowers and red geum shout at each other for attention. From one end to the other, the gauzy shades of colour melt into each other along the border that runs the length of the wall. It faces south, 'as all the best borders should,' according to Head Gardener John O'Driscoll. 'This is a great bed,' he continues, well pleased with his charge, 'it keeps going right through to the first frosts.'

The summerhouse in the centre of the walled garden was copied faithfully from an old photograph, which shows Olive Pakenham as a tiny girl sitting inside the original building with her nanny. A copy of this photo is now on the wall of the recreated summerhouse. Outside the summerhouse, the original hoops of an old croquet set are still arranged around the lawn, conjuring up a picture of genteel, turn-of-the-century croquet parties. A salvaged window from the house was turned into a folly, which draws the visitor across to a central pond and yew walk. The pond dates to the 1780s and was so overgrown when restoration began that full-sized trees had to be removed from it. Delicate white water lilies now decorate the water.

The rose garden is mostly made of new hybrid tea roses, old roses climbing over obelisks and swags meeting on ropes. It features a pergola of local stone and Irish oak.

Luke Dodd designed the Alphabet Walk. This is an *allée* of beech trees, with two serpentine lengths of hedging spanning the width of the garden. It contains a series of semicircular niches or bays, each waiting for a piece of alphabetically appropriate sculpture. It may be some years before the niches are filled with sculptures, but the idea is clever, and even unadorned the *allée* is handsome.

In the last year the restoration of the vegetable garden began. This included major work on the old glasshouses, which had all but disintegrated since the 1930s. The final feature is an unusual Georgian teahouse, the first-floor tearoom of which is reached by an outside staircase. As the saying goes, when we begin to build follies it is God telling us that we have too much money. Repairing them is probably a sign that the work is nearing completion.

GARDENING CLUBS

ROSCOMMON FLOWER AND GARDEN CLUB, THE

The Roscommon club meets on the fourth Monday of the month, between October and May, in the Abbey Hotel in Roscommon town at 8pm. The meetings occasionally cover flower-arranging but concentrate mainly on gardening topics. Meetings comprise talks by visiting and local speakers, slide shows and demonstrations. In May an outing to a large garden is arranged and at Christmas a show is arranged in conjunction with local nurseries and garden centres. New members and visitors are always welcome.

NURSERIES AND GARDEN CENTRES

ARDCARNE GARDEN CENTRE

Ardcarne, Boyle, County Roscommon; Tel: +079 67091.

ARDCARNE GARDEN CENTRE

Lanesboro Road, Roscommon town, County Roscommon; Tel: +0903 27700.

HAWTHORN NURSERY

Lisheen, Strokestown, County Roscommon; Tel: +078 33734.

MULVEY'S GARDEN CENTRE

Hodson Bay Road, Kiltoon, County Roscommon; Tel: +0902 94288.

COUNTY SLIGO

Sligo is a wonderful county. Benbulben is an incredibly powerful sight, an inspiration to artists and writers through the centuries, and can be seen from all parts of the county. The climb up to Queen Medb's tomb on top of Knocknarea is rough, but it is worth it for the reward of breathtaking views of Donegal, Achill Island and the Nephin mountain range in County Mayo. Dramatic seas and beautiful beaches, such as Rosses Point, deliver big Atlantic rollers for surfers. Beside Enniscrone beach, the Kilcullen family has been offering seaweed health baths since 1912. The tombs at Carrowmore, spread across several fields, make up a huge Megalithic cemetery. There are over thirty tombs here, ranging from simple stone mounds to chamber tombs that the determined can crawl into. Sligo town is spoilt for art, with both the Sligo Art Gallery in the WB Yeats' Memorial Building and the Model Arts Centre. For Yeats enthusiasts, the name of Yeats is omnipresent, from Drumcliff Church to just about every location in the county. A scenic Yeats drive covers a 250-kilometre route, with brown quill-and-inkstand signs taking in all the William Butler and Jack Yeats sites.

GLENWOOD

Carrowmore Road, County Sligo; Tel: +071 61449 ▪ **Contact:** Frank and Anna McKiernan ▪ **Open:** for the first two weeks in August, daily, 2pm–6pm; otherwise write for an appointment ▪ **Entrance fee** ▪ **Directions:** leave Sligo on the Carrowmore Road. Turn left at the sign for Carrowmore Horse Centre and travel for just over 3km. The house, a redbrick building, is on the right-hand side, very close to the Carrowmore Megalithic tombs.

The McKiernans's three-quarter-acre garden hits you with a bang. It is a burst of colour in the middle of the fields – wild yellows, oranges, pinks and every other colour in the spectrum. It is overwhelmingly a flower garden, filled with begonias, penstemons, petunias, dahlias, gladioli and big beds of red roses. A little lily pond sits demurely in the midst of the loudly colourful beds.

The McKiernans began gardening on this site in 1984, and since then it has featured on a number of television gardening programmes as well as winning several Shamrock awards. This is high-maintenance horticulture, not for the faint-hearted or work-shy. There are so many pots, tubs, hanging baskets and elaborate, almost candelabra-like container holders, carrying a great number of baskets full of petunia, begonia, lobelia and aubrieta, that they fill every spot not already the site of a border or rockbed. Each tub and box needs constant care throughout summer to keep it looking as it should, and the care lavished on them in this garden is extraordinary. Height is brought into the garden with trees like cherry, cordylines and lines of topiarised conifers.

For those planning a flower garden, Glenwood is a must – there is plenty of invaluable advice and ideas to be gleaned from the McKiernans's beautiful garden.

GARDEN CENTRES

GALLAGHER'S GARDEN CENTRE

Ballymote, Tobercurry, County Sligo;
Tel: +071 85513.

GREEN LEAF GARDEN CENTRE

Strandhill Road, Sligo, County Sligo;
Tel: +071 62321.

GLYNN'S HOUSE AND GARDEN

Pearse Road, Sligo, County Sligo; Tel:
+071 60060.

WATERGLADES GARDEN CENTRE

Tobernalt, Sligo, County Sligo; Tel:
+071 60445.

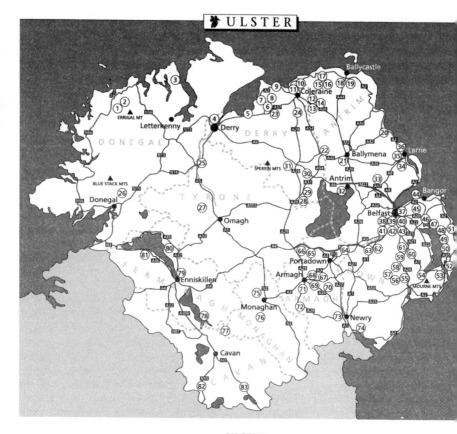

ULSTER

COUNTY ANTRIM

Antrim is the holiday county of Northern Ireland, blessed with magnificent natural advantages. The wild North Sea dominates the north and east coasts and the long coast road (A2) presents the tourist with some of the most spectacular sights on the island. The Giant's Causeway is a World Heritage Site and nature reserve, while the nearby Carrick-a-Rede rope bridge is a memorable experience for anyone with a good head for heights. The Glens of Antrim, a string of hills running inland from the east coast, rise impressively over lush, fertile and sheltered valleys. Along the coast there are a number of quaint villages, like Glenarm and Cushendall, and just outside Larne is the Carnfunnock Country Park. As well as managing many historic properties, the National Trust maintains a series of paths and walks throughout Northern Ireland. In Antrim, it maintains two coastal paths along the north coast that take in some of the most beautiful scenery on the island.

The north's capital city, Belfast, has been undergoing a heady rejuvenation since the ceasefires and peace talks of the last few years. Cafés, shops and restaurants are opening throughout the city and the tourists are returning once more to rediscover one of Ireland's most delightful and hospitable cities. New buildings, such as the beautiful new Waterfront Theatre and Ormeau Baths Art Gallery, have enlivened the urban landscape and the cultural life of the city. In addition, Belfast is home to a great number of parks which are of interest to gardeners. The Botanic Gardens, Grovelands and Sir Thomas and Lady Dixon Park are immensely popular with natives and visitors alike, and are filled with horticultural delights. Malone Park, which lies by the River Lagan and is attached to the late Georgian mansion in Barnett Demesne, is a lovely place to walk in the spring when the daffodils, rhododendrons and azaleas are blooming. The larger park is also a popular place for orienteering. Belfast Castle is set in the middle of Cave Hill Country Park, a large park incorporating a substantial wood, a big adventure playground for children and a garden themed around cats. County Antrim represents all hues of gardening, from the best urban plots to the best sprawling country estates.

ANTRIM CASTLE GARDENS

Clotworthy Arts Centre, Randalstown Road, Antrim, County Antrim; Tel: +094 428000 ■ **Contact:** the Administrator ■ **Open:** all year round, every day, twenty-four hours; groups welcome and guided tours available ■ **No entrance fee,** apart from organised guided tours ■ Supervised children welcome; please note, dogs on leads ■ **Special features:** art gallery, telephone for details of opening hours ■ Managed by Antrim Council ■ **Directions:** the entrance is off the Randalstown Road (A6), about 150m from the Ballymena Road (A26).

The gardens at Antrim Castle are unique in Northern Ireland. Along with Killrud-dery in County Wicklow, they are the only remaining example on the island of a style of gardening almost completely wiped out by later tastes and fashions. In the 1600s this style, which was born and developed in France and Holland, began to infiltrate these islands. These gardens spoke of grandeur, importance, power and confidence, and involved the creation of large and elaborate water features. Vistas or views were created across the land by cutting long *allées* or paths through woods and avenues of trees. Particularly in the French gardens, this enabled the garden to spill out into the land beyond and thus appear even bigger than it was. An important feature of the fashion was order and symmetry. Symmetrically arranged walks and *allées* made of pleached trees, often lime trees (*Tilia x. europaea*), trained like hedges on stilts, were developed to create interesting walks between features. The French designer André Le Nôtre is the most renowned gardener in this style. His designs for King Louis IV at Versailles and Les Tuileries are the best-known of these gardens.

In the mid-1600s, Sir Hugh Clotworthy, and later his son Sir John (the first Vis-count Masserene), created an impressive Anglo-French garden at their lands in County Antrim, which were attached to the new manor house on the site of an older fortified castle. The garden was made up of ornamental canals, a parterre garden, a round pond and an ancient motte. This gargantuan creation was executed at a time when the country around was in a state of civil chaos, making the achievement of their fine garden even more remarkable. Sir Hugh built the castle in 1613 and be-tween that date and 1662, amid the arrival of Oliver Cromwell, violently resisted plantations and civil war, he and Sir John completed the beautiful gardens. Today the castle is gone, burnt in a huge fire that swept through the buildings during a grand ball in 1922. The arts centre is located in the buildings that were once the stable block, converted to living accommodation after the fire and subsequently occupied by the Clotworthy family until 1956.

The gardens cover over twenty-six acres and surround the arts and visitors' centre. It was intended that the visitor be awed by the size, style, manpower and wealth em-ployed in creating the spectacle of these gardens, and this visitor was certainly awed. The main feature of the garden is the parterre. It is an immaculately laid-out vision of white pea gravel, ruler-straight box-edged beds and yew topiary, divided by wide paths and straight lines. Within the box beds there is herbaceous planting of primula, ber-genia, eryngium, dianthus, lysimachia and herbs, many of which are true to period. A smart series of pleached limes stands at one end of the parterre, surrounded by fine, tall hornbeam hedges and tall yew. These are all well maintained and look like differ-ent shades of green curtain or wall.

The long canal and cascades are beautiful and impressive, filled with lilies and lined with more clipped lime and hornbeam. A pet cemetery is flanked by a suitably sombre grove of huge yew trees. There is a round pond at the end of one of the tree-lined avenues. The trees are in the style of other seventeenth-century 'wildernesses', planted in blocks of ordered lines.

A most unusual feature is the motte. A motte is a man-made hill on top of which a fortification is built. The Normans introduced these to Ireland and the country is still littered with the banked-up remains. The crowning fortifications were always built of wood and therefore disintegrated, leaving no trace for archaeologists. The motte at Antrim Castle was cleverly incorporated into the garden design, rising up impres-sively in the middle of the garden to create a viewing mount. A spiral path leads up the little hill, bringing the viewer up to enjoy the best view of the gardens. Unfortunately, at the moment, and for the foreseeable future, it is wrapped in locked fencing while conservation work is carried out. Anyone wishing to climb the motte can hire a key at the arts centre for a deposit of stg£5 (refundable on return of key).

Please note that caution is necessary when visiting the park. It is a big city garden and should be visited with company: it is far too isolated to visit alone.

BALLYHIVISTOCK HOUSE

Ballymoney, County Antrim; Tel: +020 741155 ▪ **Contact:** Mr D Stewart-Moore ▪ **Open:** May–July, strictly by appointment only, telephone for a booking; groups welcome ▪ **Entrance fee** donated to charity ▪ Supervised children welcome ▪ **Special features:** a breathtaking man-made lake ▪ **Directions:** 1.5km from Bushmills on the B66, turn at the sign on the right for North Antrim Turkeys.

Ballyhivistock is part of a network of fine gardens in and around Benvarden Estate. Mr Stewart-Moore bought the house back in the 1960s for the thousands of crocuses that grew in the front lawn. By now the numbers must be up in the hundreds of thousands. In any case, there are masses and masses of them to cheer up the late winter and early spring, like a sprinkling of beads all over the turf. The visit begins with a walk along the path through the woodland that fronts and sides the handsome, double-fronted house. The woods, made up of purple beech, cherry and lime, lead down to the lake.

Mr Stewart-Moore has been gardening at Ballyhivistock since the 1960s when, and it is hard to believe this, the area was a field, soggy and boggy. He became tired of losing tractors to its soppy soil and thus the idea of a lake came about – it now looks as though it has been here forever. White foxgloves flower in the damp, speckled shade until August, as do the shuttlecock ferns whose self-seeded offspring are everywhere. The lakeside is deeply planted with trilliums and orchids, lilies and candelabra primulas in great runs. Bergenia, Lady's mantle and hosta sweep along, interrupted only by impressive patches of Himalayan blue poppies (*Meconopsis grandis*), which Mr Stewart-Moore is particularly adept at growing. In fact, he opens the garden briefly at the end of May so that visitors may view the poppies. There are also great masses of tall *Primula denticulata* all around the lake along with mourning widow (*Geranium phaeum*). The lake is inhabited by neat little white call ducks and koi carp, and growing by the water is rich purple willow gentian, which mixes well with *Meconopsis betonicifolia* and kirengeshoma, a beautiful perennial with healthy leaves, yellow flowers, rotund buds and dark stems – one of the great have-it-all perennials. Work is ongoing around the lake and one of the new additions is a minuscule island, again stone-edged and planted with ferns and hellebores surrounding a huge beech tree. There are also more marsh orchids, primulas and a spindle tree (*Euonymus europaeus*) with *Tropaeolum speciosum* through it.

The path travels on to the old walled garden, or what remains of it – a semicircular wall and long herbaceous border. A substantial wisteria was the only plant here when Mr Stewart-Moore took over. This is now being trained over a pergola, along with a pink *Clematis montana*. Leaving the main front and side gardens for the smaller, more intimate areas around the buildings, behind the house is an earthen mound of unknown origin, possibly older than the house itself; maybe a fairy hill or a viewing mound. This intriguing little hill overlooks a rockery with a good collection of alpines, like trout lilies (*Erthroniums*), violets and other low-growing things.

The final treat at Ballyhivistock is a secret garden. Once a barn used as a pheasant house, it is now roofless but houses the most sheltered of tropical gardens, sporting exotic Chilean bellflowers (*Lapageria rosea*), tree ferns, *Lilium giganteum*, large-leafed rhododendron and pots of small and varied ferns. This is 'the jungle', a damp, warm and exotic place with a glass starry wall made by Mr Stewart-Moore's daughter, which looks like an Indian mirror pattern. A dark laburnum walk with underplanting of hellebores leads out of the secret garden. All in all, Ballyhivistock is an impressive country garden with style and exceptional plants.

BALLYLOUGH HOUSE AND GARDEN

Bushmills, County Antrim; Tel: +020 731219 ▪ **Contact:** Mr and Mrs RS Traill ▪ **Open:** during the summer months, by appointment only ▪ **Directions:** from the A26 at Ballymoney, turn right onto the B66 for Dervock, 2.5km from Bushmills. The garden is on the right-hand side with a blue-and-white cottage and stone gateway marking the entrance.

The walled garden at Ballylough is a lovely, relaxed place; a bit loose and all the nicer for it. Both husband and wife work together on this laid-back summer garden. 'This used to be divided into twenty-seven beds,' explains Mrs Traill, who says that the garden was, as it sounds, too messy. The twenty-seven beds have been taken out one by one, making a better-looking, more solid garden structure. The walled garden covers two and a half acres. Leaving it, the path travels out towards a small lake via a plantation of beech and copper beech underplanted with bluebells. The wildflower meadow holds more than twenty-nine different wildflowers, including pyramidal orchids, wild strawberries, violets, purple and white bugle, scabious and butterwort.

Off the main wall, near the gate into the walled garden, is an interesting and unusual series of low walls with different house leeks (*Sempervivum*), sedums and wall plants. There are trellises everywhere with roses over them, including a wildly enthusiastic *Rosa* 'Rambling Rector'. Some of the prettier flowers scattered through the randomly placed beds are small potentilla, with creamy-white flowers and silver, hairy leaves, red salvia, different varieties of angel's fishing rods (*Dierama*) and balloon flowers (*Platycodon*). There is a little bed of double primroses and beside it one of the other stars is the collection of hellebores. These do well, says Mrs Traill, because the minute January comes she chops off every dead leaf, which prevents mice or slugs taking the flowers. She does this on the advice of an old gardener and says it pays off.

In the greenhouse a 150-year-old vine produces delicious muscat grapes and is heavy with fruit. Rows of beans share the rest of the greenhouse space with a *Solanum crispum* 'Glasnevin', which is chopped back to nothing every year 'and it loves it', repaying the hacking with vigorous growth and plenty of flowers

Mrs Traill has her favourite plants, like *Campanula lactiflora,* and as favourites they are indulged and allowed to raid other beds. 'When something else dies it just crops up and I leave it,' she says, and it is easy for her to forgive such a happy, pretty self-seeder. The Traills's garden is a delight and they are enthusiastic gardeners, full of stories about their garden and valuable gardening tips for the interested visitor.

Ballybogey, Ballymoney, County Antrim; Tel: +020 741331 ■ **Contact:** Mr and Mrs Hugh Montgomery ■ **Open:** June–August, Tuesday–Sunday and bank holidays, 1.30pm–5.30pm; groups may book in advance for tours in May and September ■ **Entrance fee** goes towards garden upkeep ■ Supervised children welcome ■ **Special features:** farm implement museum; unusual twenty-seven-metre-long iron bridge that was built by the family in 1878 ■ **Directions:** from the main Belfast–Coleraine road, take the B62 ring road toward Portrush. At Ballybogey turn right and follow the B67 for 2.5km. Just before the bridge over the River Bush turn right and go through the iron gates.

Benvarden, which lies by the River Bush, houses one of the oldest continuously cultivated walled gardens on the island. The two-and-a-quarter-acre walled garden appears on maps going back to 1788 and is a model of its type, still worked impressively. However, there was a garden here prior to that, dating back to the 1600s. The Montgomery family has been living and gardening here since 1798.

In the walled garden, many new plantings have been added since the beginning of the 1990s. Unusual double rows of box hedging enclose the herb and flowerbeds. These long runs are clipped higher on the outside, framing the series of beds within like subsets. Around the outer walls are deep herbaceous borders filled with all the usual garden flowers: classic spires of delphiniums, irises and campanula rise and fall in waves of soft, pretty colours along the length of the garden walls. The divisions in the garden also include a radiating rose garden, which is edged in rough stone that travels out from a central fish pond with a small fountain. A pergola with wisteria and herbs sits beside a glasshouse full of ripening peaches and grapes. Everywhere there are arches covered in scented roses. There is a good mixed border of hydrangea, abutilon, roses, fuchsia and rhododendron. An old tennis court and summerhouse sit

The bridge over the River Bush at Benvarden, County Antrim.

ready for an old-fashioned tennis party. Also within the walled garden is an interesting item – the restored garden bothy. This is where the garden boy in charge of stoking the hothouse boilers would have slept.

The area within the walled garden has been divided into well-defined plots. Separated from the leisured world of tennis parties is the vegetable garden, where huge beds are railed in military fashion and filled with neat rows of box, like stout, low, green walls. Regimental lines of strawberries march along the beds of lettuce in matching colour rows and peas stand to attention on parade. To actually pick anything from these sumptuous rows would feel like a crime. The fat tomatoes in the greenhouse, guarded by marigolds, are almost as perfectly arrayed. There are asparagus beds, apples on the walls and a lovely sundial dating to 1705.

Beyond the walled garden is the parkland, which includes a walk down through yew, copper beech, pines, rhododendron and willow to a woodland pond planted around with ferns and other damp-loving plants. The path continues on toward the River Bush, which is spanned by an elegant ninety-foot iron bridge that was built in 1878 by an ancestor of the Montgomerys, one Robert Montgomery.

THE BOTANIC GARDENS

Botanic Avenue, Belfast, County Antrim; Tel/Fax: +090 324902; e-mail: maxwellr@belfastcity.gov.uk ▪ **Contact:** Reg Maxwell ▪ **Open:** throughout the year, during daylight hours ▪ **No entrance fee** ▪ Supervised children welcome; please note, dogs on leads ▪ **Special features:** guided tours of the palm house and tropical ravine can be arranged; Victorian open days; concerts and garden parties in the summer months ▪ **Directions:** the gardens are about 0.5km from the city centre. Leave the Dublin Road, travelling south onto Botanic Avenue. The gates to the park are at the end of Botanic Avenue.

The Belfast Botanic Gardens are wonderfully well situated right in the centre of the city, close to Queen's University and the main shopping areas. As a result, the gardens are frequently visited, by visitors and natives alike, for leisurely walks, a quick short-cut, summer sunbathing as well as the more obvious pastime of plant studying.

The gardens were founded in 1828 following an upsurge of interest in botany and horticulture, which was fuelled by the thousands of new species being brought to Europe from the Americas and the Far East by plant hunters and explorers. The first large task undertaken in the new botanic gardens was the creation of a pinetum, a plantation of pines and conifers, as well as a collection of deciduous trees, mainly varieties of oak. These were laid out between 1838 and the 1850s and included trees like the newly discovered swamp cypress (*Taxodium distichum*) and a Douglas fir (*Pseudotsuga menziesii*), the sky-scraping false hemlock, brought to England only a few years before by one of the bravest plant collectors in history, David Douglas. The remains of these collections still stand today in front of the Ulster Museum, which is situated in the grounds of the gardens.

In 1839, a palm house was built to a design by the architect Sir Charles Lanyon (*see* Ballywalter Park, County Down). This was one of the first curvilinear glasshouses ever built and the work was carried out by Richard Turner, who modified the original design to make it more practical. ('Curvilinear' refers to the placement of the glass panes, arranged at angles to maximise the absorption of the rays of the sun.) The

Belfast palm house preceded the curvilinear ranges in both Kew Gardens and the Dublin Botanic Gardens. Some of the original plants placed in the palm house in the mid-nineteenth century still thrive today, including a heady *Rhododendron fragrantissimum*. The palm house is currently in the middle of vital restoration work.

However, in relation to glasshouses, Belfast's greatest claim to fame is the tropical ravine, built in the 1880s by the then curator Charles M'Kimm; it was built to resemble a sunken glen. Visitors enter by a door and walk through the warm damp-house on a raised mezzanine that overlooks the huge plants growing in the ravine below. This is a real jungle, steamy and hot, and still includes plants from the original Victorian layout. The dombeya is one of its famed plants, flowering in February and emitting the smell of caramel. There are orchids, tree ferns, bromeliads, sugar cane, papyrus and cinnamon. The plants are well illustrated and the ravine is one of the most breathtaking sights to be seen in any Irish garden.

The best walks through the park lead deep into the middle of the garden and take in the great double borders of herbaceous perennials on one side and multiple varieties of swishing grasses on the other. Parallel to these is another double bed, even deeper, mixed on one side and largely herbaceous on the other. There is also a substantial rose garden.

The Botanic Gardens in Belfast are unlike those in Dublin, where education is a very important aspect of the work being carried out. The Belfast gardens are more of a pleasure ground than an educational facility. This is quite simply a good-looking, friendly, busy and wonderfully well used city park.

BROCKLAMONT HOUSE

2 Old Galgorm Road, Ballymena, County Antrim; Tel: +025 641459 ▪ **Contact:** Mr and Mrs Louis and Margaret Glynn ▪ **Open:** by appointment only; groups welcome ▪ **Entrance fee** donated to charity and goes towards garden upkeep ▪ Supervised children welcome; please note, dogs on leads ▪ **Special features:** meals can be arranged, but must be booked in advance; the garden holds seventy types of snowdrop ▪ **Directions:** leaving Ballymena town on the A42 to Portglenone, the garden is 0.75km outside the town on the right-hand side and marked by big iron gates, which stand opposite the exit from Ballymena Academy.

The house on Old Galgorm Road is Victorian and sits on a two-and-a-half-acre garden that is worked skilfully by Mrs Margaret Glynn. She is a talented and enthusiastic gardener with a feel both for plants and for design – a rare combination.

Enter through the wonderful old gates, past a little gravel garden and carpets of *Viola labradorica*, corsican mint, little campanulas, sedums and little cushions of hepaticas. Close by the house are troughs, loads of troughs, all perfect, like rows of Lilliputian gardens, full of very small alpine plants and tastefully displayed rock plants. Set into the patio are yet more troughs, very cleverly used, chunky pots and gravel beds with more alpines. There is just one splash of colour here – a vibrant red poppy in the gravel.

Running out from the house an old walled garden has been converted and is now a patio and terrace that catches plenty of sun. The patio divides the herbaceous border on one side from the annual border on the other. Someone called the two borders the Botticelli garden, as it is all scent and colour and voluptuousness, and this description gives Mrs Glynn great pleasure. Mixed poppies, cosmos, periwinkles and osteospermum vie with each other for admiration. This is the only part of the garden where straight lines are allowed.

Mrs Glynn's favourite plants are irises, hellebores, geraniums and ferns. She has built a special little fernery leading down to a pool overlooked by acers, euonymus and *Geranium* 'Ann Folkard'. By this bridged pool a lovely wedding cake tree (*Cornus controversa* 'Variegata') and a white hydrangea make a combination to die for. Beyond this area open lawns fall away from the house, reigned in by a low clipped hedge of lonicera, and on out to a little woodland where primulas run riot under the trees, with trilliums, gunnera and aquilegia. Mrs Glynn's latest project is a hosta bank in a dry, shaded area of the woods, under the trees.

One last thing: remember to ask to see the compost system. This is the most impressive, smart and tidy-looking system I've ever encountered, comprising long, deep bins held in by galvanised metal walls. One bin is filled with newly composted material beginning its rot-down, while the other is filled with sweet-smelling, dark-brown compost ready to go to work in the garden. We would all do well to take a leaf out of this organic book.

CARNFUNNOCK COUNTRY PARK

Larne, County Antrim; Tel: +028 270541 ■ **Contact:** Alison McKeegan, Park Manager ■ **Open:** daily; groups welcome ■ **No entrance fee**, but there is a parking charge ■ Supervised children welcome ■ **Special features:** family attractions, including miniature train and maze; children's play area; nine-hole golf course plus driving range ■ **Directions:** travelling from Larne to Glenarm on the A2, the park is on the left, just outside of Glenarm.

With views out over the Antrim Coast, the two-acre walled garden of the Carnfunnock Estate has been newly planted and designed in contemporary style. Run by the Larne Borough Council as a public amenity, Carnfunnock Country Park is, somewhat unusually, a garden without a house. The garden is laid out in a pattern that is heavy on shrubs and good hedging, with a network of walks and a big circle of hornbeam. A Time Garden with a fascinating collection of different sundials has been arranged within the walls. The sundials are set within the separate hedged rooms and provide a visual chart of the progress of time-keeping instruments over the centuries. They all operate in diverse and sometimes unfathomable ways. One clever example is made of marble slabs set into the grass; several others are wall-mounted and a good number are the more usual free-standing sculptural types.

One of the gardens is a little room made up of box beds filled with penstemon and nicotiana, each with a central tall cordyline, once again hedged in with more fat hornbeam hedges. There are some brilliant colour mixes, such as red begonia bedding in front of blue lobelia.

Children will enjoy the big hornbeam maze – complete with a helpful viewing stand to aid escape. There is also a wildlife garden and walk. The gardens have been made accessible to wheelchairs with concrete paths.

Lose the children in the maze. Place the Thomas the Tank Engine fans on the tiny train. Send teenagers to the golf range, then escape to the garden and everyone can meet for a walk by the sea when they are finished. Carnfunnock Estate is a lovely place for a family day out.

The prettiest sundial from among a fascinating collection of garden timepieces at Carnfunnock Country Park in Larne, County Antrim.

50 CASTLEHILL PARK

Off Castlehill Road, Stormont, Belfast; Tel: +090 763665 ▪ **Contact:** Mrs Joan Christie ▪ **Open:** April–September, weekends, by appointment only; groups welcome ▪ **Entrance fee** donated to the National Trust ▪ **Supervised children welcome** ▪ **Special features:** teas available to small groups by prior arrangement ▪ Member of National Trust ▪ **Directions:** Castlehill Road runs between Upper Newtownards Road and Massey Avenue. Castlehill Park is halfway along on the Stormont side.

Mrs Christie was the BBC Ulster Gardener of the Year 1999. When I visited her garden she was preparing to go to London where she was to design a garden for the UK finals of the competition: 'Everyone else in the competition was glad I won because I don't think any of the other entrants wanted to go to London,' she explained as she led the way around her own exquisite, small town garden. At Castlehill Road she has effortlessly incorporated a number of different gardens within her plot and the description below will in no way do justice to the seamless, clever style of her work.

Forty years ago Joan Christie began building this garden, having arrived to a plot overgrown with huge evergreens, 'which were just so depressing we ripped them out'. She then began to put in pretty flower borders, a little pond, paths, good shrubs and, of course, the sculptures and standing stones.

The garden opens with a little woodland area filled with bluebells, snowdrops and other spring flowers. A pineapple broom (*Cytisus battandieri*) flowers happily in the shade where it does better than its partner out in the sun. In the woods there is a little retreat seat in which to sit and look out onto the garden. From here, step into the open where a *Magnolia liliiflora nigra* flowers from March to August. Like all good gardeners, Mrs Christie never gets too romantic about any one plant and is planning on uprooting a forty-year-old rhododendron in the interest of improving the little woodland area it is crowding out right now.

In one area there is a huge circle of elm framing a small acer and a white arum lily. Elsewhere she used the old stump of a long dead climber, blacked up and underplanted with black grass. Everywhere there are interesting little eye-catchers, for example, stones grouped together with succulents growing between them. Nearby a slab stone bench backs onto a great clump of sharp acanthus. A fine flowering eucryphia stands on one of the garden boundaries, alongside the many camellias raised from cuttings and an unnamed Slieve Donard seedling rhododendron. I loved the old shrub rose called 'Moonlight' with its soft white flowers.

There are little gravelled areas carpeted in tiny black pansies, all looking up together: 'Some years they all come out like that and some years they just don't appear.' Beside these is a real star of a plant: a tall, blackish angel's fishing rod (*Dierama*). I really enjoyed this garden and its diversity, but also the contemporary, modern feel of Mrs Christie's design.

CHAMBRELLY

5 Ballygowan Road, Larne, County Antrim; Tel: +028 272989 ▪ **Contact:** Rita O'Lynn ▪ **Open:** June–October, Monday–Sunday, telephone in advance for an appointment; groups welcome ▪ **Entrance fee** donated to the National Trust and the Heart Foundation ▪ Supervised children welcome; please note, dogs on leads ▪ **Special features:** teas are available to groups by prior arrangement ▪ **Directions:** travelling from Larne to Belfast, drive 3km beyond the end of the dual carriageway and turn left. The house is third on the right.

Mrs O'Lynn's modern bungalow at Chambrelly is barely visible under the network of creeping and climbing plants, roses, clematis and honeysuckle. There are hanging baskets, big ones, bursting with colour. Pots and tubs are scattered everywhere on the ground in front of the house. The gravel is set with hebe, potentilla, small rowan trees, hydrangea, ceanothus and lilies. Even the electricity post has been commandeered as an opportunity for climbers to do their thing. The overall effect is stunning: a mass of growth and colour, textures and mixtures.

The garden has only been up and running since the mid-1990s, but the O'Lynns work in it every day, almost full-time. This effort has produced an amazingly abundant garden, full of interest and surprise – like upturned boats used to make little arbours and arches covered in golden hop (*Humulus lupulus*). A walk of lupins, which Mrs O'Lynn calls the 'lupin lane', leads behind the house, into the garden and up onto a stone plateau that looks out over a sea of shasta daisies on one side and geraniums on the other. Mrs O'Lynn likes to use large patches of a single plant; over the little hill she has planted a great mass of cheery-looking, open-faced cosmos. She does everything with a real sense of punch. Mediterranean gardens and grass gardens are being developed alongside a grove of special trees, such as embothrium.

Expansion into the wilds beyond the garden began in 1999 when Mrs O'Lynn started to create a woodland walk and duck pond. She has already been a winner in the Antrim and Derry category of the Shamrock All Ireland Gardens Competition 1998, and at this rate she will undoubtedly garner many more tributes for her exquisite garden.

ULSTER • COUNTY ANTRIM

55 CLOVERHILL PARK

Belfast; Tel: +090 763782 ■ **Contact:** Mrs Esther Chapman ■ **Open:** by appointment only ■ **Directions:** Cloverhill Park is off the left-hand side of Massey Avenue, near the back gates to Stormont Castle.

The garden at Cloverhill Park is concentrated to the back of the house and really is an urban secret garden. A terrace is flanked by a wall simply dripping with *Cotoneaster procumbens*, moulding itself like a hard, green rock to whatever shape it meets. This display fronts a table-height spring rockery where the little delicacies are at just the right height for one to inspect and get a nose into – much the best way to inspect tiny alpines and rock plants.

From the terrace the garden leads down through a ravine. The ravine is sided by a steep bank that is divided into unusual, stone-fenced pockets, each holding small woodland plants: blue and white bells, scillas and snowdrops. This leads on to a fernery, which the Chapmans's children used to call 'the jungle', with Japanese painted fern and bright variegated hostas. The path back up to the rest of the garden is made of simple stepping stones through the bed. Mrs Chapman calls this the 'goat track', and she scrambles up through it like the most agile mountain goat.

Leaving this area leads you up to an orchard, which Mrs Chapman says is in need of spraying but adds that 'I haven't time to be spraying apple trees so what apples are there, we eat.' The unsprayed apple trees are being called into service as a trellis for a whole network of clematis, which she hopes will become a clematis walk in time. The greenhouse came down in a storm, but rather than lamenting it she used the base for nursery beds, in an admirable instance of mend-and-make-do.

Then it's on down to the grass walk. Mrs Chapman explains that the vegetable plot had become a bit too much work and so it was replaced with the grass garden. This is a great sweep of grasses of every description and size currently being inserted into the old lawn, which is being replaced gradually with boulders and gravel. Facing this long sweep is a herbaceous border, lovely in itself but competing for attention with the grass garden.

Advancing years are putting no curb on Mrs Chapman's expansionist tendencies as she continues to elbow out her three-quarter-acre garden. At the moment it is slowly moving outwards, taking over a new area that will eventually be a shady garden. Mrs Chapman works the garden herself, seeking help only with the lawn, and it stands as a testament to the energy and flair of an extraordinary tiny lady.

THE COTTAGE GARDEN PLANT CENTRE

154 Ballyrobert Road, Ballyclare, County Antrim; Tel: +093 22952 ■ **Contact:** Joy and Maurice Parkinson ■ **Open:** 1 May–15 October, Wednesday–Friday, 11am–7pm; Saturday, 11am–5pm; Sunday, 2pm–5pm; groups welcome ■ **Entrance fee** goes towards garden upkeep ■ Supervised children welcome; please note, dogs on leads ■ **Special features:** plant nursery, open 17 March–31 October, same times as above; winter nursery, open 16 November–March, Saturday, 11am–5pm; teas are available by prior arrangement only ■ **Directions:** just under 1km from the centre of Ballyrobert village, on the main Ballyclare Road. The centre is opposite the entrance to the golf club.

The Parkinsons have been gardening on this site for seven years. It is a cottage garden, attached, appropriately enough, to a very pretty old farm cottage. Lined out in front of the house are great healthy beds of herbaceous cottage plants: delphiniums, asters, irises, hollyhocks and violas. The beds are divided by colour and the more effective of these is the 'hot' bed, which is filled with a profusion of reds and wines, including chocolate cosmos (*Cosmos atrosanguineus*) – a plant to get children interested in gardening if ever there was one. All of the beds are very clearly labelled and are divided by wide grass paths. There is a well-tended box garden and a dovecote. Looking beyond the boundary of the garden to the wilds of rushes and weeds from which the Parkinsons wrested their garden, one can only marvel at their achievement. In addition to the cottage garden they have set up a little lake garden, a formal garden in the shape of a Celtic cross, a wildflower area and wild grass area.

A pretty nursery is attached to the garden. I particularly liked the way the herbaceous and cottage plants on sale were colour-grouped – a very attractive way to present plants that makes it easy to choose plants according to how you would like to coordinate any particular bed. This imaginative diversity and attention to detail make the garden and nursery very pleasurable to explore.

DRUMNAKEEL HERB GARDEN

Ballycastle, County Antrim; Tel: +020 763350 ▪ **Contact:** the Manager ▪ **Open:** throughout the year, Saturday–Sunday, 10am–6pm; May–September, Monday–Friday, 10am–6pm ▪ **No entrance fee** ▪ Supervised children welcome ▪ **Special features:** groups should book teas in advance; fresh herbs, vinegar, honey, jam and other local produce for sale ▪ **Directions:** situated on the road between Ballycastle and Cushendall.

This is a small herb garden, laid out formally in straight lines and grids. Beds of the usual herbs and salads are grown alongside more unusual things, like Good King Henry (*Chenopodium bonus henricum*) – also called Lincolnshire asparagus – an easy-to-grow salad crop, saffron, angelica, lovage and medicinal herbs, such as pulmonaria, yarrow and clary. Drumnakeel is a working garden that supplies herbs to the restaurants and hotels of County Antrim. Visit and see the plants growing, buy some herbs and have a cup of tea in the cosy cottage tearoom.

GLENARM CASTLE

Glenarm, County Antrim; Tel: +028 841203 ▪ **Contact:** Adrian Morrow or Cherry Robinson ▪ **Open:** 13–14 July each year, when plants are sold, teas are available and a crafts day is held; groups welcome ▪ **Entrance fee** goes towards garden upkeep ▪ Supervised children welcome; please note, dogs on leads ▪ **Special features:** crafts stalls; highland games and Strongest Man competitions ▪ **Directions:** Glenarm is on the A2, north of Larne. The castle is in the village. There are special parking facilities at the castle for disabled drivers.

Glenarm has been the home of the McDonnell family, earls of Antrim, since the seventeenth century. The front of the castle looks out over parkland and pleasure grounds and there are viewing points, balustraded and wrapped in roses. Stone steps lead down to an avenue of limes, beside a castellated wall complete with arrow holes and steps up to mock battlements and a tunnel. On the other side of the avenue is a great bank of ferns and at one end of the wall the barbican gate leads to the town.

The walled garden dates back to the mid-eighteenth century and covers four acres. This is a textbook walled garden: a model of order with neatly arranged beds of well-matched colours, lovingly tended and cared for. By the gate is a bed full of reds – pink love-lies-bleeding, pink everlasting sweet pea, ruby cosmos, red pheasant berry and cotinus – all rich, opulent colours to get the visitor in a good mood. In the wide beds, large flowering buddleia and tree peony are repeated over the length of the wall to give a sense of unity. Fruit trees are set into the lawn in the middle of the beds. Then more beds of purples, with *Papaver orientale* 'Patty's Plum', pale-pink fuchsia and purple pansy, blood-red roses and more purple poppies and salvia, toned down a little by hazy-bluish catmint (*Nepeta*).

A view through the clipped hedges at Glena in County Antrim.

Remaining within the walls of the larger garden, the vegetable garden is off to the side of the flowerbeds, another well-ordered place complete with gardener's cottage and potting sheds. A huge fig tree stands in place of one of the old greenhouses, which is now long dismantled. There are still great lengths of greenhouses, full of vines, peaches, climbers and almost iridescent blue plumbago.

This walled garden is full of surprises. A mirroring double border of silvers, blues, yellows and variegated foliage leads down to a central sundial surrounded by a tall yew circle. The sundial is in fact in the middle of a huge clump of fennel underplanted with borage and creeping golden thyme, but these are not apparent from outside the yew circle. The centre of each yew section leads out to a view. One of these is a clever serpentine *allée* of beech hedging leading to another feature – a beech circle with a raised pond that again leads off to another short beech avenue. Every time the visitor thinks they have seen the full extent of this garden, yet another pretty feature appears from around the corner.

The garden is not yet finished: there is still a lot of planting going on and a meadow area with standard trees and cut grass paths is one of the latest projects. This is a singular walled garden: ambitious, clever and attractive.

GROVELANDS

Stockman's Lane, Belfast, County Antrim; Tel: +090 320202 ▪ **Contact:** Alex McNeill ▪ **Open:** daily, until dusk, opening hours change every two to three weeks; groups welcome ▪ **No entrance fee** ▪ Supervised children welcome; please note, dogs on leads ▪ **Special features:** small exhibition gardens ▪ Managed by Belfast City Council ▪ **Directions:** situated in Musgrave Park, by the side of Musgrave Hospital, in the southeast of the city. Musgrave Park, which contains Grovelands, is situated on the left of Stockman's Lane if you are travelling from Balmoral Avenue. It is easiest to enter it from the grounds of Musgrave Park Hospital.

Grovelands is a gorgeous, secluded garden, just off one of Belfast's busiest roads. It comprises a set of display gardens, including seasonal bedding, heather gardens, conifer beds and herbaceous borders, all set against runs of lawn, alpine beds and raised beds at a perfect height for a disabled gardener. Paths run in serpentine fashion in and around large stands of rhododendron, which look good from early spring right up to mid-summer and are particularly popular with wedding groups. Apart from the wheelchair-accessible paths, there is a network of grass paths, with stone steps that seem to grow out of the hilly lawns to join them to each other. Grass paths wander blindly into rough, tall, wildflower meadows and circles of beech trees. There are banks of conifers and heathers and long mixed beds with red geum, varieties of hardy geranium and welsh poppies, which have also migrated into the conifer beds where they lighten up the green considerably.

At the front of the garden is an attractive Japanese area with a bridged pond full of huge koi carp and well-matched cut-leaf acers, chaenomeles and marginal green plants. The stone-cobbled paths are encroached on every side by low-growing variegated grass, creeping white nettle and London pride (*Saxifraga x. urbium*). Nearby, a greenhouse full of tiny cacti and succulents leads out to a little formal box garden, where the box frames different aquiligea, like 'Nora Barlow', as well as English marigolds, purple pansies and tulips.

Deep within the garden is the bog garden, a gorgeous, sunken place within a circle of stone-walled banks. Euphorbia and shuttlecock ferns run around the edge, while hosta, astilbe, iris and gunnera grow enthusiastically in the damp grass below.

Grovelands is a pleasant, varied garden. The garden's boundary is marked by very attractive double hedges. The outer, beech hedge changes colour through the year and this is fronted by a rich green yew hedge. These contrast with each other well and muffle the traffic sounds and smells from the road beyond the garden.

54 KILREA ROAD   ♿

Portglenone, County Antrim; Tel: +025 821420 ▪ **Contact:** Mr Robert Gordon ▪ **Open:** May–September, Monday–Friday, by appointment only; groups welcome ▪ **Entrance fee** donated to charity ▪ Supervised children welcome ▪ **Directions:** leave Portglenone on the A42, travelling west. Turn right for the Kilrea Road and travel 0.5km. The garden is on the left, with a stone gateway.

Mr Gordon started his garden in 1966 with three flowerbeds. In 1970 he joined the Belfast branch of the Alpine Garden Society and, as with many people who discover enthusiasm and knowledge in one place, his career as a gardener took off. His garden is now one that other gardeners speak of with respect and not a little envy. He has been featured on BBC gardening programmes several times and throughout the island his fans speak warmly of his achievements. Enquiring as to the size of the garden

I was told 'over a quarter of an acre', and sure enough it is over a quarter of an acre – I would guess about five or six times over that modest estimate! Robert Gordon works this large space himself, all day, every day.

A scree bed was being remade when I visited. It looked good, but he nevertheless felt it had done its job and grown beyond usefulness. Showing no mercy, he was about to give it the chop and replace it with younger, fresher plants. Robert has a selection of fine trees dotted throughout the garden in groves: Serbian spruce (*Picea omorika*), southern beech (*Nothofagus*), Brewer's weeping spruce (*Picea breweriana*), tulip tree (*Liriodendron tulipifera*), false acacia (*Robinia pseudoacacia*) and tupelo (*Nyssa sylvatica*). In from the trees, galtonia, white phlox, *Codonopsis* and metre-high Nepalese poppies (*Meconopsis napaulensis*) make incredibly good-looking plants. Effusive beds of American white poppies, spiky-stemmed *Meconopsis horridula*, blue gentians and *Actaea alba*, a lovely plant with porcelain-white berries and black eyes, absolutely cry for attention. Mr Gordon works on clay soil, which holds moisture, and he takes advantage of this by growing damp-loving poppies that repay the compliment by growing up to two metres high. The candelabra primulas and irises love it too.

Throughout the garden there are peonies with seedheads like little jewel boxes, hellebores, snowdrops and a spiny sea holly (*Eryngium alpinum*). Self-seeded eucalyptus trees are regularly pollarded to expose the juvenile, good-looking leaves and foliage. Out on the drive the back of a bed is seen to be full of yet more poppies, primulas, a fine snowball tree and a California poppy tree (*Romneya coulteri*). On the other side of the drive is a golden acer and a Himalayan birch (*Betula utilis jacquemontii*) with a peachy-cream bark. The stream garden, which runs alongside and parallel to the driveway, is full of trilliums, more primula and strange, alien-looking arisaema.

Robert Gordon has arranged the garden so that there are vistas in all directions. Looking through one group of trees a view of something even more attractive pulls the eye, and the browser, off in another direction. An alpine-house stuffed with wonderfully arranged gravel-dressed pots full of little treasures, from the sublime to the even more sublime, finishes off the visit. Mr Gordon is the perfect host, generous with advice and information on his fine garden.

SCREE BED

A scree bed is an imitation of a very specialised habitat where the top 15cm or so is made up of small broken stones and rocks. This free-draining layer means that the 'necks' of the plants do not sit in damp soil, while the roots enjoy a cool, damp run. In the wild, scree beds are found on mountain tops.

LESLIE HILL FARM

Ballymoney, County Antrim; Tel: +027 666803 ▪ **Contact:** James and Elizabeth Leslie ▪ **Entrance fee** goes towards garden upkeep ▪ Supervised children welcome; please note, dogs on leads ▪ **Special features:** adventure playground; gift shop; petting zoo; farm machinery museum; rare-breed farm animals; coachman's house; replica Victorian farm pay office; groups must book meals in advance ▪ **Directions:** signposted from the A26, 1km from Ballymoney.

Leslie Hill is one of those great-day-out gardens. Old farm buildings house ancient and strange farm machinery, rare-breed farm animals and a petting zoo. An authentic recreation of the Victorian farm pay office and the old coachman's house, maintained as they were when the last inhabitant vacated, will be of interest to all ages.

Leslie Hill Farm has been open for ten years, but the garden was only brought into the equation in the mid-1990s. It involved the same old story as many other gardens on the island: the walled garden was neglected for sixty years and is now being worked by a tiny number of workers. So far the Leslies have two-thirds of the area in the walled garden restored. The greenhouses and hothouses date back to the 1760s and it is hoped that these will be rebuilt at some time soon. Classically, the longest of the garden walls is the sloped south-facing wall. An old palm-house once stood here, but standing in its place today is a pergola with a mass of pale-pink, sweetly perfumed *Rosa* 'Albertine' scrambling over it.

The garden, having been redesigned, is now worked solely, and impressively, by Mr and Mrs Leslie – a far cry from the teams of gardeners that once tackled the work. In their restoration work the Leslies dug down through the layers of debris to find the old paths. They then reinstated these carefully. A debate ensued as to whether or not they should faithfully recreate the old knot garden bed. In the end they resisted this idea and instead went for a softer, looser system of mixed and herbaceous beds.

Simple and effective schemes are in evidence everywhere. Down the middle of the garden is a good bed with blood-red roses edged by the grey-blue pallor of catmint. The long, wall-backed bed of *Anemone* 'Honorine Jobert' is a fine sight for anyone who likes this delicate-looking, tough-as-nails plant. This bed runs to almost nineteen metres in length. Close by is a sloped herb garden and an interesting little beech-hedged room that plays with the slopes and angles of the ground and has a contemporary feel to it. The garden is sloped in two ways, which gives it a strange, lop-sided, parallelogram-like feel. A really handsome central bed fronts rows of espaliered apples, and there is a Victorian rockery with a little central raised throne-like seat.

There are nature trails laid out around the park, accompanied by some fine trees, among them red oak, beech and cypress, as well as Norway maple and Noble fir. The wood floor is well covered with wood anemone, scilla, primrose, violet and ferns, snowdrops, aconites and bluebells. The names of the walks are charming, including the Holly Walk (which has no holly trees) and the darkly named Forbidden Walk. A lake bordered by flag irises, sedges, rushes and water plantain greets you at the end of one of the walks. The wildflowers and hedgerow plants are well protected and encouraged in this lovely park.

Leslie Hill is an enjoyable garden, set in grounds that will undoubtedly prove popular and educational for the whole family. The Leslies are still expanding and plan a bamboo room next.

MAGHERINTEMPLE

51 Churchfield Road, Ballycastle, County Antrim; Tel: +020 762234 ※ **Contact:** Mrs FC Casement ※ **Open:** May–August, Monday–Sunday, 2pm–5pm, by appointment only; small groups welcome ※ **Entrance fee** donated to the National Trust ※ Supervised children welcome ※ **Directions:** leave Ballycastle by the Glenshesk Road, then take the first turn left (approximately 1km). Magherintemple is 2.5km along Churchfield Road.

Magherintemple is a fine old blackstone house with a very special walled garden attached to it. Mrs Casement works this one-acre walled garden herself; indeed, like many of the best gardeners, she knows her plot intimately and would not trust it to anyone less acquainted with it. She started working the garden in 1972 when, as with so many, she inherited a mess of daisies, moss and not lawn but 'grass'. During the Second World War, Mr Casement's aunt lived in the house. She filled the house with children from an evacuated orphanage and used the garden to provide the fruit and vegetables needed to feed her young charges. After the war, the old lady 'sort of thought she gardened, but the place was in need of serious work,' explains Mrs Casement, who has personally put in that work for nearly twenty-eight years. She worked on the garden bit by bit, taking the longer borders a section at a time. Mrs Casement's garden is now famed among garden visitors. Although she was never formally trained, her years of enthusiasm have invested her with knowledge which, added to her natural flair, makes hers a special garden. Walking through it, past the chickens (including a daft bird who is terrified of everything, even its own mother, unfortunately), is a rewarding trip.

A little stream travels the length of the plot, allowing the planting of damp-loving plants in a good number of places and lending the sound of water and occasional glimpses of it. A mossy path meanders companionably beside a long border. This two-and-a-half-metre-wide bed looks even wider because it backs onto shrubs and fruit bushes. This bed is particularly handsome, filled with plum-coloured day lilies, penstemon, lavatera, blue cerinthe and catmint. There is a wide variety of penstemons; Mrs Casement thinks they are hybridising. There are big splashes of purple verbena and pink crocosmia, and around the corner is a lovely blue dayflower or widow's tears (*Commelina coelestis*). A new, small, pale sedum called 'Appledore' is the current favourite in this bed. Mrs Casement loves new things and manages to fit lots of them in without comprising the venerable countenance of this beautiful old garden. In the middle of all this is a series of beehives for the neighbours' bees; spoilt, lucky bees to live in this garden.

At the bottom of the garden, close to the lower wall, is the rock garden where a tigridia grows, a very tender plant but surviving in its sheltered spot and showing off tropical-looking flowers. The other enjoyable inhabitants here include pineapple-scented sage (*Salvia elegans*), 'Scarlet Pineapple', a good artemisia with white leaves and black stems, black-leafed lysimachia and shamrock pea (*Parochetus africana*) with tiny blue flowers. Also down here in the walled garden is the bog garden, which is an unusual affair: a damp and tropical place with a sunken pool of blue poppies, hostas, *Primula denticulata*, arum lilies (*Zantedeschia aethiopica*) and Pacific Coast irises. One of the remarkably good plants here is the Indian rhubarb (*Darmera peltata*), sporting huge leaves on two-metre-high stalks. This area looks best when you stand above it in late May or early June. Once upon a time this bog garden was a pond, but it sprung a leak and ceased working so Mrs Casement let the soil that seeps in with the stream stay put. This provided the humus necessary to make it a great growing area; sheltered and safe from the worst the weather might throw at it.

Back up the garden is a path of creeping Jenny, belts of bergenia and more blue poppies. Outside the main garden there is a smaller anteroom of sorts, called the box garden, where the stumps of three old elms have been clothed in strawberries and poppies. Along the wall of this garden is an old rose, holly, hydrangea and red, fringe-flowered *Berberidopsis corallina,* aptly named the coral plant.

177 MALONE ROAD

Belfast, County Antrim; Tel: +090 682274 ■ **Contact:** Dr and Mrs Hawkins ■
Open: May–June, 6pm–8pm and weekends, by appointment only; groups
welcome ■ **Entrance fee** donated to the National Trust ■ Supervised children
welcome ■ **Directions:** travelling south on the Malone Road, number 177 is on the
right-hand side.

On the busy Malone Road, behind a big screen of eucalyptus, ash, cherry, yew and
rhododendron, lies Mrs Hawkins's garden. She has been gardening here since the late
1980s, putting in some wonderful shrubs, trees and fine beds of flowers. Sweeps of
fritillaries, meconopsis and hellebores start the garden off in spring, flowering under a
big rhododendron. The house itself is clothed in climbing dicentra, wisteria, pineapple broom (*Cytisus battandieri*) and Virginia creeper.

The garden was originally an old strip farm, one of many that ran between the parallel Malone and Lisburn Roads. Strip farms once existed in great numbers, providing
householders with enough land to produce food, keep fowl and maybe even a pig or
two. The contours of these farms can be seen clearly on any map of Belfast. Nowa-
days, they make a decent-sized urban garden. This agricultural heritage bequeathed
Mrs Hawkins a well-worked, highly conditioned soil that she enjoys to this day. The
rhododendrons and roses love the good conditions, obligingly thriving for her. Running down the side of the garden are bamboo, tall grasses and more rhododendron, as
well as a fine pergola covered with winter jasmine and the large, white flowers of
Clematis 'Marie Boissolet'.

At the bottom of the garden, what was once the children's football patch is now
put to work as a bog garden populated with arum lilies. A pond is surrounded by blue
lacecap hydrangea and white *Hydrangea paniculata grandiflora*. A stone area full of
pebbles beside the pond is planted up beautifully with blue salvia, white phlox, blue
geranium, little asters and campanula.

O'HARABROOK

Bann Road, Ballymoney, County Antrim; Tel/Fax: +027 666273 ■ **Contact:** the
Cramsie family ■ **Open:** annual open days when plants are for sale, telephone for
dates; teas provided on open days, groups must book in advance; groups welcome
by prior arrangement, but big coaches will not fit up the avenue ■ **Entrance fee**
goes towards garden upkeep ■ Children welcome, but be wary of lake ■ **Directions:** take the B66 from Ballymoney toward Garvagh. Travel for 2.5km, passing
Enagh Road on the right. The gates for O'Harabrook are on the right-hand side.

The garden at O'Harabrook begins at the gate with a most extraordinary avenue of
beech set into a wider wood; it is worth a visit for the avenue alone. The trees are wonderfully tall, mature and slender. Along the drive the ruins of a Quaker school could
pass for a Gothic folly or the curve in an ancient castle, and there is a burial ground
called the Lambs' Fold.

The estate comprises a garden, a walled garden, woods, walk and lake and covers
about ten acres. It has been gardened continuously for over 100 years by the Cramsie
family. The garden around the house is attractive and the house itself, with a beautiful old conservatory, is covered in grand-scale wisteria and surrounded by a sprawl of

ULSTER • COUNTY ANTRIM

Looking across the naturalised daffodils that sheet the lawns in front of the house at O'Harabrook, County Antrim.

herbaceous plants, pots and shrubs. The conservatory is a delicate edifice, built in 1898. There are rhododendrons in banks around the house and a run of clipped yew over which the trees, including a big monkey puzzle tree (*Araucaria araucana*), bulge and hang. There are informal mixed beds set into the lawn.

The lake, which was created recently, is a beautiful feature and lies just down from and behind the house. However, the lake cannot be seen from the house because it is surrounded by a wide planting of mature trees – tall oaks and beech trees with owls flying between their branches. Beneath the bracken there are networks of meandering paths. In spring, great masses of daffodils spread out along the slope down from the house to the lake and trees.

Out to the front of the house, by the driveway, an avenue of yew trees marks the walk to the walled garden. The walled garden is a beauty, full of old-fashioned flowers like shasta daisies, tall angelica and mallow and arches everywhere covered in roses. The big border is filled with phlox, mallow, lychnis and gloriously scented mint. The old glasshouse has been planted up with primula, hosta, ferns, roses and pretty blue cornflowers. In the thriving vegetable garden nasturtium softens the lines of vegetables. The gravel garden is held together with mossy stone edgings. Ferns, oregano and thyme, under penstemons and crocosmia, provide more great herby scent and colour.

REDCOT

35 Kings Road, Belfast; Tel: +090 796614 ▪ **Contact:** Mr Knox Gass ▪ **Open:** May–September, by appointment only, telephone for booking; groups welcome ▪ **Entrance fee** donated to the Ulster Gardens Scheme ▪ Supervised children welcome ▪ **Directions:** will be supplied on confirmation of booking.

Redcot is a lovely garden. It was started back in 1888 and continued, according to the original design, until the 1950s when the property was taken over by non-gardeners. Mr Knox Gass took on the garden in 1997 and has been restoring it ever since, coaxing it back to its original shape and appearance.

The garden to the front of the house is made up principally of rhododendrons, mature shrubs and trees. This looks very smart but gives nothing away of the truly wonderful garden behind the house. The planting by the house is spectacular – a great wisteria covers the main section of the back wall. This is underplanted with fascicularia, roses and self-seeding geraniums, big echiums and fremontodendron, white abutilon and *Melianthus major*, all adding up to a glorious cram. A bit of a path divides it from a patio full of geraniums, more grasses, callistemon, wallflowers and euphorbias. Like many of the best gardens, it looks easy and natural but couldn't be more complicated and complex.

Out from the house the delights continue. There are lawns surrounded by large beds of mixed shrubs and herbaceous perennials. A path leads under a pretty acer and past a huge flowering phormium into a little room of pulmonaria, aquilegia, perennial honesty and meconopsis. The path moves back up past a yew hedge and into the double border. This border starts at one end with blue echinops, campanula and veronica, running through the purple of goat's rue and down to pink sedums, stock, anemone, honesty and red astrantia. On the other side are big patches of catmint, crocosmia and lilies.

At the bottom of the garden there is a little blue bench for relaxing and enjoying the spectacle of colour, the mature trees and the house beyond. By now, perched on the bench, the visitor is on the edge of the woods. This is something of a surprise in the middle of Belfast, to say the least – a wild wood sloping down and away from the main garden. In here are subtle green trees, ferns and ivies. Little paths trip down through the huge acer and oak trees, stumbling into a really wild garden, full of tall grass, cow parsley, buttercups, nettles, thistles, geraniums and docks. This area is simply run through with the mower to create 'paths'. Native trees like rowan, oak, birch and hawthorn encircle it.

At this point, the visitor feels that this must be the full extent of the garden. Nothing more could possibly be expected of a town garden, could it? But to assume this would be to underestimate the capabilities of Mr Knox Gass. The garden again progresses on, this time to a wet garden with more than a touch of the tropics. Huge-leaved hostas, gunnera, bamboos, monster grasses and rodgersia, wild orchids and cimicifuga blend with the sound of a running stream, which is just audible in the background. Leaving this beautiful area, no doubt fully in awe at this stage, you clamber back up the hill to the top garden and pass through a wonderful fernery full of the finer and rarer plants of *Adiantum capillus-veneris*, shuttlecocks, tatting fern or Lady fern (*Athyrium filix-femina*) and a *Dicksonia antarctica* tree fern. Then the path hits the open to reveal a cottage garden with exuberant cosmos, dahlia, shasta daisies and other cottage garden flowers alongside rows of vegetables.

Redcot is not simply a garden, it is a lesson in horticulture, juxtaposed habitats and admirable style.

THE ROUNDHOUSE ⚓

42 Benvarden Road, Ballymoney, County Antrim; Tel: +020 741469 ▪ **Contact:**

ULSTER • COUNTY ANTRIM

Mrs N Montgomery ▪ **Open:** April–May, by appointment only; groups welcome ▪
Entrance fee goes towards garden upkeep ▪ Supervised children welcome ▪
Directions: the garden lies 2.5km along the B67 from Ballybogey to Ballycastle.
About 100m before the bridge over the River Bush and the entrance to Benvarden
Estate, look for white gates and a picnic area on the right.

Two tall beech trees announce the entrance to the Roundhouse, named after a little,
semi-round house in Mrs Montgomery's garden. This was once a gate lodge standing
by the drive into the big house, but it became sidelined over the years. About to be
listed as a protected building, it provides the garden with an impressive and enviable
feature.

Mrs Montgomery has lived in the new house set in the middle of this garden for
over thirty years. In that time she has turned her plot from a mass of rushes and wild
raspberries (which grew very well, incidentally) to a handsome, substantial garden.
But she is quick to acknowledge her debt to a farmer friend who kindly turned the soil
five times for her in order to ready it for planting. 'We have very heavy acid clay soil
with no worms at all,' Mrs Montgomery says in a lament over the conditions she
works in. She also claims that the garden has gone to the bad in the last few years. I
suspect she is a serious perfectionist, because the garden is a treat.

The Roundhouse covers two acres, and while Mrs Montgomery decided at the age
of seventy that she no longer wanted to cut grass, she continues to do all the other
garden work herself. She says that the 'wiggly paths' which wander through the
garden were never designed but simply determined by the shape of the general plant
growth: 'I certainly was not being clever or anything like that,' she continues. Nonetheless, the shape and style of the garden is really attractive, wiggles included. Full of
trilliums, trout lilies (*Erythroniums*) and rhododendrons, this is very much a spring
garden. There are impeccable lawns edged by weaving beds of flowers and shrubs,
which spill out over the grass and push back into the mature pines that surround the
garden and give it its strong sense of secluded shelter. Drifts of hellebores and
Solomon's seal, hosta, white aconitum and gunnera edge the wandering paths. The
well-tended lawn and an occasional, precisely shaped topiary hedge, made from hornbeam and Portugal laurel (*Prunus lusitanica*) and box cubes, balances and restrains
the exuberance and informality of the other planting. A remarkable double sweep of
hornbeam hedge, grown two metres high and at angles to each other, suggests the beginnings of a maze. These hedges are like a huge sculpture to be viewed from the
house: 'My mother saw something like it in a gardening magazine and we thought it
would be nice here. We grew it in hornbeam because it is so much more hardy than
beech and it only needs clipping once a year, in February.'

SIR THOMAS AND LADY DIXON PARK ♿ 🐕

Upper Malone Road, Belfast, County Antrim; Tel: +090 320202 ▪ **Contact:** Alex
McNeill ▪ **Open:** all year round, daylight hours, telephone to confirm specific
times ▪ **No entrance fee** ▪ Supervised children welcome; please note, dogs on
leads ▪ **Special features:** rose displays ▪ Managed by Belfast City Council ▪ **Directions:** located south of the city on the Upper Malone Road. You will see signposts
to your right as you travel south.

THE WORLD FEDERATION OF ROSE SOCIETIES

The World Federation of Rose Societies awarded Sir Thomas and Lady Dixon Park the title of World's Best Rose Garden in 2000. In a competition between eight of the world's top rose gardens, which included gardens in the USA and Japan, the Belfast park, which carries over 32,000 rose bushes, was voted overwhelmingly the winner. The park's gardeners, along with everyone in the Rose Society, were justly delighted with the honour.

For many people, rose gardens are not the easiest of gardens to love. The blooms are always beautiful, it is true, and the scent and variety of the flowers find few non-takers, but beds of hybrid tea roses with ugly legs are being planted less and less these days and the words 'beautiful' and 'rose bush' rarely sit happily together. Old shrub roses do have a more acceptable overall shape and can look well even out of bloom, but in general we grow roses for the bloom rather than the whole plant. That said, the long runs and large beds of roses in Sir Thomas and Lady Dixon Park are a better experience than most. As a city park, however, it is big and, like other big parks, really shouldn't be visited by people walking by themselves as it can be very isolated.

The 130-acre park is attractive and hilly, with great sweeps of lawn rising and falling in hills and hollows and a great surrounding of mature mixed trees. The rose beds have been planted in long swathes of single colours, so the viewer is saved from the jelly-and-custard sight that one is often subjected to in a rose garden. Here the beds roll and flow up and over the hilly lawns in the park, looking like long, coloured ribbons stretched across the grass. There are camellia beds, a Japanese garden and a pond garden, as well as a yew walk and long sauntering trails through the trees and park.

The rose garden is well divided out into beds of hybrid teas, cluster-flowered specimens, climbers and ramblers. The Royal National Rose Society has a display bed of roses, which achieved special merit in competition. These are useful to study before planting up a rose garden of one's own. The Dickson and McGredy rose beds celebrate the enormous achievements of two Northern Ireland families – the Dicksons and the McGredys – who between them have contributed and continue to contribute to our knowledge of roses. These are filled with roses bred and introduced by these two famous families of the rose business. Both families have been working with roses since the 1870s and both are now in their fifth generation.

THORNLEA

1 Upper Cairncastle Road, Larne, County Antrim; Tel: +028 272152 ▪ **Contact:** Mrs Martha Castles ▪ **Open:** occasionally during the summer months for open days, telephone for annual dates; groups welcome ▪ **Entrance fee** donated to charity ▪ Supervised children welcome; please note, dogs on leads ▪ **Directions:** leave Larne town centre via Roddens Road and go as far as the Highways Hotel. Turn right into Cairncastle Road and Thornlea is on the corner, on the right-hand side.

Mrs Castles started this three-quarter-acre garden twenty-five years ago. She had been working a two-acre plot, but decided that it was too difficult to maintain alone and so she 'downsized'. She moved from her older, bigger house and built a small cottage next door with a smaller garden that has stunning views over Larne harbour.

Mrs Castles is currently embarking on a policy of 'groundcover'; the appeal of low-maintenance becomes stronger as the years advance. There are beds of lysimachia and lilies, geraniums and violas, all completely covering the ground and knotting through each other. There are beds of golden thyme and, further up, a bank of drumstick-flowered persicaria or polygonum – these are things that just need trimming. Pots of tulips, daffodils, lilies and sometimes fuchsia are sunken into the beds. The idea behind this is that the beauty of the flowers and the beds need not be paid for by ugly, dying leaves. When the flowers go over to the other side, Mrs Castles simply lifts the pots and the dying plant can be replaced with something fresh and flowering.

Below the house, and visible from its big picture windows, a circular lawn is surrounded by low heathers, Corsican mint (*Mentha requienii*), scabious, primroses and roses. A low wall holds up a bed of bergenia, Lady's mantle (*Alchemilla mollis*) and low-growing campanulas. Vinca, another great groundcover plant, is used widely out by the gate and under the cherry trees. In the centre of the garden a little arch with pink roses leads to a pond edged with camomile, cyclamen and little pinks, more thyme, sisyrinchium and thrift. This pond was where the children learned to swim. When the children grew up it was transformed into a fish pond, until the heron ate all the fish, and now it holds lilies.

Mrs Castles has a great talent for cuttings and a whole bank at one side of the house is made up of plants grown from cuttings. Another feature is her hanging baskets filled with parsley and scallions. As someone who dislikes hanging baskets, I could only admire hers. The baskets are placed hanging by the door, within easy grabbing distance from the kitchen.

This is a lovely mish-mash garden. It gives great ideas for low-maintenance gardening for those who are too harrassed by work or age to take on the daily labours of the rigorous gardener.

GARDENING CLUBS AND SOCIETIES

BALLYMENA HORTICULTURAL SOCIETY

The Ballymena Horticultural Society meets on the first Monday of the month at 7.30pm in Dunclug School, Doury Road, Ballymena, for lectures, slide shows and gardening discussions. It is a busy club with an active membership. In the summer several garden visits are arranged, both locally and further afield. A spring show is held in May. They hold no meeting in January. New members are welcome to come along to meetings.

COLEMAN'S NURSERY GARDEN CLUB

Contact: Richard Fry, Coleman's Nurs-ery, 6 Ballyclare Road, Templepatrick, County Antrim; Tel: +094 432513.

Coleman's Nursery holds an exhibition of fuchsias from June to the end of October that should be visited by anyone interested in these beautiful plants. The Nursery Garden Club meets between eight and nine months of the year for lectures and demonstrations. The dates for meetings change from year to year.

CREGAGH AND DISTRICT GARDENING SOCIETY

The society meets on the fourth Tuesday of the month at 8pm at Cregagh library, on Cregagh Road in southeast Belfast. Their annual programme is made up of lectures, slide shows, talks and question-time sessions. Two garden visits are arranged during the summer; one of these is an evening outing. There are no meetings between June and August. The society is over fifty years old and still thriving. It welcomes visitors and new members to the monthly meetings. Cregagh is affiliated to the Rose Society of Northern Ireland, and members are entitled to attend the Rose Society's monthly meetings (*see* Irish Rose Society of Northern Ireland).

GILNAHIRK HORTICULTURAL AND CIVIC SOCIETY

The society meets from September to April, on the first Wednesday of each month, in the Tullycarnet Bowling Pavilion, Kingsland Park, Belfast. Visitors are welcome to all meetings, where a wide range of gardening topics is aired. A competition table is set up at each meeting for items such as the best Hallowe'en fruit arrangement, best home-grown vegetables and best wildlife photographs.

GREENMOUNT COLLEGE OF AGRICULTURE AND HORTICULTURE

Contact: Graeme Cross, 22 Greenmount Road, Antrim, County Antrim; Tel: +094 426666.

Greenmount College is Ulster's agricultural college, running courses on all aspects of horticulture. It is also part of the Royal Horticultural Society/Colleges Partnership Programme. This means that the RHS use Greenmount throughout the year for lectures, demonstrations and practical workshops on gardening.

INVER GARDEN CLUB

Contact: Inver Garden Centre, 4 Browndod Road, Larne, County Antrim; Tel: +028 276351.

An informal garden club that was founded in the 1980s. The club holds one meeting per month, with talks on seasonal topics. One or two garden trips are organised each year.

IRISH FUCHSIA SOCIETY, THE

See appendices for details.

IRISH ROSE SOCIETY OF NORTHERN IRELAND

The Rose Society meets between September and April, on the second Wednesday of the month at 7.30pm, at Malone House in Barnett Demesne on the Malone Road, Belfast. Supper is provided at the society's sociable meetings. In July, usually during the second or third week of the month, the renowned annual rose show is held in Sir Thomas and Lady Dixon Park. Contact the society for annual dates.

MONEYREA GARDENING SOCIETY

The Moneyrea society is an active society, meeting on the first Thursday of each month at 7.45pm, in the Old National School, Moneyrea, Newtownards, County Antrim. The meetings take the form of lectures, slide shows and demonstrations. In May a garden visit is organised. The society rests between June and August. New members are most welcome.

NORTH ANTRIM HORTICULTURAL SOCIETY

Contact: Mr K Bacon, 6 Downview Park, Ballymoney, Belfast BT53 6AE.

NORTHERN IRELAND BONSAI SOCIETY, THE

The society meets on the second Friday of the month, at Cregagh library on Cregagh Road in the southeast of the city. Each meeting begins with a 'sick bonsai' clinic, when owners of wilting and miserable bonsai can bring their ailing plants to be doctored and pampered a little. Remarkably, there is no charge for this wonderful service, but I think joining the society would show suitable thanks. Lectures, followed by question-and-answer sessions, are also part of the monthly meetings.

NORTHERN IRELAND VEGETABLE GROUP, THE

Contact: C Holmes (Hon. Secretary), 4 Milebush Drive, Carrickfergus, County Antrim; Tel: +093 364197.

The Northern Ireland Vegetable Group was set up to encourage the growing of fruit and vegetables by amateur gardeners. It is a leader in the promotion of growing and showing vegetables. The group meets every month at 7.30pm in the Harmony Hill Arts Centre, Clonmore House, 54 Harmony Hill, Lisburn, County Antrim. Membership is very reasonable and the talks include subjects like the propagation of specific vegetables and preparation of crops for showing. Quizzes and slide shows are also held. They are very welcoming to new members.

ROYAL HORTICULTURAL SOCIETY

Contact: for information write, enclosing a SAE, to: the Reception Desk, Ulster Museum, Belfast Botanic Gardens, Belfast BT9 5AB.

A series of lectures is run by the RHS in cooperation with the Irish Garden Plant Society (*see* appendices) in the Ulster Museum Lecture Theatre at Belfast Botanic Gardens. The lectures are varied and informative, ranging from 'The History of Italian Gardens' to 'Science in the Garden', 'Pests of Northern Ireland Gardens' and 'Diseases of Northern Ireland Gardens' – informative, if somewhat depressing topics.

NURSERIES AND GARDEN CENTRES

ARCHES GARDEN CENTRE, THE

2 Horsepark, Magheragall, Lisburn, County Antrim; Tel: +092 622380.

BALLYMONEY GARDEN CENTRE

1 Greenhill Road, Ballymoney, County Antrim; Tel: +027 664848.

CARNCAIRN DAFFODILS

Carncairn Lodge, Broughshane, Ballymena; Tel: +025 861216 ▪ **Contact:** the Reade family.

Old and new varieties of daffodil bulbs, from one of the island's most renowned breeders.

CONVERY'S ISLAND NURSERIES

Kilrea Road, Portglenone, County Antrim; Tel: +025 221797.

EURO FLOWERS

95–97 Boucher Road, Belfast, County Antrim; Tel: +090 664866.

HILLMOUNT NURSERY CENTRE

56–58 Upper Braniel Road, Gilnahirk, Belfast BT5 7TX; Tel: +090 448213.

HILLSIDE NURSERY CENTRE

328 Doagh Road, Newtownabbey, County Antrim; Tel: +090 863161.

INVER GARDEN CENTRE

4 Browndod Road, Larne, County Antrim; Tel: +028 276351.

LANDSCAPE CENTRE, THE

24 Donegore Hill, Dunadry, near Templepatrick, County Antrim; Tel: +094 432175.

LOGWOOD MILL GARDEN CENTRE

8 Logwood Road, Ballyclare, County Antrim; Tel: +093 322242.

WOODLAWN GARDEN CENTRE

360 Saintfield Road, Belfast BT8 7SJ, County Antrim; Tel: +090 401777.

COUNTY ARMAGH

County Armagh is the smallest of the northern counties, but it has played an important role in the history of Ireland: the city of Armagh is the ecclesiastical capital for both the Church of Ireland and the Roman Catholic Church. This means that the city has an abundance of museums and historic sites, making it worthy of a day trip for anyone interested in history and heritage. The county is bordered by the River Bann to the east and by Lough Neagh to the north, and is crisscrossed by scores of small rivers. There are interesting trails around Slieve Gullion for those who enjoy a bracing walk in the brisk northern air. As for the gardener's lot, County Armagh shares predominantly acid drumlin soil with its southern neighbours across the border. The hills are much used for growing apples and the orchards are beautiful when they blossom in late spring; Armagh is sometimes called the Orchard of Ireland.

ARDRESS HOUSE

64 Ardress Road, Portadown, County Armagh; Tel/Fax: +038 851236; e-mail: uagest@smtp.ntrust.org.uk ▨ **Contact:** the Administrator ▨ **Open:** at Easter, ring to confirm times; April–May and September, Saturday, Sunday and bank holidays, 2pm–6pm; June–August, every day, except Tuesday, 2pm–6pm; groups welcome ▨ **Entrance fee** donated to the National Trust ▨ Supervised children welcome; please note, dogs on leads ▨ **Special features:** walks for the visually impaired can be arranged; Georgian Sunday in September; Apple Blossom day in May, ring for annual dates; large playground ▨ Member of National Trust ▨ **Directions:** Ardress House is 13km from Portadown on the Moy Road (B28).

Ardress House was built as a farmhouse in the seventeenth century, and in the eighteenth century it was improved and enlarged by its owner, the architect George Ensor, who created a neo-classical-style manor house. The house and grounds are filled with fine furniture and paintings, old farm implements and rare-breed livestock.

Upon entering the main gate you travel through a working apple orchard and a short drive leads up to the house, which stands on a slightly raised plateau overlooking the sloping lawn. The side wall of the house bows inwards and around and holds various classical busts set into niched arches. These are guarded by clipped bay trees in pots and large containers of blue agapanthus and pelargoniums baking in the suntrap. The architectural style is very clean and disciplined.

The gardens are simple and elegant and in perfect keeping with the stylish restraint of the pale-pink Georgian house. The planting proper begins as the wall trails away from the house into a mass of creepers. Along this wall is a fine border, about seventy-five metres long, full of beautiful herbaceous plants and flowering shrubs: lacecap hydrangeas, phlox, the red-leaved *Cotinus coggygria*, berberis, laburnum, anemone and roses. Behind these climbing roses, vines and clematis run seven metres high up the wall.

When you reach the end of this border the little rose garden becomes visible. Stepping down a small stone stairway edged with a variety of shrubs, the path leads you in amongst the roses. The variations in colour and leaf texture in this little shrub area work brilliantly. Glossy, almost waxy, dark-green choisya leaves nestle against silver, feather-like artemisia leaves, downy, greyish-purple sage and more wine-coloured cotinus leaves – all meshing together superbly. The roses are held in by low lavender hedges. In the centre is a sundial, its base attended by blue iris and small-leaved bergenia. One of the borders of the rose garden is an old stone wall fronted by soft, grey-blue catmint (*Nepeta*), creeping rosemary (*Rosmarinus officinalis* 'Prostratus') and roses trained lightly over the stone. A low yew hedge encloses the garden on the other three sides. The garden is about to undergo major surgery when the old bushes are replaced by new plants, mostly old Irish varieties of roses although the exact varieties have yet to be decided upon. This rose garden is one of my favourite small garden rooms on the island, and is an inspiration for anyone thinking of creating an intimate formal garden.

The surrounding parkland sweeps off and away to the hills in the distance. There are some good woodland walks through the park.

THE ULSTER GARDENS SCHEME

The National Trust is the State-run organisation that cares for and runs many of the most renowned houses, gardens and demesnes in Northern Ireland. It is a body whose work is well known to anyone who visits gardens. For the past thirty years the Trust has run two garden-visiting schemes in order to raise money for the upkeep and restoration of some of the gardens in its care. Operating under the title of the Ulster Gardens Scheme, they have done much to encourage the gardeners of Northern Ireland to show their gardens publicly, and in so doing have contributed to the constantly rising standards of Northern Ireland's gardens.

The main scheme involves a well-scattered selection of otherwise private gardens that hold open days during the summer, welcoming the public into their gardens. These are busy, bustling occasions and draw huge numbers of visitors who enjoy the gardens, plant stalls and teas. The thirty-year-old project is hugely popular. The fact that the Trust works with a different selection of gardens each year ensures a high level of interest year in, year out among garden visitors and day-trippers.

In the last five years the Trust has also introduced a By Appointment scheme. This is a more relaxed affair, made up of a slowly revolving selection of twenty or so gardens that open right through the summer, by appointment.

There is considerable status in being invited by the Trust to join one of its schemes, so even though some people might worry a little about privacy or possible damage to their garden, most gardeners are quite willing to join in, guaranteeing the body a regular income for important garden restoration work. For the Ulster Gardens Scheme brochure, which also includes information about plant sales, garden shows, fairs and organised garden walks, contact the National Trust at Rowallane, Saintfield, County Down; Tel: +097 510721.

THE ARGORY

Derrycaw Road, Moy, Dungannon, County Armagh; Tel: +087 784753; Fax: +087 789598; e-mail: uagest@smtp.ntrust.org.uk ▪ **Contact:** the Administrator ▪ **Open:** March, Sunday, 2pm–5pm; April–May and September, Saturday–Sunday, 2pm–6pm; June–August, Monday–Sunday (closed Thursday), 2pm–6pm; bank holidays, 2pm–6pm; groups welcome ▪ **Parking fee** ▪ Supervised children welcome; please note, dogs on leads ▪ **Special features:** vintage vehicle rally in April; craft fairs in August and December; programme of walks; tours of the historic house ▪ Member of National Trust ▪ **Directions:** well signposted from the M1 travelling towards Dungannon. Leave the motorway at exit 13 and follow the signs.

The Argory is a fine Victorian house surrounded by beautiful woodlands, oak plantations, lawns, yew walks and two formal gardens. Built in 1824 by the Bond family, the house, laundry, stableyards, coach houses and an acetylene gas plant have all been maintained beautifully by the National Trust. It has the appearance of a household preserved in aspic, patiently waiting for the Victorian inhabitants to return.

The Pleasure Garden begins with a great sweep of lawn adjacent to the house and stableyards. An impressive mixed border wraps around the lawn, its strength derived not from colour or flower but from leaf and foliage, shape and colour contrasts. Shiny bergenia forms a low collar along the edge of the bed. Above this are waves of big, dark-veined rodgersia, strappy agapanthus and sharp acanthus leaves. There are touches of subtle purple courtesy of buddleia, occasional clumps of geranium and the blue puffs of agapanthus to set off the foliage. Out on the lawn two huge yew arbours into which one can sit stand four square, like Darth Vadar's helmet. The lawn has a ha-ha and a path leading down to the woods. It looks out over two quaint little stone summerhouses with interesting Chinese-style windows. The whole garden overlooks a pretty stretch of the River Blackwater, where huge herons stalk about looking for fish. There is also a lime tree walk down here, shading the riverbank.

The second of the formal gardens is a small rose and sundial garden. This is a perfect domestic-scale garden, held in by box and yew walls. The roses are all pale pinks and whites, standards and patio varieties. Delicate and pretty are the words that best describe this flower-filled room, and the scents from the roses and from the fragrant lavender lining the walls are intoxicating.

The woods at the bottom of the garden are currently being restored, as many of the trees at the Argory were felled during the Second World War and fearless rhododendron marched into the clearings. This has had to be grubbed out in order to allow new young trees to develop. While still something of a work in progress, the woods are very handsome and make a fine afternoon's walk.

10 CASTLE DRIVE

Richhill, County Armagh; Tel: +038 871326 ▪ **Contact:** Mr and Mrs Shah ▪ **Open:** May–September, by appointment only; groups welcome ▪ **Entrance fee** donated to the National Trust ▪ Supervised children welcome; please note, dogs on leads ▪ **Special features:** refreshments are available to groups by prior arrangement ▪ **Directions:** leave the Armagh–Portadown road (A3) at Stonebridge roundabout. Travel on Legacorry Road toward Richhill for just over 1km. The garden is behind the old demesne wall, to the right of the road, just at the 30mph sign. Turn right and right again to reach Castle Drive.

The Shahs's garden is a very small town garden, compact but brimming with great plants, elegant statuary and curious little features. It has an incredible amount of character. Attached as it is to a modern house, the temptation to create a country cottage garden was rightly resisted, and the garden has a modern style that suits its urban surroundings.

The space is divided into several small areas with fences and gates separating and joining them. This adds to the air of surprise in the garden. Constantly changing heights confuse the perspective and make it more fun, as well as affording opportunities for different sorts of planting schemes. Meandering paths lead around shrubs and standing stones, tall clumps of New Zealand flax (*Phormium tenax*), bamboo and small dry stone walls. Several small ponds are hidden within the garden rooms. Ornaments, sculptures, pots and stones are strategically placed and stone-paved sitting areas are filled with pots of succulents and hostas. In the courtyard are several big clematis, sharing the space with pots of bamboo. Among the taller trees and shrubs is an outstanding autumn-flowering eucryphia. Much of the garden's charm is due to the sparing use of good trees, but there is no shortage of flowers here. Sky-scraping hollyhocks (*Alcea rosea*), potentilla and greeny-cream flowering virgin's bower (*Clematis cirrhosa*) are just some of the stars.

The Shahs have married a lot of modern ideas with more traditional plants. Mrs Shah particularly loves pots and there are pots everywhere throughout the garden. Well-tended pots always indicate just how hard a gardener works, particularly in summer when attention has to dwindle only for a moment for pots to begin to look ragged, drought-struck and generally miserable. Mrs Shah's, however, are first rate. Because space is at a premium and their first love is for ornamental gardening, there are no vegetables these days, but Mrs Shah does grow delicious plums, tayberries, raspberries, blackberries, currants and apples.

I have met people who enjoy their neighbours' gardens, but the folk who live next door to number 10 have gone one better, showing their approval by allowing the Shahs to extend into their gardens on either side. The land-strapped Shahs have, of course, obliged. Any tips for small-scale gardeners? Mrs Shah is a member of the Irish Garden Plant Society (*see* appendices) and has found it a useful club for small-plot gardening. Having seen her small garden, I would have to recommend joining them.

DERRYMORE HOUSE

Bessbrook, Newry, County Armagh; Tel: +030 838361 ▪ **Contact:** the Administrator ▪ **Open:** Easter weekend, 2pm–5.30pm; May–August, Thursday–Saturday, 2pm–5.30pm; groups welcome, by appointment only ▪ **Entrance fee** donated to National Trust ▪ Supervised children welcome ▪ **Special features:** unusual thatched manor house ▪ Member of National Trust ▪ **Directions:** off the main Newry–Camlough road (A25). Bessbrook is 3km from Newry.

Derrymore House is a beautiful *cottage orné*, and the biggest thatched manor house in Ireland. Isaac Corry, Newry's representative in the Irish Parliament for thirty years, built the house in 1776. It is an unusual building: a symmetrical and largely classical single-storey house topped off with a thatched roof. There were several of these thatched houses in Ireland as early as the mid-eighteenth century. Later in that century the numbers would increase and more elaborate cottages, such as Swiss Cottage in County Tipperary and Lord Bantry's Lodge in Glengarriff, County Cork, would be built. However, Derrymore remains a handsome and impressive model of this architectural period.

The landscaping around the quaint, peach-coloured house was carried out by John Sutherland, one of the most celebrated disciples of 'Capability' Brown, the renowned eighteenth-century landscaper (*see* box, Lancelot 'Capability' Brown, p.214). Today some good young planting of rowan, sycamore and silver fir, alongside the older mature parkland trees, surrounds the house. A small, cottage-style garden stands to the side of the building. This is a classic, flowery, colourful plot with soft planting that anchors the house into the land. Climbers like jasmine and roses are lightly encouraged to play along the walls of the house. Some island beds, planted with potentilla, hydrangea and ferns, stand in front of the house, set into the sloped lawns.

GLENCOURT

29 Legacorry Road, Richhill, County Armagh; Tel: +038 870137 ✳ **Contact:** Kathleen Clendinning ✳ **Open:** Easter–September, Sundays, 2pm–5pm, apply in writing; groups welcome ✳ **Entrance fee** in the form of voluntary donations, which are given to the National Trust ✳ Supervised children welcome ✳ **Directions:** from Armagh take the Portadown Road (A3) for 6km. At the Stonebridge roundabout, take the road for Richhill. The road rises uphill over a crest, and halfway down the hill is the Fairline factory on the left and two houses side by side on the right. After the second house, there is a laneway, turn sharp left into it. In the laneway there is a showroom on the left, pass it and continue on to the Private Entrance sign, which marks the garden entrance.

The Clendinnings started their Legacorry Road garden in 1946, when the plot was just a field. The transition stage between field and fine garden came via a tennis court. These days the garden rules supreme and the tennis court is overshadowed, with dangerous intent, by some fine conifers. Tennis players may not be happy but aesthetically it is perfect, and I suspect the trees will win whatever battle ensues.

A well-designed pond stands close by the house, which is a good idea for several reasons. Many of us put in ponds to encourage wildlife, and where better to observe it from than a well-positioned window? Also, for those worried about children and safety, keeping both child and pond within sight and easy reach makes good sense. 'The pond works well,' says Mrs Clendinning, 'but it took a long time to get it to work.' For anyone keen to have water in the garden this is worth bearing in mind. Good ponds take a lot of effort to perfect. Clouded water and rampant duckweed are only some of the obstacles to achieving a crystal-clear pool.

Shamelessly promiscuous candelabra primulas flounce around the edge of the water, hybridising from purple and white to various shades of pink. They love the damp, wet conditions and it shows. Hostas and lilies enjoy the wet also and squeeze themselves in between the primulas. Around the building, gravel and stone paths are heavily planted with hummocks of alpines that invite a hands-and-knees inspection.

A helpful and obviously talented son-in-law took a chainsaw to the once columnar

Leyland cypress (*Cupressocyparis leylandii*) walk that travels up the garden from the house. He turned them into superb, flat-topped, almost sculptural, columns. This avenue leads past a little island bed of expansionist alpines and creepers and on further to the mature trees and rhododendrons that border the back of the garden. There were once beds of spring heathers, but they involved too much work, so Mrs Clendinning rooted out a number of them in favour of ferns, which mind themselves and look beautiful. Beside this path a little sphinx seat, surrounded by black pansies and black grass (*Ophiopogon planiscapus* 'Nigrescens'), is very stylish. I suspect that this is one of those more walked-past than sat-upon seats.

Glencourt is an enjoyable garden, full of clever and well-executed planting. One thing that caught my eye was what Mrs Clendinning called her 'greedy garden'. This is a bed full of the things she just couldn't resist acquiring, but has no room for. What indulgence!

GOSFORD FOREST PARK

Markethill, County Armagh; Tel: +037 551277 ■ **Contact:** the Head Forester ■ **Open:** Monday–Sunday, 10pm–sunset, ring in advance to confirm; groups welcome ■ **Entrance fee** ■ Supervised children welcome; please note, dogs on leads ■ **Special features:** rare-breed farm animals and ornamental fowl; nature trail; deer park; accommodation is available in the form of a caravan park; groups can book refreshments in advance ■ **Directions:** travel 11km from Armagh. The park is signposted on the left.

Gosford Forest Park, formerly the Gosford Demesne, is attached to an unusual nineteenth-century castle built in a Norman-revival style, similar to Glenstal Abbey in County Limerick (which is closed to the public). The Gosford Estate covers almost 500 acres just south of Armagh city, and plays host to rare-breed farm animals, a walled garden, an arboretum and many acres of woodland and marked trails. Jonathan Swift, author of *Gulliver's Travels*, is associated with Gosford, as he spent several months staying here as a guest of the Acheson family, who owned the estate in the eighteenth century. Indeed, Swift mentioned the place in his work and to this day there is a feature called the Dean's Chair, where the poet is thought to have sat and mused.

The walled garden has been laid out in lawn, flowering shrubs and a lily pond. Inner walls divide the space into smaller, more intimate sections, providing extra shelter for some of the more tender plants. The acid soil accommodates sizeable planting of rhododendron, azalea and eucryphia. The shrubs are arranged in big beds, mixing acer and azalea handsomely.

Outside the garden's walls the arboretum, which was laid out in the 1820s, stretches out, displaying baby monkey puzzle trees (*Araucaria araucana*), gigantic wellingtonia (*Sequoiadendron giganteum*), Atlas or blue cedars (*Cedrus atlantica Manetti*), a big, black walnut tree (*Juglans nigra*), *Cedrus deodara*, the Himalayan fir (*Abies spectabilis*) and the Noble fir (*Abies nobilis*). The trees are all well labelled and well cared for, and the collection continues to grow. Among the giant specimens, young Brewer's weeping spruce (*Picea breweriana*), as well as other special trees, are being planted all the time.

Markethill, County Armagh; Tel: +038 871679 ■ **Contact:** Mrs Roberta Barron ■
Open: July–August, by appointment only; groups welcome ■ **Entrance fee**
donated to charity ■ Supervised children welcome; please note, dogs on leads ■
Special features: groups can book refreshments in advance ■ **Directions:** travel
from Armagh city on the A51 to Hamiltonsbawn. Approximately 6km outside
Armagh, take the left turn opposite the sign for Redrock. The garden belongs to the
second bungalow in the laneway.

Mrs Barron has created a pretty, modern country garden around her bungalow,
looking out over the rolling Armagh landscape. The surroundings are quite idyllic and
Roberta Barron has sensibly kept the heights in her half-acre garden low so that she
can enjoy the landscape beyond. Even the trees in her garden – rowan, laburnum and
apple – are small and compact.

One long, sweeping bed surrounds the garden, creating an interesting walk
around the perimeter. The planting is mixed, incorporating a wide variety of plants
that provide a rolling flow of colour and height, texture and scent. A goodly number
of conifers ensures that there is something to look at in the garden all year round.
There is always so much here to see: heather and potentilla, broom and lavatera, hebe,
white lupins and foxgloves mix with delphiniums and low conifers, cotinus and osteospermum in a great informal salad. To the front of the house there is a lot more herbaceous planting in a cottage-style bed, and the high summer favourites, such as opium
poppies and lavender, take over where the spring bulbs leave off. A beautiful recumbent ceanothus with hardy geranium through it is particularly pretty. Stepping stones
through the bed lead out to a grove of apple trees. Mrs Barron is an effortless colour
matcher and she has arranged some striking mixes, like purple aconitum with matching aquilegia, or blue omphalodes with drumstick primulas.

KEADY RECTORY

Crossmore Road, Keady, County Armagh; Tel: +037 531230 ■ **Contact:** Rev Dr
WG Neely ■ **Open:** during the summer months, strictly by appointment only;
groups welcome ■ **Entrance fee** donated to charity and goes towards garden upkeep ■ Supervised children welcome; please note, dogs on leads ■ **Special
features:** large parties only may book meals, must be booked in advance ■ **Directions:** as you enter the village of Keady, coming from Armagh, go past the fire
station. Crossmore Road is the first turn on the right.

Keady Rectory garden is a great jumble of plants. There has been a garden on this spot
since 1775. The Reverend took it over from his mother sixteen years ago and the
planting you see today is largely his work. The old rectory house sits on a ledge on the
steep hillside overlooking Keady village, with a gravel apron in front of it. The garden
falls down and away in steps from this vantage point.

Immediate to the front door are a huge cordyline and a great array of potted shrubs
and herbaceous plants. Among these are small acers, architectural acanthus, acid-
yellow inula and a spread of mint, as well as ground-covering and creeping thymes,
self-seeding violas and succulents, all moving out across the drive in a determined

fashion. This is called the pot garden. Beyond the pot garden and the gravel drive is a jungle of roses, rhododendron and abutilon.

The garden then falls down in three levels toward the fields of cows below. A path picks its way down between rampant camellia and liquidambar, yellow *Clematis tangutica* with small, almost sponge-textured, bell-shaped flowers, and complementary, lemon-coloured *Buddleia x. weyeriana*. Repeated scatterings of rodgersia, geranium and *Campanula lactiflora* grow into each other down the slope in easy knots. It is necessary to watch out for the pond in the middle of this mass of plants. Two kittens playing together failed to notice it and they both landed in the water, much to their surprise and vexation. Around the little pond there are lots of mixed grasses in a variety of colours, heights and textures. An *Acer griseum* with a peeling, rusty bark is underplanted by patches of tiny winter cyclamen.

To the back of the house is a courtyard garden. This is a sheltered, sunny, dry place. The concrete in here is softened by different varieties of creeping thyme and violas. A golden mulberry stands in one corner. The roses are the creamy, loose-flowering 'Little White Pet', and the creamy 'Dunwich' rose with its single, scented flower.

The overall feel of Keady is that of a relaxed place. Its good looks depend, sensibly, on flowering shrubs and easy perennials, like geraniums, violas and scented herbs. The Reverend, in spite of his seven-day-a-week job, has managed, in his particular way, to create and maintain a beautiful garden. One way he has achieved this is by keeping the plants most in need of care, watering and watching in the pot garden, in front of the house. This is commonsense practice for time-strapped gardeners.

NÍ EOGHAIN LODGE

32 Ennislare Road, Armagh, County Armagh; Tel: +037 525633 ▪ **Contact:** Mrs Kathleen McGeown ▪ **Open:** May–September, Wednesday–Sunday and bank holidays, 2pm–6pm; groups welcome ▪ **Entrance fee** donated to charity ▪ Supervised children welcome ▪ **Special features:** bed and breakfast accommodation available; refreshments available to groups, but must be booked in advance ▪ **Directions:** from Armagh take the Keady Road (A29) for 4.5km. Turn left opposite a row of cottages, onto Ennislare Road. Take the second turn left, and the garden is on the right. Look for the signposts.

Kathleen McGeown has been working the garden at Ennislare Road for seventeen years. She is an extraordinarily hard-working gardener. Toiling away by herself, every year she pushes out in a new direction, adding another feature, a huge new bed of one description or another, a willow arbour, a rose pergola or a sculptural project. While the garden currently covers two acres, I suspect this information may date quickly; Ní Eoghain is less of a garden than an empire. Its marvellous virtues have recently been recognised by those in the know: in the Shamrock All Ireland Gardens Competition 1999, Ní Eoghain took first prize in the Armagh and Down category, and in 2000 it won first prize in the Antrim, Armagh and Down category.

At the front of the house is the oldest part of the garden, featuring a good collection of evergreen shrubs and some quirky wooden sculptures, in particular a strange-looking creature carved in cedar who stares boldly at arriving visitors. The walls of the house would have to be dug out from under the ivy and other climbers

Rowallane, County Down. Vibrant colour on the huge natural rockery created by Hugh Armytage Moore in the twentieth century.

The view of the house from the Italian garden at Mount Stewart, County Down. The bay lollipops and pyramids were bought in Switzerland in the 1920s by Edith, Lady Londonderry as a job lot for £99.

The charming Mairi garden at Mount Stewart, created for the baby Lady Mairi, from winning on the St Leger. In the fountain, the bronze elfin creature sitting among the water-spouting lilies is modelled on the baby girl, who was brought for a daily turn around *her* garden.

Plants in Susan Tindall's garden at Timpany, County Down.
ABOVE: Kniphofia, hesperis and delphiniums.

LEFT: Shell-pink oriental poppies (*Papaver orientale*).

RIGHT: *Meconopsis betonicifolia*, the oriental blue poppy.

The little lily pond and spouting fountain, surrounded by a cartwheel formation of rose beds on a fine sunny day in the walled garden at Benvarden, County Antrim.

A mass of fragrant lilies in Chambrelly, County Antrim.

The tiny gate lodge guarding the Bishop's Gate at Downhill Castle and Mussenden Temple in County Derry. This gate leads into the informal garden created in 1910 by Lady Bruce, a descendant of Bishop Hervey who built Downhill Castle.

The formal rose garden at The Argory, County Armagh.

The snow lantern in Lorna MacMahon's garden, Ardcarraig, in County Galway. The centrepiece of the Japanese wood and water garden, it was transported with enormous difficulty through the woody and hilly site.

A secluded spot in the terracotta pot garden at Ardcarraig.

Veratrum californicum growing in Mr Acheson Aiken's garden,
Drumadravey, County Fermanagh.

Ben Aughlin seen from Florence Court, County Fermanagh, which is the home of the famous Florence Court yew.

that are so heavily planted against them. Mrs McGeown is fond of topiary and, apart from box pyramids and balls, she is in the middle of pruning or 'grooming' a little box Jack Russell. He will be ready to take over from his elderly, real-life counterpart in guarding the house when the time comes.

Moving around to the back of the house and into the greater garden leads one past an all-blue courtyard garden of solanum, convolvulus, *Clematis alpina*, aubrieta, lobelia and a pergola groaning under a big *Rosa filipes* 'Kiftsgate'. A *Clematis montana* piggybacks a flowering cherry, extending interest as the clematis flower takes over where the cherry blossom leaves off. A Japanese garden next door hides the oil tank behind a cleverly constructed bamboo fence. Herbs are kept by the back door for easy access – a lesson for those who put the herb garden miles from the house and kitchen. Plant the herbs by the kitchen and no one need travel down the garden on a wet night with a torch looking for bay leaves and arrive back with a nice big clutch of viburnum leaves for the stew!

Parts of the garden are like a jungle, with lush, dense planting, particularly near the south-facing house wall, which is home to a fruiting kiwi (*Actinidia deliciosa*), canna lilies and a pineapple broom – all plants which need heat and decent shelter. An old swing and seat have been taken over completely by the twining leaves of golden hop (*Humulus lupulus* 'Aureus') and honeysuckle. At the back of the garden a new area of herbaceous beds is in development. The lawn sinks away at this point down to the bottom of the garden, interrupted by a growing collection of specimen trees, such as tulip tree (*Liriodendron tulipifera*). This tree is just over fifteen years old and Mrs McGeown is still waiting patiently for it to flower.

SUMMERHILL LODGE

22 Summerhill, Lurgan, County Armagh; Tel: +037 881789 ▪ **Contact:** Dean Roland Hutchinson ▪ **Open:** June–July, afternoons, by appointment only, contact Dean Hutchinson by telephone to arrange a visit; groups welcome ▪ **Entrance fee** donated to charity ▪ Supervised children welcome; please note, dogs on leads ▪ **Special features:** teas can be booked by prior arrangement; plants for sale, particularly in May and June and particularly penstemon; only 1.6km from Waringstown, the 2000 winner of the Britain in Bloom and Ulster in Bloom competitions ▪ **Directions:** coming from Belfast, travel through the town of Lurgan and turn left onto Gifford Road. The garden is about 0.5km along on the left – it is the only building standing on the left-hand side.

Although it is hard to believe when walking through it, the Hutchinsons's garden was a completely flat field just seven years ago. Now it is an expanse of wide, well-tended lawns, backed by deep beds of tall herbaceous perennials, flowering shrubs and small trees. This makes it a wonderful place to visit for anyone starting out, but may also depress the beginner at the thought of how long it will be before their new garden shows any promise.

The Dean is a gardener of great talent, with the greenest of green fingers, who had been gardening long before he came to Summerhill. When he acquired this one-and-a-half-acre site, the Dean began by working in reverse. He landscaped and began creating the garden before work on the house had even begun. Working with John Campbell of the Landscape Centre in Donegore, he began by planting a windbreak in the shape of double hedges of beech and hornbeam, to give the garden the shelter it would need. He then brought in forty tonnes of rock and stone to create huge water features, ponds and a rockery. It was only when these massive undertakings had been completed that planting began. Many people who have had a design worked out for them find that as they begin to put it in place, various factors conspire to change it, sometimes radically. Dean Hutchinson found this and only partially implemented the first plan – the site and his own tastes dictated otherwise.

The beds are full of colour and variety, mostly mixed, using shrubs, perennials and annuals together. The Dean particularly loves penstemon, pointing out fine plants of 'Rich Ruby' and 'Mother of Pearl' as favourites from among the scores of varieties he carries. Dahlias and diascias are other favourites and he grows a great number of each. He particularly loves the single orange *Dahlia* 'Moonfire', with its rich black foliage. There are long runs of trellis with huge roses and climbers running rampant through and over them. Many of the mature shrubs are so big that plans are afoot to grub them out. The Dean feels they need to be replaced with young, new and different plants. Among the condemned are a very fine *Corokia cotoneaster* (wirenet bush) and a beautiful Jerusalem sage (*Phlomis fruticosa*). Obviously, to be a good gardener is to be a tough gardener!

All year round the garden has good displays of everything, from the beds and pond to the vegetable and fruit gardens and the very busy propagation house. Dean Hutchinson propagates all his own plants, and in such abundance that he supplies the towns of Lurgan, Moira and others with bedding for their award-winning municipal displays. Driving on through Moira after the visit I was able to enjoy more of the Dean's gardening skills in the village's elaborate, traffic-stopping floral displays. The garden has been open to the public (with admission donated to charity) for five years, and last year alone the Dean welcomed 1,100 visitors on his charity open day.

GARDENING CLUBS AND SOCIETIES

ARMAGH GARDENING CLUB, THE

Contact: Mrs Kathleen McGeown; Tel: +037 525633.

The Armagh club meets from September to April, on the fourth Wednesday of the month at 8pm, in the Community Centre on Dobbin Street in Armagh city. They hold an annual garden competition for members, the winner of which receives a perpetual cup.

PORTADOWN AND DISTRICT HORTICULTURAL SOCIETY, THE

Contact: Mrs Madge Brown; Tel: +038 336843.

NURSERIES AND GARDEN CENTRES

DOBBIN'S GARDEN CENTRE

16 Dobbin Street, Portadown, County Armagh; Tel: +038 357094.

SERGEANT'S GARDEN CENTRE

Vicarage Road, Portadown, County Armagh; Tel: +038 339549.

COUNTY CAVAN

County Cavan is situated on the border with County Fermanagh and shares a landscape as lake- and river-filled as its northern neighbour. The southern twists of the River Erne and the Shannon-Erne waterway, on its way to Carrick-on-Shannon, run from Belturbet in the northwest corner of the county right across its western flank. A string of lakes scattered about enjoy a good reputation throughout Europe among anglers and coarse fishermen. The sparsely populated and lightly farmed hills and lakelands are perfect for walking and hiking. Its 'virgin territory' quality can be attributed to the fact that, like its neighbours, it is largely made up of hard-to-work drumlin land. All in all, County Cavan has an appealing, unspoilt mien.

LAKE VIEW GARDENS

Mullagh, County Cavan; Tel: +046 42480; Fax: +046 42406; e-mail: jshack@ indigo.ie ※ **Contact:** Daphne or Jonathan Shackleton ※ **Open:** May–September, Friday–Sunday and bank holidays, by appointment to small groups only; guided tours can be given if the owners are available and a request has been made in advance; groups welcome, but numbers must be limited so ring in advance to confirm ※ **Entrance fee** ※ Supervised children welcome ※ **Special features:** plants for sale, including rare and unusual herbaceous perennials ※ **Directions:** leave Mullagh on the Virginia Road (R194) and travel for 3.2km. Turn left at the lake opposite the turn for Cross. The house is the second entrance on the right.

Overlooking Mullagh Lake, the walled garden at Lake View has been restored by the well-known Shackleton family. The Shackletons are one of the country's best-known gardening families, due largely to their work on the famous Beech Park gardens in Clonsilla, just outside Dublin (*see* County Dublin). Daphne and Jonathan Shackleton moved to Lake View five years ago and took over the substantial old farmhouse and its neglected walled garden. Since then, Daphne Shackleton has carried out a great amount of work, introducing many special and unusual plants brought from the Clonsilla garden.

In Mullagh, grey limestone walls enclose the two-acre, roughly square garden, which stands on a slope facing the sun. The whole emphasis is on flowers – herbaceous beds arranged in colour blocks stretch off in all directions, edged with moss-covered stones. The beds line out in a regular but not military order. If you stand to one side of the garden and look over the whole space, you are treated to a rising and falling wave of colour, shade and texture.

A light framework of trees and trellises exists for structure and to provide some sheltered spots. A rustic pergola, weighted down by different clematis, stands behind a bed of roses and peonies edging onto the lawn. However, most of this garden is made up of a simple, glorious mass of flowers, and to walk between the beds is to get lost in a colourful perfume shop. The main herbaceous border is deep and well stuffed. *Celmisia semicordata* sits at the front, snug beside *Viola cornuta,* one of the simplest and prettiest violas. Love-in-a-mist (*Nigella damascene*), a self-seeding champion, knits other plants together and tall, slim verbena sidles in towards the back wherever the love-in-a-mist leaves space. Big clumps of different varieties and shades of crocosmia range along the length of the border. Wigwams of sweet peas sit beside agapanthus and rich purple geum. Steely-blue grasses, tall, striped stipa grass and phormium vary the textures. The beds are so full that it is easy not to take in

Daphne and Jonathan Shackleton's new flower garden at Lake View in County Cavan.

all the plants. White and purple aconitum, day lilies, echinops, chocolate cosmos, a variety of alliums and white dahlias are worked together effectively. There are opium and oriental poppies everywhere and in every shade of pink, from the watery shell-pink of 'Perry's White' to the richest, shockingly vibrant pinks and plums in full double and single blooms. A red border filled with blood-red 'Bishop of Llandaff' dahlias, *Heliotrope arborescens* 'Marine', with aubergine-coloured flowers, red lilies and tall red lobelia make up the most sumptuous scrum of colour. Tree lupins and other flowering shrubs provide a backdrop to the dizzying array of flowers.

A damp, shady bed by the stone wall holds exotic-looking *Arisaema candidissimum*, Solomon's seal (*Polygonatum hirtum*) and *Anemonopsis macrophylla,* with its black stems and delicate pink, shade-loving flowers. The wall behind the bed has been almost completely covered and coloured green by moss. At one end of the garden, standing in the sun, is an old park bench with rows and rows of ancient horse shoes hanging over its back-board. These shoes, all dug out from the beds, bear testament to the enormous amount of digging and heavy labour the Shackletons have put into their garden. The vegetable beds are located at the back of the garden, set out in neat rows and occasionally cheered along by young rose bushes.

The surrounding land at Lake View is organically farmed, so in the summer months watch out for the wildflower meadows approaching the garden freely. Attached to the garden is a small, specialist nursery, where plants seen in the garden and often unavailable elsewhere can be bought. The entire garden is organic and it will enthuse new gardeners, and those thinking of converting to organic methods, to see such healthy, vital growth achieved without recourse to herbicides and pesticides. Today, some of the very best flower gardens on the island are being worked organically, with such success that they challenge the notion of working any other way. A few examples are: Graigueconna, Festina Lente, Valclusa and Wren's Wood in County Wicklow, Butterstream in County Meath, Clonaveel in County Fermanagh and Carnival in County Cork.

Lough Gowna, County Cavan; Tel/Fax: +043 83285; e-mail: bkoston@hotmail.ie
⬧ **Contact:** Bridget Koston ⬧ **Open:** all year round, Monday–Sunday, 2pm–6pm ⬧
No entrance fee ⬧ Not suitable for children; please note, dogs on leads ⬧ **Special features:** groups can book teas in advance; garden produce, cut flowers, vegetables and fruit for sale ⬧ **Directions:** leave the Cavan–Athlone road for Lough Gowna. In the village, turn right opposite the Catholic church. The garden is on the left.

Sunnyside is a pretty, acre-sized garden, divided into a number of small rooms. The site is hilly and windy, but these small divisions go a long way toward softening the effects of the Cavan gales. Within the hedged rooms and enclosures, surrounded by a trellis covered in climbers, the Kostons have made a *potager* full of vegetables and flowers arranged in attractive rows and beds. Like the Shackletons at Lake View, they are keen on organic methods, and practice an interesting form of recycling: the beds have been cleverly edged with upturned wine bottles sunk into the ground. Green, blue and gold glass sparkles in lines alongside the leeks and parsley. The bottles are filled with soil before being set into the ground, and they make a surprisingly tough edging, as well as putting the empty bottles to good use.

This is a garden made for the enjoyment of the Koston family and their guests – one of the very few places where tables and benches set into the middle of the sweet peas and runner beans are actually regularly used for sitting at and on. Weather permitting, this is where tea and a rest from the weeding is enjoyed. The tea-table faces down the garden and towards the hills beyond – the Kostons's 'borrowed landscape' – so their hard work can be enjoyed and admired.

GARDEN DESIGNERS

DAPHNE LEVINGE SHACKLETON

Garden Design, Mullagh, County Cavan; Tel: +046 42480; Fax: +046 42406; e-mail: jshack@indigo.ie

Daphne Levinge Shackleton specialises in restoring old country house and cottage-style gardens. She also advises on ecological planting. Examples of her design work include: Ballindoolin Garden (*see* County Kildare) and Loughcrew Historic Gardens in Oldcastle (*see* County Meath). Also *see* Lake View above.

NURSERIES AND GARDEN CENTRES

CAVAN GARDEN WORLD

Dublin Road, Cavan; Tel: +049 328888.

COUNTRY GARDEN CENTRE, THE

Cavanageeragh, Carrickmacross, County Cavan; Tel: +042 9661300.

PERGOLA NURSERIES

Virginia, County Cavan; Tel: +049 8547559.

COUNTY DERRY

County Derry stretches from the west and the Inishowen Peninsula, where it noses in on County Donegal, across to the River Bann in the east. Derry city, famous for its besieged walls and handsome Guild Hall, is a bustling place, increasingly popular with backpackers and students and home to one of the finest art galleries on the island: the Orchard Gallery. Lough Foyle and the Antrim coast dominate the north of the county and seaside towns like Portrush are populous, busy places. The most memorable place on Derry's north coast is the area around Castlerock, where the eccentric Frederick Hervey, earl of Bristol and bishop of Derry, built Mussenden Temple, perched on a cliff above the beach, for his cousin, Mrs Mussenden. The temple is included in all Northern Ireland Tourist Board literature, but no picture does justice to the situation of the classical temple – well worth a visit to see for yourself. The A2 coast road from the Donegal border down to Warrenpoint, a town bordering County Louth, is scenic, unhurried and a good touring road. The Glenshane Pass in the Sperrin Mountains makes a useful base for walking and hiking. There are many marked trails both here and through the mountain range, which runs right through the county. The soil in Derry is mainly acidic and fertile and there is a large number of gardens worth visiting, as well as a vibrant gardening culture.

BLACKHILL HOUSE

5 Crevolea Road, Blackhill, Coleraine, County Derry; Tel: +070 868377 ▪ **Contact:** Mrs Rae McIntyre ▪ **Open:** May–June, by appointment only to groups of ten or less ▪ **Entrance fee** donated to the National Trust ▪ Not suitable or safe for children ▪ **Special features:** refreshments are available, but must be booked in advance ▪ **Directions:** travel from Coleraine towards Garvagh for about 11km, until the turn for Crevolea Road appears discretely on the left (a horseshoe-shaped road). The house is first on the right if you take the first turn, and third on the left if you take the second turn.

Rae McIntyre's garden covers just under an acre in a picturesque area of mountain, woods and marked trails, near the village of Garvagh in the north of the county. Rae moved into Blackhill House in the 1970s and, like many non-gardeners, she wanted to have a garden but had no desire to actually work in one. But that was to change. 'So I started to garden very reluctantly, and it just took me over completely,' says Rae of her now-serious gardening habit. She has been toiling enthusiastically and avidly collecting plants ever since. Today she is well known as the regional correspondent for *Irish Garden* magazine. When Rae started work at Blackhill House, there were hints of what had once been an 'amazing garden', dating to the 1920s. That was long gone, however, so she razed the existing garden to the ground and started from scratch to create her own flower garden.

Rae's is what one might call a colour garden; she loves and understands colour deeply. The house straddles two long wings of the garden. To one side stands a lawn, surrounded by three stone-edged, colour-defined beds. In one bed reddish tulips emerge through rust-coloured euphorbia bracts in an inspired plant combination. Another happy mix is pink tulips with *Paeonia latiflora* 'Bowl of Beauty' and *Aquilegia* 'Nora Barlow', heuchera and autumn-flowering sedum. Because Rae matches all plants according to colour, strays occasionally appear in an unwanted shade, so a good deal of transplanting takes place within the garden walls. 'The plants tremble when they see me coming,' she laughs, undaunted at the prospect of moving plants at any time of the year. The trick is to have a well-manured and watered hole ready for the uprooted victim. Another important rule is to keep the transplant well watered for a good time after the move. Bigger plants and shrubs need close attention for two growing seasons.

Her white garden is a successful spot made of variegated honesty and dead nettle (*Lamium maculatum* 'White Nancy'), hellebores, variegated box, libertia, white tulips, celmisia and astelia. One noticeable plant here is a white willowherb: 'I bought it at Wisley and brought it carefully home on the plane and now I wish I hadn't. It's a complete thug and it spreads everywhere,' says Mrs McIntyre. As thugs go, however, it is pretty acceptable. Also in the white bed is an almost white *Rhododendron yakushimanum*, coupled with great big healthy clumps of false Solomon's seal (*Smilacina racemosa*), a fragrant, plume-like flower that grows like weeds in this spot. Next door bloodroot (*Sanguinaria canadensis*), what Rae calls 'the wretched mouse plant', also flowers white and is growing enthusiastically.

I loved the rich black tulips in the blue bed, tucked in beside blue poppies, acanthus, mauve roses and a mauve peony. The garden's inhabitants grow at a very healthy rate, although sometimes they can be a little too eager – a pergola being torn apart by rampant but lovely *Rosa filipes* 'Kiftsgate' is evidence of this. Little collections of ferns, a nursery bed to bring ailing plants back to health and a Mediterranean garden in the old stackyard finish off this interesting, crammed landscape.

BROOK HALL ARBORETUM

65 Culmore Road, Derry City, County Derry; Tel: +071 351297; e-mail: candr@iol.ie ▪ **Contact:** David Gilliland ▪ **Open:** all year round, by appointment only; groups welcome ▪ **Entrance fee** goes towards garden upkeep ▪ Supervised children welcome; please note, dogs on leads ▪ **Special features:** holds the national collection of escallonias, plus collections of conifers and hardwoods ▪ **Directions:** take the A2 out of the city in the direction of Culmore and Greencastle. After two roundabouts, look for two giant anchors on the right-hand side of the road, which mark the garden entrance.

In the late eighteenth century, successful Derry merchants erected a string of handsome villas along the banks of the River Foyle. Brook Hall is considered by some to be the finest of these, standing in a landscaped park with good views of the river. History is draped across the garden like a creeping vine – there is an aged yew that is said to stand over the remains of a French officer who died during the Siege of Derry in 1689.

It is the arboretum for which Brook Hall is renowned. This was started in 1929 by

Commander Frank Gilliland and continues to be expanded today by his cousin, David, an enthusiastic expert and tree-lover. The grounds of the arboretum cover thirty acres across a slope down to the River Foyle, and are part of a garden that dates back to 1780. (Some parts of the walled garden date even further back, to the 1600s.) Soon after the arboretum had been planted it was left to its own devices. When David Gilliland came along in 1959 to begin managing what he calls 'the choc-a-bloc place', he began by taking things out to improve the spacing between each tree. Conservation work on the garden is ongoing.

The collection of trees in the arboretum is like a cabinet of curiosities and several trips at different times of the year would be needed to appreciate it properly. It boasts specimens like Chinese red birch (*Betula albosinensis*), planted in 1937, which is a tree with everything: an unusual shape, decorative catkins, autumn colour and a good bark. Mr Gilliland reckons that the huge wellingtonia (*Sequoidendron giganteum*) at Brook Hall was the first in Ireland, having come from the famous Arnold Arboretum in Chicago via Kew Gardens in London. However, Birr Castle's specimen came to Ireland around the same time and naturally there is a gentlemanly dispute about which was, in fact, the first.

Wandering through the trees is a pleasure. To one side is a beautiful southern beech (*Nothofagus*), which was frost-damaged but is growing back. Close by, a pink *Rhododendron arboreum* unfurls its first buds inside the tree, which necessitates a hunt to find the flowers. Another beauty is *Rhododendron fictolacteum*, with furry orange underleaves and white-yellow flowers. Mr Gilliland advises that JM Gault, a rhododendron nurseryman (*see* p.359), stocks versions of this lovely plant. Among the large number of rhododendrons growing in the garden, *Rhododendron brachysiphon* or *maddenii* is planted in numbers: 'It has a good habit and leaves, but the flowers are vulgar, like cabbages,' Mr Gilliland says.

One surprising treat is a *Cupressocyparis leylandii*, grown as a specimen. Leylandii is not a bad tree, but it is much maligned because of the way it is used by poor gardeners as fast-growing hedging. In these circumstances it invariably grows too tall too fast, and stands like big dull ghosts, casting unwanted shade over the gardens of next-door neighbours. The story behind this particular tree is that it was smuggled to Ireland in 1937 in a tooth mug by an aspiring plant hunter. The man thought he had discovered something special, only to find that his discovery was no discovery at all – the tree was already in the country and growing at a great rate.

Further along the walk is a Chinese dogwood (*Cornus kousa var. chinensis*), whose creamy bracts had fallen when I saw it and been replaced with ripening, strawberry-like fruits. In the autumn its leaves colour a wonderful, strong red. This is another candidate for the tree-that-has-it-all award.

Apart from work in the arboretum, the walled garden was totally congested when Mr Gilliland started work here. In recent years he has cleared it out and has filled it with a collection of camellia, magnolia and bamboo. The walls have been used to accommodate varieties of clematis, wisteria and ceanothus. Out of the walled garden, the track leads on to the pond and a growing escallonia collection. Down here a eucalyptus swooned in the face of Hurricane Debbie, and fell over the brook after which the house is named. Allowed to grow on its side, it is still a beautiful tree and an object lesson in the virtue of waiting to see if a 'disaster' is really the catastrophe it appears to be.

Gardeners have always shared stock, and here a Lebanese oak (*Quercus libani*) given to the garden by Thomas Pakenham (*see* Tullynally Castle, County West-meath) is growing happily. In the same vein, on the day I visited, tiny specimens of auricula were being exchanged with Seamus O'Gaoithin from Glenveagh in Donegal. In the world of horticulture, sharing rare plants is vital. Working on the principal that you should never keep all your eggs in one basket, exchanges increase the chance of multiplying stock and lower the chance of pests or disease killing off the few plants in existence.

DOWNHILL CASTLE AND MUSSENDEN TEMPLE

Mussenden Road, Castlerock, County Derry; Tel: +070 848728 ■ **Open:** garden open all year round, Monday–Sunday, dawn–dusk; Mussenden Temple open April–June and September, weekends and bank holidays, 12–6pm; July–August, Monday–Sunday, 12–6pm; groups welcome ■ **No entrance fee** ■ Children must be well supervised due to cliff-top location; please note, dogs on leads ■ **Special features:** accommodation in the form of camping facilities is available ■ Member of National Trust ■ **Directions:** 8km west of Coleraine, on the coast road (A2).

If you decide to visit the gardens at Downhill Castle, arrive from the west on the A2 rather than from the east. From this approach the scenery is awe-inspiring. I would also recommend lingering until dusk to see the sun sink over Mussenden Temple, which lies at the very edge of the North Sea on one of the most beautiful deserted beaches on the island.

Frederick Hervey, earl of Bristol and bishop of Derry, created the demesne at Downhill between 1777 and 1788. He was an enthusiastic builder and in its heyday Downhill was an imposing black limestone house, surrounded by an elaborate collection of replicas of classical buildings, a walled garden, the famous temple, ha-has and several different gardens. Today, however, the house is in ruins, the architectural replicas are nearly all gone and the walled garden has vanished – apart from the ice house and dovecote, which are of more interest to the historian or archaeologist than the gardener. Only one of the stone cats on the Lion's Gate survives. (The name is misleading, as these were in fact leopards from the bishop's coat of arms.)

However, the rotund Mussenden Temple, perched out on the cliff, is still magnificent, showing the bishop's mania for the circular form. He built the temple on a line with the central axis of the house and named it indiscreetly after his cousin, Mrs Mussenden. The views out to sea from the temple, which was used as a library, are breathtaking – but so too is the wind that sweeps around it. Stories are told of how the servants had to crawl from the house up to the temple on hands and knees in the howling northerly winds to prevent being blown over the cliff. The bishop is reputed to have had a particularly rotten sense of humour, so this sight was possibly part of his enjoyment of the building.

Today the gardening glory of Downhill is the three-acre garden by the Bishop's Gate entrance to the estate, which was created by Lady Bruce in 1910. This garden fell into ruin and was restored by Jan Eccles, a warden who came to look after the place in the 1960s and stayed until the 1990s. Jan Eccles's garden is hilly, floral and informal, a singular place that looks natural and melts into the surrounding mature sycamores. A bog area in the middle of the mixed garden, full of flowering primulas, cowslips, flag irises and wild orchids, is one of the prettiest gardens of its type. Toward the ruined house, wild and flowering cherry and leycesteria border the walk. There are benches placed everywhere, as well as ruined statuary and bits of architectural salvage from the old manor house, showing that the chipped top of an old Doric column set into a lawn can be as beautiful in its own way as a perfect monument. The cottage is a little Gothic gem, covered in ivy, flame creeper (*Tropaeolum speciosum*), cotoneaster, ferns and mind-your-own-business (*Soleirolia soleirolii*). The planting around it is colourful and pretty.

DRENAGH

Limavady, County Derry; Tel: +077 722649; e-mail: dfl@drenagh.com ▪ **Contact:** Sheelagh McCausland ▪ **Open:** May–September, Monday–Friday, 2pm–6pm, by appointment only; groups welcome ▪ **Entrance fee** ▪ Supervised children welcome ▪ **Special features:** accommodation is available in one wing of the house, ring for details ▪ **Directions:** the gate lodge is on the north side of the main A37 road from Coleraine to Limavady, about 1.5km before Limavady.

With a tree surgeon in the husband-and-wife team who work the garden here, the trees at Drenagh obviously look their best, well-tended and smart, and as the estate and park date back to the 1700s, there is no shortage of aged beech and oak to attend to. The house you see today is not the original, but is the result of improvements in the early 1830s by the architect Charles Lanyon. It is an imposing-looking building, standing unadorned, flat and simple before a wide sweep of gravel and lawn.

Having worked with the renowned English gardener Beth Chatto, Mrs McCausland has a background in gardening and has been working on Drenagh for several years with her husband, Conolly. They have restored and altered it a little, as it has been altered so many times over its 300-year history. When the work began there were stretches of rose beds around the house: 'I removed the rose arbours because the mature trees were getting in their way,' explains Mrs McCausland. Indeed, she has moved much, including a great many rhododendrons and camellias, from amongst the general mass of trees siding the lawns. These uprooted plants now make up a camellia and rhododendron walk a little way from the house. A smart, manicured, minimalist look is more in keeping with the McCauslands's feelings about the garden. 'Getting the edges of gravel drives and paths absolutely perfect and keeping the grass looking good is what makes a place like this look right,' says Mrs McCausland. Today, the only flowers to be seen are splashes of crocosmia where the wood and lawn meet. Close by the house there is a little cottage garden, with a pale-pink wall covered in wisteria, pink hydrangea and pink roses, all in faded and watery shell-pinks. The whole picture is extremely effective and very simple. Meanwhile, in the walled garden, the pigs are working hard and eating their way through years of growth. The long-term hope is that it might be restored to its former glory.

This is a garden about big statements and grand sweeps, mature trees and impressive vistas. An exception to the rule is always welcome, and here the exception is in the moon garden, a feature Drenagh is well known for. At the time of visiting it was being replanted with all-white herbaceous plants, such as agapanthus, anemone, roses and alliums, hesperis and white Jacobs's ladder (*Polemonium caeruleum var. album*). To one side is a round window or gate – the moon gate – that frames the little garden and lends a view out to the woodland garden beyond. Little niches in the walls of the moon garden were once used to hold straw beehives.

The moon gate leads out to the Italian garden. This is balustraded and looks out over a little pond with two tiny bridges. In May and June it is quite stunning to look down onto the bridge, water, lush foliage and fresh, new rodgersia, ferns and spring flowers. The pond is actually a stream put in by Conolly's grandmother in 1968, but it looks older than that. It is possible for the sure-footed visitor to get down to the bottom of the Italian garden by way of a set of rough stone steps, but it is not necessary, as this enchanted, secluded part of the garden can be enjoyed just as well from the balustrade, before emerging out into the open parkland once more.

HILL COTTAGE

40 Duntibryan Road, Draperstown, County Derry; Tel: +079 628266 ▪ **Contact:** Kathleen McKeown ▪ **Open:** one charity day per year, telephone early in the summer for the annual date; also opens for groups, by appointment only ▪ **Entrance fee** donated to the Lifeboat Service ▪ Supervised children welcome ▪ **Special features:** teas can be booked by prior arrangement ▪ **Directions:** leave the village of Tobermore by the Draperstown Road (B41) at the church. Drive on until you see a bus shelter on the right, and take the turn at the shelter. The house is second on the left and signposted Hill Cottage.

The McKeown family bought Hill Cottage in 1960. Initially the garden was used to grow potatoes and vegetables for the family. Then, in 1975, the McKeown sisters, Kathleen and Mary, began to work the garden, and by the 1980s it was open to the public for charity. Set in the rolling Derry countryside, the garden at Hill Cottage is a charming country garden, still worked by Kathleen and Mary.

The original field hedges of mixed and native wild rose, thorn and ivy were cleverly maintained and trained to chest level so that the view of the 'God-given landscape' – the Sperrin Mountains – could be enjoyed. The women removed some sods from the bank under the hedge and planted the base with white Jacob's ladder (*Polemonium caeruleum var. album*), London pride (*Saxifraga x. urbium*) and bluebells. This hedge joins the garden seamlessly with the surrounding fields.

The long, one-acre site is divided into three areas, centering on a substantial lily pond. Around the edge of the pond, rough stone slabs have been colonised by Corsican mints, thyme, ground-hugging cotoneaster and 100 tiny self-seeded plants. Water in a garden is always an attraction, but moving water is the most desirable, creating a sweet background music. A low stone waterfall throws a stream of water into the pond, spraying the ferns, hostas and primulas. A little 'cottage' at the bottom of the garden, once a pig-sty, is now painted in cheerful colours and sports window boxes, a picket fence and a collection of tiny antique iron glue pots, old pumps and garden implements.

The loveliest pictures in the garden are those created by the frame of an arch cut in a tall *Cupressocyparin leylandii* hedge, which divides the back garden into two rooms. From one side you catch a glimpse of old-fashioned, fat, purple aquilegia or a heavily fruiting Victoria plum. In another direction round beds of liquorice-smelling fennel and monkshood (*Aconitum*), or crown imperial lilies and a fine weeping pear can be spotted through the frame of golden foliage. Elsewhere, another pretty arch was made from old church windows. This leads out to the front garden where, in front of the immaculate cottage, beds of double opium poppies, honeysuckle and ivy romp. A low beech hedge holds in shiny bergenia, leeks and red, splashy oriental poppies. The greenhouse is here too, like a glass treasure chest, surrounded by peonies and roses, and is stuffed with tomatoes and bedding waiting to go out for the summer. Everything about Hill Cottage garden is domestic, unpretentious and very attractive.

28 KILLYFADDY ROAD

Magherafelt, County Derry; Tel: +079 632180 ▪ **Contact:** Mrs Ann Buchanan ▪ **Open:** all year round, Tuesday–Saturday, telephone in advance during the winter months; groups welcome ▪ **Entrance fee** donated to charity ▪ Supervised children welcome, swing available to amuse them ▪ **Special features:** refreshments can be arranged for parties if booked in advance ▪ Member of Dúchas, the Heritage Service; National Trust; Landmark Trust ▪ **Directions:** leaving Magherafelt on the Moneymore Road, turn left opposite the petrol station and go 1.6km. The garden is clearly signposted.

A clue to the enthusiasm for gardening at Killyfaddy Road is a sign that reads: 'Garden on both sides of the road'. The Buchanans moved to their new house in 1971 and started gardening immediately. By the mid-1980s expansion to a plot across the road was necessary: 'We never intended to grow on that spot,' Mrs Buchanan explains with the innocence and puzzlement of the truly addicted. The rate at which they work the garden meant that expansion was inevitable, however, and no doubt it will continue into the surrounding fields over the next few years.

The second garden, across the road, is mostly herbaceous plants, which Mrs Buchanan really loves, but then Mrs Buchanan is an unashamed plant-lover. As a result, the garden's overall style is adapted to accommodate the plants rather than the other way around, yet the garden is no untidy jumble. In a garden with so much herbaceous planting, the dreaded task of staking could be a big job and an even bigger headache. Not so at Killyfaddy Road. Ann Buchanan plants everything cheek-by-jowl, 'and so everything holds everything else up,' she smiles, as though it were that simple. Monarda, larkspur, agapanthus, Michaelmas daisies and foxgloves, still flowering like mad at the end of August, make up one stuffed bed, where they do indeed all hold one another upright.

If something looks good in this garden, the Buchanans leave it as it is: 'A variegated tropaeolum appeared a few years ago in the garden and it self-seeds around like anything.' This is not a problem because, as Ann Buchanan concedes, 'It's a bit of a weed but a good weed.' A *Hoheria sexstylosa* and a pittosporum are fighting for space close by. Both were grown from seed and the principle of survival of the fittest will decide the outcome. A fine woody area is underplanted with little hellebores, hosta, cautleya and primulas in the damp soil. Out in the meadow garden marsh orchids and fritillarias mass enviably. The garden covers just over an acre but the division of the space makes it look as though it could be much larger.

The whole garden is worked organically. Mr Buchanan keeps bees. The hives were planted around with mountain ash, cotoneaster and roses, with an opening made strategically to direct and aim the bees' flight path out of the way of the garden. This means that all garden workers, legged and winged, can go about their business in peace. In the middle of this part of the garden is a pond, or 'puddle' as Ann calls it, full of water snails and sticklebacks, with waterside planting of iris and *Potentilla palustris*. Deep purple-blue willow gentian contrasts richly with airy white gypsophila beside the pond. There are paths everywhere, but interestingly most can't be used in the summer because the plants take over.

In the main garden, back on the other side of the road, an island of *Pratia pendunculata*, which Ann calls 'an upmarket weed', makes a good lawn. It sits like a sea of pale blue stars in the grass. This is something only rarely seen, and it is a pity because it is such a beautiful little plant. The reason it is not used so much is most likely that for a tiny plant it has empire-building tendencies. This side of the garden has more shaded areas, but it also has its own 'sunset strip', with a view of the sunset and fields beyond. A path leading up to the sunset seat is cleverly blocked at several points by clumps of herbaceous plants to prevent it from being too easy to see. There are hellebores and wildflowers under the trees, including a spread of pyramidal orchids. No plants grow too tall here, however, because 'the cows like to reach over the fence to eat whatever is on offer. They eat everything,' says Ann. Teasingly just out of their reach are scabious, borage, shasta, *Fritillaria meleagris* (snake's head fritillaries), daisies and red rose campion (*Lychnis coronaria*). A barley sugar tree (*Cercidiphyllum japonicum*) is one of the best trees to plant in a garden frequented by children – its leaves smell of barley sugar when crushed in the hand.

Like all the best gardeners, the Buchanans never stop working their plot. Even as she stops to talk, Ann is deadheading day lilies. The garden came second in the Antrim and Derry category of the Shamrock All Ireland Gardens Competition 1999, having come third in 1998. It must be due a win by now.

25 LOUGHAN ROAD

Coleraine, County Derry; Tel: +070 344981 ▪ **Contact:** Mrs and Mr AG Kennedy ▪ **Open:** June–August, by appointment only; small groups welcome ▪ **Entrance fee** donated to charity and goes toward garden upkeep ▪ Not suitable for children ▪ **Directions:** travelling from Coleraine on the Belfast Road, turn right at Damehead School and the sign for Loughan. About 1.6km along, turn right at the T-junction. The house is 100m along on the right, with a small courtyard to the front.

In 1976, when the Kennedys arrived at Loughan Road, there were just five plants in the long, steep, narrow, riverside garden. Mrs Kennedy's grandfather had been a nurseryman and so, with gardening in her genes, she began working the plot in 1988. Hers is not an easy site, but Mrs Kennedy was not daunted. 'I want a plant, so I find a place for it,' is her philosophy, and for her it works on a very steep garden that falls down into the River Bann – literally. When the river floods, the bottom one-third of the garden disappears under water. Rather than letting this interfere with the garden, Mrs Kennedy used the flood water by instigating a bog garden of primula and native boggy plants, as well as *Lobelia x. speciosa*. A frog pond has cardinal flower (*Lobelia cardinalis*), so-called for its red stems and flowers, growing in the water, where it is well protected from the slugs.

In making a wildflower garden on the riverbank, Mrs Kennedy had to get rid of the perennial weeds first. She obviously couldn't use weedkiller by the river, so she did what she calls 'a Bob Flowerdew on it'. This involved smothering the weeds by laying lengths of old carpet on the soil and leaving it in place for nearly a year. These blanket measures effectively killed off the tough perennial weeds. Once the unwanted weeds had been evicted she simply encouraged those wildflowers she wanted to see there. (For the unenlightened, Bob Flowerdew is one of the great advocates of organic gardening today. In his writings, television and radio appearances he recommends the use of old carpets, scrap and recycled household objects as part of a green and environmentally safe way of gardening.)

Back up and away from the riverbank, the house is perched on top of the hill and overlooks the garden and river. Marching up toward the house in terraces are arrays of tall, blood-red hollyhocks, clematis, alpine strawberries and asparagus. The asparagus grows happily in the flowerbed, flowering with bauble-like seedheads right through the winter and providing delicious shoots for the dinner table. Also here are lovely blue poppies. Other edibles in the garden include redcurrants. These grow on such a slope that it would take an experienced climber – or Mrs Kennedy – to harvest them. This is not a tightly planned garden, but it has a great deal of character.

MILLBANK

171 Roemill Road, Limavady, County Derry; Tel: +077 766632 ▪ **Contact:** Mr and Mrs Patrick and Veronique Agnew ▪ **Open:** May–September, Monday–Friday, 2pm–6pm, by appointment only; small groups welcome ▪ **Entrance fee** ▪ Supervised children welcome ▪ **Special features:** craft shop ▪ **Directions:** in Limavady town centre, turn left at the War Memorial on the Derry side onto Roemill Road and continue on, passing the Gorteen House Hotel on the left. Turn left at the sign for Cahan's Rock, and take the left fork. Millbank is the first house on the right.

When the Agnews came to live at Millbank, a large villa at the edge of Limavady, in 1998, the two-acre garden was in a bad state. Since then they have carried out a huge amount of work, turning the long site into several different and interesting gardens. 'We did have a good base of trees to work with, but apart from that it has been a pick-axe job,' says Mrs Agnew of the hard-won garden.

Arriving at the house down a gravel drive, the first garden visited is the intimate, plant-stuffed area near the house and stone outbuildings. 'You wouldn't want to be too civilised,' is Mrs Agnew's feeling about gardening, and the garden is not over-civilised. Tulips, roses and artichokes under elders, philadelphus and *Rosa* 'Roseraie de l'Haÿ' run into each other easily. The greenhouse is almost sunken below a mat of snow-in-summer (*Cerastium tomentosum*), phlomis and tiny euphorbia. This is a mass of flower and exuberant growth with big euphorbia, honesty and aquilegia self-seeding everywhere in the gravel. A great scrambling red rose, periwinkle (*Vinca minor*) and spiky teasels give the area a country feel. A snake of matt-green leaves and the lime, fluffy flower of Lady's mantle (*Alchemilla mollis*) border the long path through this part of the garden, past a bandaged tamarisk tree that testifies to the Agnews's love for the garden's residents: the tree cracked and broke in a recent storm, but the patient is now happily on the mend.

A path leads past the house and down a dark, snug, shrub-lined route into the second part of the garden. This was a field when the Agnews took over, but now it is a big pond garden in a naturally terraced lawn. They don't like the pond until May, because it is fed from a spring that doesn't fill it properly until late spring. Around the water's edge, red mimulus, bog bean and ranunculus compete for attention.

Further on from the pond is 'the last mucky corner' – a lovely little beech grove garden that Patrick Agnew was working the day I visited. The trees here only appeared ten years ago. They grow about a metre apart, slim and elegant. Patrick was building interesting little stone features and mounds among the trees. There's no shortage of stones on the site and Patrick is not short of attractive uses for them. It is intriguing how a distance of a very few kilometres can make for such variations in soil type – the Agnews work wet, stony clay while fellow gardener Doreen Moody (*see* Wheatfields, p.357), who lives just up the road, is on sand and gravel.

Mrs Agnew's four sons recently made her a new garden path for Mother's Day and she planted it up with rubus, argyranthemum and euphorbia. At the top of the garden and farthest from the house a ledged bed of evening primrose and poppies was arranged so that it would be best seen from below. White foxgloves and orange poppies, white violas and osteospermum are planted along two walks that travel one above another. It is hard to take your greedy gaze off these and look over the pond and gradations of lawn below. Up on the ledge that overlooks the pond and wood area is a pretty sunny area, with an unusual teasel hedge and scabious tumbling out on the path, freely allowed to 'do its thing'.

25 MOUNTSANDEL ROAD

Coleraine, County Derry; Tel: +070 542112; e-mail: amyan@gn.apc.org ※ **Contact:** Professor Amyan MacFadyen ※ **Open:** April–September, by appointment only; groups welcome ※ **Entrance fee** donated to the National Trust ※ Supervised children welcome; please note, dogs on leads ※ **Special features:** groups may book teas by prior arrangement ※ **Directions:** Mountsandel Road is 0.5km south of the town centre, opposite the old Coleraine Hospital.

Professor MacFadyen's garden is a very unusual hillside plot in the town of Coleraine. The remarkable professor started the garden proper in 1988 on this sheltered two-and-a-half-acre site swooping down to the River Bann. It is a wonderful garden, full of healthy, well-coordinated plants. Stepping into the garden one of the first sights is *Rosa* 'Mme Isaac Pereire'. Professor MacFadyen grows 100 rose varieties in his garden, but he does so subtly – his is not a show-off's garden straining to proclaim its great collection at every turn. Nonetheless the roses are everywhere, knotted in between flowers and shrubs, scrambling opportunistically over and through every opening. 'Rambling Rector' climbs up one apple tree, while sweet, white 'Bobbie James' takes on another. The professor doesn't prune these tree-supported roses, and even points indulgently to a big *Rosa filipes* 'Kiftsgate' that managed to pull an apple tree down. He refuses to complain, even about such a bold rose. In fact, his only complaint is that the big chestnut tree in his garden, once denuded annually of its conkers by young boys, no longer attracts raiding parties. It saddens him that boys don't want to play conkers anymore.

In the vegetable and fruit garden a small number of high-bush blueberries produce over a hundredweight of fruit in a season. These are delicious and easy to grow, as long as they have good acid soil. The professor organises a 'pick-your-own' day with his raspberries and blueberries once a year for charity. Sweet pea, pumpkin and courgette surround a handsome walnut tree in the centre of this area. 'I planted the tree thirty-two years ago, but it did nothing until five years back,' explains the professor, counselling patience. He is a keen conservationist and grows a number of rare plants for seed for the Henry Doubleday Research Association, including 'Daniel's Defiance' runner beans. He encourages lacewings by filling small boxes with straw to attract aphids for them. They then oblige by staying on and eating more aphids. Admiring the beautiful, fringed, flowering climber *Berberidopsis*, the professor explains that in Chile it is grown for making baskets.

At the bottom of the garden is a field where horses used to graze. When they vacated, alders and sycamores sprang up, creating a natural wood which has been gently encouraged along. Down here, enjoying the shade and the riverside damp, are meconopsis and shuttlecock ferns. There is a small stream at the bottom of the garden, bridged several times before it enters the river. An authentic *Geranium* 'Johnson's Blue' self-seeds everywhere. This is a flower that is constantly mixed up and mistaken: those seeking the elusive real thing, enquire within.

BERNADETTE O'HAGAN'S GARDEN

24 Littlebridge Road, Moneymore, County Derry; Tel: +086 737600 ▪ **Contact:** Mrs Bernadette O'Hagan ▪ **Open:** all year round, Monday–Saturday, 9.30am– dusk, by appointment only (telephone in advance); groups welcome, by appointment only ▪ **No entrance fee** ▪ Supervised children welcome ▪ **Special features:** very good nursery attached to garden ▪ **Directions:** leave the M1 and travel through Stewartstown and on towards Coagh. About 8km from Stewartstown, take the left turn signposted for Moneymore and 3km along you'll see the sign for the garden centre. The house is on the left.

Twenty years ago Bernadette O'Hagan moved into a new house in Moneymore, surrounded by a plain plot of land, and began to work the place with a vengeance. The result is a fine garden and a collection of plants that invites a great amount of study. From three well-cut box plants, shaped like round loaves of bread, to the perfect arrangement of trees, grasses and annuals in well-placed pots and gravel beds, her garden is a series of well-designed areas filled with a huge variety of plants.

Bernadette is a fanatical gardener and plantswoman and has been all her life. She can mark out her life in plants. Some of the plants in her immaculate garden are specimens she has had since childhood, such as the little horned *Viola cornuta* and a *Primula* 'Wanda', both inherited from her father's garden. 'Even when I was small, I only ever read plant books,' she explains as we walk along one of the gorgeous, stuffed beds and she points out another old friend that came with her from childhood: soldiers and sailors (*Pulmonaria officinalis*). Further along, the snowdrop tree (*Halesia carolina*), a white, bell-flowered shrub that her mother gave her, enjoys pride of place in the middle of a fine, varied shrub bed.

'Impeccable' is the word that best describes the runs of smartly matched and tended shrubs, like golden philadelphus, crinodendron and a lovely blue-tipped abies that resides at the front of the garden. The shrub beds are divided by serpentine grass paths which lead visitors through changes in foliage, flower and shade so that they can enjoy and get close to as many plants as possible. Plants in the garden are accommodated grandly; Bernadette even built a garage in order to house a huge golden hop. She combines good plants with good taste, for example, placing a white azalea and a variegated hosta together, or a huge, white-flowering *Clematis* 'Alphabet' beside a red cut-leaf acer.

Bernadette has a talent for training plants and, as well as numerous millimetre-perfect box and yew pyramids, balls, loaves of bread and corkscrews, there is a pyracantha trained as a standard ball and an impressive wisteria in a large pot, dripping flowers from its lollipop trunk. Thankfully for visiting gardening enthusiasts, she started a nursery about ten years ago from where she sells plants taken from her garden, so that others can benefit from her immense talent. Not only that, but you can also benefit from the vast knowledge she has gleaned over the years, as there is a plaque standing next to each plant, displaying useful tips and invaluable information.

SPRINGHILL

20 Springhill Road, Moneymore, Magherafelt, County Derry; Tel/Fax: +086 748210; e-mail: uspent@smtp.ntrust.org.uk ▪ **Contact:** the Administrator ▪ **Open:** April, May, June and September, weekends and bank holidays, 2pm–6pm; pre-booked tours can visit throughout June, except Thursday; July–August, Monday–Sunday (except Thursday), 2pm–6pm; groups welcome ▪ **Entrance fee** donated to the National Trust ▪ Supervised children welcome; please note, dogs on leads ▪ **Special features:** costume museum and rooms to visit in the 300-year-old house; plant fair in May; Wellbrook Beetling Mill; Teddy Bears' Picnic in June; walks for the visually impaired can be arranged; meals for groups should be booked in advance ▪ Member of National Trust ▪ **Directions:** the house is 1.6km from Moneymore village, near Cookstown, on the Moneymore–Coagh road (B18).

'Good' Will Conyngham, a soldier who made a name for himself as one of the defenders of the walls during the Siege of Derry, built the house at Springhill when he married Anne Upton in 1680. The marriage settlement required that he build 'a convenient house of lime and stone, two storeys high with the necessary office houses'. He fulfilled the brief and subsequent generations of Conynghams and Lenox-Conynghams lived in and enlarged the original house over the centuries. Their tenure of the house terminated in 1957 when the house and all its contents were left to the National Trust; it can now be visited by the public. Along with its costume museum, the house is filled with the furniture, paintings and everyday living items from the family's 300-year occupation, making Springhill a marvellous mixed venue for a family day out.

The house Will Conyngham built is a somewhat unusual but handsome white-washed building, with deep slate roofs, curved gable ends and clean, simple lines. At the front of the house is a forecourt and planted on one side of this is a myrtle (*Luma apiculata*), the orange bark of which stands out against the white wall. Four big, rounded cones of bay, joined by low walls of box, march out from the house, past the sort of well-raked gravel that would do a Japanese garden proud. The effect is formal and minimalist. That restraint is loosened around the outbuildings, where climbing roses and spreading rosemary (*Rosmarinus officinalis* 'Prostratus') soften the white walls and anchor the house.

Back at the house and just off the courtyard car park is a sloped, narrow, walled garden with a path sideplanted with regularly spaced standard Irish junipers (*Juniperus communis* 'Hibernica'). Between these tidy, bluish columns are violet-coloured willow gentian, viola and penstemon. Yellow climbing roses and yellow lilies stand against the wall on the other side of the path. This path leads down to a camomile lawn surrounded by stone paths and herb beds on stone banks. Different varieties of mint, rue, artemisia, sage and tansey scent and softly colour the beds. Tansey is an incorrigible spreader, but here it was prevented from spreading and expanding too far by sunken corrals of slate.

Over the walls, towering beech and oak invite the walker out of the garden to the park, but not quite yet. The route leads into another, much bigger walled garden. A slate sundial stands in the middle, on a rough, ancient-looking stone plinth, surrounded by hostas and more day lilies. The whole area is wrapped around with herbaceous borders full of white phlox, in front of purple clematis, pink Japanese anemone and yellow potentilla with yellow day lilies growing through it. The planting is simple, in keeping with the no-nonsense, handsome old house. The beds work well, filled with generous blocks of individual plants.

An entrance from the front of the house passes the garden and leads out through a small, Gothic, arched doorway to a set of steps covered in roses and Chilean potato vine *(Solanum crispum)*. From here a gunnera-lined pond on the edge of the woods can be seen. Taking another route, a fine walk of young beech trees will make an impressive feature over the next fifty years or so. This beech avenue strays off towards a folly that stands above the house on a slight hill. Following this path reveals several other paths into and through the woods.

STREEVE

Limavady, County Derry; Tel: +077 766563 ▪ **Contact:** June and Peter Welsh ▪ **Open:** by appointment only; groups welcome ▪ **Entrance fee** ▪ Supervised children welcome ▪ **Special features:** light lunches are available, but must be booked in advance ▪ **Directions:** Streeve is next door to Drenagh, on the Limavady–Coleraine road (A37).

Until a few years ago, Streeve, the Welshs's beautiful redbrick home near Limavady, was a range of barns, a forge and a tractor shed belonging to Drenagh, the big house next door. This changed in 1986 when Streeve House was restored by June and Peter. Work on the garden started in a modest way in 1996, working out from one house wall and into the fields. Paddy Bowe, a garden historian and a lecturer on Victorian gardens, drew up a plan for the new garden, which Mrs Welsh wanted to lay out close to the house. Consequently, the chief area of the garden is domestic and small-scale. It fits well along the length of the house and is divided into small rooms by waist-high hedging. The larger, mature trees are held at bay in the distance, framing the views and forming boundaries for the outer garden.

A line of irises sunbathing on the wall welcomes the visitor into the pretty, south-facing garden. Box plants were planted in low hedges as surrounds to the flowerbeds, and these have matured beautifully. One box cone in the middle of each bed adds vertical structure and formality to the colour-blocked beds, which have been planted with single-colour herbaceous perennials. Pink, white, yellow and bronze were the base colours, but June Welsh is now modifying this scheme a little by relaxing the rule and allowing other colours to slip into the tight divisions. The result is both ordered and very pretty. The ideas of a designer, it should be remembered, are there to be customised and personalised by the owner who knows the space intimately.

Warming themselves on the redbrick walls of the house, honeysuckle, jasmine and old roses reach upwards with their feet tucked into lavender and pineapple sage. This prevents the ugly sight of bare-legged roses and creates the sort of plant-cram that deprives weeds of breathing space. Further along the path is a small rose garden with obelisks and arches for the roses to ascend. Again, not to be too purist, a *Clematis* 'Jackmanii' adds to the variety. The clove-scented 'Blush Noisette' is one of Mrs Welsh's favourites here, a very old rose that was first bred in France in 1817. Creamy and strong-scented *Rosa* 'Yvonne Rabier' grown through a crab apple in the centre is as pretty as anything.

The next little garden is a frame yard for the plants awaiting their turn to flourish in the main garden. There is a yew hedge around this area that will only grow to just over a metre high, enclosing it and finishing off the room effect. Down in the kitchen garden some imagination was used in creating walls of peas, a hornbeam hedge and artichokes. These three are immovable. Everything else is rotated within the beds to keep the vegetables healthy and vigorous.

Away from the house the structure of the garden loosens and some lovely walks and arches have been set out in the lawns, which stretch up to a cuttings garden and some groves of mature maples. This area was once a rubbish dump from which, Mrs Welsh explains, enormous quantities of old bottles and scrap are still being dug out. Bergenia is used here as a weed-suppresser; Mrs Welsh is a great believer in hiding the weeds with plants, and plenty of them.

In every garden there is room for a bit of the wild stuff and Mrs Welsh's is no exception. There is one final flowerbed of wild reds out beyond the trees, well away from the house. The colour red travels and draws itself in toward the viewer, which is why many people find it best to plant it off in the distance. Out here on the edge of the garden, the exotics – mad-coloured dahlias, ruby-coloured *Nicotiana sylvestris*, flamboyant varieties of hemerocallis and *Crocosmia* 'Lucifer' – disport themselves happily. The bold ones are kept at bay, but they are kept.

WALWORTH GARDEN   ♿

45 Walworth Road, Ballykelly, County Derry; Tel: +077 762671 ▪ **Contact:** Brian and Noreen Brown ▪ **Open:** end June–end July, Friday–Sunday, 2pm–5pm, but visitors must ring ahead for an appointment; also charity open days when an entrance fee applies; groups welcome ▪ **No entrance fee,** except on charity open days ▪ Supervised children welcome ▪ **Directions:** located on the Limavady–Derry road (A2), about 5km west of Limavady, on the edge of Ballykelly village. Walworth is opposite the Droppin' Well pub.

The old walled garden at Walworth was both redesigned and replanted in 1989. The one-and-a-half-acre plot is gardened by the Brown family with occasional extra help – some of which I met in the shape of a team of boys from the village who were raking gravel paths in the walled garden with admirable energy in advance of a garden open day. It is a very good-looking garden and appears more mature than its ten years, but given its situation beside the fine old house and pretty stone outbuildings this is not surprising.

Entering from a courtyard through a gate in the wall, the sense of anticipation is well rewarded by a truly lovely, old-fashioned country garden. An old slate roof, full of white doves sleepily sunning themselves, overlooks it all. Paths through the garden are edged cleverly with upturned slates bedded into the gravel. Sedum and saxifrage are encouraged to interlace these Lilliputian slate 'walls'. Great patches of house leeks (*Sempervivum*), little Welsh poppies, mixed geraniums, mint and Lady's mantle (*Alchemilla mollis*) run unchecked, self-seeding everywhere within the beds and on the paths.

The first big herbaceous border encountered begins as a white border with pale, papery rock rose flowers (*Cistus*), hydrangea, apple mint and cream-coloured variegated hosta. The mood then moves toward bolder, darker colours: red scabious, lavatera, geums and other strong-coloured herbaceous plants. The outer path in this rectangular walled garden runs parallel to the walls and continues around to the next border – a strong confection of red, purple and yellow. At the centre of the garden a pond surrounded by a circular room-within-a-room of hedging, trellis and rose arches feels almost like a maze. Standing in this circle one of the views is out towards a line of pleached limes that dissects the garden, dividing the ornamental areas from the productive areas. Pleaching involves creating what looks like a giant hedge on stilts. The trees are wired in to each other with a frame and shaped strictly to give a strong, regimental look. In this case the limes are set on top of a raised bank.

The levels and slope of Walworth Garden are deceptive, and it is something of a surprise to find that the lower one-third of the garden is sunken. This is an area of fruit trees, with plums and cherries lined out around a platform. Outside the walled garden, a side garden contains two huge tulip trees (*Liriodendron tulipifera*), flowering cherries and acers, ranging around a large square of lawn.

WHEATFIELDS

119 Seacoast Road, Limavady, County Derry; Tel: +077 762674 ▪ **Contact:** Doreen Moody ▪ **Open:** at any time, but only by advance appointment and only to individuals; write for an appointment ▪ **Entrance fee** donated to charity ▪ Supervised children welcome; please note, dogs on leads ▪ **Special features:** plants occasionally sold for charity ▪ **Directions:** travel downhill on the High Street in Limavady and cross over the River Roe. Turn right off the road onto the B119. Drive for approximately 1km until you pass a tiny village of redbrick houses. Wheatfields is on the right, set back but visible from the road.

Doreen Moody is a renowned gardener, known both to readers of *Irish Garden* and to BBC Radio Ulster listeners. She lives in a splendid redbrick house that dates to the early 1700s. Situated in the countryside near Limavady, it is idyllically surrounded by fields of sheep, with oak, red chestnut and beech trees guarding the house from the road. Mrs Moody's grandfather told her that these 'guardian' trees were bought in 1926 for the garden, but a mistake led to the plain white variety being planted inside and the red ones being placed out in the park; Mrs Moody likes them where they are. Under these trees, sheets of crocus and snowdrops cover the ground in the spring, alongside erythroniums, fritillaries and double forms of wild anemone and cow parsley or Queen Anne's lace (*Anthriscus sylvestris*).

This is a garden with a great sense of history and continuity. Mrs Moody remembers her father-in-law gardening the place for many years and, aware of the importance of continuity, the apple trees she planted many decades later were taken from cuttings from older fruit trees. 'I felt I would like to keep the things that were here, here,' she says simply. With this in mind, cuttings were also taken from the roses planted by her father-in-law in 1909. (Her father-in-law died in 1964 and Doreen took over the work then.) Plants grown from cuttings and seeds are to be found throughout the garden. Doreen has a particularly useful tip for propagating golden or variegated shrubs: choose the palest spot on the plant for cuttings and the young plants will grow in the desired bright shade. This works with everything from golden box and privet (*Ligustrum*) to iris and golden day lilies (*Hemerocallis*).

Wheatfields is filled with interesting plants and it is a pleasure to visit and to listen to Doreen talk about the place: 'My type of gardening is experimenting. I was never trained, but I always loved flowers for the house and I found that I spent too much money on them, so I thought I'd start to grow them, and my interest took off from there.' Her interest has created a classic garden, the sort of just-tamed flower-filled heaven that both gardeners and non-gardeners adore. Around the house there is a variety of garden rooms with colour-matched beds of old pink roses, pink honesty (*Lunaria annua*) and pink foxgloves. Given a long leash, the plants oblige by showing taste in self-seeding, for example, a rich pink bloody cranesbill (*Gladiolus communis subsp. byzantinus*) from Donegal and Bowles's golden grass all landed together by happy, stylish coincidence – organic serendipity.

Redbrick paths and posts act as colour-coordinated sculptures and leaning posts for roses and clematis. These break up the space into intimate areas, stuffed with plants such as little orange double poppies and fair maids of France (*Ranunculus aconitifolius*). In a small pond area, the scent of a miniature lilac is almost overpowering. Roses with ornamental strawberries at their feet squash up against libertia and variegated flag iris. Big beds run around the edge of the garden in colour blocks. In one area, yellow tree peonies, golden privet, syringa and corkscrew hazel brighten up the trees. Elsewhere cornus, white goat's rue, white cherry and tree lupin make up a good white shrub border. *Rosa* 'Twin Bridges' was a gift from an old lady up the road. A great number of Doreen's plants have associations with old people and old gardens, like a big clump of *Lilium pyrenaicum*, one of the Turk's cap lilies, which was given to Mrs Moody as part of a bunch of flowers and has now returned to its roots in the truest sense of the phrase.

Throughout the garden, under trees, there are large numbers of healthy hostas that are grown from seed: 'They do well here because my frogs kill the slugs.' As a result, Doreen has no great hatred for slugs, apart from the ones that come through the cat flap seeking the cat's milk; apparently, slugs love milk. As the garden is completely green, with no herbicides or pesticides at all, there is a great amount of wildlife, including lizards.

GARDENING CLUBS AND SOCIETIES

CITY OF DERRY AND DISTRICT HORTICULTURAL SOCIETY

Contact: Miss Joan Little; Tel: +071 43878.

COLERAINE HORTICULTURAL SOCIETY

Contact: Derrick Turbitt, 16 Swilly Road, Portstewart, County Derry; Tel: +070 833963.

The Coleraine Horticultural Society meets

from September to April on the fourth Tuesday of each month at 7.45pm, at the Coleraine campus of the University of Ulster. Meetings mostly consist of talks given by invited speakers. A spring show is held in April and during the summer garden visits are arranged. New members are always welcome.

HEATHER SOCIETY

Contact: Mr J Bradley; Tel: +079 642323.

MID-ULSTER FLORAL ART SOCIETY

The Mid-Ulster Floral Art Society meets from September to May, on the first Tuesday of each month, at 7.30pm in Maghera Primary School. The club, as its name suggests, is largely a floral art club, but they also hold gardening talks and in the summer they arrange garden visits abroad as well as local trips.

ROE VALLEY GARDENING SOCIETY

The Roe Valley Gardening Society meets from September to February, on the last Thursday of each month, at 7.30pm in the Leisure Centre in Limavady. Regular plant sales are held, and two summer trips are arranged each year. New members are welcome. Visitors may attend occasional meetings for an admission charge.

SOUTH DERRY GARDENING CLUB

Contact: Mrs Ann Buchanan; Tel: +079 632180.

The South Derry Gardening Club meets all year round, on the second Thursday of each month, in Maghera Primary School. The club is small but very active. In August they hold a barbecue. Summer garden visits are arranged and an annual flower show is held in September.

NURSERIES AND GARDEN CENTRES

LIMAVADY GARDEN CENTRE

25 Tyler Road, Limavady, County Derry; Tel: +077 763472.

MID-ULSTER GARDEN CENTRE

35 Station Road, Maghera, County Derry; Tel: +079 642324.

NELSON'S FLOWERS

Maghera, County Derry; Tel: +079 642653.

NESS NURSERIES

234 Glenshane Road, Derry, County Derry; Tel: +071 301285.

RHODODENDRON AND AZALEA NURSERY (JM GAULT)

Cahery House, 84 Broad Road, Limavady, BT49 OQH; Tel: +077 722610.

A specialist nursery stocking a huge number of hardy hybrid, dwarf, Yakushimanum and species rhododendrons, as well as azaleas. A plant list is available in return for a charity donation.

RICHFIELD NURSERY AND GARDEN CENTRE

Tel: +071 301800.

ROSSMORE GARDEN CENTRE

Cookstown Road, Dungannon, County Tyrone.

TREE TOPS GARDEN CENTRE

Curran Road, Castledawson, County Derry.

COUNTY DONEGAL

Donegal is a magnificent county; there are many people who would holiday nowhere else. It is rugged, sparsely populated and mostly untamed. Its mountains, lakes and beaches, cliffs and coast drives are among the most striking natural beauty spots on the island. In Donegal it is easy to feel that you are in the land that time forgot, where life is lived at a different pace – a far cry from the stressful lives of the bigger cities. For those interested in Irish language and culture, there is a substantial Gaeltacht area around Falcarragh, one of the northernmost parts of the county. For anyone keen to explore the natural beauty of the place, there are many walking trails, including the longest trail in Ireland, the Ulster Way, which passes through the Derryveagh and Bluestack Mountains. The Inishowen Peninsula, Glenveagh National Park and the Glengesh Pass are truly spectacular places to walk and drive. However, a good deal of time must be set aside for travelling, as the roads are, to be charitable, slow. There are only a small number of gardens to be visited in Donegal, but they are each very special and should not be missed.

ARDNAMONA

Lough Eske, County Donegal; Tel: +073 22650; e-mail: info@ardnamona.com ▪ **Contact:** Kieran and Amabel Clarke ▪ **Open:** all year round, daily, 10am–5pm, telephone to book; groups welcome ▪ **Entrance fee** ▪ Supervised children welcome; please note, dogs on leads ▪ **Special features:** rhododendron garden – visit in April or May to see the rhododendrons in full bloom; tearoom snacks are available, but must be booked in advance ▪ **Directions:** from Donegal town take the N15 to Letterkenny. After 5km take a small turning on the left marked 'Harvey's Point and Lough Eske'. Go straight on for 7km. Look for a gate lodge and white gates on the right.

Ardnamona is a rhododendron-lover's garden. It is a naturalistic, wild garden, filled with rhododendron and specimen trees. People who know say that the plantations here are the nearest one will get in Ireland to the natural rhododendron woods in the high Himalayas or in China. The place certainly has a wild feel to it. Walking around, it is easy to get lost in the middle of so many wonderful trees, and the guide leaflet does little to keep one on track.

The Wray family built the house in the 1840s and laid out the first gardens. It was the fashion at that time to devote separate areas of a garden to a particular type of planting, like a rosarium for roses or an arboretum for trees or, in this case, a pinetum for conifers. The Ardnamona pinetum was planted up with monkey puzzle trees (*Araucaria araucana*), coast redwood (*Sequoia sempervirens*) and oriental spruce (*Picea orientalis*). It was largely the next owners of the house, the Wallace family, who put in the rhododendrons in the 1880s. This makes the Ardnamona collection one of the longest established in Ireland.

Along the wooded drive is an unusual dry stone wall that backs onto and banks up the slope behind it. Water draining off the slope runs down the wall, making it a man-made waterfall. Pennyroyal and tiny ferns, violas and primroses have colonised the cracks between the stones. The stonework in this wall is beautifully executed and worth studying. The magnificent trees are ranged around the garden in groves and in sizes not usually seen in Ireland; *Rhododendron arboreum* and *Rhododendron falconeri* reach up to nineteen metres high in places. Many of the plants are parent stock of the rhododendrons in Glenveagh (*see* p.363).

The garden has not always been worked however, and between the 1950s and 1980s the whole place fell into serious neglect. Rescue arrived in 1990 in the shape of Kieran and Amabel Clarke. Much of their work has involved a battle with the national weed collection of wild *Rhododendron ponticum*, knotweed and crocosmia. I am glad to say that the Clarkes are winning the battle, slowly but surely. Ardnamona was designated a National Heritage Garden in 1991. This has given the brave Clarkes even more encouragement to continue the salvation and conservation of the magical garden, in between tending to their guests in the charming old house.

BALLYDAHEEN GARDEN

Ballydaheen, Portsalon, County Donegal ▪ **Contact:** David and Mary Hurley ▪ **Open:** May–September, Monday–Thursday and Saturday, 10am–3pm; apply by post for appointment; groups welcome ▪ **Entrance fee** donated to the Lifeboat Service ▪ Supervised children welcome ▪ **Special features:** private access to the Seven Arches caves ▪ **Directions:** the garden is well signposted and lies 1.6km outside Portsalon and 2km from Portsalon Golf Club. Park on the road, 100m up from the garden.

The garden at Portsalon overlooks Lough Swilly on the north Donegal coast. It spreads out around the Japanese-influenced house that David and Mary Hurley built for themselves at the beginning of the 1990s. The garden is divided into separate, large and spacious rooms, alternately designed by husband or wife and differing considerably from each other, like duelling gardens. Fine gateways, made by a local craftsman, separate some of the rooms from each other. Indeed, the re-building of dry stone walls and old outbuildings on the site has relied heavily on local crafts. David Hurley is particularly interested in this aspect of building a garden.

There is a great array of good statuary throughout the space, including some lovely stone urns that are placed to pull the eye across the lawns. A fine-sized pond close by the house is well planted up and full of tadpoles (although the pondside sign warns of crocodiles!). The lawns are like bowling greens, edged to perfection. The borders are very light on colour – in keeping with the Japanese influences seen all over the garden. All the plants that we associate with tender climates, such as tree ferns, paulownia and Mexican pines (*Pinus cembroides*), do surprisingly well here in the cold north of the North, and in a landscape very different to the forest-like shelter of Glenveagh (*see* p.363). Surprisingly, the Hurleys don't have to wrap their tree ferns in winter. David is very pleased with the progress of his young garden: 'We overplanted the garden when we started because we expected a loss of thirty percent of the plants to salt spray and wind, but we only suffered ten percent losses and so now the garden is completely overstocked. We have no frost here out on the sea at all. The microclimate is wonderfully favourable.' This happy outcome is not without its drawbacks, however – David is now in the process of thinning the ever-healthy beds.

While there is no frost, the Hurleys have to deal with wild salt winds on the seaside site. So one of the main jobs to be done when setting up the garden was the planting of windbreaks. A fine, tight, tidy hedge of New Zealand daisy bush (*Olearia*) does the job nicely. This is always a good seaside plant, as is New Zealand flax (*Phormium tenax*), which has also been planted liberally in this garden.

David loves bamboo and highly recommends the plants sold at Peter Stam's nursery in Waterford (*see* Nurseries and Garden Centres, County Waterford). The bamboos have been planted in walks and groves and the sea breezes creeping through them create gentle rustling sounds. Stream gardens, rose gardens, a good herb garden and heather beds fill the other rooms. David is in charge of the 'food department', as he describes the walled vegetable plot where he grows his favourite early-cropping French waxy potatoes – which cannot be bought in Ireland – among the more usual peas, cabbages and salad crops.

The planting and development of the garden is ongoing and at the moment a circular rhododendron walk is in the process of being laid out. The Hurleys put in six hours a day each on the garden and it shows. The glory of the garden, however – not to detract from the enormous amount of work the Hurleys put in – is the Seven Arches. This is the name given to a remarkable set of interlocking caves, which are reached via stairs that lead down from the bottom the main garden. The Seven Arches are the water feature to beat all water features.

GLEBE HOUSE AND GALLERY

Churchill, County Donegal; Tel: +074 37071; Fax: +074 37521 ▪ **Contact:** the Administrator ▪ **Open:** Easter, contact for annual dates; May–September, Saturday–Thursday, 11am–6.30pm; groups welcome ▪ **Entrance fee** ▪ Supervised children welcome ▪ **Special features:** art gallery ▪ Member of Dúchas ▪ **Directions:** 18km from Letterkenny on the R251.

If you have travelled as far as Glenveagh, it would be a great pity not to finish your visit with a trip to Glebe House and Gallery nearby. There must be something in the air in this part of Donegal that imparts a sense of philanthropy to its inhabitants; Glebe House was the home of artist and collector Derek Hill, who left his home and considerable art collection to the Irish nation. The Hill Collection includes works by Pablo Picasso and Oskar Kokoshka.

The garden at Glebe can be spotted from the road as it circumnavigates the lake. Huge gunnera and rodgersia leaves stand out against the bare, wild Donegal landscape, enticing the traveller in from a distance. Once in the garden, there are sunny banks with groves of the soft or woolly tree fern (*Dicksonia antarctica*) and tree ferns sheltered by hardier trees and shrubs. Rough, round boulders glowering on the grass are reminders that this is a tamed garden set into a very harsh landscape.

The house is fronted by a low wall of clematis, honeysuckle and jasmine, as well as big flowering peonies. The open summerhouse or veranda at the side of the house is quite unusual, with steps up to the jasmine-surrounded window; its ornate wrought ironwork is very striking. Under an arch and around the lawn the route leads into a more intimate cottage garden with beds of herbaceous plants and hybrid tea roses. Little gravel paths take you down a level into a courtyard full of clematis, hydrangea and a great number of big hostas, single red dahlias and, by the house, more large shrubs up against the wall. A little garden of herbs and soft fruit, known as Grace McDermot's garden, is filled with strawberries and red, black and white currants. A quite surreal feature is a beech tree with a brick wall built into a hole in it; a reminder to the garden visitor that there is another aspect to Glebe House, namely the art collection in the gallery.

GLENVEAGH GARDENS AND NATIONAL PARK ◉ ♿

Churchill, Letterkenny, County Donegal; Tel: +074 37088/+074 37090; Fax: +074 37072; website: www.heritageireland.ie ▪ **Contact:** Carmel Brady ▪ **Open:** 17 March–first Sunday in November, daily, 10am–6.30pm; October, closed every Friday; last admission at 5pm; guided tours available; groups welcome ▪ **Entrance fee** gives access to interpretive centre, park and garden ▪ Supervised children welcome ▪ **Special features:** video and interpretive centre; an excellent book outlining the history of the castle, garden, landscape, geology, wildlife and trails in Glenveagh can be bought at the interpretive centre ▪ Member of Dúchas ▪ **Directions:** 24km northwest of Letterkenny on the Churchill–Dunlewy road, well signposted.

The nineteenth-century castle at Glenveagh sits in the middle of a 36,000-acre demesne of rocky hills, mountains, lakes and woods. It is the biggest single protected area of Irish land, with seventeen miles of fencing, its own red deer herd and a small herd of Kerry cows. Until 1980 it was privately owned by an American gentleman, Mr Henry McIlhenny (related to the Tabasco McIlhenny's), for whom Glenveagh was a summer residence. Here he entertained society and celebrity friends, such as Grace Kelly (Princess Grace of Monaco), and Greta Garbo. Mr McIlhenny took the basic outline and planting of the pleasure grounds, first laid out by the Adair family in the 1850s, and with his talented head gardener, Matt Armour, turned Glenveagh into the incredible feat of gardening it is today. Sean O'Gaoithin is the current head gardener, whose task it is to maintain and improve the splendid garden. Fortunately for Glenveagh, it continues to be worked by a man with a passion for the place; I think Messrs McIlhenny and Armour would approve.

A shelter belt of Scots pine (*Pinus sylvestris*) around the castle and lake gives the gardens a favoured microclimate. The effects of this, combined with the remains of the Gulf Stream and the northerly aspect, gives sturdier and hardier growth to the plants here than on the west coast further south in Kerry and Cork. Alpines, Chinese and Himalayan plants all thrive. But it's not all good news. The garden faces northwest and in winter there are many parts of the garden that receive no sun at all during the day. These areas include part of the walled garden – the *jardin potager*.

The *jardin potager* covers one acre and is the only state-run walled garden in the Republic. 'In here we grow everything from seed,' explains Sean. 'We are trying to maintain traditional practices in the garden,' he continues, adding that one of the aims of working a garden like Glenveagh is to maintain its old cultivars and grow the sort of rare and unusual vegetables that are losing ground all the time in the wider world. Part of this mission is seen in the collection of old Donegal roses collected from

**A stone pineapple – a traditional symbol of hospitality –
at Glenveagh, County Donegal.**

cottages around the county and now assembled in the walled garden among the other, more refined herbaceous plants, clipped yew hedges, fruit trees and *orangerie*. The *jardin potager* is at its best between July and August. Matt Armour worked in Glenveagh for fifty years and Sean is quick to point out the great debt he owes to the man with whom he was lucky enough to work when he first arrived at the garden. A particularly pretty single dahlia named after Matt Armour lives in the walled garden as a lasting memorial.

Outside the walled garden, the pleasure grounds are tropical in feel and brimming with tree ferns, rhododendrons, eucryphia, hoheria and the fragrant, magnolia-like flowers of *Michelia doltsopa*, a Chinese relative of magnolia, as well as other tender plants. Glenveagh is visited by a wonderful amount of rain that gives a steamy, damp, glistening look and feel to the place.

In 1996 a seed-collecting expedition was made to China's Yunan province, which brought a whole range of new plants to Ireland. These were distributed among all the big collections on the island. Among the recipients were the JFK Arboretum in County Waterford, Fota in County Cork, the Botanic Gardens in Dublin, Rowallane in County Down, Muckross in County Kerry and Glenveagh. The results of Glenveagh's share of the treasure were planted in 1999 in a new Chinese garden down by the lake. This is an open heathland garden and includes new miniature rhododendrons.

Sections of the woods are being restored and renewed by intelligent hacking back of the old azaleas in order to refresh them. This is proving very effective and the results can be appreciated in some places. It is interesting for the visitor to see this sort of work in progress as it gives a good idea of what is required to keep a large garden from running wild and getting lost in the overgrowth that is quick to take hold given any opportunity.

An impressive set of sixty-seven steps leads up through the woods to a Belvedere, or viewing garden, set out with large Italian terracotta pots. It was laid out in front of the upper glen and Lough Veagh and the view out over the castle, gardens and lake from here is an unforgettable sight. The other features within easy walk of the castle are the rose garden and the Swiss walk, so named simply because it reminded Mr McIlhenny of Switzerland. The Belgian walk has a more substantial background, however, as it was created by recuperating Belgian soldiers during the First World War. The Italian garden is intimate, full of eighteenth-century statuary, paved with Donegal slate and planted around with rhododendron and pieris. By the castle is a Tuscan garden with griselinia hedging and marble busts of Roman emperors and their wives. None of these look as incongruous as one might think, in wet, northern Donegal.

Glenveagh is, understandably, a hugely popular place to visit, catering for 90,000 visitors annually. But it is of such a size that it feels peaceful, even at the height of the summer. There are guided tours available, but it is also possible to take an information leaflet and visit alone, taking a picnic and waterproofs. Walking the gardens and the huge surrounding wood and mountainous park could easily fill a day for the family. The castle is also well worth visiting. It is reminiscent of a Bavarian hunting lodge, with wonderfully extravagant décor, particularly the pinkest of pink bedrooms where Garbo and Kelly stayed on their visits. It was indeed a fortunate day when Mr McIlhenny generously gave this treasure to the Irish nation.

Nurseries and Garden Centres

ALCORN GARDEN CENTRE

Hazelwood House, Loughnagin, Letterkenny, County Donegal; Tel: +074 21541.

BONNER ENGINEERING (Ornamental gates and railings)

Churchill, on Letterkenny Road, County Donegal.

FLOWER POT, THE

Cresslough, County Donegal.

FLOWERS AND THINGS

Main Street, Stranorlar, County Donegal; Tel: +074 32752.

GALLAGHER'S GARDEN CENTRE

Churchill, County Donegal; Tel: +074 22510.

GARRY'S GARDEN CENTRE AND PET STORE

Tel: +074 27559.

LOUGHSIDE GARDEN CENTRE

Rathmelton Road, Letterkenny, County Donegal.

RAPHOE GARDEN CENTRE

Raphoe, County Donegal; Tel: +074 45257.

COUNTY DOWN

County Down, and particularly the Ards Peninsula, is known as one of the warmest, driest areas in Northern Ireland, recording hours of annual sunshine comparable with the south coast. The county, with its largely acid soil, is home to a clutch of the most renowned gardens on the island: Mount Stewart, Rowallane, Castle Ward, Seaforde and Castlewellan. Between them these heavyweights could fill a week of garden visits. Looming over the county, the Mourne Mountains rise up from Carlingford Lough in a series of rounded, handsome peaks skirted by great stone walls. (Advice to visitors: take the ferry over to Strangford from the pretty village of Portaferry). The Ulster Way treads between the tallest peaks, passing near the Silent Valley. Just off the scenic coast road (A2), near Newcastle, lies Murlough Nature Reserve and the beautiful Tyrella beach. Out on the Ards Peninsula, near Mount Stewart and the Temple of the Winds, is the ruin of Grey Abbey, a Cistercian abbey with a little physic garden. There is no shortage of ruined castles and historic sites in the county, from Narrow Water Castle on the outskirts of Warrenpoint to Castlewellan village and smart-looking Hillsborough, the Brontë homestead in Rathfriland, and Down Cathedral, where the patron saint of Ireland, St Patrick, is buried.

BALLYWALTER PARK

Ballywalter, Greyabbey, Newtownards, County Down; Tel: +042 758264; Fax: +042 758818; e-mail: enp@dunleath-estates.co.uk ▪ **Contact:** Mrs Sharon Graham ▪ **Open:** all year round, by appointment only; groups welcome ▪ **Entrance fee** goes towards garden upkeep ▪ Supervised children welcome ▪ **Special features:** teas can be booked by prior arrangement; 'pick-your-own' fruit and vegetables scheme during the summer ▪ Member of Historical Houses Association ▪ **Directions:** turn off the A20 at Greyabbey. Take the Ballywalter Road (B5) and turn right at the T-junction. Continue on to the gate lodge on the right-hand side.

Out on the windy Ards Peninsula, Ballywalter Park demesne was built in the mid-1800s by the English architect Charles Lanyon for the Mulholland family, later the lords Dunleath. The gardens are chiefly a landscape park made up of woods, park trees, walks and rides and impressive stands of rhododendron, including several rare varieties, such as *Rhododendron falconeri* and *Rhododendron sinogrande*, with huge leaves and creamy-yellow flowers, rendering the park most attractive in spring. A walled garden contains pillars for a rose walk and a great range of glasshouses. For fruit-lovers, a 'pick-your-own' strawberries, raspberries, gooseberries, currants and vegetables scheme is operated on the farm side of the estate during the summer months.

In front of the Italianate palazzo and large ornate conservatory a beautiful series of streams cuts through the park. These gently meandering, bridged waterways, edged by huge gunnera leaves, were also designed by Charles Lanyon to complement the house. Informal plantings of ferns, rodgersia and primula edge the water. This is a romantic spot, well kept and well maintained.

BEECHGROVE

Castlewellan Forest Park, Castlewellan, County Down ▪ **Contact:** Mr Sam Harrison, Head Forester (now retired) ▪ **Open:** month of May, by appointment only, apply in writing; also for occasional charity days (see local press for details); groups welcome ▪ **Entrance fee** donated to charity ▪ Supervised children welcome ▪ **Directions:** set within the forest park in the village of Castlewellan. The house is the first turn left inside the gates.

Sam Harrison, now retired, was head forester at Castlewellan Park and Arboretum for many years, and has worked his own garden within the grounds of the national arboretum for fifteen years. Naturally, given his day job, there are some great specimen trees in his garden, like the most handsome Roblé beech (*Nothofagus obliqua*),which stands beside a little wooden sundial and hammock house that he built himself, which is covered in *Clematis armandii*. His pride and joy is the *Juniperus recurva* 'Castlewellan': 'That tree put up with three upheavals and three trips before it came here, but it will not have to move again.'

Sam arranged the garden in peninsulas of trees and shrubs that jut onto the lawn, making a walk around the one-acre garden a pleasant, zigzagging affair. Because of this, the garden, which covers just less than two acres, feels like it's twice that size. 'I try to plant the scented plants with the prevailing winds,' he says, giving away another of his clever gardening ideas.

A rounded frog pond is surrounded by hosta, pieces of sculpture, ferns and hypericum, and the pond's overflow feeds a damp area of primulas and hostas. Close by is a bronze sculpture modelled on two hands and oak leaves from the garden, which stands bathed in the lovely scent of a pineapple broom (*Cytisus battandieri*). This is the work of Betty Newman Maguire, the sculptor known to Dubliners for her wonderful recreation of a Viking longship on the quay by Christchurch Cathedral.

An old rockery steps down toward the front of the house. A little trickle of water runs its length, fringed by tatting ferns, a dwarf lilac and a spread of barbary cotoneaster (*Cotoneaster dammeri*), which closely contours the ground by a little humped bridge midway along the rockery and over the stream. The fuchsia-flowering currant (*Ribes sanguineum*), blooms prettily against the wall. This was one of the plants brought back from North America in the 1820s by the intrepid plant hunter David Donglan.

This is an all-year garden in which the only spots of colour come from the berries and flowers of plants like poppies, potato vine (*Solanum crispum*), leptospermum, *Viburnum bodnantense* and cotoneaster. For all its virtue, Sam is not too precious about the garden and the proof of this is the presence of a three-hole golf course amid his glorious creation.

NICK BURROWES'S GARDEN

34 Dunlady Road, Dundonald, County Down; Tel: +090 486324 ▪ **Contact:**

Nick Burrowes ▪ **Open:** June–July, by appointment only; groups welcome ▪ **Entrance fee** donated to charity ▪ Supervised children welcome; please note, dogs on leads ▪ **Special features:** nursery selling plants and herbs from the garden ▪ **Directions:** travelling from Belfast, pass the Ulster Hospital and turn left at the third set of traffic lights. The garden is 1.6km along the Dunlady Road.

Nick Burrowes's garden is an informal, relaxed, child-friendly garden on a sunny hill that looks across at Scrabo Hill and Tower. The garden rises up from the back of his house in a riot of shrubs and herbaceous perennials, vegetables and herbs. The beds weave through a children's golf course, where the holes are named after Thomas the Tank Engine and his many friends. The small people of the Burrowes family also enjoy a unique climbing frame designed along the lines of the Giant's Causeway.

Nick created the garden in the mid-1990s and propagated most of the plants himself, building up a collection of mints, which are now dispersed among the beds. These include the sweet little *Prostanthera rotundifolia* with bell-shaped, purple flowers. The garden design is simple – almost like one large hillside bed with wide paths cut through it. The genius of the garden is the plant combinations: in one bed blue lobelia, variegated golden euonymus, white creeping nettle and a rich, dark, gloss-leaved pittosporum reside together attractively. Next door, mounds of mint soften tall onion spikes, big poppies, alstroemeria and huge angelica leaves. Masses of colour, wonderful leaves and the glorious smells of thyme, rosemary, apple, spearmint, onions and roses leave the senses reeling and satiated upon departing the garden. A small working nursery beside the plot also allows visitors to bring home a few pots of herbs as a souvenir of a good visit.

Anyone who feels they can't have a garden because they have children should take a look at what the Burrowes have achieved. Children benefit greatly from garden environments, and all the nature classes in the world will never teach them as much as having their own experimental plot will; Nick's six-year-old boy knew more about mint and its varieties than most adult gardeners I have met. Walking around with these two gardeners – Nick and his son – is a most entertaining and informative experience, particularly in relation to the herbs. One of the things I learned was that wormwood (*Artemisia*), when dry-fried and then lit, will rid a house of houseflies. Vegetables, children, a working nursery, chickens, flowers, a round of golf and a toy car parked neatly in the undergrowth – quite simply, I loved this garden.

CARRAIG BEAG

1 Cloughey Road, Portaferry, County Down; Tel: +042 728777 ▪ **Contact:** Mrs Daphne Wallace ▪ **Open:** May–end August, by appointment only; groups welcome ▪ **Entrance fee** donated to the National Trust ▪ Supervised children welcome ▪ **Directions:** approaching Portaferry from Kircubbin, there is a gate lodge to Nugent Estate on the right, take the next road on the left at Demesne View and then the first left at the crossroads. The house is first on the right.

Mrs Wallace's garden stands on the inland side of the harbour village of Portaferry, at the tip of the Ards Peninsula. Mrs Wallace is a real plantswoman and a keen collector, and she has worked single-handedly to create this jewel of a garden since she took it on as a plain grass site in 1989. When she began the three-quarter-acre plot was very difficult to work due to its light, stony soil. On top of that, it suffers from southwesterly winds which cross the garden, whipping and wind-burning the plants throughout winter.

The first impression of the garden is that there is a certain order, but this is only just discernible through an abundance of bloom, fruit, leaf and scent. The planting schemes are soft and informal. Big clumps of *Dahlia* 'The Bishop of Llandaff' are partnered with red scabious, purple pansies and red-flowering oregano. In later summer the reddening leaves of a Chinese dogwood (*Cornus kousa var. chinensis*) and cautleya stretch out the colour bands. In the large front bed that surrounds the circular lawn, abutilon, ceanothus and eucryphia stand over a collar of blue campanula and geranium. Chocolate cosmos, pheasant berry (*Leycesteria formosa*) and ice plants (*Sedum*) give the effect of a warm, layered look to the wide bed.

Reluctantly leaving this area, one is drawn around to the side of the house, past a selection of miscanthus grasses, phormium, peony and a young tulip tree (*Liriodendron tulipifera*), through a little fence and gate and into a completely different garden. Here, Mrs Wallace's enthusiasm is let loose and given free rein. An assortment of beauties all compete for attention: black-berried Solomon's seal, white mop-head hydrangea and pale-pink French honeysuckle (*Hedysarum coronarium*) add up to a flowerfest. The beds are divided and linked by curving paths. Distractions abound. Arches accommodate roses, clematis and climbing dicentra. Then there are little cordoned-off areas, surrounded sometimes by trellis, also swagged in roses. The series of ponds and fountains near the house is almost lost under the luxurious growth of marginals, grasses and hostas. The garden visit finishes off nicely with a scree bed full of creeping mints, house leeks, saxifrage and mats of little alpines.

CASTLE WARD

Strangford, Downpatrick, County Down; Tel: +044 881204; Fax: +044 881729; e-mail: ucwest@smtp.ntrust.org.uk ▪ **Contact:** Mike Gaston, Property Manager, or Alastair McCorry, Head Gardener ▪ **Open:** house and garden open April, May, September and October, weekends and bank holidays, 1pm–6pm; June–August, daily, 1pm–6pm; grounds open all year round, dawn–dusk; groups welcome ▪ Entrance fee donated to the National Trust ▪ Supervised children welcome; please note, dogs on leads ▪ **Special features:** cottages to rent for longer visits; shop; farm museum; rare-breed animals; children's playground; theatre facilities; caravan site; jetty; a Viking invasion occurs each June, ring for dates and times; Castle Ward opera performance, ring for details ▪ Member of the National Trust ▪ **Directions:** travel on the A25 for 11km from Downpatrick or for 3km from Strangford. The garden is well signposted from either approach.

For some reason, Castle Ward is not very well known. There seems to be little explanation for this, given its many attractions and its perfect position on one of the finest garden trails on the island, which incorporates Rowallane, Mount Stewart, Seaforde and Castlewellan.

The house at Castle Ward is an extraordinary place, seemingly the result of a disagreement between Bernard, Viscount Bangor, and his wife, Anne, who could not agree on an architectural style for their home. Their accommodating, anonymous architect created a compromise whereby the back of the house was designed in the

The big stands of cordyline at Castle Ward in County Down. These trees were part of an older, Victorian garden design, which can still be studied from an 1850s watercolour by Mary Ward that is on display in the house.

Gothic, 'Strawberry Hall' style, according to Anne's tastes, while the front of the house reflected her husband's more sober, neo-classical preferences. To this day, the guides attest that women seem to take to the Gothic façade while men prefer the classical style. The house, which was bult in the 1760s, overlooks Strangford Lough and is set in parkland filled with architectural features, including a temple set high on a hill over a massive man-made lake, replete with swans from central casting and several artificial islands. The 700-acre demesne also includes woods, farmyards and landscaped gardens.

The main garden lies well below the house, which stands on a ledge overlooking the pleasure grounds. A sunken lawn garden centres on a circular pond with a little statue of *Neptune*, whose modesty is guarded by a porpoise. Above this the walled walk is planted with cordyline, trachycarpus, embothrium, pittosporum and clianthus, under which are healthy *Bergenia stracheyi*, *Sisyrinchium striatum*, melianthus, aconitum and roses.

The garden today has changed from the original eighteenth-century design. 'We have some of the original plans,' says gardener Alastair McCorry, 'but the garden has evolved quite a bit and today the style is mainly Victorian.' Proof of this is found in an 1850s painting by Mary Ward, which depicts the gardens and still hangs in the house. The Irish yews that dominate one side of the sunken lawn can be seen in the painting, as can the banks and cordylines that now take up so much space. 'The garden went on to become a rose garden and many of the older visitors to the garden today complain that the roses are gone,' continues Alastair. With only one gardener and voluntary help, the roses were taken out about twenty years ago and replaced by easily managed shrubs and perennials. One interesting development in this garden is a new 'yew' hedge. This is actually a hedge of podocarpus – an experiment going well.

Out of the formal garden are the pleasure grounds, a Victorian rock garden and a pet cemetery where the names of the interred animals are spelled out in snowdrops. Among the groves of specimen trees one of the more important is possibly the biggest griselinia in these islands, with a girth of almost three metres, which stands almost unnoticed beside two gangly, adolescent, 150-year-old Wellingtonia (*Sequoiadendron giganteum*).

Seven acres of lawn have been planted with drifts of daffodils. One walking route out through the park (not explored by nearly enough visitors), is that leading toward the original Audley's Castle and past a temple, ice house and lake. This path goes past a large grove of yew; once upon a time a walk through these was likened to walking through a cathedral. However, in desperate need of rejuvenation, these have been pruned back very hard and it will be a number of years before they return to their former grandeur. A new avenue of limes leads to where a previous Ward home in the Queen Anne-style once stood, with views of Strangford Lough and Scrabo. A walled garden close by is now empty, but it remains a fine edifice with a fairly rare and intact semicircular wall at one end. Alastair was delighted to find one of the old men who had worked here as a young boy. This man was able to draw up a plan of the walled garden as it was in the early twentieth century. Should the chance to restore the garden present itself, Alastair will now have an authentic base from which to work.

Castle Ward is the most complete estate in the care of the National Trust in Northern Ireland, surrounded by seven miles of walls, with an old laundry, farm, corn mills, pleasure grounds and meadows. The old farmyard is a popular place for school groups and it contains watermills, animal pens (now used for rare-breed animals) and walks along 'cattle creeps' – once used to keep the cattle out of view as they were moved around the estate. The walks continue out to the lough; when I visited a Viking longboat was parked here at a boathouse, making ready for a re-enactment of a raid on the estate.

A fine garden, interesting historic estate walks, an impressive working yard, a collection of rare farm animals and the Vikings – if the family can't find a full day's enjoyment at Castle Ward, there can be no hope for them.

CASTLEWELLAN FOREST PARK

Castlewellan, Newcastle, County Down; Tel: +043 778664 ▪ **Contact:** Michael Lear ▪ **Open:** all year round, every day, 10am–dusk; groups welcome ▪ **Entrance fee;** parking charge for cars and coaches ▪ Supervised children welcome; please note, dogs on leads ▪ **Special features:** tearoom serving snacks open from Easter to September, groups should book refreshments in advance; guided tours and forest park walks can be booked; fishing permits available; conference centre in castle ▪ **Directions:** situated in the village of Castlewellan.

The Annesley family moved to Castlewellan, north of the Mourne Mountains, in the mid-1700s, and between that time and the 1960s they built, gardened and created a demesne of outstanding beauty in the hilly landscape of south County Down. In 1967 the grounds were acquired by the Northern Ireland Forest Service and opened as a national arboretum.

Castlewellan, set beside the pretty tied village of the same name, was built by the

Annesley family in the late eighteenth century. As it stands today, it is an amalgamation of features from each of the subsequent centuries. The house dates only to 1856, but the walled garden was created in 1740 when the family first arrived. In 1874 the fifth Lord Annesley began to develop the arboretum, initially confining his work to the twelve-acre walled area but over the years moving out to the greater parkland. He realised that Castlewellan's favourable microclimate, created by the shelter provided by Slieve Donard, would allow him to plant exotics in his garden. It was he who planted many of the more unusual trees and shrubs that grace the estate today. Planting continued through the years, and under the care of the forestry service the arboretum has grown to over 100 acres. It is acknowledged to be one of the most outstanding tree and shrub collections in Europe, and is a regular attraction for enthusiasts from all over the world.

The Annesley garden is the focal point of Castlewellan. This is the above-mentioned walled garden, which dates back to 1740 when it was built as a kitchen garden, alongside pleasure grounds. The walled garden is glorious. It is built on a slope and contains yet more fine trees – at one point the visitor stands, like an ant, under a huge pair of Wellingtonia (*Sequoiadendron giganteum*) that measured twenty-three metres in 1973 (they are due to be re-measured soon). A few steps past these, one overlooks the garden and treetops of rare conifers, rhododendron and maples from Japan. A number of plants carry the name of the garden, including the much-loved *Juniperus recurva* 'Castlewellan' and the much less loved *Cupressocyparis leylandii* 'Castlewellan Gold'. There are so many beautiful trees to appreciate here. In May, the fire bush (*Embothriums coccineum*) from Chile dazzles the garden with bright red flowers. Later in the year a walk of eucryphias produces a mass of creamy-white flowers more beautiful than the best cherry blossom. Podocarpus and southern beech are also planted in numbers.

The large walled garden is divided into two gardens and separated by a gate that is guarded by two huge, wobbly Irish yews. In the top, smaller garden a double border of *Paeonia lutea*, geranium, yellow iris echium, poppies and day lilies rises up to a fountain and pond surrounded by mixed ferns and the gaudiest azaleas in a range of dazzling shades. The mixed border continues uphill, backed by yew hedges. Colourful runs of London pride, rodgersia and acanthus share the bed with two huge eucalyptus trees. At the top of the hill is a little lavender garden and a pergola draped with *Vitis coignetiae*, a spectacular vine.

Castlewellan is a space in which the visitor is constantly distracted and side-stepped by one great tree after another. Attempting to admire the famous Castlewellan juniper, one is pulled away by a gorgeous weeping *Cedrus deodara* 'Pendula', with one-metre-long branches, and a big Algerian fir (*Abies numidica*). Great topples of yew line the paths and the huge west Himalayan spruce (*Picea smithiana*) is only one of fifty varieties of picea in the garden. Outside the walls, spring gardens of heathers and dwarf conifer, autumn tree walks, ponds and cherry groves are only some of the many attractions. There is a good day's work to be spent trying to see the full extent of Castlewellan.

CLOONEAVON

62 Rostrevor Road, Warrenpoint, County Down; Tel: +041 773608 ▪ **Contact:** Mrs MK Moore ▪ **Open:** Easter weekend–end September, 2pm–6pm ▪

Entrance fee donated to the hospice movement and goes towards garden upkeep ▪ Supervised children welcome; please note, dogs on leads ▪ **Directions:** travelling on the A2, Clooneavon is midway between Rostrevor and Warrenpoint on the right-hand side after the Ross Monument (a tall obelisk). The house is above the road – look for the signposts.

Clooneavon is a delightful garden, worked by Mrs Moore and Gerry Shields, her gardener, who has gardened here for many of his sixty-five years and rightly regards the place as his own. The garden looks out over a field of cows, and beyond that to Carlingford Lough and the port town of Warrenpoint. In the front garden stands of rhododendron drift downhill in subtle shades of mauve, plum and pale pinks that blend together in unusual combinations, rarley tried by other growers. A plum-flowering specimen looked particularly beautiful on the day I visited, still laden with flower it stood over what looked like a plum carpet made of recently fallen petals.

The house stands above the garden on a raised bank over an apron of gravel, with a wide collar of dianthus, hazy-blue catmint (*Nepeta*) and berberis with ferns and sea thrift (*Armeria*) shot through it. A lovely iron veranda, delicately threaded with wisteria and clematis, decorates the double bow-fronted villa. For some reason, Mrs Moore's aristocratic-looking mixed breed dogs enjoy watering the clematis while steadfastly ignoring a job that actually needs doing – rabbit-chasing – but she is forgiving of their misplaced help. The lower garden boundary is planted with particularly beautiful tall beech trees, which obligingly cast their shade away from the garden, endearing themselves even more. Rough, round stones have been used to edge all the beds; these are all the product of thorough digging.

Facing the building, to the right-hand side of the house, is a more intimate garden set out on long parallel ledges of *Hydrangea paniculata* and beds of peonies and iris. Sunken newt and frog ponds are edged with old stone flags and sprinkles of water lilies adorn the different ledges. Steps down past fringes of leathery bergenia lead to a tall shrub border of red crinodendron, tree peonies, potentilla and flame-red embothrium. This garden seems to have been made with the pleasure of the walker in mind. Lichen-covered paths pass well-made old stone retaining walls which hold up beds of anthemis, dicentra and sweet-smelling rosemary. The walled garden at the end of one of these lovely walks, houses lines of artichokes, salads, a collection of guinea fowl and a huge, three-metre-high yucca growing from the tiniest bucket imaginable.

To the left-hand side of the house, the sunny side, a wall plant called hibbertia stands out. This beautiful yellow-flowering climber was a gift from a couple Mrs Moore met in Devon many years ago. They had brought it back from New Zealand. Every year, from May to autumn, it displays its pretty yellow blooms; the curator of the Botanic Gardens in Belfast was due to come and inspect the lovely plant on the day I visited the garden. Next to it in a pretty colour complement is a healthy billardiera with bell-shaped purple and lime flowers, to be followed later on by shiny purple berries.

At the bottom of the hill that runs down from the front of the house, *Rhododendron* 'Loderi Venus' takes pride of the place in the border; its pale-pink, scented flowers are a dream: 'I thought it was dead so I stripped the bark and gave it a dose of Epsom salts and it's wonderful,' says Mrs Moore. Meanwhile, next door, a big *Rosa filipes* 'Kiftsgate' is running riot over a dead cherry tree. Mrs Moore is a big believer in

Epsom salts for whatever ails a plant, using a handful in a bucket of water to bring the patient back to health. With the results of her ministrations plainly in view, a stall selling 'the cure' outside her gate could make someone their fortune.

14 DRUMNACONNELL ROAD

Saintfield, County Down ▪ **Contact:** Mrs Sally Taylor ▪ **Open:** June–July, by appointment only, apply by letter; small groups and individuals welcome ▪ **Entrance fee** donated to charity ▪ Supervised children welcome ▪ **Directions:** take the Ballynahinch Road from Saintfield. Turn left just past the 30mph sign onto the Drumnaconnell Road. The house is second on the left, up a rough track that is almost 0.5km long.

Set in the rugged hills outside Saintfield, Drumnaconnell is a mature country garden of shrubs, flowers, vegetables and an apple orchard. The old garden, taken over by Sally Taylor a few years ago, was long known as a great rhododendron garden. She has widened its scope, adding herbaceous planting and some native tree and shrub species.

Altogether, the garden covers fourteen acres and includes a wildlife sanctuary. It is an easy, relaxed garden that boasts considerable style. Working it herself, Sally has managed to achieve a natural feel by incorporating old stone walls and wild hedgerows with rarefied planting of drimys, camellia, Chilean fire bush (*Embothrium coccineum*) and ribbonwood (*Hoheria*). A little hazel wood and some willow sculptures have been created and they are drawn together by mown paths into the big wildflower meadow.

In the new gardens close by the house, vegetables, herbs and flowers grow happily together – borage, beans, artichoke and mint grow beside crocosmia, ferns, poppies and roses. The beds spill out onto the paths, and wild strawberries and polygonum, lambs' ears (*Stachys byzantina*) and primulas must be stepped over gently. In the middle of one herbaceous bed an apple tree stands with its branches weighed down by small logs on strings. Bending the spurs of old apple trees encourages them to fruit in the same way that pulling out the branches of a rambling rose horizontally encourages more flower. If the branches are allowed to grow straight upwards, flower and fruit will be borne only at the very end or top of each branch. Training the branch out so that more of its length reaches a level height encourages more leaf, flower and fruit production. The most pleasing aspect of Sally's garden is that it fades gently into the surrounding, wild, stony farmland beyond. The transition is natural and gentle and makes the garden sit well in its surroundings.

The garden continues to expand. Sally is bringing in the services of a big saddle-back pig called Melissa from County Waterford (who has already done some good work in a friend's Cavan garden). Melissa will grub out the bracken in a little dell that will then be planted up with low-growing rhododendrons and vine maples (*Acer circinatum*).

GARY DUNLOP'S GARDEN

The Grange, 35 Ballyrogan Park, Newtownards, County Down; Tel: +091 821451 ▪ **Contact:** Mr Gary Dunlop ▪ **Open:** weekends and evenings in the summer, by appointment only; telephone for an appointment either at about 8am or after dark;

groups welcome ▪ **Entrance fee** donated to charity ▪ Children and dogs admitted if well supervised, but please note that this is not a garden for a family outing ▪ **Special features:** houses the national collections of euphorbia, celmisias and crocosmia ▪ **Directions:** will be given upon confirmation of appointment.

Mr Dunlop's garden covers about three acres and is situated on an exposed site at the northern end of the Ards Peninsula. The garden is well planted, perhaps one might even say stuffed. This is a serious plantaholic's delight – at every turn there are colourful specimens to study and to fall in love with. Woodland plants and bulbs are grown in the terraced and raised beds. Shrubs, including a good number of azalea varieties, range along the paths in colourful waves. At the highest point in the garden is a natural rock garden that houses Mr Dunlop's national collection of celmisias. Great rock formations, both natural and man-made, create an excellent backdrop for the plantings of both the ordered collections and the informal mixed beds. The views from the celmisia rock encompass the whole of County Down, the Mournes, the Isle of Man and Scotland.

A separate garden, covering half an acre, faces south. This contains a collection of South African plants, like crocosmia, agapanthus, angel's fishing rods (*Dierama*), kaffir lilies (*Schizostylis*), and watsonia, phormium, phlox and euphorbia. Throughout the garden well-placed, attractive statuary has been used to frame views and redirect the visitor towards yet another combination of plants. Many of the sculptures are oriental or oriental-influenced, but they look remarkably well in the rocky landscape. Thriving plants encroach on little paths and the walker must pick their way gingerly through beds of agapanthus and red hot pokers (*Kniphofia*), allium and penstemon. A place to study.

GREY ABBEY PHYSIC GARDEN

Greyabbey, County Down; Tel: +042 788585 ▪ **Contact:** the Administrator ▪ **Open:** April–September, Tuesday–Saturday, 10am–7pm, Sunday, 2pm–6pm; groups welcome, but must book in advance ▪ **Entrance fee** goes towards garden upkeep; school groups go free ▪ Supervised children welcome; please note, dogs on leads ▪ **Special features:** monastic ruins; interpretive centre ▪ **Directions:** situated in the middle of Greyabbey village, on the A20 south of Mount Stewart Gardens.

In the Middle Ages, abbeys, monasteries and religious houses created many of the most important early gardens in Europe. The monks ran orchards, kitchen gardens and medicinal or physic gardens to feed and care both for themselves and for their visitors. At the Cistercian abbey of Grey Abbey, the monks would have been as self-sufficient as their brethren throughout Christendom.

The physic garden at Grey Abbey is a small garden laid out in the grounds of the twelfth-century abbey. Historical records and archaeological information on the make-up of physic gardens were called on to help in the design. The results of these investigations is a plot created along the lines of a medicinal herb garden of the Middle Ages, but it is of necessity only an interpretation of what such a garden might have been like, because no actual gardens of the sort remain intact anywhere. Each bed was designed for practicality, holding a single herb and fenced in by woven wicker hurdles. They make a simple but pretty overall picture of usual and unusual herbs.

A small information centre is attached to the garden where the medicinal uses for each of the various herbs are explained. I particularly noted that mugwort wards off evil, and rue can be used against witches and the plague. But betony must take a bow as it can cure forty-seven different diseases – and that's not to be sneezed at!

GUINCHO

69 Craigdarragh Road, Helen's Bay, County Down; Tel: +090 486324 ▪ **Contact:** Nick Burrrowes, Head Gardener (see Nick Burrowes's Garden, pp.367–368) ▪ **Open:** April–September, by appointment to groups only (groups must number more than fifteen persons); for charity days (see local press or National Trust Garden Scheme leaflets for details) ▪ **Entrance fee** donated to charity ▪ Supervised children welcome; please note, dogs on leads ▪ **Special features:** garden-propagated plants for sale; tea available to groups, but must be booked in advance ▪ **Directions:** from the main Belfast–Bangor road, take the Craigdarragh Road to Helen's Bay. The garden is 0.5km along on the left-hand side.

The gardens at Guincho form one of the greatest private gardens on the island. They cover an area of twelve acres and were started in 1948 by Mrs Vera Mackie, but look nothing like their relatively young age might suggest. Guincho suggests to the visitor that it has been here for twice the number of years, particularly in the case of the four acres of woodland. The gardens are substantial in many ways, full of variety, beautifully maintained and a pleasure to visit.

Made up of huge sweeping lawns wrapped by a wide collar of woods, Guincho is a grand-scale garden. The woods contain and shelter long walks through rodgersia and hellebores, ferns and hydrangea, all under the canopy of pine, eucryphia, cordyline and rhododendron. These winding, mossy paths open every so often onto a huge expanse of lawn, letting in daylight and granting the walker a vista across the garden, taking in one of the well-designed combinations of plants, such as a huge silver fir beside a large patch of gunnera or a sea of blue hydrangea.

The path passes a huge cryptomeria that looks like a monster climbing-frame and must at some time have been a one-tree adventure playground for children. Continuing along, there is a stream garden in another clearing that looks like a tropical setting with tree ferns and trachycarpus, and on again to another wood of oak, ash, horse chestnut, beech and sweet chestnut. The paths rise and fall at the side of the stream, leading down eventually to a grove of large-leaved rhododendron and tree ferns. You emerge from the wood to a cultivated area of lawns edged with myrtle and willow, with a collar of geranium, osteospermum, *Fascicularia pitcairnifolia* and cotoneaster draping over a stone wall. Among the special plants found at Guincho are a lovely *Rehderodendron macrocarpa*, rare in Ireland, with white, creamy flowers and shiny, tapered leaves, and the purple-leaved elder *Sambucus nigra* 'Guincho Purple'), a wonderful shrub, with blackish-purple leaves and pale-pink flowers, found by Mrs Mackie while walking in the Scottish highlands in the 1960s.

Running around the smaller, more domestic-sized lawns near the house are beautiful, sometimes unusual small trees and flowering shrubs with climbers pushing their way through them. A series of tiny gardens come upon the visitor as a surprise. Some are sunken, some are circled by tall architectural walls of phormium, some by hedges. Small lily ponds marked by mop-head bays and topiary in pots hide in these rooms. One lovely touch is the slim arch of cotoneaster wound tightly around and over the front door. Virginia creeper, ceanothus, geranium and black grass also play around the front of the house.

In 1982 the garden was designated as a garden of outstanding historical importance. This may seem odd, given its youth, but the well selected, wide range of plants grown in the garden will continue to mature, producing an ever more beautiful collection as the decades march on. There are not many substantial gardens on the island of this young age and with so much promise.

THE HEATHERS

9 Portaferry Road, Greyabbey, County Down; Tel: +042 788351 ▪ **Contact:** Betty Brittain ▪ **Open:** May–September, by appointment only; groups welcome ▪ **Entrance fee** donated to charity ▪ Supervised children welcome ▪ **Directions:** situated on the A20, at the edge of the village of Greyabbey, on the road to Portaferry.

The house and garden at Portaferry Road slope out toward Strangford Lough and the croaking of seagulls is the predominant sound in this small, interesting, seaside garden. A little woodland area by the drive leads the visitor out into the garden, and once inside the main garden dense planting – inventive and varied for a seaside situation – is worked well into the wild, windy setting.

The house is completely covered in creepers, sweet pea, Virginia creeper, clematis and honeysuckle. Planted close in by the house there are lush clumps of Japanese anemone, arum lilies, rowans dripping with berries and hardy geraniums in shades of pink and soft purple. The garden is run through with gravel paths that rise, fall and wind their way through it. Rough stone steps lead around corners and down into little sheltered pockets that protectively house tender plants. Hydrangeas, both mop-head and lacecap, grow in profusion, and there are flowering cherry and crab apple trees. Trellis and fencing hems in roses, fuchsia and herbaceous plants. Mrs Brittain's garden is a very enjoyable seaside garden with great character and prettiness.

LISDOONAN HERBS

98 Belfast Road, Saintfield, County Down; Tel: +090 813624 ▪ **Contact:** Barbara Pilcher ▪ **Open:** Wednesday and Saturday mornings, 9am–1pm; at other times by appointment only ▪ **No entrance fee**, but guided tours must be booked in advance and a fee is charged for the tour ▪ Supervised children welcome; please note, dogs on leads ▪ **Special features:** nursery; classes on all aspects of herbs are held occasionally, telephone for details ▪ **Directions:** on the road to Belfast, 5km outside Saintfield, on the left-hand side. Look for the signposts.

Lisdoonan Herbs is a wonderful small nursery full of the smells of herbs, medicinal and culinary. It is run by Barbara Pilcher, who is well-known for her expertise and knowledge of herbs. (She advised on planting at the physic garden at Grey Abbey.) The small and well-stocked nursery can be visited to see growing the plants which Barbara sells, and they are pure pleasure. A small wood and a rock garden run alongside the beds of herbs. The garden has a fairly wild and barely tamed feel that suits it well. Barbara describes her growing methods as 'environmentally friendly', and she uses a minimum of non-organic treatments. She practices serious recycling and makes her own compost.

MAGILL'S GARDEN

1 Ballytrustan Road, off Ballyhoran Road, Downpatrick, County Down ▪ **Contact:** Veronica and Raymond Magill ▪ **Open:** May–June, by appointment only, apply in writing; groups welcome ▪ **Entrance fee** donated to the National Trust ▪ Supervised children welcome ▪ **Special features:** the garden is located in a quarry ▪ **Directions:** will be given with an appointment.

The Magills's remarkable garden was created in 1950 on the seven-acre site of an old quarry outside Downpatrick. The garden is divided into several areas, including rock gardens, island beds of specimen trees and shrubs, an alpine rock garden, runs of climbing roses, a pine and rhododendron wood, a sunken garden and a small walled garden. It is essentially a spring and early summer garden, and it carries a great number of rhododendron and azaleas, evident immediately at the entrance and drive, which is bordered by big colourful specimens of both.

The pine wood is where the garden takes off. This feature started out as a simple wood. Mr Magill felt that a path through it would improve the place, and then decided that the path needed a little something to border it, and so the rhododendrons began to creep in. Long runs of tall pines cast a light shade on a big selection of rhododendrons, such as yellow 'Saffron Queen', 'Blue Peter' and 'Garnet', with its red buds and pink flowers. Further along, a semicircular laburnum grove with red hawthorn is a very bold statement. In a clearing close by, groups of alpines are set together as a constant reminder to Mr Magill of his many mountain travels.

The quarry floor that provides the setting for the garden makes up a true wildflower garden. No lawn grass was ever sown in this area. However, continuous cutting of the greenery that grew naturally on the quarry floor eventually produced a lawn full of wildflowers. Needless to say, this area is never weeded and is cut only twice during the growing season, to let the seedheads drop to the ground thus ensuring next year's seeds and continuing the cycle.

In the sunken garden a Judas tree (*Cercis siliquastrum*) shelters in the frost-free microclimate along with a pale lilac abutilon, planted in 1964. At almost forty years old, this normally short-lived shrub is something of a record-breaker. Good specimens of New Zealand holly (*Olearia macrodonta*), a huge *Ceanothus arboreus* 'Trewithen Blue,' planted only fifteen years ago, and a red grevillea also live in this area. Altogether there are seventeen 'rooms' in Mr Magill's garden, tied together with just under a kilometre of paths. The garden requires a long visit, or perhaps two for full appreciation, and the informative Mr Magill will talk entertainingly about his impressive creation.

MOUNT STEWART

Newtownards, County Down; Tel: +042 788387/788487; Fax: +042 788569; e-mail: umsent@smtp.ntrust.org.uk ▪ **Contact:** the Administrator ▪ **Open:** March, Sunday, 2pm–6pm; April–September, daily, 11.00am–6pm; October,

Saturday–Sunday, 11am–6pm; November–December, Saturday–Sunday, 2pm–5pm; Temple of the Winds is open April–October, Saturday–Sunday, 2pm–5pm; please note, the tearoom may be closed during the year 2001 for restoration, telephone in advance to confirm ✷ **Entrance fee** donated to the National Trust ✷ Supervised children welcome; please note, dogs on leads ✷ **Special features:** guided tours of Mount Stewart House available; garden fair held in May when plants from the garden are for sale; jazz concerts in the garden throughout the summer months; the Temple of the Winds ✷ Member of the National Trust ✷ **Directions:** situated on the A20 between Newtownards and Portaferry.

Everything about Mount Stewart is aimed to impress: its size (seventy-eight acres), the enormous variety within its many gardens, the care employed in its upkeep, the wit of the design, even the standard of the guided tours (a retired geology professor conducted a tour on the day I visited, adding interesting geological footnotes to the general garden information). There is also the great wealth that went into the creation of the garden. Critics have said that the garden was manured with money, but it cannot be denied that Mount Stewart is an achievement worthy of the World Heritage Site title bestowed on it in 1999.

Two of the stone creatures from the well-known Dodo Terrace at Mount Stewart in County Down. These animals represent the members of the Ark Club (founded by Edith, Lady Londonderry), once a circle of powerful figures in English politics.

Mount Stewart House, an impressive pile in honey-coloured stone, is somewhat unusual. It does not stand in splendid isolation on a lawn or on a wide spread of gravel as many great houses do, nor is it advertised by a smart but restrained terrace garden. Mount Stewart House is different. Standing just 100 metres from the wide steps that lead up to the front door, one might as well be standing in a jungle. The house vies for notice with the vegetation. Tall, peeling eucalyptus, elegant conifers and seas of variegated phlox, pink, waving anemones, great Florence Court yews, cordylines, the most wonderful clipped bays, irises and a thousand other plants distract from the house magnificently.

The garden was designed by Edith, Lady Londonderry, in the 1920s, when she arrived to live in Mount Stewart, a place she declared damp and depressing, situated as it was between the Irish Sea and Strangford Lough on the Ards Peninsula. Employing first twenty, then another twenty and yet another twenty gardeners and ex-servicemen to turn her ideas into reality, she created an extraordinary series of formal gardens. These were broken up into large 'rooms' with ingenious divides. In one instance, a huge leyandii (*Cupressocyparis leylandii*) hedge is cut with nail scissors' perfection into a series of arches to look like a huge green viaduct. This wraps itself around the Spanish and smart Italian gardens. In a glorious bit of whimsy, the latter was designed in colour and shape to mirror the ceiling of the breakfast room in the house.

Another of the gardens is surrounded by the most remarkable yew hedge on top of which romp devils, hunters, the whole Londonderry family in a boat, riders on horseback and stags – all fashioned from yew and racing around the top of the circular hedge. There are now only ten of these characters left but there were originally thirty; it must be a difficult job to keep them in shape. The hedge surrounds Mount Stewart's most famous feature: the shamrock garden with its huge red hand of Ulster picked out in red bedding, begonias and double daisies and set into gravel. The hand is set off against a green topiary harp, which towers four and a half metres over it.

The most romantic of all the gardens is the Mairi garden, built from the winnings made on a horse called Polemarch who won the St Leger in 1921. This fact is inscribed into the wall of the garden (although some well-intentioned accountancy vandal tried to insert the letter 'd' in Leger). The Mairi garden was created for Edith's daughter, Lady Mairi, to take her daily turn around in the pram. A little bronze fountain incorporates a statue of the baby girl and sprays water in a haphazard way that should please children a lot more than their parents, who might find themselves sprayed by the little imp. The original layout of this garden was drawn up by the well-known English gardener Graham Stuart Thomas, who planned it as a rose garden. The roses never quite worked however, and the planting was replaced by a blue-and-white garden that does work. White potentilla, galtonia, alliums, buddleia, lambs' ears and veronica mix with blue echiums, monkshood (*Aconitum*), campanula and more veronica.

The warm damp climate, once thought to be Mount Stewart's drawback, allows the growing of tender plants in the gardens, and the place has more than a touch of the tropics about it. Tree ferns, fruiting kiwis (*Actinidia chinensis*), acacias and olive trees all grow happily in the temperate climate.

There are wonderful statues of gryphons, turtles, crocodiles and dodos scattered throughout the ark garden. These are references to a political and family in-joke, but they also appeal to the uninitiated. Children should also like the lines of great bay umbrellas and drums flanking the house. These were bought for £ 99 8s 9d as a job lot in the 1920s.

Mount Stewart is a full day's visit and it might even be two if you really want to study the individual gardens and then take in the lake and woodland walks as well as the famed Temple of the Winds overlooking the lough. While it is a fine idea to take a guided walk, the specimens are clearly marked and identified, so an unescorted browse can be just as enjoyable and instructive.

THE OLD CURATAGE

6 The Square, Hillsborough, County Down; Tel: +041 773608 ※ **Contact:** Basil and Mary Glass ※ **Open:** May–end June, 2pm–5pm; small groups welcome ※ **Entrance fee** donated to Victim Support ※ Supervised children welcome ※ **Directions:** situated opposite the Market House on Main Square.

Mary Glass's garden is entered from a little courtyard at the side of her pretty Georgian townhouse in the middle of Hillsborough. From a hilly, long, narrow plot she has made an intimate and secluded flower garden, cleverly using a small space to its fullest potential.

The garden begins on a little terraced area that overlooks the whole vista. Large pots of vinca and camellia have been arranged around the area and a vigorous climbing *Rosa* 'Albertine' rises six metres up the wall, throwing out masses of pale-pink, scented flowers. Clematis and buddleia in shades of purple sit cheek-by-jowl, while white oriental poppies top off the area beautifully. Then, a step leads down to a secret garden, which really is very secret and is divided by angular walls of trellis. These prevent the length of the garden being seen all at once. The trellises are clothed in more clematis, honeysuckle and roses and in early to mid-summer the smells and colours are wonderful. The roses include a selection of David Austin roses, along with other favourites like blood-red *Rosa* 'Danse du Feu', which does very well in shade, and pink climbers *Rosa* 'Handel' and *Rosa* 'Aloha', both of which carry beautifully scented flowers.

This being a small garden, when a boundary hedge, which was taking up nearly a metre of space, was removed,the entire length of the garden was freed up and now swathes of cotoneaster and clematis earn their living in flower and berries over the whole year. Along the length of the wall raised triangular beds add interest, planted with peony, mallow and other herbaceous plants to add summer colour. This garden is a very good example of the best use of limited space and should provide inspiration – and a challenge – to those who garden small spaces.

QUEEN MARY HOUSE

13 Rowreagh Road, Kircubbin, County Down; Tel: +042 738705 ※ **Contact:** Mrs Elinor McCracken ※ **Open:** occasional open days (see local press for details); May–August, by appointment only ※ **Entrance fee** donated to charity ※ Supervised children welcome; please note, dogs on leads ※ **Directions:** just under 1km out of Kircubbin, on the Portaferry Road. The house is on the right, up a laneway occupied by three houses.

The first thought that might strike you about Queen Mary House is that it doesn't look very queenly. A smart 1930s modern house, Mrs McCracken explained that it was so named because someone felt it looked like the Queen Mary liner, beached on the shore with its porthole windows. The garden matches the house, with strong lines and a contemporary style. As a seaside garden, sitting on the edge of Strangford Lough, its salt wind-tolerant plants are made to work well.

Elinor McCracken is a natural gardener, although she denies it. Along with her husband, known as 'the Planner', she has fashioned a garden from four and a half acres of rough, sandy, rush-, dune grass- and gorse-covered soil, working around the huge boulders that spike out of the earth all over her garden. She explains that there is no depth of soil and that the rock is hard to work, but the results of her labours are impressive. The garden was started only nine years ago, but putting in five hours a day brings returns. It is a pure pleasure to walk around the island beds, natural stone ponds, down secret gullies and into little pocket gardens and private areas, each with its own character. In one of these little pocket gardens, bamboo and decking transports the visitor to the Far East. Close by, the plants around one of the ponds – huge gunnera, flag irises and primula – give a feeling of lush, wet jungle.

There is a pretty little *potager* fenced into its own spot close to the house, supplying the kitchen with vegetables and herbs. The revolving summerhouse is Elinor's pride and joy. This ingenious device, attached to a revolving hinge, allows her to sit out and enjoy her handiwork on the windiest days, facing whatever way the sun is shining – but not until her five hours have been put in!

ROWALLANE GARDEN

Saintfield, Ballynahinch, County Down; Tel: +097 510131; Fax: +097 511242; e-mail: uroest@smtp.ntrust.org.uk ▪ **Contact:** the Administrator ▪ **Open:** 17 March–October, Monday–Friday, 10.30am–6pm; weekends, 12.00–6pm; November–17 March, Monday–Friday, 10.30am–5pm; tearoom open April–August ▪ **Entrance fee** donated to the National Trust ▪ Supervised children welcome; please note, dogs on leads ▪ **Special features:** walks for the visually impaired can be arranged; houses the national collection of penstemon ▪ Member of the National Trust ▪ **Directions:** 1.5km south of Saintfield, off the A7.

The Reverend John Moore built the house here in the 1850s, outside Saintfield, south of Belfast. Reverend Moore began a garden around his home, including a strange set of 'monuments' and stone thrones and boulders that line the drive under large rhododendrons. Today, Rowallane covers fifty acres of wonderfully landscaped gardens, rhododendron plantations, woods, rock and walled gardens.

In 1903, Hugh Armytage Moore, a man deeply interested in plants, inherited the property and started growing some of his special plants in the yards and fields of his late uncle's farm. From then until the mid-1950s Mr Moore set about creating a huge, elaborate plantsman's garden. Rowallane is renowned as a spring garden, when vast numbers of daffodils and rhododendrons burst into flower. Mr Moore subscribed to all the great plant-hunting expeditions and he planted rhododendron seeds from these, creating a large collection of special specimens. They reach their flowering peak in May. The rhododendrons, usually grown under a canopy of trees, are grown here in the open. The passion of the Moores for plants is reflected in the impressive and accurate labelling of all of the plants throughout the garden – a welcome and helpful aid to visitors.

The rock garden was created by relieving a huge outcrop of the local stone, called whinestone, of its soil and scrub. Pockets were then filled with acid soil and planted up with meconopsis, including the locally bred *Meconopsis x sheldonii* 'Slieve Donard', gentians, primulas, bulbs, erythroniums, celmisias, heathers and leptospermum over moss-covered rocks. To the side of the house, a series of huge yew cones takes two weeks to clip every summer.

In the outer walled garden *Chaenomoles* 'Rowallane' and a variety of lacecap hydrangeas are stationed. Large wisteria and a *Hoheria sexstylosa* stand by the entrance to the outer walled garden and the greenhouse. The walled garden covers two acres and varies between strictly clipped box-enclosed beds of penstemon to looser beds of great tumbling piles of peony and bergenia, inula and camellia. At the gate of the walled garden are the dates 1828–1883. In fact, throughout the garden there are dates scattered around, pointing intriguingly to landmarks in the garden's history.

SEAFORDE GARDENS

Seaforde, near Downpatrick, County Down; Tel: +044 811225; Fax: +044 881370 ▪ **Contact:** Mr Patrick Forde ▪ **Open:** January–December, Monday–Saturday, 10am–5pm, Sunday, 1pm–6om; closed for Christmas and the New Year period; groups are welcome and guided tours can be arranged in advance ▪ Entrance fee ▪ Supervised children welcome ▪ **Special features:** butterfly house; nursery specialising in rare and unusual plants, particularly specimens from wild, collected sources; specimen sales are held in autumn; houses national collection of eucryphias; group talks on plant- and seed-collecting ▪ **Directions:** situated on the Belfast–Newcastle road. Look out for the signposts in the village of Seaforde.

The gardens at Seaforde date back to the 1750s, but it was in the nineteenth century that a lot of the mature trees seen in the garden today were planted, including the wellingtonias and Monterey pines. The garden is made up of a walled garden encompassing five acres, which is divided into two sections: one of the sections holds the nursery full of rare and interesting shrubs. Many of these specimens are the fruits of Patrick Forde's numerous seed-collecting expeditions abroad, particularly to Vietnam. There is also an incredible butterfly house to occupy the non-gardeners. This tropical butterfly house is set in a huge greenhouse that is planted like a jungle to house hundreds of colourful butterflies. These fly freely about, settling on branches and leaves, camouflaging themselves only to surprise visitors by suddenly taking flight in front of them. There are also reptiles, such as lizards, and exotic insects found roaming about the house. The squeals of delight and surprise from children fill the place, adding to the sense of excitement and adventure.

The main body of the garden was at one time formal, laid out in the type of smart beds most often found in walled gardens. This format had descended into a wilderness of bramble and laurel until the mid-1970s when Patrick Forde took it in hand and began to bring the garden back to a presentable state. He planted a maze of hornbeam in 1975, now a wonderfully large, handsome puzzle out of which one can be directed from the overlooking tower, after spending a suitable time. Then the garden proper begins. A serious gardener, Patrick Forde holds the national collection of eucryphias, with twenty-three species and hybrids. He says that between them it is possible to see the blooms over a great spread of months in the summer and autumn.

The garden is well laid-out in groves of eucryphia, rhododendron and large shrubs with roses growing through them, huge echiums, mimosa and melianthus. It's not hard to get lost in this charming place, coming across the eucryphia walk in the process with its laden-down branches full of white flowers. Scattered through the woodland garden are surprise clumps of large, sweet-scented white *Lilium* 'Casa Blanca' and tree ferns. The path leads eventually into a clearing where a damp, wet area and pond garden is positively infested with primula. The place is full of rarities, like an unnamed rose that was collected in Bhutan, on the border between China and India, which has strange, orange, hairy hips.

MR CD STEWART'S GARDEN

7A The Square, Hillsborough, County Down; Tel: +092 682608 ▪ **Contact:** Mr CD Stewart ▪ **Open:** May–July, strictly by appointment only; small groups welcome ▪ **Entrance fee** donated to charity ▪ Supervised children welcome ▪ **Special features:** accommodation available, ring ahead for details and to book ▪ **Directions:** on the main square in Hillsborough town.

Mr Stewart's garden is another good example of a small town garden. Although it is set in the grounds of an eighteenth-century townhouse, the garden is quite young. Mr Stewart began working on it in the early 1990s when he moved into the house. The garden lies on a slope with good views and has plenty of steps, a terrace, a small vegetable plot and a pond. It represents a very clever division of a small space: there are five sections or rooms filled with a good range of plants, old and climbing roses, specimen trees and shrubs in pots, stone troughs of alpines and a selection of herbaceous perennials. He is particularly proud of the pots of well-travelled and aged begonias on the terrace. They are fifty years old and were bought from Ireland to Britain by his father; carried from house to house around Britain, until finally ending up back in Ireland half a century later.

Usefully, Mr Stewart provides visitors with a list of the plants he grows for those wishing to study the garden in a bit more detail, and he provides accommodation, which might be of use for an even more protracted study of the garden. Hillsborough is a very pretty place to stay.

TIMPANY NURSERY AND GARDEN

77 Magheratimpany Road, Ballynahinch, County Down; Tel: +097 562812 ▪ **Contact:** Susan Tindall ▪ **Open:** May–September, Tuesday–Saturday, 10.30am–5.30pm, Sunday, 2pm–5pm, by appointment only; closed Monday, except bank holidays; groups welcome ▪ **Entrance fee**, but children go free ▪ Supervised children welcome ▪ **Special features:** specialist alpine nursery; refreshments available by prior arrangement ▪ Member of Dúchas; the National Trust; the Landmark Trust ▪ **Directions:** take the Newcastle Road from Ballynahinch, then take the Ballymaglave Road to the right after the Millbrook Hotel. Take the first left onto the Magheratimpany Road. The garden is up this road on the left.

Susan Tindall has been working her garden for twenty-six years. She brought the place from a state of wilderness to its current glory: a handsome garden in which one can see many of the plants she sells in her nursery, displayed to great effect. The herbaceous beds are full of lilies, crocosmia, day lilies (*Hemerocallis*) and rudbekia. Tumbles of the very best flowers jostle each other for attention in attractive patterns. There are wonderful plantings of trees, large and small, giving the appearance of a very mature garden. The fine rockery and alpine bed is well raised so that its treasures can be inspected, nose close, in their full glory. There are seductive, sweet little cyananthus with fine, blue, star flowers, *Gaultheria miqueliana* 'Pink Champagne' with pink-tinged white berries and scutellaria with white flowers and black stems. Little mounds of mat-forming alpines are tucked into every crevice and crack. The nursery is famed among gardeners in Ulster, and in the minds of many hers is one of the few truly pioneering nurseries in Ireland. (Write for a mail order catalogue.)

GARDENING CLUBS AND SOCIETIES

BALLYNAHINCH GARDENING CLUB

The club meets from September to April, on the third Tuesday of each month. (This changes when Easter and St Patrick's Day fall close to or on that date). The venue is the library in Ballynahinch and the meetings begin at 8.15pm. During the summer months several outings are arranged, some in the evening. New members are always welcome.

BANBRIDGE GARDENING CLUB

Contact: Mr Alfie Fyfie (Secretary); Tel: +040 622554.

The club meets on different Tuesdays of the month at the Methodist Church Hall in Banbridge. From November to May the meetings are held indoors, with guest speakers, lectures and slide shows. From June onwards evening garden visits are arranged. They mount an annual show on the second Saturday in September, at the Banbridge Presbyterian Hall. A plant and cake sale is held on the first Saturday in June.

COMBER AND DISTRICT HORTICULTURAL SOCIETY

The Comber Society meets at 7.45pm on the second Tuesday of each month between October and April in the Comber Primary School on Darragh Road. The club celebrates its seventieth anniversary in 2001, and it has a large, active membership, with over 250 participants. Meetings include slide shows, lectures and demonstrations. They hold a summer show on the second Saturday in September. An evening outing is organised for the second Tuesday in May, and on the second Saturday in June a day trip is arranged. One five-day trip abroad is usually arranged each year. (In 2000 this trip was to the gardens of Paris). Go along for more details.

NEWCASTLE AND DISTRICT GARDENING SOCIETY

Contact: Russ Whatmough (Hon. Secretary), Clock House, 1 Manse Road, Dundrum, County Down.

The society meets in the audio-visual room of the Newcastle Leisure Centre, Main Street, Newcastle, at 7.30pm on the first Wednesday of each month from September to April. Illustrated talks by a visiting speaker and a competition are regular activities. New members are always welcome. An annual dinner is organised in the spring. The annual show is held in late August. Garden visits are held during the summer. Plant sales and exchanges between members are occasionally arranged.

NORTHERN IRELAND DAFFODIL GROUP

Contact: Mr Richard McCaw (Secretary), 77 Ballygowan Road, Hillsborough, County Down.

The Northern Ireland Daffodil Group meets through the winter months at Balance House, near Lisburn. The group is dedicated to the furtherance of daffodil breeding, conservation and promotion. The Belfast Spring Show is where their work can be seen. New members are most welcome to join.

NURSERIES AND GARDEN CENTRES

BALLYDORAN BULB FARM

Killylinchy, Newtownards, County Down; Tel: +097 541250.
Mail order only, contact for a catalogue.

CARRIGDALE NURSERY

2 Carrigs Road, Newcastle, County Down; Tel: +043 723795.

DICKSON NURSERIES

Milecross Road, Newtownards, County Down; Tel: +091 812206 ■ Mail order service available.

Dicksons are among the island's leading rose-breeders. A list of the roses bred for sale to the public is available. The 2000 list included seventy-six hybrid tea, floribunda, patio and shrub roses.

DONAGHADEE GARDEN CENTRE

34 Stockbridge Road, Donaghadee, County Down; Tel: +091 883603.

FLAGSTAFF NURSERY

Flagstaff Road, Newry, County Down; Tel: +030 267755.

GILLESPIES'S NURSERY

47 Ballyhenry Road, Comber, Newtownards, County Down; Tel: +091 872369.

GREENBANK NURSERY

62 Ballygowan Road, Saintfield, Ballynahinch, County Down; Tel: +097 591381.

SAINTFIELD NURSERY

58 Belfast Road, Saintfield, County Down; Tel: +090 814331.

TEMPLE GARDEN CENTRE

88 Carryduff Road, Bailies Mills, Lisburn, County Down; Tel: +092 638318.

TWO LIONS GARDEN PLANTS

80 Killough Road, Downpatrick, County Down; Tel +044 612195 ■ **Open:** strictly by appointment only.

A comprehensive collection of herbaceous perennials, along with a smaller list of ferns and shrubs. For those unable to travel to Down, a comprehensive list can be had of all of the festivals and shows attended by the owner each year. Write for details.

WOODHALL NURSERY

125 Hillsborough Road, Ballynahinch, County Down; Tel: +097 562459.

COUNTY FERMANAGH

An enormous area of County Fermanagh is under water. Two lakes, Upper and Lower Lough Erne, joined together by the winding River Erne and cradling more than 100 islands, run the length and breadth of the county. Fermanagh is mountainous, sparsely populated and stunningly beautiful. Like much of the west of Ireland, gardening on this magnificent landscape seems almost superfluous. Apart from the obvious water-based activities, the Marble Arch Caves are well worth visiting. These are a collection of caverns and caves near Florence Court. The Palladian mansion at Florence Court, once home to the Cole family, earls of Enniskillen, is a perfectly preserved house, as is its close neighbour, Castle Coole. Both houses boast large, landscaped parklands that are also well worth seeing. Crom Estate covers over 1,400 acres of nature trails. This is an important conservation area, with boat-hire and pike-fishing facilities. Much of the soil in Fermanagh is hard drumlin clay, the result of ancient glacial action, yet there are some great gardens to visit and an active gardening club scene. Unfortunately, since my visit to Fermanagh there have been two sad losses from that scene: Hunter's Moon, Major Wilkinson's beautiful post-World War Two garden on the edge of Enniskillen, and Jill Scott's Clonaveel, a great organic garden. I sincerely hope these two fine gardens, the former created by the late Major and his wife and the latter by Jill Scott (who has moved on to create a whole new garden), find new owners who may open their gates again.

Clonaveel in County Fermanagh (now closed).

CROM ESTATE

Newtownbutler, County Fermanagh; Tel: +067 738174; Fax: +067 738118; e-mail: ucromw@smtp.ntrust.org.uk ■ **Contact:** the Administrator ■ **Open:** 17 March–end September, Monday–Saturday, 10am–6pm, Sunday, 12-6pm; groups welcome ■ **Entrance fee** charged per car and donated to the National Trust ■ Supervised children welcome; please note, dogs on leads ■ **Special features:** visitor centre; boat hire at jetty; coarse fishing and angling; overnight woodland hide; conference and lecture facilities; refreshments available in tearoom, but large groups should book in advance ■ Member of National Trust ■ **Directions:** situated on the shores of Upper Lough Erne, off the A34, just out of Newtownbutler. Crom Estate is well signposted.

The Northern Ireland Tourist Board leaflet advertises Crom as a garden, but strictly speaking it is a wildlife sanctuary. There is a walled garden marked Private and a cottage garden marked Private. However, Crom is one of Ireland's most important nature reserves and conservation areas. It covers almost 800 hectares (1,977 acres) and boasts walks, islands, ruins and woodlands stretching along the shores of Upper Lough Erne. Among the animals and creatures on the estate there are rare butterflies, pine martens and the largest heronry in Ireland.

DRUMADRAVEY

Lisnarick, Irvinestown, County Fermanagh; Tel: +068 621257 ■ **Contact:** Mr E Acheson Aiken ■ **Open:** May–September, by appointment only; groups welcome ■ **Entrance fee** donated to charity of visitor's choice ■ Supervised children welcome ■ **Special features:** particularly fine collection of herbaceous plants ■ **Directions:** leave Irvinestown by the road to Lisnarick. The house is 4km along on the right-hand side with stone gates.

'All I can tell you is that the thing is in a mess,' says Mr Acheson Aiken, whose aim was to get his garden 'right for the millennium'. The garden is the sort of 'mess' poorer gardeners dream of at night and covet during the day. It's a classic turn-of-the-century, substantial country garden, worked by a man with a passion for herbaceous perennials. Mr Acheson Aiken has been gardening this plot for fifty years. He doles out information entertainingly about some of his favourite plants as he walks along, and he has a lot of favourites, among them a gorgeous, pale, variegated lysimachia that has, as he says, 'everything going for it – good leaves, flower, habit, the lot'.

Drumadravey holds over 2,000 varieties of hardy herbaceous perennials, many of which are to be found in two impressive, twenty-seven-metre-long borders. Great manor houses and castles aside, I cannot think of any other fifty-four-metre-long borders. Walking through these well-planted beds is a pleasure for the visitor and obviously for Mr Acheson Aiken, despite its lack of perfection. The aspect of the garden is favourable, even for delicate plants like watsoni, which doesn't normally grow well in northerly Fermanagh. The shelter of mature trees also protects another little beauty in the middle of the bed: a ginger plant (*Cautleya robusta*). For all the garden's advantages, it also has its limitations: 'I don't grow roses. This soil here is no good for roses and they just don't do well,' says Mr Acheson Aiken. But what it lacks in roses

THE FLORENCE COURT YEW

The common yew is a native Irish tree. While the vast majority of yew trees we see today are cultivated plants, there are some ancient, wild trees growing in parts of the Burren in County Clare and Killarney in County Kerry. These yews (*Taxus baccata*) have a lax spreading habit – the branches grow out in an easy, open fashion. But there is an interesting variation on the Irish yew called the Florence Court yew.

In the mid-1700s a man called George Willis, a worker in Florence Court in County Fermanagh, was walking in the hills close to the estate. He came across two small plants that were unmistakably yew trees, but different in habit to known specimens. These had shoots that grew erect and upwards, in a manner something like the Italian cypress. Willis dug up the two plants and brought them home, planting one in his garden and giving the other to his master, Viscount Enniskerry. Over the next few decades cuttings were taken from the plants and distributed around the country. In the early 1800s these became commercially available to the public. This new form of the common yew was named *Taxus baccata f. fastigata*.

Yew grows in both male and female forms. The Florence Court yew is female and therefore can only be propagated by cuttings, so the countless numbers of Irish *Taxus baccata f. fastigata* found today all over the world are the daughter plants of that first venerable mother tree, which can still be seen in the grounds of Florence Court today.

the garden makes up in blooms of every other description There are several varieties of trillium, blue willow gentian and the hard-to-grow Chatham Island lily. Six varieties of cimicifuga, thirty of peony and a bulb garden with a huge number of spring-flowering bulbs sees the list mounting up. One great sight is the huge clump (covering three metres by seven and a half metres) of *Kniphofia* 'Mt Etna', which, he says, 'flower themselves sick. They're great things altogether.'

In the greenhouse that stands behind the house and away from the colourful borders an array of pineapple lilies (*Eucomis*) are growing in such abundance that Mr Acheson Aiken spends much time seeking accommodation for the surplus plants. Their exotic, tall flowers are like huge, waxy, green, yellow and pink hyacinths. Leading out of the greenhouse is one of the newer areas: a small Japanese garden with miniature cut-leaf acers and grasses set into gravel. This is a restrained area in comparison with the exuberance of the wonderful borders.

The vegetable garden, which lies at the furthest reaches of the garden and is well hedged in, is organically worked and weed-free, thanks to a flame-thrower that is used to burn off weed growth. A flame-thrower used a few times a year can be an excellent organic method of weed-killing, both in the vegetable garden and on paths and drives.

We finished the visit looking at a beautiful *Podophyllum*. This is a deadly poisonous plant, but has interesting-looking fleshy fruits that are apparently delicious. However, I thought better of it and didn't try one.

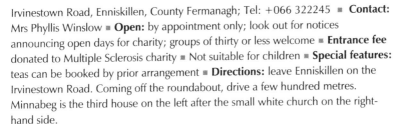

Irvinestown Road, Enniskillen, County Fermanagh; Tel: +066 322245 ▪ **Contact:** Mrs Phyllis Winslow ▪ **Open:** by appointment only; look out for notices announcing open days for charity; groups of thirty or less welcome ▪ **Entrance fee** donated to Multiple Sclerosis charity ▪ Not suitable for children ▪ **Special features:** teas can be booked by prior arrangement ▪ **Directions:** leave Enniskillen on the Irvinestown Road. Coming off the roundabout, drive a few hundred metres. Minnabeg is the third house on the left after the small white church on the right-hand side.

Minnabeg is a new garden on the site of a tennis court that once belonged to a larger garden. It covers about one acre and Mrs Winslow has only been working it since 1984. It's a real flower garden, bursting with colour and bloom, particularly pink and purple, with big mop-head hydrangea and many different shades of phlox and primula. It was actually designed so that there would be no grass to cut. Mrs Winslow does not like cutting grass, not because it takes up time – hers is a very high-maintenance garden – but rather because grass is a bit of a bore as far as she is concerned. Instead of lawns there are gravel paths between the mixed, herbaceous and alpine beds. The plants spill out onto the gravel in a natural sprawl, making the whole effect look rather easier to achieve than it actually is. Beds of rhododendron underplanted with primula create floor-to-sky walls of colour. One flower Mrs Winslow has almost given up on is the tulip; the grey squirrels dig up and devour the bulbs. Instead she grows some in pots and tubs close to the house as these can be protected from the 'tree rats', as another gardener unkindly described them. The garden, like that of its neighbour, leads right down to Lough Erne, but it also has its own little lake, a ten-metre by twelve-metre pool with a waterfall, filled with trout and roach.

The levels rise and fall around beds of flowers and elegant small trees. Hard landscaping in the shape of paths and steps are widely but subtly used. Beds of hostas, day lilies, tall, creamy arum lilies, bergenia and roses sport together, while a background of mature trees gives the garden a toned-down, softened and mature air. In the shade of the trees a royal fern (*Osmunda regalis*) grows big and healthy beside *Geranium endressii* and *Geranium macrorrhizum*. White creeping dead nettle is used as bright ground cover. All these plants do well in dry shade – a good tip as for most gardeners dry shade is the worst of all situations because it's hard to grow anything well.

There were numerous large trees on the site, but Mrs Winslow suffered more than her fair share of damage in the storms of Christmas 1997. The loss of twelve good pines and beech trees initially caused all sorts of trouble, not least with knocked fences. But for the optimistic Mrs Winslow it was a blessing, albeit in heavy disguise, opening up new areas to light and new planting possibilities and schemes, and even a new summerhouse.

Churchill, County Fermanagh; Tel: +090 543037 ▪ **Contact:** Angela Reid or Bernie Canning ▪ **Open:** April–September, Tuesday–Saturday, 10am–6pm, Sunday, 2pm–6pm; groups welcome ▪ **Entrance fee** ▪ Supervised children welcome; please note, dogs on leads ▪ **Special features:** castle ruins ▪ Managed by the Department of the Environment ▪ **Directions:** signed off the Enniskillen–Beleek road (A46).

Tully is a seventeenth-century tower house castle with a restored garden, unique on the island in style and period. The castle belonged to Sir John Hume, the largest landowner in Fermanagh in the 1600s. In 1641 Rory Maguire set out to recapture the land where Hume's castle stood, which had once been the Maguires's land and castle. Everyone was killed in the ensuing battle and the castle went to ruin.

The garden, which ebbs away from the front of the castle shell, has now been restored to that period. Low box hedges encircle beds of bluish-grey rue, tall umbels of angelica, violets, geranium, marigolds, deep-blue cornflowers and some shrub roses. Wattled hazel fences enclose beds, effectively holding in the plants. It is a surprising garden, inspiring for those with a small garden and a desire to do something a little different.

GARDENING CLUBS AND SOCIETIES

ERNE FLOWER-ARRANGING SOCIETY

Contact: Mrs Phyllis Winslow (President), Minnabeg, Irvinestown Road, Enniskillen, County Fermanagh.

The Erne society meets on the first Monday of each month. Contact Mrs Winslow for the venue (*see* opposite page, Minnabeg). In November a special show is held with well-known demonstrators in aid of various local charities. The membership count stands at around 100, and the club is a quarter of a century old. New members are welcome.

FERMANAGH GARDENING SOCIETY

The society meets on the third Tuesday of each month in the library at Enniskillen at 8pm. There are about seventy members in the club and it is a very active group. Speakers are brought in to talk on different topics each month. Plant sales are held in October. In April an annual daffodil show is held. In May an outing is arranged. New members and visitors are always welcome. Call along to a meeting to join up.

NURSERIES AND GARDEN CENTRES

ASHWOOD NURSERIES AND GARDEN CENTRE

Sligo Road, Enniskillen, County Fermanagh; Tel: +066 322243.

CRAIGVILLE GARDEN CENTRE

Sligo Road, Enniskillen, County Fermanagh; Tel: +066 326004.

FLORAL VALLEY GARDEN CENTRE

Main Street, Fivemiletown, County Fermanagh; Tel: +089 521164.

MANOR GARDEN CENTRE

Drumgoon Manor, Maguiresbridge, County Fermanagh; Tel: +067 721217.

COUNTY MONAGHAN

Monaghan is a lake-filled county; Castleblayney has been called 'the Killarney of the North' due to the number of lakes seeping through it. Lough Muckno alone devours over 900 acres, and recently played host to the European Coarse Fishing Championships. The county is shot through with hilly, varied and interesting scenery – places such as Rossmore Forest Park are good venues for walkers. The soil in Monaghan is mainly acid brown clay and it is either blessed or cursed, depending on one's point of view with regard to drumlins. These low, elongated hills, created by ancient glacial action, produced the earth Patrick Kavanagh famously called the 'stony grey soil of Monaghan', which, for gardeners, translates as: hard to work and manipulate. In spite of producing problems for gardeners, the drumlins also contribute to the arresting scenery, which makes for interesting touring.

HILTON PARK

Clones, County Monaghan; Tel: +047 56007; Fax: +047 56033 ▪ **Contact:** John and Lucy Madden ▪ **Open:** May–August, visits are strictly by appointment to groups only ▪ **Entrance fee** goes towards garden upkeep ▪ Supervised children welcome ▪ **Special features:** refreshments are available by prior arrangement; hotel accommodation available ▪ **Directions:** situated on the Scotshouse Road. Leave Clones, taking the right fork at the Lennard Arms Hotel, and travel for 5km. Hilton Park is on the right.

Travelling up a 1.5km-long drive provides teasing glimpses of the house, which is fronted by 200 metres of yew hedge battlements. This hedge is the longest of its kind in the country, 'guarding' a smart croquet lawn and a very stately Georgian house complete with classical porticos.

Hilton Park has been home to the Madden family since the 1730s. It is known primarily for its oak woods, which hold exceptionally tall trees for plants grown so far north, but there is a lot more to be seen than woods. As with so many big houses, there have been several gardens on this site since the 1690s, for which the current Maddens, Lucy and John, unearthed documentation when they began work here several years ago. The Maddens have discovered wonderful mysteries about the older gardens, including work by the well-known family member 'Premium' Madden, one of the founder members of the Royal Dublin Society (RDS) and one of the great 'improving' landowners of his time. Another of the Maddens who added to the garden was the Victorian John Madden, who brought many of the then popular North American trees to Hilton Park. These trees are still growing in the estate today. The current Maddens are no less interesting: Lucy Madden is known in her own right as an author and expert on the potato and its history.

Visiting Hilton today, the first feature you see is a Victorian garden. To the side of the house the lawns drop down dramatically to a perfect Maltese cross design made of yew and box. This is a parterre garden, designed by Ninian Niven, the renowned

CROP ROTATIONS

If one vegetable is grown in the same place year after year the soil will quickly begin to accumulate viruses and pests with a penchant for that particular vegetable. What you are effectively doing is erecting an advertising billboard telling, for example, the carrot root fly that this is where the carrot restaurant is. The nutrients required by the crop will also become depleted over time. What one should aim to do is avoid growing a crop, or its relatives, in the same spot two years in a row. Instead, rotate them from bed to bed. The soil will be kept healthier and more balanced, and dinner hunts will not be made too easy for the pests and bugs. Keep notes from year to year marking where each type of vegetable was last grown.

Vegetables for rotation are divided into the following groups. You should mark out the area for vegetables into four corresponding areas: A, B, C and D.

Year 1: Potatoes – Plot A
Year 2: Legumes (pea and bean families) – Plot B
Year 3: Brassicas (cabbages) – Plot C
Year 4: Roots (carrots, parsnips, onions and leeks) – Plot D

Then you simply rotate the areas of occupation: in year two, legumes go to Plot A, brassicas go to Plot B, roots go to Plot C and potatoes go to Plot D, and so on.

designer who worked in the middle years of the nineteenth century (*see* Iveagh Garden, County Dublin). The pattern in box and yew is seen to best advantage from the house above it.

Set in behind the house, the herbaceous borders are deep and full of tall plants – four-metre-high grasses, buddleia and rust-red sunflowers. A huge stone wall covered in figs, roses and clematis backs the bed with its strong lines and bold colours. The walk leads into the herb garden. This is a compact garden, inspiring for small-scale gardeners. Anchored on a stone ledge, one negotiates it by way of little paths that are almost impossible to get through at the height of summer due to the overflow of billowing catmint, chives, parsley, dill and borage. Hundreds of bees busy themselves working in the middle of this lovely sight. This whole area is backed by low hornbeam hedges and bordered on the outside by shade-loving hostas, primulas and hellebores.

From the herb garden and herbaceous borders the paths lead down through the trees and woods to the huge natural lakes. These are alive with wildlife; I nearly stepped on several lazy frogs. The lakes are naturally planted up with yellow flag iris, sedge and bullrushes. The woods leading to and from the lake are charming, filled with fine big native trees as well as rhododendrons and specimens of North American trees, such as Douglas fir (*Pseudotsuga menziesii*), and coast redwood (*Sequoia sempervirens*). There are two lakes, a summerhouse clothed in roses, an island and a lovers' walk to saunter through. The older, romantic, eighteenth-century parkland really is beautiful – a treat for all walkers, not just lovers.

The farm and gardens at Hilton Park are all worked biodynamically. Biodynamic gardening is cultivation based on methods that prevent the soil from being leached of nutrients; the aim is sustainability. This involves considered rotation of crops, good timing in planting, the use of green manure and companion planting for its help in combating pests without restoring to the use of pesticides and chemicals. Biodynamic gardening is related to organic gardening, but it differs in the emphasis it places on different methods of working the soil.

LEGACORRY HOUSE

Emyvale Road, County Monaghan; Tel +047 81402; e-mail: lega@eircom.net ■ **Contact:** Mrs Sheila Murphy ■ **Open:** April–October, by appointment only; groups welcome ■ **Entrance fee** donated to charity ■ Supervised children welcome; please note, dogs on leads ■ **Special features:** teas available, but must be booked in advance ■ **Directions:** leave Monaghan town on the N2. Pass the Four Seasons Hotel and travel through two crossroads. Just under 5km from the town, the garden is first on left-hand side and visible from the road. Grey iron gates and a line of beech trees mark the entrance.

The hilly drumlins of Monaghan provide the backdrop to Sheila Murphy's country house and garden. The old Georgian house, with an impressive run of steps leading up to it, stands on the side of a hill outside Monaghan town, surrounded by an attractive garden. The garden is Sheila's labour of love, worked on for several hours everyday, despite family, job and house renovations. 'I'm a plantswoman, not a planner and I feel that is where I fall down, really,'says Sheila at the outset. It is true that the hand of design has been lightly laid on the place, but that is to its advantage as it is fine, well-loved and well-tended garden. Sheila knows her garden well. She has been working it for thirty-two years in various ways, starting gently, as many people do, when the children were small: 'But I only really got going about ten years ago and since then I've been giving it three full days a week.'

The house stands above two raised alpine beds with small rock plants like auricula pasque flowers (*Pulsatilla vulgaris*), which I love for their hairy leaves and stalks and nodding, pale-purple flowers. Snake's head fritillaries and tonnes of aubrieta and bugle (*Ajuga reptans*), with its wrinkled, shiny, dark-green leaves and little rich purple flower spikes, fill the long lengths of rock; an uncomplicated but effective scheme. To the side of the house is a yard filled with pots of heathers, nasturtiums, everlasting sweet pea and tulips. A large-sized white *Clematis montana* shares the farmyard and stall walls with a monster cotoneaster, which attracts legions of bees and butterflies in the summer and feeds the birds with berries in the winter.

The wood garden to the front of the house sits under a light canopy of tall, slim beech trees, which barely shade the ground in the spring – the season in which this space is at its best. This area was once the old gravel drive that led to the house and the plants seem to like the well-drained, gravely soil left in its wake. On the wood floor are double primroses, anemone and, later on in the year, hard-to-grow blue poppies (*Meconopsis grandis*) take over. Healthy flowering shrubs provide a more permanent sight and a variegated red-bloomed *Rhododendron ponticum*, called 'Blousy Betty' (not an official name), stands proudly among its companions. A minuscule stone shed standing over a stream is visible through the winter and early spring, but later in the year becomes well smothered by golden hop. *Humulus lupulus* stands over the stream. This stream is called a *siogh* (pronounced shock) and is planted up with iris, drumstick primula, spirea and other marginals. The paths through the wood garden are made of unedged, rough gravel, which slips gently out into the planting of bright blue omphalodes and hebe on either side. Mrs Murphy loves sedges and grasses and everywhere between the shrubs and herbaceous plants there are mixed grasses, like stipa. The garden soil is generally alkaline, but to her great pleasure there is one pocket of acid soil in this wood garden, where some delicate Japanese acers and a white rhododendron are getting along happily.

By the driveway and visible from the main garden, Mrs Murphy has planted some scented shrubs and some eye-catching plants, such as snowy mespilus (*Amelanchier*), with a gorgeous scented white flower and rusty leaves in spring which change to red in autumn. Looking across the garden one immediately sees a fine-looking *Viburnum carlesii* 'Aurora'. A mixed bed up by the side of the house starts with an *Acer palmatum* 'Ozakazuki' and *Cotinus coggygria* laced through by the bright red *Clematis* 'Vino'. I was very impressed to see how mature this bed was after only two years of growth. It really doesn't take very long for a flower border to pad out if it is given a decent start in life. The delphiniums in this bed were staked good and early in the year, before anything got the chance to flop or sprawl untidily. (It is important to stake those plants that need it in the spring while the plants are around eight to twelve inches high. This gives plenty of time and space for the plants to grow, to cover their unsightly sticks, canes or supports, and yet to be well secured against rain and wind in the summer. Furthermore, at this time of the year it is an easy job, unlike the mammoth task it becomes if left until later.) The mixed bed is filled with hardy geraniums, including 'Mrs Kendall Clarke' and a wonderful double pink variety that has thus far eluded identification by Mrs Murphy. Penstemon, heuchera, potentilla, roses, red-hot pokers and aconites form a pleasant froth of colour. Anthemis is pointed out as extra-special, and Mrs Murphy declares them so good they 'flower themselves to death every year'. Her hollyhocks from France are among her favourite flowers: a memory of holidays. Even at the height of the summer it is possible to get into and work the bed because there are paths leading in and around it at several intervals.

A New Zealand garden by the side of the house enjoys the shelter afforded it by the drumlin rising above, and it returns the compliment with a display of hoheria, callistemon, drimys and a variegated myrtle. This is a spot that feels noticeably warmer than every other spot in the garden. There is always a more favourable spot in every garden, which will treat tender plants with just that bit of extra spoiling if you can find it.

In the vegetable garden, which lies to the rear of and close by the house, lavender hedges were dismissed when they refused to perform well and will be replaced by more useful and well-behaved parsley edging. Among the courgettes, leeks, peas and runner beans, are raspberries, loganberries, plums and blueberries, but unfortunately the hares love them as much as the Murphys do and make regular daring raids to carry away the loot. These aren't the only cute menaces to contend with, rabbits also stalk the garden for edibles. Sheila Murphy's two Burmese cats are champion rabbit-catchers, and they do more than their fair share of keeping the bunnies at bay. So now her only problem is the invading sheep from the field next door. 'Those sheep chomp everything,' she says in exasperation, frowning at the black faces that peer shortsightedly through the hedge from the field beyond. Hares, sheep, rabbits, invading cattle and horses – the hazards of gardening in the countryside would defeat most townspeople.

Monaghan, County Monaghan ▪ **Open:** all year ▪ **No entrance fee** ▪ **Directions:** situated 3.5km from Monaghan town, on the Newbliss Road (R189).

The attractions at Rossmore are the lake and its walks, the walled garden and an old yew walk. Travelling up an avenue of big beech trees that tower over a carpet of naturalised white wood anemone or 'wooden enemies' and an iris-filled stream, the entrance to the park at Rossmore is perfect. By the stream *Rhododendron ponticum*, the bane of many a great garden and woodland in this country, looks far too lovely to be a pest.

Like many old estates around the country, Rossmore is long past its sell-by date as one of the great gardens. All that is left is the ghostly remains of the garden features, and even more ghostly remains of the house – a raised platform above the lawns with a few bits of castle stone marking the spot. Majestic stone steps leading up a blank grass plateau where the gravel house would once have stood look slightly absurd. Unfortunately, it is not possible to get into the walled garden, but from without the iron gates there is a view of the box and yew hedging and topiary within. Wandering along the half-forgotten paths, rustic stone bridges – once a feature for the young things of the house to gambol over – peep shyly out from the overgrowth. This being County Monaghan, the drumlin terrain is very hilly and it makes for very enjoyable rising and falling walks through the woods: you find yourself ensconced at the bottom of a canyon of trees, then a few steps more and you are rising above the level of the trees and looking out over the countryside for miles. I would recommend Rossmore as a good walking and picnicing spot.

GARDENING CLUBS

MONAGHAN FLOWER AND GARDEN CLUB

The club meets on the second Tuesday of each month, from September to April. At the moment their venue is roving so check in the local newspaper on the Thursday before the second Tuesday of the month for the latest meeting place. The club divides its activities fairly evenly between flower-arranging and gardening, sometimes covering both areas in a single meeting. They organise several garden visits, including one big trip to an event like the Chelsea or Hampton Court flower shows. The members are very active and the club has been in existence for seventeen years.

NURSERIES AND GARDEN CENTRES

BALLY GA TAIG

Corlat, Shantonagh, Castleblayney, County Monaghan; Tel: +042 9745530.

CHURCH VIEW GARDEN CENTRE

Dublin Road, Castleblayney, County Monaghan; Tel: +042 9740937.

LOUGH EGISH GARDEN CENTRE

Lough Mourne, Castleblayney, County Monaghan; Tel: +042 9745930.

MARRON GARDEN CENTRE,

Clones Road, County Monaghan; Tel: +047 81225.

ULSTER • COUNTY MONAGHAN

COUNTY TYRONE

County Tyrone is a wild county, more akin to counties Donegal and Fermanagh to the west and north than to its tamer eastern neighbour, County Armagh. The Sperrin Mountains are marked out with many walking trails, and there are scenic drives from Omagh up to Glenelly Valley and Sawel Mountain. The Ulster American Folk Park, which documents emigration history, is a popular visit for families and school tours, as is the Ulster History Park.

BARONS COURT GARDEN

Newtownstewart, Omagh, County Tyrone; Tel: +081 661683; Fax: +081 662059 ■ **Contact:** RWL Scott ■ **Open:** April–September, by appointment only; groups welcome ■ **Entrance fee** goes towards garden upkeep ■ Supervised children welcome ■ **Directions:** Barons Court lies 5km from Newtownstewart on the B84 to Drumquin. Signed from the main Omagh–Derry road (A5).

Set down on the bank of a tributary of the River Strule, Barons Court House and Garden is first seen, unusually, from above, as the drive rolls downhill toward it through fields of sheep. The landscape of this smart, riverside garden must, therefore, work both from ground-level and from above.

The garden at Barons Court, as is usual in large demesnes, is divided into two. The house stands beside the river and is surrounded by the first section: fine terraced gardens, sunken and densely planted with a wide variety of shrubs and trees on one side. White flowering hoherias and red acers, and buddleia with crocosmia underneath work in simple, bold foliage combinations. Looking up the hill away from the house you see a collection of rhododendrons set in among the ash and beech trees, which colour the hill in spring. Directly in front of the house is a lawned terrace linked to another by a herbaceous border, all pinks and purples with several varieties of campanulas, shades of purple and peacock-blue delphiniums, plume poppies and phlox. This is a very classic summer border. Beside it a *potager* or ornamental vegetable garden, arranged in French style – smart, formal and symmetrical – looks across the river to the parkland beyond.

The second garden – the pleasure ground – is the romantically named flower wood garden. This is a place overrun with pheasants, looking strangely comic in the sort of numbers they make up here; they follow visitors, keeping their distance and stopping when the walker stops. The flower wood garden is made up of tall pines which create a light canopy far above, letting in more than enough light for groves of flowering shrubs and small trees to thrive below. But the treats here are the fine specimen trees and shrubs, including a variegated golden yew beside a reddening acer and a still lime-green ash tree. Everywhere there are wonderful colour contrasts, like those found in a collection of acers and dogwoods, including a *Cornus kousa* with drooping and colouring leaves and a fine little *Crataegus laevigata* 'Rosea Flore Plena'.

The woods also hold unexpected elements to delight the explorer. Walking along, one suddenly comes upon a boggy area of iris and astilbe – a surprise in this area.

Then there is a little maze of sorts being grown at the centre of the woods. The paths are simply cut into the rough grass in a naturalistic style. This place is only very slightly tamed. The cow parsley, foxgloves, mallow, thistles, wild roses and wild cherry are just as well catered for as the more rarefied plants. It is a very enjoyable, wild, colourful garden.

FOX LODGE

Leckpatrick Road, Strabane, Ballymagorry, County Tyrone; Tel: +071 882442 ▪
Contact: Brian Mooney ▪ **Open:** one charity open day per year, fee donated to the Ulster Gardens Scheme; May–September, by appointment only; groups welcome ▪ **Entrance fee** donated to charity ▪ Supervised children welcome ▪
Directions: leave Strabane and travel 5km towards Derry on the A5. Go through Ballymagorry. Take first right turn and travel 100m, Fox Lodge is up on the hill, fourth house on the left-hand side.

Brian Mooney has been working this garden since 1969 and it has gradually expanded over the years in response to his demands for space. Right now it covers two acres, but probably not for long. This garden is one man's happy obsession, so it continues to spread according to his whims and fancies. 'We took a chunk off the neighbours' land and then we kept just kept acquiring,' explains Brian, thankful that he has obliging neighbours who appreciate his garden. Indeed some of the boundary hedges have moved from the first boundary to the second and the third, and look good enough to move again if it were required of them. This sounds as though it might not be a great way of life for the plants, but tree nurseries regularly dig up and disturb the root-balls of trees. It makes the eventual removal into a container less traumatic, and it also leads to good development of tiny feeding roots important to healthy growth.

As a mountain-walker, Brian's love of mountain and alpine plants is evident in the garden and he has made raised peat beds to accommodate his alpines, most of which he grows from seed. There is a special pleasure in growing plants from seed, a sense of achievement, particularly if it's hard-to-grow plants like celmisias, succulents and campanulas. With his love of hills and wilds, Brian's garden reflects and echoes these places, so there are no blousey beds full to bursting with colour, no beds of gladioli or dahlias. The colours here are less obvious, and leaf colour, texture and shape juxtaposed with rock and water are what make it attractive. Water is Brian's other great love, and his garden has several ponds. He tries to recreate *lochans* and stony areas to add to the effect. A series of linking ponds all lead down to a bog garden filled with skunk cabbage, rodgersia, primula and generous swathes of hardy geranium. The steps down to the pond are carpeted with *Cotoneaster horizontalis*.

A vegetable garden leads off to the woodland area where shaded beds of trilliums and spring bulbs have been planted under oak trees. There is a natural and informal feeling to the garden and the vistas are tremendous. Brian's feelings about garden design are simple: 'No matter where you are in the garden you should be in a quandary as to which way you should go next.'

At the top of the garden there are more spring bulbs and fritillaries planted under willow, alder, ash and a variety of oaks. These trees provide welcome shelter and the birch walk is also very handsome. All this edges out onto the fields where curious cows saunter up to nose in, but not quite close enough to get at the white *Viola cornuta*. A traditional sod-stone boundary wall was interestingly restored in the last five years or so adding to the garden, even at its edges.

Gardening Clubs and Societies

OMAGH GARDEN SOCIETY, THE

Contact: Mr WJE Dukelow (Secretary), 17 Birchwood, Omagh, County Tyrone.

The Omagh Garden Society meets at 8pm in the Silver Birch Hotel on the fourth Tuesday of each month, every month apart from December. Talks, slide shows and demonstrations are given at these meetings and a sales table of plants is generally set up. During the summer, garden trips are organised. New members are always welcome and meetings are open to non-members for a very small admission fee. Coffee evenings and members' nights are also organised.

Nurseries and Garden Centres

CLOON LANDSCAPE AND GARDEN CENTRE

14 Monegal Road, Castlederg, County Tyrone.

DUNCAN, BRIAN, NOVELTY AND EXHIBITION DAFFODILS

Knowehead, 15 Ballynahatty Road, Omagh, County Tryone; Tel: +082 242931.

Along with Tyrone Daffodils (*see* opposite), Brian Duncan's is known as one of the best places for daffodil enthusiasts. The nursery can be visited by appointment only, but look out for occasional openings in aid of the National Trust. A mail order catalogue offers a great number of specialities, including modern exhibition hybrids and more unusual specimens.

EVERGREEN NURSERY

37 Knockmoyle Road, Omagh, County Tyrone; Tel: +082 242020.

TYRONE DAFFODILS

90 Ballynahatty Road, Omagh, County Tyrone; Tel: +082 242192.

One of the island's best-known daffodil-growers, stocking exhibition cultivars and reliable garden hybrid daffodils. Mail order catalogue available. Just to whet your appetite, the 1999 catalogue contained 300 cultivars.

AUTHOR'S CHOICE

TEN FAVOURITE GARDENS

Below is a list of ten of my favourite gardens. They are ten of the most beautiful places on the island, each of them special; gardens that display the skill and talent of, in some cases, generations of teams of talented gardeners and, in other cases, the singular style of one gifted amateur. I love and covet them all. But nonetheless they are today's list. Ask me tomorrow and I might choose another ten.

* Airfield, County Dublin
* Annes Grove, County Cork
* Ardcarraig, County Galway
* Glenveagh, County Donegal
* Kilmokea, County Wexford
* Primrose Hill, County Dublin
* Ram House Garden, County Wexford
* Redcot, County Antrim
* Rowallane, County Down
* Style Bawn House, County Wicklow

THE BEST WALLED GARDENS

* Ballinlough Castle and Gardens, County Westmeath
* Beaulieu House and Garden, County Louth
* Beech Park, County Dublin
* Benvarden Garden, County Antrim
* Birr Castle, County Offaly
* Camas Park, County Tipperary
* Glenveagh, County Donegal
* Lake View, County Cavan
* Lismore Castle, County Waterford
* Primrose Hill, County Dublin

THE BEST TINY GARDENS

* 10 Castle Drive, County Armagh
* Doolin Crafts Gallery and Garden, County Clare
* Fairfield Lodge, County Dublin
* An Féar Gorta, County Clare
* Heatherset, County Wexford

* Medina, County Dublin
* Shanganagh, County Dublin
* The Watergarden, County Kilkenny

THE BEST FLOWER GARDENS

* Butterstream, County Meath
* The Dillon Garden, County Dublin
* Drumadravey, County Fermanagh
* Lake View, County Cavan

THE GARDENS WITH THE MOST GLORIOUS SETTING

* Bantry House and Gardens, County Cork
* Cashelane, County Cork
* Dunloe Hotel, County Kerry
* Glanleam House and Garden, County Kerry
* Glenveagh, County Donegal
* Powerscourt Gardens and House, County Wicklow

THE BEST WILD GARDENS

* Annes Grove, County Cork
* Creagh Gardens, County Cork
* Wren's Wood, County Wicklow

THE TEN BEST GARDENS FOR CHILDREN

Many of the gardens in this book are private gardens whose owners open them so that they might share their beauty with other gardeners and interested people. These gardens are not designed to provide The Great Family Day Out and, in general, they are unsuited to children – the presence of ponds, streams and other features may prove too attractive and therefore too dangerous for small visitors. That said, if you have a child who is actually keen on gardening, you might raise this with the owner when booking. Nonetheless, there are a great number of public gardens included in this book and these do cater for children. The ten gardens listed below are particularly good and actively welcome children, both within family groups and on school tours. These gardens have been designed to include and entertain all the children in your family.

Ballindoolin House and Garden
(*see* County Kildare)
Rare-breed animals are always popular with children, as well as those less interested in the gardening side of a visit. Ballindoolin has some wonderful, strange and exotic breeds of hens, ducks, pigs and cattle. The nature walk is quite organised and is a good venue for school tour groups during the spring and summer terms. A leaflet provides a useful guide to the flora and fauna to be found on the trail; this will be helpful for the inevitable project back at school. Ballindoolin also boasts an excellent restaurant and tearoom.

Ballymaloe Cookery School Gardens
(*see* County Cork)
The maze at Ballymaloe is still in its infancy and so it will do little to baffle anyone bigger than toddler size, but it will grow. The gardens are positively crawling with fancy fowl of every variety, from tiny little blackbirds sporting headgear like Philip Treacy hats to large, fat hens with bell-bottom-trouser feathers. Their scattered presence will do much to encourage children to keep up with the group as they hunt to spot the next flock or gaggle emerging from under a tomato bush or wading through a puddle in the path. Other features that will keep children interested are the silly sculptures – scarecrows, wirework ducks and huge willow dragons – that are dotted about the garden. Finally, a restaurant serving delicious ice cream and with a play area outside is a great carrot to dangle in front of small eyes and weary legs.

Carnfunnock Country Park
(*see* County Antrim)
A mature maze, with a standing platform from which 'escape instructions' can be shouted, is the centrepiece at Carnfunnock. The non-gardeners can amuse themselves by hopping on board the miniature train and chugging through the fields, taking in a round of crazy golf and finishing off with a shell hunt on the beach just beyond the garden. The collection of strange sundials might interest older children. A tearoom and picnic area are available.

Celbridge Abbey
(*see* County Kildare)
Celbridge Abbey was laid out with the entertainment of children in mind. It is a place where they are not just tolerated but made to feel welcome. A great playground, alive with the roars and squeals of happy children, is set in the middle of the garden. There are interesting and educational themed nature walks picked out around the grounds, which encounter a model railway and quirky sculptures dangling from trees. A big outdoor tearoom is another bonus. This is always an easier place to feed children than the indoor variety, where cake on the ground is a bother – outside, cake on the floor means an opportunity to invite sparrows along for a spot of lunch.

Ewe Art Centre
(*see* County Cork)
The chance to take part in a pottery-making session is something novel for children and adults to do on holiday, particularly when the weather is less than clement. When visiting the garden on a sunny day, children will enjoy playing hide-and-seek with the sculptures dotted through the small plot. Add to this the fact that the seaside is on the doorstep and a good day out is guaranteed.

Grove Gardens
(*see* County Meath)
The *menagerie* at Grove is spectacular. Scattered through the garden is a host of beasts, from demonic-looking black goats with huge horns to pot-bellied pigs, emus and ostriches, snowy and barn owls, lemurs and all manner of exotic birds, including albino peacocks. Grove Gardens is usually filled with children not knowing quite where to look next. Also tearooms with outdoor and indoor seating.

Larchill Arcadian Gardens
(*see* County Kildare)
The animal farm at Larchill has the look of something designed by a child's mind. Goats act as sentries on their own battlements and the pigs live in little castles. For the adults, this is a *ferme orné* or ornamental farm – an eighteenth-century entertainment and diversion for the wealthy landowner and his guests, which combined pretty and unusual animals within an aesthetically pleasing landscape filled with follies and other features. Larchill is the only intact *ferme orné* in the country and it is a place that children will find very appealing. The stories about the family who owned Larchill, and who staged mock battles and jousts among themselves and their guests on the forts built on the lake, will also enchant. A tearoom, gift shop and occasional rare-breed sales in the summer make it an unusual day out.

Leslie Hill Farm
(*see* County Antrim)
A great, big, old-fashioned farmyard with a petting farm full of all sorts of animals to feed and stroke. There are pony-and-trap rides, weird and unusual farm implements from the last century, an adventure playground and the old coachman's house, which has been preserved as it was at the turn of the 1900s. Nature trails and a tearoom top off a visit to Leslie Hill. This would make a particularly good venue for school trips.

Lodge Park Walled Garden and Steam Museum
(*see* County Kildare)
The Steam Museum in Lodge Park will provide education and entertainment for children and those adults averse to gardening, as well as somewhere more interesting than a café in which to shelter from the rain. But there is a café as well, and a gift shop with lots of Thomas the Tank Engine things. Fat Controller toothbrushes are particularly recommended.

Seaforde Gardens
(*see* County Down)
The maze at Seaforde is large and formidable and will provide the family with a great run-around. The Butterfly Farm is fascinating – children of all ages will adore walking freely through the large hothouse, where thousands of multicoloured insects flutter. The hoots of surprised laughter from children as what they thought was a bit of tree bark comes suddenly to life and flies past them are proof of a good time. A big tearoom is also on hand to distract them.

THE TWENTY BEST NURSERIES
One of the growing pleasures of gardening in Ireland today is the fast-rising number of specialist nurseries and propagators providing plant-lovers with rare, unusual and hard-to-get plants. All of these nurseries, both established and fledgling, have one thing in common: owners who really love and understand plants. It's a far cry from the dark days only a few years ago when it was all but impossible to find special plants. In addition to straightforward nursery sales, the rise of mail order plant-buying is a real blessing for gardeners who live far from their favourite source of choice plants

and seeds. Well-packed plants travel surprisingly well by post and there are many gardeners who now swear by mail order. Below is my personal list of twenty great nurseries.

Annes Grove Plants

Middle Lodge, Annes Grove, Castletownroche, Mallow, County Cork; Tel: +022 2681/086 8291467 ▦ **Contact:** Rosamund Henley ▦ **Open:** 17 March–30 September, Monday–Saturday, 10am–5pm; Sundays, 1pm–6pm ▦ **Directions:** situated 1.6km from Castletownroche on the Fermoy/Mallow/Killarney road. Well signposted.

Rosamund Henley has been selling plants from the walled garden at Annes Grove for the past two years. She grows a range of less common herbaceous perennials along with a small range of shrubs and trees, many propagated from plants growing in the famed Annes Grove garden (see County Cork). Among the long list of plants stocked are five varieties of astrantia, twelve of salvia, seven of sedum, four of thalictrum, six of meconopsis and an ever-changing range of other perennials. Plant list available on request.

Ballydoran Bulb Farm

Killylinchy, Newtownards, County Down; Tel: +097 541250 ▦ **Contact:** Mr Harrison.

The Harrisons are part of the small band of well-known, specialist breeders of daffodils and narcissi in Northern Ireland. They operate by mail order only and their catalogue includes a large number of new and recently bred award-winning varieties of daffodil. Write or telephone for a catalogue.

Conneff, Sydney

3 Ardagh Court, Blackrock, County Dublin; Tel/Fax: +01 2887625 ▦

Contact: Sydney Conneff ▦ **Open:** beginning March–end October (excluding 1–18 August), Thursday and Friday, 12pm–5pm; by appointment only at other times ▦ **Directions:** travelling down Newtownpark Avenue from Foxrock, turn left onto Newtown Park and left again into Ardagh Park. Ardagh Court is left off Ardagh Park.

Sydney Conneff supplies many of the great gardens of Ireland, as well as a large number of keen amateurs, with over 400 unusual and high quality herbaceous perennials from a tiny, suburban, back-garden nursery. In the most recent catalogue there are twenty-two varieties of geranium, six of agapanthus, nineteen of aster, twelve of campanula, six of canna, twenty-three of hosta and twelve of lily. The operation works largely through mail order and, in addition to the main catalogue, a bulb list is made available each year. Mail order service available all year round, catalogue £1.

Dacus Plants

PO Box 5326; e-mail dacus@indigo.ie ▦ **Contact:** Carl Dacus.

Carl Dacus is well-known among gardeners, particularly those with an interest in alpine plants. He stocks a large selection of alpines and perennials. Many of the seeds come from the wild, particularly from collecting expeditions to Chile, the Himalayas, China and South Africa. This is a mail order only and a catalogue is available from the PO box number given above.

Dickson Nurseries

Milecross Road, Newtownards, County Down; Tel: +091 812206 ▦ **Directions:** situated 16km southeast of Belfast, off the A20.

Dickson Nurseries is among the island's leading rose-breeders. Their contribution in the field is so important that it led to the rose garden in Sir Thomas and Lady Dixon Park in Belfast being partially named after the family firm (*see* County Antrim). A descriptive list of the roses bred for sale to the public is available. The list includes seventy-six hybrid tea, floribunda, patio and shrub roses bred by the nursery. Mail order service available.

Duncan, Brian, Novelty and Exhibition Daffodils

Knowehead, 15 Ballynahatty Road, Omagh, County Tyrone; Tel: +082 242931 ▪ **Contact:** Brian and Elizabeth Duncan ▪ **Open:** by appointment only ▪ **Directions:** approaching Omagh from Ballygawley, pass the big electricity pylons on the right and you will see the S-bend bridge over the river on the left. Travel on 400m and take the first turn off the road after the bridge, signposted Ballynahatty Road and 'Integrated School'.

Along with Tyrone Daffodils, Brian Duncan is known as one of the best sources on the island for daffodil enthusiasts. The mail order catalogue offers an extensive number of specialities, including modern exhibition hybrids and unusual specimens of daffodil.

Dunlop's Garden and Nursery, Gary

The Grange, 35 Ballyrogan Park, Newtownards, County Down; Tel: +091 81045.

Gary Dunlop holds the national collections of euphorbia, crocosmia and celmisia. He runs a small, part-time, mail order nursery selling plants, some of which are the fruits of his plant research activities. Write for a plant list.

Fuchsia Nursery, The

Ballinaboola, County Wexford; Tel: +051 428252 ▪ **Open:** beginning April–end September, Tuesday–Saturday, 10am–5pm; Sunday and bank holidays, 2pm–5pm ▪ **Directions:** situated off the main Wexford–New Ross road. Turn at the sign opposite the Horse and Hound pub. Well signposted. The Fuchsia Nursery stocks over 1,000 varieties of fuchsia in a riot of colour and scent. Enthusiastic and helpful staff will spend any amount of time with a customer. The prices are terribly reasonable and even gardeners generally blind to the charms of fuchsias will go home with something newly fallen-in-love-with. Some unusual herbaceous plants stocked also.

Hardy Plant Nursery

Ridge House, Ballybrack Crossroads, Ballybrack, County Dublin; Tel: +01 282 6973/088 2785614 ▪ **Open:** end August–end October, Saturdays, 9am–5pm; if visiting any other day, please telephone in advance ▪ **Directions:** situated at the Ballybrack Crossroads, opposite the Jet service station, about 4.8km from Bray.

Set in the fine grounds of Ridge House, the Hardy Plant Nursery is one of the most exciting places in the country to buy hardy perennials. They stock a wonderful array of usual, rare and interesting perennials, all of which are arranged tantalisingly in the small nursery. The plants can be bought either by mail order or on one of the nursery's open days. The best advice for the undisciplined would be to stick with the mail order, as the temptations on show are more than a weak plantaholic can bear. The 2000/2001 catalogue contains good descriptions of the plants for sale and includes twenty-seven varieties of geranium, five of digitalis, eight of hemerocallis, nine of lobelia, nine of primula and eight of salvia.

Herb Garden, The

Forde-de-Fyne, Naul, County Dublin; Tel: +01 8413907; e-mail: herbs@

indigo.ie ▪ **Contact:** Denise Dunne ▪ **Directions:** take the Naul exit off the Balbriggan by-pass. At the village, turn right at Killen's pub and after that take the first left, first right and first left. The nursery is on the left and signposted.

Denise Dunne has made quite a reputation for herself as an organic grower of herbs over the past few years in her small nursery on the back roads in north County Dublin. As well as selling plants to a number of the great gardens, she also sells a range of herb oils, salads and herbs to the public at the Temple Bar food market in Dublin. She grows over 200 different herbs. Plant list available.

Irish Country Garden Plants

Upper Irey, Ballyfinn, County Laois; Tel: +0502 55343 ▪ **Contact:** Assumpta Broomfield ▪ **Open:** by appointment only; telephone in advance ▪ **Directions:** leave Portlaoise by the Mountmellick Road. At the edge of Portlaoise take the turn for Ballyfinn to the left and travel for 7km. Turn left at the sign for Irish Country Garden Plants. The nursery is 1.5km along.

Assumpta Broomfield is an enthusiastic plantswoman who runs a part-time nursery propagating hard-to-find and unusual herbaceous perennials and shrubs. She will be known to garden visitors as one of the gardeners responsible for the replanting of the new double borders at Altamont (*see* County Carlow). The list changes regularly, so contact her for an up-to-date plant list.

Iverna Herbs

Glenmalure, Rathdrum, County Wicklow ▪ **Contact:** Peter O'Neill.
Mr O'Neill grows and sells over 200 varieties of herbs, both culinary and medicinal, from his County Wicklow nursery. His extensive catalogue is very informative and witty. Among the plants

for sale are ten varieties of mint, five of oregano, three of rosemary and nine of thyme. Mail order service only, write for a catalogue.

Lisdoonan Herbs

98 Belfast Road, Saintfield, County Down; Tel: +090 813624 ▪ **Contact:** Barbara Pilcher ▪ **Open:** Wednesday and Saturday mornings all year round; at other times strictly by appointment only ▪ **Directions:** located on the road to Belfast, just outside Saintfield, on the left-hand side.

Lisdoonan Herbs is an excellent small nursery, full of the smells of herbs, run by Barbara Pilcher, a gardener well-known for her expertise and knowledge of herbs. She advised on the planting at the Grey Abbey Physic Garden (*see* County Down). In addition to the herbs in the nursery, she also holds classes on herbs. Contact for a full plant list.

Rhododendron and Azalea Nursery

Cahery House, 84 Broad House, Limavady, County Derry; Tel: +077 722610 ▪ **Contact:** JL and MN Gault; please telephone in advance for an appointment ▪ **Directions:** situated 2.3km from Limavady on the A37 and well signposted.

The Gault family runs a specialist rhododendron and azalea nursery. They carry a large number of hardy, hybrid, dwarf, yakushimanum and species rhododendron. Friendly as well as knowledgeable, they do not operate a mail order service but can deliver in some circumstances. Their catalogue is available for stg£1, which is donated to charity.

Seaforde Nursery

Seaforde, near Downpatrick, County Down; Tel: +044 811225; Fax: +044 881370 ▪ **Contact:** Patrick Forde ▪ **Open:** Monday–Saturday, 10am–5pm;

Sunday, 1pm–6pm; closed Christmas and New Year ❊ **Directions:** situated in the middle of Seaforde, on the Belfast–Newcastle road, and well signposted.

Seaforde Nursery is attached to Seaforde Gardens in south County Down. Patrick Forde runs a specialist nursery selling plants propagated from his fine garden. Many of these are raised from seeds collected by him on expeditions to China and Vietnam. The plant list is chiefly made up of trees and shrubs and includes many varieties of sorbus, camellia and eucryphia, of which Seaforde holds the national collection. A great number of rhododendron, magnolia and hydrangea is also stocked. Contact the nursery for their catalogue.

Stam's Nursery

The Garden House, Cappoquin, County Waterford; Tel: +058 54787; e-mail: stam@iol.ie ❊ **Contact:** Peter Stam ❊ **Open:** by appointment only ❊ **Directions:** situated in the village of Cappoquin.

Stam's is a highly recommended specialist nursery with a comprehensive range of bamboos in all sizes for use in garden or greenhouse. They stock nearly 100 varieties of ground-covering, medium and tall bamboos. The important feature of many of Stam's plants is that they are grown outside, in the ground. This makes them more suited to Irish conditions than imported, indoor plants – an important point to remember when buying large, expensive plants. A range of the rarer conifers, like dacrydium and podocarpus, several varieties of tree ferns, banana trees, palms, grasses, eucryphias, rhododendrons and azara are also stocked. A full plant list is available on request.

Terra Nova Plants

Dromin, Kilmallock, County Limerick; Tel: +063 90744/087 6758160 ❊

Contact: Deborah Begley ❊ **Open:** by appointment only ❊ **Directions:** travel to Bruff and leave it by the Kilmallock Road. Travel 2.4km, then turn right at the crossroads and follow signs for 'Martin Begley Glass'.

Deborah Begley has a great flair for growing plants. She has been selling from her small garden nursery only since 1999, but she has already gained a reputation among plant-lovers. Deborah grows plants mainly from seeds gathered from all over the world on expeditions to which she subscribes. Part of the strength of her nursery is that everything she sells has been tried and tested by her in her own Limerick garden. The mail order list runs to seven typed pages. It includes a changing selection of plants, including several varieties of papaver, lysimachia, eryngium, geranium, codonoposis, aconitum and dianella. Write for the mail order list.

Timpany Nurseries

77 Magheratimpany Road, Ballynahinch, County Down; Tel: +097 562812; e-mail: timpany@alpines.freeserve.co.uk ❊ **Contact:** Susan Tindall ❊ **Open:** between May and August, Tuesday–Saturday, 10.30am–5.30pm; Sunday, 2pm–5pm; closed Monday, except bank holidays ❊ **Directions:** travelling on the Newcastle Road from Ballynahinch, take the Ballymaglave Road to the right after the Millbrook Hotel. Then take the first left onto the Magheratimpany Road. The nursery is up this road, on the left

Susan Tindall sells a great range of plants. Although she specialises in alpines and herbaceous plants, she also stocks a number of shrubs. Her list runs to sixteen tightly typed pages and is an exciting one for plantaholics, with thirty-two varieties of saxifrage, sixteen of anemone, nine of campanula, seven of celmisia, nine of cyclamen, seven of gentian, three of leucojum, seven of meconopsis, eleven of phlox and a staggering 175 varieties of primula. Timpany has a great and well-deserved reputation among gardeners. Contact for a mail order catalogue and plant list.

Two Lions Garden Plants

80 Killough Road, Downpatrick, County Down; Tel: +044 612195 ▪ **Contact:** Norres Perceval-Maxwell ▪ **Open:** by appointment only ▪ **Directions:** leave Downpatrick on the Killough Road. At the edge of the town, at the Downe Hospital, is a five-armed junction with traffic lights. Take the Killough Road at this junction. About 3.2km along the road is a bungalow on the left. Immediately past the gates is a rough laneway. Two Lions is at the end of the laneway. Mrs Norres Perceval-Maxwell single-handedly runs a small plant centre outside Downpatrick. She sells her plants at most garden fairs and festivals held throughout the island each summer. In addition, she sells from the nursery by appointment. The list of plants includes alpines, herbaceous perennials, herbs, ferns, trees, shrubs and climbers and it changes regularly.

Tyrone Daffodils

90 Ballynahatty Road, Omagh, County Tyrone; Tel: +082 242192 ▪ **Contact:** Clarke and Desmond Campbell ▪ **Open:** by appointment only ▪ **Directions:** approaching Omagh from Ballygawley, pass the big electricity pylons on the right and you will see the S-bend bridge over the river on the left. Travel on about 400m and take the first turn off the road, after the bridge, signposted Ballynahatty Road and Integrated School.

Tyrone Daffodils is one of the island's best-known daffodil-growers, stocking a very big range of exhibition cultivars and reliable garden hybrid daffodils. Their annual catalogue contains, on average, about 300 cultivars and a mail order service is available. Contact for their comprehensive plant list.

COUNTRY MARKETS

THE COUNTRY MARKETS OF IRELAND

The Country Markets movement is a co-operative organisation which was set up in Ireland nearly fifty years ago. It is a national movement, with markets in almost every county. These usually open on one or two mornings a week, selling farm, garden and food produce. Many of the producers sell organic vegetables and fruit. Seedlings, trays of bedding plants, shrubs, herbaceous plants, pots of herbs and seasonal cut flowers can all be bought at extremely reasonable prices. My personal favourites are the cut flowers, and as the selection changes every week according to season, it allows me to keep the house full of flowers without pulling my own few stalks from the garden.

COUNTRY MARKETS IN THE REPUBLIC

COUNTY CARLOW
Bagenalstown, Kilcarrig Street: Saturday, 8.30am.

COUNTY CAVAN
Ballyjamesduff, Main Street: Saturday, 9.30am.

COUNTY CLARE
Ennis, Friary Hall: Friday, 8.30am.

COUNTY CORK
Bandon, South Main Street: Friday, 1pm.
Ballincollig Community Centre: Friday, 10am.
Carrigaline, GAA Hall: Friday, 9.30am.
Cobh, Atlantic Inn: Friday, 10.30am.
Douglas, ICA Hall: Thursday, 2pm.
Fermoy, Youth Centre: Friday, 3pm.
Macroom, Sports Centre, Castle Grounds: Tuesday, 11am.

COUNTY DONEGAL
Donegal Car Park, Town Centre: Friday, 9.15am.
Ramelton, Town Hall: Friday, 11am.

COUNTY DUBLIN
Blanchardstown, Community Centre: Friday, 10.30am.
Balbriggan, Town Hall: Friday, 9.30am.
Fingal, Old School, Dublin Road: Friday, 10.30am.
Kilternan, Golden Ball: Saturday, 10.30am.
Raheny, Scout's Den: Friday, 9.30am.

COUNTY GALWAY
Cleggan, Market House: Wednesday, 11.30am.
Portumna,Town Hall: Friday, 11am.
Tullycross*, Marian Hall: Tuesday, 8pm.

COUNTY KERRY
Ballyheigue, Community Centre: Sunday, 3pm.
Killarney, Parochial Hall: Friday, 11am.
Killorglin, CYMS Hall: Friday, 11am.
Tralee, Dúchas House: Thursday, 2pm.

COUNTY KILDARE
Kilcock, St Joseph's Hall: Friday, 9am.
Naas, Moat Club: Friday, 10.45am.

COUNTY KILKENNY
Ballyragget, CYMS Hall: Friday, 9.30am.
Kilkenny, Market Yard: Friday and Saturday, 8.30am.

COUNTY LAOIS
Mountrath, Macra Hall: Friday, 1pm.
Portlaoise, Macra Hall: Friday, 10.30am.
Rathdowney, Community Centre: Friday, 1.30pm.

COUNTY LEITRIM
Manorhamilton, Gilbrides, Main Street: Saturday, 11am.
Mohill, Green's Restaurant: Friday, 10.30am.

COUNTY LIMERICK
Limerick, St Augustine's Hall: Friday, 8.30am.

COUNTY LONGFORD
Granard, Market House: Friday, 9am.
Longford, Main Street: Friday, 11am.

COUNTY LOUTH
Ravensdale, Community Centre: Saturday, 11am.

COUNTY MAYO
Ballina, Market Square: Friday, 9.30am.

Castlebar, Town Hall: Friday, 9.30am.
Mulranny, Amenity Centre: Tuesday, 11am.
Westport, Town Hall: Thursday, 9.30am.
COUNTY MEATH
Duleek, Parish Centre: Friday, 10.15am.
Kells, Parish Hall: Friday, 10am.
Navan, Banba Hall, Fair Green: Friday,
   12.30pm.
Oldcastle, Masonic Hall: Friday, 10am.
Slane, Parochial Hall: Friday, 10am.
Trim, Town Hall: Friday, 2pm.

COUNTY OFFALY
Tullamore, The Shambles: Friday, 10am.

COUNTY ROSCOMMON
Boyle, Bridget Street: Friday, 10am.
Sligo, Market Yard Store: Friday, 10am.
Strandhill, Dolly's Cottage: June, weekends,
   3pm; July–August, daily, 10am

COUNTY TIPPERARY
Cahir, Community Centre: Friday, 10.30am.
Fethard, Town Hall: Friday, 8.30am.
Nenagh, New Institute, Friar Street: Friday,
   10.30am.
Roscrea, Abbey Hall: Friday, 2.30pm.
Thurles, Confraternity Hall: Friday, 3pm.

COUNTY WATERFORD
Dungarvan Scout Hall, Mary Street: Friday,
   1.15pm.
Waterford, St Olaf's Hall: Friday, 8.30am.

COUNTY WESTMEATH
Ballynacargy, Parish Hall: Friday, 10am.
Castlepollard, Connie's Bar: Friday,
   10.30am.
Mullingar, Community Centre: Friday,
   10.30am.
Multifarnham, Community Hall: Friday,
   9.15am.
Kinnegad, Old School: Friday, 9am.

COUNTY WEXFORD
Enniscorthy, IFA Centre: Friday, 9am.
Gorey, St Michael's Place: Saturday, 9am.
Wexford, Bull Ring: Friday and Saturday,
   9am.

COUNTY WICKLOW
Arklow, Masonic Hall, Ferrybank: Saturday,
   10.30am.
Blessington, Band Hall: Saturday, 2.30pm.
Kilcoole, St Patrick's Hall: Saturday,
   10.30am.

*denotes summer markets only

THE COUNTRY MARKETS OF NORTHERN IRELAND

The Country Markets movement was set up in 1991 in Northern Ireland. As a young venture it continues to grow and develop, so I have included a contact name for enquiries regarding new developments, and also because some markets are only held occasionally and on alternate days.

Contact: Lucinda Hughes, The Beeches, 63 Tobermore Road, Draperstown, County Derry BT45 7HJ.

COUNTRY MARKETS IN NORTHERN IRELAND

COUNTY ANTRIM
Gracehill, The Moravian Church Hall: first
   and third Fridays of each month,
   10.30am–11.30am.
Ballyclare, Ballylinney Hall: Saturday,
   2pm–4.30pm.
Belfast, St Agnes's Parish Hall, Ballydown-
   fine: first Saturday of each month,
   12–1.30pm.
Ballymena, Methodist Church Hall: Saturday, all day.

COUNTY ARMAGH
Armagh, The Shambles: alternate Saturdays,
   9am–5pm.
Killylea, Armagh: alternate Saturdays,
   9am–5pm (note: closed October,
   February, January and March).

COUNTY DERRY
Magherafelt, Workspace, Rainey Street:
   Friday, 11am–1pm.
Limavady, 81 Main Street: alternate Satur-
   days, 11am–3pm.
Garvagh, Clyde's Shop, Main Street: alter-
   nate Fridays, 10.30–11.30am; Saturday,
   10.30am–1pm.
Drumahoe, YMCA Hall: alternate Wednes-
   days, 7pm–8pm.
Derry, St Columba's Park House: Thursday,
   10am–3pm.
Derry, Irish Street Community Centre: Satur-
   day, 12–2pm.

COUNTY DOWN
Hillsborough, Downshire Hall, Ballynahinch
Street: alternate Saturdays, 2pm–4pm.
Ballynahinch, Community Centre, Windmill
Street: Thursday, 10.30am–12pm.
Portaferry, Market House, The Square:
Saturday, 12–2pm; Friday, 7pm–9pm.

COUNTY TYRONE
Cookstown, The Old Railway Station/Tourist
Office: Friday, 12–2pm; Saturday,
12–2pm; Thursday (occasion-
ally),12–2pm; Wednesday (occasionally),
12–2pm.

Cookstown, Loughry College, Thursday,
7pm.
Wellbrook, Beetling Mill: Saturday (occasionally), 2–5pm; Sunday (occasionally),
2–5pm.
Molesworth, Church Hall: Wednesday
(occasionally), 7pm–9pm.
Omagh, Scout and Guide Hall, Campsie
Road: alternate Fridays, 11am–1pm.
Omagh, St Joseph's Hall: Saturday,
10am–2pm.
Strabane, Methodist Church Hall: Friday,
11am–5pm.

GARDENING SOCIETIES
OF IRELAND

ALPINE GARDEN PLANT SOCIETY (AGPS, Ireland)

The Alpine Garden Plant Society was founded in 1929 and has over fifty-nine branches throughout Britain and Ireland. There are branches in Cork, Dublin and Belfast. The society's aims are similar to those of the Irish Garden Plant Society, but the Alpine Garden Society deals with alpines only.

One of the great advantages of joining is that members can avail of the Annual Seed Distribution Scheme. This gives access to seeds shared out among society members. Choices can be made from nearly 5,000 species, many of them not easily available elsewhere.

The society publishes books on alpine gardening, along with a quarterly bulletin. Trips to the mountain regions of the world are occasionally arranged. Advice can be obtained on growing alpines and dealing with the problems peculiar to these plants. Shows are arranged annually and entry to these is free to members.

Within a season the programme of activities will usually include several talks, a number of garden visits, a show and a lunch. As with all horticultural clubs and societies, the subscription charge is extremely reasonable.

CORK GROUP

Contact: Hester Forde, 15 Johnstown Park, Glounthaune, County Cork; Tel: +021 353855.
Note: the Cork group of the Alpine Garden Plant Society incorporates the Hardy Plant Society.

DUBLIN GROUP

Contact: Carl Dacus (Vice Chairperson), Ivanhoe, 28 Spencer Villas, Glenageary, County Dublin; Tel: +01 2809602; or George Sevastopulo (Secretary), 21 Evora Park, Howth, County Dublin; Tel: +01 8324598.

Meetings of the Dublin group take place at the Institute of Engineers of Ireland, 22 Clyde Road, Dublin 4, generally at 8pm. Talks are given approximately eight times a year and many guest speakers come from overseas.

ULSTER GROUP

Contact: Mrs Marion Bill (Secretary), 6 The Chase, Templepatrick, Ballyclare, BT39 0JT; or Mr Harold McBride, 10 Waverly Avenue, Lisburn, BT28 1JS; Tel: +092 662122.

IRISH FUCHSIA SOCIETY (IFS)

The Irish Fuchsia Society was set up in 1992. It holds meetings both in Dublin and Belfast and, as a result, the membership is growing steadily. Meetings are held monthly, apart from July and December. These include lectures, slide shows and hands-on workshops and demonstrations. Non-members may attend on payment of a small entrance fee. An annual show is held in the first week in September at the Belfast venue.

DUBLIN BRANCH

Contact: Nick Egan (Vice Chairperson); Tel: +01 8351836.

The Dublin Group meets once a month in the Community Lending Library, Artane, Dublin 5. Telephone for dates.

BELFAST BRANCH

Contact: David Walsh (Chairperson); Tel: +090 797242.

The Belfast meetings are held on the third Thursday of the month, at 8pm, at the Hillmount Nursery Centre, 58 Upper Braniel Road, Gilnahirk, Belfast BT5 7TX.

IRISH GARDEN PLANT SOCIETY (IGPS)

The Irish Garden Plant Society is the only group in Ireland affiliated to the National Council for the Conservation of Plants and Gardens (*see* end of entry for further information*) – an independent group set up in 1978 by gardeners in Great Britain. Membership is open to anyone living in Ireland or overseas who is interested in the work of the society. Members include amateur gardeners, nurserymen, professional horticulturalists, botanists and others. The subscription is paid on 1 May each year.

Lectures and workshops are held between September and May in Dublin, Cork and Belfast, and occasionally in other centres, sometimes in association with local garden societies. The 2000 fixture list of the IGPS included picnics and garden visits to three private and two public gardens, ten talks, slide shows, demonstrations and two plant sales. A quarterly newsletter is sent to all members free of charge, as well as a copy of any other publications that appear during the membership year. The newsletter includes details of forthcoming IGPS events, future meetings, requests and notes on books and plants. Articles are diverse and interesting and range from essays on the reclassification of plants to Victorian gardening techniques and reports on garden visits and trips abroad. The editor of the newsletter is Sally O'Halloran.

MOOREA, the society's journal, was named in honour of Sir Frederick and Lady Moore. Sir Frederick was the famous early twentieth-century curator of the Botanic Gardens at Glasnevin and a noted gardener. The journal was first published in 1982 and is sent to all members. It contains papers on the history of Irish gardens and garden plants, as well as information on gardening in Ireland, botanical notes and book reviews. Plant sales and exchanges are organised at various times of the year at different venues.

DUBLIN

Contact the society, by letter only, at: The National Botanic Gardens, Glasnevin, Dublin 9.

CORK

Regional queries can be made to: Kay Burke (Hon. Secretary), Parkhurst, Victoria Road, Cork; Tel: +021 310041.

BELFAST

Queries for Northern Ireland: Patrick Quigley, 24 Areema Drive, Dunmurry, Belfast BT17 0QG; or Anne Carter, 86b Balmoral Avenue, Belfast BT9 6NY.

* Details on the National Council for the Conservation of Plants and Gardens (NCCPG) may be obtained from: The RHS Garden, Wisley, Woking, Surrey GU23 6QB, England.

ROYAL HORTICULTURAL SOCIETY OF IRELAND (RHSI)

The RHSI was founded over 150 years ago. It aims to encourage a better awareness of gardening and gardens in Ireland both among its members and the general public. It encourages the growing of a wide range of garden plants to improve the environment and to conserve species. One of the great advantages of joining the RHSI, as with any gardening society, is the knowledge picked up when gardening enthusiasts get together.

Talks and lectures are arranged to teach better gardening skills and knowledge. These are always given by gardeners known for their skill and learning. The talks are held in an informal and relaxed atmosphere, with cups of tea liberally supplied to supplement the chat. Visits to private gardens throughout the country are arranged in the spring and summer.

As an example, previous fixture lists have included garden visits, talks, demonstrations, plant sales and shows, coffee mornings and cake sales.

Three newsletters per year are sent to members. These are informative and keep members up to date, and include articles by specialists, tips on techniques and methods and lists of books recently acquired by the RHSI library. Subscribing members are allowed to use the society's library, both to borrow from and for reference book study.

The annual subscription covers admission to all the society's talks, garden visits, shows and plant sales. Send sub. for membership to: The Secretary, The Royal Horticultural Society of Ireland, Swanbrook House, Bloomfield Avenue, Donnybrook, Dublin 4; Tel: +01 6684358 (Tuesday to Thursday, mornings only).

DESIGN AND LANDSCAPE

GARDEN AND LANDSCAPE DESIGNERS' ASSOCIATION (GLDA)

An increase in disposable income coupled with (and usually related to) a decrease in disposable time, a shortage of ideas about what to do with the boundless acres or handkerchief-sized back yard, and, just possibly, the cachet of being able to say that Helen Dillon or Verney Naylor were 'in to do the garden' has seen the numbers of garden and landscape designers rocket in the past few years. The sheer number of companies and individuals offering landscaping, maintenance and garden design services is formidable and with every passing year the number increases, making it hard for the uninitiated to know quite where to look for a qualified, reliable and capable person or company to help them create a garden.

This is where the Garden and Landscape Designers' Association come in. The GLDA is a useful organisation that aims to help the public easily identify a group of professionals who will satisfy their customers and bring credit to the profession of garden and landscape designers by guaranteeing a high standard of work. The association produces a brochure that should go some way to helping anyone thinking of employing a garden designer. This briefly outlines the sort of questions one should ask when thinking of employing a professional. The leaflet makes the case for employing a garden designer or landscape architect; it lays out the range of services a good designer will offer a client; it gives an indication of design costs; and finally provides a full list of the services which members of the association will provide.

Separate to this, the GLDA produces another leaflet with fairly comprehensive information on all members of the association. These are the designers whose work has been assessed and has met with the requirements of a panel of horticultural experts. The details given on each member include their qualifications, awards won, the full range of services offered, the sort of clients they work best with (for example, hotels, corporate or private clients) and contact addresses. A brief description of their particular mode of working is given, alongside information on the geographical area within which they work.

In addition, the GLDA runs an organisation called Friends of the GLDA. This is an association for amateur gardeners and anyone interested in gardens and design. Friends receive a newsletter four times a year, with information about the various courses, lectures and workshops run by the association.

Contact: 73 Deerpark Road, Mount Merrion, County Dublin; Tel: +01 2781824; Fax: +01 2835724. Contact them for copies of the two information brochures.

ASSOCIATION OF LANDSCAPE CONTRACTORS OF IRELAND (ALCI)

Once your garden design is complete, you may want to call in the professionals to carry out the physical work of landscaping and planting. This is where the landscape contractor comes in, and ALCI can provide you with a list of its members who undertake all types of landscaping work, from small to commercial projects.

Contact, Southern region: Evert Verveen, Glenealy Landscape Centre, County Wicklow; Tel: +0404 44789; Fax: +0404 44796; e-mail: everveen @eircom.net

Contact, Northern region: May Ringland, 3 Plantation Road, Lisburn, County Antrim, BT27 5BP; Tel/Fax: +092 672140; e-mail: alci-north@aol.com; website: www.alci.org.uk

NATIONAL GARDEN EXHIBITION CENTRE (NGEC)

Another route to take for someone looking to find a garden designer is to visit the National Garden Exhibition Centre in Kilquade (*see* County Wicklow). The centre is made up of nineteen exhibition gardens in a range of styles. What makes these gardens of use to someone requiring professional help is that each is accompanied by a comprehensive list of designers, contractors, artists, sculptors and providers. A full-colour catalogue containing all contact information about all gardens can be bought at the centre.

OUTDOOR CRAFTS

There will always be a place in Irish gardens for traditional statuary, old stone urns, peeing cherubs, spouting dolphins and other garden ornaments. Tastes change slowly, but they are changing, gradually and increasingly. The influences from contemporary art are beginning to seep into the world of gardens.

Meanwhile, on the ground, a small number of gardeners are bringing something more contemporary into the garden.

The changes can be seen to a very small extent in the developing style of ornament being sold in garden centres. But, by and large, contemporary style is experienced first in more go-ahead gardens, places like: Lismore Castle Gardens in Waterford, where the selection of outstanding works includes pieces by Cork artist Eilis O'Connell and British sculptor Antony Gormley; Shekina Sculpture Garden in Wicklow, home to the work of a varied collection of Irish and Irish-based sculptors; and Kilfane Glen in Kilkenny, where British artist David Nash and the renowned American artist James Turrell can be studied along with a number of others.

Acquiring contemporary art for the garden is not straightforward, but listed below are a few of the routes one might take to find contemporary art or craft.

CRAFTS COUNCIL OF IRELAND

The Crafts Council of Ireland has a long registry of craftsmen and women working in a range of areas. Their offices are situated in the Crescent Yard, The Parade, Kilkenny. For information, contact: Tel: +056 61804; e-mail: ccoi@craftscouncilofireland.ie

NATIONAL GARDEN EXHIBITION CENTRE (NGEC)

The work of a number of stained-glass artists, sculptors, thatchers and potters can be seen and studied at the National Garden Exhibition Centre in Kilquade (*see* County Wicklow).

ARTS COUNCILS

The Arts Council at 70 Merrion Square, Dublin (Tel: +01 6180200), or the Arts Council of Northern Ireland, The Malone Road, Belfast (Tel: +090 385200), will also be able to put you in touch with the details of artists working in the field of outdoor sculpture. In particular, enquire from time to time about upcoming sculpture symposia being held in Ireland. These give a wonderful opportunity to meet with and see the work of anything up to a dozen sculptors at one time.

SCULPTURE SOCIETY OF IRELAND (SSI)

The Sculpture Society of Ireland is the main representative body for sculptors in this country. They will provide lists of artists and information about upcoming exhibitions and events through which the work of a huge number of artists can be seen. Over the years they have also been responsible for the Sculpture in Context exhibitions at Fernhill Garden, Malahide Castle and Kilmainham Jail, all in Dublin. This series of exhibitions has been held with the aim of letting the public see the possibilities of sculpture in gardens and has been responsible for many people's discovery of the uses for art in gardens.

Finally, seek out sculptors at exhibitions in the public galleries and arts centres throughout the island. Ask the curators for information on local artists. Contact the County Arts Officer for information on local activities. Find out when art colleges hold their annual degree shows, and if you see an attractive piece of work, remember, you can often negotiate to pay for an expensive work in instalments. There is a saying about buying art: it is always too expensive the day before you buy it, but never the day after you bring it home.

Examples of places where you can see contemporary art in a garden setting:

- Shekina Sculpture Garden
  (*see* County Wicklow)
- The National Garden Exhibition Centre (*see* County Wicklow)
- Kilfane Glen and Waterfall
  (*see* County Kilkenny)
- Cork University Campus
- Liss Ard Foundation
  (*see* County Cork)
- Lismore Castle Gardens
  (*see* County Waterford)

INDEX OF GARDEN NAMES

GENERAL INDEX

APPENDIX

O'Brien Press Walking Guides

THE MOURNES WALKS
Paddy Dillon

Explore the Mourne Mountains in the company of walking expert Paddy Dillon. Visit the quiet corners where the history, heritage, wildlife and stillness of the area can be enjoyed. Examples of routes include: the High and Low Mournes as well as the Kingdom of Mourne; the Silent Valley circuit; the old smuggling route of the Brandy Pad; Warrenpoint and Rostrevor; as well as lesser-known outlying trails, such as the Castlewellan Loanans.

Paperback £5.99/€7.61/$9.95

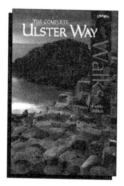

THE COMPLETE ULSTER WAY
Paddy Dillon

The Ulster Way, the longest marked walking trail in Britain or Ireland, takes the walker through all the most beautiful parts of Northern Ireland, from mountain landscape at the Mournes to seascapes at the Giant's Causeway and the Antrim coast, as well as lakeland and pastoral lands. This is a long walk, planned to take in virtually all of Northern Ireland, normally done in small sections. Illustrated with maps, photographs and drawings.

Paperback £9.99/€12.68/$16.95

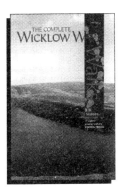

THE COMPLETE WICKLOW WAY
JB Malone

The Wicklow Way is a signposted walking trail that leads from Marlay Park in south Dublin over the hills and glens of Wicklow. County Wicklow is renowned for its great beauty and variety, its place-names conjuring images of breathtaking vistas: Glencree, Glenmalure, Glendalough, Powerscourt, Lough Dan, Annamoe and Laragh. Contents include several step-by-step walks, shorter walks and variations (for the beginner), eighty-three detailed maps, what to wear, bus routes and car parking, safety notes.

Paperback £5.99/€7.61/$9.95

KERRY WALKS
Kevin Corcoran

Twenty walks spread throughout beautiful and wild Kerry, including a special section on Killarney – one of the most popular destinations in Ireland. The walks take in some of the most stunning scenery to be found in Ireland, in places like Kenmare, Killarney, Dingle, Iveragh Peninsula and North Kerry. Caters for all levels of walkers and types of terrain, from mountains, beaches and islands to river and lakeside walks. Illustrated with the author's drawings.

Paperback £6.26/€7.95/$9.95

WEST CORK WALKS
Kevin Corcoran

Experience the rugged wildness of one of Ireland's most beautiful regions. *West Cork Walks* details ten different walks, giving clear instructions and maps for each, approximate length of time they should take, equipment required, notable features, etc. Casual strollers, family groups, ramblers and serious walkers are all catered for. The walks include: the Gearagh (near Macroom), Ballyvourney, Gougane Barra, Castlefreke, Lough Hyne (near Skibbereen), Mizen Head, Priest's Leap (near Glengarriff), Glengarriff and Allihies

Paperback £5.99/€7.61/$9.95

WEST OF IRELAND WALKS
Kevin Corcoran

Explore the counties of Clare, Galway and Mayo in the company of a wildlife expert. The West of Ireland offers a huge choice of landscape to the walker: mountain peaks, woodland, bogs and lakes, sandy beaches, the strange limestone plateaux of the Burren and the stark, stony beauty of Connemara. The walks include: the Cliffs of Moher; the Burren; Sliabh Eilbhe; Blackhead; Abbey Hill; Inishmore; Aran Islands; Casla Bog; Errisbeg Mountains (Roundstone); Maumturk Mountains; Kylemore Abbey; Killary Harbour; Cong; Lough Nadirkmore (Party Mountains); Tonakeera Point; Croagh Patrick.

Paperback £5.99/€7.61/$9.95

O'Brien Press City Guides

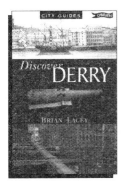

DISCOVER DERRY
Brian Lacey

This is the fascinating story of Derry, in words and pictures, from the sixth century to the present day. It explores key historical events, including the founding of the Early Christian Church, the first English invasion in 1566, the 'siege of Derry', the Apprentice Boys' rebellion, and the effects of the Troubles. The city's most interesting buildings and landmarks are visited, including: the city walls, the Guildhall, the Memorial Hall, the Tower Museum and St Columb's Cathedral.

Paperback £9.99/€12.68/$16.95

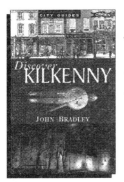

DISCOVER KILKENNY
John Bradley

Kilkenny is Ireland's foremost medieval town. Founded in the sixth century, the town has greatly influenced the course of Irish history. This book explores the history of Kilkenny, including: the founding of the Early Christian monastery, the coming of the Normans, the witchcraft trial of Alice Kyteler and the Confederation of Kilkenny. It also visits the town's most significant buildings and landmarks, including: Kilkenny Castle, St Canice's Cathedral, Rothe House and the Shee Alms House.

Paperback £9.99/€12.68/$16.95

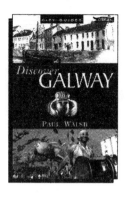

DISCOVER GALWAY
Paul Walsh

Galway is one of Ireland's best-loved and most visited towns. Its fascinating history stretches back to the twelfth century. This book explores events such as the coming of the Anglo-Normans and their subsequent settlement, the lives of the townspeople over the centuries, architecture, religion and politics, the 'Tribes of Galway', etc. It also provides a guide to the places and buildings of interest, including St Nicholas's Church, Lynch's and Blake's Castles, the Cathedral, Eyre Square, the Spanish Arch and Fish Market, the Claddagh and the University College.

Paperback £10.20/€12.95/$16.95

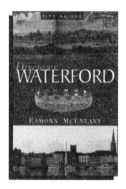

DISCOVER WATERFORD
Eamonn McEneaney

Waterford is Ireland's oldest city, pre-dating all of the northern European capitals, except London and Paris. It was founded in AD914 by Ragnall, a Viking pirate, and was subsequently involved in some of the most significant events in Irish history. Forging close ties with the Crown, the town was essential to the success of the English in Ireland. Alongside the story of its development, the historic buildings of the town are explored, including: Reginald's Tower, the French Church, the medieval undercrofts, the bishop's palace and the semi-lunar tower.

Paperback: £10.20/€12.95/$16.95

THE GOLDEN BOOK – IRELAND

Frances Power
Photos: Ghigo Roli

Over 200 stunning photographs of Ireland, north and south, featuring historic places, monuments, breathtaking scenery, the people, fairs and festivals.

Each photograph is accompanied by informative text on the history, legends, lives and customs of the island. This is a county-by-county tour, taking in all the major tourist attractions – the Rock of Cashel, the Cliffs of Moher, the Giant's Causeway, Trinity College, Bunratty Castle – as well as illustrating unique features for which the Irish landscape is famous, such as thatched cottages, stone walls and round towers. Also available in French, Gernan, Italian and Spanish.

Paperback: £8.99/€11.41/$12.95

Send for our full-colour catalogue